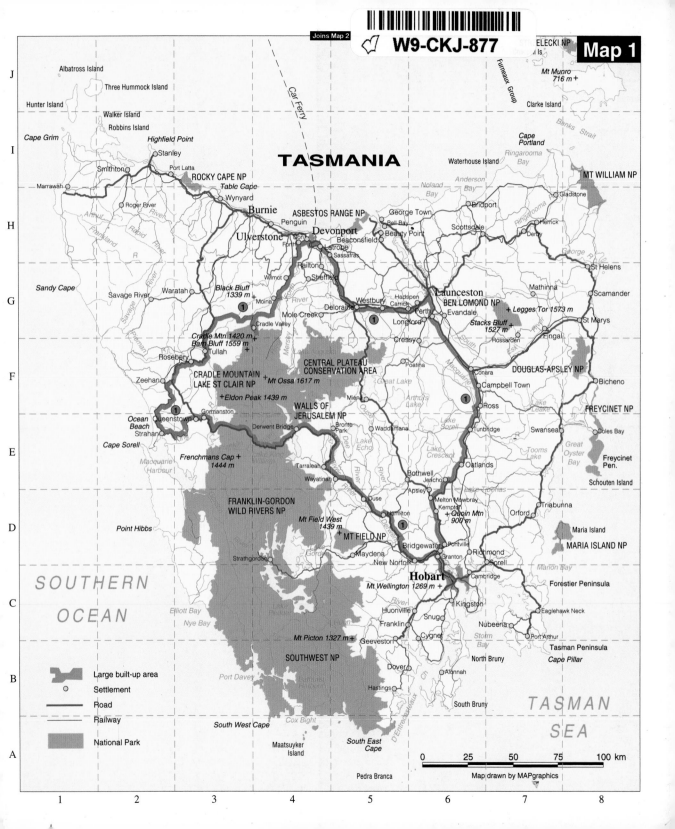

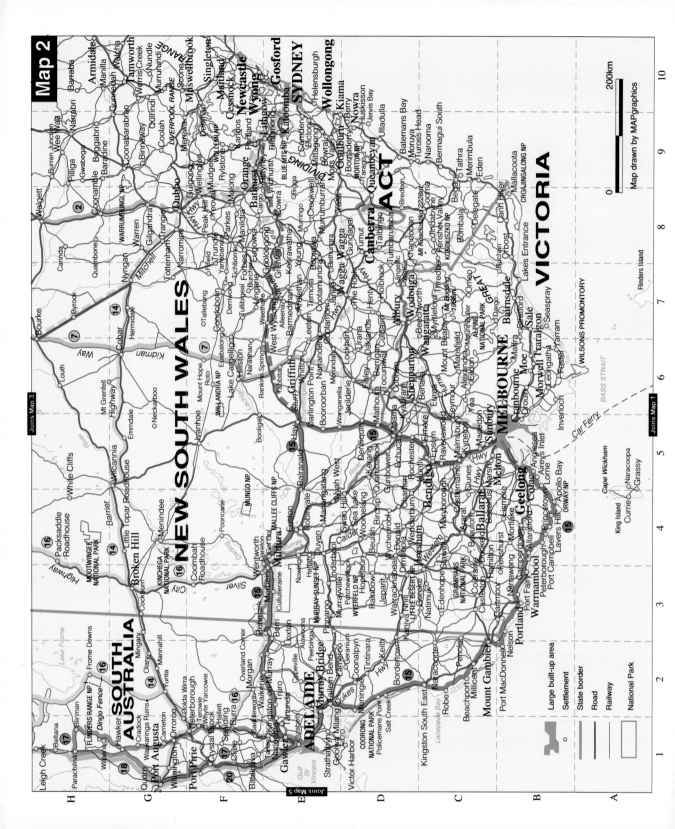

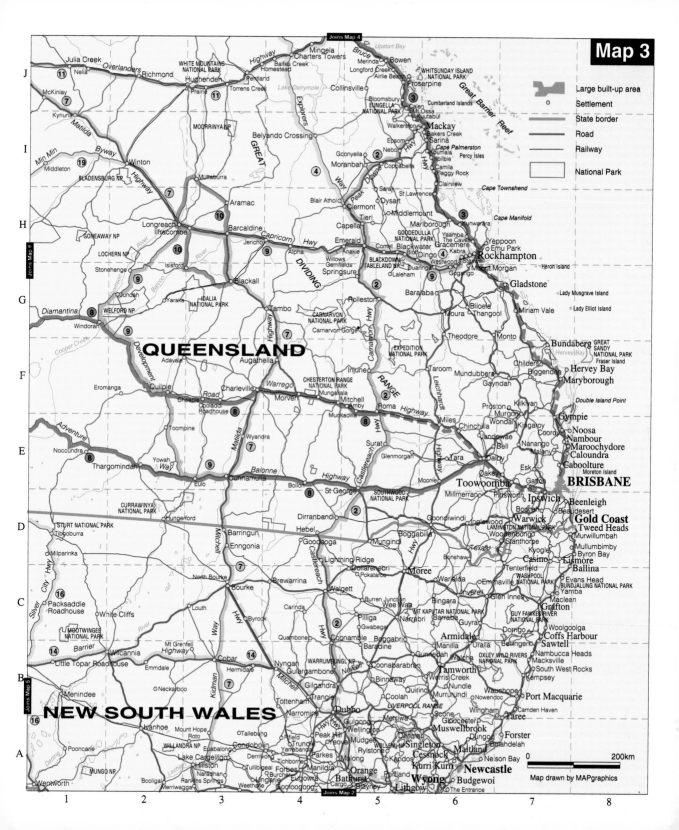

Map 3

Legend:
- Large built-up area
- Settlement
- State border
- Road
- Railway
- National Park

QUEENSLAND

NEW SOUTH WALES

Map drawn by MAPgraphics

0 — 200km

Joins Map 4

Joins Map 2

Joins Map 5

Joins Map 6

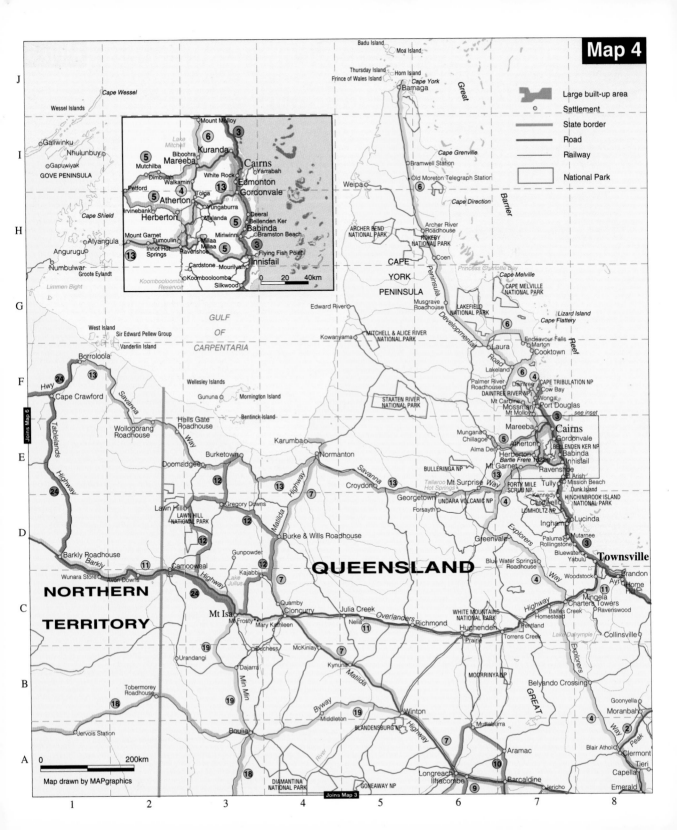

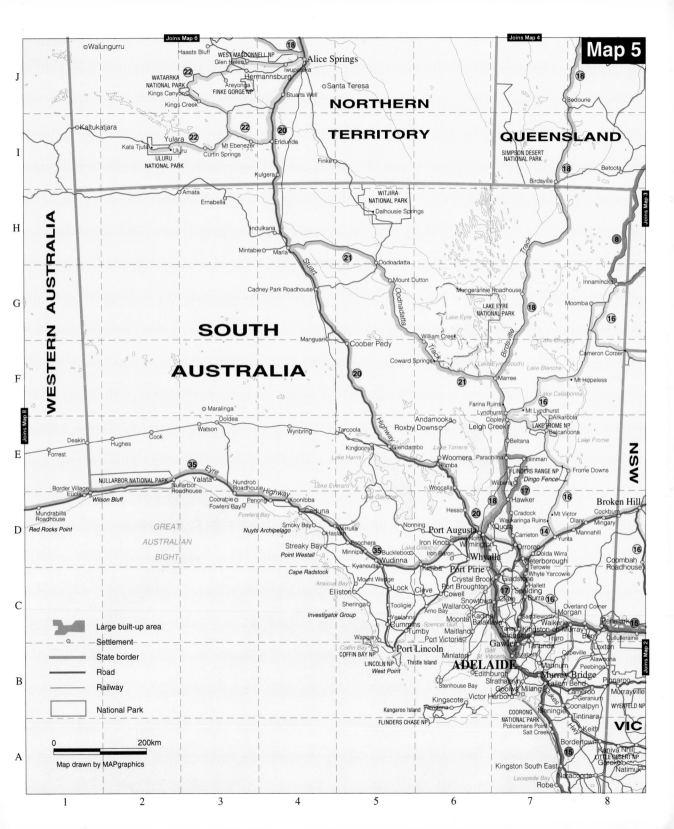

Map 5

NORTHERN

TERRITORY

QUEENSLAND

SOUTH

AUSTRALIA

WESTERN AUSTRALIA

NSW

VIC

Walungurru

Haasts Bluff
WEST MACDONNELL NP
Glen Helen
Alice Springs
Iwupataka
WATARRKA
NATIONAL PARK
Hermannsburg
Kings Canyon
Areyonga
FINKE GORGE NP
Santa Teresa
Kings Creek
Stuarts Well

Kaltukatjara
Yulara
Mt Ebenezer
Eridunda
Kata Tjuta
Uluru
Curtin Springs
ULURU
NATIONAL PARK
Finke

Kulgera

Amata
Ernabella
WITJIRA
NATIONAL PARK
Dalhousie Springs

Indulkana
Simpson Desert National Park
Bedourie
Betoota
Birdsville

Mintabie
Marla
Oodnadatta
Innamincka

Cadney Park Roadhouse
Mount Dutton
Mungerannie Roadhouse
Moomba

Manguari
Coober Pedy
William Creek
LAKE EYRE
NATIONAL PARK
Cameron Corner

Coward Springs
Lake Eyre (South)
Lake Blanche
Mt Hopeless

Marree
Lake Callabonna

Maralinga
Farina Ruins
Lyndhurst
Mt Lyndhurst
Arkaroola
Ooldea
Copley
LAKE FROME NP
Balcanoona
Watson
Tarcoola
Andamooka
Roxby Downs
Leigh Creek
Lake Frome
Wynbring
Glendambo
Beltana

Deakin
Hughes
Cook
Kingoonya
Lake Torrens
Woomera
Parachilna
Blinman
Forrest
Lake Harris
Pimba
FLINDERS RANGE NP
Frome Downs
Dingo Fence

Border Village
NULLARBOR NATIONAL PARK
Yalata
Woocalla
Wilpena
Eucla
Nullarbor
Roadhouse
Hawker
Broken Hill
Wilson Bluff
Coorabie
Penong
Koonibba
Hesso
Cradock
Mt Victor
Cockburn
Mundrabilla
Roadhouse
Fowlers Bay
Ceduna
Nonning
Port Augusta
Quorn
Carrieton
Olary
Mingary
Red Rocks Point
Smoky Bay
Wirrulla
Stirling North
Wilmington
Yunta
Mannahill

GREAT
AUSTRALIAN
BIGHT
Streaky Bay
Haslam
Iron Knob
Orroroo
Point Westall
Minnipa
Wudinna
Iron Baron
Golda Wirra
Coombah
Roadhouse
Cape Radstock
Kyancutta
Kimba
Whyalla
Peterborough
Whyte Yarcowie
Mount Wedge
Buckleboo
Port Pirie
Terowie
Anxious Bay
Lock
Cleve
Gladstone
Hallett
Elliston
Cowell
Crystal Brook
Spalding
Investigator Group
Sheringa
Tooligie
Snowtown
Clare
Burra
Arno Bay
Wallaroo
Overland Corner
Morgan
Yeelanna
Moonta
Kadina
Saddleworth
Waikerie
Cummins
Tumby
Balaklava
Penfold
Wangary
Port Victoria
Maitland
Tarlee
Kingston-on-Murray
Berri
Culluleraine
Coffin Bay
COFFIN BAY NP
Port Lincoln
Minlaton
Truro
Loxton
LINCOLN NP
West Point
Gawler
Tanunda
Thistle Island
Elizabeth
Capeville
Peebinga
Kingscote
ADELAIDE
Mannum
Alawoona
Pinnaroo
Stenhouse Bay
Edinburgh
Strathalbyn
Maannum
Lameroo
Murrayville
Kangaroo Island
Penneshaw
Victor Harbor
Goolwa
Milang
Tailem Bend
Geranium
WYENFELD NP
FLINDERS CHASE NP
COORONG
NATIONAL PARK
Meningie
Coonalpyn
Tintinara
Policemans Point
Keith
Salt Creek
Bordertown
Kaniva Nhill
LITTLE DESERT NP
Kingston South East
Naracoorte
Gerako
Natimuk
Lacepede Bay
Robe

Legend:
Large built-up area
Settlement
State border
Road
Railway
National Park

0 — 200km

Map drawn by MAPgraphics

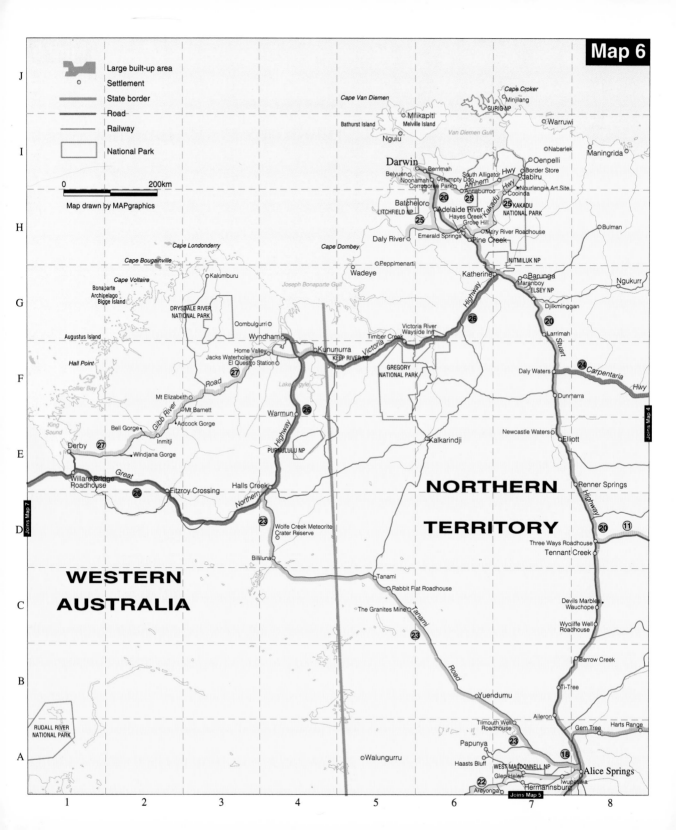

Map 6

Legend
- Large built-up area
- Settlement
- State border
- Road
- Railway
- National Park

0   200km

Map drawn by MAPgraphics

WESTERN AUSTRALIA

NORTHERN TERRITORY

J
I
H
G
F
E
D
C
B
A

1 2 3 4 5 6 7 8

Joins Map 7
Joins Map 4
Joins Map 5

Cape Van Diemen
Cape Croker
Minjilang
GURIG NP
Milikapiti
Melville Island
Bathurst Island
Warruwi
Nguiu
Nabarlek
Maningrida
Oenpelli
Darwin
Berrimah
Border Store
Belyuen
South Alligator Hwy
Jabiru
Noonamah
Humpty Doo
Arnhem
Nourlangie Art Site
Corroboree Park
Annaburroo
Cocinda
Batchelor
KAKADU
Adelaide River
NATIONAL PARK
LITCHFIELD NP
Hayes Creek
Grove Hill
Mary River Roadhouse
Bulman
Emerald Springs
Pine Creek
Daly River
NITMILUK NP
Cape Londonderry
Cape Dombey
Cape Bougainville
Peppimenarti
Wadeye
Katherine
Barunga
Ngukurr
Kalumburu
Maranboy
ELSEY NP
Cape Voltaire
Joseph Bonaparte Gulf
Bonaparte Archipelago
Bigge Island
Djilkminggan
DRYSDALE RIVER NATIONAL PARK
Augustus Island
Oombulgurri
Larrimah
Victoria River Wayside Inn
Hall Point
Wyndham
Timber Creek
Daly Waters
Carpentaria Hwy
Collier Bay
Home Valley
Jacks Waterhole
Kununurra
El Questro Station
KEEP RIVER NP
Dunmarra
Mt Elizabeth
GREGORY NATIONAL PARK
Warmun
Lake Argyle
King Sound
Mt Barnett
Newcastle Waters
Elliott
Bell Gorge
Adcock Gorge
Kalkarindji
Derby
Inmitji
Gibb River
Willare Bridge Roadhouse
Windjana Gorge
PURNULULU NP
Renner Springs
Great
Northern Hwy
Fitzroy Crossing
Halls Creek
Three Ways Roadhouse
Wolfe Creek Meteorite Crater Reserve
Tennant Creek
Billiluna
Tanami
Devils Marbles
Wauchope
Rabbit Flat Roadhouse
Wycliffe Well Roadhouse
The Granites Mine
Barrow Creek
RUDALL RIVER NATIONAL PARK
Ti-Tree
Yuendumu
Tanami Road
Aileron
Tilmouth Well Roadhouse
Gem Tree
Harts Range
Papunya
Walungurra
Haasts Bluff
WEST MACDONNELL NP
Alice Springs
Glen Helen
Iwupataka
Areyonga
Hermannsburg

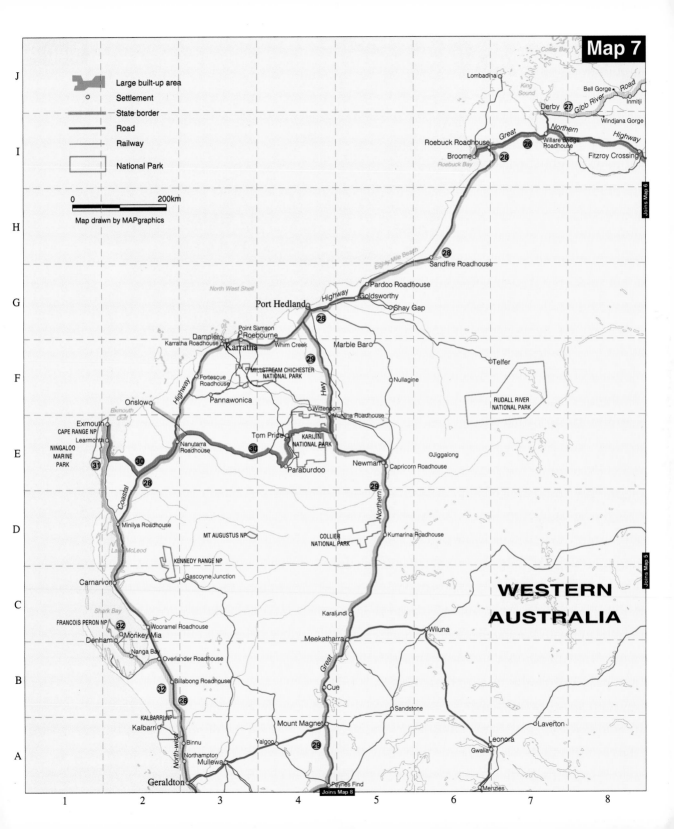

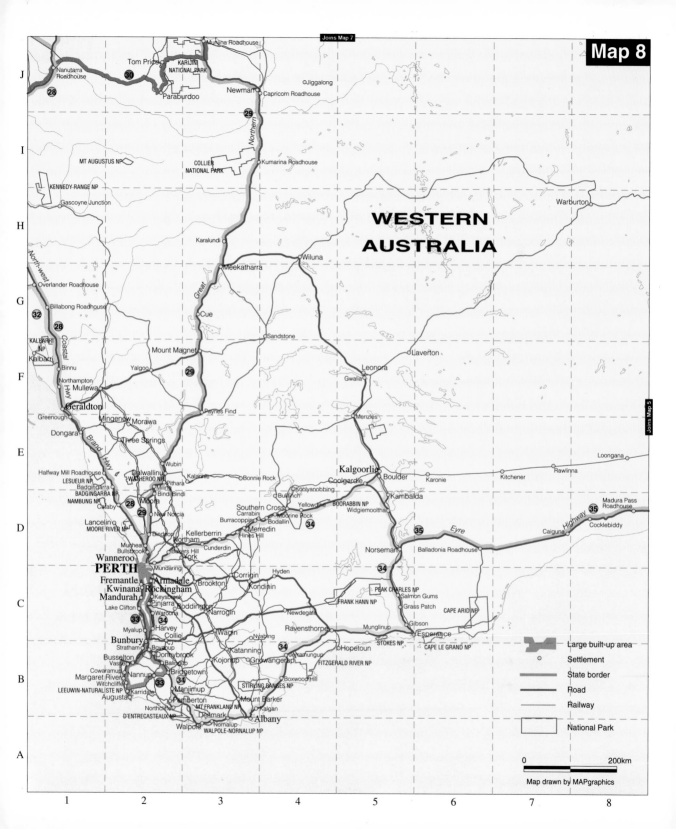

Map 8

Joins Map 5

WESTERN AUSTRALIA

Nanutarra Roadhouse
Tom Price
KARIJINI NATIONAL PARK
30
Munjina Roadhouse
28
Paraburdoo
Newman
Jiggalong
Capricorn Roadhouse

J

29

MT AUGUSTUS NP
COLLIER NATIONAL PARK
Kumarina Roadhouse
Warburton

I

KENNEDY RANGE NP
Gascoyne Junction

H
Karalundi
Wiluna

North-west
Overlander Roadhouse
Meekatharra

G
32 28
Billabong Roadhouse
Cue
Sandstone

Coastal
KALBARRI NP
Kalbarri
Binnu
Mount Magnet
Laverton
Leonora
Gwalia

F
Northampton
Mullewa
Yalgoo
29
Paynes Find
Menzies

Geraldton
Greenough
Mingenew Morawa
Loongana

E
Dongara
Three Springs
Wubin
Kalgoorlie
Coolgardie
Boulder
Karonie
Kitchener
Rawlinna

Brand Hwy
Halfway Mill Roadhouse
LESUEUR NP
Badgingarra
BADGINGARRA NP
NAMBUNG NP
Dalwallinu
WATHEROO NP
Miling
Bindi Bindi
Kalannie
Pithara
Bonnie Rock
Bulfinch
Koolyanobbing
Yellowdine
BOORABBIN NP
Widgiemooltha
Kambalda
Madura Pass Roadhouse
35

D
Cataby
Moora
New Norcia
Carrabin
Bodallin
Merredin
Hines Hill
Southern Cross
Mt Marie Rock
34
35
Eyre
Caiguna
Cocklebiddy
Lancelin
MOORE RIVER NP
28 29
Bindoon
Kellerberrin
Burracoppin
Norseman
Balladonia Roadhouse

Muchea
Bullsbrook
Bakers Hill
York
Cunderdin
34

Wanneroo
PERTH
Mundaring
Corrigin
Hyden

C
Fremantle
Kwinana
Mandurah
Armadale
Rockingham
Keysbrook
Brookton
Kondinin
PEAK CHARLES NP
FRANK HANN NP
Salmon Gums
Grass Patch
CAPE ARID NP

Lake Clifton
Pinjarra
Wagora
Boddington
Narrogin
Newdegate
Gibson

Myalup
Harvey
Collie
Wagin
Nyabing
Ravensthorpe
Munglinup
STOKES NP
Esperance

Bunbury
Donnybrook
Balingup
Katanning
Gnowangerup
Jarramungup
FITZGERALD RIVER NP
CAPE LE GRAND NP

B
Busselton
Vasse
Stratham
Boyanup
Bridgetown
Kojonup
Boxwood Hill
Hopetoun

Margaret River
Cowaramup
Witchcliffe
LEEUWIN-NATURALISTE NP
Augusta
Nannup
33 34
Manjimup
STIRLING RANGES NP

Karridale
Pemberton
Northcliffe
MT FRANKLAND NP
Denmark
Mount Barker
Kalgan
Albany

D'ENTRECASTEAUX NP
Walpole
Nornalup
WALPOLE-NORNALUP NP

A

Legend

Large built-up area
Settlement
State border
Road
Railway
National Park

0   200km

Map drawn by MAPgraphics

1   2   3   4   5   6   7   8

Australian Road Trips

Australian Road Trips

Ian Read

LITTLE HILLS PRESS

Text by Ian Read
©Little Hills Press, Reprinted 2002

Editor and designer: Mark Truman
Publisher: Charles Burfitt

Maps by MAPgraphics

Photo Credits: All photographs by the author except
pages 170, 179 by Eduard Domin, page 254 by Gonzalo de Alvear and
pages 378, 380, 385, 391 by Noel Clegg

Cover design concept by Artitude
Printed in Korea

Australian Road Trips
ISBN 1 86315 169 9

Little Hills Press
Sydney, Australia

www.littlehills.com
info@littlehills.com

DISCLAIMER
Whilst all care has been taken by the publisher and authors to ensure that the
information is accurate and up to date, the publisher does not take responsibility
for the information published herein or the consequences of its use. The
recommendations are those of the author, and as things get better or worse, with
places closing and others opening, some elements in the book may be inaccurate
when you arrive. Please inform us of any discrepancies so that we can update
subsequent editions.

Contents

Road Trips

Connecting Routes

Practical Information

How to Use This Book

Australian Road Trips provides travel details and descriptions of the countryside over most of the main, secondary and tourist roads throughout northern, western and inland Australia, as well as a circuit of Tasmania. These roads have been divided into 35 Road Trips.

The Road Trips are of two basic types: linear routes running from point A to point B, for example Adelaide to Darwin; or loops starting or finishing from the same, or a not too distant town. They have been designed to 'flow' in the direction most commonly taken by long distance travellers leaving from the populated areas of southern Australia.

All Road Trips (except Tasmania) are connected so that travellers can follow 'cross-country' routes. The Road Trip notes have been designed to be read in *both directions*. Simply read in the reverse order (distances given in the road trip notes run in both directions) and follow the specific directions, given in italics, which usually follow immediately after the main directions (not in italics).

Most of the Road Trips are presented so that they are read from *top to bottom* when travelling away from the populated south-east corner of the continent, and read from *bottom to top* when travelling to the south-east corner. For those travellers completing the 'around Australia drive' the top-to-bottom order is continued around Western Australia and back across the Nullarbor.

To find a specific Road Trip, refer to either the *Index of Road Trips* or to the *maps*.

The Road Trips

Each Road Trip has an introductory section featuring:

- Distance and a suggested minimum number of days required.
- General description of the road trip.
- Climatic information (maximum and mininum temperatures, rainfall, best time to travel).

- Distances from capital cities, and along the road route.
- Details about individual road routes (or areas) and any specific warnings pertaining to that road route. A special warning is given if distance between fuel supplies is *over 200 kilometres*.

Road Trips are *subdivided into one day's travel*. This day should be considered the absolute minimum of time required, if you wish to have more than a cursory overview of the features of that day's travel.

Each day's travel has an introductory section featuring:

- Name of the road or roads.
- Day number and title.
- Grade of the route, or portions thereof (see information about route gradings below).
- Total distance between settlements mentioned in the title.
- Intermediate distances between towns, townships, major road junctions, and features of scenic interest. Also, approximate travel times expressed in hours and minutes are given.
- Average number of vehicles per day (averaged over the whole year). Note that any road with 30 or less vehicles per day is considered *remote* - heed special warnings. While remote routes may seem busy during school holidays or the tourist season, there may be very few or no vehicles some days during the summer/ monsoon season.
- Regions traversed.

Details of the Day's Travel

Here you will find descriptions of the countryside and information about the tourist features along that route. This book concentrates more on the landscape than on town-based tourist features (though these are listed too.)

The daily information includes:

- A **star rating** (*) of especially worthy towns, townships, scenic or tourist features (see information about star ratings below)

- **Towns and townships**, their altitude (a few are approximate) and population (some smaller townships are estimates). Towns given in CAPITALS offer full town facilities; towns and townships given in 'lower case' offer limited facilities. There is also a brief description of that settlement and its tourist features. In addition, basic services information (accommodation, store, fuel) is provided. Connecting road trips are given in italics. All settlements providing fuel are in bold.

- Between each settlement are **details** about the countryside, and places or points of interest, presented in order of travel. *Intermediate distances* are given, in kilometres, in both the forward and reverse direction between the two towns making up that day's travel (eg *156/75*). Distances are given for intermediate settlements, major road junctions, rest areas, and specific tourist features.

- **Directions**, where required, are given as bold compass points (**N**, **S**, **NE** etc) and intended only as general indications - always follow road signs. Instructions that do not appear in italics refer to the normal reading of the road trip, eg "Turn **N** for Mackay", while directions referring to the Reverse reading are written in italics, eg "*Turn **W** onto Peak Downs Hwy for Walkerston*". Directions for Side Trips and detours are common to both readings, and do not appear in italics eg "Turn **N** for Carnarvon Gorge - see Side Trip below." Arrows denote the beginning (▾) and end (▴) of each day.

- In some instances there are **Side Trips** to major or interesting tourist sites. Distances, road gradings and special warnings are provided; these distances are not included in the day's total distance.

- **Accommodation** details are provided at the end of each day's travel, and at some intermediate towns or settlements. Details include name, location, phone number and approximate price range (including GST). Accommodation types include hotels, motels and caravan parks. In caravan park listings, 'site' refers to a powered site (unpowered sites are usually $2-$5 cheaper); 'van' refers to an on-site caravan, park cabin or chalet, with prices increasing accordingly. These listings are examples only and not necessarily all that is available. Unlisted accommodation may include other hotels, motels, backpackers, serviced apartments, holiday flats, bed & breakfasts, and farmstays.

The Rest of the Book

The **Before You Go** and **On The Road** sections contain some travel hints, preparing your vehicle and yourself, and any permits or licences required, such as for camping, fishing or fossicking. As well there is information on road conditions, travelling etiquette, nasty animals and plants, environmentally-sound bush camping, and what to do if you break down or get lost.

In the **Appendices** you will find details of tourist offices and visitor centres, a list of recommended books, a glossary of unusual terms, web sites to visit, and a suggested list of tools, spares, personal requirements, camping equipment and food.

The Route Gradings Explained

Each days' road trip has been graded in order to give the traveller an idea of the road conditions likely to be encountered. These gradings are based on the type of road surface, vehicle suitability and driver experience, and are representative of *dry weather conditions*. The gradings indicate the typical conditions for that section of the route, not necessarily the best or worst.

Grade One
(All vehicles)

Virtually all highways and major tourist roads are Grade One.

- Two or more lane bitumen highway in fair to very good condition. Some roads may be subject to flooding.

- Suitable for all vehicles and caravans.
- Beware of stock grids on outback roads.
- Exercise caution when passing or overtaking road trains.

Grade Two
(All vehicles; caravans with care)
Commonly found in the outback as secondary or tourist roads.

- Single-width bitumen road in fair to good condition.
- Extra care required when passing or overtaking as the wheels on one side will need to run on gravel verges; beware of jagged bitumen edges, windscreen breakages, narrow stock grids.
- Slow down when approaching other vehicles; completely leave the bitumen when passing road trains.
- Some roads may be subject to flooding. Exercise caution in wet weather as road verges may be muddy. Take care on narrow causeways.
- Suitable for all vehicles, and caravans with care.

Grade Three
(2WD usually okay - enquire after rain; caravans with extreme care)
Mostly unsealed outback roads that normally provide good travelling conditions when dry.

- Two-lane unsealed road in fair to good condition, generally well-maintained in normal (dry) periods.
- Surfaces vary from constructed gravel roads to graded natural formations. Heavily used (especially after school holidays, race meetings) or irregularly maintained roads may be pot-holed, uneven or corrugated. Loose gravel and sandy creek crossings will be encountered.
- Exercise care at stock grids.
- Slow down when approaching other vehicles, to reduce dust hazard and windscreen breakages.

- Some routes may be subject to flooding; all routes may be impassable in wet weather. Always check in advance after heavy rains or the monsoon as road surfaces may be washed out or scoured. Creek and river crossings could prove difficult at this time.
- Suitable for conventional vehicles with care; or extreme care if towing a caravan, or in adverse conditions.
- A good clearance is desirable; small cars may need modifications.
- *In remote areas enquire locally before proceeding, especially in summer or during wet weather.*

Grade Four
(4WD recommended; 2WD with extreme care and experience; not suitable for caravans)
Most are outback roads that receive little maintenance, or Grade 3 roads after heavy rains. Not recommended for inexperienced 2WDers.

- One or two-lane unsealed and irregularly maintained road or track.
- Conditions may be rough, rocky, pot-holed, corrugated, washed out, sandy, and there may be high centre mounds of gravel, large bulldust holes, etc. Creek crossings are often rocky, sandy or washed out.
- Exercise extreme caution at stock grids.
- Routes offer fair travelling after grading, but quickly degenerate with passing traffic. All routes subject to flooding and may be impassable in wet weather, even to 4WDs.
- Slow down when approaching other vehicles to reduce dust hazard and windscreen breakages.
- Suitable only for experienced drivers of conventional vehicles with extreme care.
- A good ground clearance is essential; 4WDs recommended if only for good clearance. Conventional vehicle modifications highly desirable (sump and fuel tank guards, undercarriage protection).

- Not recommended for caravans; passable with trailers towed by a 4WD.

- *Always enquire locally before proceeding and inform someone of your travel intentions.*

Grade Five
(Strictly 4WD)

- Unsealed and unconstructed track receiving little or no maintenance. Routes negotiate soft and high sand dunes, deeply rutted sections of track, or boggy terrain; otherwise conditions are similar to Grade Four routes.

- All routes subject to adverse wet weather conditions; detours and route finding may be required.

- Suitable only for high clearance 4WDs.

- *Always enquire locally before proceeding and inform someone of your travel intentions.*

The Star Ratings Explained

A number of features within towns or across the countryside have been rated by a system of stars. This rating is personal, based on the author's experiences. A feature or town with no stars is not meant to be a poor reflection on that feature or town; it simply means that on a road trip with limited time, a long stay is not necessarily warranted. The ratings are as follows:

No star Feature of interest

* Feature of interest; worth making a point of seeing if you are in the area. These features are relative to the area they are in.

** Impressive feature; worth going out of your way to see.

*** Outstanding feature; see at all costs.

Road Trip Index

Road Trip 1
The Tassie Loop

Devonport-Cradle Valley-Strahan-Queenstown-Hobart-Launceston-Deloraine-Devonport
Total Distance: 826km
Suggested Travelling Time: 4 days

> *Discover the best of wild and historic Tasmania*
> See Hobart the capital, tranquil Launceston, the rainforests and glaciers of spectacular Cradle Mountain-Lake St Clair National Park, the tourist centres of Zeehan and Strahan, and the historic little towns along the way.

The Tassie Loop

This road trip takes the traveller through the heart of the wild mountains of the West Coast, across the Central Plateau to Hobart, through the Midlands with its English-style landscapes, on to pretty Launceston, then back to the ferry terminal at Devonport. Though the island state has a lot to offer, this excursion takes in the very best of all that is wild or historic in Tasmania. Note that the main tourist season (December to March) will require advanced bookings for accommodation and tours in many places.

The Climate

Many people will find that Tasmania is a cool place. While hot days are not unknown they are uncommon, and any warm days will be followed by cool ones, at any time of the year. The best time to visit Tasmania is mid-summer to mid-autumn. Most days are mild to warm (low to mid-twenties) with the odd hot day thrown in. Generally nights are cool (low teens). This time of the year provides the most stable weather with more than a few clear, sunny days. Nonetheless rain is always a possibility, especially in the mountains or in the west coast region. Carry wet- and wind-proof clothing at all times.

Late autumn and spring can be good times to visit with cool to mild days (mid-teens) and cool to cold nights (5C to 8C), although showery weather is common, especially in the mountains and in the west. Winters are cold with sub-teen days and freezing nights. The mountains are very cold at this time with snow and ice conditions. The west coast is then cold and damp.

Capital City Connections

Tasmania can be reached from the mainland via the *Spirit of Tasmania*, which departs Monday, Wednesday and Friday nights from Station Pier, Beach Road, Port Melbourne, Victoria. Journey time is approximately 14.5 hours. Arrival time in Devonport is around 9am depending on weather conditions.

Ship departs from Spirit of Tasmania terminal, off The Esplanade, East Devonport.

The Route
Distances in kilometres

	Intermediate	Total
Devonport	0	0
Cradle Valley	77	77
Strahan	154	231
Queenstown	40	271
Hobart	257	528
Launceston	198	726
Devonport	100	826

B19/C132/A10/B27/A10 (Lyell Highway)
Devonport-Cradle Valley-Strahan-Queenstown-Hobart

Tasmania's road are numbered, with A roads being the most important. The route described is virtually all sealed. It passes through mountainous country for the most part and can be narrow and twisty. This means that travelling times are slower than on the mainland. Slow down! Each day's travel should be considered the minimum time required for a cursory look at the major tourist features.

DAY ONE

DEVONPORT

7

Don

9

Forth

23

Wilmot

26

Cradle Valley turnoff

7

Cradle View

Cradle Mtn-Lake St. Clair NP

5

Cradle Valley

16

Cradle Valley turnoff

26

A10 Highway junction

37

Rosebery

1:30

1:45

Warnings: travel slowly on narrow and twisty mountain roads. Beware of wildlife, especially at night. During ther cooler months severe winter conditions (snow, blizzards) may close the road - heed local advice.

DAY 1: DEVONPORT-STRAHAN via Cradle Valley

Roads to Take: Bass Highway, B19, C132, A10, B27
Grade 1 around Devonport/A10 and B27
Grade 2 (along C132; short unsealed section near Cradle Valley)
Total Distance: 231km (3:50)
Intermediate Distances:

	Km	Hours
Devonport-Cradle Valley	77	(1:30)
Cradle Valley-Zeehan	108	(1:45)
Zeehan-Strahan	46	(0:35)

Regions Traversed: The North-West/Central Highlands/West Coast

Spirit of Tasmania Terminal: leave via The Esplanade, follow the signs towards Devonport, loop onto the Bass Highway crossing Mersey River bridge (if required, the exit for Devonport centre is immediately after the bridge), exit left onto Middle Road, turn right into Stony Rise Road (B19) and proceed **W** to Don. (*0/231*)

DEVONPORT (Alt 8m; Pop 25400): large regional centre and sea port set between the Mersey and Forth rivers. Worth seeing: Bluff Lighthouse* built in 1889, Tiagarra* (Tasmanian Aboriginal Culture & Art Centre), Tasmanian Maritime & Folk Museum* and Home Hill historic residence. Full town facilities. (*2/229*) If you are leaving from the city centre, proceed along Steele Street then turn into Don Road and continue **W** to Don.

Accommodation
Argosy Motor Inn, Tarleton St (2kmE), ©03 6427 8872, ◐$70-$90
Edgewater Motor Inn, 2 Thomas St, ©03 6427 8441, ◐$65

Gateway Inn, 16 Fenton St (1kmW), ©03 6424 4922, ◐$110-$130
Bay View Holiday Village, 2 Caroline St, East Devonport, ©03 6427 0499, ◐Site: $18 Van: $50-$65
Devonport Vacation Village, 20 North Caroline St, East Devonport, ©03 6427 8886, ◐Site: $15 Van: $45-$60

Don: small township on the edge of Devonport. The Don River Railway and Museum** is of interest. Store, fuel. (*7/224*)
Proceed **W** under the underpass along Forth Road (B19) to Forth township. *Follow the signs E to Devonport.*

Forth: interesting township located on the Forth River. Store, fuel. (*16/215*)
Turn **S** onto C132 for Wilmot. *Head E for Devonport.*
Hilly country offers good views*, especially along the lower reaches of the Forth River.
Lower Wilmot: locality. (*30/201*)

Wilmot (Alt 265m; Pop 285):* interesting small village. The historic store* is worth seeing. Store, fuel. (*39/192*)

Mountainous country offers glimpsed views. The hillslopes support forests.
Moina (Alt 637m): locality. (*46/185*)
Undulating country presents a wild face, especially on the Middlesex Plains.
Cradle Valley turnoff: (*65/148*) Turn **S** for Cradle Valley. *Turn E for Wilmot.*

Cradle View (Alt 870m): small settlement; store, fuel, campground - walking trails. (*72/159*)

Cradle Mountain - Lake St Clair National Park: large park preserving some of the best glaciated country in Australia as well as World Heritage rainforests and landscapes. Be prepared for cold, wet and windy conditions at any time, especially when walking or during the cooler months. Also expect cloud - totally clear days are rare.

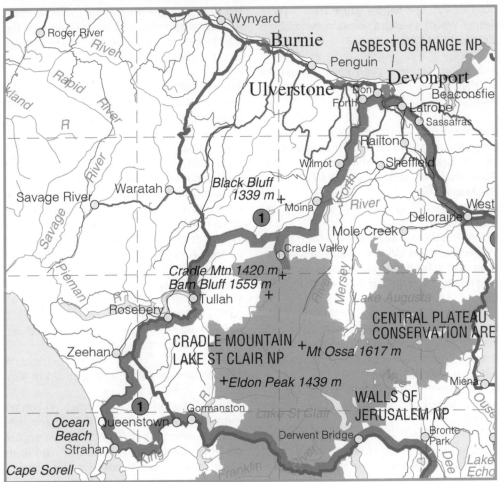

Detail of MAP 1

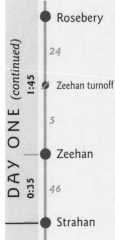

DAY ONE (continued)

Rosebery

1:45

24

Zeehan turnoff

5

Zeehan

0:35

46

Strahan

Pencil Pine (Alt 800m): location of Cradle Mountain Visitors Centre* and Ranger Station. Numerous walking trails. Accommodation. (74/157)

Cradle Valley (Alt 914m):** small settlement set in a fantastic setting. Old Waldheim Hut** worth seeing. Walking trails. Accommodation. (77/154)

Dove Lake: the end of the road. This site offers probably the most easily accessible glaciated mountain view*** in Australia. Cradle Mountain (1544m) dominates the scene with Mt Campbell (1248m) on the right and Marions Lookout (1223m) on the left. The pine trees are pencil pines. Numerous walks from here - heed

all warnings. (79/152) Return to Cradle Valley turnoff and the C132.

Cradle Valley turnoff: (93/138) Turn W for the A10 and Zeehan. Turn S for Cradle Valley.
Mountainous country offers occasional good views*.

A10 road junction: (119/122) Turn S for Tullah and Zeehan. Turn E for Cradle Valley.
Mountainous country provides some good views*.

Tullah (Alt 152m; Pop 700): small town set scenically between two hydro-electricity lakes.

DAY TWO

	Strahan
37	
0:40	A10 Highway junction
3	
	QUEENS-TOWN
RA 88	Cradle Mtn-Lake St Clair NP
RA	Derwent Bridge
45	
	Tarraleah
34	
	Ouse
17	
	Hamilton
35	
	NEW NORFOLK
17	
	Granton
21	
	HOBART

1:10 / 2:20

Good views*. The narrow gauge train** (Wee Georgie Wood) is worth a ride. Accommodation, store fuel. (*142/89*)

Hilly country offers good views over Lake Rosebery. Mt Murchison (1257m) lies to the south.

Rosebery (Alt 140m; Pop 1600): originally an old gold mining town located between Mt Black and Mt Read (1128m). Mine tours available. Accommodation, stores, fuel. (*156/75*)

Accommodation
Plandome Hotel, Agnes St, ©03 6473 1351, ○$45-$65

From Rosebery a short 8km drive leads to Williamsford*, an old zinc mining settlement. From here a 1.5 hour walk leads to the 113m high Montezuma Falls* set deep within the rainforest.

Mountainous country provides occasional good views*. Rainforests line the road. En route, the Renison Bell tin mine is passed. There is a lookout* just west of Rosebery.
Zeehan turnoff: (*180/51*) Turn **W** onto the B27 for Zeehan and Strahan. *Turn **N** onto the A10 for Rosebery.*

Zeehan (Alt 172m; Pop 1130):** interesting old silver mining town well worth visiting. It currently houses the workers of Renison Bell mine. Numerous historic buildings*. The West Coast Pioneers Memorial Museum* is well worth seeing. Accommodation, stores, fuel. (*185/46*)

Accommodation
Heemskirk Motor Hotel, Main St (1.5kmSE), ©03 6471 6107, ○$70-$90
Cecil Hotel, Main St, ©03 6471 6221, ○$100
Treasure Island West Coast Caravan Park, Hurst St (1kmNE), ©03 6471 663, ○Site: $18 Van: $40-$70

From Zeehan a 7km scenic drive* leads to the Spray Silver Mine Workings*.

Undulating country supports buttongrass plains and provides mountain views* including Mt Zeehan (701m).

Henty Dunes* line the road on the west. There is picnic area and a walking trail through the 30m high dunes to the exposed (no swimming) Ocean Beach. (*217/14*)

Strahan (Alt 7m; Pop 600):** old mining port town, nowadays a tourist centre. Numerous old buildings*, especially along The Esplanade. The Visitors Centre houses the West Coast Reflections display*. A foreshore track* leads to Regatta Point. In the Peoples Park, a walking trail* leads through rainforest to Hogarth Falls. Cruises are available on Macquarie Harbour, up the Gordon River and to the old convict settlement of Sarah Island. The newly reconstructed Abt Wilderness Railway** to Queenstown should be seen. Accommodation, stores, fuel. (*231/0*)
*Head **N** on the B27 for Zeehan.*

Accommodation
Strahan Motor Inn Motel, Jolly St (1kmN), ©03 6471 7160, ○$85-$135
Strahan Village Cottages Motel, The Esplanade, ©03 6471 7191, ○$105-$150
Strahan Caravan & Tourist Park, Innes St (1.5kmW), ©03 6471 7239, ○Site: $18 Van: $40-$75

West of Strahan lies Ocean Beach* (12km return) a good place for birdwatching and sunsets; no swimming though. South-west (turn off Ocean Beach Rd) an unsealed road leads 15km to Macquarie Heads* via Swan Basin*. Picnic area, camping available.

▲

DAY 2: STRAHAN-HOBART via Queenstown

Roads to Take: B27, A10 (Lyell Highway)
Grade 1
Total Distance: 297km (4:10)
Intermediate Distances:

	Km	Hours
Strahan-Queenstown	40	(0:40)
Queenstown-Derwent Bridge	88	(1:10)
Derwent Bridge-Hobart	169	(2:20)

Regions Traversed: West Coast, Central Highlands, The South-East

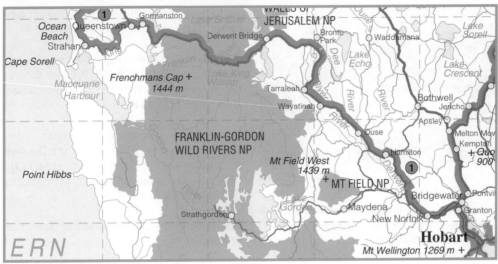

Detail of MAP 1

Strahan (Alt 7m; Pop 600):** old mining port town. For more information see Day 1. (**0/297**) Head **NE** on the B24 for Queenstown.

Hilly country provides occasional views. The route passes through forests and rainforests. A10 Highway junction: (**37/260**) Turn **E** for Queenstown. *Turn **S** for Strahan.*

QUEENSTOWN (Alt 129m; Pop 3350):* interesting old gold and copper mining town surrounded by bare, colourful hillslopes**, a result of past mining activities. Plenty to see: historic buildings*, Galley Museum*, good views from Spion Kop Lookout* (Bowes St), Chairlift ride** across the barren hills, Mt Lyell mine tours, and the Iron Blow Lookout* which overlooks an original open cut mine. The Abt Wilderness Railway** from Strahan is well worth seing. Full town facilities. (**40/257**)

Accommodation

Westcoaster Motor Inn, Batchelor St (1kmN), ©03 6471 1033, ✪$90
Silver Hills Motel, Penghana Rd (1kmN), ©03 6471 1755, ✪$85
Mt Lyell Motor Inn, 1 Orr St, ©03 6471 1511, ✪$50-$60

Queenstown Cabin and Tourist Park, 17 Grafton St (2kmS), ©03 6471 1332, ✪Site: $16 Van: $35-$65

Hilly country provides fantastic views over bare hillslopes. Very colourful late in the afternoon or early in the day. On the side of Mt Owen is a lookout.

Gormanston (Alt 366m): old mining locality. (**45/257**)

Hilly country supports forests and rainforests. Good views* overlooking the hydro Lake Burbury. **Rest area** nearby.

Cradle Mountain-Lake St Clair National Park: World Heritage listed park preserving some of Australia's finest wilderness country.

Nelson Falls:* stop here for a short walk along a nature trail to Nelson Falls, set deep within the rainforest. (**60/237**)

Hilly country covered in forests.

Donaghys Lookout:** a short walk leads to a superb viewpoint overlooking Tasmania's southwest wilderness country. The obvious peak is Frenchmans Cap (1444m). The Collingwood River is 250m below.

Frenchmans Cap trackhead: this walk is for well-prepared and experienced bushwalkers only. A short walk* from the road leads to the Franklin River. (**97/200**)

Derwent River, Tas

Franklin River Nature Trail:* pleasant picnic area by the river. Walking trail. (*100/197*)
Hilly country offers good views* as the route skirts Mt Arrowsmith (981m) and Mt King William (1324m). Two lookouts on this section.
Lake King William, a hydro lake, lies adjacent to the road.

Derwent Bridge:* small township attractively located on the Derwent River. Accommodation, store, fuel. (*128/169*)
   Turn **NW** for the 12km return drive to **Cynthia Bay** (Alt 735m) on Lake St Clair**, a glacial lake surrounded by spectacular mountains. Walking tracks lead along the lake, and to Mt Rufus (great views**). Lake cruises* are available. Additional walks can be done at northern end of lake - heed all weather warnings. Accommodation, kiosk.

Undulating country offers good views* as the route crosses the Central Plateau. Frost hollows and woodlands are common.
Bronte Park turnoff: (*154/143*) A short distance **N** is **Bronte Park*** (Alt 675m), a locality offering accommodation. Popular with fishers. **Rest area** adjacent.
Undulating country supports some small glacial lakes (Bronte Lagoon/Brady Lake/Lake Binney) located near the road. Trout fishing, boating and canoeing are available, but heed weather warnings. **Rest area** at Tungatinah Lagoon.
Hilly country supports forests where the route crosses the Nive River valley.

Tungatinah-Tarraleah Power Station: hydro-power stations located near the road.

Tarraleah (Alt 589m; Pop 500): small hydro town, located just **E** off the A10, which services the nearby power stations. Accommodation, stores, fuel. (*173/124*)

Hilly country supports eucalypt forests.
Lookout* provides good views of the Derwent River valley and Waytinah Lagoon. (*184/113*)
Hilly country supports forests with grazing country further east.

Ouse (Pop 150): small rural township. Store, fuel. (*207/90*)

Lawrenny: farming locality.

Hamilton (Alt 85m; Pop 150):* small country town set among rolling hills. Historic buildings*. Accommodation, stores, fuel. (*224/73*)

Lookout* provides good views overlooking the Derwent River valley.
Hilly country supports farmlands.
Gretna: farming locality. (*241/56*)
Rosegarland: farming locality. (*243/54*)
Undulating country supports farmlands*. Hop farms and oast houses are common.
Hayes: farming locality.

NEW NORFOLK (Alt 30m; Pop 6200):* sizeable country and historic town. Numerous historic buildings*. The Oast House museum* and the Old Colony Inn (museum) are worth seeing. Other interesting buildings include St Mathew's Church (1823), Tasmania's oldest, and the Bush Inn, Australia's oldest continuously licenced pub. Full town facilities. (*259/38*)

Accommodation
Bush Inn, 49 Montague St, ©03 6261 2011, ❂$55
New Norfolk Caravan Park, The Esplanade (1.5kmN), ©03 6261 1268, ❂Site: $15 Van: $35-$45

Undulating country offers good views* of the Derwent River estuary and nearby farmlands.

Granton: small township on the junction of the A10 and Highway 1. Store, fuel. (**276/21**) Head **S** on Highway 1 for Hobart. *Turn* **W** *onto the A10 for New Norfolk.*

South of Granton the route follows the Northern Outlet and Brooker Highway into Hobart, passing through Hobart's northern suburbs. Good views* overlooking the Derwent Estuary.

HOBART (Alt 10m; Pop 129000):** state capital of Tasmania situated on the Derwent River estuary. Interesting historic city with many things to see and do. The CBD has many historic buildings* dating from the 1830s (take a walking tour), the Tasmanian Museum and Art Gallery*, the Allport Library and the Museum of Fine Arts. Nearby Constitution Dock** should not be missed (great views; old seaport atmosphere) and the Maritime Museum of Tasmania* is close by. Salamanca Place** has some excellent colonial architecture (markets on Saturday morning); also here is the science centre and theme park Antarctic Adventure. Up the hill lies Battery Point**, probably the best preserved Georgian-style suburb in Australia; see Arthur Circus*, Kelly Steps*, St George's Anglican Church and Van Dieman's Land Folk Museum*. Just east of the CBD is the Royal Tasmanian Botanic Gardens** with great views. Full town facilities. (**297/0**) Head **N** on Highway 1 for Granton.

Out of the city centre are many sights worth visiting. Mt Wellington, a high peak rising behind Hobart, offers great views** (take warm clothing whatever the weather down below, this mountain is 1270m high and alpine!). Walking trails on the mountain lead to the summit. En route the montane village of Fern Tree** is worth a stop. At the foot of the mountain is the Cascade Brewery** (Australia's oldest) set in a wonderful location. Mt Nelson, in the southern suburbs, also offers good views*. Ten kilometres south of Hobart, on the Channel Highway, is the Taroona Shot Tower* (48m high tower offering good views). A little further on is King-

Victoria Dock, Hobart, Tas

ston, an outer suburb of Hobart, where there is good swimming and boating, and the Commonwealth Antarctic Division Headquarters which has a great Antarctic display*.

Accommodation

Hobart Mid-City Hotel, 96 Bathurst St, ✆03 6234 6333, ✪$110-$150

Mayfair Motel, 17 Cavell St, ✆03 6231 1188, ✪$85-$105

Fountainside Motor Inn, Cnr Brooker Hwy/Liverpool St, ✆03 6234 2911, ✪$85-$110

Marquis of Hastings Hotel/Motel, 209 Brisbane St, ✆03 6234 3541, ✪$80

Welcome Stranger Hotel, Cnr Harrington/Davey Sts, ✆03 6223 6655, ✪$65

Brunswick Hotel, 72 Liverpool St, ✆03 6234 3737, ✪$55

Treasure Island Caravan Park, Main Rd, Berriedale (9kmN), ✆03 6249 2379, ✪Site: $16 Van: $40-$70

Elwick Cabin and Tourist Park, 19 Goodwood Rd, Glenorchy (7kmN), ✆03 6272 7115, ✪Site: $16 Van: $35-$65

Sandy Bay Caravan Park, 1 Peel St, Sandy Bay (1.5kmS), ✆03 6225 1264, ✪Site: $17 Van: $40-$60

Highway 1 (Midland or Heritage Highway)
Hobart-Launceston
This major route connects Hobart with Launceston and the northern coast. It is a relatively fast highway for Tasmania, by-passing many historical towns en route - these towns should

not be missed. The countryside is mostly farmed and settled, with many areas having a cultivated 'English' appearance. Always in the background though are Tasmania's brooding mountains. Take your time to enjoy this countryside.

Warnings: take care of increased traffic north of Hobart/south of Launceston.

DAY 3: HOBART-LAUNCESTON via Ross

Road to Take: Heritage Highway 1
Grade 1
Total Distance: 198km (2:45)
Intermediate Distances:

	Km	Hours
Hobart-Oatlands	84	(1:20)
Oatlands-Ross	38	(0:30)
Ross-Launceston	76	(0:55)

Regions Traversed: The South-East, Midlands

▼

HOBART (Alt 10m; Pop 129000):** state capital of Tasmania. For more information see Day 2. (*0/198*) From Hobart the route follows the Brooker Highway and Northern Outlet to the south of Granton. Good views* overlooking the Derwent Estuary.

Granton: small township on the junction of the A10 and Highway 1. Store, fuel. (*21/177*) Proceed **N** on Highway 1 for Brighton. *Proceed **S** on Highway 1 for Hobart.*

Derwent River estuary is crossed by a long causeway and bridge. Good views*.
Bridgewater turnoff: (*23/175*) Turn here for **Bridgewater**, a large town on the northern side of the Derwent River estuary. Full town facilities.

Brighton/Pontville (Pop 1125): small farming township. Nearby Pontville* (2km north) is an old convict garrison township. Jordon River bridge* is worth seeing. Accommodation, stores, fuel. (*26/172*)

Undulating country supports farmlands. Good views. En route the localities of Manalore, Bagdad and Dysart are passed. Mangalore Teir rises to the west.

Kempton (Alt 198m; Pop 340):* old colonial township, located just off the highway, dating from the 1820s. Historic buildings* including St Mary's Anglican Church. **Rest area** nearby. Store, fuel. (*49/149*)

Melton Mowbray (Alt 183m): farming locality just west of Highway 1. Black Tier (775m) is located further out to the west. (*55/143*)
Hilly country offers good views. Spring Hill (574m) lies to the west.

Jericho (Alt 400m; Pop 340): farming township located just **W** off the highway. Store, fuel. (*71/127*)

Oatlands (Alt 432m; Pop 550):** interesting historic town located just **E** of the highway and well worth visiting. The town contains numerous fine examples of Georgian architecture**, best viewed on a walk around. Callington Mill* is also worth seeing. Next to the town is the Lake Dulverton wildlife sanctuary. **Rest area** nearby. Accommodation, stores, fuel. (*84/114*)

Hilly country supports farmlands. Scenic vistas*. **Rest area** at Vincent Hill. The localities of Antill Ponds, Woodbury and Tunbridge are passed en route. Note the scattered rocks piled up in the fields.

Ross (Alt 180m; Pop 280)**: small historic garrison township located just **E** of the highway and well worth visiting. See Ross Bridge** (third oldest in Australia and one of the prettiest), numerous historic buildings* and visit the Tasmanian Wool Centre museum*. Accommodation, stores, fuel. (*122/76*)

Undulating country offers good views*. Mt Augusta (328m) lies to the west.

DAY THREE

HOBART
21
Granton
5
Brighton/ Pontville
1:20
23
Kempton
RA
22
Jericho
13
Oatlands
RA
0:30
38
RA
Ross
10
Campbell Town
RA
0:55
47
Perth
19
LAUNCESTON

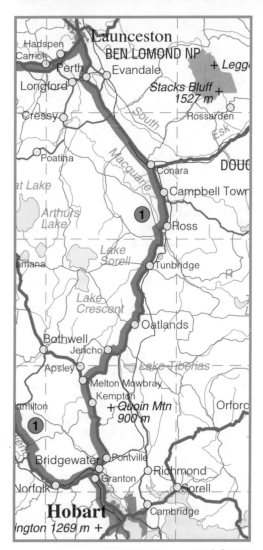

Detail of MAP 1

Campbell Town (Alt 186m; Pop 880):** former garrison town. Many historic buildings** including Campbell Town Inn*, St Luke's Church, the Grange, Foxhunters Return, and the Red Bridge*, all dating from the late 1820s to the 1840s. The Heritage Highway Museum* is worth seeing. Picnics are possible at Wardlaw Park. Accommodation, stores, fuel. (*132/66*)

Low rises and plains (this is Tasmania's flattest countryside) support grazing and farming. Dis-

tant views. Localities past en route include Conara (old railway junction), Cleveland (old coaching township, worth a quick look), and Epping Forest. **Rest area**. (*144/54*)

Evandale turnoff: (*176/22*) Turn **E** for the 10km return trip to Evandale** (Pop 850), Tasmania's best preserved town, with historic buildings dating back to the 1820s. (It is possible to rejoin Heritage Highway at Bredalbane via Western Junction.)

Perth (Pop 1550):** historic old garrison town dating from the 1830s. Accommodation, stores, fuel. (*179/19*)

Low rises support farmlands; distant views.
Breadalbane: locality. Evandale Road joins here. (*185/13*) Head **N** for Launceston. *Head **SE** for Evandale via Western Junction, otherwise stay on Highway 1 for Perth.*

LAUNCESTON (Alt 24m; Pop 67000):** regional centre and Australia's third oldest city (1805) located on the Tamar River. Plenty to see in the CBD: historic buildings such as Macquarie House*, Old Umbrella Shop*, Queen Victoria Museum and Art Gallery*, and the Johnstone and Wilmot Warehouse. Good parks include City Park**, Princess Square*, Royal Park, Punchbowl Reserve (rhododenrons) and Windmill Hill Reserve. Just out of the CBD is Pennyroyal World (rides, cruises), and Cataract Gorge** with walking trails and a chairlift*. Full town facilities. (*198/0*) *Head **S** on Highway for Breadalbane.*

Accommodation
Colonial Motor Inn, 31 Elizabeth St (1kmS), ©03 6331 6588, ●$95-$135
Parklane Motel, 9 Brisbane St (1kmE), ©03 6331 4233, ●$75-$80
Mews Motel, 89 Margaret St (2kmSW), ©03 6331 2861, ●$65-$75
Tasmania Hotel, 191 Charles St, ©03 6331 7355, ●$60-$65
Sandors On The Park Hotel, 3 Brisbane St (1kmNE), ©03 6331 2055, ●$70-$95
Treasure Island Caravan Park, 94 Glen Dhu St (2kmS), ©03 6344 2600, ●Site: $18 Van: $40-$65

Road Trip 1

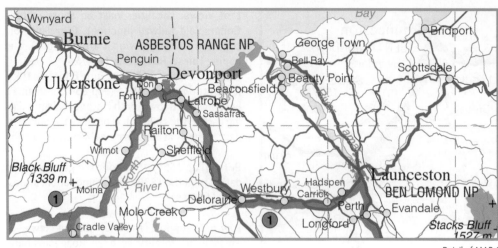

Detail of MAP 1

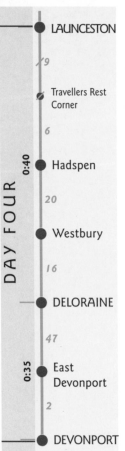

DAY FOUR

0:40

0:35

LAUNCESTON

9

Travellers Rest
Corner

6

Hadspen

20

Westbury

16

DELORAINE

47

East
Devonport

2

DEVONPORT

DAY 4: LAUNCESTON-DEVONPORT
via Deloraine

Roads to Take: Highway 1, B54
Grade 1
Total Distance: 100km (1:15)
Intermediate Distances:

	Km	Hours
Launceston-Deloraine	51	(0:40)
Deloraine-Devonport	49	(0:35)

Regions Traversed: The North-West

▼

LAUNCESTON (Alt 24m; Pop 67000):** regional centre. For more information see Day 3. (*0/100*) Head **S** to the Hobart/Devonport intersection and then turn **W** for Devonport.

Travellers Rest Corner: (*9/91*) Turn **W** for Hadspen onto the B54. *Turn **N** for Launceston.*

Hadspen (Pop 1500):* part residential suburb/ part historic town. Some historic buildings including Hadspen Gaol* and Red Feather Inn*. A short distance west is Entally Historic House. Accommodation, stores, fuel. (*15/85*)

Carrick: historic locality. Worth seeing is the very photogenic Carrick Mill*. (*20/80*)

Low rises support farmlands. Mountain views to the south.

Hagley: farming locality. Stay on the B54 for Deloraine. *Stay on the B54 for Hadspen.* (*30/70*)

Westbury (Alt 183m; Pop 1300):* old town with many historic buildings* including White House*. Accommodation, stores, fuel. (*35/65*)

Undulating country exhibits attractive farmlands. Southward mountain views, including towards the Cluan Tiers.

DELORAINE (Alt 235m; Pop 2100):* attractive country town situated on the Meander River. Good views* of the Great Western Tiers. Numerous historic buildings*. Several galleries and arts and crafts outlets. The town park is pleasant for picnics. Full town facilities. (*51/49*) Join the Highway 1 **N** for Devonport. *Join the B54 **E** for Hadspen.*

This town is a good base to visit Trowunna Wildlife Park* (14km west along Mole Creek Road) and Mole Creek Karst National Park* (about 40km west along Mole Creek Road) - great limestone caves with tours available.

Accommodation
Mountain View Country Inn, 144 Emu Bay Rd, ☎03 6362 2633, ✪$75-$95
Apex Caravan Park, 51 West Pde, ☎03 6362 2345, ✪Site: $14

Undulating country passes through grazing lands and eucalypt forests. The localities of Elizabeth Town and Sassafras are passed en route. Farmlands offer good views*.

East Devonport: suburb of Devonport. (**98/2**) Follow the signs to the *Spirit of Tasmania* terminal. Ship desparts Tuesday, Thursday and Satur-day evenings. Arrival time in Melbourne is around 8.30am. Continue on for Devonport.

DEVONPORT (Alt 8m; Pop 25400): large regional centre. For more information see Day 1. (**100/0**) *Follow the signs S onto Highway 1 for Deloraine.*

▲

Road Trip 2
The Great Inland Way

Gilgandra-Mackay
Total Distance: 1494km
Suggested Travelling Time: 5 days

> *Strike a path from country New South Wales to coastal Mackay*
>
> See the opal town of Lightning Ridge, scenic Roma, the impressive Carnarvon Gorge, Rainworth Fort near Springsure, and the sugar town of Mackay.

The Great Inland Way
(Castlereagh/Carnarvon/Dawson/Gregory/ Peak Downs Highways)

The Great Inland Way provides southern Australians with the short path to central and northern Queensland. Taking this road trip will give travellers a sense of the vastness of Australia's inland. Flat plains with long stretches of straight road are interrupted occasionally by undulating country, with the countryside becoming quite mountainous in the vicinity of the Carnarvon Ranges. Vast tracts of cropping country and cleared grazing lands are peppered at intervals by western-style towns.

For travellers with time to spare, the towns and townships along the way have much to offer: the Lightning Ridge Opal Fields, Roma's grand and elegant buildings, Springsure's delightful setting, Clermont's intriguing history. This route also provides ready access to Central Queensland's best natural features, contained within the Carnarvon National Park. It is readily accessed by southern Australians via the Newell Highway at Gilgandra. Travellers from south-east Queensland can travel along the Warrego Highway to Roma.

The Climate

The cooler season between May and September is the ideal time to visit. Maximum temperatures are generally mild to warm (around 24C) with the odd cooler or warmer day thrown in. Nights are cool to cold, with minimum temperatures around 5C, dropping to freezing in mid-winter. Either side of the cooler months, higher temperatures will be experienced. Generally days are clear and sunny with virtually no rain.

Summers are hot, and sometimes humid, with maximum temperatures in the low to mid-thirties. Nights too are often warm and may be uncomfortable. Summers are also the time for rain or showers. During wetter periods, summer rains can be intense, and the wet weather often extends well into autumn.

Capital City Connections
Distances in kilometres
SYDNEY-GILGANDRA
via Great Western/Mitchell/Newell Highways

	Intermediate	Total
Sydney	0	0
Bathurst	207	207
Dubbo	205	412
Gilgandra	65	477

MELBOURNE-GILGANDRA
via Hume/Goulburn Valley/Newell Highways

	Intermediate	Total
Melbourne	0	0
Narrandera	422	422
Gilgandra	459	881

BRISBANE-ROMA
via Warrego Highway

	Intermediate	Total
Brisbane	0	0
Toowoomba	129	129
Miles	211	340
Roma	141	481

The Route
Distances in kilometres

	Intermediate	Total
Gilgandra	0	0
Lightning Ridge	289	289
Roma	426	715
Emerald	397	1112

| Clermont | 106 | 1218 |
| Mackay | 276 | 1494 |

Castlereagh/Carnarvon Highways
Gilgandra-Rolleston

The route crosses the vast plains of north-west New South Wales and the plains and low rises of the Western Downs of south-central Queensland, country given over to broadacre-cropping farmlands. In the right light, or the right place, one can feel the immensity of this near-outback country and appreciate its grandeur. North of Injune, the countryside changes to one of forested hills and rugged sandstone escarpments as the route traverses the Carnarvon Ranges.

Warnings: beware of stock and kangaroos at night; avoid night travelling if at all possible. Roads subjected to flooding.

DAY 1: GILGANDRA-LIGHTNING RIDGE via Walgett

Road to Take: Castlereagh Highway (Great Inland Way)
Grade 1
Total Distance: 289km (3:20)
Intermediate Distances:

	Km	Hours
Gilgandra-Coonamble	95	(1:10)
Coonamble-Walgett	116	(1:20)
Walgett-Lightning Ridge	78	(0:50)

Average Vehicles per Day: 350 south of Lightning Ridge
Regions Traversed: North-West Plains

▼

GILGANDRA (Alt 278m; Pop 5150):* interesting agricultural town characterised by its many windmills. Worth seeing: Gilgandra Observatory* (privately owned), Gilgandra Museum*, Rural Museum* (in Cooee March Memorial Park), Hitchen House Museum*, Orana Cactus World, flora and fauna reserve. Tourist drives. Full town facilities. (*0/289*) *Connecting Route A connects.*

DAY ONE
- GILGANDRA
- 51
- 1:10
- Gulargambone
- 44
- COONAMBLE
- RA
- 1:20 / 116
- WALGETT
- 72
- 0:50 / Lightning Ridge turnoff
- 6
- LIGHTNING RIDGE

Accommodation
Cooee Motel, Cnr Newell Hwy/Hargraves St, ©02 6847 1511, ○$50-$70
Orana Windmill Motel, 40 Warren Rd, ©02 6847 2404, ○$60-$70
Castlereagh Motor Inn, Newell Hwy (2.5kmE), ©02 6847 2697, ○$50-$60
Bungalow Motel, 19 Castlereagh St, ©02 6847 1271, ○$45-$55
Gilgandra Lodge Motel, 178 Warren Rd (2kmW), ©02 6847 2431, ○$50
Gilgandra Rotary Caravan Park, Newell Hwy, ©02 6847 2423, ○Site: $15 Van: $35-$50
Rest-a-While Caravan Park, 108 Miller St (1kmN), ©02 6847 2252, ○Site: $12 Van: $30-$35
Barneys Caravan Park, Castlereagh Hwy (2kmN), ©02 6847 2636, ○Site: $13 Van: $25-$30

Plains and low rises support wheat and cereal cropping. Good eastwards views towards the Warrumbungle Ranges (afternoons best).

Gulargambone (Alt 225m; Pop 500): small agricultural town with some appeal. A good spot for picnics on the banks of the Castlereagh River. Accommodation, stores, fuel. (*51/238*)

Plains support cereal cropping and grazing. Very attractive area after the winter rains. Distant views to the south-east towards the Warrumbungle Ranges.

COONAMBLE (Alt 180m; Pop 3000):* attractive agricultural and grazing town with many interesting buildings. A walk along the main street is pleasant. The historical museum is worth seeing. Full town facilities. (*95/194*)
Accommodation
Castlereagh Lodge Motel, 79-81 Aberford St, ©02 6822 1999, ○$60
Coonamble Motel, Castlereagh St, ©02 6822 1400, ○$55-$65
Cypress Motel, Castlereagh Hwy (1kmS), ©02 6822 1788, ○$55-$60
Riverside Caravan Park, Castlereagh Hwy (1kmS), ©02 6822 1926, ○Site: $12 Van: $35

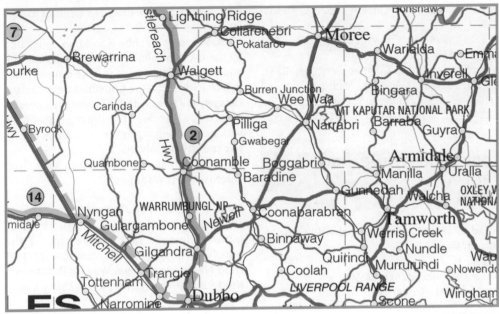

Detail of MAP 3

Plains support grasslands with some low trees. Those with a drooping crown are most likely weeping myalls, a type of acacia. The small semi-erect shrubs, with somewhat twisted trunks about two to three metres high, are warrior bushes. Wheat farms occupy the southern plains. **Rest area**. (*158/131*)
Castlereagh River* crossing reasonably pleasant. (*164/125*)
Plains support wide tracts of grassland. Broad views.

WALGETT (Alt 132m; Pop 2400): interesting grazing town with an outback appearance. Good fishing on the adjacent rivers (licence required). A sizeable Aboriginal population means some cultural displays and activities are available - enquire locally. Worth noting are the levee banks which encircle the town. Full town facilities. (*211/78*)

Accommodation
Walgett Motel, 14 Fox St, ©02 6828 1355, ✪$55-$65
Coolabah Motel, 95 Wee Waa St, ©02 6828 1366, ✪$65-$80

Floodplains of the Namoi and Barwon Rivers exhibit river red gum-lined banks.
Plains support vast tracts of sparse eucalypt woodlands with a grassy understorey. The country north of the Barwon River has an outback 'feel' to it.
Lightning Ridge turnoff: locality only; no facilities. (*283/6*) Turn **E** for Lightning Ridge (6km). *Turn **S** for Walgett.*

LIGHTNING RIDGE (Alt 115m; Pop 2700):** commonly referred to as 'The Ridge'. Interesting opal mining town well worth visiting (spend a day here at least). Much to see and do including fossicking in official areas, noodling (ask first), opal showrooms, artesian bore baths* (yum), bottle house museum*, mine tours and visits, precious stone fossicking area, the Big Opal, and more. If exploring the diggings watch your step; there are many open shafts. When you get sick of opals, wander the town as there are many characters to meet. Full town facilities. (*289/0*)

Accommodation
Black Opal Motel, Opal St, ©02 6829 0518, ✪$70

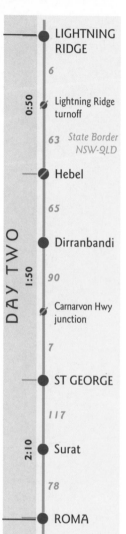

LIGHTNING RIDGE

6

Lightning Ridge turnoff

63 *State Border NSW-QLD*

Hebel

65

Dirranbandi

90

Carnarvon Hwy junction

7

ST GEORGE

117

Surat

78

ROMA

0:50 · 1:50 · 2:10

DAY TWO

Lightning Ridge Motel, Onyx St, ©02 6829 0304, ♥$70
Wallangulla Motel, Cnr Morella/Agate Sts, ©02 6829 0542
Crocodile Caravan & Camping Park, Morella St, ©02 6829 0437, ♥Site: $12 Van: $40
Lightning Ridge Caravan Park, Harlequin St, ©02 6829 0532, ♥Site: 14 Van: $35-$50

DAY 2: LIGHTNING RIDGE-ROMA
via St George

Road to Take: Castlereagh Highway (Great Inland Way)
Grade 1
Total Distance: 426km (4:50)
Intermediate Distances:

	Km	Hours
Lightning Ridge-Hebel	69	(0:50)
Hebel-St George	163	(1:50)
St George-Roma	194	(2:10)

Average Vehicles per Day: 150 near Angledool
Regions Traversed: North-West Plains, Western Downs

LIGHTNING RIDGE (Alt 115m; Pop 2700):** interesting opal mining town. For more information see Day 1. (*0/426*)

Lightning Ridge turnoff: locality only; no facilities. (*6/420*) Turn **N** for Hebel. *Turn **E** for Lightning Ridge (6km).*
Coocoran Lake:* normally dry lake located west of the road.
Low rises with occasional rocky outcrops support low eucalypt woodlands. Occasional fair views from the tops of rises. Elsewhere are small stony plains. The rises are typical of the opal-bearing country in this district.
Weetalibah Creek:* picnic area.
Jim Harper bridge (Narran River*) is a bush camping and picnic area.
New Angledool*, a short distance off the road, is an interesting small locality of historic build-

---

ings. Worth a quick look. No facilities except for a phone.
Plains* support shrubby woodlands dominated by the eucalypt bimble box with mulga in the understorey. Other trees include cypress pines (which look a little like Christmas trees), belahs (straggly tall trees without leaves; their needles are actually branchlets), and wilga (squat trees with dense overhanging crowns). Quite attractive country hereabouts.
State border between New South Wales and Queensland. (*64/362*)

Hebel (Alt 150m; Pop 20):* small grazing township and former customs post. Historic buildings. A pleasant spot for a picnic by the waterhole. Accommodation, store, fuel. (*69/357*) Head **NE** on Great Inland Way for Dirranbandi. *Head **S** on Castlereagh Hwy for Lightning Ridge.*

Plains (with some recent clearings) support tracts of eucalypt woodlands with a shrubby understorey. These woodlands are rather attractive in the late afternoon light.

Dirranbandi (Alt 172m; Pop 450): small grazing and cropping town. Accomodation, stores, fuel. (*134/292*)
Accommodation
Dirranbandi Motel, Cnr Moore/Richardson Sts, ©07 4625 8299, ♥$65
Dirranbandi Caravan Park, 13 Railway St, ©07 4625 8350, ♥Site: $12 Van: $25-$30

Noondoo: railway siding. Plains to the west recently cleared for cropping. (*154/272*)
Plains virtually completely cleared for agriculture. Cotton cropping is common south of St George (irrigation farms in this area). Further south the land is given over to broadacre wheat farms.
Carnarvon Highway junction: (*224/201*). Turn **NW** for St George. *Turn **S** for Dirranbandi.*

ST GEORGE (Alt 201m; Pop 2500): pleasant agricultural and grazing town located on the banks of the Balonne River* (attractive area, picnic facilities, fishing). Interesting town for a wan-

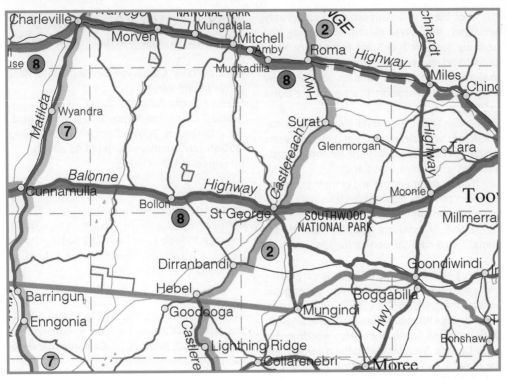

Detail of MAP 3

der. Murals* are worth seeing, as is the Unique Egg* (Balonne Sports Store - have a look). Attractive bauhinias* line Victoria Street. Full town facilities. **(231/194)** *Road Trip 8 connects. Stay on Carnarvon Hwy heading* **NE** *for Surat. Stay on Carnarvon Hwy heading* **SE** *for Dirranbandi.*

Accommodation

Merino Motor Inn, 78 Victoria St, ©07 4625 3333, ©$75-$85

Balonne Motel, 52 Victoria St, ©07 4625 5155, ©$60-$65

Kamarooka Tourist Park, 56 Victoria St, ©07 4625 3120, ©Site: $14 Van: $35-$50

St George Tourist Park, 221 Victoria St, ©07 4625 5778, ©Site: $12 Van: $25

Farmlands support small hobby farms.

Low rises (offering only fair views) support extensive tracts of either mulga shrublands and/or eucalypt woodlands occasionally interspersed with clearings given over to grazing.

Donga Creek:* small creek crossing with shady waterholes. Hereabouts northbound travellers will see their first (small) bottle trees; bean trees also become increasingly common.

Historic Site:* site of Rosehill Mail Change Station. There is a monument and picnic area. Fair views. **(306/119)**

Farmlands occupy generally cleared undulating country and low rises. Grazing and cropping is common. Fair views including a low flat-top range visible to the east.

Surat (Alt 250m; Pop 480):* attractive small town located on the banks of the Balonne River* (picnic facilities and river walks). Many photogenic historic buildings to see, as well as the Cobb and Co Museum*. Enquire locally about fossil localities in the area, and access to Beranga Lagoon to view the waterlilies (Febuary to May). Accommodation, stores, fuel. **(348/78)**

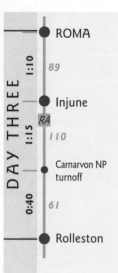

DAY THREE

ROMA	
1:10	89
Injune	
1:15 RA	110
Carnarvon NP turnoff	
0:40	61
Rolleston	

Plains of black soil support eucalypt grassy woodlands with areas cleared for grazing and cropping. Just north of Surat is a winery while four kilometres north of town are some original corduroys*, lengths of sandalwood laid over boggy ground to support coaches in the horse and buggy days.

Undulating country exhibits eucalypt shrubby woodlands with clearings for grazing and some cropping. Near the Condamine turnoff is an attractive cypress pine woodland*.

Farmlands support grazing and cropping country. Lookout* provides reasonable views over farmlands surrounding Roma.

Warrego Hwy junction: (**423/3**) Turn **W** for Roma. *Turn* **S** *onto Carnarvon Hwy for Surat.*

ROMA (Alt 300m; Pop 6770):* large grazing and agricultural town with many photogenic buildings. A park on the eastern edge of town contains the Old Lenroy Slab Hut*, The Big Rig*, Duck Pond and bottle trees. Also worth seeing is Bottle Tree Avenue* (Wyndham Street) and the Clay Mural (Cultural Centre). Full town facilities. (**426/0**) *Road Trip 8 connects. /Head* **E** *on Warrego Hwy for Carnarvon Hwy turnoff.*

Accommodation

Overlander Homestead Motel, Warrego Hwy, 07 4622 3555, ✪$85
Starlight Motor Inn, 20B Bowen St, ✆07 4622 2666, ✪$80
Bottle Tree Gardens Motel, 22 Bowen St, ✆07 4622 6111, ✪$65
Bryants Motel, Cnr Bowen/Gregory Sts, ✆07 4622 3777, ✪$75
Palms Motel, 6 Bowen St (1.5kmE), ✆07 4622 6464, ✪$45
Villa Holiday Park, Injune Rd (1kmN), ✆07 4622 1309, ✪Site: $22 Van: $40-$60
Roma Big Rig Van Park, 4 McDowall St, ✆07 4622 2538, ✪Site: $16 Van: $28-$55
Palms Caravan Park, 6 Bowen St (1.5kmE), ✆07 4622 6464, ✪Site: $12 Van: $25

DAY 3: ROMA-ROLLESTON
via Injune and Carnarvon Gorge

Road to Take: Carnarvon Developmental Road (Great Inland Way)
Grade 1 Roma-Rolleston direct
Grade 3 Carnarvon National Park access road
Total Distance: 260km Roma-Rolleston direct (350km via Carnarvon Gorge) (3:05 direct)
Intermediate Distances:

	Km	Hours
Roma-Injune	89	(1:10)
Injune-Carnarvon NP turnoff	110	(1:15)
Carnarvon NP turnoff-Rolleston	61	(0:40)

Average Vehicles per Day: 250 north of Injune
Regions Traversed: Western Downs, Central Highlands

ROMA (Alt 300m; Pop 6770):* large grazing and agricultural town. For more information see Day 2. (**0/260**) Head **N** on Carnarvon Developmental Road for Rolleston.

Bungil Creek:* picnic area at crossing. (**18/242**)
Undulating country offers fair to reasonable views, especially in the more hilly areas. Eucalypt and cypress pine woodlands are common, although many large areas are cleared for grazing or, just north of Roma, cropping.

Cutting:* the road slices through some low sandstone hills. Noteworthy as this is one of the main intake beds of the Great Artesian Basin. (**39/221**)

Mt Eumamurrin: low hill rising above the general level. Just north are views to the north-west towards high flat-top hills, including Mt Hutton (940m).

Bymount East: locality only; no facilities save for a country school. (**59/201**)

Great Dividing Range* marked by a sign and a slightly higher than usual rise in this undulating country.

Gunnewin: locality marked by a few houses and a ruin. No facilities. (**73/187**)

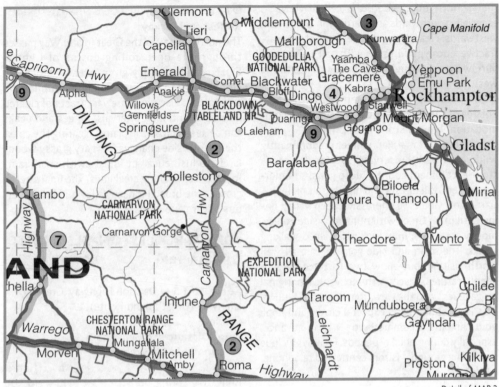

Detail of MAP 3

Injune (Alt 389m; Pop 395):* small grazing and timber town with some character. Interesting pub. Worth stopping for a while to absorb the atmosphere. Accommodation, stores, fuel. (**89/171**)

Hilly country offers fair views*. Ironbark and cypress pine woodlands are common, with some large clearings given over to grazing.

Low ranges offer good views* of wild country. Eucalypt and cypress pine woodlands are common. Numerous rivers have their source hereabouts.

Ranges form part of the spectacular Carnarvon Range. A very scenic area* with numerous clifflines, eucalypt forests on hillslopes and ironbark woodlands on the flats. Keep an eye out for bottle trees and softwood scrubs (dry rainforests*) on the western side of the road. Forms part of the Moolayember Gorge section of Carnarvon National Park.

Moolayember Creek: a narrow valley. Great views* of clifflines and tall forests. **Rest area** is a good spot for picnics. (**174/86**)

Undulating country has been cleared for grazing. Good to excellent views*, especially southwards towards escarpment country and prominent white sandstone clifflines. Eastwards are views* of the Expedition Range escarpments. Remnant bottle trees are visible in paddocks.

Carnarvon National Park turnoff: locality only; no facilities. (**199/61**) Turn **W** for Carnarvon Gorge - see Side Trip below.

Side Trip
Carnarvon Gorge access road (Grade 3) 90km return
Warning: unsealed road subjected to flooding and may be impassable in wet weather; road surface may be rough - allow plenty of time.

Undulating country has been mostly cleared for grazing - good views*.

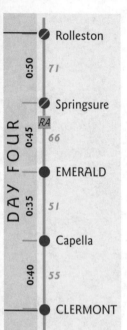

DAY FOUR

0:50	Rolleston
71	
0:45 RA	Springsure
66	
0:35	EMERALD
51	
0:40	Capella
55	
	CLERMONT

Hilly country offers good to excellent views**, especially southwards and Carnarvon Gorge road westwards. Near the escarpment country are attractive eucalypt forests* with tall palms and burrawangs. Consuelo Peak (1174m) lies to the west.

Oasis Lodge: private accommodation located outside of the park. An attractive area*. Accommodation, limited store, fuel. (37/8)

Carnarvon National Park: large, predominantly wilderness park preserving spectacular sandstone escarpment country, deep gorges, rainforest pockets, tall forests and high basalt plateaux. Carnarvon Gorge:** impressive deep valley lining Carnarvon Creek with numerous side gorges, mostly accessible from well maintained walking tracks. The main and side gorges** are all well worth visiting, but allow two to three days to see all features. Also worth seeing are Aboriginal art galleries* and the view from Boolimba Bluff**. This is a popular park; expect a crowd and book your camping accommodation well in advance, especially during holiday periods. Facilities include a camping ground, visitors centre and telephone. (45/0)

Undulating country supports ironbark, belah (shaggy looking trees) and gum woodlands partially cleared for grazing. Fair views.

Plains and low rises support eucalypt woodlands and paddocks cleared for grazing. Views to low and distant ranges.

Low ranges* line the road for a short distance, offering good views. The prominent hill at the southern end is Mt Ceres (436m).

Rolleston (Alt 206m; Pop 130):* small grazing and agricultural township. Interesting buildings. Pleasant park at the top end of town. An attractive area on the nearby Comet River*. Accommodation, stores, fuel. (260/0) Head **S** on Carnarvon Hwy for Roma.

Accommodation
Rolleston Hotel-Motel, Cnr Warrijo/Comet Sts, ℗07 4984 3288, ✆$60
Rolleston Caravan Park, Comet St, ℗07 4984 3145, Site: ✆$12

Dawson/Gregory/Peak Downs Highways
Rolleston-Mackay
The northern part of the Great Inland Way passes through the open rolling downs of Central Queensland, country given over to broadacre cropping. Crops include sorghum, sunflowers and cotton. Elsewhere are vast tracts of cleared grazing country. At intervals, ranges and peaks can be seen across the plains. Nearing the coast the countryside changes from dry grassy woodlands to lush eucalypt forests with small rainforest patches along creeklines. The final stretch crosses the broad Pioneer Valley and its numerous sugar cane farms.

DAY 4: ROLLESTON-CLERMONT via Emerald

Roads to Take: Dawson Highway, Gregory Highway (Great Inland Route)
Grade 1
Total Distance: 243km (2:50)
Intermediate Distances:

	Km	Hours
Rolleston-Springsure	71	(0:50)
Springsure-Emerald	66	(0:45)
Emerald-Capella	51	(0:35)
Capella-Clermont	55	(0:40)

Average Vehicles per Day: 600 south of Clermont
Regions Traversed: Central Highlands

Rolleston (Alt 206m; Pop 130):* small farming township. For more information see Day 3. (0/243) Head **W** on Dawson Hwy for Springsure.

Low rises support vast cleared tracts of black soil downs given over to cropping and grazing. Distant southwards views to sandstone escarpments. Westward views towards the Staircase Range. Some tracts of eucalypt grassy woodlands remain. At night the glowing lights from large coal mines can be seen to the north.

Ranges* provide good eastwards views. These sandstone escarpments are known as the Staircase Range. The countryside is either partially

cleared for grazing or supports ironbark woodlands with zamia palms in the understorey.
Lookout:* good eastwards views overlooking the black soil downs and eastern slopes of the Staircase Range. Three kilometres east is an original cutting* of the first road over the range. (*49/194*) Low hills provide an attractive outlook.

Springsure (Alt 332m; Pop 950):* interesting historic town set among rocky hills and ranges. Some old photogenic buildings can be seen, including the Springsure Hospital. The Rich Memorial Park* (giant windmill, museum) is also worth seeing. A short distance away (20km return along Wealwandangie Road) is Rainworth Fort**, a collection of old buildings and historic items that is well worth seeing. To the west lies the Minerva Hills National Park**, a small park preserving tracts of rugged uplands, rocky outcrops, clifflines and scenic viewpoints. Access is via the Dendle Scenic Drive, which leads off Tambo Road and is 30km return - road partially unsealed and sometimes rough. Accommodation, stores, fuel. (*71/172*) Head **N** on Gregory Hwy for Emerald. *Head SE on Dawson Hwy for Rolleston.*

Accommodation
Springsure Zamia Motel, 27 Charles St, ©07 4984 1455, ©$65
Springsure Roadhouse and Caravan Park, 86 William St, ©07 4984 1418, Site: ©$10 Van: $25-$55

Virgin Rock:* impressive rocky bluff overlooking Lion's Park. **Rest area**. (*75/168*)
Undulating country supports tracts of eucalypt woodlands with some clearings given over to grazing. Occasional good views westwards and southwards to nearby ranges. Some rocky outcrops can be seen, especially just north of Springsure.
Fernlees: locality composed of a few houses; no facilities except a telephone. (*99/144*)
Low rises virtually totally cleared for cropping and grazing. Fair southwards views towards distant ranges.
Gindie: locality only; no facilities. Settlement comprises a few houses and a silo. (*115/128*)

EMERALD (Alt 180m; Pop 10000): large, busy urban-looking town supporting the surrounding agricultural, grazing and irrigation farming industries as well as housing miners from nearby coal mines. The railway station* is of interest. Also worth seeing is the Pioneer Cottage* and fossilised tree* (at the town hall). Picnic area on the east side of town, with botanic gardens* nearby. Full town facilities. (*137/106*) *Road Trips 4 and 9 connect.*

Accommodation
The Emerald Meteor Motel, Cnr Opal/Egerton Sts, ©07 4982 1166, ©$95-$110
A & A Lodge Motel, Clermont St, ©07 4982 2355, ©$70-$80
Motel 707, Ruby St, ©07 4982 1707, ©$60
Emerald Star Hotel-Motel, Cnr Clermont/Egerton Sts, ©07 4982 1422, ©$55
Emerald Cabin and Caravan Village, 64 Opal St, Site: $20 Van: ©$30-$60
True Blue Gums Caravan Park, Andrews Rd (1kmSE), ©07 4982 2387, Site: ©$15
Lake Marboon Holiday Village, Lake Maraboon (18kmSW), ©07 4982 3677, ©Site: $15 Van: $50-$65

A short distance to the south is Lake Maraboon*. This small settlement, connected with the adjacent Fairbairn Dam, has a low-key resort set beside the impounded lake, with picnic facilities, boating, and more. Camping and accommodation available.

Low rises offer some fair views across country cleared for cropping and grazing. Elsewhere are patches of eucalypt woodlands.
Lookout* (or rather a vantage point) provides a broad but distant vista (binoculars help) of the Peak Range, a series of remnant volcanic plugs and lava flows rising above the slightly undulating Peak Downs. (*186/57*)

Capella (Alt 230m; Pop 1000):* small agricultural and grazing town with some appeal. Pioneer Village* is of interest. There is a pleasant picnic area by the railway station. Accommodation, stores, fuel. (*188/55*)

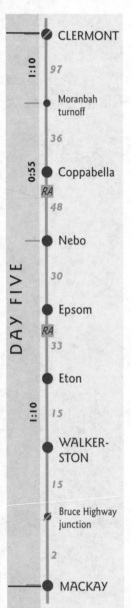

Road Trip 2

CLERMONT

1:10

97

Moranbah
turnoff

36

0:55

Coppabella

RA

48

Nebo

30

Epsom

RA

33

Eton

15

WALKER-
STON

15

Bruce Highway
junction

2

MACKAY

DAY FIVE

Accommodation

Bottlebrush Motel, 12 Abor St, ☏07 4984 9752, ✸$70-$75
Capella Motel, Slider St, ☏07 4984 9177, ✸$55
Capella Van Park, Langton St, ☏07 4984 9615, ✸Site: $13 Van: $25

Low rises and downs have been mostly cleared for cropping (typically sunflowers) and grazing. Distant eastward views towards the dramatic Peak Range.

CLERMONT (Alt 267m; Pop 2800):* interesting agricultural, grazing and coal mining town located just **S** off the highway. Many things to see including Hoods Lagoon/Ivan Bettridge Park**, which features a 1916 flood memorial, a hairy nose wombat sculpture and the 'piano in the tree'. Visit the amazing Historical Society Museum** and stroll past old buildings, the courthouse and the railway station. Enquire locally about fossicking sites. Full town facilities. (**243/0**) Road Trip 4 connects. /Head **S** along Gregory Hwy for Emerald.

Accommodation

Leo Hotel-Motel, Cnr Capella/Douglas Sts, ☏07 4983 1566, ✸$45
Grand Hotel-Motel, Capella St, ☏07 4983 1188, ✸$65
Clermont Motor Inn, Cnr Box/Capella Sts, ☏07 4983 3133, ✸$70
Clermont Caravan Park, Haig St, ☏07 4983 1927, ✸Site: $15 Van: $25-$35

A short distance along the Copperfield Road (12km return) lies the remains of the old copper mining settlement of Copperfield**. Features include the old Copperfield store* (containing old stock), cemetery (two kilometres further south) and Copperfield chimney** - best seen at dawn or dusk and very photogenic.

▲

DAY 5: CLERMONT-MACKAY via Nebo

Road to Take: Peak Downs Highway
Grade 1

Total Distance: 274km (3:15)
Intermediate Distances:

	Km	Hours
Clermont-Moranbah turnoff	97	(1:10)
Moranbah turnoff-Nebo	85	(0:55)
Nebo-Mackay	92	(1:10)

Average Vehicles per Day: 750
Regions Traversed: Fitzroy Basin, Central Coast

CLERMONT (Alt 267m; Pop 2800):* coal mining and farming town. For more information see Day 5. (*0/274*) Head **NE** along Peak Downs Hwy for Moranbah.

Low rises offer sweeping views across cleared country given over to cropping.
Wolfang Peak:* prominent volcanic peak rising above the undulating black soil lowlands. Part of the Peak Range National Park. Limited facilities; marked trails, good views. Definitely worth a look. (*36/238*)
Undulating country offers fair to good views across country given over to grazing and cropping. Elsewhere are tracts of grassy eucalypt woodlands.

Moranbah turnoff: roadhouse. Store, fuel. (*97/177*) A 26km return journey provides access to Moranbah (Alt 210m; Pop 7500), a large modern mining town servicing the Goonyella, Riverside and Peak Downs coal mines. Mine tours available. Full town facilities.

Undulating country has been partially cleared for grazing.

Coppabella (Alt 210m): small farming township. Store, fuel. **Rest area** nearby. (*133/141*)

Undulating country and low hills support tracts of grassy eucalypt woodlands with some clearings given over to grazing.

Nebo (Alt 195m; Pop 150):* interesting grazing township. Photogenic buildings, especially the pub. The deeply entrenched and mostly dry Nebo Creek lies at the end of the main street. It is worth deviating off the highway for a quick look around. Accommodation, stores, fuel. (*181/93*)

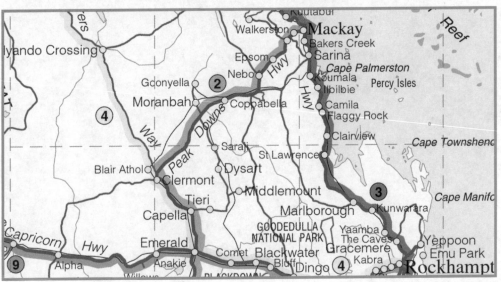

Detail of MAP 3

Undulating country and low hills offer fair to good views towards distant forest-clad ranges. The land is partially cleared for cattle grazing. Elsewhere are grassy eucalypt forests. Occasionally grass trees can be seen.

Low hills* rise above the road offering reasonable views. Westwards lies the prominent flat-top hill of Mt Fort Cooper (528m).

Epsom (Pop 5):* interesting bush pub set within a grassy valley. Accommodation, fuel. (*211/63*)

Ranges* offer fair views of eucalypt forests and rainforest patches along creeklines. The observant will see some cypress pines to the west of the ranges. This range, the Conners, forms a distinct boundary between the lush Pioneer Valley and the drier cattle country inland. **Rest area**. (*230/44*)

Eton (Alt 32m; Pop 300): small farming township surrounded by grazing lands and sugar cane fields. Accommodation, stores, fuel. (*244/30*)

Plains and low rises support sugar cane farms. Good views.

WALKERSTON (Alt 21m; Pop 1250): sugar cane farming town and residential area. Full town facilities. (*259/17*)

Plains support sugar cane farms.

Bruce Highway junction: (*274/2*) Turn **N** for Mackay. *Turn W onto Peak Downs Hwy for Walkerston.*

MACKAY (Alt 5m; Pop 59000): large regional centre and sugar town. For more information see Road Trip 3, Day 1. (*276/0*) *Road Trip 3 connects.*

Road Trip 3
The Tropical Coast

Rockhampton-Cape Tribulation
Total Distance: 1209km
Suggested Travelling Time: 6 days

Skirt the western fringe of the Great Barrier Reef

See the tropical towns of Rockhampton, Townsville and Cairns, the Whitsundays, Kuranda's scenic railway and skyway, Mossman Gorge, the Innisfail waterfront, the beaches of Bowen, Paronella Park, Mt Bartle Frere, the pristine Daintree National Park, and Cape Tribulation.

The Tropical Coast

The Queensland coast is Australia's holiday coast. A combination of sunny days, azure seas, coral reefs, an attractive hinterland and winter warmth means the Queensland coast receives numerous visitors.

Do not be fooled though; the Queensland coast is not one long green verdant strip. Parts of the coast lie parallel to a predominantly south-easterly air stream, meaning that those sections of the coast can be quite dry. These areas are known as the dry tropics. Such country lies between Rockhampton and Sarina, Proserpine and Townsville, and over much of Cape York Peninsula. Though perhaps not as attractive as the wet tropical areas that lie inland from Mackay, and between Townsville and Cooktown (the true Wet Tropics), the dry tropics are, on the whole, sunnier.

The Queensland coast offers the traveller much to see and do: snorkling on the Great Barrier Reef, walking through World Heritage Rainforests, talking scenic drives and enjoying languid holidays at beach resorts.

The Climate

The Queensland coast is generally a warm to hot place. Summer maximums, around 32C on the coast (hotter inland, up to 36C) are moderated by the nearness to the sea. The trade-off humidity is high enough to be uncomfortable. Nights too can be unpleasant, with minimums around 23C. Coupled with these high temperatures is the likihood of intense rain periods and the threat of tropical cyclones.

The southern cool season (April to October) is the time to visit the Queensland coast. Daytime temperatures at either end of this period can still be hot (up to 30C) but without the humidity. The nights are pleasantly mild to warm. Mid-winter can experience many warm days (around 26C) coupled with the odd mild day (24C with a cool wind). Nights tend to be mild (around 17C). Rainfall at this time is usually just sporadic showers.

Capital City Connections

Distances in kilometres
SYDNEY-ROCKHAMPTON
via Pacific/Bruce Highways

	Intermediate	Total
Sydney	0	0
Hexham	157	157
Coffs Harbour	380	537
Ballina	214	751
Coolangatta	110	861
Brisbane	98	959
Maryborough	255	1214
Gin Gin	117	1331
Rockhampton	272	1603

SYDNEY-ROCKHAMPTON
via New England/Burnett Highways

	Intermediate	Total
Sydney	0	0
Maitland	166	166
Tamworth	203	369
Tenterfield	298	667
Toowoomba	201	868
Nanango	142	1010
Gayndah	161	1171
Biloela	245	1416
Rockhampton	140	1556

Road Trip 3

MELBOURNE-ROCKHAMPTON
via Hume/Goulburn Valley/Newell/Leichhardt
Highways

	Intermediate	Total
Melbourne	0	0
Shepparton	179	179
Narrandera	243	422
Parkes	274	696
Dubbo	119	815
Moree	379	1194
Miles	333	1527
Theodore	220	1747
Rockhampton	208	1955

The Route
Distances in Kilometres

	Intermediate	Total
Rockhampton	0	0
Mackay	334	334
Bowen	190	524
Townsville	203	727
Cairns	344	1071
Mossman	75	1146
Cape Tribulation	63	1209

Bruce Highway
Rockhampton-Townsville

This section of the Bruce Highway passes through the dry tropics of the Queensland coast as well as the lush countryside between Camila and Proserpine. This route gives access to a number of features: the Hibiscus Coast north of Mackay, the glorious Whitsunday Islands and hinterland, Bowen's delightful beaches, the Burdekin region, as well as Townsville. It is a well trafficked route though one does not have to travel far off the highway to find peace and solitude.

Warnings: road subject to flooding. Beware of numerous sugar-cane railway level crossings, and slow moving cane traffic between Camilla and Proserpine.

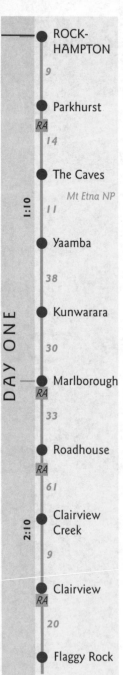

DAY ONE

ROCK-
HAMPTON
9

Parkhurst
RA
14

The Caves
Mt Etna NP
11

1:10

Yaamba
38

Kunwarara
30

Marlborough
RA
33

Roadhouse
RA
61

2:10

Clairview
Creek
9

Clairview
RA
20

Flaggy Rock

DAY 1: ROCKHAMPTON-MACKAY
via Sarina

Road to Take: Bruce Highway
Grade 1
Total Distance: 334km (3:45)
Intermediate Distances:

	Km	Hours
Rockhampton-Marlborough	102	(1:10)
Marlborough-Sarina	196	(2:10)
Sarina-Mackay	36	(0:25)

Average Vehicles per Day: approx 3000
Regions Traversed: Capricornia, Central Coast

ROCKHAMPTON (Alt 10m; Pop 65000):* large regional centre and beef capital of Australia, located on the Fitzroy River. Worth seeing: Quay Street* (numerous historic buildings), Fitzroy River area (picnic areas, river tours available), Heritage Walk (historic buildings), Botanic Gardens and Zoo**, Kershaw Gardens** (devoted to Australian plants), The Spire* (marks the Tropic of Capricorn), Dreamtime Cultural Centre* (museum displays, Darambal indigeneous culture), the railway line running down Denison Street, historic Archer Park railway station*, and numerous cattle statues* around the city. A few kilometres out of town is Mt Archer** which has excellent views and walking trails. On the coast (but not covered in this book) are the resort towns of Yeppoon (access to Great Keppel Island), Keppel Sands and Emu Park. Full town facilities. (0/334) *Road Trips 4 and 9 connect. Connecting Route B connects.* Head **N** along Bruce Hwy for Marlborough.

Accommodation
Cattle City Motor Inn, 139 Gladstone Rd, ©07 4927 7811, ✪$95-$110
Sun Palms Hotel-Motel, 160 Gladstone Rd, ©07 4927 4900, ✪$85-$95
Ambassador on the Park Motel, 161 George St, ©07 4927 5855, ✪$80-$120
Central Park Motel, 224 Murray St, ©07 4927 2333, ✪$65-$80

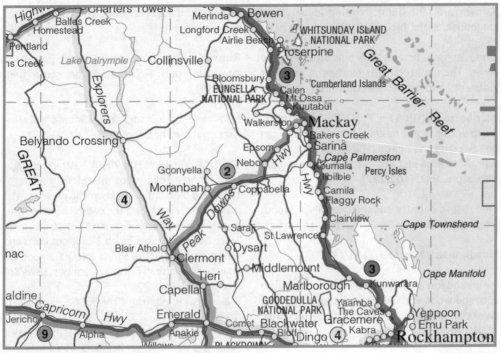

Detail of MAP 3

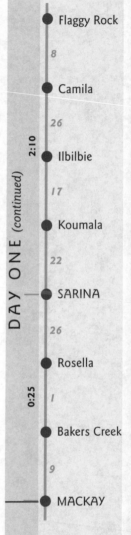

DAY ONE (continued)

2:10

- Flaggy Rock

  8

- Camila

  26

- Ilbilbie

  17

- Koumala

  22

- SARINA

  26

- Rosella

0:25   1

- Bakers Creek

  9

- MACKAY

The David Motel, 209 Musgrave St, ©07 4927 4333, ●$55

A1 Motel North, 30 Main St, ©07 4922 4251, ●$50

Lodge Motel, 100 Gladstone Rd, ©07 4922 5322, ●$55

Criterion Hotel-Motel, Cnr Quay/Fitzroy Sts, ©07 4922 1225, ●$40-$55

Big 4 Tropical Wanderer Holiday Village, 394 Yaamba Rd (Bruce Hwy), ©07 4926 3822, ●Site: $22 Van: $50-$90

Southside Holiday Village, Lower Dawson Rd, ©07 4927 3013, ●Site: $18 Van: $35-$65

Rambles Motor Village, Bruce Hwy, North Rockhampton, ©07 4928 2084, ●Site: $19 Van: $45-$65

Municipal Riverside Caravan Park, Reany St, North Rockhampton, ©07 4922 3779, ●Site: $14

Parkhurst (Alt 31m): outer suburb of Rockhampton. Stores, fuel. **Rest area** nearby. (*9/325*)

Undulating country supports tracts of grasslands given over to grazing. Distant views.

The Caves (Alt 59m): small township. Nearby are two limestone cave systems: Cammoo Caves* and Olsens Capricorn Caves*. Accommodation, store, fuel. (*23/311*)

Mt Etna:* prominent limestone peak. Nearby is the Mt Etna National Park*, a small park preserving limestone caves, a bat colony and dry rainforest. Tours are available with short walks possible. No camping.

Milman: farming locality; no facilities. (*30/304*)

Yaamba (Alt 19m): small township. Store, fuel. (*34/300*)

Undulating country supports eucalypt grassy open forests and woodlands given over to grazing. Plains have been cleared for grazing. Good views* to a rugged mountain range in the east.

Kunwarara (Alt 48m): farming locality and roadhouse. Store, fuel. (*72/262*)

Undulating country and low hills provides good views. The countryside is clothed in eucalypt grassy open forests and woodlands.

Marlborough (Alt 87m; Pop 100):* small grazing township. Some interesting old buildings can be seen, and the historical museum is worth a visit. **Rest area** just out of town. Accommodation, store, fuel. (*102/232*)

Undulating country supports eucalypt woodlands. Some clearings are given over to grazing.

Roadhouse: store, fuel. (*135/199*)

Plains and low rises are clothed in eucalypt forests and woodlands. Paperbark trees line some creeks. Clearings are used for grazing. **Rest area**. (*164/170*)

Clairview Creek: small roadhouse. Fuel. (*196/138*)

Clairview (Alt 9m): one of the very few townships located right on the coast; excellent sea views*. Good fishing off Clairview Beach. Accommodation, store, fuel. **Rest area** nearby. (*205/129*)

Undulating country supports eucalypt forests and woodlands. Conners Range is visible to the west. Northwards the land has been cleared for sugar cane farming.

Flaggy Rock (Alt 24m): farming locality and roadhouse. Fuel. (*225/109*)

Camila (Alt 17m): small sugar cane farming township. Accommodation, store, fuel. (*233/101*)

Undulating country supports grazing and sugar cane. Westward views towards the Conners Range.

Ilbilbie (Alt 40m): small sugar cane township and roadhouse. Store, fuel. (*259/75*)

Farmlands of sugar cane and grazing; westward mountain views*.

Koumala (Alt 30m): small township with an interesting pub. Accommodation, store, fuel. (*276/58*)

Farmlands support sugar cane. Some small rainforest patches hereabout.

SARINA (Alt 18m; Pop 9000):* attractive sugar cane farming town with interesting buildings. There is a pleasant park down the centre of the main street. Nearby are the coastal beach settlements of Sarina Beach, Grasstree Beach, Campwin Beach and Armstrongs Beach. Numerous inlets and waterways (including Sarina Inlet) are good for boating and fishing. Full town facilities. (*298/36*)

Accommodation

Sarina Motor Inn, Bruce Hwy, ☎07 4943 1431, ✪$55-$65

Tramway Motel, 110 Broad St (Bruce Hwy North), ☎07 4943 1262, ✪$55-$65

Sarina Palms Caravan Village, 11 Heron St, ☎07 4956 1892, ✪Site: $12 Van: $20-$30

Undulating country supports sugar cane farms and grazing. Reasonable views.

Alligator Creek: farming locality. Nearby is a mangrove-lined estuary. Accommodation.

Farmlands support sugar cane and grazing.

Rosella (Alt 11m): small township and roadhouse. Store, fuel. (*324/10*)

Bakers Creek (Alt 6m; Pop 680): small farming town. Accommodation, store, fuel. (*325/9*)

MACKAY (Alt 5m; Pop 59000):* large sugar town and regional centre. Pleasant main street and mall. See the artworks in Victoria Street. Queens Park*, including its orchid house, is worth seeing. Follow the heritage walk to see historic buildings. Numerous sandy beaches, caravan parks and low-key resort townships are located within 15 kilometres of Mackay (Bucasia, Eimeo Beach, Dolphin Heads, Blacks Beach, Shoal Point) along a sealed access road about three kilometres north-west of town on the Bruce Highway. Access to Brampton Island, Lindeman and Hamilton Islands**, and others, from Mackay Harbour. Full town facilities. (*334/0*) Road Trip 2 connects.

Accommodation
Country Plaza Motel, 40 Nebo Rd, ✆07 4957 6526, ◆$70
Golden Reef Motel, 164 Nebo Rd, ✆07 4957 6572, ◆$55
Sun Plaza Motel, 35 Nebo Rd, ✆07 4951 2688, ◆$55-$65
City Gates Motel, 9 Broadsound Rd (Bruce Hwy), ✆07 4952 5233, ✎$50
Mia Mia Motel, 191 Nebo Rd, ✆07 4952 1466, ◆$50
Tropic Coast Motel, 158 Nebo Rd, ✆07 4951 1888, ◆$45
Andergrove Caravan Park, Beaconsfield Rd, North Mackay, ✆07 4942 4922, ◆Site: $16 Van: $35-$45
Beach Tourist Park, 8 Petrie St, Illawong Beach (4km), ✆07 4957 4021, $20, ◆Van: $ 45-$65
Central Tourist Park, Cnr Malcomson/Evans Sts, ✆07 4957 6141, ◆Site: $14 Van: $30-$40
Tropical Caravan Park Melanesian Village, Bruce Hwy (5.6kmS), ✆07 4952 1211, ◆Site: $17 Van: $30-$45
Premier Caravan Park, 152 Nebo Rd (2.5kmS), ✆07 4957 6976, ◆Site: $14 Van: $30-$35

▲

DAY 2: MACKAY-BOWEN
via Proserpine

Road to Take: Bruce Highway
Grade 1
Total Distance: 190km (2:10)
Intermediate Distances:

	Km	Hours
Mackay-Proserpine	124	(1:25)
Proserpine-Bowen	66	(0:45)

Average Vehicles per Day: 3000
Regions Traversed: Central Coast

▼

MACKAY (Alt 5m; Pop 59000):* large regional centre. For more information see Day 1. (*0/190*)

Farleigh (Alt 40m; Pop 260): sugar mill township and outer suburb of Mackay. Good views* southwards overlooking the Pioneer River valley. Accommodation, stores, fuel. (*9/181*)

The Leap: locality and interesting pub* set within partially cleared rainforests. Accommodation. (*20/170*)

Hilly country provides good views*, especially when travelling southwards, of high hills and rocky outcrops. Keep a look out for hoop pines* which gives this countryside a distinctive look. Scenic countryside hereabouts.

Kuttabul (Alt 38m): small township. Accommodation, store, fuel. **Rest area** nearby. (*32/158*)

Mt Ossa/Mt Pelion (Alt 11m): twin farming townships. Store, fuel. (*44/146*)

Hilly country is quite scenic, especially near Murray Creek*.

Calen/Kolijo (Alt 23m; Pop 250): twin sugar and farming townships with some interesting old buildings*. Accommodation, store, fuel. (*52/138*)

Pindi Pindi: farming locality; no facilities. (*58/132*)
Yalboroo: sugar cane farming locality. No facilities. (*66/124*)
Undulating country provides excellent views** westwards towards the bold granite bluffs of the Clarke Range, an escarpment of high mountains, ranges and bluffs. Elsewhere are eucalypt forests and woodlands given over to grazing and some cropping.

Bloomsbury (Alt 46m): small highway and sugar cane township. Roadhouses. Store, fuel. (*82/108*)

Plains and low hills offer good views* toward mountains to the west (Clarke Range) and east. Land is either cleared for sugar cane or supports wetlands where water lilies may be seen.

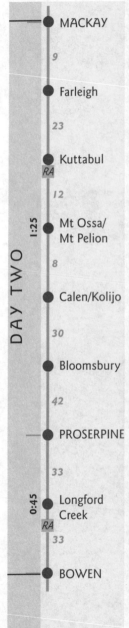

DAY TWO

1:25

0:45

MACKAY	
9	
Farleigh	
23	
Kuttabul *RA*	
12	
Mt Ossa/ Mt Pelion	
8	
Calen/Kolijo	
30	
Bloomsbury	
42	
PROSERPINE	
33	
Longford Creek *RA*	
33	
BOWEN	

PROSERPINE (Alt 11m; Pop 2850): sugar cane town with character. Interesting pubs and other buildings. A narrow main street. The nearby sugar mill has tours. Turn off here for the Whitsundays. Full town facilities. (*124/66*) Turn **E** for Whitsundays - see Side Trip below.

Accommodation
A & A Motel, Main St, ©07 4945 1288, ©$45
Whitsunday Palms Motel, Bruce Hwy, ©07 4945 1868, ©$45
Anchor Motel Whitsunday, 32 Herbert St, ©07 4945 1200, ©$40
Golden Cane Caravan Park, Bruce Hwy (8kmN), ©07 4945 1540, ©Site: $12 Van: $30-$40

Side Trip
Whitsunday (Airlie Beach/ Shute Harbour) Road (Grade 1) 72km return
Hilly country offers good views* overlooking sugar cane farms, patches of rainforest and eucalypt forests.
WHITSUNDAY (Alt 10m): formerly the settlements of Cannonvale and Airlie Beach, which today could be considered suburbs. Cannonvale is primarily residential and has many town facilities while Airlie Beach is still the resort centre and holiday settlement.
Cannonvale: a suburb of Whitsunday. Full town facilities.
Airlie Beach:** popular resort town with great views** overlooking Airlie Bay. Good sunset views* from Mandalay Point. Countless facilities and good tourist shopping. This is the place to be and be seen. Numerous tourist attractions, including coral gardens. Whale watching between July and September and turtle hatching in January. Numerous other holiday attractions. Full town facilities.
Accommodation
Island Gateway Caravan Resort, Cnr Shute Harbour/Jubilee Pocket Rds, ©07 4946 6228, ©Site: $20 Van: $35-$65
Airlie Cove Resort Park, Cnr Shute Harbour/Ferntree Rds, ©07 4946 6727, ©Site: $20 Van: $40-$95
Whitsunday Wanderers Resort Caravan Park, Shute Harbour Rd, ©07 4946 6446, ©Site: $17

Mountain Valley Caravan Park, Manooka Dr (2.5kmE), ©07 4946 6402, ©Site: $15 Van: $45

Hilly country provides good views* of rainforests and mixed forests that are part of Conway National Park. The picnic area is very attractive. Numerous bushwalks.
Shute Harbour:* port facility and resort settlement. Provides water access to the incredible islands of the Whitsunday Group***. Unfortunately views of the islands are very limited - try the residential road heading up the hill near the large car park, where you should catch glimpses between the houses on top of the ridge. Good views* around the wharf area (note the extreme tidal range!) overlooking inlets and the rugged range opposite. Accommodation, store, fuel.
Accommodation
Coral Point Lodge Motel, Harbour Ave, ©07 4946 9500, ©$80-$90
Shute Harbour Motel, Shute Harbour Rd, ©07 4946 9131, ©$55-$80
Flame Tree Tourist Village, Shute Harbour Rd, ©07 4946 9388, ©Site: $14 Van: $30-$60

Foxdale: small farming locality; no facilities. Countryside hilly hereabouts. (*131/59*)
Plains provide excellent views* of the attractive Mt Dryander (820m). Countryside partially cleared for grazing, otherwise supports eucalypt or paperbark woodlands with pandanus along creeklines. The plains southwards support sugar cane.

Longford Creek (Alt 15m): small roadhouse facility. Store, fuel. (*157/33*)

Plains and low hills offer good views. Countryside supports eucalypt woodlands given over to grazing. A few kilometres south of the Bowen turnoff is a **rest area**. A short walk through the scrub provides excellent views** overlooking Edgecombe Bay and the immense bulk of Gloucester Island. Good walking at low tide*. This is one of the few places where the coast can be seen from the highway.
Don: locality only. Turnoff for Bowen. (*187/3*)

BOWEN (Alt 3m; Pop 8,500):** interesting grazing and irrigation town with plenty of character. The saltworks at the entrance to the town are very photogenic in the right light. Numerous murals* are in the town centre, 22 in total at last counting! Interesting historic museum. Excellent views from Flagstaff Hill**. Also worth seeing is Dalrymple Point (nice island views) and Mullers Lagoon (birdwatching, plant displays, botanical gardens). Three kilometres to the north are the Bowen Beaches including the Queens Beach area. Definitely worth visiting are Horseshoe Bay** and Rose Bay. Excellent scenery of small bays and beautiful granite outcrops, with numerous walking tracks and lookouts**. Full town facilities. (*190/0*)

Accommodation
Castle Motor Lodge, 6 Don St, ©07 4786 1322, ✆$70
Pearly Shell Motel, 2 Don St, ©07 4786 1788, ✆$50
North Australian Hotel-Motel, Cnr William/Herbert Sts, ©07 4786 1244, ✆$50
Coral Coast Caravan Park, Cnr Soldiers/Horseshoe Bay Rds, ©07 4785 1262, ✆Site: $18 Van: $30
Queens Beach Caravan Park, 160 Mount Nutt Rd, ©07 4785 1313, ✆Site: $15 Van: $25-$55
Tropical Beach Caravan Park, Howard St, ©07 4785 1490, ✆Site: $16 Van: $30-$50

DAY 3: BOWEN-TOWNSVILLE via Ayr

Road to Take: Bruce Highway
Grade 1
Total Distance: 203km (2:15)
Intermediate Distances:

	Km	Hours
Bowen-Ayr	118	(1:20)
Ayr-Townsville	85	(0:55)

Average Vehicles per Day: 3000
Regions Traversed: Burdekin-Townsville district

BOWEN (Alt 3m; Pop 8,500):** interesting grazing and irrigation town. For more information see Day 2. (*0/203*)

Don: locality only. Turnoff for Mackay/Townsville. (*3/200*)

Delta (Alt 9m): farming locality. Roadhouse, fuel. (*5/198*)

Merinda (Alt 8m; Pop 200): scattered irrigation township. Store, fuel. (*6/197*)

Hilly country offers excellent views* of high and bare granite mountains. Eucalypt grassy woodlands are common.
Plains support sparse grassy eucalypt woodlands given over to cattle grazing. Vast views*, especially to distant high granite mountains which are often enshrouded or capped with cloud, especially Station Hill (Cape Upstart) to the north.

Guthalungra (Alt 13m): small grazing township. Store, fuel. **Rest area** nearby. (*42/161*)

Gumlu (Alt 14m): small grazing and farming township. Store, fuel. (*59/144*)

Plains are mostly cleared for farming. Broad vistas.

Inkerman (Alt 7m): sugar cane township. **Rest area** nearby. Accommodation, store, fuel. (*93/110*)

HOME HILL (Alt 11m; Pop 3300): sugar cane and irrigation town with some charm. Sugar mill nearby. Museum. Full town facilities. (*106/97*)

Burdekin River: broad impressive river crossed by a long combined rail and road bridge**. Very photogenic.

AYR (Alt 10m; Pop 8600):* large sugar and irrigation town with some character. Worth stopping for a short while. The pleasant park is good for picnics. Nearby Alva Beach has a boat ramp and picnic facilities. Ayr Nature Display* is worth seeing. Full town facilities. (*118/85*)

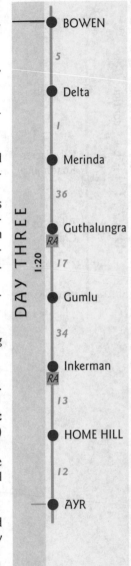

DAY THREE   1:20

BOWEN
5
Delta
1
Merinda
36
Guthalungra   RA
17
Gumlu
34
Inkerman   RA
13
HOME HILL
12
AYR

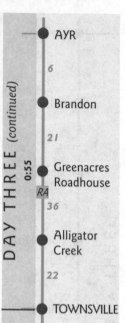

DAY THREE (continued) 0:55

- AYR
- 6
- Brandon
- 21
- Greenacres Roadhouse
- RA
- 36
- Alligator Creek
- 22
- TOWNSVILLE

Accommodation

Ayr Max Motel, 4 Edward St, ✆07 4783 2033, ✪$55

Ayrline Motel, 129 Edward St, ✆07 4783 1100, ✪$55

Tropical City Motor Inn, Cnr MacMillan/McKenzie Sts, ✆07 4783 1344, ✪$55

Silver Link Caravan Park, 34 Northam Rd, ✆07 4783 3933, ✪Site: $17 Van: $40-$55

Burdekin Cascades Caravan Park, 230 Queen St, ✆07 4783 1429, ✪Site: $14 Van: $30

Brandon (Alt 9m; Pop 900): interesting small sugar town with a narrow main street. Accommodation, stores, fuel. (**124/79**)

Plains offer northbound travellers excellent views* of Mt Elliot massif. Land supports either grassy eucalypt woodlands or has been cleared for sugar cane.

Greenacres Roadhouse: store; fuel. (**145/58**)

Mt Elliot (l342m) forms an incredible bulk obvious to northbound travellers. Prominent bluffs and rainforest patches can be seen. The adjacent lowland plain offers good views*. Eucalypt shrubby open forests dominate the countryside. **Rest area**. (**154/49**)

Wetlands occupy a portion of Bowling Green Bay National Park. Glimpsed views overlooking salt flats. Keep an eye out for the turnoff (**175/28**) to the Mt Elliot section of Bowling Green Bay National Park, where you can camp, bushwalk and swim.

Alligator Creek (Alt 11m): small spread out township set among low hills. Crocodile farm. Roadhouse. (**181/22**)

Hilly country offers fair views to the imposing bulk of Mt Elliot. A low rise offers northbound travellers a distant view of Townsville. Eucalypt grassy woodlands dominate the landscape. Else-

where, small plains have been cleared chiefly for hobby farms.

TOWNSVILLE (Alt 3m; Pop 140000):** Australia's largest tropical city. There is much to see and do including the Great Barrier Reef Aquarium**, the Omnimax Theatre** and Museum of Tropical Queensland** (all three features are located in the one complex), Castle Hill Lookout** (highly recommended), The Strand** (beachside parks and interesting tropical mansions), Flinders Mall, the historic buildings* of Flinders Street East, Town Common Environmental Park* (bird-watching) just north of the city, Queens Gardens*, Anderson Park* (botanic gardens), Palmetum** (palm botanic gardens), and various museums including Townsville Museum. Numerous tours including reef tours are available. Full town facilities. (**203/0**) *Road Trip 11 connects*.

Offshore lies Magnetic Island***, a 'high' island of pretty bays, great coral reefs and unlimited tourist facilities. The island is virtually the cheapest and most accessible of the Great Barrier Reef islands. Vehicle ferries are available.

Accommodation

South Bank Motel Inn, 23 Palmer St, South Townsville, ✆07 4721 1474, ✪$100-$120

Cedar Lodge Motel, 214 Nathan St, ✆07 4775 7800, ✪$70-$85

A1 Motel, 107 Bowen Rd, ✆07 4779 3999, ✪$55

The Strand Motel, The Strand, ✆07 4772 1977, ✪$65-$75

Adobi Motel, 86 Abbott St, ✆07 4778 2533

Banjo Paterson Motor Inn, 72 Bowen Rd, ✆07 4725 2333, ✪$65-$80

Sun City Caravan Park, 119 Bowen Rd, ✆07 4775 7733, ✪Site: $17 Van: $30-$50

Coconut Glen Van Village, 910 Ingham Rd, ✆07 4774 5101, ✪Site: $18 Van: $35-$60

Magnetic Gateway Holiday Village, Bruce Hwy, ✆07 4778 2412, ✪Site: $17 Van: $55

Town & Country Caravan Park, 16 Kings Rd, ✆07 4772 1487, ✪Site: $16 Van: $30-$50

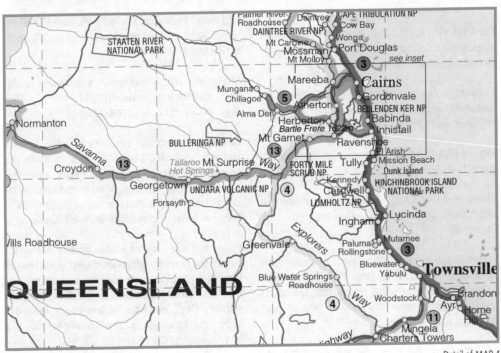

Detail of MAP 4

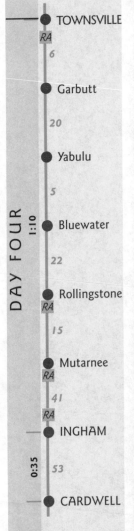

TOWNSVILLE

RA

6

Garbutt

20

Yabulu

5

Bluewater

22

Rollingstone

RA

15

Mutarnee

RA

41

RA

INGHAM

53

CARDWELL

DAY FOUR   1:10   0:35

Wet Tropics

Bruce Highway: Townsville-Cairns
Captain Cook Highway: Cairns-Mossman
Daintree/Cape Tribulation Road: Mossman-Cape Tribulation

Rising abruptly from the coastal lowlands, the highest mountains in Queensland intercept moist on-shore winds for most of the year, resulting in this part of the country receiving the highest rainfall in Australia. A large variety of rainforests grow as a result of the rainfall and rich soils. This region has recently become known as the Wet Tropics. While rainforests characterise the countryside, much of the lowlands has been cleared for sugar cane farming, giving this region its second characteristic identity. The Wet Tropics is a land of green lushness and spectacular beauty, set beside an azure sea brimming with coral reefs. The area attracts many visitors and supports a close network of settlements.

Warnings: route between Townsville-Cairns is very busy during the tourist season with limited overtaking opportunities. Beware of sugar cane trains and trucks (all of which move slowly) on this and other Wet Tropic routes. Beware of the twisty road between Cairns-Port Douglas turnoff and the narrow, twisty road between Daintree ferry-Cape Tribulation.

DAY 4: TOWNSVILLE-TULLY via Ingham

Road to Take: Bruce Highway
Grade 1
Total Distance: 205km (2:15)
Intermediate Distances:

	Km	Hours
Townsville-Ingham	109	(1:10)
Ingham-Cardwell	53	(0:35)
Cardwell-Tully	43	(0:30)

Average Vehicles per Day: 3,000 south of Ingham
Regions Traversed: Townsville district, Wet Tropics

TOWNSVILLE (Alt 3m; Pop 140000): large tropical city. Full town facilities. For further information see the notes above. (*0/205*)

Garbutt: suburb of Townsville. The ribbon development extends for some distance along the highway. **Rest area** nearby. (*6/199*)

Yabulu (Alt 16m): small township. Roadhouse, store, fuel. (*26/179*)

Bluewater (Alt 12m): small farming, residential and holiday settlement. Roadhouse, store, fuel. (*31/174*)

Plains support tracts of melaleuca forests with some land cleared for grazing. Occasional views to high ranges in the west. Notice that the countryside changes from dry to wet tropics near Rollingstone.

Rollingstone (Alt 22m; Pop 50): small farming township. Sugar cane is grown north of here. Pleasant **rest area**. Accommodation, store, fuel. (*53/152*)

Mt Spec Road turnoff: (*63/142*) Turn **W** for Paluma.

Side Trip
Mt Spec Road
(Grade 2 - narrow and twisty) 36km return
Paluma National Park: interesting park preserving a lengthy tract of the Seaview Range escarpment and its rainforests and eucalypt forests.
Big Crystal Creek: attractive national park camping area located at the end of a side road that passes through sugar cane farming country. Swimming is available. (*4/14*)
Paluma Range:** impressive escarpment with occasional great views**. Rainforests, eucalypt forests and patches of bare granite can be seen. Hoop pines* are visible near Little Crystal Creek. Interesting stone bridge* here with a picnic area.
Paluma (Alt 900m; Pop 50): small hill station settlement set within upland rainforests. Spectacular eastward views from nearby McClellands **

and other lookouts. The botanic walk* is of interest. Paluma offers galleries, tearooms. Accommodation. (*18/0*)

Mutarnee (Alt 15m): small sugar cane township. Roadhouse, store, fuel. Nearby is a **rest area** at Crystal Creek. (*68/135*)

Bambaroo: sugar cane locality of a few houses and a school. (*81/124*) Four kilometres to the north is the turnoff to Jourama Falls, a popular area supporting eucalypt forests and rainforest-lined creeks. Picnic areas, short walking trails to falls and lookouts, swimming holes. Camping is available.
Plains and low rises have been mostly cleared for sugar cane farming. Good views westwards toward high ranges. Uncleared country supports eucalypt woodlands, melaleuca forests and rainforest patches. **Rest area** near Frances Creek. (*98/107*)
Toobanna: small sugar cane farming locality of a few houses. (*102/103*)

INGHAM (Alt 12m: Pop 5700):* sizeable sugar cane town. It is worth stopping a while to appreciate this place. A wide main street and Italian cultural influences makes this a sugartown with a difference. The coastal Taylor and Forrest beaches offer good swimming. Full town facilities. (*109/96*)
Accommodation
Ingham Motel, 62 Townsville Rd, ©07 4776 2355, ○$55-$95
Herbert Valley Motel, Bruce Hwy, ©07 4776 1777, ○$55
Palm Tree Caravan Park, Bruce Hwy, ©07 4776 2403, ○Site: $17 Van: $40-$45

Lookout:** great views (unfortunately marred by power lines, busy highway traffic and lack of parking spaces - take extra care crossing road if travelling north) overlooking Hinchinbrook Island and Channel, and vast mangrove formations. The area below is often referred to as Australia's Everglades. (*125/80*)
Hilly country (Cardwell Range) supports rainforests and eucalypt forests. This is virtually the

only hilly country between Townsville and Cairns along the highway.

Lumholtz National Park:* highway traverses a small portion of this large park. This section preserves rainforest and eucalypt forests. North of the park (15 kilometres south of Cardwell) is the start of the Dalrymple Gap Walking Track crossing the Cardwell Range - a permit is required and there is no camping, but the reward is good views overlooking Hinchinbrook Island. Low rises, partially cleared for grazing in the north, support dense melaleuca (paperbark) forests. Eastwards, some mangrove formations may be seen.

CARDWELL (Alt 7m; Pop 1400):* attractive small town spread out along the Hinchinbrook Channel waterfront. Great views** looking towards the spectacular Hinchinbrook Island. Offshore are the national park islands** of Hinchinbrook, Goold and the Family Group; camping available, permit required. Access via charter boat from Cardwell. Make local enquiries regarding the Cardwell Forest Drive. Accommodation, stores, fuel. (*162/43*)

Accommodation

Marine Hotel-Motel, Victoria St, ©07 4066 8755, ○$55-$70
Lyndoch Motor Inn, 215 Victoria St, ©07 4066 8500, ○$55
Cardwell Sunrise Village, 43A Marine Pde, ©07 4066 8550, ○Site: 18 Van: 40-$70
Kookaburra Holiday Park, 175 Bruce Hwy, ©07 4066 8648, ○Site: $15 Van: $35-$80

Hinchinbrook Channel and Barge, Cardwell, QLD

Cardwell Van Park, 107 Roma St, ©07 4066 8689, ○Site: $13 Van: $35-$50

Kennedy (Alt 9m): small grazing and farming township. Store, fuel. (*172/33*)

Plains and occasional low rises have been mostly cleared for sugar cane farming and grazing. Some westward views towards distant ranges. **Rest area**. (*178/27*)

Murrigal: farming locality. (*188/17*) Turnoff here for the Murray Falls State Forest Park, set at the foot of the Kirrama Range. The main feature is Murray Falls*, a series of cascading waterfalls flowing over granite boulders. Very scenic. Swimming, walking trails, picnic area, camping.

Euramo (Alt 9m): small sugar cane and farming township. Accommodation, store, fuel. (*196/9*)

Silky Oak (Alt 10m): small township. Store, fuel. (*199/6*)

TULLY (Alt 16m; Pop 3100):* sugar town and Australia's wettest settlement located at the foot of Mt Tyson. Although not a tourist town, it is still worth seeing. The nearby sugar mill, under heavy cloud-ladened wet skies, makes an interesting photographic subject. Full town facilities. (*205/0*)

Accommodation

Tully Motel, Bruce Hwy, ©07 4068 2233, ○$60-$70

DAY 5: TULLY-CAIRNS
via Innisfail

Road to Take: Bruce Highway
Grade 1
Total Distance: 139km (1:45)
Intermediate Distances:

	Km	Hours
Tully-Innisfail	52	(0:35)
Innisfail-Babinda	29	(0:20)
Babinda-Gordonvale	35	(0:25)
Gordonvale-Cairns	23	(0:25)

DAY FOUR (continued)

● CARDWELL
10
● Kennedy
RA
24
0:30
● Euramo
3
● Silky Oak
6
● TULLY

Road Trip 3

DAY FIVE

● TULLY	
15	
● El Arish	
RA	0:35
29	
● Mourilyan	
8	
● INNISFAIL	
22	
● Miriwinni	0:20
7	
● BABINDA	
8	
● Bellenden Ker	
6	
● Deeral	0:25
6	
● Fishery Falls	
15	
● GORDON-VALE	

Average Vehicles per Day: 3500 north of Tully
Regions Traversed: Wet Tropics

TULLY (Alt 16m; Pop 3100): sugar cane farming town. Full town facilities. For more information see Day 4. (*0/139*)

Mission Beach turnoff (southern end): (*2/137*) Turn **E** for Mission Beach - see Side Trip below.

Side Trip
Mission Beach road
(Grade 1) 36km loop road
Low hills support attractive rainforests. Some areas are cleared for sugar-cane farming.
Tam O'Shanter State Forest:** a preserved area of lowland fan-palm forest and cassowary habitat well worth seeing. Short unsealed access is west of the South Mission Beach turnoff. Interesting walking trails, especially the Licuala Walk.
Wongaling Beach: residential and tourist settlement.
Mission Beach area (Alt 3m,; Pop 2500):** attractive and popular tourist destination. Area extends from Bingil Bay in the north to South Mission Beach in the south. Behind lies rainforest-clad hills. Off-shore lies Dunk** and Bedarra Islands** and adjacent reefs - access by water taxi from Mission Beach, Wongaling and Clump Point. Also off-shore are some national park islands where camping available with a permit. Accommodation, stores, fuel.
Accommodation
Mackays Mission Beach Motel, 7 Porter Prom, ©07 4068 7212, ●$65-$100
Mission Beach Hideaway Holiday Village, ©60 Porters Prom, 07 4068 7104, ●Site: $18 Van: $40-$75
Beachcomber Cocout Village, Kennedy Esp, Mission Beach South, ©07 4068 8129, ●Site: $18 Van: $45-$120
Dunk Island View Caravan Park, 175 Reid Rd, ©07 4068 8248, ●Site: $16 Van: $55
Tropical Hibiscus Caravan Park, Cassowary Dr (3kmS), ©07 4068 8138, ●Site: $15 Van: $35-$55

Kennedy Walking Track:** starts at South Mission Beach, 7km of great coastal views and attractive rainforests. No swimming due to the presence of estuarine crocodiles.
Clump Mountain National Park: small park preserving tropical rainforests. Walking tracks provide good views from Bicton Hill*.
Lacey Creek Forest Walk:* attractive walk through the rainforests. Swimming holes and picnic facilities available.

Mission Beach turnoff (northern end). (*15/124*) *Turn here for Mission Beach* - see Side Trip above. Hilly country supports tracts of rainforest.

El Arish (Alt 20m; Pop 320): small sugar cane farming town located just off the highway. Interesting and photogenic pub*. Accommodation, stores, fuel. (*15/124*)

Plain has been mostly cleared for sugar cane farming. **Rest area**.
Low rises and plains have been mostly cleared for sugar cane farming. Occasional westward views towards distant ranges. **Rest area**. (*30/109*)
Moresby: locality; no facilities except for a school. (*38/101*)

Mourilyan (Alt 12m; Pop 500): attractive sugar cane farming town and sugar mill. Australian Sugar Museum* is worth seeing. Accommodation, stores, fuel. (*44/93*)

INNISFAIL (Alt 8m; Pop 8150): interesting and sizeable sugar cane and agricultural town set upon low hills. Worth pulling off the highway to see the Johnstone River waterfront area* and scenic esplanade, Warrina Lakes and Botanic Gardens*, Canecutters Statue, Good Counsel Catholic Church* (very impressive), the Joss House*, and heritage walk. Good fishing hereabouts in the river, estuary and off-shore. Full town facilities. (*52/87*) *Road Trip 5 connects.* Turn **SW** for South Johnstone Road and Paronella Park - see Side Trip below).
Accommodation
Barrier Reef Motel, Bruce Hwy, ©07 4061 4988, ●$70-$85

Walkabout Motel, 20 McGowan Dr, ©07 4061 2311, ©$50
Carefree Motel, 14 Owen St, ©07 4061 2266, ©$50
August Moon Caravan Park, Bruce Hwy (4kmS), ©07 4063 2211, ©Site: $16 Van: $30-$50
Mango Tree Caravan Park, 2 Couche ST (2kmS), ©07 4061 1656, ©Site: $14 Van: $25-$55

Side Trip
South Johnstone Road
(Grade 1) 44km return
Wangan: small township. Store, fuel.
South Johnstone (Alt 18m):** very pretty sugar cane milling town. Interesting and photogenic buildings. The sugar cane railway line* runs down the main street. Large sugar mill. Accommodation, stores, fuel.
Undulating country supports sugar cane farms, banana plantations set amidst rainforest patches. Good views*.
Mena Creek: attractive small township. Adjacent is the Mena Creek Environmental Park* (waterfall, picnic area and suspension bridge). Next door is Paronella Park***, an amazing example of a landscaped gardens, follys and outbuildings set around a tropical 'castle'. This idiosyncratic feature should not be missed. Accommodation, store, fuel.

Low hills have been cleared for sugar cane farms. Low rises support dense lowland rainforests. Interesting railway bridge over the Russel River. Low rises offer good views* across sugar cane farms to the towering rainforest-clad ramparts of Mt Bartle Frere. At 1611m it is Queensland's highest mountain and before you is the greatest hillslope in the state.
Josephine Falls turnoff: (**72/67**) Turn here for Josephine Falls*, an attractive cascading waterfall at the end of a short walking track that wends through the rainforest. Situated in the Wooroonooran National Park. No camping but picnic facilities are available. This is the start of the Mt Bartle Frere and Broken Nose walking tracks (experienced walkers only).

Miriwinni (Alt 23m; Pop 220): small township. Accommodation, stores, fuel. (**74/65**)

BABINDA (Alt 11m; Pop 1400): interesting sugar cane farming town. Photogenic buildings in the main street* (off the highway) and an interesting sugar mill. Full town facilities. (**81/58**)

Bellenden Ker (Alt 14m): sugar cane farming locality. Occasional views* (when the clouds lift) of Bellenden Ker, Queensland's second highest mountain at 1582m. The summit is the wettest place in Australia. Store, fuel. (**89/50**)

Undulating country and small plains provides some of the best lowlands scenery** in the Wet Tropics, extending between Innisfail and Gordonvale. Countryside mostly cleared for sugar cane farming and grazing, though many rainforest pockets remain. Spectacular views westwards toward the high Bellenden Ker Range. Good views eastwards across open country towards the lower Graham and Thompson ranges.

Deeral (Alt 9m): small sugar cane farming township notable for the incredibly steep rainforest-clad hillslope rising to the west. Nearby, at Deeral Landing, boat tours run to the Frankland Islands. Camping available - permit required. Store, fuel. (**95/44**)

Fishery Falls (Alt 20m): farming township. Accommodation, store, fuel. (**101/38**)

Mulgrave River: deep, dark tropical river estuary lined with rainforests. Beware of estuarine crocodiles. (**115/24**)
Walshs Pyramid:** high conical hill (921m) devoid of rainforest due to open rock slabs of granite. This interesting landmark is Australia's highest free-standing mountain.

GORDONVALE (Alt 19m; Pop 2400):* attractive sugar cane farming town with photogenic buildings, located just off the highway. It also forms part of the Cairns suburban area. Worth seeing: Mulgrave sugar mill (tours available), and

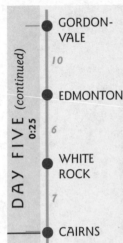

DAY FIVE (continued) 0:25

GORDON-VALE

10

EDMONTON

6

WHITE ROCK

7

CAIRNS

the Mulgrave Rambler Station and Visitors Centre* (train rides). Full town facilities. (*116/23*) *Road Trip 13 connects.*

Plains have been cleared for sugar cane farming and suburban development. Good views towards the rainforest-clad Isley Hills in the west.

EDMONTON (Alt 17m): basically a Cairns suburb and sugar cane farming town. Full town facilities. (*126/13*)

WHITE ROCK (Alt 19m): Cairns suburb. Full town facilities. (*132/7*)

CAIRNS (Alt 3m; Pop 101000):** large tropical city with a laid-back feel. Most people here are holiday-makers, backpackers, retirees, escapees, and those who serve them - there are even a few locals as well. Much to see and do. The town centre* area is pleasant to walk around. The Esplanade** and its night markets* are well worth experiencing. The adjacent mud flats (Cairns centre has no beach) have interesting bird life at low tide. Numerous shopping arcades and tourist shops can be perused, and the Cairns Museum* may be an option for those interested. Numerous other holiday attractions are available. Full town facilities. (*139/0*) *Road Trips 5, 6 and 13 connect. /Head S on Bruce Hwy for Gordonvale.*

Further out from the city centre there is the Flecker Botanic Gardens** (walking tracks), Mt Whitfield Environmental Park* (walking tracks, good views), the mangrove boardwalk* (off airport road - take insect repellent), scenic railway*** and skyway*** to Kuranda, Tjapukai Aboriginal Cultural Centre**, scenic drive through West Cairns, Brimsmead to Redlynch (mostly suburbs with backdrops of rainforest-clad hills), scenic drives to Crystal Cascades* and Barron Gorge**, swimming at the northern beaches, and a scenic drive* to Copperlode Dam. Numerous land-based tours available.

Offshore pleasure craft provide tours and access to many Great Barrier Reef features: Green Island***, a true coral cay, Fitzroy Island*, a 'high' island (national park camping available -

permit required), Michaelmas Cay** and the Outer Reef**. Accommodation is available on Green Island and Fitzroy Island.

Accommodation

All Seasons Cairns Village Resort, Cnr Bruce Hwy/Anderson St, ©07 4054 7700, ✪$85

Cairns Angler, 287 Lake St, ©07 4031 1666, ✪$85-$105

High Chaparral Motel, 195 Sheridan St, ©07 4051 7155, ✪$85-$95

Beltana Motel, 380 Mulgrave St, ©07 4054 3777, ✪$55-$75

Cairns Queens Court, 167 Sheridan St, ©07 4051 7722, ✪$60-$85

Rainbow Inn Motel, 179 Sheridan St, ©07 4051 1022, ✪$70-$110

Tree Tops Lodge Motel, 7 Tanner Cres, ©07 4039 9599, ✪$65-$75

A1 Motel, 211 Sheridan St, ©07 4051 4499, ✪$65

Cairns Motor Inn, 187 Sheridan St, ©07 4051 5166, ✪$60-$80

Carns Coconut Caravan Resort, Cnr Bruce Hwy/Anderson Rd, Woree, ©07 4054 6644, ✪Site: $24 Van: $50-$100

Cool Waters Caravan Park, Brinsmead Rd, Brinsmead, ©07 4034 1949, ✪Site: $20 Van: $55-$65

First City Caravilla Caravan Park, Kelly St, Earlsville (3kmS), ©07 4054 1403, ✪Site: $20 Van: $50-$75

White Rock Caravan Park, Skull Rd, White Rock (6kmS), ©07 4036 2523, ✪Site: $13 Van: $40

Woree Caravan Park, 664 Bruce Hwy, Woree, ©074054 1305, ✪Site: $15 Van: $30-$55

DAY 6: CAIRNS-CAPE TRIBULATION via Mossman

Roads to Take: Cook Highway, Daintree Road, Cape Tribulation Road
Grade 1 Cairns-Daintree
Grade 2 Daintree-Cape Tribulation
Total Distance: 138km (2:30)

Intermediate Distances:

	Km	Hours
Cairns-Mossman	75	(1:10)
Mossman-Cape Tribulation	63	(1:20)

Average Vehicles per Day: 3,200 south of Mossman
Regions Traversed: Wet Tropics

CAIRNS (Alt 3m; Pop 101000):** large tropical city with a nice laid-back feel. Plenty to see and do on the mainland or the Great Barrier Reef. For further information see the notes above. (*0/138*) Head **N** on Captain Cook Hwy for Craiglie.

En route from Cairns are access roads to the suburbs and beaches of Yorkeys Knob, Holloways Beach and Machans Beach*.

SMITHFIELD: new suburban development. Full town facilities. (*13/125*)

Plain supports sugar cane farms and urban development. Good views* westwards towards Kuranda Range.

Palm Cove (Alt 3m; Pop 2000):* northernmost of Cairns' northern suburbs. Resorts and a nice beach. Accommodation, store, fuel. (*25/113*)

Ellis Beach:** beautifully located beachside camping ground and rainforest-lined road. Accommodation, store. (*28/110*)
Hilly country** offers some of Australia's best coastal scenery (from Ellis Beach to south of Craiglie). Slow, curvey road offers good views along a wild coastline. Elsewhere, rainforests close in. Occasional vantage points (pull overs) offer excellent views, especially Rex Lookout** just north of Wangetti; likewise Red Cliff Point* south of Wangetti.
Wangetti: small beachside locality; no facilities. Nearby is Hartley Creek crocodile farm*. (*39/99*)

Craiglie (Alt 10m): sugar cane farming township, nowadays virtually a suburb of Port Douglas. Store, fuel. (*61/77*) Turn **E** for Port Douglas - see Side Trip below.

Side Trip
**Port Douglas Road
(Grade 1) 12km return**
PORT DOUGLAS (Alt 4m; Pop 2500):** very popular tourist town which still retains some of its original charm. Good views from Flagstaff Hill*, nautical museum. Numerous tourist facilities: shops, cafes, resorts and more. Offshore access to Agincourt Reef** and Low Isles**. Full town facilities.
Accommodation
Port Douglas Motel, 9 Davidson St, ©07 4099 5248, ●$80-$95
Coconut Grove Motel, 58 Macrossan St, ©07 4099 5124, ●$60-$85
Four Mile Beach Caravan Park, 2 Reef St, ©07 4098 5281, ●Site: $20 Van: $30-$60
Pandanus Van Park, 97-107 Davidson St, ©07 4099 5944, ●Site: $14 Van: $50-$65
Tropic Breeze Van Village, 24 Davidson St, ©07 4099 5299, ●Site: $18 Van: $55

Rex Highway junction: locality only; no facilities. (*70/68*) *Road Trip 4 Connects.* Continue **N** for Mossman. *Continue SE for Craiglie.*

MOSSMAN (Alt 10m; Pop 1850): sugar cane farming town with an interesting main street. Sugar mill tours available as well as a scenic train ride* (the Bally Hooley). Nearby are Newell and Cooya beaches. A kilometre south of town is Mossman Gorge**, virtually the only accessible part of the Daintree National Park. Swimming, walking tracks through the rainforest and vantage points. No camping. Expect a crowd. Full town facilities. (*75/63*)
Accommodation
Demi-View Motel, 41 Front St, ©07 4098 1277, ●$65-$75
Mossman Bicentennial Caravan Park, Foxton Ave (1kmN), ©07 4098 2627, ●Site: $17

Miallo: farming township. Store, fuel. (*84/54*)

Plain mostly cleared for sugar cane farming. Good views westwards toward the rainforest-clad Main Coast Range (Mt Carbine Plateau).

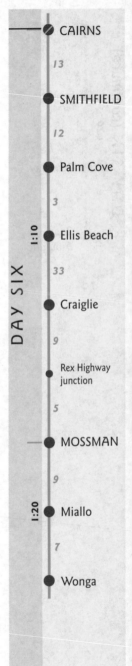

Road Trip 3

DAY SIX

CAIRNS

13

SMITHFIELD

12

Palm Cove

3

1:10

Ellis Beach

33

Craiglie

9

Rex Highway junction

5

MOSSMAN

9

1:20

Miallo

7

Wonga

DAY SIX *(continued)*

1:20

- Wonga
  - 9
- Daintree turnoff
  - 12
- Cow Bay
  - 26
- *Cape Tribulation*

Wonga (Alt 2m): beachside settlement located within sugar cane country. The beach is attractive. Camping available. Store, fuel. (*91/47*)

Accommodation

Pinnacle Village Holiday Caravan Park, Vixies Rd, ©07 4098 7566, ⊕Site: $17 Van: $50-$75

Plain supports sugar cane farms. Scenic view* of mountains to the north including Thornton Peak (1374m).

Daintree turnoff: (*100/38*) Proceed straight on for Daintree - see Side Trip below. Turn **N** for Daintree River ferry and Cape Tribulation. *Turn* **E** *for Mossman.*

Side Trip
Daintree Road
(Grade1) 22km return

Daintree (Alt 4m; Pop 100):* interesting grazing and sugar cane township nowadays mostly given over to tourism. Located within the attractive Daintree River valley. Museum and river cruises**. Accommodation, store, fuel.

Daintree River: crossed by a ferry (fee payable). If heading north, wait a short time while the rest of the ferry traffic tears off, then you can have the first section of the route to yourself. Good views** from the ferry. Nearby facilities include tour offices, a cafe and interesting river tours**. Expect a crowd. Beware of estuarine crocodiles. (*105/33*)

Lookout** on top of Alexandra Range offers great views overlooking Daintree River. Rainforests hereabouts are very attractive. Warning: narrow, winding road - take care.

Cow Bay (Alt 20m): new spread out settlement servicing tourists with rainforest resorts, restaurants, tours and the like. A short distance away (12km return) is Cow Bay Beach,* which has a seaside picnic area and pleasant beach walking. Accommodation, store, fuel. (*112/26*)

Accommodation

Cow Bay Hotel, Cape Tribulation Rd, ©07 4098 9011, ⊕$90
Rainforest Retreat Motel, Cape Tribulation Rd, ©07 4098 9120, ⊕$35-$80
Rum Runner Rainforest Village, Cape Tribulation Rd (8kmN), ©07 4098 9015, ⊕Site: $17 Van: $30

Thornton Beach:* attractive beach with small island offshore. Beach walking. A short distance to the north are the 'bouncing stones'. Interesting kiosk. A short distance south is a store selling fuel. The adjacent area supports small farms and rainforest resorts. Nearby Palm Road is worth visiting. Cleared land offers great views** towards Thornton Peak (1374m). (*123/15*)

Maardja Boardwalk:** highly recommended. Interesting rainforest and mangrove forest walk. Popular but worth taking your time.

Noah Head:* national park beachside camping area.

Noah Range: interesting drive through the rainforest*. Great views eastwards**.

Cape Tribulation National Park: preserves sections of World Heritage rainforests, mangroves, swamps and upland heaths. Information is available in Cape Tribulation.

Cape Tribulation (Alt 3m):** furthermost point north for the family sedan. An interesting area of rainforests, reefs and spectacular countryside. Boardwalks, lookouts and beach walking. This is a popular area. Scattered throughout the rainforest is a tourist village with resorts and cafes. Camping available. Store; no fuel (at time of visit). (*138/0*) *Road Trip 4 connects.*

Accommodation

Ferntree Rainforest Motel, Camelot Cres, ©07 4098 0000, ⊕$275
Pilgram Sands Holiday Park, Cape Tribulation Rd (2kmN), ©07 4098 0030, ⊕Site: $15 (unpowered) Van: $80

Road Trip 4
Queensland's Hinterland

Cape Tribulation-Rockhampton
Total Distance: 1429km
Suggested Travelling Time: 4 days

> *Wind through the Hinterland,*
> *where the outback meets the reef*
>
> See the historic villages of Mt Molloy and Mt Garnet, World Heritage rainforests, attractive Ravenshoe, The Crater at Mt Hypipamee National Park, the old gold mining township of Charters Towers, and Queensland's highest road.

The Queensland Hinterland

Running parallel to the Queensland coast, and extending up to 200 kilometres into the interior, the Queensland hinterland is a combination of outback rangelands, recently developed broadacre farming country, and the upland tropical grazing and farming country of the Atherton Tableland.

South of Belyando Crossing, the native vegetation has been cleared over the past 30 or more years - massive land clearances still occur here. In some places this area presents a raw face to the traveller: solitary bottle trees stand amid grassy downlands, the bare soil of broadacre croplands lies under a droughty sun. During good seasons these drastically altered landscapes can appear benign, even attractive in the right light, and one can appreciate the enormity of this countryside. Vast views from the tops of hills run from one's feet to distant ranges, a mere line of purple somewhere near the horizon.

North of Belyando Crossing, vast tracts of remaining native vegetation soften the landscape. Elsewhere are wild ranges and tablelands, unaltered and unchanged, providing pristine environments for the traveller to enjoy. The towns and townships too offer plenty of interest. Many still possess an air of the pioneering spirit that settled this countryside. And they are friendly places too.

The Climate

The cooler season between May and September is the ideal time to visit. Maximum temperatures are generally mild to warm (around 24C), with the odd cooler or warmer day thrown in. Nights are cool to cold, with minimum temperatures around 5C, dropping to freezing in mid-winter. Higher temperatures will be experienced either side of the cooler months . Generally, days will be clear and sunny with virtually no rain.

Summers are hot, and sometimes humid, with maximum temperatures in the low to mid-thirties. Nights too are often warm and may be uncomfortable. Summers are also the time for rain or showers. During wetter periods, summer rains can be intense, and the wet weather often extends well into autumn. At such times, access may be difficult due to flooding.

Note that at altitude, such as on the Atherton Tableland, summer temperatures (and humidity) are moderated (28C - 30C). In winter they are moderated too, with beautiful warm, sunny days (around 23C) but with cold nights (down to freezing).

Capital City Connections

Distances in kilometres
SYDNEY-ROCKHAMPTON
via Pacific/Bruce Highways

	Intermediate	Total
Sydney	0	0
Hexham	157	157
Coffs Harbour	380	537
Ballina	214	751
Coolangatta	110	861
Brisbane	98	959
Maryborough	255	1214
Gin Gin	117	1331
Rockhampton	272	1603

SYDNEY-ROCKHAMPTON
via New England/Burnett Highways

	Intermediate	Total
Sydney	0	0
Maitland	166	166

Road Trip 4

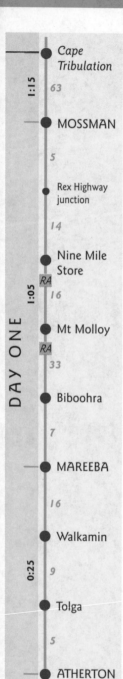

DAY ONE	●	*Cape Tribulation*	
1:15		63	
	●	MOSSMAN	
		5	
	●	Rex Highway junction	
		14	
	●	Nine Mile Store	
1:05	RA	16	
	●	Mt Molloy	
	RA	33	
	●	Biboohra	
		7	
	●	MAREEBA	
		16	
	●	Walkamin	
0:25		9	
	●	Tolga	
		5	
	●	ATHERTON	

	Intermediate	Total
Tamworth	203	369
Tenterfield	298	667
Toowoomba	201	868
Nanango	142	1010
Gayndah	161	1171
Biloela	245	1416
Rockhampton	140	1556

MELBOURNE-ROCKHAMPTON
via Hume/Goulburn Valley/Newell/Leichhardt Highways

	Intermediate	Total
Melbourne	0	0
Shepparton	179	179
Narrandera	243	422
Parkes	274	696
Dubbo	119	815
Moree	379	1194
Miles	333	1527
Theodore	220	1747
Rockhampton	208	1955

The Route
Distances in Kilometres

	Intermediate	Total
Cape Tribulation	0	0
Mossman	63	63
Mareeba	75	138
Ravenshoe	82	220
Charters Towers	457	677
Clermont	376	1053
Emerald	106	1159
Rockhampton	270	1429

Atherton Tablelands
Cape Tribulation-Ravenshoe

The Atherton Tablelands is a district mostly cleared for farming and grazing. It supports a number of settlements as well as providing access to numerous waterfalls, lakes, escarpment views and World Heritage rainforests. Travellers to the Wet Tropics and Atherton Tablelands could easily spend a week here exploring its many delights. The route between Mossman and Ravenshoe described below is via the Rex Highway (and Peninsula Development Road) to Mareeba, the Kennedy Highway to Atherton and

the junction of the Tumoulin Road, then via the Tumoulin Road (double-width bitumen all the way) to Ravenshoe.

Warnings: Routes leading to or from the Atherton Tableland are steep. Note that many roads on the Atherton Tableland are narrow bitumen and very curvy. Take care on soft verges after rain.

DAY 1: CAPE TRIBULATION-RAVENSHOE
via Mossman, Mareeba

Roads to Take: Cape Tribulation-Daintree Road, Rex Highway, Kennedy Highway, Tumoulin Road
Grade 2 Cape Tribulation-Daintree
Grade 1 Daintree-Ravenshoe
Total Distance: 220km (3:30)
Intermediate Distances:

	Km	Hours
Cape Tribulation-Mossman	63	(1:15)
Mossman-Mareeba	75	(1:05)
Mareeba-Atherton	30	(0:25)
Atherton-Ravenshoe via Tumoulin	52	(0:45)

Average Vehicles per Day: 1,000 south of Mossman
Regions Traversed: Wet Tropics, Atherton Tableland

Cape Tribulation (Alt 3m):** For more information see Road Trip 3, Day 6. (*0/220*) *Road Trip 3 connects.*

For information about the route between Cape Tribulation and Mossman see Road Trip 3, Day 6.

MOSSMAN (Alt 10m; Pop 1850): sugar cane farming town. For more information see Road Trip 3, Day 6. (*63/157*)

Rex Highway junction: locality only; no facilities. (*68/152*) *Road Trip 3 connects.* Turn **S** for Mareeba. *Turn* **NW** *onto Captain Cook Hwy for Mossman.*

Detail of MAP 4

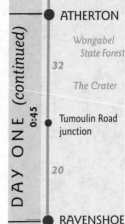

Lyons Lookout* (there is another lookout nearby) offers good views overlooking the sugar cane farms of the Mossman River valley and the coastal ranges beyond.

Nine Mile Store: store, fuel. (*82/138*)

Hilly country forms the eastern escarpment of the Great Dividing Range. Good views* are occasionally glimpsed from within the rainforest-clad slopes. Further south, the rolling hilly country has been mostly cleared for grazing. Some eucalypt forests and rainforest patches remain. Good views* toward Heights of Victory (1227m) and Mt Frazer (1156m) in the west, and Black Mountain to the south east.

Rumula: farming locality, accommodation. (*87/133*)

Julatten: farming locality with a few houses and a school. (*89/131*)

Abattoir Swamp: small environment park and bird hide - famous bird watching area. A short distance to the north is the Hunter Creek **rest area**.

Peninsula Development Road junction. (*94/126*) Continue **S** for Mareeba. *Continue **N** for Mossman.*

Mt Molloy (Alt 389m; Pop 150):* old mining township with some character, nowadays a farming settlement. Interesting buildings, some old ruins and an historic cemetery. Just north of the town is the Rifle Creek rest area where camping

and swimming is available. Accommodation, stores, fuel. (*96/124*)

Undulating country supports eucalypt woodlands with occasional views to distant ranges. Anthills common. North of Biboohra is a reservoir impounding a section of the Mitchell River.

Biboohra (Alt 391m): small irrigation farming township. Sugar cane and rice farms surround the settlement. About 5km west is the Mareeba Tropical Savanna and Wetland Reserve*, a reserve featuring lagoons and tropical woodlands; walking trails, picnic areas; no camping. Store, fuel. (*131/89*)

MAREEBA (Alt 404m; Pop 17300): sizeable agricultural, grazing and service centre with some character. The annual rodeo one of the largest in Australia. Interesting heritage museum*. Also worth seeing is The Beck Museum south of town. Full town facilities. (*138/82*) *Road Trips 5 and 6 connect.*

Accommodation
Jackeroo Motel, 340 Byrnes St, ©07 4092 2677, ✪$65

Mareeba Motel Golden Leaf, 261 Byrnes St, ©07 4092 2266, ✪$120

Riverside Caravan Park, Egan St, ©07 4092 2309, ✪Site: $12 Van: $25-$35

Road Trip 4

Farmlands support irrigated crops and pastures. Fair to reasonable views.

Walkamin (Alt 593m): small irrigation-based township. Just north of the settlement is Nardellos Lagoon while to the south is the Jump-Up, which forms the northern boundary of the Atherton Tableland proper. Fair northward views overlooking the irrigated country. Store, fuel. (*154/66*)

Tolga (Alt 750m; Pop 800): small agricultural town with tourist facilities and craft shops. Also see the Tolga Railway Station Museum*. Accommodation, stores, fuel. (*163/57*)

ATHERTON (Alt 752m; Pop 9950): sizeable agricultural and grazing town set at the foot of the eucalypt-clad Great Dividing Range. Walking trail on nearby Baldy Mountain*. Nearby are Hallorans Hill Environmental Park* (picnic facilities) and Hasties Swamp National Park (no facilities). Full town facilities. (*168/52*) *Road Trip 13 connects.*

Accommodation

Hinterland Motel, 44 Cook St, ©07 4091 3311, ✪$60
Atherton Motel, Maunds Rd (2kmN), ©07 4091 1500, ✪$65
Wrights Motor Inn, Sims Rd, (2.5kmN), ©07 4095 4141, ✪$55
Mountain View Van Park, 152 Roberts St, ©07 4091 4144, ✪Site: $14 Van: $50
Atherton Woodlands Tourist Park, 141 Herberton Rd, ©07 4091 1407, ✪Site: $15 Van: $55
Atherton Caravan Park, Yungaburra Rd (3kmE), ©07 4091 1099, ✪Site: $15 Van: $50-$65

Wongabel State Forest: interesting botanic walk*. **The Crater**:** highly recommended main feature of the small Mt Hypipamee National Park. The Crater is a very deep sheer-sided hole, a 58 metre drop to the lake below. A viewing platform provides awesome views. Elsewhere are attractive walking tracks passing through upland rainforests. Picnic facilities available but no camping. (*194/26*)

Hilly country supports remnant rainforest patches. **Herberton Road junction**: locality only; no facilities. (*197/23*) Herberton lies **NW**. Continue **S** for Tumoulin Road junction. *Continue N for Atherton.*
Tumoulin Road junction: locality only; no facilities. (*200/20*) Turn **W** for Ravenshoe. *Turn N for Atherton.*
Hilly country offers good views over cleared farming and grazing lands. Just west of the Tumoulin Road turnoff is the highest main road in Queensland* (marked by a sign).
Tumoulin: small farming locality (Queensland's highest settlement) of a few houses set within grazing country. This is the terminus of historic steam railway running from Ravenshoe (weekend afternoons). No facilities. (*214/6*)

RAVENSHOE (Alt 914m; Pop 1200):** interesting and attractive town with some photogenic buildings; Queensland's highest town. Centre of a small community of alternative lifestylers. Worth seeing: Little Millstream Falls* (off Tully Falls road), arts and crafts shops, historic steam train** (Ravenshoe-Tumoulin; weekend afternoons) and old railway station precinct, Koombooloomba Visitors Centre* (historical displays), Ravenshoe Historical Museum. Accommodation, stores, fuel. (*220/0*) *Road Trips 5 and 13 connect.*

Accommodation

Club Hotel-Motel, Grigg St, ©07 4097 6109, ✪$55
Tall Timbers Motel, Kennedy Hwy, ©07 4097 6325, ✪$55

Explorers Way
(Gregory Developmental Road)
Ravenshoe-Emerald
The Explorers Way between Ravenshoe and Charters Towers is mostly a scenic road passing through a variety of rugged landscapes, or traversing quite attractive grassy woodlands. The Charters Towers-Clermont road (Gregory Development Road) is a good sealed short-cut between far north Queensland and central Queens-

land. Though not particularly scenic, it passes through interesting outback country south of Charters Towers.

Warnings: this is an outback route - take care on narrow bitumen sections - keep the speed down. Remember that verges will be soft after rain. Beware of stock and kangaroos at night; avoid night driving if at all possible. Road subject to flooding. Road of two-lane width south of Belyando Crossing.

DAY 2: RAVENSHOE-CHARTERS TOWERS via The Lynd

Roads to Take: Gulf Developmental Road, Gregory Developmental Road (Explorers Way)
Grade 2
Total Distance: 457km (6:05)
Intermediate Distances:

	Km	Hours
Ravenshoe-Mt Garnet	47	(0:35)
Mt Garnet-Gulf Dev. Rd junction	68	(0:55)
Gulf Dev. Rd junction-The Lynd turnoff	92	(1:15)
The Lynd turnoff-Greenvale	52	(0:40)
Greenvale-Charters Towers	200	(2:40)

Average Vehicles per Day: 250 north of Charters Towers
Regions Traversed: North-East Highlands, Burdekin-Belyando Basin

RAVENSHOE (Alt 914m; Pop 1200):** interesting and attractive town. For more information see Day 1. (**0/457**)

Millstream Falls turnoff: (**5/452**) Turn **S** for the short drive to Millstream Falls*, an attractive waterfall (said to be the widest in Australia but only during the wet season) that is well worth seeing. Walking trails and gorge views. On the drive in, note the change in vegetation from dry woodlands on granite to moister woodlands (taller trees) on basalt. The falls are the centrepiece of a small national park of the same name;

no camping. World War II ruins are at the turnoff. En route to the falls is a short unsealed road that leads to Army Pools, an area of small waterfalls and swimming holes (not during high water).
Hilly country (with some minor clearings) offers fair to reasonable views. The countryside supports attractive eucalypt woodlands. A pleasant roadside **rest area** (very popular) is west of Millstream Falls turnoff. Keep an eye out for marked World War II sites.

Innot Hot Springs:* township set beside a creek which bubbles up very hot water. The creek is shallow (no swimming) but wading in the warm sands is pleasant (take care that you are not scalded). The nearby caravan park offers thermal pools (fee payable). Worth a quick look at least. Ask here about access to the nearby Mt Gibson fossicking area (permit required; 4WD recommended). Accommodation, store, fuel. (**15/442**)

Undulating country supports shrubby and grassy eucalypt woodlands.

Mt Garnet (Alt 671m; Pop 400):* old mining town with plenty of character. Interesting buildings. Old mine ruins can be found in the district, as well as fossicking sites - enquire locally. The town is located on the edge of outback rangelands. Accommodation, stores, fuel. (**47/410**)

Accommodation
Mt Garnet Motel, **Kennedy Hwy**, ©07 4097 9249, ©$50
Mt Garnet Caravan Park, **Kennedy Hwy**, ©07 4097 9249, ©Site: $14

Undulating country supports shrubby eucalypt woodlands. Near Mt Garnet are small land clearances.

Forty Mile Scrub National Park:* interesting park preserving remnant rainforest vegetation. These dry rainforests, or evergreen vine thickets, are typical of the vegetation that existed eons ago. Trees include white beans and bottle trees, as well as vines. Walking trail. **Rest area** adjacent. (**113/344**)

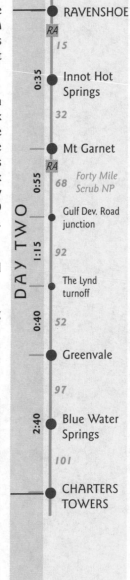

Road Trip 4

RAVENSHOE
RA
15
0:35 — Innot Hot Springs
32
Mt Garnet
RA
0:55 — 68 — *Forty Mile Scrub NP*
— Gulf Dev. Road junction
1:15 — 92
— The Lynd turnoff
0:40 — 52
Greenvale
97
2:40 — Blue Water Springs
101
CHARTERS TOWERS

DAY TWO

Gulf Developmental Road junction: locality only; no facilities. (*115/342*) Road Trip 13 connects. Continue **S** for Greenvale. *Continue **N** for Mt Garnet.*

Low rises support grassy eucalypt woodlands. Plains and low rises support quite scenic tracts of grassy eucalypt woodlands*. Basalt outcrops can be seen at intervals. Keep an eye out for the occasional patch of dry rainforest growing out of these basalt outcrops.

Court House Hotel, Charters Towers, Qld

The Lynd turnoff: (*207/250*) Two kilometres **SW** is **The Lynd** (Alt 610m; Pop 5), a small roadhouse. Accommodation, limited store, fuel. Undulating country supports grassy eucalypt woodlands. The area is dotted with basalt ridges. The countryside around here constitutes the Great Dividing Range* (marked by a sign).

Greenvale (Alt 450m; Pop 100):* former nickel mining town that today services tourists. A modern town with pleasant surroundings. Nearby Miners Lake* is an interesting wetland. Accommodation, stores, fuel. (*259/198*)
Accommodation
Three Rivers Hotel, Redbank Dr, ✆07 4788 4222, ◉$60
Greenvale Caravan Park, 3 Kylee Crt, ✆07 4788 4155, ◉Site: $14 Van: $45

Undulating country supports grassy eucalypt woodlands.
Low hills and flat-top ranges provide good views*. Spinifex grows on the hillsides. Small anthills can be seen.
Range* of rocky hills is quite scenic. Near Christmas Creek turnoff (1km east) is a rocky outcrop* supporting a patch of dry rainforest. The railway formation is part of the old Greenvale-Townsville railway.

Clarke River:* entrenched river crossing, and old telegraph station (no access). (*315/142*)
Low hills and rocky outcrops provide occasional views towards Mt Fullstop Range and Mt Oweenee.

Blue Water Springs Roadhouse (Pop 2): rustic roadhouse with some appeal. Accommodation, fuel. (*356/111*)

Plains and low rises support grassy eucalypt woodlands.
Basalt River crossing:* interesting spot. (*376/81*)
Plains* support tracts of attractive grassy eucalypt woodlands. At intervals, long but low ridges of basalt can be seen. These basalt walls* are the remains of old lava flows.
Fletcher Creek:* delightful camping spot by an attractive waterhole. Note the old basalt stonework on the road bridge. Nearby is the Dalrymple National Park* that preserves the remains of the old Dalrymple township. Little to see except for the cemetery, old fences and mine sites. (*412/45*)
Undulating country supports grassy eucalypt woodlands.

CHARTERS TOWERS (Alt 307m; Pop 9000):** old gold mining township with plenty of character. Worth at least half a day (more is better) for exploration. There are numerous historic and photogenic buildings - even residential streets have interesting structures. Worth seeing: main street and its buildings including the old stock exchange**, City Hall* and Pfeiffer House*; Zara Clarke Museum*, old Venus Battery* (fee); Lissner Park*; Centenary Park*, Buckland's Hill Lookout* (great views). Full town facilities. (*457/0*) *Road Trip 11 connects./Continue **N** along Gregory Developmental Road for Greenvale.*

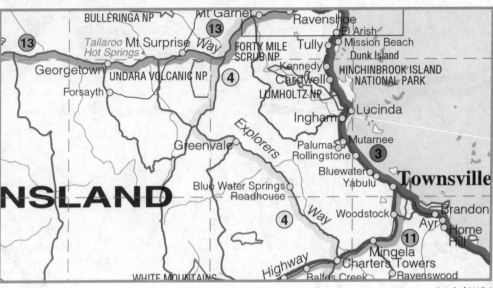

DAY THREE

CHARTERS TOWERS

2:40

199

Belyando Crossing

RA

1:55

177

CLERMONT

Detail of MAP 4

Accommodation

Charters Towers Heritage Lodge, 79-97 Flinders Hwy, ©07 4787 4088, ✪$70

Cattlemans Rest Motel, Cnr Bridge/Plant Sts, ©07 4787 3555, ✪$70

Country Road Motel, Flinders Hwy, ©07 4787 2422, ✪$50

Hillview Motel, Flinders Hwy, ©07 4787 1973, ✪$60

Park Motel, 1 Mosman St, ©07 4787 1022, ✪$70-$85

Dalrymple Tourist Van Park, Lynd Hwy (2kmN), ©07 4787 1121, ✪Site: $15 Van: $40-$55

Charters Towers Caravan Park, 37 Mt Leyshon Rd, ©07 4787 7944, ✪Site: $15

Mexican Tourist Park, 75 Church St, ©07 4787 1161, ✪Site: $13 Van: $30-$40

DAY 3: CHARTERS TOWERS-CLERMONT
via Belyando Crossing

Roads to Take: Gregory Developmental Road (Explorers Way)
Grade 2
Grade 1 Belyando Crossing-Clermont

Total Distance: 376km (4:35)
Intermediate Distances:

	Km	Hours
Charters Towers-Belyando Crossing	199	(2:40)
Belyando Crossing-Clermont	177	(1:55)

Average Vehicles per Day: 150 north of Clermont
Regions Traversed: Burdekin-Belyando Basin, Central Highlands

CHARTERS TOWERS (Alt 307m; Pop 9000):** old gold mining township. For more information see Day 2. (*0/376*) Head **SW** out of town for 2km along the Flinders Hwy then turn **S** onto Gregory Developmental Road for Belyando Crossing.

Undulating country supports eucalypt woodlands. Near Charters Towers are low, rocky hills giving the landscape a semi-arid appearance.
Low ranges offer occasional good views. Numerous rocky outcrops and gullies. Low eucalypt woodlands common.
Policeman Creek* crossing riverbank vegetation displays lush tropical growth. (*37/339*)
Low rises and plains support tracts of eucalypt woodlands. Some minor land clearances are given over to grazing.

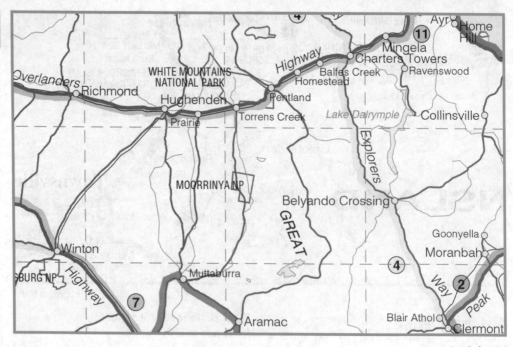

Detail of MAP 4

Sandplain supports a semi-arid landscape of stunted eucalypts and spinifex. Small anthills can be seen.

Cape River* exhibits a wide sandy river red gum-lined bed with waterholes during the dry season. Limited access. (*113/263*)

Low rises support eucalypt woodlands interspersed with acacia woodlands and dominated by blackwoods. Blackwoods are readily distinguished by their black trunks.

Low hills offer occasional fair views of range country lying to the west. Eucalypt woodlands common.

Blackwood National Park: limited facilities including a camping area. Small park preserving blackwood woodlands.

View: good westward view of an unnamed range, available from atop a rise a short distance east of Blackwattle Creek. The range exhibits remarkable bedding features*. (*179/197*)

Belyando Crossing (Alt 200m; Pop 5): roadhouse facility with some character. **Rest area** adjacent. Accommodation, limited store, fuel. (*199/177*)

Accommodation

Belyando Crossing Caravan Park, Gregory Dev. Rd, ©07 4983 5269, ✪Site: $14

Belyando River: attractive river crossing. River red gum-lined sandy river bed and waterholes during dry season. Adjacent floodplain supports eucalypt woodlands.

Low hills support acacia woodlands and spinifex. Fair views.

Low rises and plains offer fair views* of distant hills. Extensive land clearances.

Low hills supporting stunted eucalypts offer fair but distant views. Westwards the rocky outcrops of Mt Rolfe can be seen.

Mazeppa National Park: small park set within an ocean of cleared land, which preserves a tract of brigalow country. No facilities. (*296/80*)

Plain, mostly cleared, exhibits some cropping.

Low rise offers a broad vista to the north.

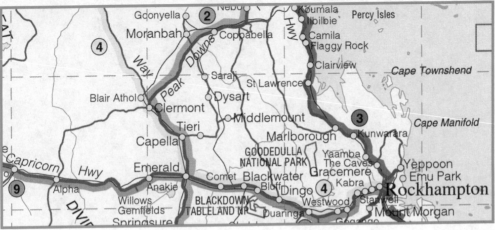

Detail of MAP 3

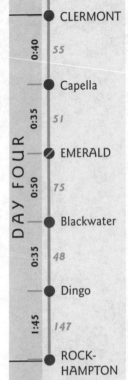

Undulating country has been partially cleared for grazing. Eucalypt woodlands dominate with ironbarks elsewhere.

Low rise signifies the Drummond Range. The landscape is mostly cleared for cropping, typically sunflowers.

CLERMONT (Alt 267m; Pop 2800):* coal mining and farming town. For more information see Road Trip 2, Day 4 . (**378/0**) *Road Trip 2 connects.*

DAY 4: CLERMONT-ROCKHAMPTON
via Emerald

Roads to Take: Gregory Highway, Capricorn Highway
Grade 1
Total Distance: 376km (4:25)

Intermediate Distances:

	Km	Hours
Clermont-Capella	55	(0:40)
Capella-Emerald	51	(0:35)
Emerald-Blackwater	75	(0:50)
Blackwater-Dingo	48	(0:35)
Dingo-Rockhampton	147	(1:45)

Average Vehicles per Day: 600 south of Clermont
Regions Traversed: Central Highlands, Capricornia

CLERMONT (Alt 267m; Pop 2800):* coal mining and farming town. For more information see Road Trip 2, Day 4. (**378/0**) *Road Trip 2 connects.*

For information on the route between Clermont, Emerald, Blackwater and Rockhampton see Road Trip 2, Day 4 and Road Trip 9, Day 5.

ROCKHAMPTON (Alt 10m; Pop 65000):* large regional centre. For more information see Road Trip 3, Day 1. (**270/0**) *Road Trips 3 and 9 connect.*

Road Trip 5
Wet Tropics - Atherton Tableland Loop

Cairns-Chillagoe-Ravenshoe-Innisfail-Cairns
Total Distance: 562km
Suggested Travelling Time: 3 days

Drive through rainforest country and sugar cane farmlands

See the popular town of Kuranda and its markets, the mining township of Chillagoe, the waterfalls near Millaa Millaa, and historic Herberton.

Wet Tropics/Atherton Tableland

Rising abruptly from the coastal lowlands, the highest mountains in Queensland intercept moist on-shore winds for most of the year, resulting in this part of the country receiving the highest rainfall in Australia. A large variety of rainforests grow as a result of the rich soils and frequent rainfall. While rainforests characterise the countryside, the lowlands have been largely cleared for sugar cane farming, the region's second characteristic identity. The Wet Tropics and adjacent Atherton Tablelands feature green lushness and spectacular beauty.

Access for southerners (anyone from south of Townsville is a southerner here) is via the coastal Bruce Highway (Road Trip 3) or the inland Explorers Way (Road Trip 4). Travellers doing a circuit of North-West Queensland usually use the Savanna Way (Road Trip 13).

The Climate

The Wet Tropics coast is generally a warm to hot place. Summer maximums, around 32C on the coast (hotter inland, up to 36C) are moderated by the close proximity to the sea. The trade-off humidity is high enough to be uncomfortable. Nights too can be unpleasant, with minimums around 23C. Coupled with these high temperatures is the likelihood of intense rain periods and the threat of tropical cyclones.

The southern cool season (April to October) is the time to visit. Daytime temperatures at either end of this period can still be hot (up to 30C) but without the humidity. Nights are pleasantly mild to warm. Mid-winter can experience many warm days (around 26C) coupled with the odd mild day (24C with a cool wind). Nights tend to be mild, around 17C. Rainfall at this time is usually in the form of sporadic showers.

Note that on the Atherton Tableland, summer temperatures (and humidity) are moderated (28C - 30C). In winter they are moderated too, with beautiful warm, sunny days (around 23C) but cold nights (down to freezing).

Capital City Connections
Distances in kilometres
SYDNEY-CAIRNS
via Pacific/Bruce Highways

	Intermediate	Total
Sydney	0	0
Coffs Harbour	537	537
Brisbane	422	959
Rockhampton	644	1603
Mackay	334	1937
Townsville	393	2330
Cairns	344	2674

MELBOURNE-CAIRNS
via Hume/Goulburn Valley/Newell/Leichhardt/Bruce Highways

	Intermediate	Total
Melbourne	0	0
Parkes	696	696
Moree	478	1194
Miles	333	1527
Rockhampton	428	1955
Mackay	334	2289
Townsville	393	2682
Cairns	344	3026

Road Trip 5

The Route
Distances in kilometres

	Intermediate	Total
Cairns	0	0
Mareeba	64	64
Chillagoe	145	209
Herberton	135	344
Ravenshoe	38	382
Millaa Millaa	30	412
Innisfail	63	475
Cairns	87	562

Atherton Tablelands/
North East Highlands Routes
**Cairns-Chillagoe-Herberton-
Ravenshoe-Innisfail-Cairns**
The tablelands, generally referred to as the Atherton Tablelands, is a district mostly cleared for farming and grazing. It supports a number of settlements as well as providing access to numerous waterfalls, lakes, escarpment views and World Heritage rainforests. Further west the countryside lies in a rainshadow, and rainforests are replaced by eucalypt forests and grassy woodlands. This upland country forms part of the rugged North-East Highlands.

Warnings: routes leading to or from the Atherton Tableland are steep and twisty. Note that some roads on the Atherton Tableland are narrow bitumen and very curvy; take care on soft verges after rain. The Mareeba-Chillagoe road is partially unsealed but in good condition. The return route, between Petford and Irvinebank, is unsealed and quite rough - 4WD recommended; travellers wishing to avoid this section can return via Mareeba and Atherton, joining the road trip at Herberton. Narrow sealed sections will be encountered between Ravenshoe and Millaa Millaa. The route between Innisfail-Cairns is very busy during the tourist season with limited overtaking opportunities; beware of sugar cane trains and trucks (all of which move slowly) on this and other Wet Tropic routes.

DAY ONE

- CAIRNS
- 13
- ⊘ Kennedy Hwy junction
- 14
- 0:55
- Kuranda
- 37
- ⊘ MAREEBA
- 36
- Mutchilba
- 11
- 2:05
- Dimbulah
- RA
- 65
- Alma Den
- 33
- Chillagoe

DAY 1: CAIRNS-CHILLAGOE via Mareeba

Roads to Take: Kennedy Highway, Burke Developmental Road
Grade 1 Cairns-Dimbulah
Grade 2 Dimbulah-Alma Den
Grade 3 Alma Den-Chillagoe (may be sealed during currency of this book)
Total Distance: 209km (3:00)
Intermediate Distances:

	Km	Hours
Cairns-Mareeba	64	(0:55)
Mareeba-Chillagoe	145	(2:05)

Average Vehicles per Day: 200 west of Dimbulah
Regions Traversed: Wet Tropics, Atherton Tableland, North-East Highlands

CAIRNS (Alt 3m; Pop 101000):** large and vibrant tropical city. For more information see Road Trip 3, Day 5. (*0/209*) *Road Trips 3 and 6 connect.*
En route from/to Cairns are access roads to the suburbs and beaches of Yorkeys Knob, Holloways Beach and Machans Beach*.

Plain supports sugar cane farms and urban development. Good views* westward towards the Kuranda Range.
Kennedy Highway junction: (*13/196*) Turn off roundabout **W** for Kuranda and Mareeba.
Henry Ross Lookout* provides excellent views from near the top of the steep rainforest-clad Kuranda Range. Below, the sugar cane farms and spreading northern suburbs of Cairns occupy the lowland plain. Beyond lies the shoals and deeper waters of the Great Barrier Reef. Access is difficult if heading up the mountain. A popular stop for tourist coaches. (*19/190*)
Hilly country* is clothed in impressive tropical rainforests. Unfortunately the busy, twisting and fairly narrow road limits areas in which to pull over.
Kuranda turnoff: (*27/182*) Drive the short distance into Kuranda.

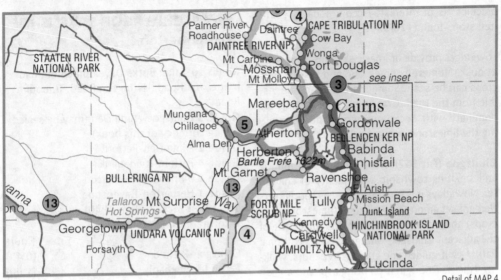

Detail of MAP 4

Kuranda (Alt 329m; Pop 750):** popular tourist town. Expect a big crowd, especially on market days. There is lots to see and do, including rainforest tours by boat and mini-trains, rainforest markets*, bungy jumping, butterfly sanctuary*, wildlife noctarium*, Kuranda railway station*, Tjapukai Dance Theatre**, Jumrum Creek Environmental Park*, numerous gift shops and restaurants. This is the terminus of the Kuranda Scenic Railway*** and the Skytrain*** (aerial cableway). A short distance away is **Barron Falls**,* centrepiece of the Barron Gorge National Park. There is an impressive waterfall (best during wet season), lookouts and brief walking tracks. A wander down to the Barron Falls railway station is worthwhile (watch for trains). No camping. Nearby is Wrights Lookout* - unsealed access) overlooking Barron Gorge. Accommodation, stores, fuel.

Undulating country supports grazing country and forested lands. Westwards are irrigated farmlands.

MAREEBA (Alt 404m; Pop 17300): sizeable agricultural, grazing and service centre. For more information see Road Trip 4, Day 1. (*64/145*) *Road Trips 4 and 6 connect.* Continue **W** along Bourke Developmental Road for Mutchilba. *Continue **E** along Kennedy Hwy for Kuranda.*

Farmlands occupy undulating to flat countryside. Irrigation is common. A variety of crops are grown, including tobacco, mangoes and avocados. Reasonable views.

Mutchilba (Alt 480m; Pop 30): small agricultural township. Store, fuel. (*100/109*)

Dimbulah (Alt 462m; Pop 350): small agricultural and irrigation town. Tobacco farming is common. Interesting main street*. Accommodation, stores, fuel. (*111/98*)

Hilly country provides good views towards distant ranges. West of Dimbulah is a good view* westwards down the Walsh River valley. Eucalypt woodlands are common. This area marks the start of the outback rangelands. **Rest area**. (*117/92*)
Petford (Alt 462m): (small former railway) locality with some character. Interesting buildings. (*144/65*)
Lappa: former railway junction marked by a couple of timber houses. (*151/58*)
Hilly country provides good views over eucalypt-clad ridges and hills.

Alma Den (Alt 493m; Pop 50):* sometimes known as 'Cowtown', as cattle often wander throughout the settlement. The railway station

Road Trip 5

DAY TWO

0:45		● Chillagoe
	65	
		◐ Petford
1:00	43	
		● Irvinebank
0:20	27	
		◐ Herberton
0:35	15	
		Kennedy Hwy junction
	3	
		Tumoulin Road junction
	20 Tumoulin	
		● RAVENSHOE

precinct* is of interest. Accommodation, limited store, fuel. (*176/33*)

Low ridges provide dramatic skylines, especially at dusk. Numerous limestone and marble outcrops can be seen. Some marble mines are visible from the road. Grassy eucalypt woodlands dominate with deciduous woodlands occupying the limestone outcrops.

Chillagoe (Alt 352m; Pop 220):** old mining and smelting township with plenty of character. Nowadays it is mostly a low-key tourist settlement set among tower karsts (limestone outcrops) and marble hillocks. This is the centre of the adjacent Chillagoe-Mungana Caves National Park** (self-guided and guided cave tours, walking tracks, Aboriginal paintings, picnic areas). Interesting buildings, some of which are photogenic. The township has a good feel and is well worth visiting, especially the Smelter ruins** (self-guided tours, phamplets available), a fascinating ruin of a large copper, lead, silver and gold smelting works dominated by high chimney stacks - photogenic, especially in the late afternoon light. Also see the Chillagoe Heritage Museum*. Accommodation, stores, fuel. (*209/0*)

Accommodation
Chillagoe Caves Lodge Motel, 7 King St, ℂ07 4094 7106, ✪$50-$60
Chillagoe Caravan Park and Roadhouse, Queens St, ℂ07 4094 7177, ✪Site: $12 Van: $40-$50
Chillagoe Caves Lodge Caravan Park, 7 King St, ℂ07 4094 7106, ✪Site: $12

Balancing Rock, Chillagoe, Qld

DAY 2: CHILLAGOE-RAVENSHOE via Herberton

Roads to Take: Burke Developmental Road, Irvinebank Road, Herberton Road, Tumoulin Road
Grade 3 Chillagoe-Alma Den (may be sealed during currency of this book)
Grade 2 Alma Den-Petford
Grade 4 Petford-Irvinebank
Grade 2 Irvinebank-Herberton
Grade 1 Herberton-Ravenshoe
Total Distance: 173km (2:40)
Intermediate Distances:

	Km	Hours
Chillagoe-Petford	65	(0:45)
Petford-Irvinebank	43	(1:00)
Irvinebank-Herberton	27	(0:20)
Herberton-Ravenshoe	38	(0:35)

Average Vehicles per Day: 200 west of Petford
Regions Traversed: North-East Highlands, Atherton Tableland

▼

Chillagoe (Alt 352m; Pop 220):** old mining and smelting township. For more information see Day 1. (*0/173*) Return **E** for Petford.

For information on the route between Chillagoe and Petford see Day 1.

Petford: old railway settlement. (*65/108*) Turn **E** for Irvinebank (4WD recommended - dry weather road only - rough and rocky between Petford and Irvinebank). If you are driving a conventional vehicle, you may prefer to take the good quality sealed road via Mareeba (turn **S**) and Atherton (turn **SW**), and rejoin this Road Trip at Herberton - a distance of 129km. *Turn **W** for Chillagoe.*
Emuford: former tin mining settlement of which little remains save for some ruins and rusted machinery. Attractive wild country hereabouts with occasional good views. (*83/90*)
Hilly country supports dry eucalypt woodlands. Many good views. Sharp, narrow gullies and broader valleys provide constantly changing

vistas. It is worth travelling slowly to appreciate the landscape.

Irvinebank (Alt 756m; Pop 120):* interesting and historic mining township set within a deep valley. Numerous old buildings, many photogenic. Picnic areas and swimming. Worth spending some time here to absorb the atmosphere. Also see Loudoun House Museum*. Accommodation, store, fuel. (**108/65**)

Jumna Creek: two plants grow here that are found nowhere else: *Acacia purpureapetala*, a wattle with purple flowers, and *Grevillea glossanenia*, a 2m high shrub with orange-red flowers.
Hilly country provides dramatic views overlooking the western ramparts of the Great Dividing Range. Eucalypt woodlands are common.
Watsonville: old mining settlement, nowadays a locality. Notable for the windmill set within the middle of the settlement's crossroads. (**127/46**)

Herberton (Alt 900m; Pop 600):* historic tin-mining town set upon numerous hills. Interesting buildings; many photogenic. Worth stopping a while to explore the town on foot. A tourist railway may by now be running over the old Atherton-Herberton line. Accommodation, stores, fuel. (**135/38**) Head **S** for Ravenshoe. Head **W** for Irvinebank.
Accommodation
Wild River Caravan Park, 23 Holdcroft Dr (3kmN), ©07 4096 2121, ○Site: $12 (unpowered)

Wondecla: small locality of a few houses. No facilities. (**138/35**)
Hilly country has been mostly cleared for grazing. Occasional westward views overlooking distant rugged ranges and outback country.
Kennedy Highway junction: locality only; no facilities. Attractive upland rainforests hereabout. (**150/23**) Road Trips 4 and 13 connect. Turn **S** for Ravenshoe. *Turn **W** for Herberton.*
Tumoulin Road junction: locality only; no facilities. (**153/20**) Road Trip 13 connects. Turn **SW** for Ravenshoe via Tumoulin. *Turn **N** for Herberton.*
Hilly country offers good views over cleared farming and grazing lands. Just west of the

Tumoulin Road turnoff is the highest main road in Queensland* (marked by a sign).
Tumoulin: small farming locality of a few houses set within grazing country. The terminus of an historic steam railway running from Ravenshoe (weekend afternoons). No facilities. (**167/6**).

RAVENSHOE (Alt 914m; Pop 1200):** interesting and attractive town. For more information see Road Trip 4, Day 1. (**173/0**) Road Trips 4 and 13 connect. /Head **N** along Tumoulin Road for Tumoulin.

DAY 3: RAVENSHOE-CAIRNS via Innisfail

Roads to Take: Kennedy Highway, Millaa Millaa Road, Palmerston Highway, Bruce Highway
Grade 2 Ravenshoe-Millaa Millaa
Grade 1 Millaa Millaa-Cairns
Total Distance: 180km (2:30)
Intermediate Distances:

	Km	Hours
Ravenshoe-Millaa Millaa	30	(0:30)
Millaa Millaa-Innisfail	63	(0:50)
Innisfail-Cairns	87	(1:10)

Average Vehicles per Day: 3500 north of Innisfail
Regions Traversed: Atherton Tableland, Wet Tropics

RAVENSHOE (Alt 914m; Pop 1200):** interesting and attractive town. For more information see Road Trip 4, Day 1. (**0/180**) Head **E** along Kennedy Hwy for Millaa Millaa turnoff.

Hilly country* offers good to excellent views. The highest hill is Windy Hill, an extinct volcano. The land is mostly cleared for farming. Note the wind farm* (giant wind generators) on the hillside. Viewpoint nearby. The towers are 45m high, and the blades are 22m long and rotate 30 times per minute.

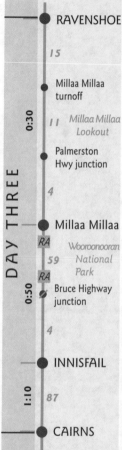

RAVENSHOE

15

Millaa Millaa turnoff

0:30   11   *Millaa Millaa Lookout*

Palmerston Hwy junction

DAY THREE   4

Millaa Millaa

RA   *Wooroonooran National Park*

59

RA

0:50   Bruce Highway junction

4

INNISFAIL

1:10   87

CAIRNS

Millaa Millaa (McHugh Road) turnoff: locality only, no facilities. (*15/165*) Turn **E** for Millaa Millaa. *Turn S for Ravenshoe.*

Milla Milla Lookout** offers excellent views northwards over the Atherton Tableland and eastwards towards the distant coastal ranges. Definitely worth visiting but bring a jumper - it's cool here. (*23/157*)

Palmerston Highway junction: locality only; no facilities. (*26/154*) Turn **E** for Millaa Millaa. *Turn S for Ravenshoe.*

Millaa Millaa (Alt 831m; Pop 350):* small farming township set among rolling hills. Eacham Historical Museum* is worth seeing. Accommodation, stores, fuel. (*30/150*)

Accommodation
The Falls Holiday Park, Malanda Rd, ©07 4097 2290, ⊙Site: $13 Van: $35-$45

Waterfall Circuit turnoff: (*32/148*) Turn here for the 15km unsealed loop road called the Waterfall Circuit. This route gives access to three pretty falls: Millaa Millaa, Zillie and Ellinjaa, all worth seeing.

Views* from on top a high hill overlook cleared farmlands, the distant Evelyn plateau (to the west) and rainforest-clad mountains (to the east). Hilly country supports excellent rainforests. Further west the countryside has been cleared for grazing.

Henrietta Creek: camping and **rest area** with picnic facilities, set within the rainforest. Start/finish of rainforest, riverside and waterfall tracks. (*56/124*)

K-Tree: roadside parking, **rest area** and start/finish of rainforest and waterfall tracks. Highly recommended is the walk to Tchupala Falls** and beyond. The rainforest** is one of the best

you will see. The falls are awesome and the track beyond is spectacular and potentially dangerous. (*59/121*)

Rest area. Nearby is a ranger station. (*61/119*)

Crawfords Lookout:* a cleared cut through the rainforest gives views to the Johnstone River gorge far below. Start/finish of rainforest walking track.

Wooroonooran National Park: this section of the park was formerly the Palmerston National Park, which preserves probably one of the finest and reasonably accessible World Heritage rainforests. Walks here are highly recommended, but take care in very wet weather. It's not as popular as other rainforests, so you may well have the place to yourself.

East Palmerston: farming locality of a few houses and a school. No facilities. Good eastward views from the tops of hills and ridges.

Farmlands occupy undulating to moderately hilly country. The land is given over to grazing, banana and tea plantations and, nearer Innisfail, sugar cane farms. Good all round views.

Bruce Highway junction: locality only; no facilities. (*89/91*) Turn **SE** for Innisfail. *Turn SW for Millaa Millaa.*

INNISFAIL (Alt 8m; Pop 8150):* interesting sugar cane farming town. For further information see the notes to Road Trip 3. (*93/87*) *Road Trip 3 connects.*

For information on the route between Innisfail and Cairns see Road Trip 3, Day 5.

CAIRNS (Alt 3m; Pop 101000):** large and vibrant tropical city. For more information see Road Trip 3, Day 5. (*180/0*) *Road Trips 3 and 6 connect.*

Road Trip 6
Southern Peninsula Loop

Cairns-Cooktown-Laura-Cairns
Total Distance: 799km
Suggested Travelling Time: 3 days

> *Pass rivers, rainforests and*
> *wilderness areas*
>
> See delightful Cooktown on the banks of the Endeavour River, the bush township of Laura, Lakefield National Park, Battlecamp Range, the Palmer and Annan Rivers, Mt Carbine, the very top of Australia at Cape York (4WD only), and the ancient Aboriginal art galleries at Split Rock.

Southern Peninsula Loop

Cape York Peninsula is a vast region that constitutes one of Australia's many 'last frontiers' , countryside that is still wild and relatively undeveloped. Contrary to popular belief, Cape York Peninsula is not one endless tract of rainforest. Mostly it is a broad, sweeping plain covered in eucalypt woodlands and dotted with anthills. There are some rainforests, though, including the largest remaining tracts of lowland rainforests in Australia, scattered along its east coast at the foot of some moderately high ranges. Elsewhere rainforests occupy narrow bands along some of the westward flowing rivers, otherwise it is mostly eucalypt and paperbark woodlands, the majority of which support a fair number of large outback stations given over to the extensive grazing of beef cattle.

The Climate

Cape York Peninsula is a warm to hot place. Summer maximums, around 34C on the coast (hotter inland, up to 40C), are moderated by the nearness to the sea. The trade-off humidity is high enough to be uncomfortable. Nights too can be unpleasant, with minimums around 23C.

Coupled with these high temperatures is the likelihood of intense rain periods and the threat of tropical cyclones.

The southern cool season (April to October) is the time to visit Cape York Peninsula. Daytime temperatures at either end of this period can still be hot (up to 30C) but without the humidity. Nights are pleasantly mild to warm. Mid-winter can experience many warm days (around 26C) while the nights tend to be mild (around 17C). Rainfall at this time is usually just sporadic showers.

Capital City Connections
Distances in kilometres
SYDNEY-CAIRNS
via Pacific/Bruce Highways

	Intermediate	Total
Sydney	0	0
Coffs Harbour	537	537
Brisbane	422	959
Rockhampton	644	1603
Mackay	334	1937
Townsville	393	2330
Cairns	344	2674

MELBOURNE-CAIRNS
via Hume/Goulburn Valley/Newell/Leichhardt/ Bruce Highways

	Intermediate	Total
Melbourne	0	0
Parkes	696	696
Moree	478	1194
Miles	333	1527
Rockhampton	428	1955
Mackay	334	2289
Townsville	393	2682
Cairns	344	3026

The Route
Distances in Kilometres

	Intermediate	Total
Cairns	0	0
Mareeba	64	64
Lakeland	186	250
Cooktown	82	332
Laura	151	483

Road Trip 6

Lakeland	66	549
Cairns	250	799

Kennedy Highway/ Peninsula Development Road

Cairns-Mareeba-Lakeland-Cooktown-Laura-Cairns

This region is one of Australia's most popular 4WD tourist destinations which, it must be said, has many locals wondering why. Most of Cape York is not particularly attractive (there are exceptions) and given the immense uniformity of many of its landscapes (stunted eucalypts, sandy soils and anthills) there is often little to see. Even vast vistas are few and far between. Nonetheless there are compensations: beautiful tracts of rainforest, attractive river crossings, pretty waterfalls, excellent coastal landscapes, ruins, indigenous cultures and, away from the main route at least, vast wilderness areas and a feeling of remoteness. Travellers taking their time will find a lot to enjoy, especially if they set up camp for a few days, or visit regions away from the main route.

Warnings: road subject to flooding. Avoid travelling at night. Due to the popularity of the Cape and its relatively busy traffic during the dry season, unsealed roads are usually badly corrugated and potholed, with occasional rocky outcrops. As such none can be recommended for the towing of caravans. Nonetheless the road is suitable to experienced drivers of conventional drive vehicles, but a 4WD is recommended. Travel before the winter school holidays is quiet and roads are in better condition (depending on how late the wet season was). Travel after this time will be rough, perhaps arduous. Virtually all roads are likely to be closed during the wet season which can extend from November to May. Always make local enquiries at this time.

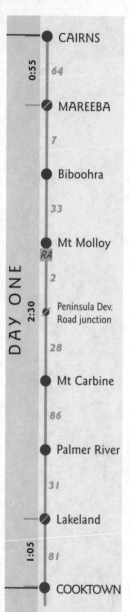

DAY 1: CAIRNS-COOKTOWN via Mareeba

Roads to Take: Kennedy Highway, Peninsula Developmental Road, Cooktown Developmental Road
Grade 3
Grade 1 Cairns-Palmer River
Total Distance: 332km (4:30)
Intermediate Distances:

	Km	Hours
Cairns-Mareeba	64	(0:55)
Mareeba-Lakeland	187	(2:30)
Lakeland-Cooktown	82	(1:05)

Average Vehicles per Day: 200 west of Mt Carbine
Regions Traversed: Wet Tropics, Atherton Tableland, North-East Highlands, Cape York Peninsula

CAIRNS (Alt 3m; Pop 101000):** large tropical city. For more information see Road Trip 3, Day 5. **(0/332)** *Road Trips 3 and 5 connect.*

For information about the route between Cairns and Mareeba see the notes to Road Trip 5.

MAREEBA (Alt 404m; Pop 17300): sizeable agricultural and grazing town. For more information see Road Trip 4, Day 1. **(64/268)** *Road Trips 4 and 5 connect.* Head **N** for Mount Molloy. Head **E** for Cairns.

Biboohra (Alt 391m): small irrigation farming township. Surrounding the settlement are sugar cane and rice farms, among others. Store, fuel. **(71/261)**

Undulating country supports eucalypt woodlands with occasional views to distant ranges. Anthills are common. North of Biboohra is a reservoir impounding a section of the Mitchell River.

Mt Molloy (Alt 389m; Pop 150):* old mining township with some character, nowadays a

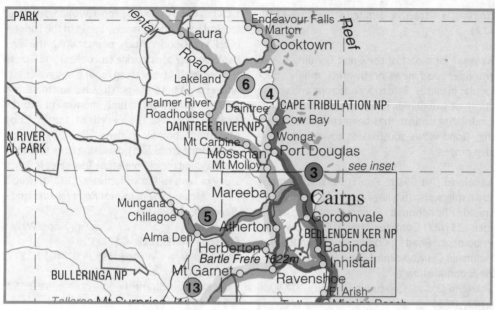

Detail of MAP 4

farming settlement. Interesting buildings. There are some old ruins and an historic cemetery. Just north of town is the Rifle Creek **rest area**, where camping and swimming is available. Accommodation, stores, fuel. (*104/228*) Road Trip 4 connects.

Peninsula Developmental Road junction: (*106/ 226*) Turn **W** for Mt Carbine. *Turn S for Mt Molloy.*

Hilly country* offers good views, especially towards the high ridge of Mt Fraser (1,155m). Eucalypt forests are common. Countryside hereabouts separates the coastal farming districts from the outback rangelands.
Many Farms: farming locality of cleared land set within a sea of eucalypt woodlands. No facilities save for a telephone. This area marks the start/end of the outback rangelands. (*126/206*)

Mt Carbine (Alt 320m):* interesting small mining township with an outback atmosphere. Nearby is Narrabullgan** (Mt Mulligan), with tours available - contact Ku Ku Djungan Aboriginal Corporation, Mareeba. Roadhouse. Accommodation, store, fuel. (*134/198*)

Undulating country and low hills support grassy eucalypt woodlands and small anthills. Occasional good mountain views.
McLeod River: attractive river crossing*; reasonable camping. (*148/184*)
Bobs Lookout:** stop here for excellent views overlooking Mt Elephant (1046m) and the Mitchell River valley. The impressive and quite barren Mt Elephant rises over 740 metres above the lowlands. Afternoons are best for photography, and full moons are not bad either. (*161/ 171*)
Ranges: good views* from high hilltops overlooking the broad Mitchell River valley. Sparse eucalypt woodlands are common. The area is known as Desailly Range.
Low hills and ranges line the road for some distance supporting tracts of ironbark woodlands. Occasional good views*, especially eastwards towards an impressive granitic range. Afternoons are best for viewing. Numerous boulders and tors can be seen.

Palmer River (Alt 440m): roadhouse settlement with some character. A small museum* contains Palmer River goldfield relics. The nearby river crossing is attractive. Limited store, fuel. (**220/112**)

Ranges* form part of the Great Dividing Range and offer good views northwards, mildly spectacular in places. Bare rocky outcrops and sparse eucalypt woodlands make up the landscape. Undulating country has been cleared for farming. Good views southwards towards impressive ranges.

Lakeland (Alt 290m; Pop 100): small farming township set with a large tract of cleared countryside. Roadhouse. Accommodation, store, fuel. (**251/81**) Continue **N** onto Cooktown Developmental Road for Cooktown. *Continue* **S** *onto Peninsula Developmental Road for Palmer River.*

Accommodation
Lakeland Downs, Cooktown Dev. Rd, ℂ07 4060 2142, ✪$55

Low hills and small plains offer fair to reasonable views. Countryside becomes wetter as one moves east, indicated by changes in vegetation: eucalypt grassy woodlands in the west and eucalypt forests in the east.
Little Annan River (The 'Little' Annan): pleasant river crossing. Downstream (watch your footing) is a deep waterworn chute and waterfalls*, worth a look. Picnic area. Camping is possible. (**303/29**)
Helenvale turnoff: locality only; no facilities. (**304/28**) A 12km return drive leads **S** to **Helenvale** (Alt 140m; Pop 20)*, an interesting bush pub (The Lions Den) and nearby eatery located in a pretty section of the partially cleared Annan River valley. Accommodation, limited store, fuel.
Black Mountain: (no facilities) centrepiece of a national park of the same name. Interesting lichen-covered boulder-strewn mountain which forms part of a longer range. Attractive countryside hereabouts. (**306/26**)
Annan River* (The 'Big' Annan): attractive estuary crossing. Mangroves and rainforests line the river. Interesting old bridge. Beware of estuarine crocodiles. (**322/10**)

COOKTOWN (Alt 2m; Pop 1300):** delightful tropical town on the muddy banks of the Endeavour River. Good vantage points along the river bank (beware of estuarine crocodiles) and Grassy Hill Lookout** (very steep road) of rugged coastline, especially to the north. Also worth seeing: riverside park with statues, monuments to the explorer Cook*, the excellent James Cook Museum**, botanic gardens, Finch Bay (beware of estuarine crocodiles), a walking track to Cherry Tree Bay, and the old cemetery. Town area is worth a day or two. Full town facilities. (**332/0**) *Head* **S** *on Cooktown Developmental Road for Lakeland.*

Accommodation
Cooktown River of Gold Motel, Cnr Hope/Walker Sts, ℂ07 4069 5222, ✪$75-$90
Sea View Motel, Webber Esp, ℂ07 4069 5377, ✪$80-$90
Seagrens Inn, Charlotte St, ℂ07 4069 5357, ✪$45-$65
Cooktown Tropical Breeze Caravan Park, Cnr Charlotte/McIvor Sts, ℂ07 4069 5417, ✪Site: $17 Van: $40-$75
Peninsula Caravan Park, Howard St (1kmS), ℂ07 4069 5107, ✪Site: $17 Van: $35-$70
Cooktown Orchid Travellers Park, Cnr Charlotte/Walker Sts, ℂ07 4069 6400, ✪Site: $18 Van: $40

DAY 2: COOKTOWN-LAURA
via Old Laura

Roads to Take: Battlecamp/Lakefield Roads (Cooktown-Laura)
Grade 4
Warning: Remote Summer Route
Total Distance: 151km (2:25)
Intermediate Distances:

	Km	Hours
Cooktown-Old Laura	123	(2:00)
Old Laura-Laura	28	(0:25)

Average Vehicles per Day: 20 east of Musgrave
Regions Traversed: Wet Tropics, Cape York Peninsula (Laura Plain)

COOKTOWN (Alt 2m; Pop 1300):** historic town. For more information see Day 1. (*0/151*) Head **W** on Battlecamp Road for Laura.

Marton (Alt 3m): small store serving the surrounding farming community. Lush, green tropical valley setting. Store, fuel. (*11/140*)

Plains provide good views* of adjacent ranges, especially to the west (wild country here). The countryside is mostly cleared for farming. Remnant rainforest patches can be seen along drainage lines, otherwise eucalypt forests.

Endeavour Falls (Alt 35m): small camping area set within a lush, green valley. Limited store, fuel. (*33/118*)

Hilly country provides good views* overlooking coastal ranges. Rainforest patches and eucalypt forests are common. This area forms the boundary to the outback country beyond.
Ranges provide excellent views overlooking sandstone ranges, valleys and wild country. One creek crossing (can be deep; take care) has an attractive small waterfall* nearby. Eucalypt forests with pandanus palms, grass trees and dry rainforest patches are common in the east, grading to eucalypt woodlands in the west.
Normanby River:* pleasant river crossing and popular camping spot.
Battle Camp Range rises above the road and provides good views* of sandstone escarpments. Vast tracts of eucalypt woodlands.
Lakefield National Park:* large park preserves vast tracts of woodlands, wetlands, and crocodile habitats. Good fishing, birdwatching and boating. Permits are required for camping.
Lake Emma turnoff: (*78/73*) Turn here for Lake Emma (4km return). Not the prettiest of lakes by the middle of the dry season (looks like a good place for mosquitoes), but undoubtedly pleasant after the wet season. Fair camping; beware of soft sand.
Horseshoe Lagoon turnoff: (*81/70*) Turn here for short drive to Horseshoe Lagoon*, a pretty la-

Horseshoe Lagoon, north-east of Laura, Qld

goon with incredible birdlife, brumbies and water lilies. Fair camping. Beware of estuarine crocodiles. A sandy 4WD loop track leads to other lagoons.
Low rises and plains support grassy eucalypt woodlands. Anthills can be seen.
Old Laura:* old station homestead and outbuildings partially restored - very photogenic. Worth a quick look at least. Nearby Laura River offers reasonable campsites. (*123/28*) Turn **S** for Laura. *Turn **E** for Cooktown.*
Plains support attractive grassy eucalypt woodlands. Anthills common.

Laura (Alt 91m; Pop 70):** bush township with plenty of character. Stop a while to enjoy the place. A visit to the pub is enjoyable. Nearby are the ruins of an old railway bridge. In June is an Aboriginal dance festival. Picnic facilities are availble at the (second) Laura River crossing. Museum. Accommodation, stores, fuel. (*151/0*) *Head **N** on Lakefield Road for Old Laura.*

Side Trip
Below is a brief description of the trip to the tip of Cape York. This popular 4WD journey is not part of the road trip, but has been included due to its popularity. The journey should only be undertaken in a 4WD during the dry season (May-November). Travel with company and take care at river crossings. Allow at least 6 days for the return journey.

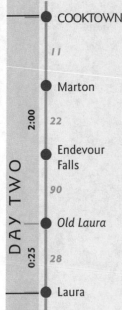

COOKTOWN

11

Marton

22

2:00

Endevour
Falls

90

DAY TWO

Old Laura

0:25

28

Laura

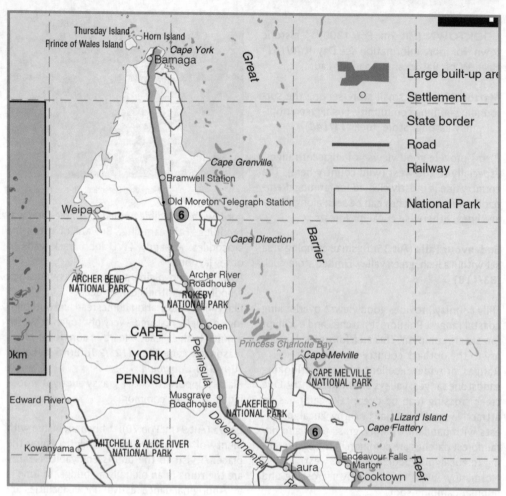

Detail of MAP 4

LAKELAND-BAMAGA
(Tip of Cape York)
via Coen

Roads to Take: Peninsula Development Road, Telegraph Road, By-Pass Roads
Grade 5
Grade 4 Laura-Weipa turnoff
Warning: Remote Summer Route. No fuel Archer River-Bamaga 392km
Total Distance: 1478km
Intermediate Distances:
Laura-Musgrave 136km

Musgrave-Coen	107km
Coen-Archer River	66km
Archer River-Weipa turnoff	49km
Weipa turnoff-Moreton Telegraph Stn	72km
Moreton Telegraph Stn-Bramwell Stn	39km
Bramwell Station-Bamaga	232km
Bamaga-Cape York	38km
Cape York-Laura	739km

Average Vehicles per Day: 75 north of Laura
Regions Traversed: Cape York Peninsula
Facilities en route:

Laura: township - accommodation, store, fuel.
Hann River: roadhouse facilities.
Musgrave: roadhouse facilities.

Coen: small town - accommodation, stores, fuel.
Archer River: roadhouse facilities.
Moreton: store, camping.
Bramwell Station: accommodation, store, camping.
Bamaga: small town - stores, fuel.
Cape York: accommodation.

DAY 3: LAURA-CAIRNS
via Lakeland

Roads to Take: Peninsula Development Road, Kennedy Highway
Grade 3
Total Distance: 316km (4:20)
Intermediate Distances:

	Km	Hours
Laura-Lakeland	66	(0:55)
Lakeland-Mareeba	186	(2:30)
Mareeba-Cairns	64	(0:55)

Average Vehicles per Day: 200 west of Mt Carbine
Regions Traversed: Cape York Peninsula, North-East Highlands, Wet Tropics

▼

Laura (Alt 91m; Pop 70):** bush township. For more information see Day 2. (*0/316*) Head **SE** on Peninsula Developmental Road for Lakeland.

Split Rock:** site of Aboriginal art galleries. Not to be missed. Small fee (honesty box) payable. Take water and wear a hat. Some climbing is involved on marked tracks - remember that it can get very hot, even in July. Excellent paintings including flying foxes, other animals and spirit Quinkin figures. Good views* overlooking sandstone ranges. Longer walks lead to more galleries. (*14/302*)
Ranges offer good views overlooking grassy eucalypt woodlands. Rugged country hereabouts. Attractive crossing of the Laura River*.
Low rises have been mostly cleared for farming. Good views towards distant ranges.

Lakeland (Alt 290m; Pop 100): small farming township. For more information see Day 2. (*66/250*)

For information about the route between Lakeland and Cairns see Days 1 and 2, and Road Trip 5, Day 1.

CAIRNS (Alt 3m; Pop 101000):** large tropical city. For more information see Road Trip 3, Day 5. (*316/0*) *Road Trips 3 and 5 connect.*

▲

Road Trip 6

DAY THREE		
		Laura
0:55	66 Split Rock	
		Lakeland
2:30	186	
		MAREEBA
0:55	64	
		CAIRNS

Road Trip 7
Matilda Country

Griffith-Karumba
Total Distance: 2457km
Suggested Travelling Time: 8 days

Waltz through Matilda Country, taking in the stockman heritage

See the agricultural town of Griffith, the historic buildings of Bourke, the town centre of Charleville, the Heritage Centre at Barcaldine, the Stockmen's Hall of Fame at Longreach, Winton's Waltzing Matilda Centre, the 'Crocodile Dundee' Hotel at McKinlay, the museum at Cloncurry, the Gulflander train at Normanton, and Kurumba Point for sunset over the Gulf of Carpentaria.

Matilda Country

The Kidman Way and Matilda Highway passes through country that is evocative of eastern inland Australia. Named after Sydney Kidman, the Cattle King, and Waltzing Matilda, Australia's unoffical national anthem, Matilda Country is a land of big skies arcing over treeless Mitchell grass plains. Most of the land is utilised for the extensive grazing of sheep and beef cattle. Towards the south, the Mitchell grass country abruptly changes into mulga shrublands, presenting another face of this part of Australia. Tourism has boomed here over the past 15 years, and although one would not travel here just for the scenery, the towns and townships make this a region worth visiting.

The Climate

The majority of travellers to the northern parts of the Matilda Country find that the cooler season between May and September is the ideal time to visit. Maximum temperatures are generally mild to warm (around 24C) with the odd cooler or warmer day thrown in. Nights can be cool though, with minimum temperatures around 5C - 10C. For those who prefer warmth, temperatures are higher either side of the cooler months. Generally days will be clear and sunny with virtually no rain.

Summers are hot, and sometimes humid, with maximum temperatures in the mid-thirties. Nights too are often warm and may be uncomfortable. Summer is also the time for rain. During wetter periods, summer showers can be intense, and the wet weather often extends well into autumn. During these times, access may be difficult due to flooding.

In the southern parts of the Matilda Country, temperatures will be correspondingly cooler, although extreme maximum summer temperatures will often be hotter than further north.

Capital City Connections
Distances in kilometres
SYDNEY-NYNGAN
via Great Western/Mitchell Highways

	Intermediate	Total
Sydney	0	0
Bathurst	207	207
Dubbo	205	412
Nyngan	166	578
Bourke	201	777

MELBOURNE-GRIFFITH
via Northern/Newell Highways/Kidman Way

	Intermediate	Total
Melbourne	0	0
Shepparton	179	179
Jerilderie	134	313
Griffith	132	445

BRISBANE-CHARLEVILLE
via Warrego Highway

	Intermediate	Total
Brisbane	0	0
Toowoomba	129	129
Roma	352	481
Charleville	265	746

The Route
Distances in kilometres

	Intermediate	Total
Griffith	0	0
Hillston	106	106
Cobar	257	363
Bourke	162	525
Cunnamulla	256	781
Charleville	198	979
Barcaldine	408	1387
Winton	281	1668
Cloncurry	343	2011
Karumba	446	2457

Kidman Way
Griffith-Bourke

Striking north-south across the heart of New South Wales, the Kidman Way provides ready access to all travellers heading to or from Queensland from Victoria or South Australia. Travellers will find plenty of interest along this route: attractive wheatlands, the largest tract of uncleared mallee country in New South Wales, old mining towns and ruins, mirage-dotted empty plains and the tranquil beauty of the lower Lachlan River.

Travellers from Victoria can access this route by either the Cobb Highway via Hay or the Newell Highway and Route 87 via Griffith. South Australians access this route at Hay via the Sturt Highway, or continue along the Mid-Western Highway to Goolgowi.

Warnings: beware of stock and kangaroos at night; avoid night driving if at all possible. Road subject to flooding, especially Lachlan River crossing north of Hillston. If in doubt make local enquiries.

DAY 1 GRIFFITH-COBAR
via Hillston

Road to Take: Kidman Way
Grade 1
Total Distance: 363km (4:05)

Intermediate Distances:

	Km	Hours
Griffith-Hillston	106	(1:10)
Hillston-Mt Hope	96	(1:05)
Mt Hope-Cobar	161	(1:50)

Average Vehicles per Day: 250 north of Mt Hope
Regions Traversed: Riverina, Western Plains (Cobar Plains)

GRIFFITH (Alt 126m; Pop 22000):* large agricultural and irrigation town. Attractive main street. Numerous tourist activities including museum, lookouts, water activities at Lake Wyangan (10 kilometres north-west), galleries, walking tracks, industrial tours and many wineries. Enquire locally. Full town facilities. (*0/363*) Head **N** on Kidman Way for Goolgowi. *Connecting Route C connects.*

Accommodation
A-Line Motel, 187 Wakaden St, ℂ02 6962 1922, ✪$65-$85
MIA Motel, Leeton Rd (2.5kmSE), ℂ02 6962 1866, ✪$65-$85
The Gemini Motel, 201 Banna Ave, ℂ02 6962 3833, ✪$75-$100
Griffith Tourist Caravan Park, 919 Willandra Ave (2kmS), ℂ02 6964 2144, ✪Site: $18 Van: $45-$65
Griffith Caravan Village, Mackay Ave (3kmE), ℂ02 6962 3785, ✪Site: $15 Van: $30-$60

Farmlands support country given over to wheat and cereal cropping. Closer to Griffith are irrigation farms.
Tabbita: railway siding. (*29/334*)

Goolgowi (Alt 123m; Pop 240): small agricultural town. Accommodation, store, fuel. (*46/317*)

Merriwagga (Alt 114m; Pop 100):* small agricultural township with some character. Accommodation, store, fuel. (*67/296*)

Farmlands support moderately large holdings given over to cereal cropping (notably wheat) and

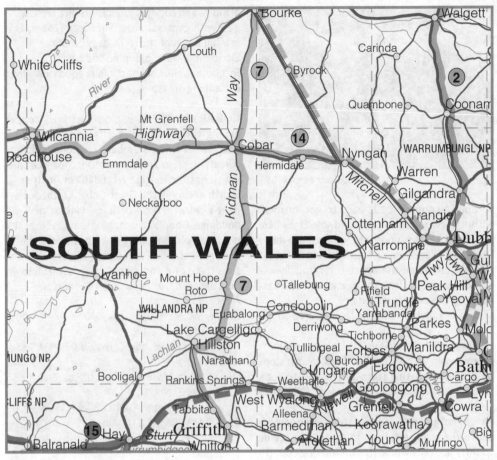

Detail of MAP 3

grazing. Vegetation remnants mostly restricted to road reserves, typically mallee eucalypts. Good eastward views* towards the Lachlan Range.

HILLSTON (Alt 123m; Pop 1000): agricultural town with character. Interesting main street. Worth seeing: Island reserve, Lake Woorabinda. Full town facilities. (*106/257*)

Accommodation

Kidman Way Motor Inn, Cnr High/Keats Sts, ©02 6967 2151, ✪$60-$80

Hillston Motel, 25 McGee St, ©02 6967 2573, ✪$55

Hillston Caravan Park, Cnr High/Oxley Sts, ©02 6967 2575, ✪Site: $15 Van: $50

Farmlands used mostly for cereal cropping and grazing occupy the countryside south of Willandra Creek. Attractive area at the Lachlan River bridge* (river red gums). Good views eastward towards the Lachlan Range. Reasonable views from the tops of rises, especially after winter rains. Northwards the route enters/exits outback country.

Matakana Mallee:* the largest remaining tract of uncleared eucalypt mallee country in New South Wales, much of which can be considered wilderness. Dominant plants are various species of whipstick mallees (short shrubby eucalypts with slender smooth trunks), beneath which grow a variety of shrubs and herbs. Good wildflower displays after rain. Do not walk here

DAY TWO 1:45

● COBAR

162

Fred Hol-
lows
Grave

● BOURKE

Mt Hope South mine ruin, NSW

without a compass; it is easy to get 'bushed' within a few metres of the roadway. Elsewhere are grassy tracts supporting cypress pine woodlands. Travellers heading south should note that they have entered the agricultural fruit fly exclusion zone - no fruit or vegetables to be carried into the zone from outside
Matakana: railway siding; no facilities. (**184/179**)

Mt Hope (Alt 183m; Pop 25):* old copper mining township with an 'outback' feel. Worth stopping to absorb the atmosphere and to look around. Accommodation, store, fuel. (**202/161**)

Ranges* of granite rise some 100 metres or more above the road, resulting in pleasantly scenic countryside. Elsewhere this undulating country provides fair views. Cypress pine and bimble box woodlands common.
Plains and low rises support tracts of grassy eucalypt woodlands interspersed with cypress pine woodlands. Some small clearings on grazing properties, occasionally utilised for wheat cropping.
Gilgunnia: old mining locality; no facilities. Worth stopping for a quick look. Some relics are visible if you poke about in the long grass. Old copper mines lie just to the north of the road junction. **Rest area**. (**254/109**)
Low rises offer good views towards the nearby Gilgunnia Range, including Mt Gilgunnia (523m). Attractive country hereabouts with cypress pine woodlands and eucalypts.
Low rises offer fair views of some minor land clearances given over to grazing. Elsewhere are tracts

of mulga and eucalypt woodlands often intermingled with cypress pines. Sheerlegs (256m) is a low hill north of the Nymagee turnoff.
Occidental Mine: old mine and ruins.
Fort Bourke Hill Lookout* offers good views over old mining areas.

COBAR (Alt 251m; Pop 5500):* busy copper mining town with some character. Interesting main street with a number of historic buildings (Great Western Accommodation, for example, which has the longest verandah* in Australia.). Worth seeing is the Great Cobar Outback Heritage Centre*. Take a heritage walk to view old buildings. Good bird watching is available at the old reservoir. Balloon launchings at the meteorological station (9am daily). Explore old mine sites (take care and do not trespass). Full town facilities. (**363/0**) Road Trip 14 connects.
Accommodation
Hi-Way Motel, Barrier Hwy, ©02 6836 2000, ✪$65
Cobar Oasis Motel, Barrier Hwy, ©02 6836 2452, ✪$65
Cross Roads Motel, 21 Louth Rd, ©02 6836 2711, ✪$60
Cobar Caravan Park, Barrier Hwy (1kmW), ©02 6836 2425, ✪Site: $16 Van: $25-$50

▲

DAY 2: COBAR-BOURKE
via Kidman Way

Roads to Take: Kidman Way
Grade 3
Total Distance: 162km (1:45)
Average Vehicles per Day: 160 south of Bourke
Regions Traversed: Western Plains (Cobar Plains, Darling River floodplain)

▼

COBAR (Alt 251m; Pop 5500):* busy copper mining town. For more information see Day 1. (**0/162**)

Low rises support tracts of mulga shrublands with occasional eucalypt woodlands. The prominent Mt Merrere (297m) rises about 100 metres above the lowlands.

Low rises offer occasional fair views overlooking vast tracts of eucalypt woodlands, (mulga) shrublands and cypress pines.

Plains support vast tracts of open grasslands with good views southward towards Mt Gunderbooka (496m). Elsewhere are gidgee woodlands and, further south, shrubby eucalypt woodlands with mulga.

Cemetery* worth looking at for its Afghan graves, and that of famous eye surgeon Fred Hollows. Adjacent is a rather poignant pet cemetery. Levee banks and a cotton gin lie nearby. (*160/2*)

BOURKE (Alt 106m; Pop 3200):* interesting grazing and irrigation town. Forget the bad press Bourke occasionally receives; many innovative programs are underway here - enquire locally. Plenty of historic buildings**, especially in Mitchell Street. Worth seeing: rebuilt old wharves* and riverside walking track* (good river fishing). West of town are the Fort Bourke Stockade, Lock, and weir. Full town facilities. (*162/0*) Head **S** on Kidman Way for Cobar.

Accommodation
Darling River Motel, 74 Mitchell St, ©02 6872 2288, ✪$60-$70
The Outback Motel, Mertin St, ©02 6872 2716, ✪$60-$70
The Port of Bourke Hotel, 32 Mitchell St, ✪$50-$60
Mitchell Caravan Park, Mitchell St (1kmW), ©02 6872 2791, ✪Site: $12 Van: $30
Kidman Camp Van & Cabin Park, Mitchell Hwy (8kmN), ©02 6872 1612, ✪Site: $16 Van: $35-$50

Mitchell/Matilda Highway
Bourke-Karumba
This major outback route provides southern Australians with an easy access to the east-west routes that penetrate the arid country of Western Queensland, as well direct access to northern Australia. Though long on straight roads and short on scenery, this route passes through typical 'Back of Bourke' country, a land rich in Euro-

pean Australia's pioneering heritage, a fact recognised by the renaming of this route to Matilda Highway. Passing mostly through mulga shrublands, and crossing treeless Mitchell grass plains, the Matilda Highway visits interesting grazing towns that seem little changed since the 1950s. Also of interest are the smaller bush townships and Longreach's Stockmen's Hall of Fame.

Travellers from the southern states can access the Matilda Highway's southern connection via either the Mitchell Highway at Bourke, or the Kidman Way from Griffith. Southern Queenslanders can reach the Matilda Highway along the Warrego Highway by travelling either directly to Augathella or by taking the slightly longer but more interesting route via Charleville.

Warnings: beware of stock and kangaroos at night. Roadkills are a hazard. Roads subject to flooding.

DAY 3: BOURKE-CUNNAMULLA via Barringun

Roads to Take: Mitchell Highway
Grade 1
Total Distance: 256km (2:50)
Intermediate Distances:

	Km	Hours
Bourke-Enngonia	95	(1:05)
Enngonia-Cunnamulla	161	(1:45)

Average Vehicles per Day: 250 north of Enngonia
Regions Traversed: Western Plains (Cobar Plains, Darling River floodplain, Warrego River floodplain)

BOURKE (Alt 106m; Pop 3200): sizeable grazing and irrigation town on the banks of the Darling River. For more information see Day 2. (*0/256*) Head **N** on Mitchell Hwy for Enngonia. *Connecting Route E connects.*

Darling River:* Australia's longest stream. Numerous billabongs in area. Eucalypt woodlands - river red gums along main channel.

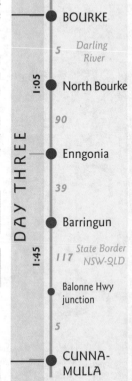

DAY THREE

BOURKE

5 · Darling River

1:05 · North Bourke

90

Enngonia

39

Barringun

1:45 · 117 · State Border NSW-QLD

Balonne Hwy junction

5

CUNNA-MULLA

North Bourke (Pop 20): small township. The old lifting span bridge* over Darling River is worth investigating. Accommodation, store, fuel. (*5/251*)

Plains north of North Bourke support open grasslands and gidgee woodlands. Keep an eye out for a dry lake just west of the highway. Note the old Government bores from the droving days. Sand plains and low ridges. Eucalypt woodlands cover the sand plains, mulga shrublands occur on the low ridges. In this region the sand plains are known as 'soft-red country', the low ridges as 'hard-red country', due to their rocky nature. Usually good springtime wildflowers* grow in the area.

Enngonia (Alt 107m; Pop 100):* small grazing township and Aboriginal community. Many old 'bush' buildings. Aboriginal enterprises worth visiting. Heritage sites* in the district - enquire locally. Accommodation, store, fuel. (*95/161*)

Plains south of Barringun form part of the Warrego River plains. Open grassland areas and low eucalypt woodlands.

Barringun (Alt 140m; Pop 10):* interesting and friendly bush pub. A couple of old wooden buildings make interesting photographic subjects. Accommodation, store, fuel. (*134/122*)

State border between New South Wales and Queensland. (*135/121*)
Plains south of Tuen are part of Warrego River floodplain. Numerous grasslands and occasional acacia stands. Tinnenburra Station, west of highway (no access), is the former encampment of displaced Kunja people. There are burial sites in area. Tuen Station: no facilities. Site of old hotel. Open grasslands provide extensive views. (*194/62*)
Low dunes south of Cunnamulla are part of Warrego River floodplain. Eucalypts and cypress pines are common.
Balonne Highway junction: (*251/5*) Turn **W** for the short drive into Cunnamulla. *Turn S for Barringun.*

CUNNAMULLA (188m; Pop 1500):* pleasant grazing town with some houses on stilts* (unusual sight for southerners), located on the banks of the Warrego River. Numerous Aboriginal sites in the area, including canoe trees near river; enquire locally. Worth seeing is the Robbers Tree in Stockyard Street, heritage trail, museum and Cunnamulla Weir (picnic area 5km south). Full town facilities. (*256/0*) Road Trips 8 and 9 connect. *Head E to Balone Highway junction for Barringun.*

Accommodation
Billabong Hotel, 5 Murray St, ©07 4655 1225, ☻$55
Warrego Hotel-Motel, 9 Louise St, ©07 4655 1737, ☻$40-$70
Oxford Hotel-Motel, Railway St, ©07 4655 1126, ☻$45-$50
Jack Tonkin Caravan Park, Watson St, ©07 4655 1421, ☻Site: $14 Van: $35-$50

DAY 4: CUNNAMULLA-AUGATHELLA
via Charleville

Road to Take: Matilda Highway (Mitchell Highway, Landsborough Highway)
Grade 1
Total Distance: 282km (3:10)
Intermediate Distances:

	Km	Hours
Cunnamulla-Charleville	198	(2:15)
Charleville-Augathella	84	(0:55)

Average Vehicles per Day: 380 south of Wyandra
Regions Traversed: Queensland's Mulga Belt

CUNNAMULLA (Alt 188m; Pop 1500):* pleasant grazing town. For more information see Day 4. (*0/282*)

Mitchell Highway junction: (*2/280*) Turn **N** for Wyandra. *Turn W for Cunnamulla.*
Plains south of Coongoola support gidgees (stinking wattle - try smelling it after rain!), low

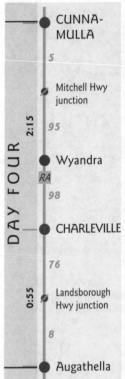

Detail of MAP 3

and sparse eucalypts, and grasslands. Occasional expansive views. Part of the Warrego floodplain.
Coongoola: old railway settlement. No facilities. (*52/230*)

Wyandra (Alt 237m; Pop 60):* small bush town with many interesting outback-style buildings. A heritage walk points out the highlights. Cows often walk down the main street. Worth trying to strike up a conversation with the locals. Accommodation, store, fuel. (*100/182*)

Low rises provide minor relief from the general flatness.
Dillalah: railway siding.
Mangalore: railway settlement set upon a grassy plain. No facilities. **Rest area** nearby. (*151/131*)

Angellala Creek crossing: interesting railway bridge adjacent to road.
Plains south of Charleville covered with bimble box and mulga.

CHARLEVILLE (294m; Pop 3900):* south-western Queensland's largest town, literally on the banks of the Warrego River. Interesting streetscapes including many large Queensland-style hotels. The town centre is worth a couple of hours' exploration. Worth seeing: Steiger Vortex Gun*, Historic House* (Alfred Street), Royal Flying Doctor Service, School of the Air, Bidjara (Aboriginal arts), National Parks Research Station* (learn about bilbies), nature walks* along Warrego River, Graham Andrews Parklands. Full town facilities. (*198/84*) Road Trip 8 connects.

Accommodation

Charleville Motel, 148 King St, ℂ07 4654 1566, ⊕$65-$75
Charleville Waltzing Matilda Motor Inn, 125 Alfred St, ℂ07 4654 1720, ⊕$50
Warrego Motel, 75 Wills St, ℂ07 4654 1299, ⊕$70
Bailey Bar Caravan Park, 196 King St, ℂ07 4654 1744, ⊕Site: $15 Van: $30-$50
Cobb & Co Caravan Park, Ridgway St, ℂ07 4654 1053, ⊕Site: $12 Van: $30-$45

Low ranges barely discernible through the trees; flat-top hills similar to the jump-ups found in the arid areas.
Undulating country with low sandstone ridges and sand plains. Covering of bimble box and mulga.
Landsborough Hwy junction: (**274/8**) Turn **N** onto Landsborough Hwy (Matilda Hwy) for Augathella. *Turn SW onto Mitchell Hwy (Matilda Hwy) for Charleville.*

Augathella (328m; Pop 540): interesting western Queensland town on the banks of the Warrego River (park and picnic area adjacent). Unusual and photogenic pub*. Grazing and timber town. **Rest area** just south of town. Accommodation, stores, fuel. (**282/0**)

Accommodation

Augathella Motel, Cavanagh St, ℂ07 4654 5177, ⊕$60-$70
Augathella Caravan Park, Cavanagh St, ℂ07 4654 5177, ⊕Site: $14

DAY 5: AUGATHELLA-BARCALDINE
via Tambo

Road to Take: Matilda Highway (Landsborough Highway)
Grade 1
Total Distance: 324km (3:35)

Intermediate Distances:

	Km	Hours
Augathella-Tambo	116	(1:15)
Tambo-Blackall	101	(1:10)
Blackall-Barcaldine	107	(1:10)

Average Vehicles per Day: 300 north of Tambo
Regions Traversed: Queensland's Mulga Belt, Mid-West.

Augathella (Alt 328m; Pop 540): small grazing town. For more information see Day 4. (**0/324**)

Plains and low rises are covered with mulga and bimble box. Extensive land clearances in this area. Occasional views to far distant ranges.
Nive River crossing:* abrupt change in landscapes here - rolling Mitchell grass plains to the north, mulga and bimble box woodlands to the south. (**73/251**)
Low rise south of Tambo (watershed between Warrego and Barcoo Rivers) offers expansive views* to the north. Rugged outliers of the Great Dividing Range are clearly visible, including Mt Windeyer. The strip of country around Tambo is probably the most scenic in the Mid-West.

Tambo (Alt 396m; Pop 400):* small grazing town on the Barcoo River, the oldest town in the Mid-West. Worth seeing: Old Post Office Museum*, heritage walk, Coolibah walk* along the Barcoo River, Woodies Store, picnic area at The Lake. Accommodation, stores, fuel. (**116/208**)

Accommodation

Tambo Mill Motel, Arthur St, ℂ07 4654 6466, ⊕$75
Club Hotel-Motel, Arthur St, ℂ07 4654 6109, ⊕$25-$50

Plains and low rises composed of black soil. Expansive areas of open Mitchell grass country, woodlands of gidgees as well as borees (attractive low acacias with silvery-grey boles). South of the Barcoo River are distant views* to sandstone ranges, outliers of the Great Dividing Range. In the afternoon light, these distant ranges can be an attractive sight.

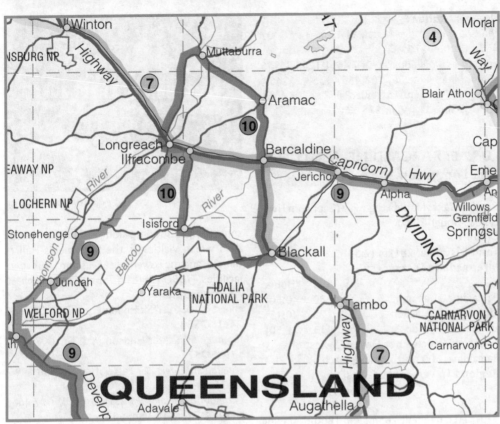

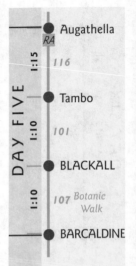

Detail of MAP 3

BLACKALL (Alt 284m; Pop 1780):* grazing town on the banks of the Barcoo River. The site of Queensland's first artesian bore. Interesting main street lined with bottle trees. Blackall Wool Scour* 5 km north of town is worth visiting. Also see the Jackie Howe Memorial (greatest shearer of them all), Ram Park*, the Black Stump* display and the original artesian bore. Full town facilities. (*217/107*) Road Trip 10 connects.

Accommodation
Blackall Motel, Shamrock St, ©07 4657 4491, ✪$60
Blackall Coolibah Motel, Matilda Hwy, ©07 4657 4380, ✪$60
Blackall Acacia Motor Inn, Shamrock St, ©07 4657 6022, ✪$70-$80
Blackall Caravan Park, 53 Garden St, ©07 4657 4816, ✪Site: $14 Van: $30-$50

Plains of black soil support a woodland of gidgees as well as other acacias. Ground cover often sown with introduced grasses. Patches of red soil country support bimble box woodlands with understorey shrubs of wilga, beefwood, etc. Botanic Walk* - interesting walk through a bimble box woodland. Numerous species of plants - most labelled. Worth an hour or so. (*317/7*)

BARCALDINE (Alt 265m; Pop 1800):* attractive town with an impressive and colourful array of pubs in the main street. Famous for the 'Tree of Knowledge'*, a site of the establishment of the Labour Party. Town worth a couple of hours exploration, especially Australian Worker's Heritage Centre**, the Outback Zoo*, the unusual Masonic Lodge, Mad Micks, and the Barcaldine Baths. Full town facilities. (*324/0*) Road Trips 9 and 10 connect. Head **S** for Blackall.

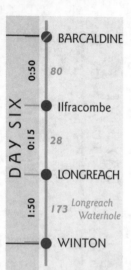

DAY SIX

BARCALDINE

0:50 — 80

Ilfracombe

0:15 — 28

LONGREACH

1:50 — 173 Longreach Waterhole

WINTON

Accommodation

Landsborough Lodge Motel, Matilda Hwy, ©07 4651 1100, ©$75
Barcaldine Motel, Box St, ©07 4651 1244, ©$55
Starlin Motel, Pine St, ©07 4651 1353, ©$45
Homestead Caravan Park, Blackall Rd, ©07 4651 1308, ©Site: $14 Van: $25-$60

DAY 6: BARCALDINE-WINTON via Longreach

Road to Take: Matilda Highway (Capricorn Hwy, Landsborough Hwy)
Grade 1
Total Distance: 281km (2:55)
Intermediate Distances:

	Km	Hours
Barcaldine-Ilfracombe	80	(0:50)
Ilfracombe-Longreach	28	(0:15)
Longreach-Winton	173	(1:50)

Average Vehicles per Day: 675 west of Barcaldine; 500 north of Longreach
Regions Traversed: Mid-West

BARCALDINE (Alt 265m; Pop 1800):* grazing town. For more information see Day 5. (*0/281*) Head **W** for Longreach along the Capricorn Hwy.

Plains of black soil covered with Mitchell grass extend from Longreach to Barcaldine. Some areas of gidgees; gidgee woodlands near Barcaldine. Wildflowers are common after rain.

Ilfracombe (Alt 214m; Pop 160):* small township with the very interesting Ilfracombe Folk Museum*. Also worth seeing is Langenbaker House*, an old teamsters cottage, Oakhampton Cottage, and the Hilton bottle collection. Accommodation, store, fuel. (*80/201*)

LONGREACH (Alt 192m; Pop 4500):* grazing town situated on the Tropic of Capricorn. Largest town in the Mid-West. Town area is worth a day's exploration. Visit the original Qantas Founders Outback Museum*, and maybe see

Railway Hotel, Barcaldine, Qld

some brolgas strolling along residential streets. Also worth visiting is the Stockmen's Hall of Fame**, and the Powerhouse Museum*. Full town facilities. (*108/173*) Road Trips 9 and 10 connect.

Accommodation

Albert Park Motel, Sir Hudson Fysh Dr, ©07 4658 2411, ©$80
Jumbuck Motel, Sir Hudson Fysh Dr, ©07 4658 1799, ©$75
Longreach Motel, 127 Eagle St, ©07 4658 1996, ©$75
Gunnadoo Caravan Park, Thrush Rd, ©07 4658 1781, ©Site: $17 Van: $55
Longreach Caravan Park, 180 Ibis St, ©07 4658 1770, ©Site: $15 Van: $20-$25

Thomson River: multi-channelled stream which flows into Cooper Creek. This is floodplain country; when in flood the river is up to 6km wide. There is a bridge over Longreach Waterhole*, from which the nearby town derives its name. This waterhole is one of the longest in Australia and river cruises are available. (*112/169*)
Plain of black soil supports a gidgee woodland, with an understorey of Mitchell grass.
Plain* of red soil provides a brief change in countryside. Vegetation includes bloodwoods, corkwoods and whitewoods.
Darr River: fair picnic/camping site by waterhole. River red gums in the area. (*139/142*)
Morella: old railway settlement; no facilities. (*174/107*)
Rimbanda: former railway siding. (*195/86*)

Plains and low rises extend between Winton and Longreach. Expansive views from the tops of rises, closed-in skylines in depressions. Ground cover of Mitchell grass, which is vibrant green after summer rains and bleached white after winter drought. Mitchell grass makes good stock feed for cattle and sheep. The low shrubby bush on plains and along drainage lines is prickly mimosa, an introduced species rapidly engulfing the Mitchell grass country. Telegraph lines and railway provide interesting perspectives* for photographers.

Chorregon: former railway settlement; no facilities. Near Chorregon is a giant windmill* on the western side of the road.(*217/64*)

Vindex Range (229m) and Forsyth Range: low range of jump-up hills visible to the west between Winton and Chorregon. Hill country locally known as 'red-top rock'. The ranges appear higher than they really are, due to open country and atmospheric conditions.

WINTON (Alt 187m; Pop 1200):** friendly grazing town. Worth a day at least for its interesting buildings and people. Take a walk around the streets to see the idiosyncratic houses, photogenic buildings and pubs, old-fashioned stores, unusual railway station and a good cafe. Saturday afternoons and evenings are perhaps the best times. Worth seeing: photogenic pubs*, Waltzing Matilda Centre*, Arno's Wall* (Vindex Street), Corfield and Fitzmaurice Store* (dinosaur diorama and mineral display), Royal Theatre (open air theatre). Just west of town (2km) is Pelican Waterhole*. Full town facilities. (*281/0*) Road Trip 19 connects.

Accommodation
Banjos Motel and Cabins, Cnr Manuka/Bostock Sts, ©07 4657 1213, ✪$55
Matilda Motel, 20 Oondooroo St, ©07 4657 1433, ✪$60
Winton Outback Motel, 95 Elderslie St, ©07 4657 1422
Matilda Country Caravan Park, 43 Chirnside St, ©07 4657 1607, ✪Site: $15 Van: $25-$50
Pelican Fuel Stop Caravan Park, Matilda Hwy, ©07 4657 1478, ✪Site: $15 Van: $20-$40

South of Winton, a 65km unsealed loop road takes visitors through the Bladensburg National Park*, a large park of former grazing leases preserving low rugged ranges, gorges, waterholes and grasslands. Good views from the tops of ranges. Camping available.

Southwards again, a 222km return journey over unsealed roads leads to Lark Quarry**, an environmental park exhibiting (under shelter) one of the world's only examples of preserved dinosaur stampede footprints. The hundreds of footprints include a carnosaur (about 3m high) confronting coelurosaurs (emu-chick size) and ornithopods (emu size) on the edge of a muddy lake. The smaller creatures then fled. This is well worth seeing. There are also walking tracks and lookouts providing views of the nearby Tully Range. No camping. Enquire locally before proceeding.

DAY 7: WINTON-CLONCURRY via Kynuna

Road to Take: Matilda Highway (Landsborough Hwy)
Grade 1
Total Distance: 343 km (3:50)
Intermediate Distances:

	Km	Hours
Winton-Kynuna	164	(1:50)
Kynuna-McKinlay	74	(0:50)
McKinlay-Cloncurry	105	(1:10)

Average Vehicles per Day: 650 north of Winton
Regions Traversed: Mid-West, North-West Queensland

WINTON (Alt 187m; Pop 1150):** interesting grazing town. For more information see Day 6. (*0/343*)

Plains and low rises support vast tracts of Mitchell grass. Fair views westwards from east of Workingham Creek towards Ayrshire Hills. Jump-ups visible on the outskirts of Winton. The

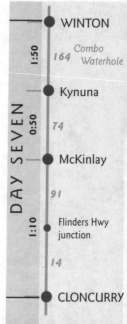

Road Trip 7

DAY SEVEN

WINTON
1:50   164   Combo Waterhole
Kynuna
0:50   74
McKinlay
91
1:10   Flinders Hwy junction
14
CLONCURRY

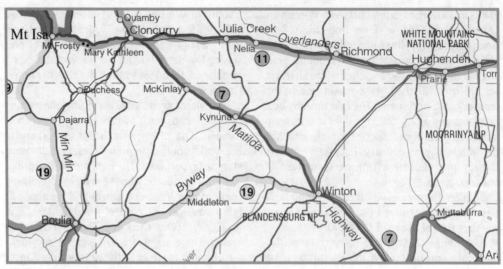

Detail of MAP 4

single-strand telephone wires date from the days when stations provided their own connections. Ayrshire Hills:* low jump-ups by the highway. Notable for being the only hills set so close to the road for hundreds and hundreds of kilometres. Worth stopping for a quick look. Good wide views from 'summits'. Be careful on the loose scree slopes. Interesting valleys. Stay near the road if exploring - avoid trespassing. (65/278) Plains and low rises support extensive Mitchell grass grasslands. Scattered low shrubs and prickly mimosas, an introduced plant.

Combo Waterhole turnoff: locality only; no facilities. (148/195) Turn S for the short, unsealed (Grade 3) drive to Combo Waterhole*, supposed site of inspiration for Banjo Patterson's poem 'Waltzing Matilda'. Interesting area with a walking track. Note the stone-built overshots, low embankments built to raise the water level of waterholes.

Kynuna (Alt 208m; Pop 25):* interesting bush township set upon a grassy plain. Photogenic pub with unusual neon sign of a blue heeler dog. Worth seeing: Matilda Expo* (Waltzing Matilda heritage). Accommodation, store, fuel. (164/179)

Jump-up* hills lie near the road. Expansive views from the tops of rises.

Plains support extensive tracts of Mitchell grass grasslands. Jump-ups are occasionally visible to the south.

McKinlay (Alt 172m; Pop 30): interesting small grazing township containing photogenic buildings. This is where you'll find the famous 'Crocodile Dundee' hotel*. Worth spending a short time here to absorb the atmosphere. Accommodation, store, fuel. (238/105)

Plains and floodplains alternate. Plains support broad tracts of Mitchell grass grasslands, floodplains support coolibah woodlands along drainage lines. Gidgees may also be seen.

Fullerton River forms a marked boundary between the Mid-West's black soils and the North-West's red soils. (281/62)

Low rises support eucalypt woodlands of white-trunked trees (possibly snappy-gums) with an understorey of spinifex. Red soil marks the end of the black soil plains for those travellers heading north-west. Reasonable westward views* from the tops of rises of jagged ridges visible on the horizon.

Flinders Highway Junction: locality only; no facilities. (329/14) Continue W for Cloncurry. *Continue SE for Winton.*

Kynuna Store, Kynuna, Qld

CLONCURRY (Alt 188m; Pop 2500):* interesting old mining town, nowadays a service centre for the surrounding pastoral industry as well as supporting new mining operations. Photogenic historic buildings. Attractive area* on the banks of the normally dry Cloncurry River. Good lookout* west of the town. The Afghan and Chinese cemeteries, and old mine workings, are worth seeing. Also take a look at the Mary Kathleen Memorial Park and Museum**, Great Australian Mine*, and John Flynn Place** (Royal Flying Doctor exhibits). Full town facilities. (343/0) Road Trip 11 connects. /Head E on Flinders Hwy (Matilda Hwy) for Winton.

Accommodation
Oasis Hotel-Motel, Ramsay St, ©07 4742 1366, ✪$60
Wagon Wheel Motel, 54 Ramsay St, ©07 4742 1866, $60-✪$70
Gidge Inn Motel, Matilda Hwy, ©07 4742 1599, ✪$95-$120
Gilbert Park Tourist Village, McIlwraith St, ©07 4742 2300, ✪Site: $15 Van: $55
Cloncurry Caravan Park, McIlwraith St, ©07 4742 1313, ✪Site: $14 Van: $30

DAY 8: CLONCURRY-KARUMBA via Normanton

Road to Take: Matilda Highway (Burke Developmental Road)
Grade 2

Total Distance: 446km (5:45)
Intermediate Distances:

	Km	Hours
Cloncurry-Burke and Wills	181	(2:15)
Burke and Wills-Normanton	195	(2:35)
Normanton-Karumba	70	(0:55)

Average Vehicles per Day: 120 north of Cloncurry
Regions Traversed: North-West Queensland, Gulf Country.

▼

CLONCURRY:* interesting grazing town. For more information see Day 7. (0/446) Head **N** along Burke Developmental Road (Matilda Hwy) for Qaumby.

Plains support small areas of Mitchell grass grasslands. Elsewhere is undulating country, low rocky hills* and the prominent Flat Top just north of Cloncurry.
Urquhart:* old railway siding of which little remains. (36/410)

Quamby (Alt 183m; Pop 5):* former grazing and mining township. Pub worth visiting. Spend a short time here to absorb the atmosphere. The big beer can* is of interest. Accommodation, fuel. (45/401)

Low ranges* line the road. Rocky outcrops and bluffs are clearly visible. Quite attractive country hereabouts. Vegetation is sparse in the overstorey, but numerous species are present. Ground cover is usually grassy. One Tree Hill visible to the west.
Plains dominated by sparse eucalypt woodlands with a ground cover of grass. In the south, plains grade into undulating country. Ranges are visible to the west.
Collulah Station turnoff. (106/340) Road Trip 12 connects.
Low rises provide fair views along the road. Eucalypt woodlands dominate the countryside. Spinifex is common. Mt Dromederry (western side) and Black Mountain (eastern side) visible from the road.

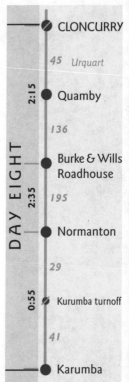

Road Trip 7

DAY EIGHT

	⊘ CLONCURRY
	45 Urquart
2:15	● Quamby
	136
2:35	● Burke & Wills Roadhouse
	195
	● Normanton
	29
0:55	✦ Kurumba turnoff
	41
	● Karumba

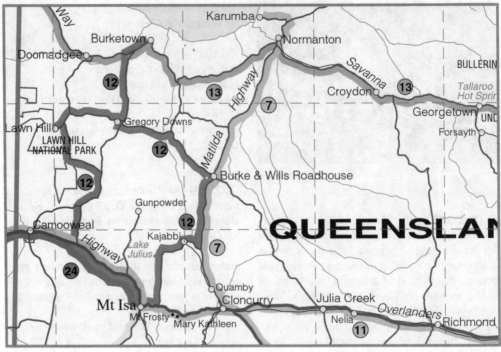

Detail of MAP 4

Plains typical of the southern reaches of the Gulf Country, consisting of hard red soil, small anthills and open eucalypt woodlands with an understorey of spinifex. Just south of Burke and Wills is an open grassland with scattered shrubs.

Burke And Wills Roadhouse (Alt 71m; Pop 5): roadhouse facility. Accommodation, store, fuel. (*181/265*) *Road Trip 12 connects.*

Plains support eucalypt woodlands with an understorey of spinifex. Good vistas* along the dead straight road.

Plains support grassy eucalypt woodlands and other trees like bauhinias.

Low rises support somewhat sparse shrubby eucalypt woodlands. Reasonable views* hereabouts. Donors Hill is visible to the east.

Plains supports shrubby eucalypt woodlands with an understorey of spinifex. Anthills are common. About three kilometres from Bang Bang Jump-Up are numerous anthills* which look like gravestones - very photogenic.

Bang Bang Jump-Up:* low escarpment separating a grassy lowland plain from a shrubby upland one. Low hills are near the road at the base of the jump-up. Good northwards views when descending the jump-up. (*268/178*)

Plains support vast tracts of open grasslands with scattered shrubs. Big sky country with southwards and westwards views to a line of jump-ups.

Flinders River* is crossed by a high and long bridge. The old causeway crossing nearby accesses good camping spots beside a beautiful waterhole*. (*313/133*)

Plains support vast tracts of open grasslands with occasional shrubs. Vast vistas.

Low rises support tracts of shrubby eucalypt woodlands, with the occassional glimpsed view between.

Normanton (Alt 8m; Pop 1150):* interesting grazing town. Stop here awhile to absorb the atmosphere. Worth seeing: Gulflander train** (local tours and weekly runs to Croydon - enquire at station), Normanton railway station** and precinct, historic buildings* (many photogenic), colourful pubs, old wharf and picnic area on Norman River (beware of estuarine crocodiles) and adjacent wetlands*, and a crocodile statue. Accommodation, stores, fuel. (*376/70*) *Road Trip 13 connects.*

Accommodation
Albion Hotel-Motel, Haig St, ©07 4745 1218, ✪$55
Gulfland Motel, Landsborough St, ©07 4745 1290, ✪$75
Normanton Caravan Park, Brown St, ©07 4745 1121, ✪Site: $13

Norman River* has picnic facilities east of the bridge. West of the bridge a side road leads to the old wharf*. Good fishing but beware of crocodiles. (*378/68*)
Wetlands* (beware of estuarine crocodiles) have numerous swamps, aquatic vegetation and amazing birdlife. Worth stopping for a look.
Plain supports a diversity of vegetation, typically eucalypts but numerous other trees as well.
Walker Creek* offers shady camp sites and a nice waterhole. Again, beware of estuarine crocodiles. (*404/42*)
Kurumba turnoff: (*405/41*) Head **W** for Kurumba - Burke Developmental Road continues **NE**. *Head* **S** *for Normanton.*

Plains support broad open treeless grasslands. Small creek crossings are mostly tidal. Nearer Karumba the plains support grassy eucalypt woodlands.

Karumba (Alt 3m; Pop 620):* prawning settlement with some appeal located on the banks of the broad Norman River estuary. Good fishing, boat ramps (beware of estuarine crocodiles). Nearby Karumba Point** (8km away) is basically a suburb of Karumba but with a seaside appeal (no swimming though - crocodiles). Excellent spot to watch sunsets** over the Gulf of Carpentaria. Some of the best sunsets in Australia can be seen from here (stay for the excellent twilight light show**). Beach walks, sea shell collecting and fishing. Accommodation, stores, fuel. (*446/0*)

Accommodation
Karumba Lodge, Yappar St, ©07 4745 9121, ✪$85
Gulf Country Caravan Park, Yappar St, ©07 4745 9148, ✪Site: $15 Van: $50
Karumba Point Tourist Park, Karumba Point Rd, ©07 4745 9306, ✪Site: $16 Van: $40
Sunset Caravan Park, Palmer Road, Karumba Point, ©07 4745 9277, ✪Site: $17 Van: $60

Road Trip 7

Road Trip 8
Mulga Country/Innamincka Loop

Roma-Dalby via Innamincka
Total Distance: 2370km
Suggested Travelling Time: 7 days

Enter the dead heart of Australia

See the Great Artesian Spa at Mitchell, Ooline Park, Cooper Creek near Windorah, the dunes west of Windorah, gibber desert landscapes, Innamincka Regional Reserve, Dig Tree, Noccundra pub, and the picturesque town of Eulo.

Mulga Country/Innamincka Loop

The Mulga Country/Innamincka Loop takes travellers deep into the desert. Between Windorah and Noccundra this is a remote road trip that crosses barren gibber plains and passes deep red dunes. The roads over this section are stony and rough and travel may be slow. Except for experienced drivers of 2WDs this is 4WD country. East of Windorah and Noccundra the roads are sealed; they cross mulga shrublands for the most part, country given over to the extensive grazing of sheep. In the easternmost sections of this tour the countryside has been cleared for grazing and cropping. Travellers undertaking this journey will enter the 'dead-heart' of Australia's arid country. Heed the warnings!

The Climate

As befits one of the driest areas in Australia rainfall in the western part of this tour is low. Nonetheless light winter showers or heavy summer thunderstorms can be expected. As well during wet periods heavy rains can close unsealed roads for weeks.

Stay out of this western area in summer. Maximum temperatures can be extreme, up to 48C

with no shade; nightimes can be very warm, around 26C. Best travel times are autumn to spring. Though some warm to hot days can be experienced either end of this period it rarely lasts for more than two to three days; generally maximums will be in the low to high twenties. Nights are generally cool. In midwinter cool days will be experienced, often with a wind. Maximums at this time are generally in the high teens; nights will be cold with occasional frosts. Springtime can be windy with the occasional duststorm.

Capital City Connections
Distances in kilometres

SYDNEY-CHARLEVILLE
via Great Western/Mitchell/Matilda Highways

	Intermediate	Total
Sydney	0	0
Bathurst	207	207
Dubbo	205	412
Nyngan	166	578
Bourke	201	779
Charleville	454	1233

MELBOURNE-CHARLEVILLE
via Northern/Newell Highways/Kidman Way/Matilda Highway

	Intermediate	Total
Melbourne	0	0
Shepparton	179	179
Jerilderie	134	313
Griffith	132	445
Bourke	525	970
Charleville	454	1424

BRISBANE-ROMA
via Warrego Highway

	Intermediate	Total
Brisbane	0	0
Toowoomba	129	129
Roma	352	481

The Route
Distances in kilometres

	Intermediate	Total
Roma	0	0
Charleville	265	265

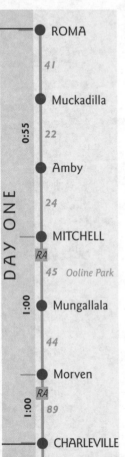

Road Trip 8

DAY ONE

ROMA

41

0:55

Muckadilla

22

Amby

24

MITCHELL
RA
45 Ooline Park

1:00 Mungallala

44

Morven
RA
1:00 89

CHARLEVILLE

Windorah	448	713
Innamincka	462	1175
Noccundra	273	1448
Thargomindah	142	1590
Cunnamulla	197	1787
St George	291	2078
Dalby	292	2370

Warrego Highway (Kenniff Byway)
Roma-Charleville

The Warrego Highway is the main east-west connection across southern Queensland joining the populated south-east corner of the state with the near outback rangelands centred in the mulga country surrounding Charleville. As such this is the route to take if heading to or from south-west Queensland, Longreach and the Mid-West, or west towards Quilpie, Windorah and Innamincka. Southern Australians can access this road trip from either the Great Inland Way at Roma, or Matilda Highway at Charleville.

Though not the most scenic of drives the Warrego Highway does pass through some interesting countryside ranging from cleared cropping lands to outback grazing country. Along the way are many settlements, each with an individual character that will be of interest to travellers, especially southern Australians unfamiliar with Queensland-style architecture.

Warnings: beware of stock and kangaroos at night, especially west of Mitchell. Roads may be subjected to flooding.

DAY 1: ROMA-CHARLEVILLE via Mitchell

Road to Take: Warrego Highway (Kenniff Byway)
Grade 1
Total Distance: 265km (2:55)
Intermediate Distances:

	Km	Hours
Roma-Mitchell	87	(0:55)
Mitchell-Morven	89	(1:00)
Morven-Charleville	89	(1:00)

Average Vehicles per Day: 750 east of Charleville
Regions Traversed: Western Downs, Queensland's Mulga Belt

▼

ROMA (Alt 300m; Pop 6770):* large grazing and agricultural town. For more information see Road Trip 2, Day 2. *(0/265) Road Trip 2 connects. Connecting Route D connects.* Head **W** for Muckadilla.

Low rises have been virtually totally cleared and given over chiefly to wheat cropping.
Hodgson: railway siding. Wheatlands and dairying are common. (*19/246*)
Bundango: railway siding. (*27/238*)

Muckadilla (Alt 358m; Pop 50): small agricultural township. Check to see if the old spa baths* have been reopened. Accommodation, store, fuel. (*41/224*)
Accommodation
Muckadilla Hotel, Warrego Hwy, ©07 4626 8318, ✪$40

Low rises support wheat cropping, sorghum, oats and the like, as well as grazing. Very little uncleared land remains. Big views from the highway, especially from the tops of rises. The landscape is dotted with low hills in the distance.

Amby (Alt 347m; Pop 90): small agricultural township and railway siding. Worth seeing: old stage coach changeover shanty and Amby Quarry, where fossils and opalised wood are sometimes found in an old lava flow. Accommodation, store, fuel. (*63/202*)

Yumba: Aboriginal heritage site*. (*84/175*)

MITCHELL (Alt 335m; Pop 1300):* pleasant grazing and agricultural town set on the banks of the Maranoa River. Neil Turner Weir* (two kilometres west - river cruises) and Memorial Park are good places for picnics. Try out the Great Artesian Spa*, see the Maranoa Cinema*, walk

Detail of MAP 3

the nature trail, and visit Kenniff Courthouse (historical displays). Full town facilities. (**87/178**)

Accommodation
Mitchell Motel, Cnr Oxford/Caroline Sts, ©07 4623 1355, ✪$60-$70
Berkeley Lodge Motel Inn, 20 Cambridge St, ©07 4623 1666, ✪$70-$80

Low rises support grazing lands. The countryside is dotted with low hills and rocky outcrops. Some uncleared remnants remain, supporting ironbark and bimble box woodlands with understoreys of mulga.
Ooline Park:* preserves one of the last stands of the rare ooline, a remnant rainforest tree. **Rest area**, good for picnics and short walks. (**122/143**)

Mungallala (Alt 424m; Pop 130): small grazing township set within a sea of cleared countryside. Interesting pub. Enquire locally about access to the Chesterton Range National Park in the nearby Chesterton Ranges, which contains caves with Aboriginal paintings. Accommodation, store, fuel. (**132/133**)

Dulbydilla: railway siding. (**149/116**)
Chesterton Range:* low range and escarpment prominent to westbound travellers. The range approximates the boundary between farming country to the east and outback grazing lands to the west.

Morven (Alt 423m; Pop 230):* small grazing town. Picnic area in the main street. Worth seeing: the mural, historic railway station* and Morven Historic Museum*. Ten kilometres south of town is the Tregole National Park,* a small park preserving ooline trees, with a walking track and picnic area. Accommodation, stores, fuel. (**176/89**)

Landsborough Highway junction: (**181/84**) Continue **W** on Warrego Hwy for Charleville. *Continue **E** on Warrego Hwy for Mungallala.*
Undulating country offers fair views along the road, especially between Lurnea and Arabella. Countryside supports extensive tracts of mulga shrublands and bimble box woodlands. The woodlands are more open on the plains, offering reasonable views. Keep an eye out for the distinctively shaped bottle trees. Outback rangelands extend westward.
Lurnea: railway siding. (**216/49**)
Sommariva: railway siding. **Rest area** located a few kilometres to the east. (**225/40**)
Arabella: railway siding. (**240/25**)

CHARLEVILLE (Alt 294m; Pop 3500): grazing town on the banks of the Warrego River. For more information see Road Trip 7, Day 4. (**265/0**) *Road Trip 7 connects. /Head **E** on Warrego Hwy for Mitchell.*

DAY TWO

2:20

3:10

- CHARLEVILLE
- 89
- Cooladdi
- 45
- Cheepie
- 76
- Quilpie
- RA
- 238 *Cooper Creek*
- Windorah

Diamantina Developmental Road (Channel Country Byway)/ Innamincka Road via Arrabury

Charleville-Innamincka

These roads were originally constructed under the beef roads program in the 1960s and 70s to provide relatively easy access to far-flung cattle stations. As road trains replaced drovers, the roads were upgraded either to single-lane bitumen standard, leading to railheads, or as maintained gravel and earth roads, connecting remote stations to tiny bush townships and the outside world.

Such roads virtually ring Queensland's Channel Country, passing through some of the most isolated and arid country in Australia. While the eastern Channel Country is one of mulga shrublands and Mitchell grass plains supporting sheep and cattle, the western part of this region is one of red sand dunes, colourful jumpups and vast, stony, arid plains. These routes traverse awe-inspiring country, where dancing mirages hover over virtually featureless plains, spaces in which one feels very insignificant. Travellers here will not only have a 'desert experience', they will return home changed.

Warnings: roads west of Windorah are impassable when wet; all roads subject to flooding. Avoid travelling at night. West of Windorah, inform a reliable person of your travel intentions and always make enquiries before proceeding. Stay out of this area in summer unless experienced; recommended convoy travel only at this time. Recommended 4WD west of Windorah unless experienced. **Note:** no fuel available between Quilpie-Windorah 238km; Windorah-Innamincka 462km.

DAY 2: CHARLEVILLE-WINDORAH
via Quilpie

Roads to Take: Diamantina Developmental Road

Grade 2
Grade 1 Charleville-Quilpie
Total Distance: 448km (5:30)
Intermediate Distances:

	Km	Hours
Charleville-Quilpie	210	(2:20)
Quilpie-Windorah	238	(3:10)

Average Vehicles per Day: 450 west of Cooladdi
Regions Traversed: Queensland Mulga Belt, Channel Country

CHARLEVILLE (294m; Pop 3500):* grazing town. For more information see Road Trip 7, Day 4. (*0/448*) Head **W** on Diamantina Developmental Road for Quilpie.

Plains support a quite dense growth of mulga, combined with eucalypts. If heading east the trees will now appear to be quite large compared to where you have come from, especially around the Ward River area.

Cooladdi (Alt 265m; Pop 6):* railway settlement and roadhouse. Interesting railway buildings. The roadhouse has plenty of character. Nearby Quilberry Creek has pleasant waterholes and camping may be possible. Accommodation, store, fuel. (*89/359*)

Paroo River: numerous depressions and a few muddy waterholes, surrounded by a eucalypt woodland. (*106/342*)
Low hills and escarpment provide a fair view over the mulga from the top of the rise. Interesting rocks can be seen beneath the cliff-line. Mulga abounds in this area.

Cheepie (Alt 255m; Pop 20):* interesting bush township; former railhead. Worth stopping here for a quick look around. Nearby Beechal Creek has a pleasant waterhole. Accommodation, fuel. (*134/314*)

Low hills (hard red country) can be glimpsed on either side of the road.

Plains support a shrubland of mulga with a grassy understorey.

Winbin Creek: numerous channels crossing a grassy plain.

Floodplain is part of the Bulloo River and supports a woodland of eucalypts.

Quilpie (Alt 197m; Pop 625): sheep and cattle grazing town. For more information see Road Trip 9, Day 1. **Rest area** with an opportunity to search for opal just west of town. (*210/238*) *Road Trip 9 connects.*

Grey Range: a complex of low hills, jump-ups, rocky gullies and stony slopes, supporting a low woodland of mulga. Low rises provide occasional views. Watershed marked by signs. A good area for short walks (do not become 'bushed'). The old telegraph lines are of interest. (*245/203*)

Eromanga Road turnoff: locality only; no facilities. (*247/201*) Eromanga lies 68km west. Head **N** for Windorah.

Undulating country supports a shrubland of mulga. Occasional fair views from the tops of rises.

Floodplains and dunes form very attractive country, especially in the afternoon light. Low gidgee trees occupy the flats while various acacias occupy the dunes.

Plains and low rises support tracts of mulga shrublands. Note the layered effect of the mulga, partly due to the fact that mulga needs both summer and winter rains to germinate and establish early growth; hence all young plants are roughly the same age.

Plains and low rises support spinifex and mulga, common east of Cooper Creek. Otherwise, grassy mulga shrublands dominate the country. The stony rises have a gibber surface.

Cooper Creek:* broad floodplain about 10km wide. Dense grasses and herbs are normally present. Numerous shallow channels. Good camping under shady trees on the main waterhole* (near the bridge). (*428/20*)

Windorah (Alt 130m; Pop 80):* small bush township with some character. Nice park and picnic area. Good views* southward at the edge

of town overlooking the Cooper floodplain. Accommodation - camping available, store, fuel. (*448/0*) *Road Trip 9 Connects.*

Accommodation
Western Star Hotel, main street, ✆07 4656 3166, ✪$40

DAY 3: WINDORAH-INNAMINCKA
via Arrabury Station

Roads to Take: Channel Country Byway, Innamincka Road
Grade 4
Grade 2 Windorah-Bedourie turnoff
Warning: Remote Route. No fuel for 462km.
Total Distance: 462km (7:25)
Intermediate Distances:

	Km	Hours
Windorah-Birdsville Dev. Rd jctn	103	(1:20)
Birdsville Dev. Rd junction-Innamincka turnoff	51	(0:45)
Innamincka turnoff-Birdsville turnoff near Arrabury	155	(2:40)
Birdsville turnoff-Innamincka	153	(2:40)

Average Vehicles per Day: 20 near Innamincka turnoff
Regions Traversed: Channel Country, Sturts Stony Desert

Windorah (Alt 130m; Pop 80):* small grazing town. For more information see Day 2. (*0/462*)

Floodplains* (part of Cooper Creek) abut the road to the south, dominated by saltbush and grasses.

Plains* support spinifex-covered dunes in some localities, otherwise broad grasslands and claypans. Sparse covering of Mitchell grass on open plains. Some dunes are quite high. A short walk* near the road is interesting. Jump-ups are visible to the west.

Plains support tracts of mulga shrublands.

Canterbury ruins:* old town site, represented by the JC Hotel ruins. Numerous artefacts surround the area; please do not disturb. Interest-

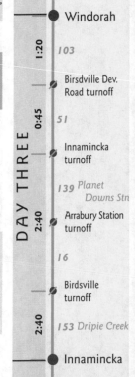

DAY THREE

Windorah
1:20   103
Birsdville Dev. Road turnoff
0:45   51
Innamincka turnoff
139 Planet Downs Stn
2:40   Arrabury Station turnoff
16
Birdsville turnoff
2:40   153 Dripie Creek
Innamincka

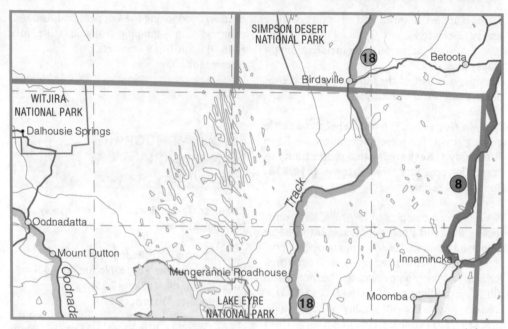

Detail of MAP 5

ing cemetery. Please investigate on foot - some vehicles have driven right over the ruins! (**78/384**)
Jump-up hills: good views* over an arid plain and surrounding jump-ups. A short walk in the vicinity (do not lose sight of the vehicle) is worthwhile. Mulga shrublands common in this area.
Plains:** very open country hereabout with jump-ups looming on the horizon. Mirages are common, appearing as hazy jump-ups floating above shimmering lakes. The jump-up north of the road junction is known as Flat Top, and the bluff west of the road junction is called Hamilton Bluff. This area is a good location for 'bitumen-only' travellers to experience a vast arid landscape (cool seasons only).
Birdsville Developmental Road junction: locality only, no facilities. (**103/359**) Turn **S** for (Birdsville) and Innamincka. *Turn E for Windorah.*
Jump-ups: interesting jump-ups rising above a vast, empty plain. Mirages may be seen.
Plains support only the thinnest veneer of vegetation in dry times. Here the gibber landscape runs from your boots to the horizon. Low jump-up hills in the distance. Aptly named as Planet Downs.

Planet Downs turnoff: locality only; no facilities. (**154/308**) Turn **S** for Innamincka. *Turn E for Windorah.*
Planet Downs Station: outstation buildings; no facilities. (**179/283**)
Haddon Corner turnoff: (**196/266**) **W** lies the point where the South Australian border turns a corner, located in an area of grassland. The rough 26km return track to Haddon Corner may prove difficult. Continue **S** for Innamincka. *Continue N for Windorah.*
Copracunda Well: stock watering place. (**205/257**)
Stony plains: vast, lonely country supporting very little vegetation during dry spells. At certain times vivid mirages** may be seen, especially near Lake Yamma Yamma.
Plains and downs of gibbers surround Arrabury Station, setting it in what must be Australia's most barren homestead location. Very sparse cover of saltbush. Creeks are lined with sparse and low growing red mulgas and bean trees.
Arrabury Station turnoff: locality only; no facilities. (**293/169**)
Birdsville turnoff via Cordillo Downs; locality only; no facilities.(**309/153**) Turn **S** onto Cordillo

Downs Road for Innamincka. *Turn **E** for Arrabury Station and Windorah.*

Sand dunes* line the road, presenting a park-like appearance. Various acacias dominate, and spinifex may be seen. A walk to the top of a nearby dune (do not lose sight of the road) will present a vista of country barely altered for eons.

Dripie Creek:* interesting creek crossing red rocks; red mulga and bean trees provide scant shade. (*369/93*)

Sand plains and outwash plains support a sparse covering of Mitchell grass.

Sand dunes to the west of the road can be seen in the distance. These dunes form part of the Strzelecki Desert. This is floodout country, stemming in part from Cooper Creek. Vast vistas*.

Plains* and downs of gibbers occasionally break out into low jump-ups. Higher jump-ups can be seen in the distance (these were once thought to be high mountain ranges!). The ugly remnant scars of seismic surveys can be seen at intervals, spoiling what is otherwise magnificent wild country. Red mulgas line the creeks and low saltbushes cover the slopes.

Innamincka Regional Reserve: large desert reserve preserving Cooper Creek, Coongie Lake wetlands, sand dunes and gibber plains. A Desert Parks Pass is required for camping and travelling on all but the main roads and Innamincka town area roads.

Innamincka (Alt 50m; Pop 10):* former droving township. For more information see Road Trip 16, Day 3. (*462/0*) *Road Trip 16 connects.*

Accommodation
Innamincka Hotel-Motel, Main St, ©08 8675 9901, ✪$70

▲

Adventure Way
(Bulloo Development Road)
Innamincka-Cunnamulla

The Adventure Way provides access from the southern Channel Country to Noccundra and Cunnamulla on the Matilda Highway. It passes through a range of landscapes: in the west an arid region of gibber plains, jump-ups and sand dunes; in the east, mulga shrublands and Mitchell grass plains.

Dripie Creek, north of Innamincka, SA

This route provides easy access between Cunnamulla, Thargomindah and Noccundra, although first-timers should take care if not familiar with narrow sealed roads. Between Innamincka and the Cooper Creek crossing west of Noccundra the road is rough; this is country only for experienced 2WDers; 4WDs are recommended.

Warnings: beware of stock and kangaroos at night; avoid travelling at night if possible. Road subject to flooding. Between Innamincka and Noccundra inform a reliable person of your intentions. Avoid summer travel unless experienced between Noccundra-Innamincka, always make local enquiries before proceeding. 4WDs recommended between Innamincka-Noccundra.

Note: no fuel available between Innamincka-Noccundra 273km.

DAY 4: INNAMINCKA-NOCCUNDRA
via The Dig Tree turnoff

Road to Take: Adventure Way
Grade 4
Grade 2 Naccowlah-Noccundra
Warning: Remote Route between Innamincka-Jackson. No fuel Innamincka-Noccundra 273km
Total Distance: 273km (4:15)
Intermediate Distances:

	Km	Hours
Innamincka-The Dig Tree turnoff	55	(1:00)
Dig Tree turnoff-Noccundra turnoff	198	(3:00)
Noccundra turnoff-Noccundra	20	(0:15)

DAY FOUR

● Innamincka

45

1:00 ⌖ Road junction

10

⌖ Dig Tree turnoff

191

3:00 ⌖ Eromanga turnoff

7

⌖ Noccundra turnoff

0:15 20

● Noccundra

Average Vehicles per Day: approximately 10-20 west of Cooper Creek
Regions Traversed: Sturt's Stony Desert, Channel Country

Innamincka (Alt 50m; Pop 10):* former droving township. For more information see Road Trip 16, Day 3. (*0/273*)

Innamincka Regional Reserve: large desert reserve preserving Cooper Creek, Coongie Lake wetlands, sand dunes and gibber plains. A Desert Parks Pass is required for camping and travelling on all but the main roads and Innamincka town area roads.
Callyamurra Waterhole turnoff: turn **N** for access to Burkes Memorial* (pleasant waterhole and camping area); Callyamurra Waterhole**: one of the largest waterholes in Australia - up to 28m deep (excellent camping but popular during the tourist season); and Innamincka Choke (approximately 30km return), a narrow reach of Cooper Creek, barely 12m wide (nearby are Aboriginal engravings and a walking track). (*5/268*)
Sand dunes* form a northern extension of the Strzelecki Desert.
Plains and low rises support gibbers and a sparse covering of herbs. Broad vistas*.
Road junction: (*45/ 228*) Turn **N** for Dig Tree turnoff. *Turn W for Innamincka.*
Cooper Creek:* wide channel and waterhole, crossed by a new bridge. (*49/224*)
Dig Tree turnoff: (*55/218*) Turn **W** for the 24km return trip to the Dig Tree**, an historic site by a waterhole on Cooper Creek where Burke and Wills' base party buried supplies on account of the explorers' long-overdue return from northern Australia. The base party left only nine hours before Burke and Wills returned! Adjacent to Dig Tree is a good carving of Burke. Located on private property - fee payable. Head **E** for Noccundra. *Head S for Innamincka.*
Plains form part of the Sturt's Stony Desert. Vast spaces abound. Expansive views from high points of distant jump-ups on the horizon.
Sand dunes and sand plains support a variety of shrubs and occasionally grasses, including spinifex.

Plains* of gibbers form an outlier of Sturt's Stony Desert. Sparsely vegetated with low growing saltbush. Awesome spaces hereabout.
Floodplain: broad plain of Cooper Creek, usually covered with a dense growth of ephemeral herbs. Coolabah trees edge waterholes polluted by cattle. (*158/115*)
Naccowlah: oil field and processing plant. No facilities. Tourists are not encouraged but help is given if required. (*178/95*)
Low rises and jump-ups: here the jump-ups literally 'jump-up' out of the plain, hence the name. 'Jump-up' mirages are common on this stretch of road. Good views* from the tops of rises. Heading east in the afternoon light makes for an attractive trip. Mitchell grass downs west of Jackson Creek.
Jackson: mining settlement which does not encourage tourists but provides help if required. No facilities. (*210/63*)
Undulating country provides pleasant views of Mulga shrublands. Occasionally beam pumps or peckers can be seen, pumping oil.
Eromanga turnoff: locality only; no facilities. Eromanga lies 156km **NE** (*246/27*) Turn **S** for Noccundra. *Turn W for Innamincka.*
Noccundra turnoff: locality only; no facilities. (*253/20*) Turn **S** for Noccundra. *Turn W for Innamincka.*
Low rises offer distant views to low ranges and jump-ups. Mulga shrublands and gidgee woodlands dominate the landscape.

Noccundra (Alt 105m; Pop 5):* small township and ruins. Interesting pub and good waterhole* camping on Wilson River. Pleasant spot to spend a day or two. Accommodation, fuel. (*273/0*) *Head N for Noccundra turnoff.*

DAY 5: NOCCUNDRA-CUNNAMULLA via Thargomindah

Road to Take: Adventure Way
Grade 2 Noccundra-Thargomindah
Grade 1 Thargomindah-Cunnamulla

Detail of MAP 3

Total Distance: 339km (4:00)
Intermediate Distances:

	Km	Hours
Noccundra-Thargomindah t/off	20	(0:15)
Thargomindah t/off-Thargomindah	122	(1:30)
Thargomindah-Eulo	129	(1:30)
Eulo-Cunnamulla	68	(0:45)

Average Vehicles per Day: 100 west of Thargomindah
Regions Traversed: Channel Country, Queensland's Mulga Belt

Noccundra (Alt 105m; Pop 5):* small township and ruins. For more information see Day 4. Head **N** for Thargomindah turnoff.

Low rises offer distant views to low ranges and jump-ups. Mulga shrublands and gidgee woodlands dominate the landscape.
Thargomindah turnoff: locality only; no facilities. (**20/319**) Turn **E** for Thargomindah. *Turn S for Noccundra.*
Wilson River:* one of the Channel Country's lesser-known streams. Water is usually present at the river crossing causeway. Country on the western side of the river is mostly stony plains and downs. (**22/317**)
Plains support an open shrubland of mulga with a grassy understorey.
Plains form the foot slopes of the Grey Range. Mulga shrublands dominate.
Grey Range:* low range of jump-up hills, tablelands, escarpments and rocky gullies. Fair views from road, but better views from nearby hills. Take care if walking as the loose screes are dangerous.
Plains support a covering of mulga with a grassy understorey; areas of grassland also present.
Plains support tracts of mulga.

Thargomindah (Alt 126m; Pop 280): small grazing town on the banks of the Bulloo River. What to see: Leahy Historical House* (museum), town bore, Cobb and Co stone crossing, heritage walk. Accommodation, stores, fuel. (**142/197**)
Accommodation
Bulloo River Hotel-Motel, Dowling St, ©07 4655 3125, ✪$45
Thargomindah Motel, Dowling St, ©07 4655 3155, ✪$55

Road Trip 8

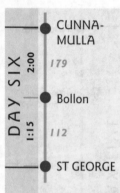

DAY SIX

CUNNA-MULLA — 2:00

179

Bollon — 1:15

112

ST GEORGE

Plains support an attractive shrubland of mulga. Numerous wildflowers grow in the understorey after rain.

Lake Bindegolly National Park:* drainage lake for numerous creeks that flow from nearby low hills. Water is often present, as are numerous birds. Lignum and canegrass is common on the lake's perimeter. Worth stopping. (**181/158**)

Leopardwood Mine turnoff: locality only; no facilities. (**210/129**) Turn here for the 8km return unsealed access road to Leopardwood Mine* opal diggings. Fossicking and mining on private leases is available (fee payable). Free camping.

Jump-ups and low rises (occasionally visible from road) form a low divide between the Paroo and Bulloo River basins. Mulga shrublands dominate.

Yowah turnoff: locality only; no facilities. (**253/86**) Yowah lies 71km **N**. *Road Trip 9 connects.* Continue **E** for Eulo. *Continue **W** for Thargomindah.*

Mud springs* look like dirty mounds a few metres high. These are natural outlets of the Great Artesian Basin. Although mostly dormant, they occasionally erupt, spewing forth mud and gases. Worth a quick look at least. (**263/76**)

Eulo (Alt 137m; Pop 80):* one of the most attractive outback townships you are likely to see. Spend an hour or two here to soak up the atmosphere. Interesting buildings, particularly the general store. Also visit the lizard race track and date farm. Local honey is available for sale. Accommodation, store, fuel. (**271/68**) *Road Trip 9 connects.*

Accommodation

Eulo Caravan Park, Eulo St, ✆07 4655 4890, ✪Site: $12

Low rises form a low divide between the Warrego and Paroo River basins. Dense mulga shrublands dominate. Some eucalypts are present. West of Cunnamulla are grasslands with areas of gidgee woodland.

CUNNAMULLA (Alt 188m; Pop 1500): grazing town. For more information see Road Trip 7, Day 3. (**0/339**) *Road Trips 7 and 9 connect.*

Balonne Highway-Moonie Highway
Cunnamulla-Dalby

The Balonne-Moonie Highway is a major east-west route crossing southern Queensland. It passes through a range of landscapes, from the semi-arid eucalypt woodlands of the east, to the mulga shrublands and open grassy plains of the west.

> **Warnings:** beware of stock and kangaroos - avoid travelling at night. Road subject to flooding.

DAY 6: CUNNAMULLA-ST GEORGE
via Bollon

Roads to Take: Balonne Highway
Grade 1
Total Distance: 291km (3:15)
Intermediate Distances:

	Km	Hours
Cunnamulla-Bollon	179	(2:00)
Bollon-St George	112	(1:15)

Average Vehicles per Day: 300 east of Cunnamulla
Regions Traversed: Queensland's Mulga Belt, Western Downs

▼

CUNNAMULLA (Alt 188m; Pop 1500): grazing town on the banks of the Warrego River. For more information see Road Trip 7, Day 3. (**0/291**) Head **E** for St George.

Floodplains form part of the Warrego River system. Areas of open grasslands and stands of gidgee trees. After rains gidgees smell like rotting flesh, hence their other name, 'stinking wattle'.

Plains support a covering of open eucalypt woodland, mostly bimble box, with an understorey of mulga.

Nebine Creek:* broad, sandy creek bed with river red gums. Worth exploring a short distance on foot. The area makes a reasonable rest/lunch break setting. (**114/177**)

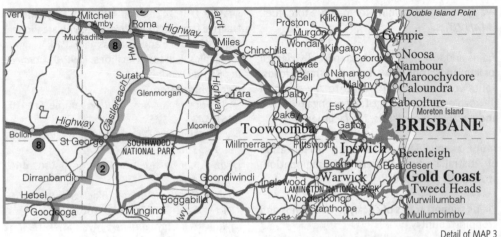

Detail of MAP 3

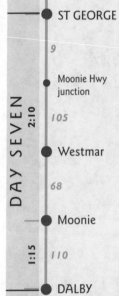

ST GEORGE

9

Moonie Hwy junction

DAY SEVEN 2:10

105

Westmar

68

Moonie

1:15

110

DALBY

Plains support a woodland of bimble box with an understorey of mulga. The trees here are taller than those further west.

Bollon (Alt 183m; Pop 100):* small grazing township. Worth seeing: koala habitat and birdwatching along Wallam Creek*, heritage centre and craft centre. Accommodation, store, fuel. (*179/112*)

Plains support a covering of belah with a grassy understorey; further east eucalypts and various acacias dominate the landscape.
Boolba: country school and locality; no facilities. (*244/47*)
Farming country: land here has been partially cleared for grazing and some cropping. Around St George are large cotton farms.
Balonne River:* forms a part of Australia's longest stream, the Murray-Darling-Culgoa-Balonne-Condamine, whose headwaters rise in the Great Dividing Range. This one stream is approximately 3750km long.

ST GEORGE (Alt 201m; Pop 2500):* grazing and cotton town. For more information see Road Trip 2, Day 2. (*291/0*) Road Trip 2 connects.

DAY 7: ST GEORGE-DALBY
via Moonie

Road to Take: Balonne Highway
Grade 1
Total Distance: 292km (3:25)
Intermediate Distances:

	Km	Hours
St George-Moonie	182	(2:10)
Moonie-Dalby	110	(1:15)

Average Vehicles per Day: 500 east of St George
Regions Traversed: Western Downs, Darling Downs

ST GEORGE (Alt 201m; Pop 2500):* grazing and cotton town. For more information see Road Trip 2, Day 2. (*0/292*) Head **E** on Carnarvon Highway for Moonie Hwy junction. *Head **W** on Balonne Hwy for Bollon.*

Moonie Highway junction: (*9/283*) Road Trip 2 connects. Head **E** for Dalby. *Head **W** for St George.*
Plains and low rises support tracts of brigalow. Extensive areas are cleared for broad-acre farming.
Alton: locality only. Nearby is Alton National Park preserving a small tract of brigalow country. (*73/219*)
Plains and low rises support brigalow and farmlands.

Westmar: small farming township. Store, fuel. (*114/178*)

Plains and low rises have been partially cleared for farmlands. Long views down the straight roads. Southwood National Park lies to the north of the road preserving a large tract of brigalow scrub and eucalypt woodlands. No facilities.

Moonie: small farming township. The location of Australia's first oil field. Accommodation, store, fuel. (*182/100*)

Plains support tracts of eucalypt woodlands and cropping country.

Plains and low rises exhibit eucalypt woodlands and some farmlands.

Lake Broadwater turnoff: (*276/16*) Turn **S** for Lake Broadwater Environmental Park (Grade 3 access, 20km return): seasonal lake (dry during droughts), camping area, walking tracks.

DALBY (Alt 342m; Pop 10200):* large and attractive farming town. Worth seeing are Pioneer Park Museum* and Thomas Jack Park* - good for picnics. Full town facilities. (*292/0*) *Connecting Route D connects.*

Accommodation
Pathfinder Motor Inn, 62 Condamine St, ©07 4662 4433, ✪$75
Myall Motel, Cnr Drayton/Myall Sts, ©07 4662 3399, ✪$60
Dalby Parkview Motel, 31 Drayton St, ©07 4662 3222, ✪$65
Pioneer Caravan Village, Black St, ©07 4662 1811, ✪Site: $15 Van: $30-$50
Myall Creek Caravan Park, Myall St, ©07 4662 4793, ✪Site: $16 Van: $30-$45

Road Trip 9
Opal Country/ Capricorn Loop

Cunnamulla-Yowah-Quilpie-Windorah-Longreach-Emerald-Rockhampton
Total Distance: 1535km
Suggested Travelling Time: 5 days

Visit opal towns and gemfields beneath big skies

See the opal town of Yowah, the historic village of Jericho, the Drummond Range, the central Queensland gemfields, and the sandstone plateau of Blackdown Tableland National Park.

Opal Country-Capricorn Loop

This is a land of big skies arcing over treeless Mitchell grass plains, land utilised for the extensive grazing of sheep and beef cattle. In the south the Mitchell grass country abruptly changes into mulga shrublands, presenting another face to this part of Australia. Herein one will find some of Queensland's opal fields. The Capricorn Highway, running between Barcaldine and Rockhampton passes through a variety of landscapes ranging from outback grazing lands, rugged ranges and broadacre farmlands.

The Climate

The majority of travellers to central inland Queensland will find that the cooler season between May and September is the ideal time to visit. Maximum temperatures are generally mild to warm (around 24C) with the odd cooler or warmer day thrown in. Nights can be cool though, with minimum temperatures around 5C - 10C. Either side of the cooler months. temperatures will be higher for those people who like warmth. Generally days will be clear and sunny with virtually no rain.

Summers are hot, and sometimes humid, with maximum temperatures in the mid-thirties. Nights too are often warm and may be uncomfortable. Summer is the time for rain or showers.

Capital City Connections
Distances in kilometres
SYDNEY-CUNNAMULLA
via Great Western/Mitchell Highways

	Intermediate	Total
Sydney	0	0
Bathurst	207	207
Dubbo	205	412
Nyngan	166	578
Bourke	201	779
Cunnamulla	256	1035

MELBOURNE-CUNNAMULLA
via Northern/Newell Highways/Kidman Way/ Mitchell Highway

	Intermediate	Total
Melbourne	0	0
Shepparton	179	179
Jerilderie	134	313
Griffith	132	445
Bourke	525	970
Cunnamulla	256	1226

The Route
Distances in kilometres

	Intermediate	Total
Cunnamulla	0	0
Eulo	68	68
Quilpie	238	306
Windorah	238	544
Jundah	95	639
Longreach	214	853
Barcaldine	108	961
Emerald	304	1265
Rockhampton	270	1535

Opal Byway

Cunnamulla-Yowah-Quilpie
This is an interesting route for those travellers who like to tinge their journeys with a mild adventure. It visits Eulo, one of the prettiest town-

Road Trip 9

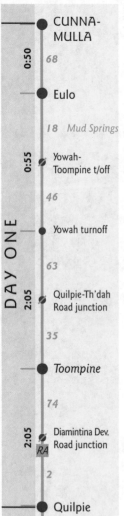

CUNNA-
MULLA

0:50

68

Eulo

18   Mud Springs

0:55

Yowah-
Toompine t/off

46

Yowah turnoff

63

Quilpie-Th'dah
Road junction

2:05

35

Toompine

74

Diamintina Dev.
Road junction

2:05

RA

2

Quilpie

DAY ONE

---

ships in the outback, the Yowah opal fields and the historic Cobb and Co bush pub at Toompine. For most of the route, mulga shrublands abound.

Warnings: sections of the road impassable when wet and subject to flooding. Avoid travelling at night. After wet weather make enquiries before proceding.

DAY 1: CUNNAMULLA-QUILPIE via Eulo

Road to Take: Opal Byway
Grade 3
Grade 2 Cunnamulla-Yowah
Total Distance: 306km (3:25)
Intermediate Distances:

	Km	Hours
Cunnamulla-Eulo	68	(0:50)
Eulo-Yowah turnoff	64	(0:55)
Yowah turnoff-Toompine	98	(1:30)
Toompine-Quilpie	76	(1:10)

Average Vehicles per Day: 50 south of Toompine
Regions Traversed: Queensland's Mulga Belt

▼

CUNNAMULLA (Alt 188m; Pop 1500): grazing town. For more information see Road Trip 7, Day 3. (*0/306*) *Road Trips 7 and 8 connect.* Head W along Adventure Way for Eulo.

Low rises form a low divide between the Warrego and Paroo River basins. Dense mulga shrublands dominate, with some eucalypts present. West of Cunnamulla are grasslands with areas of gidgee woodland.

Eulo (Alt 137m; Pop 80):* one of the most attractive outback townships you are likely to see. Spend an hour or two here to soak up the atmosphere. Interesting buildings including the general store, lizard race track and date farm. Local honey is available for sale. Accommodation, store, fuel. (*68/238*)

Paroo River:* attractive waterholes and shady eucalypts.

Mud Springs:* outlets of the Great Artesian Basin. They normally appear as a dirty brown mound a few metres high. With pressure build-up, the springs explode and mud begins to ooze. The blue mud turns green in the air, then dries to a brown colour. Beneath the surface the mud is moist and sticky. (*76/230*)

Jump-up forms a relatively high hill; reasonable views.

Yowah/Toompine turnoff: (*86/220*) *Road Trip 8 connects.* Turn N for Yowah. *Turn E for Eulo.*

Plains support mulga shrublands. Coolabahs and gidgees are found on the nearby Yowah Creek.

Yowah turnoff: (*132/174*) Turn SW for Yowah - see Side Trip below. *Turn E for Eulo.*

Side Trip

Yowah Road
(Grade 2) 46km return

Yowah (Alt 205m; Pop 150):** area of low ranges, tablelands and jump-ups covered by mulga shrublands and given over to opal mining. Mines are scattered over a few kilometres. A permit is required for prospecting. This is an interesting settlement with plenty of character. It is worth spending a day or two in the area. A lookout is four kilometres east of town, but access is unsealed. Store, fuel, camping area with hot bore baths.

Low rises support mulga shrublands.

Jump-ups: range of low stony hills covered with mulga; occasional views. Interesting area to explore on foot for an hour or two. Stay near the road or you might get lost.

Quilpie-Thargomindah Road junction: locality only; no facilities. (*195/111*) Turn N for Quilpie. *Turn E for Yowah and Eulo.*

Plains support mulga shrublands.

Toompine (Alt 169m; Pop 4):* former Cobb & Co staging post in virtually original condition. Enquire here about access to nearby opal diggings. Hotel only; emergency fuel may be available. (*230/76*)

Plains support mulga shrublands with an understorey of grasses. Quite attractive in the afternoon light. Minor areas of stony ground.

Detail of MAP 3

Floodplain at Bulloo River crossing supports eucalypts and acacias (gidgees).

Low rises offer fair views. Mulga shrublands are common.

Diamintina Development Road junction: **rest area** with chance to look for opal chips. **(304/2)** *Road Trip 8 connects. Turn* **E** *for Quilpie. Turn* **S** *for Yowah and Eulo.*

Quilpie (Alt 197m; Pop 625):* grazing and shire town with many streets named after birds. Worth seeing: Quilpie Museum and Vistors Centre, Lake Houdraman* (6km north on Adavale Road), opal shops, Amy Johnson landing site, Mary McKillop Memorial, St Finbarrs Catholic Church. Accommodation, stores, fuel. **(306/0)** *Road Trip 8 connects. Head* **W** *for Quilpie-Thargomindah Road junction.*

Accommodation
Quilpie Motor Inn, Brolga St, ©07 4656 1277, ✪$60

Imperial Hotel/Motel, Cnr Brolga/Buln Buln Sts, ©07 4656 1300, ✪$55-$65
Channel Country Caravan Park, Chipu St, ©07 4656 2087, Site: $15 Van: ✪$30-$50

▲

Diamintina Developmental Road/ (northern section of Channel Country Byway
Quilpie-Windorah-Longreach
Development roads were mostly constructed under the beef roads program of the 1960s and 70s to provide relatively easy access to far-flung cattle and sheep stations. As road trains replaced drovers, roads were upgraded either to single-lane bitumen standard leading to railheads, or as maintained gravel and earth roads, connecting remote stations to tiny bush townships and the outside world. This route passes through mulga shrublands and Mitchell grass plains supporting sheep as well as cattle.

DAY TWO 3:45

Quilpie

238

Windorah

Warnings: roads subject to flooding. Avoid travelling at night. Exercise caution on single-lane bitumen Quilpie-Windorah, Jundah-Longreach - edges may be soft after rain. **Note:** no fuel Quilpie-Windorah 238km.

DAY 2: QUILPIE-WINDORAH
via Kyabra Creek

Roads to Take: Diamantina Development Road
Grade 2
Total Distance: 238km (3:45)
Average Vehicles per Day: 450 west of Cooladdi
Regions Traversed: Queensland Mulga Belt, Channel Country

Quilpie (Alt 197m; Pop 625): sheep and cattle grazing town. For more information see Day 1. (**0/238**) Head **W** along Diamintina Developmental Road for Windorah.

For details of the route between Quilpie and Windorah see Road Trip 8, Day 2.

Windorah (Alt 130m; Pop 80):* small bush township with some character. For more information see Road Trip 8, Day 2. (**238/0**) Road Trip 8 connects.

DAY 3: WINDORAH-LONGREACH
via Jundah

Road to Take: Channel Country Byway
Grade 3
Grade 2 Jundah-Longreach
Total Distance: 309km (4:45)
Intermediate Distances:

	Km	Hours
Windorah-Jundah	95	(1:30)
Jundah-Stonehenge	65	(1:00)
Stonehenge-Longreach	149	(2:15)

Average Vehicles per Day: 60 north of Stonehenge
Regions Traversed: Channel Country, Mid-West

Windorah (Alt 130m; Pop 80):* small grazing township. For more information see Road Trip 8, Day 2. (**0/309**) Head **N** for Winton-Jundah Road junction.

Windorah-Jundah Road junction: (**6/303**) Turn **N** onto the unsealed road for Jundah. *Turn **S** for Windorah.*
Plains support an expanse of mulga shrublands with a spinifex understorey in some areas.
Thomson River:* multi-channelled stream and floodplain supporting a grassland. Tree-lined waterholes. Scenic area. (**90/219**)

Jundah (Alt 146m; Pop 100):* grazing township of some interest. The pretty park is good for picnics. Historic museum. Accommodation, store, fuel. (**95/214**) Proceed **N** on the sealed road for Stonhenge. *Head **W** for Windorah.*

Jump-ups form low rocky ranges covered with grassy mulga shrublands. Quite an attractive area. Fair view from the top of a steep rise overlooking wild country. En route is Swanvale Lookout* and **rest area** - good views.
Plains support a low woodland of gidgees with areas of mulga shrublands.

Stonehenge (Alt 165m; Pop 30):* bush pub and grazing settlement with interesting buildings, located just **W** off the main road. Accommodation, limited store and fuel. (**160/149**)

Jump-ups* rise suddenly from the plains. Good views* from the top looking north-east. The open area near the top of the ascent/descent is worth investigating: gnarled gidgees appear to grow from expansive rock sheets and look like huge bonsais, beneath are shallow caverns (watch your head!) following a drainage line. Westward, rock sheets break away into shallow valleys.

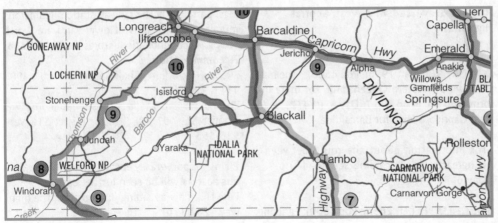

Detail of MAP 3

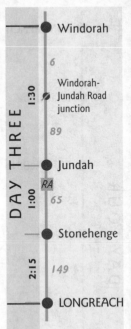

Plains provide expansive views, especially to the jump-ups in the south. Fair covering of Mitchell grass.

Lochern National Park turnoff: (**209/100**) Turn **W** for the 65km return Grade 3 unsealed road to Lochern National Park*, a park preserving Thomson River waterholes, mulga country and grasslands. Good camping at Broadwater Hole*. Birdwatching.

Plains and low rises support vast expanses of Mitchell grass and occasional boree woodlands. Gidgees and coolabahs line the main creeks.

LONGREACH (Alt 192m; Pop 4500):* the major town of western Queensland. For more information Road Trip 7, Day 6. (**309/0**) *Road Trips 7 and 10 connect. Head S on Thomson Developmental Road for Stonehenge.*

Central Hotel, Longreach, Qld

Matilda/Capricorn Highway

The Matilda/Capricorn Highway is the main east-west route through Central Queensland, joining Longreach and Barcaldine to Rockhampton. The countryside varies from settled agricultural and grazing districts to outback rangelands, the vegetation ranging from eucalypt woodlands in the east to acacia woodlands and grasslands in the west. This highway gives access to the scenic Blackdown Tableland, the Central Highlands gemfields, and the outback rangelands of the Mid-West.

Warnings: road subject to flooding; beware of stock and kangaroos at night.

DAY 4: LONGREACH-EMERALD via Barcaldine

Roads to Take: Matilda Highway, Capricorn Highway
Grade 1
Total Distance: 412km (4:45)
Intermediate Distances:

	Kilometres	Hours
Longreach-Barcaldine	108	(1:05)
Barcaldine-Alpha	136	(1:30)
Alpha-Anakie	124	(1:40)
Anakie-Emerald	44	(0:30)

Average Vehicles per Day: 1000 west of Emerald

Regions Traversed: Mid-West, Central Highlands

DAY FOUR

LONGREACH

28

1:05 Ilfracombe

80

BARCALDINE

83

1:30 Jericho

85

Alpha

1:40 92

Anakie

0:30 44

EMERALD

LONGREACH (Alt 192m; Pop 4500):* the major town of western Queensland. For more information see Road Trip 7, Day 6. (*0/412*) Head **E** on Capricorn Hwy for Barcaldine.

For information about the route between Longreach and Barcaldine see Road Trip 7, Day 6.

BARCALDINE (Alt 265m; Pop 1800):* grazing town. For more information see Road Trip 7, Day 5. (*108/304*) *Road Trip 7 connects.*

Plains support tracts of acacia woodlands with grassy understoreys as well as sparse eucalypt woodlands. Westwards, Barcaldine's 36.5 metre high water tower can be seen.
Lochnagar: railway siding. (*144/268*)
Alice: railway siding. Nearby is the Alice River and its rail and road bridges. The rail bridge is of minor interest. (*159/253*)
Plains support mixed eucalypt and acacia woodlands with an understorey of low shrubs. Wildflowers may be seen in spring (not all years).

Jericho (Alt 350m; Pop 150):** town retains many buildings and the atmosphere of an outback bush settlement. Most of the picturesque buildings** are still in use; do not trespass. Also worth seeing is the Crystal Trumpeters*. Enquire here about access to Blacks Palace** (one of the most impressive Aboriginal art galleries in Queensland - permission is required for entry). Accommodation, stores, fuel. (*191/221*)

Low hills represent the crossing of the Great Dividing Range. Plains to the west support low eucalypt woodlands with spinifex in the understorey.
Beta: railway siding.

Alpha (Alt 351m; Pop 500):* pleasant small grazing town with some interesting photogenic build-

ings, particularly the railway station. Numerous murals and the Native Flower Farm are worth seeing. Accommodation, stores, fuel. (*276/136*)

Accommodation
Alpha Hotel/Motel, Shakespeare St, ℂ07 4985 1311, ◉$60
Alpha Caravan & Villa Park, Cnr Capricorn Hwy/ Hooper St, ℂ07 4985 1337, ◉Site: $16 Van: $30-$55

Plains support grassy eucalypt woodlands. Various acacias will be seen further east.
Pine Hill: railway siding just north of the highway. (*242/170*)
Hannams Gap: highest point on the road and railway at around 524 metres altitude. Occasional good views* overlooking rugged mountain country clothed in dry eucalypt woodlands. Northwards the countryside is especially wildlooking. Find somewhere safe to park and enjoy the scenery. (*304/108*)
Drummond Range:* high and wild range which many people mistake for the Great Dividing Range. It is not - it merely separates the Belyando River basin to the west from the Nogoa River Basin to the east. Many good views. Keep an eye out for a lookout* to the north of the road; the railway line is clearly visible.
Medway Creek: interesting railway bridge* and site of a major train disaster.
Bogantungan (Alt 336m):* small railway township set among the foothills of the Drummond Range. The locals call it 'Bogan'. Stop a while and enjoy this sleepy settlement. Interesting Railway Museum*. (*316/96*)
Hilly country forms the foothills of the Drummond Range. Occasional good views*. Eucalypt woodlands are common.
Willows turnoff: (*341/71*) Turn **S** for the short drive to **Willows** (Alt 245m; Pop 400)*, a gemfield area with plenty of character set among low hills. The settlement is characterised by idiosyncratic dwellings: brick, timber, corrugated iron and billy boulder (the local rock) houses. Spend some time here meeting the locals. Photographic opportunities. Fossicking areas are available, particularly for sapphires found close

to the surface. Bird life is common. Accommodation, store, fuel.

Glenalva: gemfield area not as developed as other areas in the district.

Anakie (Alt 251m; Pop 100): interesting and friendly township located just south of the highway. The pub is worth visiting to met Gemfield characters and to absorb the atmosphere. This gateway settlement is the place to come for fossicking information. and to see the Big Sapphire. Accommodation, store, fuel. (*368/44*)

Turn **N** for a short journey into the heart of the gemfields. Nine kilometres away is **Sapphire** (Alt 260m; Pop 700)*, a settlement of scattered dwellings and minesites. Enquire locally about fossicking sites. There are gemstone shops and galleries to visit. Between Sapphire and Rubyvale keep an eye out for some weirdness*: buried vehicles, overloaded cars and odd buildings. Stores, fuel. Another 8km further on is **Rubyvale** (Alt 280m; Pop 550)*, an idiosyncratic mining settlement with many old buildings. Worth seeing is the walk-in mine* and museum. Gemstone shops, galleries and the like. Fossicking sites* - enquire locally. Accommodation, stores, fuel.

Undulating country supports eucalypt woodlands, partly cleared for grazing. Fair views. Low rises support cotton farms. Distant views from the tops of rises.

EMERALD (Alt 180m; Pop 10000): large agricultural and coal mining town. For more information see Road Trip 2, Day 4. (*412/0*) *Road Trips 2 and 4 connect.*

DAY 5: EMERALD-ROCKHAMPTON
via Dingo

Road to Take: Capricorn Highway
Grade 1
Total Distance: 270km (2:55)

Intermediate Distances:

	Km	Hours
Emerald-Blackwater	75	(0:45)
Blackwater-Dingo	48	(0:35)
Dingo-Rockhampton	147	(1:35)

Average Vehicles per Day: 1500
Regions Traversed: Central Highlands, Capricornia

EMERALD (Alt 180m; Pop 10000): large agricultural and coal mining town. For more information see Road Trip 2, Day 4. (*0/270*)

Plains and low rises given over to grazing and cropping on mostly cleared land. Black soil is common. Irrigated crops can be seen east of Emerald.

Comet (Alt 167m): small grazing and farming township. Accommodation, stores, fuel. (*40/230*)

Low hills supports tracts of eucalypt woodlands. Plains and low rises offer broad vistas overlooking cleared grazing land.

BLACKWATER (Alt 186m; Pop 8000): large coal mining town. The tall water tower can be seen for some distance. Pleasant park for picnics. Full town facilities. (*75/195*)

Accommodation
Black Diamond Motel, Capricorn Hwy, ☏07 4982 5944, ✪$85
Capricorn Hotel Motor Inn, Cnr Taurus/Arthur Sts, ☏07 4982 5466, ✪$60
Bottletree Motel and Caravan Park, Cnr Capricorn Hwy/Littlefield St, ☏07 4982 5611, ✪$55 Site: $14

Plains and low rises have been cleared for grazing. Great southwards views* towards the prominent western escarpment of the Blackdown Tableland/Shotover Range.

Bluff (Alt 170m; Pop 600):* interesting small grazing and railway town. Accommodation, store, fuel. (*94/176*)

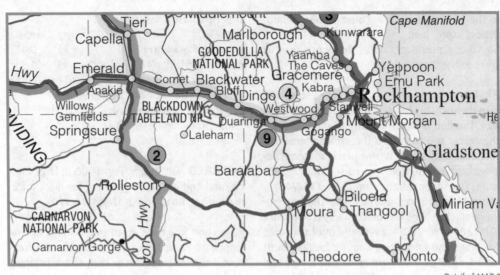

Detail of MAP 3

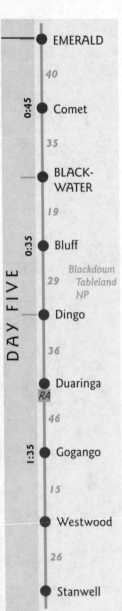

DAY FIVE

EMERALD

40

0:45 · Comet

35

BLACK-
WATER

19

0:35 · Bluff

29 · *Blackdown Tableland NP*

· Dingo

36

· Duaringa
RA

46

1:35 · Gogango

15

· Westwood

26

· Stanwell

Hilly country offers reasonable views of eucalypt woodlands. Prominent escarpment known as The Bluff.

Blackdown Tableland National Park turnoff: (**110/160**) Turn **S** for the 50+km return drive (take care on the narrow gravel road) to Blackdown Tableland National Park**, a park that preserves a high-standing (600m) sandstone plateau ringed by sheer cliffs and rent with deep gorges. Supports eucalypt forests, heathlands, waterfalls and Aboriginal rock art. Camping is available at Mimosa Creek**, a delightful camping area set along a pretty creek. Numerous walking trails here and elsewhere.

Undulating country partially cleared for grazing. Prominent escarpment to the south, forming the edge of the Blackdown Tableland.

Dingo (Alt 116m): small grazing township with some interesting buildings. Accommodation, stores, fuel. (**123/147**)

Undulating country partially cleared for grazing. Southward views to Dawson Range.

Duaringa (Alt 86m; Pop 340):* interesting bush town with rustic dwellings. Worth a quick look.

Accommodation, store, fuel. **Rest area** nearby. (**159/111**)

Dawson River crossing: pleasant area.

Undulating country supports grassy eucalypt woodlands dominated by ironbarks.

Gogango Range offers good views*.

Gogango (Alt 80m): grazing township; interesting buildings. Accommodation, stores, fuel. (**205/65**)

Low ranges support tracts of eucalypt woodlands. Good views*.

Westwood (Alt 156m): grazing township. Accommodation, stores, fuel. (**220/50**)

Wycarbah: locality. The nearby mining lease at Mt Hay Gemstone Tourist Park allows people to fossick* for 120 million year old thundereggs - picnic area, camping. Mt Hay lies south of the road. (**231/39**)

Undulating country offers fair views. Flagstaff Hills is visible to the south, Native Cat Range and Mt Candlelight (434m) are visible to the north.

Stanwell (Alt 42m): small township. Accommodation, store, fuel. (**246/24**)

Kabra (Alt 28m): small farming township. Cargoogie Mountain (191m) lies to the north. Store, fuel. (**254/16**)

Gracemere (Alt 9m; Pop 1250): small town on the edge of Rockhampton. Large cattle stockyards. Accommodation, stores, fuel. (**261/9**)

ROCKHAMPTON (Alt 10m; Pop 65000):* large regional centre. For more information see Road Trip 3, Day 1. (**270/0**) *Road Trips 3 and 4 connect.*

DAY FIVE *(continued)*
1:35

Stanwell

8

Kabra

7

Gracemere

9

ROCK-
HAMPTON

Road Trip 10
Mid-West Loop

Longreach-Isisford-Blackall-Aramac-Muttaburra-Longreach
Total Distance: 618km
Suggested Travelling Time: 2 days

Stand in the wide grazing country of the Mid-West

See the historic villages of Ilfracombe and Aramac, the Barcoo River waterhole at Isisford, and the large dinosaur replica at Muttaburra.

Mid-West Loop

The characteristic features of the Mid-West are broad undulating plains composed of dark-grey clay-like soils, generally referred to as black soils. This type of country is sometimes called 'rolling downs'. Much of this land is treeless, covered with a sward of Mitchell grass, a tussocky herb which grows up to a metre high. Elsewhere are woodlands of various acacia trees, principally gidgees and borees, and shrublands of prickly mimosa, an introduced acacia. The Mid-West is evocative of eastern inland Australia. It is a land of big skies arcing over treeless Mitchell grass plains, land utilised for the extensive grazing of sheep and beef cattle.

The Climate

The majority of travellers will find that the cooler season between May and September is the ideal time to visit. Maximum temperatures are generally mild to warm (around 24C) with the odd cooler or warmer day thrown in. Nights can be cool, with minimum temperatures around 5C - 10C. People who like warmth with prefer travelling during the higher temperatures either side of the cooler months. In general, days will be clear and sunny with virtually no rain.

Capital City Connections
Distances in kilometres
SYDNEY-LONGREACH
via Great Western/Mitchell/ Matilda Highways

	Intermediate	Total
Sydney	0	0
Nyngan	578	578
Bourke	201	779
Cunnamulla	256	1035
Charleville	198	1233
Barcaldine	408	1641
Longreach	108	1749

MELBOURNE-LONGREACH
via Northern/Newell Highways/Kidman Way/
Matilda Highway

	Intermediate	Total
Melbourne	0	0
Griffith	445	445
Cobar	257	702
Bourke	162	864
Cunnamulla	256	1120
Charleville	198	1318
Barcaldine	408	1726
Longreach	108	1834

BRISBANE-LONGREACH
via Warrego/Matilda Highways

	Intermediate	Total
Brisbane	0	0
Toowoomba	129	129
Roma	352	481
Charleville	265	746
Barcaldine	408	1387
Longreach	108	1495

The Route
Distances in kilometres

	Intermediate	Total
Longreach	0	0
Isisford	117	117
Blackall	123	240
Barcaldine	107	347
Aramac	67	414

| Muttaburra | 85 | 499 |
| Longreach | 119 | 618 |

DAY ONE 1:40 1:10 0:15

LONGREACH

28

Ilfracombe

89

Isisford

123

BLACKALL

107

BARCALDINE

1:15

Matilda Highway/Outer Barcoo Byway (Ilfracombe-Blackall-Isisford Road)

Longreach-Isisford-Blackall-Barcaldine

The Outer Barcoo Byway offers travellers a mostly narrow-sealed alternative route between Longreach and Blackall via Isisford, a quiet alternative to the Matilda Highway. It passes through Mitchell grass plains and attractive boree woodlands. During or after wet weather always make enquiries before proceeding.

Warnings: road subject to flooding and may be impassable after rain. Avoid travelling at night - kangaroos and stock are a hazard.

DAY I: LONGREACH-BARCALDINE
via Isisford, Blackall

Road to Take: Matilda Highway, Outer Barcoo Byway
Grade 2 Ilfracombe-Isisford
Grade 3 Isisford-Blackall (may be sealed during currency of this book)
Total Distance: 347km (4:20)
Intermediate Distances:

	Km	Hours
Longreach-Ilfracombe	28	(0:15)
Ilfracombe-Isisford	89	(1:10)
Isisford-Blackall	123	(1:40)
Blackall-Barcaldine	107	(1:15)

Average Vehicles per Day: 100 north of Isisford
Regions Traversed: Mid-West

LONGREACH (Alt 192m; Pop 4500):* grazing town situated on the Tropic of Capricorn. For more information see Road Trip 7, Day 6. (*0/347*) *Road Trips 7 and 9 connect.*

Ilfracombe (Alt 214m; Pop 160):* grazing township. For more information see Road Trip 7, Day

6. (*28/319*) *Road Trips 7 and 9 connect. Turn **S** for Isisford. Turn **W** for Longreach.*

Plains support extensive tracts of Mitchell grass with areas of gidgee woodlands. Vast views* across the black soil plains from the tops of low rises. Undulating country supports quite dense growths of acacia shrublands. Borees are common. The ground is strewn with gibbers, locally known as gidgee stones.

Isisford (Alt 210m; Pop 130):* interesting small shire township. Many photogenic buildings. Worth stopping to explore and soak up the atmosphere. Nearby Barcoo River* waterhole is an attractive area. Oma Waterhole, 16km west, offers fishing and swimming. Accommodation, store, fuel. (*117/228*) Turn **E** onto Blackall-Isisford Rd for Blackall. *Turn **N** for Ilfracombe.*

Plains and low rises support open tracts of Mitchell grass, gidgee woodlands along drainage lines and occasional boree woodlands (those low trees with silvery boles) on low rises. Distant views* to far-off jump-ups to the south. En route is the Isis Downs Shearing Shed, the largest in Australia. Tours are available, make local enquiries.

BLACKALL (Alt 284m; Pop 1780): grazing town. For more information see Road Trip 7, Day 5. (*240/107*) *Road Trip 7 connects.* Turn **N** onto Matilda Hwy for Barcaldine. *Turn **W** onto Blackall-Isisford Rd for Isisford.*

For information on the route between Blackall and Barcaldine see Road Trip 7, Day 5.

BARCALDINE (Alt 265m; Pop 1800):* grazing town. For more information see Road Trip 7, Day 5. (*347/0*) *Road Trips 7 and 9 connect.*

Muttaburrasaurus Way

Barcaldine-Longreach via Muttaburra

The partially sealed route between Barcaldine and Longreach via Aramac and Muttaburra (the

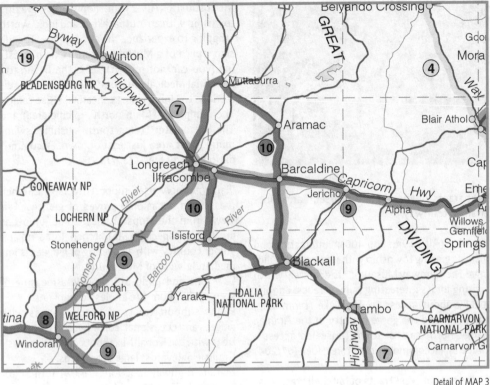

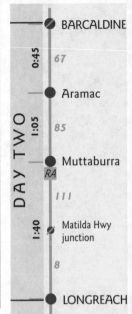

Detail of MAP 3

Muttaburrasaurus Way) is recommended as an alternative route to the Matilda Highway. It provides a quiet alternative, giving access to the historic township of Aramac and the 'outback' township of Muttaburra. Always seek local advice after rain.

Warnings: always make enquiries during or after rain; black soils plains are impassable to all traffic when wet. Routes subjected to flooding. Avoid travelling at night.

DAY 2: BARCALDINE-LONGREACH
via Aramac/Muttaburra

Road to Take: Muttaburrasaurus Way
Grade 3 Muttaburra-Longreach
Grade 2 Barcaldine-Muttaburra
Total Distance: 271km (3:30)

Intermediate Distances:

	Km	Hours
Barcaldine-Aramac	67	(0:45)
Aramac-Muttaburra	85	(1:05)
Muttaburra-Longreach	119	(1:40)

Average Vehicles per Day: 100 west of Aramac
Regions Traversed: Mid-West

BARCALDINE (Alt 265m; Pop 1800):* grazing town. For more information see Road Trip 7, Day 5. *(0/271)* Head **N** on Muttaburrasaurus Way for Aramac.

Plains and low rises support tracts of Mitchell grass. Eastwards are vast views to far-off tree-lined creeks and distant ranges. South of Aramac, a prominent jump-up lies on the north-west horizon. The keen, very observant traveller might

Old Garage, Aramac, Qld

spot traces of the old and disused Barcaldine-Aramac tramway.

Aramac (Alt 219m; Pop 400):* interesting and historic grazing township with photogenic buildings. The Tramway Museum** is definitely worth visiting for its interesting railway relics. Enquire locally about access to The Lake (swimming, camping) and the gorge country of the Aramac Range north-east of town (unsealed access - Grade 3). Accommodation, stores, fuel. (**67/204**)

Plains support vast tracts of Mitchell grass. Distant views westwards towards jump-up ranges. Small tract of acacia woodlands near Torrens Creek turnoff.
Floodplain supports an attractive river red gum woodlands. Pleasant waterholes* after floods.

Muttaburra (Alt 213m; Pop 160):* grazing township with an 'outback' feel and look. Worth stopping to experience the atmosphere. The full size replica of a Muttaburrasaurus* is interesting (you can not miss it), as is the Dr Arratta Memorial Medical Museum**. Ask locally for directions to Union Hole (a shearers' strike camp), The Pumphole* (4km north - picnic area) and The Broadwater* (6km south - fishing, swimming). **Rest area** just east of town. Accommodation, store, fuel. (**152/119**)

Plains and low rises support tracts of Mitchell grass with occasional groves of gidgees. Fair views from the stops of rises. Some jump-ups are visible, especially Mt Mitchell. Jump-up and gibber country with a covering of gidgees is immediately west of Muttaburra.
Low hills and jump-ups provide a measure of scenic relief from the endless clay plains.
Plains support tracts of Mitchell grass with gidgees and occasional leopardwoods (those low trees with the leopard-like spots on their trunks).
Cramsie Saleyards: large stockyards.
Matilda Highway junction: (**263/8**) Turn **SE** for Longreach. *Turn **N** for Muttaburra.*

LONGREACH (Alt 192m; Pop 4500): sizeable grazing town. For more information see Road Trip 7, Day 6. (**271/0**) *Road Trips 7 and 9 connect. Head **NW** for Muttaburra via Cramsie Saleyards.*

Road Trip 11
Overlanders Highway

Townsville-Tennant Creek
Total Distance: 1546km
Suggested Travelling Time: 5 days

Head into sweeping savanna plains

See the historic villages of Ravenswood and Camooweal, the Leichardt Range, the Burdekin River, White Mountains National Park, Torrens Creek, the Isa Ridges, the large mining town of Mt Isa, the picnic area of Clem Walton Park, and the broad space of the Barkly Tableland.

Overlanders Highway
(Flinders Highway)

The Overlanders Highway crosses Australia's savanna country. Broad sweeping grasslands, low rocky ranges, old mining and grazing towns combined with warm winter days all add up to numerous travelling delights. Features are scattered in this outback environment, but by taking your time, the enormity of space and the diversity of plant and animal life becomes apparent. This is a region to be savoured, a place for you to slow down and become part of the landscape.

The Climate

North Quensland is very warm to hot throughout the year. Summers are normally wet, with monsoonal rains filling waterholes and flooding streams. Combine this with warm, sticky nights and you will discover that the time to visit is during the dry season between April and October. Early in the season the days are still hot (low to mid-thirties) but the landscape is green and the waterholes are full after the wet season. As the dry season progresses, daytime temperatures fall (high twenties with the odd hot day) and nights are mild (low teens). Rainfall is very low or non-existant, and that means endless sunny days. Some of the cooler days might be a bit windy though. Later in the dry season the temperature climbs again, then hot, dry days become the norm.

Capital City Connections
Distances in kilometres
SYDNEY-TOWNSVILLE
via Pacific/Bruce Highways

	Intermediate	Total
Sydney	0	0
Coffs Harbour	537	537
Brisbane	422	959
Rockhampton	644	1603
Mackay	334	1937
Townsville	293	2230

SYDNEY-CLONCURRY
via Great Western/Mitchell/Matilda Highways

	Intermediate	Total
Sydney	0	0
Bourke	779	779
Barcaldine	408	1641
Winton	281	1922
Cloncurry	343	2265

MELBOURNE-CLONCURRY
via Hume/Goulburn Valley/Newell/Kidman/Matilda Hwys

	Intermediate	Total
Melbourne	0	0
Griffith	445	445
Charleville	454	1233
Bourke	525	970
Barcaldine	859	1829
Winton	281	2110
Cloncurry	343	2453

The Route
Distance in Kilometres

	Intermediate	Total
Townsville	0	0
Charters Towers	135	135
Hughenden	243	378
Julia Creek	256	634
Cloncurry	134	768
Mt Isa	118	886
Camooweal	189	1075

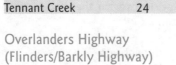

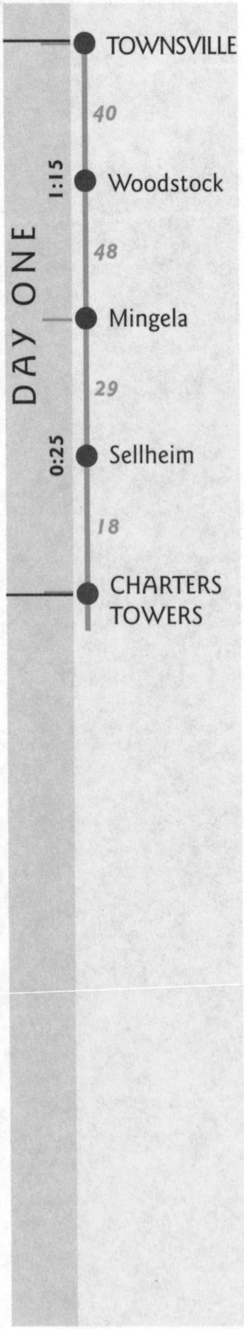

Three Ways	447	1522
Tennant Creek	24	1546

Overlanders Highway
(Flinders/Barkly Highway)
Townsville-Mt Isa

This major east-west route provides ready access to all major north-south roads as well as to a number of interesting towns. Most travellers tend to travel this route as fast as legally possible, which is a shame for there is much to see and do. While there are lengthy stretches of straight roads traversing black soil plains (the enormity of the space appeals to some) there is also a wide range of other scenic delights. These include the spectacular range country between Townsville and the Leichhardt Range, the wildflower displays of the White Mountains National Park, and the richly red jagged mountains, bluffs and ranges of the Isa Uplands between Cloncurry and Mt Isa. En route are a numbering of interesting towns, each deserving at least half a day's exploration, particularly Charters Towers, Richmond and Cloncurry, as well as a number of townships which beg a short stop at least: recommended are Torrens Creek, Prairie, Maxwelton, Nelia and Gilliat.

Warnings: beware of stock and other animal life at night. Road subjected to flooding. Take care on twisty and hilly sections of highway between Cloncurry-Mt Isa. Unsealed access to features between Cloncurry-Mt Isa are mostly rough; in wet weather make local enquiries before proceeding. Avoid westward travel after about 4pm, as the incoming sun is hazardous for driving.

DAY 1: TOWNSVILLE-CHARTERS TOWERS
via Mingela

Road to Take: Overlanders Highway (Flinders Highway)
Grade 1
Total Distance: 135km (1:40)

Intermediate Distances:

	Km	Hours
Townsville-Mingela	88	(1:15)
Mingela-Charters Towers	47	(0:25)

Average Vehicles Per Day: 1,500 east of Charters Towers
Regions Traversed: Townsville district, Burdekin-Belyando Basin

TOWNSVILLE (Alt 3m; Pop 140000): large tropical city. For more information see Road Trip 3, Day 3. (*0/135*)

Plains, mostly cleared for grazing, offer good views towards the Hervey Range to the west and Mt Elliot to the south. On the western edge of Townsville are high hills featuring an access road to Mt Stuart**, where grand views overlooking Townsville and Cleveland Bay can be enjoyed.

Woodstock (Alt 64m; Pop 50): small spread-out farming township. Accommodation, store, fuel. (*40/95*)

Plains occupy narrow valleys set between high hills. Good to spectacular mountain views**, especially eastwards towards the massive bulk of Mt Elliot (1342m). The plains are either draped in eucalypt woodlands or cleared for farming and grazing. A small **roadhouse** (fuel) is located between Reid River and Woodstock.
Reid River: small locality of a few houses, railway station and interesting railway bridge*. There is an old World War II airfield* nearby - visitors welcome; enquire locally. No other facilities, save a telephone. (*61/74*)
Plains (partly cleared) offer spectacular views** of surrounding high mountains.
Hilly country* ascends/descends a rugged, granite-strewn escarpment (the Hervey/Leichhardt Range) which forms the boundary between the interior tablelands and coastal lowlands. Good views* towards the prominent Bluff. Countryside hereabouts becomes drier moving inland.

Mingela (Alt 290m; Pop 50): small grazing township located just off the highway. Accommoda-

Left margin (route map)

Road Trip 11

DAY ONE

TOWNSVILLE
40
1:15
Woodstock
48
Mingela
29
0:25
Sellheim
18
CHARTERS TOWERS

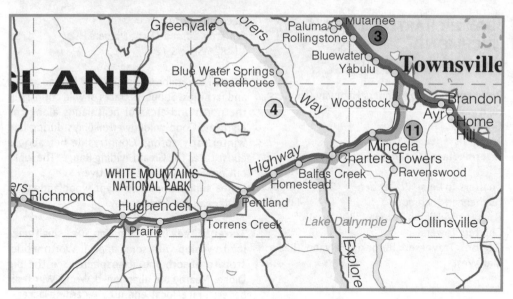

Detail of MAP 4

tion, store, fuel. (**88/47**) Turn **S** for Ravenswood via the Burdekin Falls Dam access road - see Side Trip below.

Side Trip
Ravenswood access road
(Grade 1) 84km return
Undulating country offers fair to reasonable views across dry eucalypt woodlands. Occasional eastward views toward the Leichhardt Range.
Ravenswood (Alt 249m; Pop 100):** interesting historic gold mining township with some character. While more touristed than it used to be there is still much to see; old buildings such as Imperial* and Railway Hotels*, Court House Museum*, St Patricks Church*, historic miners cottages*, as well as old mines and works. Beware of mine shafts. Enquire locally about fossicking sites. 5km east is the White Blow Environment Park* (interesting quartz outcrop). A short distance further east is a lookout* overlooking the Leichhardt Range. Accommodation, store, fuel. (**130/89**)

Accommodation
Top Camp International Resort, Burdekin Falls Dam Rd (2kmN), ✆07 4770 2188, ○$55-$70
Top Camp International Caravan Park, Burdekin Falls Dam Rd (2kmN), ✆07 4770 2188, ○Site: $14 Van: $50

Undulating country offers fair to reasonable views of distant ranges. Eucalypt woodlands are common, with some clearings along the road.
Burdekin River:* very large river during the wet season crossed by a long and high bridge. Interesting long railway bridge* to the south. Tracks lead off the highway onto the river banks, but beware of soft sand. Camping area and caravan park nearby. (**114/21**)

Sellheim (Alt 256m): small locality dominated by an army camp and roadhouse. Store, fuel. (**117/18**)

CHARTERS TOWERS (Alt 307m; Pop 9000):** old gold mining township with plenty of character. For more information see Road Trip 4, Day 2. (**135/0**) *Road Trip 4 connects.*

DAY 2: CHARTERS TOWERS-RICHMOND
via Hughenden

DAY TWO

CHARTERS TOWERS

42

Balfes Creek

31

Homestead

RA

42

2:50

Pentland

White
40   *Mountains*
         NP

Torrens Creek

46

Prairie

42

HUGHENDEN

RA

1:15

112

Richmond

Road to Take: Overlanders Highway (Flinders Highway)
Grade 1
Total Distance: 355km (4:05)
Intermediate Distances:

	Km	Hours
Charters Towers-Hughenden	243	(2:50)
Hughenden-Richmond	112	(1:15)

Average Vehicles Per Day: 700 west of Charters Towers
Regions Traversed: Burdekin-Belyando Basin, Mid-West

▼

CHARTERS TOWERS (Alt 307m; Pop 9000):** old gold mining town. For more information see Road Trip 4, Day 2. (*0/355*)

Plains and low rises support grassy eucalypt woodlands. Near Charters Towers are low hills and rocky outcrops offering fair views.
Powlathanga: railway siding; no facilities. (*32/323*)

Balfes Creek (Alt 327m; Pop 20): roadhouse facility and railway siding. Accommodation, store, fuel. (*42/313*)

Plains support grassy eucalypt woodlands.

Homestead (Alt 344m): small grazing township. Store, fuel. (*73/282*)

Plains support tracts of grassy eucalypt woodlands. Northwards the escarpment country of the Lolworth Range can be seen.
Kimburra: railway siding; no facilities. Nearby is a roadside **rest area**. (*88/267*)

Pentland (Alt 403m; Pop 400):* small grazing town with some appeal. Interesting buildings. Accommodation, store, fuel. (*115/250*)

Accommodation
Pentland Caravan Park, Flinders Hwy, ©07 4788 1148, ✪Site: $ 12

White Mountains National Park:* limited access and facilities. Supports tracts of wild country in the north and areas of heathlands along the highway. Good wildflower displays during late winter/early spring. Countryside hereabouts constitutes the Great Dividing Range. The lookout provides a good perspective.
Plains support open eucalypt woodlands with spinifex in the understorey.

Torrens Creek (Alt 466m; Pop 50):* small grazing township with some appeal. Worth a brief stop to absorb the atmosphere. See the Big Didge. Nearby are abandoned World War II air bases; make local enquires regarding access. Accommodation, store, fuel. (*155/200*)
Accommodation
Exchange Hotel, Flinders Hwy, ©07 4741 7342, ✪$35
Exchange Hotel Van and Camping Park, ©07 4741 7342, ✪Site: $12

Plains support sparse low grassy eucalypt woodlands, grading eastwards into eucalypt woodlands with a spinifex understorey (unusual for this part of the world).

Prairie (Alt 432m; Pop 30):* small grazing township with character. Worth stopping to absorb the atmosphere. A visit to the butcher's is rewarding. Accommodation, store, fuel. (*201/154*)

Flat-top hills* form an outlier of the vast basalt tableland which lies to the north. Mt Arthur, north of the road at Jardine Valley, rises about 70 metres above the valley. The area is fairly scenic in the right light. Acacia woodlands are common.

HUGHENDEN (Alt 325m; Pop 1500):* interesting grazing town. Worth seeing is the replica of the 14 metre long Muttaburrasaurus skeleton at the Dinosaur Display and Museum**; also fossil displays and historical memorabilia. There

Grand Hotel, Hughenden, Qld

is another Muttaburrasaurus replica in Stansfield Street. Also visit Robert Grey Memorial Park, rotunda and drinking fountain, and the Landsborough and Walker blazed coolabah tree (next to the showgrounds). Full town facilities. (*243/112*)

Accommodation
Royal Hotel, Moran St, ©07 4741 1183, ✪$70
Wrights Motel, 20 Grey St, ©07 4741 1677, ✪$40-$50
Hughenden Rest-Easi Motel, Flinders Hwy, 07 4741 1633, ✪$60
Hughenden Rest-Easi Caravan Park, Flinders Hwy, ©07 4741 1633, ✪Site: $14
Allan Terry Caravan Park, Resolution St, ©07 4741 1190, ✪Site: $15 Van: $30

Dunluce: railway siding; no facilities. (*277/78*)
Plains and low rises supports vast tracts of Mitchell grass. Low plateau visible on the skyline to the north. Some acacia shrublands will be seen. Near Hughenden the soil appears blacker, the grasses more yellow; eastwards are flat-top hills and ranges.
Marathon: railway siding; no facilities. **Rest area** nearby. (*307/48*)
Plains offer the usual views of Mitchell grass and prickly mimosas. If heading west after sunset the lights* of Richmond hover on the skyline, visible up to 30 kilometres away.

Richmond (Alt 214m; Pop 800):** if you spend time in only one town west of Charters Towers make it this one, a grazing town with plenty of character and characters. Many interesting, historic and photogenic buildings* including the Strand Theatre, O'Sullivans Drapery and Richmond Stores. Visit Kronosaurus Korner** for its world renowned fossil displays; Lions Park* for views over the Flinders River, old machinery displays, and a collection of spherical 'moon rocks'*; pioneer cemetery; sandalwood mill; and two interesting churches. **Rest area**. Enquire locally about access to the Woolgar gold mining district. Accommodation, stores, fuel. (*355/0*)

Accommodation
Midway Motel, Flinders Hwy, ©07 4741 3192, ✪$70
Entrikens Pioneer Motel, Goldring St, ©07 4741 3188, ✪$70
Richmond Caravan Park, Flinders Hwy, ©07 4741 3772, ✪Site: $14 Van: $50

DAY 3: RICHMOND-MT ISA via Julia Creek

Road to Take: Overlanders Highway (Flinders Highway)
Grade 1
Total Distance: 396km (4:35)
Intermediate Distances:

	Km	Hours
Richmond-Julia Creek	144	(1:45)
Julia Creek-Cloncurry	134	(1:30)
Cloncurry-Mt Isa	118	(1:20)

Average Vehicles per Day: 450 west of Cloncurry
Regions Traversed: Mid-West, North-West Queensland

Richmond (Alt 214m; Pop 800):* interesting grazing town. For more information see Day 2. (*0/396*)

Undulating country offers vast views from the tops of rises. Expect the usual Mitchell grass and prickly mimosas.
Maxwelton (Alt 170m):* old township that has seen better days, consisting of some ruins and

Road Trip 11

DAY THREE

Richmond
RA
1:45   144
RA
Julia Creek
1:30   RA
134

CLONCURRY
Mt Frosty
Sun Rock
1:20   118   Poison Hole
Warrigal Waterhole

MT ISA

Road Trip 11

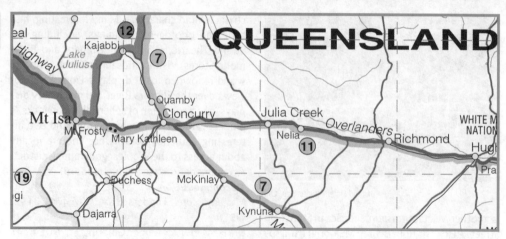

Detail of MAP 4

a few occupied houses. Worth a look. No facilities except a phone. (*48/348*)

Plains support extensive tracts of grasslands with tree-lined creeks on the horizon. Numerous tributaries and ana-branches of the Flinders River form scattered wetlands* after the monsoon. **Rest area**. (*49/357*)

Nelia turnoff: (*97/299*) Turn **N** for Nelia, an interesting old township* of a hall, some houses and ruins lying just off the highway. Worth a quick look, but do not trespass. No facilities except a phone.

Plains support grasslands. Next to the large bridge over Alick Creek is the old river crossing offering some shade, a passable spot for a picnic.

Plains and low rises support vast tracts of Mitchell and other grasses. The small shrubby bushes are prickly mimosa. Julia Creek's wine-glass water tower is visible to the west. Occasional vast views. **Rest area**. (*143/253*)

Julia Creek (Alt 125m; Pop 600): grazing and trucking centre. Small block of interesting buildings. McIntyre Museum worth a look. Accommodation, stores, fuel. (*144/252*)

Accommodation

Julia Creek Motel, Flinders Hwy, ©07 4746 7305, ✪$65

Gannons Motel, 36 Burke St, ©07 4746 7103, ✪$55

Julia Creek Caravan Park, Old Normanton Rd, ©07 4746 7108, ✪Site: $13

Plains support tracts of Mitchell grass with areas of acacia shrublands. Large attractive waterhole* at the Eastern Creek crossing (*165/231*). Eastwards, the Julia Creek watertower is visible for some distance.

Plains support vast tracts of Mitchell grass. Eastbound travellers will appreciate the wide open spaces and expansive views.

Low rises and plains will come as a relief to those travellers heading west (no more Mitchell grass or black soil plains). Red soils support a low eucalypt woodland with a spinifex understorey. Fair views westwards from the tops of rises. **Rest area**. (*214/182*)

Matilda Highway junction: locality only; no facilities. (*264/132*) *Road Trip 7 connects.*

CLONCURRY (Alt 188m; Pop 2500):* interesting grazing town. For more information see Road Trip 7, Day 7. (*278/118*) *Road Trip 7 connects.*

Ranges* support sparse eucalypt woodlands with an understorey of spinifex. Good views of rocky bluffs and ridges. Just west of the Normanton turnoff is the Rotary Lookout*, providing good views over the Cloncurry district.

Memorials: near Corella River is a memorial to Burke and Wills. A short distance further west is a far more interesting memorial* to the Kalkadoon and Mitakoodi people, who were displaced by European occupation. The memorial also commemorates the battle of Battle Mountain between the Kalkadoons and state troopers, one of the fiercest fights in the guerilla war against the Aborigines. (*322/74*)

Clem Walton Park turnoff. (*331/65*) Turn **S** for the 6km return unsealed (Grade 3) road to Clem Walton Park*, a very pleasant area on the banks of Corella River and adjacent to Corella Dam. Patches of tropical vegetation are backed by high, rocky cliffs. A good spot for birdwatching and picnicking. Popular with the locals on weekends. Spectacular country* hereabouts. Bottle trees line the road at intervals.

Mary Kathleen turnoff. (*341/55*) A short sealed access road leads **N** to Mary Kathleen*, a former uranium mining town of which little remains. It is an interesting area nonetheless, where you can see the old streets and the open cut mine a short distance to the north.

Range country* hereabouts is quite spectacular with sharp, jagged skylines. Very colourful in the late afternoon light.

Mt Frosty turnoff. (*348/48*) A rough, unsealed (Grade 4) 6km return track leads **S** to Mt Frosty*, an old limestone quarry partly filled with water. Good swimming, but it's not called Mt Frosty for nothing. No shallows. Surrounding area is good for fossicking and is often called a gem-seeker's paradise.

Sun Rock:* worth visiting, a pleasant area 200 metres off the road (plus a further 150 metres walking). Explore the rocky outcrops and study the Aboriginal paintings. The access track is unsealed - look for it between a deep gully and road cutting. (*349/47*)

Poison Hole turnoff. (*365/26*) A rough (Grade 4) 14km return track leads **N** to Poison Hole*, an abandoned mine 100 metres wide and just as deep. Follow the walking track into the hole. Water, undrinkable and coloured bright green, partly fills the mine. The disused mine and processing equipment are quite photogenic.

Ranges* offer good views of rocky bluffs and ridges. Countryside is clothed in eucalypt wood-lands with a spinifex understorey. Keep an eye out for bottle trees easily recognisable by their bulbous trunks.

Warrigal Waterhole turnoff. (*348/7*) A rough 6km return track (Grade 4) **S** accesses Warrigal Waterhole*, an interesting rockhole located in a dry, sparsely vegetated valley. Contains Aboriginal paintings.

MT ISA (Alt 356m; Pop 22200):** large mining town and regional centre; one of the outback's major towns. Mt Isa Mine is one of the largest underground mines in the world, and its chimney stacks and slag heaps dominate the skyline. Mining includes silver, lead, copper and zinc. Plenty to see: Mount Isa Mines* above and underground tours, Riversleigh Fossil Display**, Kalkadoon Tribal Centre and Cultural Keeping Place**, City Lookout* (day and night visits recommended), Lake Moondarra* (15km north), plus Tent House, Frank Aston Underground Museum**, Royal Flying Doctor Service, School of Distance Education, John Middlin Mining Display*, Lake Moondarra, and more. Worth a day or two in the area. Full town facilities. (*391/0*) *Road Trips 12, 19 and 24 connect. /Head **E** on Overlanders Hwy for Julia Creek.*

Accommodation

Copper City Motel, 105 Butler St, ©07 4743 2033, ✪$70

Inland Oasis Motel, 195 Barkly Hwy, ©07 4743 3433, ✪$55-$70

Waltons Motor Court Motel, 23 Camooweal St, ©07 4743 2290, ✪$90

4th Avenue Motor Inn, 20 Fourth Ave, ©07 4743 3477, ✪$70

Townview Motel, 116 Kookaburra St, ©07 4743 3328, ✪$45-$90

Riverside Tourist Caravan Park, 195 West St, ©07 4743 3904, ✪Site: $18 Van: $65

Sunset Caravan Park, 14 Sunset Dr (1.6kmN), ©07 4743 7668, ✪Site: $15 Van: $20-$60

Copper City Caravan Park, 185 West St, ©07 4743 6447, ✪Site: $15 Van: $40-$50

Barkly Highway
Mt Isa-Three Ways

West of Mt Isa, vast expanses of Mitchell grass form the Barkly Tableland - big sky country. Further west lies a vast semi-arid landscape described by many travellers as dreary - slow down and enjoy the space.

Warnings: beware of stock and kangaroos at night; avoid night travel if at all possible. Road may be subject to flooding. Exercise caution on the less than adequate bitumen between Mount Isa and Camooweal; there are numerous dips, blind crests, floodways and jagged edges, although the road may be improved during the currency of this book.

DAY 4: MT ISA-BARKLY ROADHOUSE via Camooweal

Road to Take: Barkly Highway
Grade 1
Total Distance: 449km (5:05)
Intermediate Distances:

	Km	Hours
Mt Isa-Camooweal	189	(2:15)
Camooweal-Barkly Roadhouse	260	(2:50)

Average Vehicles per Day: 200 east of Avon Downs
Regions Traversed: North-West Queensland, Barkly Tableland

▼

MT ISA (Alt 356m; Pop 22200):** large mining town and regional centre. For more information see Day 3. (*0/449*)

Low ranges offer reasonable views. **Rest area**. (*5/444*)
Hilton Mine: large mine complex clearly visible from the road. (*19/430*)
Ranges* rise above the road; good views from the tops of crests. Rocky outcrops and bluffs are quite common. Ranges support a sparse eucalypt woodland with a spinifex understorey.

Gunpowder turnoff: locality only; no facilities. (*44/394*) Gunpowder lies 83km **N**. Proceed straight ahead.
Undulating country supports eucalypt woodlands (mainly bloodwoods) with an understorey of spinifex.
Yelvertoft Road junction: locality only; no facilities. (*118/331*) *Road Trip 12 connects.*
Undulating country supports eucalypt woodlands, typically bloodwoods. Some acacias are present. Spinifex understorey.
Plains support eucalypt woodlands with an understorey of spinifex, grading westward into expansive tracts of Mitchell grass grasslands. This is the eastern edge of the Barkly Tableland.

Camooweal (Alt 233m; Pop 360): interesting grazing town. Small community of Alyawarre people. Freckleton's Store* is worth seeing, as is the old shire hall. Good opportunity to photograph cattle-carting road trains. Museum* and information is available at at the Barkly Tableland Heritage Centre. Also see the old cemetery and the town mural. Nearby waterholes on the Georgina River (west of town) offer fair shade for a picnic. Accommodation, stores, fuel. (*189/260*)
Accommodation
Camooweal Roadhouse Motel, Barkly Hwy, ©07 4748 2155, ✪$65
BP Camooweal Driveway, Barkly Hwy, ©07 4748 2137, ✪$60

An unsealed 40km return trip leads from Camooweal to the Camooweal Caves National Park, preserving a broad expanse of Mitchell grass above countless cave systems. Do not venture into these caves unless properly equiped and experienced. Camping is available.

State Border between Queensland and the Northern Territory. This also marks a time zone boundary - add 1/2 hour heading west; subtract 1/2 hour heading east. (*202/247*)
Plains support vast tracts of Mitchell grass grasslands during good seasons. Vast views from tops of rises. Mirages may be seen; oncoming traffic may appear greatly distorted.

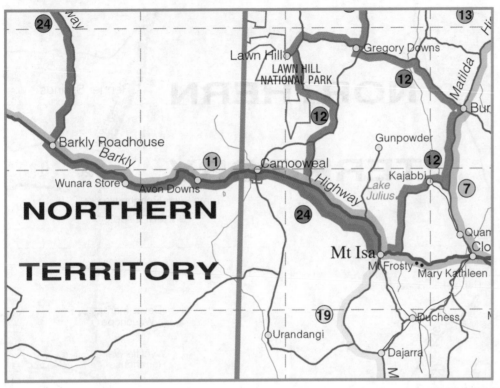

Detail of MAP 4

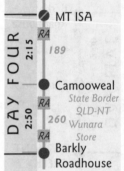

Avon Downs: locality and police station. No other facilities. Emergency fuel may be available. **Rest area**. (*258/191*)

Plains support vast tracts of Mitchell grass grasslands during good seasons, vast tracts of nothing but small gibbers during droughts. Worth stopping (well off the road) just to experience the enormity of the space. If you stop in a gibber area*, start looking at the stones - there's a good chance you won't leave in under half an hour! Coolabah trees dot the main drainage lines. Low rise offers broad views. Eucalypt woodland with spinifex understorey is common.

Soudan Station: working cattle station, no facilities. The station buildings and plant are clearly visible from the road. Ranken River crossing is of minor interest. (*309/140*)

Plains supporting bloodwoods and spinifex contrast dramatically with the empty black soil country further east. Black soil supports Mitchell grass grasslands during good seasons. **Rest area**. (*325/124*)

Low rises offer fair views of bloodwoods and spinifex.

Barry Caves ruin:* former roadhouse facility of which there is little to be seen, save for numerous rusted car parts. Worth a quick look. (*352/97*)

Wunara Store:* small community of Wakaya people. Well worth visiting for its artefacts and bush garden. Store. (*356/93*)

Wonorah ruin:* former telegraph repeater station of which little remains save for building foundations, scraps of building materials and piles of junk. Worth a quick look. Fair view from a low rise upon which a ruin is situated. Country to the south is an uninhabited sand dune desert. (*399/50*)

Plains support sparse eucalypt woodlands with a spinifex understorey. Bloodwoods common; corkwoods may be seen. Plains are sandy. Coun-

DAY FIVE

Barkly
Roadhouse

RA

2:00   *187 Frewena ruin*

RA

Three Ways

0:15   *24*

TENNANT
CREEK

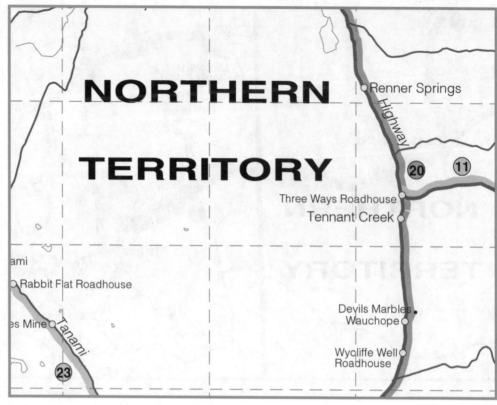

Detail of MAP 6

tryside south of the highway forms part of Wakaya Aboriginal Land. **Rest area**. (*409/40*)

Barkly Roadhouse (Alt 244m; Pop 5): roadhouse facility. (*449/0*) *Road Trip 24 connects*.
Accommodation
Barkly Homestead Motel, Barkly Hwy, ✆08 8964 4549, ✪$75
Barkly Homestead Caravan Park, Barkly Hwy, ✆08 8964 4549, ✪Site: $18

DAY 5: BARKLY ROADHOUSE-TENNANT CREEK
via Three Ways

Road to Take: Barkly Highway
Grade 1
Total Distance: 211km (2:15)

Intermediate Distances:

	Km	Hours
Barkly Roadhouse-Three Ways	187	(2:00)
Three Ways-Tennant Creek	24	(0:15)

Average Vehicles per Day: 200 west of Barkly Roadhouse
Regions Traversed: Barkly Tableland

Barkly Roadhouse (Alt 244m; Pop 5): roadhouse facility. For more information see Day 4. (*0/211*)

Plains support tracts of eucalypt woodlands with a shrubby understorey.
Frewena ruin:* old roadhouse ruin. Although there is little to see at first sight, poking about in the grass will elicit signs of previous occupation. The area is surrounded by a relatively open Mitchell grass grassland. **Rest area** nearby. (*56/155*)

Old Tennant Creek Telegraph Station, NT

Low rises formed on sandstone support spinifex and a few bloodwood trees. Vast views. Rises elevated about 30 metres above the plains. Country hereabout crosses Waramungu Aboriginal Land. **Rest area**. (*116/95*)

Plains support vast tracts of sparse eucalypt woodlands, notably bloodwoods, with an understorey of spinifex.

Three Ways (Alt 328m; Pop 25): interesting roadhouse. For more information see Road Trip 20, Day 7. (*187/24*)

For information on the route between Three Ways and Tennant Creek, see Road Trip 20, Day 7.

TENNANT CREEK (Alt 377m; Pop 3500): interesting mining and Aboriginal town. For more information see Road Trip 20, Day 7. (*211/0*)

Road Trip 12
Lawn Hill Loop

Mt Isa-Burke & Wills-Gregory Downs-Burketown-Lawn Hill-Mt Isa
Total Distance: 1052km
Suggested Travelling Time: 4 days

> *Hike through the stunning gorges of Lawn Hill National Park*
>
> See the scenic Lake Julius, historic Gregory Downs, the Leichardt and Gregory Rivers, Campbell Camp, the Riversleigh fossil outcrop, Adels Grove, and the superb waterfalls and walking tracks within Lawn Hill National Park.

Lawn Hill Loop

The Lawn Hill area is in part of Australia's savanna country, lying on the edge of the Barkly Tableland escarpment where it abuts the lowlands of the Gulf Savanna. Broad sweeping grasslands, low rocky ranges, old mining and grazing townships combined with warm winter days all add up to numerous travelling delights.

The Climate

North-West Queensland is very warm to hot throughout the year. Summers are normally wet with monsoonal rains filling waterholes and flooding streams. As such, land transport may not always be possible. Combine this general inaccessibility with warm, sticky nights and you will discover that the time to visit here is during the dry season between April and October. Early in the season the days are still hot (low to mid-thirties) but the landscape is green and the waterholes are full after the wet season. As the dry season progresses, daytime temperatures fall (high twenties with the odd hot day) and nights are mild (low teens). Rainfall is now very low or non-existent, resulting in endless sunny days. Some of the cooler days might be a bit windy though. Later in the dry season the temperature climbs again, then hot dry days become the norm

Capital City Connections
Distances in Kilometres
SYDNEY-MT ISA
via Great Western/Mitchell/Matilda/Barkly Highways

	Intermediate	Total
Sydney	0	0
Nyngan	578	578
Charleville	655	1233
Mt Isa	1150	2383

BRISBANE-MT ISA
via Warrego/Matilda/Barkly Highways

	Intermediate	Total
Brisbane	0	0
Roma	481	481
Longreach	698	1179
Cloncurry	516	1695
Mt Isa	118	1813

ADELAIDE-MT ISA
via Highway One/Stuart/Barkly Highways

	Intermediate	Total
Adelaide	0	0
Port Augusta	312	312
Coober Pedy	536	848
Kulgera	411	1259
Alice Springs	273	1532
Three Ways	531	2063
Mt Isa	636	2699

The Route
Distances in kilometres

	Intermediate	Total
Mt Isa	0	0
Kajabbi	117	117
Burke & Wills	115	232
Gregory Downs	145	377
Burketown	117	494
Gregory Downs	117	611
Lawn Hill	97	708
Mt Isa	344	1052

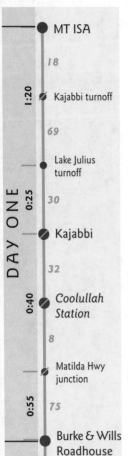

DAY ONE

●	MT ISA
	18
1:20 ⊘	Kajabbi turnoff
	69
⊘	Lake Julius turnoff
0:25	30
⊘	Kajabbi
	32
0:40 ⊘	*Coolullah Station*
	8
⊘	Matilda Hwy junction
0:55	75
●	Burke & Wills Roadhouse

Lake Julius/Kajabbi Road
Mt Isa-Burke & Wills Roadhouse

Travelling north from Mt Isa is an alternative unsealed route that leads through attractive rangelands via Lake Julius and the historic town of Kajabbi. This route is normally accessible to conventional vehicles driven with care during the dry season.

> **Warnings:** beware of stock at night; night travelling not recommended. Roads subjected to flooding. Unsealed route impassable after rain - make local enquiries before proceeding.

DAY 1: MT ISA-BURKE AND WILLS via Kajabbi

Roads to Take: Lake Julius-Kajabbi Road, Matilda Highway
Grade 3
Warning: Remote Route
Total Distance: 232km (3:20)
Intermediate Distances:

	Km	Hours
Mt Isa-Lake Julius turnoff	87	(1:20)
Lake Julius turnoff-Kajabbi	30	(0:25)
Kajabbi-Matilda Hwy junction	40	(0:40)
Matilda Hwy jctn-Burke & Wills	75	(0:55)

Average Vehicles per Day: less than 30
Regions Traversed: North-West Queensland, Gulf Savanna

▼

MT ISA (Alt 356m; Pop 22200):** Interesting mining town and regional centre. For more information see Road Trip 11, Day 3. (*0/232*) *Road Trips 11, 19 and 24 connect.*

Kajabbi turnoff: (*18/214*) *Road Trip 11 connects.* Turn **N** for Lake Julius and Kajabbi. *Turn **W** for Mt Isa.*
Low hills offer good views*. Low eucalypts and spinifex are common.
Undulating country: good views* to distant ranges. Sparse eucalypt woodlands and spinifex

with gidgees on the drainage lines. Numerous quartz blows*.
Ranges line the road exhibiting rocky bluffs, jagged skylines, rocky pinnacles and striking ridges. Views abound from the tops of rises*. Very attractive area, photogenic in early morning and late afternoon light. Sparse eucalypt woodlands are common.
Lake Julius turnoff: (*87/145*) Turn **W** for the 22km return journey to Lake Julius*, a dam and reservoir on the Leichhardt river set within attractive range country*. Boating is allowed on the lake, canoe hire, fishing recommended. Walking tracks, lookout, gold fossicking and a fauna sanctuary are all located here. The Recreation Camp offers basic accommodation and camping. Low ranges line the Leichhardt River valley*. An attractive area. Sparse eucalypt woodlands with spinifex are common.

Kajabbi (Alt 154m; Pop 30):* interesting old township well worth visiting, pleasantly situated on the banks of the Leichhardt River. The old pub* should be seen; stick around long enough to talk to the locals. A memorial opposite the pub pays tribute to the Kalkadoon people. Old railway relics and ruins*. Nearby is a craft cottage. Enquire here about directions to Mt Cuthbert and Dobbyn (4WD recommended). Accommodation, fuel. (*117/115*) Continue **N** for Burke and Wills. *Continue **S** for Mt Isa.*

Coolullah Station: working cattle station; no facilities. (*149/83*) Turn **E** for Matilda Hwy junction. *Turn **S** for Kajabbi.*
Matilda Highway junction: no facilities. (*157/75*) *Road Trip 7 connects.* Turn **N** for Burke and Wills Roadhouse. *Turn **W** for Coollulah Station.*

For information on the route to Burke and Wills Roadhouse see Road Trip 7, Day 8.

Burke And Wills Roadhouse (Alt 71m; Pop 5): roadhouse facility. For more information see Road Trip 7, Day 8. (*232/0*) *Road Trip 7 connects.* Turn **S** onto Burke Developmental Road for Kajabbi.

▲

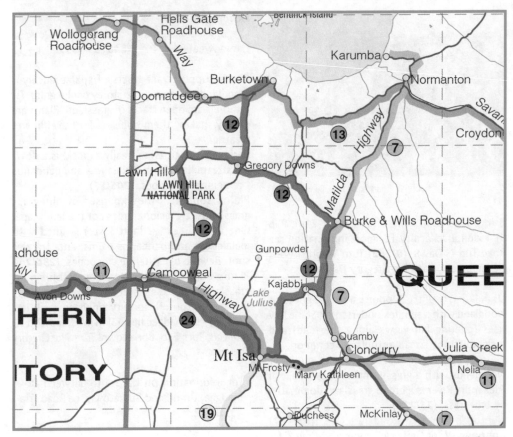

Detail of MAP 4

Wills Developmental Road

Burke & Wills-Gregory Downs-Burketown
This route will take the traveller through a vast region of expansive grasslands and treed savannas, crossing wide plains, passing low hills, en route to one of North-West Queensland's most delightful places: Lawn Hill National Park. This route also provides access to historic Burketown. Note that in the wet season nearly all land-based transport ceases, except along the sealed roads - even these routes are susceptible to flooding.

Warnings: beware of stock at night; travelling at this time is not recommended. Take care on narrow bitumen as verges may be soft after rain. Roads subject to flooding. On unsealed roads make local enquiries before proceeding, especially just before, during or after the wet season, or after rain at any time.

DAY 2: BURKE & WILLS-BURKETOWN
via Gregory Downs

Road to Take: Wills Developmental Road
Grade 4
Grade 2 Burke & Wills-Gregory Downs
Total Distance: 262km (3:30)
Intermediate Distances:

	Km	Hours
Burke & Wills-Gregory Downs	145	(1:45)
Gregory Downs-Burketown	117	(1:45)

Average Vehicle per Day: 40 west of Burke & Wills Roadhouse
Regions Traversed: Gulf Savanna

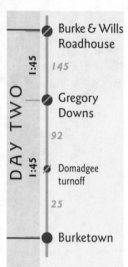

DAY TWO

- Burke & Wills Roadhouse
  - 1:45
  - 145
- Gregory Downs
  - 92
  - 1:45
- Domadgee turnoff
  - 25
- Burketown

Burketown bore, Burketown, Qld

Burke And Wills Roadhouse (Alt 71m; Pop 5): roadhouse facility. For more information see Road Trip 7, Day 8. (*0/262*) Turn **W** onto Wills Development Road for Gregory Downs.

Undulating country supports a sparse eucalypt woodland with a spinifex understorey. Some low rises (offering fair views along the road) and rocky outcrops. Small anthills are common.
Plain supports extensive tracts of eucalypt woodlands with a grassy understorey. West of Alexandra River is a broad grassland dominated by bluegrass. (*23/239*)
Nardoo-Burketown Road junction: (75/187) Continue **W** for Gregory Downs. *Continue* **E** *for Burke and Wills.*
Leichhardt River:* interesting river crossing. Good views* of the river from the high level bridge (beware of traffic). The waterholes look ominous (there may be estuarine crocodiles here) but are lined with a tropical gallery forest. A shady woodland of tall gums line the high banks and adjacent flood flats. Incredible bird life on the river. Reasonable camping. (*82/180*)
Plain supports extensive tracts of grassy eucalypt woodlands.

Gregory Downs (Alt 77m; Pop 10):* interesting bush settlement of a pub, small store, a hall and a few houses. Accommodation, limited stores, fuel. (*145/117*) Stay on Wills Developmental Road heading **N** for Burketown. *Stay on Wills Developmental Road heading* **E** *for Burke and Wills.*

Accommodation
Gregory Downs Hotel-Motel, Gregory Downs-Camooweal Rd, ⓒ07 54846163, ⊙$70

Plains support vast tracts of sparse eucalypt woodlands with an understorey of bluegrass. At intervals are open tracts of grassland. Plains are of clay, making them hopeless for travel in wet weather.
Barkly River* crossing (really a creek) is a flowing stream lined with melaleucas and pandanus - remember the crocs. (*205/57*)
Plains support wide expanses of bluegrass grasslands. Occasional trees dot the landscape. One Mile Creek* (Albert River) is lined with melaleucas and pandanus palms, an attractive spot. Beware of estuarine crocodiles. (*236/26*)
Plains support wide expanses of bluegrass grasslands dotted at intervals with low trees.
Domadgee turnoff: locality only; no facilities. (*237/25*) Domadgee lies 93km **W**. *Road Trip 13 connects.* Turn **E** for Burketown. *Turn* **S** *for Gregory Downs.*

For information on the route between Domadgee turnoff and Burketown see Road Trip 13, Day 2.

Burketown (Alt 6m; Pop 235):* interesting and historic town. For more information see Road Trip 13, Day 2. (*262/0*) *Road Trip 13 connects. Head* **W** *to Domadgee turnoff.*

DAY 3: BURKETOWN-LAWN HILL
via Gregory Downs

Roads to Take: Wills Developmental Road, Lawn Hill Road
Grade 4
Total Distance: 214km (3:25)
Intermediate Distances:

	Km	Hours
Burketown-Gregory Downs	117	(1:45)
Gregory Downs-Lawn Hill	97	(1:40)

Average Vehicles per Day: 50 south of Burketown
Regions Traversed: Gulf Savanna, Barkly Tableland

Burketown (Alt 6m; Pop 235)* interesting and historic town. For more information see Road Trip 13, Day 2. (*0/214*)

For information on the route between Burketown and Gregory Downs see Day 2.

Gregory Downs (Alt 77m; Pop 10):* interesting bush settlement. For more information see Day 2. (*117/97*) Head **W** for Lawn Hill. *Head **N** for Burketown.*

Gregory River:** very attractive river lined with tall melaleucas. The river flows virtually all year and is crystal clear. It is fed by limestone springs from the nearby Barkly Tableland. Good camping on the riverbanks. (*120/94*)
Plains support vast tracts of grassy eucalypt woodlands.
Low hills provide good westwards views* towards Constance Range (347m) and lesser ranges to the north and south. Attractive country hereabouts. The countryside supports sparse eucalypt woodlands with a spinifex understorey.
Lawn Hill Homestead: no facilities. (*194/20*) Head **S** for Adels Grove. *Head **E** for Gregory Downs.*
Road junction: (*202/12*) Turn **SW** for Adels Grove. *Turn **N** for Gregory Downs.*

Adels Grove (Alt 138m; Pop 5): small tourist facility offering camping and bushwalks. The former exotic garden* located on Lawn Hill Creek's flood flats is worth seeing: cool, shady and very attractive. Canoeing is available on Lawn Hill Creek*. This is a much quieter area than the adjacent national park. Limited stores, fuel. (*208/6*)

Lawn Hill National Park:** large national park of predominantly wilderness country located on the eastern escarpment of the Barkly Tableland. The principal areas of interest are the gorges**

centred on Lawn Hill Creek. Towering 60 metre sandstone bluffs stand above crystal clear waterholes teeming with fish. Swimming and canoeing is highly recommended. Waterholes are lined with tropical gallery rainforests* and palm forests. Also of interest are tufa dam waterfalls**, spectacular walking tracks, lookouts, splendid wildlife including freshwater crocodiles, Aboriginal paintings and photogenic semi-arid vegetation, making this an area well worth visiting. Camping, bushwalking, canoeing and swimming are available, but be warned: this is a popular park during the dry season so expect a crowd. Campsites need to be booked well in advance. Park information, displays and telephone; no other facilities. (*214/0*)

Isa/Riversleigh Byway
Lawn Hill-Mt Isa

This route crosses the rugged uplands of North-West Queensland and the eastern Barkly Tableland, taking the traveller through a region of treed savannas and low ranges. It provides access to Riversleigh (world famous for its fossils) and Lawn Hill National Park, the scenic wonder of North-West Queensland. It is only passable to travellers during the dry season. Conventional-vehicle drivers will need to exercise extreme caution - 4WD recommended. In the wet season nearly all land-based transport ceases, except along the sealed roads - even these routes are susceptible to flooding.

Warnings: beware of stock at night; night travelling is not recommended. Roads subjected to flooding. On unsealed roads make local enquiries before proceeding, especially just before, during or after the wet season, or after rain at any time.
Note: no fuel between Adels Grove-Mt Isa 338km

DAY THREE

Burketown

25

1:45   Domadgee turnoff

92

Gregory Downs

77 Gregory River

Lawn Hill Homestead

8

1:40   Road junction

6

Adels Grove

6 Lawn Hill NP

Lawn Hill

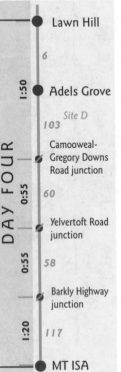

Lawn Hill

1:50

6

Adels Grove

Site D

103

DAY FOUR

0:55

Camooweal-
Gregory Downs
Road junction

60

0:55

Yelvertoft Road
junction

58

1:20

Barkly Highway
junction

117

MT ISA

DAY 4: LAWN HILL-MT ISA
via Riversleigh

Road to Take: Isa-Riversleigh Byway
Grade 4
Warning: Remote Route. No fuel for 338km.
Total Distance: 344km (5:00)
Intermediate Distances:

	Km	Hours
Lawn Hill-Camooweal/Gregory Downs Rd jctn	109	(1:50)
Camooweal/Gregory Downs Rd jctn-Yelvertoft Rd junction	60	(0:55)
Yelvertoft Rd jctn-Barkly Hwy jctn	58	(0:55)
Barkly Hwy jn-Mt Isa	117	(1:20)

Average Vehicles per Day: 20 near Thorntonia Station
Regions Traversed: Barkly Tableland, North-West Queensland

Lawn Hill: national park settlement. Park information, displays and telephone; no other facilities. (*0/344*) Head **N** for Adels Grove.

Adels Grove (Alt 138m; Pop 5): small tourist facility. For more information see Day 3. (*6/338*)

Road junction: (*12/332*) Lawn Hill Homestead lies north. Continue **SE** for Mt Isa. *Continue **SW** for Adels Grove.*
Undulating country and low hills offer delightful scenery. Hills are covered with spinifex. The intervening flats are mostly grassy.
Site D:** a readily accessible site offering visitors the opportunity to see some of the world-famous Riversleigh fossils in situ (ie old fossils embedded in limestone rock). The nearby information board explains all. Interesting limestone ridges hereabouts; note the rough weathered texture of the rocks. Good views* from the top of the ridge (watch your footing). (*73/271*)
Campbells Camp:* located a short distance off the road is a private tour bus operator's camp

on the Gregory River that allows camping for travellers. Birdwatching, walking trails, canoeing, and more are availble.
Gregory River:* fast-flowing river crossing over a concrete causeway (not as bad as it looks outside of the wet season). The river flows virtually all year due to the constant seepage from the limestone bedrock within its headwaters. Rainforest and tall melaleucas line the watercourse. Camping is available on the western side. (*75/269*)
Riversleigh Station: working cattle station in attractive range country. No facilities. (*77/267*)
Low ranges support a sparse eucalypt woodland with a spinifex understorey. Very attractive country with good views* from the tops of rises. Beware of severe rocky outcrops.
Camooweal-Gregory Downs Road junction: locality only; no facilities. (*109/235*) Turn **S** for Mt Isa. *Turn **W** for Lawn Hill.*
Hilly country lines the road supporting sparse eucalypt woodlands. Quite attractive in the afternoon light.
Yelvertoft Road junction: locality only; no facilities. (*169/175*) Turn **S** for Mt Isa. *Turn **E** for Lawn Hill.*
Plains support vast tracts of eucalypt woodlands.
Barkly Highway junction: locality only; no facilities. (*227/117*) *Road Trips 11 and 24 connect.* Turn **E** for Mt Isa. *Turn **N** for Lawn Hill.*
Undulating country supports eucalypt woodlands (mainly bloodwoods) with a spinifex understorey. Ranges line the road presenting good views* of rocky outcrops, narrow valleys, stony ridges and bluffs. Sparse eucalypt woodlands dominate the landscape. Spinifex is common.
Hilton Mine: large mine complex. (*325/19*)

MT ISA (Alt 356m; Pop 22200):** large mining town and regional centre. For more information see Road Trip 11, Day 3. (*344/0*) *Road Trips 11, 19 and 24 connect.*

Road Trip 13
Savanna Way

Borroloola-Cairns via Normanton
Total Distance: 1412km
Suggested Travelling Time: 6 days

> ## See the highlights of Australia's Gulf Country
>
> See King Ash Bay, the Albert, Robinson and Gilbert rivers, Leichardt Falls, the historic villages of Croydon and Mt Surprise, Newcastle Range, Curtin Fig, the Tallaroo Hot Springs, Lake Barrine, Wollogorang and Escott Stations, Hells Gate, the Undara Lava Tubes, and the scenic Gillies Highway.

Savanna Way

Hugging the southern coastline of the Gulf of Carpentaria, the Gulf Savanna is a monsoonal region that exhibits two faces depending on the time of the year. During the wet season, which is of variable length and intensity, the landscape is green, characterised mostly by tall grasses which either form expansive grasslands in their own right or constitute a dense understorey beneath widespread woodlands. The rivers and creeks run at this time, closing roads and blocking access, as well as refilling waterholes left low or dry after a lengthy dry season. It is the dry season landscape that most travellers see in the Gulf Savanna, a time of virtually no rain (save for a rare cool outbreak from the south), warm temperatures, and scenery that gradually changes from green to brown as the dry season progresses. Creeks and rivers stop flowing (except for some like the Gregory River which flows continuously, fed by spring water held in the limestone beds of the adjacent Barkly Tableland), waterholes shrink and perhaps dry up, and the grasses of the understorey or plains wilt.

The Climate

North Queensland is very warm to hot throughout the year. Summers are normally wet with monsoonal rains filling waterholes and flooding streams. As such, land transport may not always be possible. Combine this general inaccessibility with warm, sticky nights and you will discover that the time to visit here is during the dry season between April and October. Early in the season the days are still hot (low to mid-thirties) but the landscape is green and the waterholes are full after the wet season. As the dry season progresses, daytime temperatures fall (high twenties with the odd hot day) and nights are mild (low teens). Rainfall is now very low or non-existent, resulting in endless sunny days. Some of the cooler days might be a bit windy. Later in the dry season the temperature climbs again, then hot, dry days become the norm.

Capital City Connections

Distances in Kilometres

SYDNEY-BORROLOOLA
via Great Western/Mitchell/Matilda/Barkly/Tablelands/Carpentaria Highways

	Intermediate	Total
Sydney	0	0
Nyngan	578	578
Charleville	655	1233
Mt Isa	1150	2383
Barkly R'house	449	2832
Borroloola	490	3322

BRISBANE-BORROLOOLA
via Warrego/Matilda/Barkly/Tablelands/Carpentaria Highways

	Intermediate	Total
Brisbane	0	0
Roma	481	481
Longreach	698	1179
Cloncurry	516	1695
Mt Isa	118	1813
Barkly R'house	449	2262
Borroloola	490	2752

ADELAIDE-BORROLOOLA
via Highway One/Stuart/Barkly/Tablelands/
Carpentaria Highways

	Intermediate	Total
Adelaide	0	0
Port Augusta	312	312
Coober Pedy	536	848
Kulgera	411	1259
Alice Springs	273	1532
Three Ways	531	2063
Barkly R'house	187	2250
Borroloola	490	2740

The Route
Distances in kilometres

	Intermediate	Total
Borroloola	0	0
Burketown	489	489
Normanton	231	720
Georgetown	301	1021
Ravenshoe	261	1282
Cairns	130	1412

Savanna Way (Wollogorang Road/ Gulf Developmental Road)
Borroloola-Ravenshoe
The Savanna Way (often spelt as Savannah Way), between Normanton and Ravenshoe, is the major east-west connection of far north Queensland and a popular route connecting up with the northern end of the Matilda Highway. Many travellers use it to make a circuit of northern Queensland. Though a typical outback highway, it does pass through a variety of landscapes that provide plenty of interest to those travellers not in a hurry. Small towns dot the road at regular intervals, some of which are deserving of at least half-a-day's exploration, especially Mt Surprise and Croydon. Other features include the Undarra Lava Tubes, Tallaroo Hot Springs and the Gulflander train.

The Savanna Way between Borroloola and Wollogorang is in good condition (take care at river crossings), but the route between Wollogorang and Normanton is rough - take extreme care in conventional vehicles. Worthy of note along this section are the Leichhardt Falls and the historic town of Burketown.

Warnings: beware of stock at night; avoid driving at this time if possible. Take care on narrow bitumen as verges may be soft after rain. Unsealed sections are normally okay when dry but may be impassable when wet; make local enquiries at this time. Road are subjected to flooding and may be closed for lengthy periods during the monsoon. Unsealed roads quickly deteriorate after monsoonal rains (scouring and washouts are common). The route between Burketown and the Northern Territory Border can be very rough with severe corrugations, washouts and bulldust holes - suitable only for experienced drivers of conventional vehicles- always make local enquiries before proceeding. Beware of estuarine crocodiles.
Note: no fuel between Borroloola-Wollogorang Station 257km; Burketown-Normanton 231km.

DAY 1: BORROLOOLA-WOLLOGORANG STATION via Robinson River

Road to Take: Savanna Way
Grade 3
Warning: Remote Route. No fuel for 257km
Total Distance: 257kms (3:30)
Average Vehicles per Day: 15 near Robinson River
Regions Traversed: Gulf Savanna

Borroloola (Alt 18m; Pop 800):* interesting settlement virtually divided into two by Rocky Creek. The older part of town lies to the south. This town was once famous for its hermits and local characters; some wild-eyed woolly types will still be seen. Good fishing on the McArthur River but beware of estuarine crocodiles. The old police station* has an interesting museum. Good views* from Trig Hill reservoir overlook-

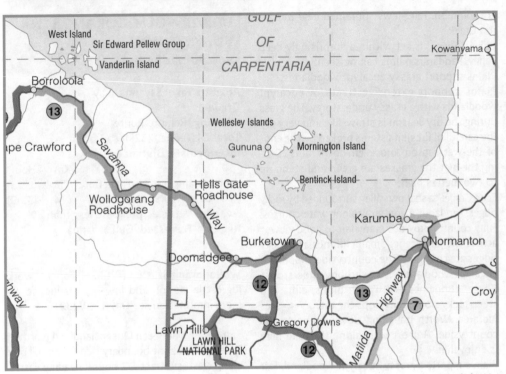

Detail of MAP 4

ing McArthur River plains. Accommodation, stores, fuel. (*723/0*) *Road Trip 24 connects.*

Accommodation

Borroloola Holiday Village, Robinson Rd, ©08 8988 6329, ©$100

McArthur River Caravan Park, Robinson Rd, ©08 8975, ©Site: $17 Van: $35-$90

A 90km Grade 3 return trip leads from Borroloola to Kings Ash Bay, a pleasant spot on the banks of the McArthur River with an attractive beach (no swimming due to crocodiles and sharks). Settlement is a fishing camp. Normally no facilities, but fuel is sometimes available. Good camping spot; limited facilities.

Narwinbi Aboriginal Land surrounds Borroloola. No permit required for entry. The land and town are home to a sizeable population of Mara, Yanyula and Garawa people.

Undulating country supports eucalypt grassy woodlands. At intervals, low stony rises (offer-ing fair views*) support eucalypt woodlands with a spinifex understorey.

Foelsche River: attractive crossing. West of the crossing, cycads can be seen. (*70/187*)

Plains support grassy eucalypt woodlands.

Lily Lagoon:* attractive waterhole supporting water lilies and numerous birdlife; approach cautiously to observe, and beware of estuarine crocodiles. Clean area; please do not litter. North of the lagoon, pandanus palms can be seen in the understorey. (*80/177*)

Plains support grassy eucalypt woodlands.

Robinson River:* attractive area away from the road crossing. The large waterhole* downstream is attractive at dawn. Beware of estuarine crocodiles.

Undulating country supports grassy eucalypt woodlands with areas exhibiting a shrubby understorey. The plain east of Robinson River supports quite tall eucalypts. Occasional low rocky ridges will be seen. Spinifex and eucalypts

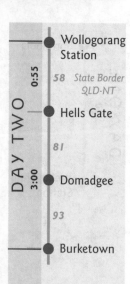

DAY TWO

0:55

58   State Border
        QLD-NT

81

3:00

93

Wollogorang
Station

Hells Gate

Domadgee

Burketown

are common. Fair views* obtained near Kangaroo Creek.

Calvert River* is set within a surprisingly deep valley. Pandanus palms can be seen.

Plains support grassy eucalypt woodlands.

Plains support extensive tracts of eucalypt woodlands with a grassy understorey. The grass during the dry season is straw-like and very dry (be careful of fires), its stems broken by the end-of-the-wet-season 'knock 'em down rains'. During the wet the grasses are green and stand up to two metres high.

Echo Gorge:* a shallow valley surrounded by rocky ridges. Pandanus palms grow along watercourses.

Hilly country provides many fair to good views* across the landscape. Small clifflines and rocky ridges are common. The countryside supports a eucalypt woodland with a shrubby understorey. Gorge* (unnamed) with high bluffs, cliffs and steep rocky slopes, envelops the road. Very scenic area. Worth travelling slowly to enjoy the countryside. A short walk along the road here is enjoyable.

Plain supports a grassy eucalypt woodland. Fair views* westward towards escarpment country marked by tabular ridges. Settlement Creek is entrenched in a deep trough and may make for a difficult crossing during the wet season.

Wollogorang Station (Alt 52m; Pop 5):* working cattle station and low-key roadhouse. Enquire here about access (4WD only) to the Gulf of Carpentaria coast - sandy beaches and good fishing (station tracks user fee payable). The roadhouse is worth a stop and there is plenty of information available here. Accommodation, store, fuel. (257/0)

Accommodation

Gulf Wilderness Lodge, Wollogorang Rd, ©08 8975 9944, ◎$80

DAY 2: WOLLOGORANG STN-BURKETOWN
via Domadgee

Road to Take: Savanna Way
Grade 3
Warning: Remote Route
Total Distance: 232kms (3:55)
Intermediate Distances:

	Km	Hours
Wollogorang Station-Hells Gate	58	(0:55)
Hells Gate-Burketown	174	(3:00)

Average Vehicles per Day: less than 30
Regions Traversed: Gulf Savanna

Wollogorang Station (Alt 52m; Pop 5):* working cattle station and low-key roadhouse. For more information see Day 1. (0/232)

State Border between Queensland and Northern Teritory. Time zone boundary: add 1/2 hour if travelling west, subtract 1/2 hour if heading east.

Plains support tracts of eucalypt woodlands with a grassy understorey. Numerous small creeks cross the road.

Dilldoll Rock:* prominent rock standing by the road. Nearby, closer to Hells Gate, is a large flat rock lying adjacent to the southern side of the road. A climb to its top (be careful of the cliff on the other side) provides interesting views* towards the escarpment. You need to get above the trees to get views in this country. These outcrops form the northern edge of the Barkly Tableland. Nearby is Buck Hill (280m).

Hells Gate (Alt 90m; Pop 2):* interesting and relaxed roadhouse facility. Good, shady camping. Enquire here about access to the Gulf of Carpentaria coast (4WD only) using station roads - good fishing. Accommodation, limited stores, fuel. (58/174)

Plains support eucalypt grassy woodlands and numerous creeks (the road often seems to be in one!). Cliffdale Creek* crossing is an attractive area.

Low rises offer fair views along the road. Westward travellers will see a prominent hill. Rises support eucalypt woodlands with an understorey of spinifex.

Kingfisher Camp turnoff: locality only; no facilities. (*123/109*) Turn **S** for the 98km (Grade 4) return journey to Kingerfisher Camp, an attractive camping area located on the Nicholson River. Features include a 5km scenic gorge with waterholes, numerous birdlife, bushwalking, scenic tours and more. Located on a working cattle station. Direct access from here to Lawn Hill National Park via Boxthorn Station - fee payable to use this route.

Plains support grassy eucalypt woodlands with many creeks.

Domadgee (Alt 47m; Pop 900): large Aboriginal settlement. Located on Jokula land, but other clans also reside here, descendants of those people displaced by the cattle industry. A permit is required to enter living areas but access to the town centre is okay (take the road nearest the river). Store, fuel. (*139/93*)

Nicholson River* crossing is of interest. Waterholes and large water-polished rocks provide features of interest.

Plains support vast tracts of grassy eucalypt woodlands.

Gregory River:* vegetation along the river banks is rather lush. Beware of estuarine crocodiles.

Tirranna Roadhouse: former low-key roadhouse facility currently closed. (*198/34*)

Gregory Downs turnoff: locality only; no facilities. (*202/25*) *Road Trip 12 connects.*

Plains support wide expanses of bluegrass grasslands dotted at intervals with low trees.

Escott Station turnoff: (*227/5*) Turn **W** for Escott Station (Alt 5m; Pop 10)*, a working cattle station and tourist facility. An attractive area, especially on the banks of the Nicholson River. Bush and waterhole camping are available. Good fishing but beware of estuarine crocodiles. User's fee allows access to many of the station's roads - enquire locally. Accommodation, fuel.

Burketown (Alt 6m; Pop 235)* interesting and historic town serving the surrounding cattle stations. Worth seeing: Old Post Office* (tourist centre and museum), Albert Hotel*, cemetery, Landsborough (the explorer) Tree*, Truganini Landing*, and the Town Bore* (very attractive and colourful with its built-up mineral deposits; be careful - it is very hot). Beyond the cemetery lie the vast saltpans* which separate the 'mainland' from the Gulf of Carpentaria's coastline. This is as close as you can get to the coast by road. Tracks cross its surface but this is not recommended. The pans are a good place to observe the roll clouds known as the Morning Glory* (September to November). Accommodation, stores, fuel. (*232/0*) *Road Trip 12 connects.*

Accommodation

Burketown Hotel, Beamer St, ©07 4745 5104, ✪$55-$95

Burketown Caravan Park, Sloman St, ©07 4745 5118, ✪Site: $15

DAY 3: BURKETOWN-NORMANTON
via Leichhardt Falls

Road to Take: Savanna Way
Warning: Remote Route. No fuel for 231km
Grade 4
Total Distance: 231km (3:45)
Average Vehicles per Day: less than 30
Regions Traversed: Gulf Savanna

Burketown (Alt 6m; Pop 235)* interesting and historic town. For more information see the notes above. (*0/231*)

Plains support tracts of bluegrass with a scattering of low eucalypts. Creek crossings are more densely vegetated. The bridge* over Albert River is worth inspecting; one local reckons estuarine crocodiles occasionally leap up onto its decking - not true but take care anyway.

Monument commemorates Frederick Walker, Commandant of a troop of Native Mounted Po-

DAY THREE   3:45

Burketown

Leichhardt Falls 225 Camp 119

Matilda Hwy junction

6

Normanton

lice, commissioned to control local Aborigines. Whether he was a great man or not would depend on one's cultural heritage.

Leichhardt Falls:* interesting low rocky falls and cascades, best seen after the monsoon. Worth stopping here for a while. Bush camping is available. Beware of estuarine crocodiles. (**70/161**)

Plains support tracts of bluegrass.

Undulating country and plains support tracts of spinifex with occasional overstoreys of low eucalypts, typically Darwin stringybarks. Minor grassland areas.

Plains support vast tracts of bluegrass. Broad vistas.

Armstrong Plain: vast clay plain supporting tracts of bluegrass.

Camp 119:* Burke and Wills' final campsite marked by a monument. Nearby is one of their blazed trees. Worth a quick look. (**193/38**)

Plains support tracts of low eucalypt woodlands with a spinifex or grassy understorey. The countryside hereabouts is the remnant of an ancient low plateau.

Matilda Highway junction: (**225/6**) Turn **N** for Normanton. *Turn W onto Savannah Way for Burketown.*

Normanton (Alt 8m; Pop 1150):* interesting grazing town. For more information see Road Trip 7, Day 8. (**0/231**) *Road Trip 7 connects.*

DAY 4: NORMANTON-GEORGETOWN
via Croydon

Road to Take: Savanna Way (Gulf Development Road)
Grade 3 (Route may be sealed during the currency of this book)
Grade 2 Croydon-Georgetown
Total Distance: 301km (3:45)
Intermediate Distances:

	Km	Hours
Normanton-Croydon	153	(2:00)
Croydon-Georgetown	148	(1:45)

Burns Philip Store, Normanton, Qld

Average Vehicles per Day: 100 west of Croydon
Regions Traversed: Gulf Savanna

Normanton (Alt 8m; Pop 1150):* interesting grazing town. For more information see Road Trip 7, Day 8. (**0/301**) Head **S** for Savannah Way (Gulf Developmental Road) junction.

Savannah Way junction: (**3/298**) Turn **E** for Croydon. *Turn N for Normanton.*

Low rise supports eucalypt shrubby woodlands. Fair eastwards view from the top of the rise.

Norman River:* attractive river crossing and picnic area. Adjacent is floodplain country. (**25/276**)

East Haydon: railway siding; no facilities. Hard to spot.

Plains support eucalypt grassy woodlands with patches of mixed woodlands.

Blackbull:* railway siding marked by a few rustic buildings. No facilities. (**93/208**)

Plains support grassy eucalypt woodlands with areas of mixed woodlands.

Plains support quite a diversity of vegetation. Mixed woodlands are common, dominated by bauhinias and various eucalypts among other species, with a layer of shrubs in the understorey. In wetter areas (low-lying country) are melaleucas (paperbarks).

Croydon (Alt 112m; Pop 150):** interesting old mining township. Many old buildings* can be seen, some quite photogenic. The colourful pub* makes a good subject in the afternoon light. Walk

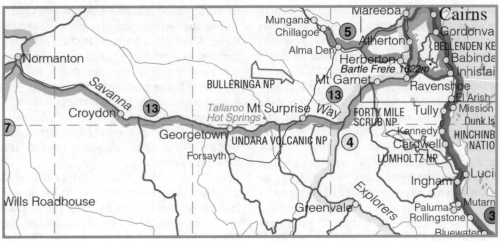

Detail of MAP 4

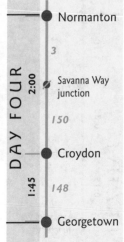

the streets and visit the general store* (it has a small museum*) and old police station. See the old government buildings*, view mining relics, take a look at the railway station precinct** (terminus of the isolated Gulflander railway**), and see the old cemetery. Tours are available. The township is worth at least a day, and an overnight stay is recommended. Enquire locally about access to old mining areas and fossicking sites. Accommodation, stores, fuel. (*153/148*)

Accommodation
Croydon Club Hotel, Cnr Brown/Sircom Sts, ©07 4745 6184, ✪$50-$60
Croydon Gold Caravan Park, Brown St, ©07 4745 6238, ✪Site: $15 Van: $35-$45

Low rises support attractive grassy acacia woodlands with granite outcrops. Low hills are visible in the distance.
Low hills and jump-ups support grassy acacia woodlands. These hills* are attractive in the late afternoon light.
Low ranges offer occasional views. Eucalypt and acacia woodlands are common. The acacias appear to be lancewood, a dense, shrubby plant about three metres high.
Undulating country supports tracts of eucalypt and acacia shrubby woodlands.
Gilbert River:* attractive river crossing with waterholes. Good picnic/camping spot on the western side at Langlo Lake with walking trails and birdwatching to enjoy. (*228/73*)
Plains support grassy acacia woodlands with areas of bauhinias. The yellowy shrub in the understorey (flowers during dry season) makes this section of the route quite pleasant.
Undulating country supports eucalypt grassy woodlands with granite outcrops. Fair views from the tops of rises.
Cumberland Chimney:* old chimney rising above the plain forms a prominent landmark. Nearby is an old dam which supports a large bird population. Reasonable camping area.

Georgetown (Alt 299m; Pop 340):* small grazing town with some character. Formerly a mining centre. Numerous old buildings, some photogenic. A pleasant small park overlooks the sandy bed (in the dry season) of the broad Etheridge River. Accommodation, stores, fuel. (*301/0*)

Accommodation
Latara Resort Motel, Gulf Dev. Rd, ©07 4062 1262, ✪$75
Midway Caravan Park, North St, ©07 4062 1219, ✪Site: $15 Van: $ 45
Goldfields Caravan Park, St George St, ©07 4062 1269, ✪Site: $14

South of Georgetown (80km return; Grade 3 road) lies the old mining township of **Forsayth** (Alt 404m; Pop 50):* railway yards* of interest,

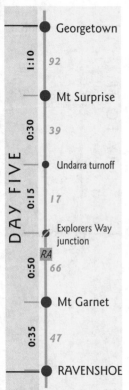

DAY FIVE

1:10	● Georgetown
	92
0:30	● Mt Surprise
	39
0:15	● Undarra turnoff
	17
0:50	Explorers Way junction
	RA
	66
0:35	● Mt Garnet
	47
	● RAVENSHOE

old buildings, scattered and preserved mining relics, and an old cemetery. Enquire locally about access to mine sites and fossicking areas. Accommodation, store, fuel. From Forsayth an unsealed (Grade 3) road leads to Cobbold Gorge**, a series of deep, narrow ravines (up to 30m deep and down to 2m narrow) etched in sandstone with cliff-lined waterholes. Tours, kiosk and camping available, and a short drive from here leads to the Quartz Blow*, a 10m high pinnacle of silica. Also from Forsayth, an unsealed (Grade 4) road leads to Agate Creek*, a fossicking area set within rugged range country where world renowned agate deposits are located. Bushwalking trails to Mushroom Rock* and The Chimney* (enquire locally). Camping available. Limited store.

DAY 5: GEORGETOWN-RAVENSHOE
via Mt Surprise

Road to Take: Savannah Highway (Great Top Road/Gulf Development Road)
Grade 2
Total Distance: 261km (3:30)
Intermediate Distances:

	Km	Hours
Georgetown-Mt Surprise	92	(1:10)
Mt Surprise-Undarra turnoff	39	(0:30)
Undarra turnoff-Explorers Way Rd jtn	17	(0:15)
Explorers Way Rd jtn-Mt Garnet	66	(0:50)
Mt Garnet-Ravenshoe	47	(0:35)

Average Vehicles per Day: 100 west of Mt Suprise
Regions Traversed: Gulf Savanna, North-East Highlands

Georgetown (Alt 299m; Pop 340):* small grazing town, formerly a mining centre. For more information see Day 4. (0/261)

Undulating country supports grassy eucalypt woodlands. Eastwards are distant views towards the Newcastle Range.

Lookout* provides good westward views overlooking the western ramparts of the Newcastle Range. Nearby Routh Creek (20/241) offers fair camping. A short distance east is another lookout* providing good views overlooking the wild Newcastle Range country to the south.
Ranges support eucalypt woodlands and offer fair to reasonable views.
Undulating country supports eucalypt woodlands with fair westward views towards the Newcastle Range.
Tallaroo Hot Springs turnoff: (51/210) Turn N for the 12km return drive to Tallaroo Hot Springs**, a treat not to be missed (follow direction signs and do not disturb nearby Tallaroo Station, a working cattle station). The hot springs have interesting tufa formations** and the entry fee includes a guided tour; well worth taking. The main feature though is a constructed pool in which you can bathe in the warm spring waters (highly recommended). A pleasant spot for a picnic (you have to walk the last few hundred metres); kiosk available. On the way in, a high basalt formation known as The Wall can be seen in the distance. No camping.
Einasleigh River:* attractive river crossing with waterholes. (56/205)
Undulating country supports grassy eucalypt woodlands with anthills. Occasional westward views towards the rugged Newcastle Range.
Jump-up forms a small rise of basalt which marks the western edge of the McBride volcanic province. Good westward views* from the top of the rise.
Low rises support grassy eucalypt woodlands. Occasional basalt outcrops are visible.

Mt Surprise (Alt 455m; Pop 65):* delightful small railway and grazing township. Stop here a while and absorb the atmosphere. The Savannahlander train* passes through here. There are two museums, including a railway museum*. Accommodation, stores, fuel. (92/169)
An 80km return drive (Grade 4) leads to O'Briens Creek topaz gemfield.

The Wall: basalt formation rising above the lowlands.

Low rises with occasional higher hills support grassy eucalypt woodlands. Outcrops of basalt appearing as low rocky mounds are commonly seen.

Undara Lava Tubes turnoff: locality only; no facilities. (*131/130*) Turn **S** for Undara Lava Tubes - see Side Trip below.

Side Trip

Undara Lava Tubes access road (Grade 3) 30km return

Undara Lava Tubes** sinuous tunnels of impressive dimensions (up to 10 to 15 metres high, 20 metres across and kilometres long) formed by the differentiated cooling within lava flows. The tubes can only be visited on guided tours. Advance bookings are essential, although casual visitors may find a spare seat but do not count on it. The tubes are definitely worth seeing, but some people are disappointed. Within the area there are pleasant walking trails of various lengths as well as lookouts. Access is possible to Kalkarni Crater* near Yarramulla. The adjacent *Lava Lodge* provides accommodation.

Undara Volcanic National Park:* new national park preserving the Undara Lava Tubes. Limited access and no camping at time of writing.

Explorers Way road junction: locality only; no facilities. (*148/113*) *Road Trip 4 connects.* Turn **N** for Mt Garnet. *Turn **W** onto Savannah Way for Mt Surprise.*

Forty Mile Scrub National Park:* interesting small park preserving remnant rainforest vegetation. These dry rainforests, or semi-evergreen vine thickets, are typical of the vegetation that existed hundreds of millions of years ago. The trees include white beans and bottle trees, and there are also vines. Walking track; **rest area** adjacent. No camping. (*150/111*)

Undulating country supports shrubby and grassy eucalypt woodlands. Near Mt Garnet are some small land clearances.

Mt Garnet (Alt 671m; Pop 400):* old mining town. For more information see Road Trip 4, Day 2. (*214/47*)

For information about the route between Mt Garnet and Ravenshoe see Road Trip 4, Day 2.

RAVENSHOE (Alt 914m; Pop 1200):** interesting and attractive town. For more information see Road Trip 4, Day 1. (*261/0*) *Road Trips 4 and 5 connect.*

Kennedy/Gillies Highways

Ravenshoe-Cairns

The Atherton Tablelands is a district mostly cleared for farming and grazing. It supports a number of settlements as well as providing access to numerous waterfalls, lakes, escarpment views and World Heritage rainforests. The route between Ravenshoe and Cairns described below is via the Kennedy Highway to Atherton, and the Gillies Highway from Atherton to Cairns.

Warnings: Routes leading to or from the Atherton Tableland are steep. Note that many roads on the Atherton Tableland are narrow bitumen and very curvy; take care on soft verges after rain.

DAY 6: RAVENSHOE-CAIRNS via Atherton

Roads to Take: Kennedy Highway/Gillies Highway
Grade 2 Ravenshoe-Herberton turnoff (Grade 1 route via Tumoulin Road - see Road Trip 5)
Grade 1 Herberton turnoff-Atherton-Cairns
Total Distance: 130km (1:55)
Intermediate Distances:

	Km	Hours
Ravenshoe-Millaa Millaa turnoff	15	(0:15)
Millaa Millaa turnoff-Atherton	36	(0:25)
Atherton-Cairns	79	(1:15)

Average Vehicles per Day: over 1000 east of Atherton
Regions Traversed: Atherton Tablelands, Wet Tropics

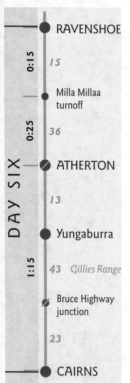

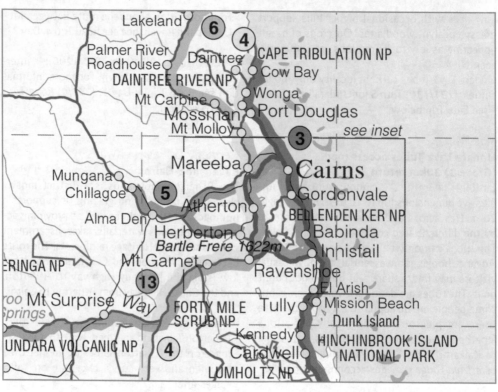

Detail of MAP 4

RAVENSHOE (Alt 914m; Pop 1200):** interesting and attractive town. For more information see Road Trip 4, Day 1. **(0/130)**

Hilly country* offers good to excellent views. The highest hill is called Windy Hill; it is an extinct volcano. The land is mostly cleared for farming. Note the wind farm* (giant wind generators) on the hillside. Viewpoint nearby. The towers are 45m high, and the blades are 22m long and rotate 30 times per minute.

Millaa Millaa (McHugh Road) turnoff: locality only, no facilities. **(15/115)** *Road Trip 5 connects. Continue **N** for Atherton. Continue **S** for Ravenshoe.*

Hilly country** supports tracts of upland rainforests and cleared dairying country. Very scenic area.

Evelyn Central: Queensland's highest locality. Store. **(18/112)**

Tumoulin Road junction: locality only; no facilities **(21/109)** *Road Trips 4 and 5 connect. Continue **N** for Atherton. Continue **S** for Ravenshoe.*

Herberton Road junction: locality only; no facilities **(22/108)** *Road Trip 5 connects.* Continue **N** for Atherton. *Continue **S** for Ravenshoe.*

Hilly country supports remnant rainforest patches.

The Crater:** highly recommended main feature of the small Mt Hypipamee National Park. The Crater is a very deep sheer-sided hole, a 58 metre drop to the lake below. The viewing platform provides awesome views. Elsewhere are attractive walking tracks passing through upland rainforests. Picnic facilities; no camping. **(27/103)**

Wongabel State Forest: interesting botanic walk*.

ATHERTON (Alt 752m; Pop 9950): sizeable country town. For more information see Road Trip 4, Day 1. **(51/79)** *Road Trip 4 connects.* Turn **E** for Yungaburra. *Turn **S** for Ravenshoe.*

The Seven Sisters: old volcanic vents rise above the surrounding farmlands.

Curtin Fig turnoff: (*63/67*) Turn **S** for the Curtin Fig** a spectacular fig tree with a curtain of aerial roots rising 15 metres. There is a short walking trail. Well worth seeing.

Yungaburra (Alt 696m; Pop 770):** historic town with plenty of character, although somewhat touristic. Numerous historic and National Trust-listed buildings - very photogenic - as well as arts and crafts stores. An interesting and impressive pub*. Nearby Lake Eacham*, an old volcanic crater, is of interest. Accommodation, stores, fuel. (*64/66*)

Accommodation
Kookaburra Lodge Motel, Cnr Oak St/Eacham Rd, ©07 4095 3222, ✪$75
Curtin Fig Motel, 16 Gillies Hwy, ©07 4095 3515, ✪$75
Lake Eacham Hotel, Gillies Hwy (2kmW), ©07 4095 3515, ✪$40-$55
Lake Eacham Caravan Park, Lakes Dr (1.2kmS), ©07 4095 3730, ✪Site: $14 Van: $45

Lake Barrine turnoff: (*72/58*) Turn **S** for Lake Barrine:** a very attractive rainforest-lined crater lake and centrepiece of a national park of the same name. Well worth visiting. Lake cruises. A walking trail circumnavigates the lake (at least walk the short distance to see the twin kauri pines*). No camping.

Danbulla State Forest Drive turnoff: (*78/52*) This dry weather unsealed road leads **N** to numerous camping spots and features including Platypus Rock, Downfall Creek, Lake Euramoo, Mobo Creek Crater*, The Chimneys and Cathedral Fig Tree**.

Gillies Range:** traversed by probably Australia's most twisty if not spectacular highway. Awesome but slow drive. There are numerous lookouts (pullovers) on the ascending (southern) side. Patches of rainforest are intermingled with eucalypt forests and bare granite boulders. Occasional good descending views into the deep Goldsborough Valley and the Bellenden Ker massif beyond.

Little Mulgrave: interesting pub* and focal point set within the sugar cane farmlands of the Mulgrave Valley. Accommodation. (*97/33*)

Mountainous country:** spectacular valley set between high rainforest-clad mountains. The many sugar cane farms are interspersed with patches of rainforest. Good river views.

Goldsborough Valley turnoff: (*101/29*) Turn **S** for an interesting 30km return journey (Grade 3 route) into the Goldsborough Valley. Worth visiting for great views, good camping, picnic spots and pleasant canoeing. An easy walk to Kearneys Falls* through rainforests.

Bruce Highway junction:(*107/23*) Gordonvale is located just off the highay. *Road Trip 3 connects.* Turn **N** for Cairns. *Turn **W** for Yungaburra.*

For details of the route between Gordonvale and Cairns see Road Trip 3, Day 5.

CAIRNS (Alt 3m; Pop 101000):** large and vibrant tropical city. For more information see Road Trip 3, Day 5. (*130/0*) *Road Trips 3, 5 and 6 connect.*

Road Trip 14
Barrier Highway Connection

Nyngan-Port Augusta via Broken Hill
Total Distance: **990km**
Suggested Travelling Time: **4 days**

Experience the delights of western New South Wales and the southern Flinders Ranges

See the mines and museums of Broken Hill, Steamtown at Peterborough, the historic villages of Canbelego and Silverton, the lookouts near Port Augusta, Mt Grenfell Historic Site, the White Cliffs opal mines Mutawintji National Park, Alligator Gorge, Hancocks lookout, and scenic Horrocks Pass.

Barrier Highway Connection

Crossing western New South Wales and eastern South Australia, the Barrier Highway provides easy access to the closest outback regions of south-east Australia. From the farming country around Nyngan, the route traverses semi-arid woodlands and mulga shrublands en route to the Darling River, passing through the copper mining town of Cobar. West of the Darling the traveller enters arid country: vast saltbush plains, distant rocky ranges, and an enormity of space, in the midst of which is the fascinating mining city of Broken Hill. The arid country continues into South Australia where rocky hills and ranges provide a scenic backdrop.

The Climate

Travellers to western New South Wales and eastern South Australia will experience a variety of weather conditions, even extremes. During summer this area records some of the highest temperatures in Australia with maximums up to the mid-forties. Normally most summer days are just hot, around 32C to 35C. Nights are generally mild (around 20C), but may occasionally be warmer.

The time to travel this part of the country is during autumn or spring. Daytime temperatures are usually mild to warm, with only the odd hot (or cool) day. Nights are generally cool. Most years there will be little or no rain in autumn, and only the chance of showers in spring. Wintertime is usually okay too, except that some days are cool (15C to 18C maximums) with cold winds. Nighttime temperatures can drop to freezing.

Capital City Connections
Distances in kilometres
SYDNEY-NYNGAN
via Great Western/Mitchell Highways

	Intermediate	Total
Sydney	0	0
Bathurst	207	207
Dubbo	205	412
Nyngan	166	578

MELBOURNE-COBAR
via Northern/Newell Highways/Kidman Way

	Intermediate	Total
Melbourne	0	0
Shepparton	179	179
Jerilderie	134	313
Griffith	132	445
Cobar	363	808

ADELAIDE-PORT AUGUSTA
via Highway One

	Intermediate	Total
Adelaide	0	0
Port Wakefield	99	99
Port Pirie turnoff	121	220
Port Augusta	92	312

The Route
Distances in kilometres

	Intermediate	Total
Nyngan	0	0
Cobar	131	131
Wilcannia	252	383
Broken Hill	192	575
Yunta	198	773
Peterborough	86	859
Port Augusta	131	990

Road Trip 14

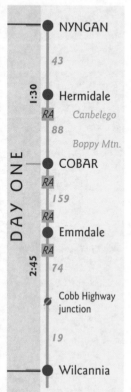

NYNGAN

43

1:30

Hermidale

RA   Canbelego

88

Boppy Mtn.

COBAR

RA

159

RA

Emmdale

RA

2:45

74

Cobb Highway
junction

19

Wilcannia

Barrier Highway/Highway 56
Nyngan-Port Augusta

Cutting a swathe across western New South Wales and north-eastern South Australia, the all-sealed two-lane Barrier Highway provides easy access for those people heading from the east coast to Central or Western Australia, the Flinders Ranges, or northward into the arid landscapes of the Corner Country. The route traverses a variety of landscapes, from mulga shrublands to saltbush plains, and provides access to the Darling River, Broken Hill and the southern Flinders Ranges.

The Barrier Highway can be accessed from the Mitchell Highway at Nyngan, the Newell Highway (via the Mitchell Highway) at Dubbo, the Kidman Way at Cobar, or directly from Adelaide.

Warning: beware of stock and kangaroos at night. Road subject to flooding.

DAY 1: NYNGAN-WILCANNIA via Cobar

Roads to Take: Barrier Highway
Grade I
Total Distance: 383km (4:15)
Intermediate Distances:

	Km	Hours
Nyngan-Cobar	131	(1:30)
Cobar-Wilcannia	252	(2:45)

Average Vehicles per Day: 500 west of Cobar
Region Traversed: Western Plains (Cobar Plains, Darling River Floodplain)

▼

NYNGAN (181m; Pop 2500): agricultural and grazing town with a shady main street. Picnic facilities on the banks of the Bogan River. Old railway station is of interest, as is the nearby museum* dedicated to the 1990 floods. Full town facilities. (*0/383*) *Connecting Route E connects.*
Accommodation
Alamo Motor Inn, Mitchell Hwy, ©02 6832 1660, ❂$55-$60
Country Manor Motor Inn, Mitchell Hwy, ©072 6832 1501, ❂$65

Riverside Caravan Park, Barrier Hwy, ©02 6832 1729, ❂Site: $16 Van: $45-$50

Miandetta: small locality of a few houses and ruins. (*20/363*)
Farming country: cleared paddocks, wheat cropping and grazing occupy this western fringe of eastern Australia's agricultural land.

Hermidale (Alt 220m; Pop 50): grazing township with plenty of character. Accommodation, store, fuel. (*43/340*)

Undulating country supports mulga shrublands and eucalypt woodlands. **Rest area.** (*77/304*)
Canbelego turnoff: locality only; no facilities. (*82/299*) Turn **S** for the 8km loop road via **Canbelego** (Alt 274m; Pop 20)* an old copper mining township and bush pub well worth visiting. Many ruins, some of which may be still occupied! Do not trespass. Accommodation, fuel.
Boppy Mountain: railway siding set beside the prominent peak of Boppy Mountain* (418m). (*87/294*)
Undulating country east of Cobar supports bimble box woodlands with an understorey of mulga. Occasional ridges and hills, the tallest being Boppy Mountain.

COBAR (Alt 251m; Pop 5500):* busy copper mining town. Full town facilities. For more information see Road Trip 7, Day I. (*131/252*) *Road Trip 7 connects.*

Undulating country provides long views as the highway cuts a swathe through a woodland of bimble box and cypress pines. Mulga occupies the occasional low ridge. Immediately west of Cobar are extensive tracts of mulga. **Rest area.** (*146/238*)
Mt Grenfell turnoff: locality only; no facilities. (*170/213*) Turn **N** here for the Mt Grenfell Historic Site - see Side Trip below.

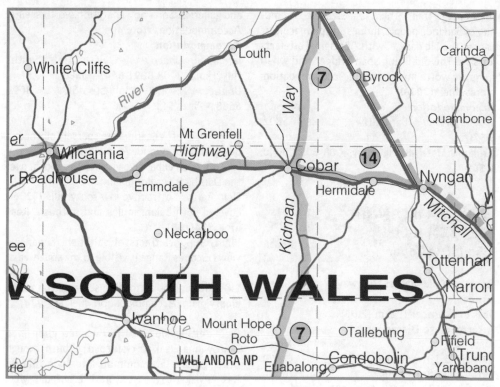

Detail of MAP 3

Side Trip
Mt Grenfell Road (Grade 3)
56km return
Mt Grenfell:** Aboriginal paintings well worth visiting. They are some of the best examples of Aboriginal art in southern Australia. Early morning is best for photographs. Interesting walking trails follow ridgelines - good views and picnic areas. No camping allowed. Warning: no services available. Make enquiries regarding conditions after rain.

Plains and low rises support bimble box and cypress pine woodlands. **Rest area**. (*186/197*)
Plains support belah and rosewood with areas of the eucalypt bimble box. **Rest area**. (*251/132*)

Emmdale (Pop 5): roadhouse facility. Camping available. Store, fuel. (*290/93*)

Plains support a low woodland of belah and rosewood. The trees with the spotted bark are called leopardwoods. **Rest area**. (*266/117*)
Maccullochs Range: low rocky range and hills covered with mulga and low-growing eucalypts. Occasional views to north across Darling River floodplain.
Cobb Highway junction: locality only; no facilities. (*364/19*) Turn **N** for Wilcannia. *Turn E for Cobar.*
Darling River floodplain: broad treeless floodplain crossed by Talyawalka Creek, an ana-branch (distributary) of the Darling River. Lush grass and wild flowers spring up after floods.
Darling River: Australia's longest river channel (the Murray-Darling), lined with river red gums.

Wilcannia (Alt 76m; Pop 900):* interesting old town and former river port. Historic stone buildings make interesting photographic subjects, from the days when this was a major river port. Take

DAY TWO

0:50

RA

118

1:15

74

Wilcannia

Little Topar

BROKEN HILL

the heritage trail*. There is a sizeable community of Barkindji people. Interesting permaculture park at the old garage, with Aboriginal artefacts for sale. The old lifting span bridge* and wharf ruins are worth investigating. Accommodation, stores, fuel. (**383/0**)

Accommodation

Wilcannia Motel, Barrier Hwy, ©08 8091 5802, ✪$70

Grahams Motel, Barrier Hwy, ©08 8091 5040, ✪$65

DAY 2: WILCANNIA-BROKEN HILL
via Little Topar

Road to Take: Barrier Highway
Grade 1
Total Distance: 192km (2:05)
Intermediate Distances:

	Km	Hours
Wilcannia-Little Topar	118	(1:15)
Little Topar-Broken Hill	74	(0:50)

Average Vehicles per Day: 500 east of Broken Hill
Regions Traversed: Far West

Wilcannia (Alt 76m; Pop 900):* old town of historic buildings. For further information see Day 1. (**0/192**)

White Cliffs turnoff: (**1/191**) Turn **N** for White Cliffs - see Side Trip below.

Side Trip

An interesting 186km return journey over good roads (only short unsealed sections) leads to the opal mining town of White Cliffs.

White Cliffs** (Alt 122m; Pop 120) is an unusual mining township insofar as most people live underground in dug-outs. Opal mine visits are possible, as is noodling on unclaimed areas (beware of shafts). Precious stones can be found in the district; enquire locally. Opal showrooms

and galleries. Solar power station worth seeing. Accommodation, store, fuel.

Accommodation

White Cliffs Underground Dug-Out Motel, Smiths Hill (1kmS), ©08 8091 6647, ✪$80

Opal Pioneer Reserve, Johnston St, ©08 8091 6688, ✪Site: $11

Plains west of Wilcannia are sparsely clothed in belah and rosewood. A low rise near the dry lake offers an expansive view to the south, over the Darling River floodplain.

Dolo Range:* attractive low rocky hills (333m) covered with belah, mulga and saltbush. **Rest area**. (**74/118**)

Plains support tracts of saltbush. Expansive views. Scopes Range is visible to the south-east.

Little Topar (Pop 5): roadhouse located on a vast, empty plain. Accommodation, fuel. (**118/74**)

Plains either side of the river red gum-lined Yancowinna Creek are clothed in saltbush, though other grasses are common after rain. Barrier Ranges visible to the west. Travellers heading west should note that they have entered the agricultural fruit fly exclusion zone - no fruit or vegetables to be carried into the zone from outside. Time zone boundary: travellers heading west gain 1/2 hour, travellers heading east lose 1/2 hour.

Mt Gipps: old former bush pub set among dry rocky hills. (**180/12**)

Barrier Ranges:* broad range of undulating country with hilly outcrops and metamorphic ridges (with interesting mica formations and 'tombstone' rock outcrops).

BROKEN HILL (Alt 304m; Pop 25000):** Mining centre (silver, lead and zinc). Poppet heads and mine dumps dominate the townscape. Interesting public buildings, grand accommodations and corrugated iron workmen's cottages. Worth seeing: Living Desert and Sculptures** (walking trails, viewpoints and impressive stone sculptures); Delprats Underground Mine Tour; surface mine tours; Geo Centre** (museum, mining and geological displays); Railway, Min-

Detail of MAP 2

eral and Train Museum**; Afghan Mosque*; School of the Air; Royal Flying Doctor Service; Whites Mineral Art Gallery and Mining Museum; Pinnacles Mine (bushwalks, displays, fossicking); Silver City Mint and Art Centre; numerous art galleries. Tours available. Full town facilities. (**192/0**) *Road Trip 16 connects.*

Accommodation

The Lodge Outback Motel, 252 Mica St, ©08 8088 2722, ✪$65

Mine Host Motel, 120 Argent St, ©08 8088 4044, ✪$85

Sturt Motel, 153 Rakow St (4kmW), ©08 8087 3558, ✪$55

Royal Exchange Hotel, 320 Argent St, ©08 8087 2308, ✪$50

Theatre Royal Hotel, 347 Argent St, ©08 8087 3318, ✪$40

Broken Hill City Caravan Park, Rakow St (3.3kmW), ✪Site: $18 Van: $35-$50

Lake View Broken Hill Caravan Park, 1 Mann St (3kmNE), ©08 8088 2250, ✪Site: $14 Van: $35-$45

Two sidetrips from Broken Hill are definitely worth considering. The first is the 46km sealed return road to Silverton (62km return if extended to Umberumberka). **Silverton** (Alt 226m; Pop 50)* is an old mining township, nowadays a tourist centre. Numerous historic stone buildings and mine workings make the area worth visiting. Interesting pub. Penrose Park is a pleasant picnic area. Numerous art galleries. Accommodation, store, fuel. A good lookout* lies a short distance to the west. Umberumberka* is a resevoir set within rocky hills.

110km away, on a Grade 1 road, is **Menindee** (Alt 61m; Pop 980), a small grazing and irrigation town situated on the Darling River. Maidens Accommodation* (where Burke and Wills stayed) is worth visiting. Other features include Ah Chungs Bakehouse, Woodsons Store, Dost Mahomets Grave and the railway bridge. Boat tours available. Accommodation, stores, fuel. Nearby is the Kinchega National Park, a superb park offering riverside and lakeside camping under the river red gums by the Darling River. Interesting self-drive tours, historic buildings and ruins, picnic areas. Worth seeing: Lake Cawndilla, Lake Menindee, Riverside Drive*, PS *Providence* remains* and the old Kinchega Woolshed**. Worth a day or two's exploration. En route the **Quondong** bush pub, set on the river red gum-lined Stephens Creek, is passed.

▲

DAY 3: BROKEN HILL-PETERBOROUGH
via Yunta

DAY TWO

2:10

0:55

●	BROKEN HILL
52	
●	Cockburn
68	
●	Olary
37	
●	Mannahill
41	
●	Yunta
64	
●	Oodla Wirra
10	
◎	Peterborough turnoff
12	
●	PETER-BOROUGH

Roads to Take: Barrier Highway, Highway 56
Grade 1
Total Distance: 284 (3:05)
Intermediate Distances:

	Km	Hours
Broken Hill-Yunta	198	(2:10)
Yunta-Peterborough	86	(0:55)

Average Vehicles per Day: 500 east of Broken Hill
Regions Traversed: Far West, The North-East

▼

BROKEN HILL (Alt 304m; Pop 25000):** Interesting mining and tourist town. For more information see Day 2. (*0/284*)

Thackaringa Hills: moderately high hills with rocky gullies and outcrops. Good views* from high points of interesting rock formations. If heading east keep an eye out for the 'broken hill' after which Broken Hill takes its name.
Burns: locality and hotel on the **state border** between New South Wales and South Australia. Accommodation. (*52/232*)

Cockburn (Pop 30): small township of stone-built houses. Accommodation, store, fuel. (*52/232*)

Mundi Mundi Plain: expansive flat saltbush plain devoid of trees.
Mingary: former narrow gauge railway siding, now ruins. Old railway water tower. (*88/206*)
Low hills and ranges surrounding Olary are part of an off-shoot of the Flinders Ranges. Interesting rocks and occasional expansive views*. Nearby are Aboriginal engravings, believed to be the oldest artworks in the world; no public access at present. Hills are clothed in sparse shrubs and saltbush.

Olary (Alt 283m; Pop 30): small township of corrugated iron and stone buildings. Worth at

Leaning telegraph pole, near Yunta, SA

least a brief stop. Pub serves good meals; popular with shearers. Accommodation, store, fuel. (*120/164*)

Mannahill (Alt 371m; Pop 30): small township set oasis-like on an empty saltbush plain. Interesting railway station. Accommodation, store, fuel. (*157/127*)

Undulating country of saltbush and rocky ridges forms part of the Olary Hills. Good expansive views*.

Yunta (Alt 303m; Pop 150): interesting township with unpaved roads (except for the highway). Attractive ridges surround the settlement, especially Tattawuppa (611m) to the north. Excellent views** of Yunta district obtained from ridge-crest on Lilydale Station road (about 10km south). Accommodation, stores, fuel. (*198/86*)
Road Trip 16 connects.

Accommodation
Yunta Hotel, Barrier Hwy, ©08 8650 5002, ●$45

Undulating country east of Oodla Wirra provides expansive views to low ranges. Low scattered trees are belahs and sugarwoods. Saltbush country east of Nackara Hill (660m).

Oodla Wirra (Alt 500m; Pop 150): small agricultural township, the last before the outback if heading east. Agricultural check-point for travellers heading west. Accommodation, store, fuel. (*262/24*)

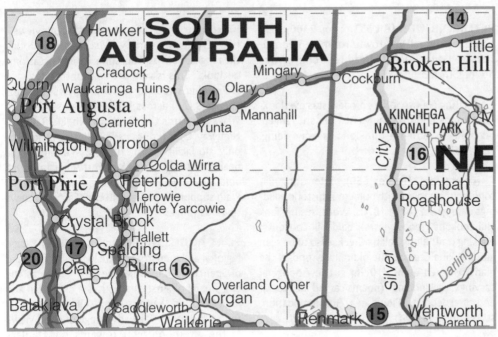

Detail of MAP 2

Farming country extends to just east of Oolda Wirra. Wheat cropping and grazing are common. The low hills and broad plains look attractive after winter rains. Remnant patches of mallee scrub on the hill slopes.

Peterborough turnoff: locality only; no facilities. **(272/14)** Turn **W** for Peterborough. *Turn **NE** onto Barrier Highway for Yunta.*

PETERBOROUGH (Alt 533m; Pop 2300):* agricultural and former railway town. Many historic buildings (especially the Town Hall), attractive main street, Ranns Museum (old stationary engines), Ivan Leys Museum (antiques, bottles, etc), Steamtown** (museum) and narrow-gauge steam train rides**, railway model sculptures*, gold battery, tourist walk, Victoria Park. At 533m, this is one of the few South Australian towns to have occasional winter snows! Full town facilities. **(284/0)** *Road Trip 17 connects. /Head **E** for Peterborough turnoff (Barrier Highway junction).*

Accommodation
Railway Hotel-Motel, 221 Main St, ©08 8651 2427, ✪$50-$75
Peterborough Motor Inn, 25 Queen St, ©08 8651 2428
Peterborough Caravan Park, 36 Grove St (1kmS), ©08 8651 2545, ✪Site: $16 Van: $30-$45

DAY 4: PETERBOROUGH-PORT AUGUSTA via Orroroo

Roads to Take: Highway 56
Grade 1
Total Distance: 131km (1:40)
Intermediate Distances:

	Km	Hours
Peterborough-Orroroo	37	(0:25)
Orroroo-Wilmington	51	(0:35)
Wilmington-Port Augusta	43	(0:40)

Average Vehicles per Day: 1000 near Peterborough
Regions Traversed: Mid-North, Flinders Ranges

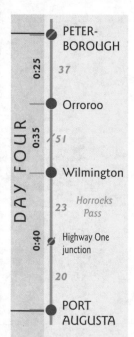

DAY FOUR

PETER-
BOROUGH

0:25 37

Orroroo

0:35 51

Wilmington

23 *Horrocks
Pass*

0:40 Highway One
junction

20

PORT
AUGUSTA

PETERBOROUGH (Alt 533m; Pop 2300):* agricultural and railway town. For more information see Day 4. (*0/131*) Head **NW** on Highway 56 for Orroroo.

Undulating country offers broad vistas overlooking farming country. Views of a distant range.
Black Rock: old farm ruins and railway siding. (*25/106*)

Orroroo (Alt 421m; Pop 650):* interesting historic cropping town with numerous historic buildings dating back to the 1870s. Worth seeing: Tank Hill Lookout* (good views); Bald Hill Lookout*; walking trail* along Pekina Creek. Also to be seen along Pekina Creek is the old railway bridge; the giant river-red gum* (10.9m girth); Aboriginal carvings; rock poems* (poems carved into rock); and coral deposits. Picnic area. Accommodation, stores, fuel. (*37/94*) Road Trip 17 connects.

Hilly country supports tracts of eucalypt woodlands. Fair views.
Plains support cropping and grazing lands. The plain, which extends to Wilmington, is called the Willochra Plain.
Willochra Creek: drainage area marked by saltbush and shrubs.
Pinda: locality only; no facilities. (*76/55*)
Main North Road junction: (*86/45*) Turn **N** for Wilmington. Turn **E** for Orroroo. Two kilometres south is the 28km return unsealed access road to the Mt Remarkable National Park* and the very scenic Alligator Gorge**.

Wilmington (Alt 324m; Pop 250):* farming township with historic buildings. Worth seeing: Aussie Relics Museum, Centenary Park (old farm machinery). Accommodation, stores, fuel. (*88/43*) Stay on Hwy 56 heading **W** for Port Augusta. *Stay on Hwy 56 heading **S** for Peterborough.*

Three kilometres to the west (off Highway 56) is the Hancocks Lookout access road, a 15km unsealed return journey. Hancocks Lookout** offers superb westward views overlooking the Flinders Ranges escarpment and upper Spencers Gulf.

Hilly country given over to grazing; scenic views*.
Horrocks Pass:* narrow twisting pass through the ranges. Bold bald hill summits and occasional outlooks. This is very scenic countryside.
Plains offer sweeping westward views* towards Spencers Gulf across saltbush plains; eastward views* towards the southern Flinders Ranges.
Highway One (Princes Hwy) junction: locality only; no facilities. The ruins of Winninowie lie nearby. (*111/20*) Turn **N** for Port Augusta. *Turn **E** onto Hwy 56 for Wilmington.*
Plain supports tracts of saltbush. Eastward views towards ranges.

PORT AUGUSTA (Alt 5m; Pop 14600):* large regional and industrial centre located at the head of Spencers Gulf, sometimes referred to as the crossroads of Australia, as it is a major rail and road junction. Saltbush and salt marshes surround the town. Take advantage of good views in the afternoon light towards the Flinders Ranges. A heritage walk passes by historic buildings. Some sites worth visiting including Wadlata Outback Centre*, Australian Arid Lands Botanic Gardens**, Royal Flying Doctor Service, School of the Air, Pioneer Museum*, Northern Power Station and two lookouts: McLellan Lookout* for views of the Gulf and Flinders Ranges, and the Water Tower Lookout*. Full town facilities. (*131/0*) Road Trips 17, 18, 20 and 35 connect.

Accommodation
Port Augusta Hi-Way One Motel, Highway One, ©08 8642 2755, ☺$70-$100
Acacia Ridge Motel Inn, 33 Stokes Tce (2kmNW), ©08 8642 3377, ☺$60-$70
Poinsettia Motel, Highway One, ©08 8642 2411, ☺$55
Port Augusta East Motel, Highway One (5kmE), ©08 8642 2555, ☺$55
Port Augusta Big 4 Holiday Park, Cnr Highway 1/Stokes Tce, (1kmW), ©08 8642 2974, ☺Site: $20 Van: $45-$90
Shoreline Caravan Park, Gardiner Ave (1.5kmW), ©08 8642 2965, ☺Site: $18 Van: $35-$55
Port Augusta Caravan Park, 9 Brook St, Stirling North (6kmE), ©08 8643 6357, ☺Site: $17 Van: $30-$45

Road Trip 15
The Southern Loop

**Melbourne-Hay-Mildura-Adelaide-
Mt Gambier-Lorne-Melbourne**
Total Distance: 2197km
Suggested Travelling Time: 7 days

Loop through Australia's southern regions, from the Murray River to the Great Ocean Road

See the capital cities of Melbourne and Adelaide, the many historic buildings of Bendigo, the Murray River port of Echuca, the Island Sanctuary at Deniliquin, the paddlesteamers at Mildura, the relaxed seaside town of Robe, Flagstaff Hill at Warrnambool, Hay Plains, the Sunraysia district, Lake Mungo National Park, Lake Cullulleraine, Blachetown Lock, the Barossa Valley, the Adelaide Hills, Tower Hill Reserve, the famous Twelve Apostles, and other features along the stunning Great Ocean Road.

The Southern Loop

Striking north from Melbourne, a number of connecting highways lead through the historic goldrush city of Bendigo before crossing the vast plains of the Murray River area and Riverina district of New South Wales. This northward leg of the road trip takes the traveller from the southern Australian coastline to the edge of the outback.

Spreading west from Hay lies the Hay Plains, a virtually dead-level saltbush-covered plain formed by the deposits of ancient rivers, the forerunners of today's Murrumbidgee and Lachlan Rivers and their distributaries and ana-branches. This country, typical of the Riverina, merges into mallee country before entering the Sunraysia irrigation district centred around Mildura.

Occupying north-western Victoria is a region of old sand dunes covered with mallee eucalypts. Sometimes referred to as 'The Mallee', this is Victoria's outback. Huge tracts of uncleared country remain as wilderness area, although along the highway the land has been cleared for the broadacre farming of wheat.

Straddling the Murray River in South Australia, the Riverland is an intensively farmed irrigation area. Crops include citrus orchards, market gardens and vineyards. The Murray River here is a majestic stream that sweeps across a broad floodplain of its own making.

Adelaide sits at the foot of the Mt Lofty Ranges, its areas of parkland and low density suburbs making this one of Australia's more interesting cities. A run over the ranges leads to the Murray River and a brief return to mallee country. En route to Mt Gambier, the highway passes The Coorong, a long, narrow lagoon, and the old port town of Robe.

The route from Mt Gambier to Melbourne follows the coastline virtually all the way, passing through the historic towns of Portland and Port Fairy. East of Warrnambool the road trip returns to Melbourne via the Great Ocean Road, taking in some of the most spectacular coastal country in Australia.

The Climate

Travellers to south-western New South Wales, western Victoria and the Adelaide/Riverland area of South Australia will experience a variety of weather conditions. Many summer days are hot, around 32C to 35C. Nights are generally mild (around 20C) but may occasionally be warmer. In the southern districts, hot summer days are replaced by mild cloudy days, sometimes with drizzle. Wintertime travel is cool to cold with maximums around 12C (in the south) to 16C (in the north), often accompanied with winds and showers. Nights are cold, sometimes with sub-zero temperatures.

The time to travel this part of the country is during autumn or spring. Daytime temperatures are usually mild to warm, with only the odd hot (or cool) day. Nights are generally cool. Except along the southern coast, in most years there will normally be little rain in autumn, and only the chance of occasional showers in spring.

Capital City Connections
Distances in kilometres
SYDNEY-HAY
via Hume/Sturt Highways

	Intermediate	Total
Sydney	0	0
Goulburn	191	191
Wagga	264	455
Hay	266	721

MELBOURNE-MILDURA
via Calder Highway

	Intermediate	Total
Melbourne	0	0
Bendigo	149	149
Ouyen	300	449
Mildura	103	552

The Route
Distances in kilometres

	Intermediate	Total
Melbourne	0	0
Bendigo	150	150
Echuca	89	239
Hay	206	445
Mildura	286	731
Renmark	153	884
Adelaide	256	1140
Mt Gambier	479	1619
Warrnambool	231	1850
Lorne	207	2057
Melbourne	140	2197

Calder/Midland/Northern/ Cobb Highways

Melbourne-Bendigo-Hay
This combination of highways takes the traveller from Australia's second largest city to the edge of the outback, via the rolling green hills of Central Victoria, past historic goldmining towns, and on to the flat plains of northern Victoria. North of the Murray River, in New South Wales, the eucalypt woodlands and farmlands merge onto the vast, treeless Hay Plains.

Travellers coming from Sydney, or the east coast, can join this road trip at Hay by using the Hume/Sturt Highways or the Great Western/ Mid-Western Highways (Connecting Route F).

Warnings: road subject to flooding. Beware of stock and kangaroos at night north of Denilquin.

DAY 1: MELBOURNE-HAY via Bendigo

Roads to Take: Calder Highway, Midland Highway, Northern Highway, Cobb Highway
Grade 1
Total Distance: 445km (5:15)
Intermediate Distances:

	Km	Hours
Melbourne-Bendigo	150	(2:00)
Bendigo-Echuca	91	(1:05)
Echuca-Deniliquin	78	(0:50)
Denilquin-Hay	126	(1:20)

Regions traversed: South-Central Victoria, Central Victorian Hills, North-Central Victoria, Riverina

▼

MELBOURNE (Alt 35m; Pop 3000000):** state capital of Victoria, set on the banks of the Yarra River (river cruises) and one of the world's great and quite intact Victorian-era cities. Many things to see and do: Rialto Towers Observation Deck** - good views, Parliament House*, Melbourne Aquarium**, Crown Entertainment Complex and Southbank* - including Melbourne Maritime Museum*, National Gallery of Victoria**, State Library and numerous other historic buildings and churches** - follow the Golden Mile Heritage Trail** (start at Immigration & Hellenic Antiquities Museum*), Old Melbourne Gaol*, Museum of Victoria*, Victoria Police Museum, Flinders Street Railway Station*, Gold Treasury Museum*, Chinatown*, and the Museum of Chinese Australian History*. Do not forget to take a tram ride**, and walk through Melbourne's laneways and arcades**. Melbourne's parks should not be overlooked, especially Fitzroy Gardens*, Treasury Gardens*, and the Alexander and Queen Victoria Gardens*. Full town facilities. (*0/445*)

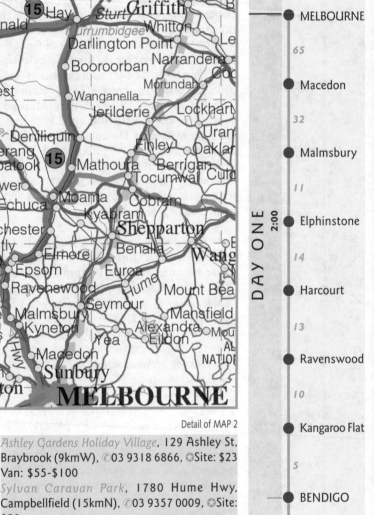

Detail of MAP 2

DAY ONE 2:00

- MELBOURNE
- 65
- Macedon
- 32
- Malmsbury
- 11
- Elphinstone
- 14
- Harcourt
- 13
- Ravenswood
- 10
- Kangaroo Flat
- 5
- BENDIGO

Accommodation

Astoria City Travel Inn, 288 Spencer St, ©03 9670 6801, ●$150

City Limits Motel, 20 Little Bourke St (1kmE), ©03 9662 2544, ●$125-$150

The Victoria Hotel, 215 Little collins St, ©03 9653 0441, ●$65-$160

City Square Motel, 67 Swanston St, ©03 9654 7011, ●$105-$120

Duke of Wellington Hotel, 146 Flinders St, ©03 9650 4984, ●$100-$130

Exford Hotel, 199 Russell St, ©03 9663 2697, ●$45-$55

Ashley Gardens Holiday Village, 129 Ashley St, Braybrook (9kmW), ©03 9318 6866, ●Site: $23 Van: $55-$100

Sylvan Caravan Park, 1780 Hume Hwy, Campbellfield (15kmN), ©03 9357 0009, ●Site: $20

Melbourne Big 4 Holiday Park, 265 Elizabeth St, Coburg (9kmN), ©03 9354 3533, ●Site: $23 Van: $50-$75

Honey Hush Caravan Park, 6 Leakes Rd, Laverton North (18kmSW), ©03 9369 2253, ●Site: $20 Van: $55-$65

Melbourne Airport Caravan Village, Ardlie St, Attwood (17kmNW), ©03 9333 1619, ●Site: $13 Van: $65-$80

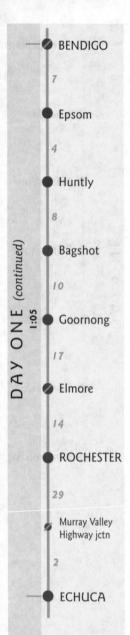

Road Trip 15

DAY ONE (continued) 1:05

BENDIGO

7

Epsom

4

Huntly

8

Bagshot

10

Goornong

17

Elmore

14

ROCHESTER

29

Murray Valley
Highway jctn

2

ECHUCA

Within a kilometre of the city centre, the following sights are worth visiting: in **Jolimont** is the Melbourne Cricket Ground* and the Olympic Museum & Gallery of Sport; in **South Yarra** see the Kings Domain, Sydney Myer Music Bowl, Pioneer Womens Memorial Garden*, historic La Trobes Cottage*, and Government House; to the west on St Kilda Road is the Shrine of Remembrance**; to the east are the Royal Botanic Gardens**, probably the best such gardens in Australia. East of the city centre, in **East Melbourne** is Cooks Cottage* and the Fire Services Museum; north of the city in **Parkville** is the Melbourne Zoo*, the Melbourne Museum* in Carlton Gardens, and the Queen Victoria Market** - the world's largest outdoor market.

Further out nearby Chapel Street**, also in South Yarra and **Prahran**, is one of Australia's great shopping 'high streets'.

If in central Melbourne, take Elizabeth Street to the north, half turn left into Flemington Road (National Highway 8), turn right onto Tullarmarine Freeway (*4/441*), proceed onto Calder Freeway (Highway 79) avoiding the airport turnoff (*13/432*) - stay on Calder Highway. The route passes through suburbs (limited access) until Taylors Lakes. *If heading towards Melbourne, just follow the Melbourne signs.*

Organ Pipes National Park turnoff: (*25/420*) Turn **N** for a short drive to this park preserving an outcrop of columnar basalt*. Picnic area.
Plains and low rises offer distant views* across the mostly treeless basaltic Keilor Plains. Distant Melbourne skyline views to the south-east. The large bulk to the north-west is Mt Macedon (1013m).
Gisborne turnoff: (*55/390*) Turn **W** for the pleasant town of Gisborne* (Alt 442m; Pop 1800) with its elm-lined streets. Accommodation, stores, fuel.
Hilly country forms part of the Great Dividing Range. Eucalypt woodlands and grazing country are common.
Mt Macedon turnoff: (*58/387*) Turn **N** for the 7km drive into **Mt Macedon** (Alt 762m; Pop

1100), an unusual town with a 'hill-station' atmosphere, spread along a steeply rising ridge. Interesting houses and beautiful private gardens - Ard Chollie** is open to the public. About 7km further on, a road leads to the summit* of the mountain - lookouts, picnic area - located in the Macedon Regional Park. Accommodation, stores, fuel.

Macedon: small town located just **E** of the highway. Accommodation, store, fuel. (*65/380*)

Ranges support eucalypt forests and woodlands. Forms the main crest of the Great Dividing Range. Woodend turnoff: (*70/375*) Turn here for the pleasant small town of **Woodend** (Alt 570m; Pop 1800). Look out for the 14km return drive to Hanging Rock**, a maze of rocky outcrops - picnic area, kiosk. Accommodation, stores, fuel. Undulating country supports grazing - good views*.
Kyneton turnoff: (*85/360*) Turn **W** for pretty **Kyneton**ial* (Alt 509m; Pop 4000). Worth seeing: Botanical Gardens* - picnic area, Mineral Springs Reserve*, old Steam Flour Mill*, Blackhill Reserve - granite outcrops, native vegetation. Accommodation, stores, fuel.
Undulating country has good views overlooking farmlands.

Malmsbury (Alt 450m; Pop 550): small historic town. Worth seeing: old bluestone railway station*, stone railway viaduct* and Bleak House gardens. Accommodation, stores, fuel. (*97/348*)

Taradale: locality. The nearby Taradale Viaduct* is interesting. (*104/341*)

Elphinstone (Pop 200): township. Store, fuel. (*108/337*)

Undulating country supports tracts of woodlands and farmlands.
Faraday: locality. (*116/329*)

Harcourt (Pop 400): small town centre for an orcharding area. Some nearby orchards and vineyards are open to the public. Nearby Mt Alexander Regional Park is worth visiting - follow the signs - picnic areas, walking trails, lookouts. Accommodation, stores, fuel. (*122/323*)

Undulating country supports farmlands. Mt Alexander rises to the south-east.

Ravenswood: small township. Store, fuel. (*135/310*) Head **N** for Bendigo. *Head* **S** *for Harcourt.*

Kangaroo Flat: old gold mining area and settlement on the outskirts of Bendigo. Store, fuel. (*145/300*)

BENDIGO (Alt 225m; Pop 70000):** very interesting and relatively intact Victorian-era gold-mining town. Numerous historic buildings including the Shamrock Hotel** and the Pall Mall historic precinct**, Colonial Bank Gallery*, Bendigo Post Office, Rosalind Park and Conservatory Gardens**, and Alexandra Fountain*. Also see Sacred Heart Cathedral* with its 100m high spire, Bendigo Art Gallery*; Central Deborah Gold Mine*, Diamond Hill historic area*, Chinese Joss House at Emu Point, Dudley historic house, Fortuna Villa historic house, Golden Dragon Museum*, Gold Mining Museum*, White Hills Botanic Gardens, Steam & Oil Preservation Group*, Bendigo Bushland Trail* - views and walks, Discovery Science and Technology Centre, and the Dja Dja Wrung Aborigibal Association Museum*. (*150/295*) Take Napier St (Midland Highway) to Epsom and Elmore. *Southbound enter Pall Mall and High St (Calder Hwy) for Kangaroo Flat and Melbourne.*

Accommodation
Homestead Motor Inn, 508 High St (Calder Hwy), ©03 5447 7455, ✪$85-$145
Tea House Motor Inn, 280 Napier St (Midland Hwy - 1.5kmN), ©03 5441 7111, ✪$70-$85
Bendigo Central Motor Lodge, 181 View St, ©03 5443 9388, ✪$60-$70
City Centre Motel, 26 Forest St, ©03 5443 2077, ✪$55-$60
Brougham Arms Hotel/Motel, 150 Williamson St, ©03 5442 3555, ✪$55

Ascot Holiday Park, 15 Heinz St, White Hills (4kmN), ©03 5448 4421, ✪Site: $20 Van: $50-$90
Gold Nugget Caravan Park, 293 Midland Hwy, Epsom (8kmN), ©03 5448 4747, ✪Site: $18 Van: $40-$80
Central City Caravan Park, 362 High St (Calder Hwy - 2.5kmS), ©03 5443 6937, ✪Site: $17 Van: $35-$60

Epsom: small town on the northern outskirts of Bendigo. Worth seeing: Bendigo Pottery* - picnic area. Accommodation, stores, fuel. (*157/288*)

Huntly (Pop 600): old mining township. The Hartlands eucalyptus factory* is worth a look. Stores, fuel. (*161/284*)

Bagshot: small township. Store, fuel. (*169/276*)

Undulating country supports farmlands.

Goornong: small township. Store, fuel. (*179/266*)

Plains and low rises support farmlands.

Elmore (Pop 850): small agricultural town on the Campaspe River. Accommodation, stores, fuel. (*196/249*) Head **N** on Northern Hwy to Echuca. *Head* **S** *on the Midland Hwy for Bendigo.*

Plains support farming country.

ROCHESTER (Alt 105m; Pop 2550):* interesting farming town with some historic buildings. Worth seeing: Random House - historic house and gardens - picnic area. Full town facilities. (*210/235*)

Plains support farmlands and grazing country. Murray Valley Highway junction: (*239/206*) Turn **E** for Echuca. *Turn* **S** *for Rochester.*

ECHUCA (Alt 96m; Pop 10000):** historic river port on the Murray River. Worth spending some time here to see Port of Echuca** - old wharf, paddlesteamers, river cruises. Also visit Sharps

DAY ONE *(continued)*

ECHUCA

2

0:50

Moama

39

Mathoura

37

DENILIQUIN

75

1:20

Booroorban

51

HAY

Magic Music House and Penny Arcade*, National Holden Museum*, Historical Society Museum*, Raverty's Motor Museum, and Murray River Aquarium**. Full town facilities. (*241/204*) Head **N** on the Cobb Hwy for Moama. *Head **W** on Murray Valley Hwy for the Northern Hwy junction.*

Accommodation

Pevensey Motor Lodge, 365 High St, ©03 5482 5166, ✪$85-$125

High Street Motel, 439 High St, ©03 5482 1013, ✪$55-$60

Big River Motel, 317 High St (1.5kmS), ©03 5482 2522, ✪$55-$65

Northern Way Caravan & Tourist Park, 75 Northern Hwy (4kmS), ©03 5482 4266, ✪Site: $15 Van: $30-$60

Echuca Caravan Park, Crofton St (1kmNW), ©03 5482 2157, ✪Site: $17

Rich River Caravan Park, Crescent St (2kmE), ©03 5482 3658, ✪Site: $20 Van: $55-$80

Murray River forms the **state border** between Victoria and New South Wales.

Moama (Alt 98m; Pop 2500): twin town of Echuca. Full town facilities. (*243/202*)

Plains support farmlands.
Barnes: locality and former railway junction.
Plains given over to farming and grazing.

Mathoura (Pop 650): small farming town. Accomodation, stores, fuel. (*282/165*)
   The main attractions lie 11km to the east (sealed road) at Picnic Point*, an old timbecutter's camp set in the river red gum forests on the Murray River. Nearby is the Moira Forest walk*, views of the Cadell Tilt* (geological fault), and a bird hide. **Warning:** do not sit, camp or picnic directly under river red gums - they drop branches without warning.

Plains support farmlands.

DENILIQUIN (Alt 91m; Pop 8000):* large rice-growing and irrigation town. Worth seeing: Police Inspector's Residence* (historic museum),

Peppin Heritage Centre (merino museum & information centre), Waring Gardens*, Pioneer Tourist Park*, town walk of old buildings, McLean Beach (swimming, picnics), Island Sanctuary* (walking trails, wildlife), Blake Botanic Reserve (walking trails). Full town facilities. (*319/126*)

Accommodation

Centrepoint Motel, 399 Cressy St, ©03 5881 3544, ✪$65-$75

Riverview Motel, Butler St, ©03 5881 2311, ✪$65

Peppin Motor Inn, Crispe St, ©03 5881 2722, ✪$60

Deniliquin Riverside Caravan Park, 24 Davidson St (1kmN), ©03 5881 1284, ✪Site: $16 Van: $50

McLean Beach Caravan Park, Butler St, 03 5881 2448, ✪Site: $16 Van: $30-$60

Plains support farmlands and grazing country.
Wanganella (Alt 82m): locality on Billabong Creek. (*360/85*)
Plains offer distant views across farming and grazing country.

Booroorban: farming township. Store, fuel. (*394/51*)

Plains support grazing country. North of The Forest Creek the broad open expanses of the Hay Plains* can be seen.
Sturt Highway junction (South Hay): (*443/2*) Proceed **N** for Hay. *Proceed **S** for Booroorban.*

HAY (Alt 94m; Pop 3000):* interesting sheep grazing town with photogenic buildings. Old Hay Gaol museum* worth visiting, as are the old Hay Railway Station, Witcombe Fountain*, Cobb and Co Coach, and the Hay Wetlands* (good birdwatching). Attractive beaches and swimming areas along the Murrumbidgee River. Full town facilities. (*445/0*) *Connecting Route F connects.*

Accommodation

Hay Motel, Cnr Cobb/Sturt Hwys, ©02 6993 1804, ✪$50-$55

Cobb Inlander Motel, 83 Lachlan St, ©02 6993 1901, ✪$60

Bidgee Motor Inn, 74 Lachlan St, ©02 6993 2260, ✪$60

Nicholas Royal Motel, 152 Lachlan St, ©02 6993 1603, ✪$65-$75

Hay Caravan Park, Sturt Hwy (2kmSE), ©02 6993 1415, ✪Site: $16 Van: $35-$75

Hay Plains Holiday Park, 4 Nailor St (1kmSE), ©02 6993 1875, ✪Site: $17 Van: $35-$75

Sturt Highway
Hay-Adelaide

This all-sealed access provides an easy and interesting route to and from the Sunraysia district, the Riverland and Adelaide, especially for those people coming from Victoria or southern New South Wales. The countryside ranges from the vast open Hay Plains, to dense mallee country west of Balranald, to irrigated country around Mildura and the Riverland, to scenic farming country in South Australia's Barossa Valley.

Warnings: beware of stock and kangaroos at night, especially between Hay and Renmark. Road subject to flooding.

DAY 2: HAY-MILDURA
via Balranald

Road to Take: Sturt Highway
Grade 1
Total Distance: 286km (3:10)
Intermediate Distances:

	Km	Hours
Hay-Balranald	128	(1:25)
Balranald-Euston	82	(0:55)
Euston-Mildura	76	(0:50)

Average Vehicles per Day: 2500
Regions Traversed: Riverina, Western Plains, Sunraysia

HAY (Alt 94m; Pop 3000):* interesting sheep grazing town. For more information see Day 1. (*0/286*) Head **S** for Sturt Highway junction.

Sturt Highway junction: (*2/284*) Turn **W** for Balranald. *Turn **N** onto Cobb Hwy for Hay.*

Plains support tracts of saltbush. Northward the tree-lined Uara Creek can be seen on the horizon. Close to Hay the plain supports eucalypt woodlands.

Plains support vast tracts of saltbush - broad vistas.

Low rise offers awesome views* of wide open space. Big sky country hereabouts.

Plains supports eucalypt woodlands in the west, saltbush plains in the east.

Yanga Lake:* pleasant spot for fishing, boating and swimming when water levels are high. **Rest area** adjacent. (*119/167*)

Farmlands support cattle and sheep grazing as well as irrigated crops.

BALRANALD (Alt 61m; Pop 1500): interesting grazing and farming town. Greenham Park* on the banks of the Murrumbidgee River is the place for a picnic. Heritage Park has information, a museum and picnic facilities. Full town facilities. (*128/158*)

Accommodation
Sturt Motel, Cnr River/Courts Sts, ©03 5020 1309, ✪$55

Balranald Shamrock Motel, Cnr Market/Mayall Sts, ©03 5020 1107, ✪$55

Balranald Caravan Park, 60 Court St, ©03 5020 1321, ✪Site: $12 Van: $25-$40

Plains and low rises support extensive tracts of mallee eucalypts. **Rest area**. (*182/104*)

Lake Benanee:* attractive lake located near the highway. Swimming, picnicking. **Rest area** adjacent. (*194/101*)

Farmlands support sheep grazing, grape and citrus growing.

Robinvale turnoff: (*207/79*) Turn **S** onto Murray Valley Highway for the 10km return trip to **Robinvale** (Alt 55m; Pop 3000)*: an attractive irrigation town on the Victorian side of the border. Bridge* crossing the Murray River is worth a look, as are the Fish Ladders and Weir* (2 kilometres south along the Sea Lake road), and the Robinvale Historic Homestead. Wineries. Full town facilities.

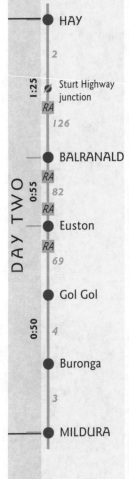

DAY TWO

HAY

2

1:25   Sturt Highway junction
RA

126

BALRANALD
RA

0:55   82
RA

Euston
RA

69

Gol Gol

0:50   4

Buronga

3

MILDURA

Euston (Alt 61m; Pop 620): small grazing and irrigation town with some appeal. Interesting old buildings*. Worth seeing: Euston Weir and Fish Ladders. Accomodation, stores, fuel. (*209/77*)

Accommodation

Euston Motel, Sturt Hwy, ©03 5026 3806, ©$60
Riverfront Caravan Park, 27 Murray Tce, ©03 5026 1543, ©Site: $16 Van: $30-$45

Plains support tracts of mallee eucalypts (quite attractive in the late afternoon light). Some land has been cleared for grazing. **Rest area.** (*248/38*)
Monak: irrigation farming district. From around this point westward you are entering the irrigation area known as Sunraysia. (*267/19*)
Farmlands are mostly irrigation farms - citrus growing.
Trentham Cliffs: farming locality - some services may be available. (*273/13*)

Gol Gol (Pop 620): irrigation town with some appeal. Accommodation, stores, fuel. (*279/7*)

Buronga (Pop 900): basically an extension of Mildura on the New South Wales side of the border. Irrigation town. Worth seeing are the Sunraysia Oasis Botanical Gardens, 5 kilometres north-west. Full town facilities. (*283/3*) Head **S** on Sturt Hwy to Mildura.

Murray River: considered to be Australia's longest river (with a single name). In fact the Murray-Darling and subsidiary channels with head-waters in Queensland are by far longer: 3750km compared to 2570km. The southern bank of river forms the **state border** between New South Wales and Victoria.

MILDURA (Alt 54m; Pop 21000):** attractive major regional centre, irrigation and holiday town. Many things to see and do including paddle-steamer cruises* on the Murray River, watching paddlesteamers pass through the lock*, picnicking in parklands at Lock 11, swimming at Apex Park sandbar, seeing the old Mildura Homestead, visiting the Psyche Bend Pumps* and Rio Vista (historic house), seeing Langtree Hall, the Pio-

neers Cottage and Golden River Zoo. Also museums and wineries. Full town facilities. (*286/0*) *Road Trip 16 connects.*

Accommodation

Riviera Motel, 157 Seventh St, ©03 5023 3696, ©$50
Vineland Motel, 363 Deakin St, ©03 5023 4036, ©$50
Kar-Rama Motor Inn, 153 Deakin St, ©03 5023 4221, ©$50-$70
Three States Motel, 847 Fifteenth St, ©03 5023 3735, ©$55-$75
Sunraysia Motel and Holiday Apartments, 441 Deakin Ave, ©03 5023 0137, ©$45-$55
New Wheatlands Motel, 433 Deakin Ave, ©03 5023 3266, ©$55-$70
Mildura Park Motel, 250 Eighth St, ©03 5023 0479, ©$50-$100
Cross Roads Holiday Park, Cnr Deakin/Fifteenth Sts, ©03 5023 3239, ©Site: $19 Van: $45-$95
Mildura & Deakin Tourist Caravan Park, Deakin Ave (Sturt Hwy), ©03 5023 0486, ©Site: $20 Van: $55-$70
Golden River Caravan Gardens, Flora Ave, ©03 5021 2299, ©Site: $20 Van: $55-$130
Desert City Tourist and Holiday Park, Calder Hwy, ©03 5022 1533, ©Site: $19 Van: $40-$85
Calder Caravan Park, Calder Hwy, ©03 5023 1310, ©Site: $18 Van: $30-$70

A 214km return trip on unsealed roads leads to Lake Mungo National Park** (look for signs back in Buronga) a world heritage area due to its archaeological significance. This is a site of some of the oldest evidence of human activity in Australia, extending back 40,000 years. Artifacts include stone tools, portions of ancient human skeletons (roughly 26,000-30,000 years old), and evidence of cremation and ritual burials. Physical features include the saltbush-covered dry lake bed of Lake Mungo* and the intricately eroded clay dune, or lunette, called the Walls of China** (afternoons are best for photography). Also of interest is the old Mungo woolshed*, Visitors Centre and the 70km self-drive trail through the park (allow for extra fuel); walking trails. Camping is available but there are no other facilities. **Warnings:** carry suffa cent fuel for your return journey. Do not proceed if wet. The route is okay for 2WDs in dry conditions.

DAY 3: MILDURA-BERRI via Renmark

Road to Take: Sturt Highway
Grade I
Total Distance: 158km (1:45)
Intermediate Distances:

	Km	Hours
Mildura-Renmark	140	(1:30)
Renmark-Berri	18	(0:15)

Average Vehicles per Day: 3000
Regions Traversed: Sunraysia, The Mallee, Riverland

MILDURA (Alt 54m; Pop 21000):** large regional centre situated in Victoria's Sunraysia district. For more information see Day 2. (*0/158*)

Plains* support irrigation farms. Very scenic. **Rest area**.

Merbein South: farming locality. Store, fuel. (*19/139*)

Plains and low rises have been mostly cleared for grazing and wheat cropping. Some small tracts of the original mallee scrub remain.

Cullulleraine: small township. A short distance north lies Lake Cullulleraine*, lined with black box and reed beds (boating, swimming). Accommodation, store, fuel. (*57/101*)

Plains and low rises support wheat farms and remnant tracts of mallee. Some of the straightest roads in Victoria are located hereabout.
Murray-Sunset National Park:* vast national park preserving tracts of mallee country.
State border between Victoria and South Australia. Time zone boundary: add 1/2 hour if heading west, subtract 1/2 hour if heading east. **Rest area**. (*115/163*)

Yamba: farming locality. Westward is an agricultural inspection station. (*125/33*)
Pike River Conservation Park:* converses part of the Pike River system, a broad floodplain of wetlands and billabongs. Good birdwatching, canoeing.

Paringa (Pop 580): small irrigation and farming town. Worth seeing: Bert Dix Memorial Park (picnics, river access) and Lock 5 sandbar (good swimming area). North of town a 60km partly unsealed return drive leads to Paringa Cliffs Lookout*, Heading Cliffs Lookout*, Murtho Forest Reserve* (swimming, picnic area) and an old pre-Federation customs house. Accommodation, store, fuel. (*136/22*)

RENMARK (Alt 20m; Pop 4250):* sizeable irrigation farming town set on the Murray River. Worth seeing: riverfront reserve* (palm trees, picnic areas), the old pumping station, Jane Eliza Landing* (park and picnic area), historic buildings including Olivewood* (includes museum), Brendl Wonder World of Wildlife, PS *Industry* - a working paddlesteamer, Rotary Park, Goat Island Sanctuary* (walking trails, koalas, canoetrees), and Paringa Park Walking Trail*. Not far away is the Bulyong Island scetion of the Murray River National Park (birdwatching, canoeing, camping - river access only). Boat tours. Full town facilities. (*140/18*) *Road Trip 16 connects.*

Accommodation
Fountain Gardens Motel, Renmark Ave, ©08 8586 6899, ©$60-$70
Ventura Motel, 234 Renmark St, ©08 8586 6841, ©$65
Citrus Valley Best Western Motel, 210 Renmark Ave, ©08 8586 6717, ©$75-$90
Renmark Riverfront Caravan Park, Riverfront (2kmE), ©08 8586 6315, ©Site: $16 Van: $30-$75
Riverbend Caravan Park, Sturt Hwy (3kmE), ©08 8595 5131, ©Site: $15 Van: $35-$55

Plain supports irrigation farms.
Big Orange Lookout:* popular tourist stop near a 16m orange-coloured sphere. (*153/5*) *Road Trip 16 connects.* Head **S** off the Sturt Hwy for Berri.

DAY THREE

MILDURA
RA
19
Merbein South
38
Cullulleraine
RA
79   *State Border VIC-SA*
Paringa
4
RENMARK
18
BERRI

1:30

0:15

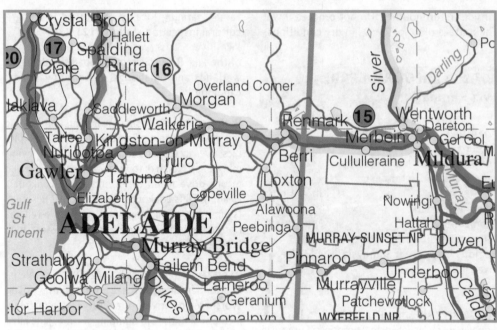

Detail of MAP 2

DAY FOUR

BERRI

13   0:10

Glossop

3

BARMERA

4

Cobdogla

7   0:15

Kingston-on-Murray

34

WAIKERIE

42   0:25

Blanchetown

52

Truro   0:40

13

Nuriootpa turnoff

BERRI (Alt 66m; Pop 3700):* pleasant and attractive irrigation town set on the banks of the Murray River. Worth seeing: Wilabalangaloo Flora and Fauna Reserve* (old homestead, museum, native vegetation and wildlife), Apex Park (picnics), Martins Bend* picnic area (on the Murray River), Jimmy James Memorial* (sculptures and installations), Berrivale Orchards, Berri Fruit Tree. Full town facilities. (*158/0*) Head **N** to the Sturt Hwy for Renmark.

Accommodation

Big River Motor Inn, Sturt Hwy, ©08 8582 2688, ✪$85

Berri Bridge Motel, Sturt Hwey, ©08 8582 1011, ✪$60-$80

Berri Resort Hotel-Motel, Riverview Dr, ©08 8582 1411, ✪$60-$110

Berri Riverside Caravan Park, Riverview Dr, ©08 8582 3723, ✪Site: 18 Van: $35-$55

DAY 4: BERRI-ADELAIDE via Blanchetown

Road to Take Sturt Highway
Grade I
Total Distance: 238km (2:50)
Intermediate Distances:

	Km	Hours
Berri-Barmera	16	(0:15)
Barmera-Waikerie	46	(0:30)
Waikerie-Blanchetown	42	(0:25)
Blanchetown-Nuriootpa	60	(0:40)
Nuriootpa-Adelaide	74	(1:00)

Average Vehicles per Day: 5000 on Sturt Highway
Regions Traversed: Riverland, Barossa Valley, Adelaide district

BERRI (Alt 66m; Pop 3700):* pleasant and attractive irrigation town. For more information see Day 3. (*0/238*) Head **W** via Glossop to Barmera where the road rejoins the Sturt Hwy.

Plain supports a dense network of irrigation farms such as vineyards, citrus groves, apricot and peach orchards.

Glossop: small irrigation community. Accommodation, store, fuel. (*13/225*)

BARMERA (Pop 1850):* attractive irrigation town set on the banks of Lake Bonney. Worth seeing: Lake Bonney* (boating, swimming), tourist drive around the lake, and the Donald Campbell Obelisk. Full town facilities. (*16/222*) Rejoin the Sturt Highway, heading **W** for Cobdogla. *Turn **SE** off the Sturt Hwy for Berri.*

Plain supports irrigation farms.

Cobdogla (Pop 300): small irrigation town set on the Murray River. The town lies just off the highway. Interesting museum*. Accommodation, store, fuel. (*20/218*)

Floodplain of the Murray River offers good views. Road passes through Moorook Game Reserve* (camping available).
Murray River:* impressive bridge crosses the river. (*25/213*)
Lookout* offers good views over the Murray River, floodplain, wetlands and lakes. (*25/213*)

Kingston-on-Murray (Alt 30m; Pop 300):* this small irrigation town set beneath river cliffs lies just off the highway. Accomodation, store, fuel. (*27/211*)

Plain supports tracts of dryland farming. Sweeping vistas.

WAIKERIE (Alt 30m; Pop 1750):* citrus orcharding town set by the Murray River and lying just off the highway. Worth seeing: Cliff-Top Lookout* (walking trail, river views), The Orange Tree* (good views), Lions Riverfront Park, Terrigal Fauna Park*, Hart Lagoon* (birdwatching and birdhide), Maize Island Conservation Park* (2km north-east). Full town facilities. (*61/177*)

Accommodation
Kirriemuir Motel, Sturt Hwy, ©08 8541 2488, ✪$75-$110
Waikerie Hotel-Motel, ©08 8541 2999, ✪$50-$55
Waikerie Caravan Park, Ramco Rd, ©08 8541 2651, ✪Site: $14 Van: $30-$50

Blanchetown Plain: vast plain given over to dryland farming and grazing. Eastbound travellers enter fruit fly exclusion zone - carry no fruit or vegetables.
Murray River:* impressive river scenes and bridge. On the floodplain just east of the bridge is Blanchetown Historic Reserve - canoe trees show scars where bark was removed for canoes. (*102/136*)

Blanchetown (Alt 30m; Pop 220):* pleasant old river township with historic buildings. Worth seeing: Lock One* (a river lock - good birdlife), and river views. Accommodation, store, fuel. (*103/135*)

Twelve Mile Plain: broad plain given over to grazing and mallee shrublands. En route the turnoff (*114/124*) **N** to Brookfield Conservation Park* is passed (6km return). The park preserves mallee scrub: typically red mallees, mallee box and yorrell, and native wildlife including the southern hairy-nosed wombats.
Hilly country forms the eastern ramparts of the Mt Lofty Range. Fair to good eastward views. The countryside is mostly cleared for grazing.

Truro (Alt 345m): small township roughly coinciding with the eastern edge of the Barossa Valley. Store, fuel. (*155/83*)

Undulating country has been mostly cleared for farming. Hawker Hill (422m) lies to the north. Mt Karinya (445m) lies to the south-east.
Old Sturt Highway (Nuriootpa) turnoff: (*168/70*) Turn **S** for the Barossa Valley town of Nuriootpa - see the Side Trip below.

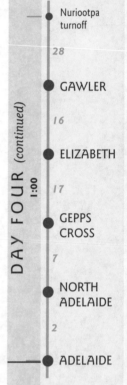

Road Trip 15

DAY FOUR (continued) 1:00

Nuriootpa turnoff

28

GAWLER

16

ELIZABETH

17

GEPPS CROSS

7

NORTH ADELAIDE

2

ADELAIDE

Barossa Valley, SA

Side Trip
Old Sturt Highway
(Grade 1) 4km+ return
Nuriootpa (Alt 275m; Pop 3300): major town of the Barossa Valley with some interesting old cottages. Worth seeing: Luhrs Pioneer German Cottage* (historic building and museum), Coulthard House museum, Penfolds and Kaiser Stuhl wineries*. Full town facilities.
Accommodation
Nuriootpa Vine Inn Hotel-Motel, 14-22 Murray St, ℗08 8562 2133, ◎$105
Barossa Gateway Motel, Kalimna Rd, ℗08 8562 1033, ◎$40
Top of the Valley Tourist Motel, 49 Murray St, ℗08 8562 2111, ◎$70-$85
Barossa Valley Tourist Park, Penrice Rd, ℗08 8562 1404, ◎Site: $16 Van: $30-$60
  Just south of town are Seppelts and Hardys wineries*, among many others, as well as the towns of **Tanunda*** (pop 3100; full town facilities) and **Angaston** (pop 1950; full town facilities) and the historic German village of Bethany** (pop 400; limited services) laid out in traditional Hufendorf (horsehoe pattern) lines. These features can be seen by following a number of tourist drives in the area.

Plains and low rises support farming country. Reasonable views.
Barrier Highway junction: locality only. (*193/45*)
Road Trip 17 connects.

GAWLER (Pop 13800): large regional town set between the North and South Para rivers; lo-cated off the Sturt Highway on a loop road (follow the signs). Some interesting old buildings. Worth seeing: Gawler Heritage Walk*, Para Para Mansion, Old Telegraph Station*. Full town facilities. (*196/42*) Proceed **SW** along Main North Road (Highway 20) for Elizabeth and Gepps Cross.
Accommodation
Prasads Gawler Motel, Cnr Main North Rd/Gawler By-Pass, ℗08 8522 5900, ◎$65-$90
Gawler Caravan Park, Main North Rd, ℗08 8522 3805, ◎Site: $16

Plains virtually cleared for grazing and vegetable gardens. Fair southward views towards Adelaide's skyscrapers and the Mt Lofty Ranges to the east.

ELIZABETH: large suburb of Adelaide. Nearby Parafield offers the Classic Jet Fighter Museum. Full town facilities. (*212/26*)
Accommodation
Downs Hotel-Motel, 212 Midway Rd, ℗08 8255 3333, ◎$55

Plain given over mostly to industrial estates. Fair eastward views towards Mt Lofty Ranges.

GEPPS CROSS: Adelaide suburb. Full facilities. (*229/9*)

From Gepps Cross, follow Main North Road into Adelaide. This route then becomes O'Connell Street then King William Road and leads directly into Adelaide's CBD.

ENFIELD & PROSPECT: Adelaide suburban areas. Full facilities.
Accommodation
Hoffmann Motel, 393 Main North Rd, Enfield, ℗08 8262 5115, ◎$65-$80

Parklands surround the city of Adelaide and North Adelaide. Attractive area.

NORTH ADELAIDE (Alt 22m):* attractive historic suburb well worth visting. Numerous photogenic buildings. Worth seeing: Lights Vision Lookout*. Full facilities. (*236/2*)

Accommodation
Princess Lodge Motel, 73 Lefevre St, ⊕08 8267 5566, ●$55-$65
Hotel Adelaide International, 62 Brougham St, ⊕08 8267 3444, ●$100
Old Adelaide Inn Motel, 160 O'Connell St, ⊕08 8267 5066, ●$115-$180

*Parklands*** lie between Adelaide and North Adelaide, spread out along the Torrens River. Good city views, excellent walking paths and picnic areas. The River Torrens Walk extends to Henley on the coast, and into the hills.

ADELAIDE (Alt 43m; Pop 1023000):** state capital of South Australia. Adelaide City is an attractive place surrounded by fabulous parklands. Worth seeing: Botanic Gardens*, Zoological Gardens*, historic buildings, Parliament House*, Old Treasury Museum*, Ayers House*, Migration Museum*, Adelaide Gaol, Adelaide Oval, Art Gallery of South Australia*, South Australian Museum*, Tate Museum* (rock collections), Adelaide Arcade*, Bradman (the cricketer) Collection (State Library), Rundle Mall, Victoria Square*, and more. Try a pie from the pie carts*. Full town facilities. (*238/0*) Road Trips 17 and 20 connect.
Grosvenor Vista Hotel, 125 North Terrace, 08 8407 8888, $95-$135
Festival Lodge Motel, 140 North Terrace, 08 8212 7877, $90
Adelaide City Parklands Motel, 471 Pulteney St, 08 8223 1444, $75-$105
City Central Motel, 23 Hindley St, 08 8231 4049, $65
Brecknock Hotel, 401 King William St, 08 8231 5467, $50
Metropolitan Hotel, 205 Rundle St, 08 8231 5471, $40
Adelaide Caravan Park, Cnr Richmond/Bruton Sts, Hackney (2kmNE), 08 8363 1566, Site: $22 Van: $40-$100
Brownhill Creek Caravan Park, Brownhill Creek Rd, Mitcham (8kmS), 08 8271 4824, Site: $20 Van: $40-$80
Levi Park Caravan Park, 69 Landsdowne Rd, Walkerville (4kmNE), 08 8344 2209, Site: $21 Van: $65-$85

Further out of town the following features are worth visiting. In the Mt Lofty Ranges: Cleland Conservation Park*, Belair Recreation Reserve*, Morialta Falls Conservation Park*, Eagle-on-the-Hill (good views*). In the suburb of **Glenelg**: take the tram* - also see the Shark Museum, HMS Buffalo - sailing ship replica, Proclamation Tree. **Port Adelaide area**: Port Adelaide precinct**, South Australian Maritime Museum*, Historic Aviation Museum*, Historic Military Vehicles Museum*, scenic cruises on the Port River*. **Wayville**: Investigator Science and Technology Centre (interactive exhibits). **Hallett Cove**: Hallett Cove Conservation Park* (geological curiousity).

▲

Princess Highway
Adelaide-Mt Gambier-Warrnambool via Robe
The Princess Highway (sometimes called Princess Highway West) is the major route between Adelaide and the South-East region of the state. The route firstly crosses the Mt Lofty Ranges (also called the Adelaide Hills) before entering upon a vast plain east of the Murray River. The highway follows the coast along an inlet known as The Coorong before entering delightful farming country around Robe (Alt Highway 1), Millicent and Mt Gambier. This southern portion of South Australia is one of green landscapes and a temperate climate.

From Mt Gambier, this road trip takes a scenic back route to Portland via Port MacDonnell and Nelson before continuing on to Warrnambool via the Princes Highway.

> **Warnings:** road subject to flooding. Take care of busy city traffic near Adelaide and across the Adelaide Hills.

DAY 5: ADELAIDE-MT GAMBIER via Kingston

Road to Take: Princess Highway
Grade 1
Total Distance: 479km (5:40)

Road Trip 15

DAY FIVE			
	●	ADELAIDE	
	6	Glen Osmond	
1:00	64		
		Murray Bridge turnoff	
	27		
0:20	●	TAILEM BEND	
	54		
	●	Meningie	
	51		
2:05	●	Policemans Point	
	9		
	●	Salt Creek	
	86		
	●	KINGSTON SOUTH EAST	
0:30	43		
	●	Robe	

Intermediate Distances:

	Km	Hours
Adelaide-Murray Bridge turnoff	70	(1:00)
Murray Bridge turnoff-Tailem Bend	27	(0:20)
Tailem Bend-Kingston	198	(2:05)
Kingston-Robe	45	(0:30)
Robe-Millicent via Beachport	89	(1:10)
Millicent-Mt Gambier	50	(0:35)

Regions Traversed: Adelaide district, Adelaide Hills, Lower Murray, The South-East

▼

ADELAIDE (Alt 43m; Pop 1023000):** state capital of South Australia. For more information see Day 4. (**0/479**)

Leaving from central Adelaide along King William St, turn left onto South Tce then half-right onto Glen Osmond Rd. Follow Glen Osmond Rd (Highway 1) to Glen Osmond where the road becomes Mt Barker Rd. *Heading into Adelaide, just follow the signs. This route passes through Adelaide's suburbs.*

Glen Osmond: Adelaide suburb set at the foot of the Mt Lofty Range. Note the old toll house* at the foot of the ranges. Accommodation, stores, fuel. (**6/473**)

Ranges form steep eucalypt-clad hillslopes. Occasional good views of this scenic area. An impressive new highway connects directly with the South-Eastern Freeway.

Hilly country supports eucalypt woodlands and scattered urban development. Cleland Conservation Park lies to the north.

Crafers turnoff: (**14/465**) Turn **N** for Crafers (an outer suburb) and the Summit Road (6km return) to Mt Lofty Lookout (727m)** - great views, especially in the morning or at night. About 2km further on (along Summit Rd) is the turnoff to Cleland Wildlife Park*.

Hahndorf turnoff: (**23/456**) Turn **N** for **Hahndorf**** (Alt 329m; Pop 1650), a very pretty German-style village. A popular tourist destination - expect a crowd. Historic buildings** can be seen

by taking a heritage walk. Numerous craft shops and galleries. Worth seeing is the Antique Clock Museum* and German Model Railway Land**. Accommodation, stores, fuel.

Hilly country supports scattered development, small farms and orchards. Good views*. Mt Barker (517m) lies to the south.

Undulating country offers sweeping views* across mostly cleared farmlands and grazing country.

Plains and low rises support farmlands and grazing country. Westward views* towards the Mt Lofty Ranges.

Murray Bridge turnoff: (**70/409**) Turn **N** for the 6km drive to **Murray Bridge** (Alt 26m; Pop 13500), a large town set on the banks of the Murray River. Worth seeing: railway and road bridges*, historic buildings, the Anglican Cathedral - Australia's smallest, and Captain's Cottage Museum. Take a river cruise on the Murray. Full town facilities.

Murray River is crossed by the Swanport Bridge, the longest bridge in South Australia.

Plains support farmlands. Sweeping views*.

TAILEM BEND (Alt 21m; Pop 1600): old railway town set on a bend of the Murray River. Worth seeing: Old Tailem Town*, a recreation of an 1880s pioneering settlement. Full town facilities. (**97/382**) Stay on the Princes Hwy as it heads **S** for Meningie.

Accommodation

Tailem Bend Motel, 39 Princes Hwy, ©08 8572 3633, ○$55

Rivers Edge Caravan & Tourist Park, Princes Hwy (2kmNW), ©08 8572 3307, ○Site: $14 Van: $25-$40

Plains support farmlands and grazing country

Ashville: farming locality. (**127/352**)

Lake Albert, an arm of Lake Alexandrina, is visible to the west.

Meningie (Alt 3m; Pop 800): small town located on Lake Albert. A popular windsurfing area. Some historic buildings*. Accommodation, stores, fuel. (**151/328**)

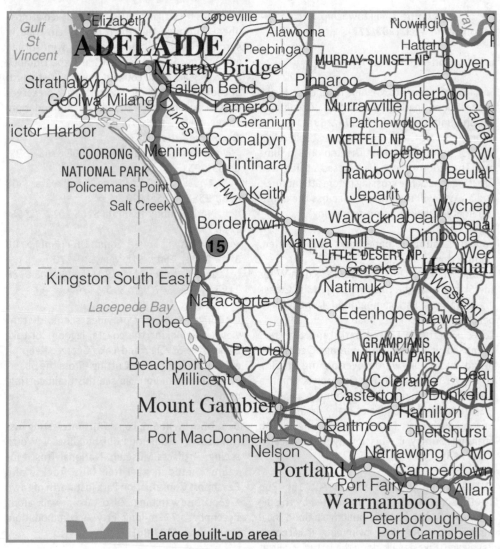

Gulf St Vincent

ADELAIDE

Elizabeth
Copeville
Alawoona
Nowingi
Peebinga
Hattah
MURRAY-SUNSET NP
Ouyen
Murray Bridge
Pinnaroo
Underbool
Strathalbyn
Tailem Bend
Murrayville
Caldal
Goolwa Milang
Lameroo
Patchewollock
Dukes
Geranium
Victor Harbor
Coonalpyn
WYPERFELD NP
Hopetoun
We
COORONG
Meningie
Tintinara
Rainbow
Beulah
NATIONAL PARK
Policemans Point
Keith
Jeparit
Wychep
Salt Creek
Warracknabeal
Donal
Bordertown
Hwy
Kaniva Nhill
Dimboola
15
LITTLE DESERT NP
Wed
Goroke
Horsham
Kingston South East
Natimuk
Western
Lacepede Bay
Naracoorte
Edenhope
Stawell
Robe
GRAMPIANS
NATIONAL PARK
Penola
Beachport
Coleraine
Beau
Millicent
Casterton
Dunkeld
Mount Gambier
Hamilton
Dartmoor
Penshurst
Port MacDonnell
Narrawong
Mo
Nelson
Camperdown
Portland
Port Fairy
Allans
Warrnambool
Peterborough
Large built-up area
Port Campbell

Detail of MAP 2

DAY FIVE (continued)

Robe

1:10   53

Beachport

36

MILLICENT

0:35   50

MT GAMBIER

Plains support tracts of farming country.

Camp Coorong: Ngarrindjeri Cultural Centre provides information about The Coorong and local Ngarrindjeri people. (161/318)

The Coorong: a lagoon some 145km long and up to 3km wide. The Coorong and adjacent Younghusband Peninsula (the sand dunes lying to the west) are preserved in The Coorong National Park. Good birdwatching, canoeing, camping, fishing - note that ocean swimming is dangerous. First glimpses* of The Coorong are just north of Magrath Flat.

Magrath Flat: locality only. From here an 8km return unsealed road leads W to Hells Gate on The Coorong. (175/304)

Low rises support paperbarks and tea-tree. Glimpsed views.

Lookouts* near the road provide broad vistas. (185/294)

Low rises offer glimpsed views. Occasional vistas across farmlands to the east.

Policemans Point: small township. Accommodation, store, fuel. (*202/277*)

Low rises offer glimpsed views.

Salt Creek: small township; roadhouse facilities. National park ranger station. Accommodation, limited store, fuel. (*211/268*)

South of Salt Creek an unsealed scenic road* runs for about 13km along The Coorong. In summer The Coorong can be crossed at Tea Tree Crossing (check the crossing before attempting), and a 4WD will then take you across the dunes to Ninety-Mile Beach (no swimming).

Low rises support paperbarks and tea-tree. Glimpsed views.

42 Mile Crossing turnoff: (*228/251*) Turn **W** for the 6km unsealed return trip to 42 Mile Crossing, a National Park campground. Dune walk to beach - no swimming.

Low rises support paperbarks and tea-tree. Glimpsed views of The Coorong. Occasional broad vistas eastwards overlooking grazing country. Further south The Coorong is simply a set of lagoons and low-lying country.

Blackford Drain: the first of many drains found in the south-east. Drains are dug to establish farming country in this low-lying landscape. (*297/188*)

KINGSTON SOUTH EAST (Alt 3m; Pop 1500):* cray-fishing port dominated by the Big Lobster*. A few historic buildings. Good local history museum*. Safe swimming at Lacepede Bay Beach, take a walk along the jetty*. Picnic at Apex Park or Len Lampit Reserve. Full town facilities. (*295/184*) Proceed straight ahead **S** for Robe on Alt Highway 1. *Continue **N** joining the Princes Hwy for Salt Creek.*

Undulating country provides vast vistas across farmlands.

Mt Benson: locality. (*319/160*)

Undulating country supports farmlands. Distant coastal views from the tops of rises.

Robe (Alt 3m; Pop 730):** interesting historic town well worth visiting. Numerous historic buildings** (walking tours) and a relaxed atmosphere, although this town is very crowded in summer. Good swimming, surfing, windsurfing and fishing. See the Obelisk* at Cape Dombey and the Beacon Hill Lookout Tower*. Just south of the town, Little Dip National Park preserves coastal features and wetlands. Accommodation, stores, fuel. (*340/139*)

Accommodation

Melaleuca Motel, 20 Smillie St, ✆08 8768 2599, ◐$65-$95

Robe Haven Motel, Cnr Hagen/Smillie Sts, ✆08 8768 2588, ◐$55-$90

Robe Hotel, Mundy Tce, ✆08 8768 2077, ◐$55-$120

Sea Vu Caravan Park, 1 Squire DR (1kmE), ✆08 8768 2273, ◐Site: $18 Van: $30-$70

Lakeside Tourist Park, Main Rd (1kmE), ✆08 8768 2193, ◐Site: $17 Van: $35-$120

Undulating country provides scenic distant views overlooking the coastal lagoons of Lake Eliza, Lake St Clair and Lake George. Keep an eye out for Woakwine Cutting - from the observation platform you can see this drain cutting, made by one man!

Beachport (Alt 5m; Pop 450):* interesting historic town. Numerous old buildings*. Worth seeing: Artifacts Museum, National Trust Museum*, midden at Three Mile Rocks, and Beachport Conservation Park just north of town - good birdwatching. Also take a walk along Beachport's 772m long jetty. Accommodation, stores, fuel. (*393/86*)

Undulating country offers god views* across farmlands and Rivoli Bay.

Rendlesham: locality. (*415/64*)

MILLICENT (Alt 19m; Pop 5100):* large commercial centre. The Memorial Gardens* are worth visiting. Jubilee Park is good for picnics. Millicent Museum** is excellent. A 13km sealed drive leads south-west to Canunda National Park*. Full town facilities. (*429/50*)

Plains support farmlands and pine forests.

Tantanoola turnoff: (**438/39**) A short (9km) loop road **S** rejoins the highway via Tantanoola, a timber township. See the stuffed Tantanoola Tiger* (a wolf) at the pub.

Tantanoola Caves: these decorative caves have regular tours. Located within the Tantanoola Caves Conservation Park. (**450/29**)

Undulating country passes through farmlands. Good views from the tops of rises.

MT GAMBIER (Alt 122m; Pop 21200):** large regional centre set at the foot of the Mt Gambier volcano, one of Australia's youngest volcanoes - the last eruption was about 4000 years ago. Many things to see and do: visit the Lady Nelson Visitor and Discovery Centre*, see the Cave Gardens* (a sinkhole in the middle of town) and Umpherston Sinkhole** with its terraced gardens, take a heritage walk*, visit Engelbrecht Cave* (guided tours), see the Old Courthouse Museum*, take a drive around Blue Lake** (blue from November to March), and take a walk to Centenary Tower** overlooking Valley Lake and Brownes Lake - walking trails* hereabouts. Full town facilities. (**479/0**)

Accommodation
Avalon Motel, 93 Gray St, ©08 8725 7200, ✪$55-$70
Arkana Motor Inn, 201 Commercial Rd East (1.5kmE), ©08 8725 5823, ✪$75-$105
Grand Central Motel, 6 Helen St, ©08 8725 8844, ✪$55-$65
Mt View Motel, 14 Davidson St (2kmNE), ©08 8725 8478, ✪$45
Blue Lake City Caravan Park, Bay Rd (2kmSW), ©08 8725 9856, ✪Site: $18 Van: $35-$75
Kalganyi Caravan Park, Cnr Penola/Bishop Rds (3kmN), ©08 8723 0220, ✪Site: $20 Van: $40-$65
Jubilee Holiday Park, Jubilee Hwy East (3.5kmSE), ©08 8723 2469, ✪Site: $17 Van: $35-$65

DAY 6: MT GAMBIER-WARRNAMBOOL
via Port MacDonnell, Portland

Roads to Take: Bay Road, Port MacDonnell-Nelson-Portland Roads
Grade I
Total Distance: 230km (2:50)
Intermediate Distances:

	Km	Hours
Mt Gambier-Port MacDonnell	28	(0:20)
Port MacDonnell-Portland	101	(1:15)
Portland-Warrnambool	101	(1:15)

Regions Traversed: The South-East, Western Districts

MT GAMBIER (Alt 122m; Pop 21200):** large regional centre. For more information see Day 5. (**0/230**)

Head **S** to Port MacDonnell along Bay Rd (past Blue Lake).

Hilly country provides good southward views*. Plains and low rises support attractive farmlands. Sweeping views.

Little Blue Lake turnoff: (**14/216**) Turn **W** onto Mt Salt Road for the 6km return unsealed drive to Little Blue Lake* (blue between November and March).

Mt Schank turnoff:** (**15/215**) Turn **E** for the short drive to Mt Schank (158m), a prominent volcanic cone rising above the plain. The last eruption was about 7000 years ago. Walking trail to the top - excellent views*. Picnic area.

Plains support farmlands.

Allendale East: small township. Notable for the sinkhole* in the middle of the road. (**22/208**)

Port MacDonnell (Alt 5m; Pop 680):* interesting historic port and crayfishing centre. Worth seeing: historic buildings*, Maritime Museum*, good views* at nearby Cape Northumberland* (at low tide old wagon tracks and petrified trees can be seen), and Dingley Dell Con-

DAY SIX

0:20	
	MT GAMBIER
	28
	Port MacDonnell
	16
	Lower Nelson Road junction
	7
1:15	Summerhill junction
	9 State Border SA-VIC
	Nelson
	69
	PORTLAND

servation Park (Adam Lindsay Gordon's Cottage). Good fishing, swimming. Accommodation, stores, fuel. (*28/202*) Head **E** for Nelson. *Head* **N** *for Mt Gambier.*

Undulating country provides good coastal views*. Ewan Ponds turnoff: (*38/192*) Travel along the unsealed Peacocks Road (6km return) to Ewan Ponds Conservation Park. Ewan Ponds* is a large pool of crystal-clear water containing caves and chambers. Snorkelling is possible (no permit required but a wetsuit is essential - obey all instructions). Walking trails. Good views* from pool landings. No camping.
Brown Beach: surfing beach. (*41/189*)
Lower Nelson Road junction: (*44/186*) Turn **E** for Nelson. *Turn* **S** *into Green Point Road for Port MacDonnell.*
Summerhill Junction: locality only; no facilities. (*51/179*) Turn **SE** for Nelson. *Turn* **W** *for Port MacDonnell.*
Piccaninnie Ponds turnoff: (*54/176*) Turn **S** for the 6km return unsealed road to Piccaninnie Ponds Conservation Park. Piccaninnie Ponds* is a very deep underwater cavern with good views* into the crystal-clear waters from the jetty - visibility is up to 40m. Diving is possible but with a permit; people have died here. Walking trails lead to beach, limestone formations and outlet channel. Camping is okay.
State Border between South Australia and Victoria. Time zone boundary: lose 1/2 hour if heading east, add 1/2 hour if heading west. (*56/174*)

Nelson (Alt 61m; Pop 200)*: delightful small town set on the lower reaches of the Glenelg River. Good estuary fishing. Delightful views. Just south of town is access to the western end of Discovery Bay National Park*: picnic area, access to Ocean Beach (swimming dangerous - good beach walking) and Estuary Beach (swimming okay) - about 8km return. Accommodation, stores, fuel. (*60/170*)
The Glenelg River* is one of the best canoeing rivers in Australia - broad and deep. It is possible to do either short day trips or overnight trips camping in the nearby Lower Glenelg National

Park*. The river is navigable for 70km between Nelson and Dartmoor. Simpsons Landing (2kmN along Nelson North Road) has launch facilities and a picnic area.

Undulating country passes through scattered farmlands and pine plantations.
Bong Bong Road junction: (*76/154*) Turn **S** for 14km return unsealed road leading to Lake Monibeong* in the Discovery Bay National Park: canoeing, swimming, picnic area, camping. A short walk leads to the beach - no swimming.
Undulating country supports pine plantations and farmlands.
Hedditch Hill offers good views*. (*90/140*)
Swan Lake Road junction: (*95/135*) A short but steep road leads **S** to Swan Lake*, a pretty lagoon, in the Discovery Bay National Park: picnicking, swimming, canoeing, camping. Walk over dunes to beach - no swimming.
Mt Richmond turnoff: (*106/124*) Turn **S** for Mt Richmond National Park*. This park preserves an extinct volcano (Mt Richmond 277m) mostly covered with sand; vegetation ranges from eucalypt forests to heathlands. Great views* of Discovery Bay and surrounding countryside. Numerous short walking trails. No camping.

Undulating country provides sweeping views across farmlands. Follow the signs at the highway junction into Portland.

PORTLAND (Alt 10m; Pop 11000):* historic port and industrial town. Many things to see and do: Portland Botanic Gardens* (old gardens, picnic area), Powerhouse Motor and Car Museum, Steam Packet Inn*, Mary MacKillop Memorial Gardens, Lions Fauna Park and Nursey, History House, Battery Point (old fort, picnic area), historic buildings*, Burswood Homestead Gardens* (Edward Henty's home), Cottage in the Gardens* (old restored house and furnishings), Customs House, Fawthorp Lagoon (tidal wetland - walkways, picnic area), and Smelter Nature Walk - good views. Full town facilities. (*129/101*) Head **N** for Narrawong and the Princes Hwy at Tyrendarra. *Head* **W** *for Nelson.*

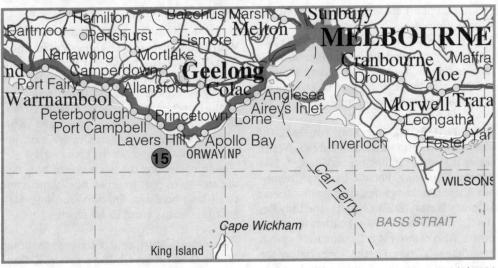

Detail of MAP 2

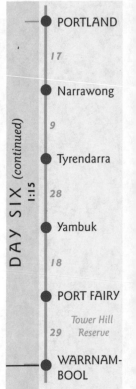

DAY SIX (continued) 1:15

- PORTLAND
  - *17*
- Narrawong
  - *9*
- Tyrendarra
  - *28*
- Yambuk
  - *18*
- PORT FAIRY
  - *Tower Hill*
  - *29* *Reserve*
- WARRNAM-
  BOOL

Accommodation

Grosvenor Motel, 206 Hurd St (1.6kmN), ©03 5523 2888, ©$65-$85

Admella Motel, 5 Otway Ct, ©03 5523 3347, ©$55

William Dutton Motel, Cnr Percy/Otway Sts, ©03 5523 4222, ©$60-$75

Portland Haven Caravan Park, 76A Garden St (1.6kmN), ©03 5523 5673, ©Site: $15 Van: $35-$55

Dutton Way Caravan Park, 50 Dutton Way (5kmNE), ©03 5523 1904, ©Site: $15 Van: $30

South of Portland take the 22km return sealed drive to Cape Nelson* for spectacular scenery and an old lighthouse.

Bolwarra South: locality. (*139/91*)
Plains offer good views across Portland Bay and the farmlands beyond.

Narrawong (Pop 880): small town located on the Surrey River. Good views* across Portland Bay. A couple of kilometres to the north (along Boyers Rd) is the Whalers Lookout* and the Sawpit picnic area. Accomodation, stores, fuel. (*146/84*)

Low rises offer sweeping views across farmlands.

Tyrendarra: farming township. Store, fuel. (*155/75*) Head **E** for Port Fairy on the Princes Hwy. Head **SW** for Narrawong along Portland Road.

Undulating country offers good views* across pleasant green farmlands. The localities of Tyrendarra East and Codrington are passed en route.

Yambuk (Pop 300): small farming township. The bluestone Yambuk Inn* is of interest. Just south of town is the pretty Yambuk Lake - fishing, boating. Store, fuel. (*183/47*)

Undulating country offers good views across farmlands.

PORT FAIRY (Alt 6m; Pop 2500):** historic old port town that should not be missed. Numerous historic buildings*, most dating from the 1840s and 50s - take the historic town walk. Other things worth seeing and doing: Port Fairy Aquarium*, Captain Mills Cottage* (probably Victoria's oldest house), Caledonian Hotel*, original milepost*, Shipwreck Walks* (walks overlooking shipwreck sites), Old Port Fairy cemetery walk, and Griffiths Island walk to muttonbird colony*. Full town facilities. (*201/29*)

Low rises support attractive farming country. Killarney: locality.

Tower Hill State Game Reserve**: (*219/11*) Take the one-way road into the Tower Hill extinct volcano crater: good views*, old quarry showing volcanic ash deposits*, crater lake*, walking trails, and natural history centre.

WARRNAMBOOL (Alt 21m; Pop 26000):* large regional centre situated on Lady Bay. Worth seeing is Flagstaff Hill Maritime Village**, Lake Pertobe - canoeing, Botanic Gardens*, numerous historic buildings including the impressive St John's Presbryterian Church*, the Lady Bay Hotel, and the Hopkins River Boathouse* among others. Also of interest is Cannon Hill* - picnic area, Granny's Grave, Fletcher Jones factory gardens* (floodlit at night), Swan Reserve*, and the Mahogany Ship Site - ask locally about this. Full town facilities. (*230/0*)

Accommodation

Norfolk Lodge Motel, 692 Raglan Pde (Princes Hwy), ✆03 5562 6455, ✪$55-$80

Riverside Gardens Motor Inn, Cnr Simpson/Verdon Sts (2.5kmE), ✆03 5562 1888, ✪$55-$80

Mahogany Motel, 463 Raglan Pde (Princes Hwy), ✆03 5562 5722, ✪$60-$80

Western Coast Motel, Cnr Raglan Pde/Bell St, ✆03 5562 2755, ✪$85-$100

Ocean Beach Holiday Village, Pertobe Rd (1.8kmS), ✆03 5561 4222, ✪Site: $25 Van: $45-$105

Fig Tree Holiday Village, 33 Lava St (1kmE), ✆03 5561 1233, ✪Site: $20 Van: $55-$85

Warrnambool Surfside Holiday Park, Pertobe Rd, ✆03 5561 2611, ✪Site: $20 Van: $50-$90

Just out of town is Logans Beach** (2kmE) for whale watching (June to October), Wollaston Bridge* over Merri River (2kmN), Thunder Point Coastal Reserve* (2kmSW) - birdwatching, walking, old middens; Warrnambool Aquarium* (2kmS) and Time and Tide Museum.

Great Ocean Road/ Anglesea Road-Princess Highway

Warrnambool-Lorne-Geelong-Melbourne

Today's drive takes the traveller along one of the great coastal routes in Australia: The Great Ocean Road. This scenic road provides tremendous views of the spectacular Port Campbell coastline, crosses the verdant Otway Ranges, and twists and turns along the rugged Otway Coast, unfolding panoramic scenes the entire way.

South of Geelong the landscape flattens out, the area given over to urban development and small land-holdings. The final run into Melbourne is across broad basalt plains.

Warnings: allow plenty of time to travel the Great Ocean Road - it is a slow drive. Take extra care in wet weather. Expect heavy traffic around Geelong and coming into Melbourne.

DAY 7: WARRNAMBOOL-MELBOURNE via Lorne

Roads to Take: Great Ocean Road, Anglesea Road, Princess Highway

Grade 1

Total Distance: 347km (5:15)

Intermediate Distances:

	Km	Hours
Warrnambool-Port Campbell	66	(0:50)
Port Campbell-Lorne	141	(2:25)
Lorne-Geelong	67	(1:00)
Geelong-Melbourne	73	(1:00)

Regions Traversed: Western Districts, Otway Coast, South-Central Victoria

WARRNAMBOOL (Alt 21m; Pop 26000):* large regional centre. For more information see Day 6. (*0/347*)

Undulating country supports attractive farmlands. Pleasant views*.

Allansford (Pop 560): small farming and cheese-making town. Worth seeing: Allansford Cheese

Twelve Apostles, Great Ocean Road, Vic

London Bridge:** former double sea arch, part of which collapsed in 1990. Lookout. (*57/293*)
The Arch:* sea arch and lookout.
Undulating country provides views across heathlands.
Two Mile Bay turnoff: (*63/285*) A short drive leads **S** through the heath to Two Mile Bay*. A walking track leads from here into Port Campbell.

Port Campbell (Alt 15m; Pop 200): small coastal resort township set on a pretty bay. Nearby Beacon Steps* provide access to the rock platform - take care. Lookout* just east of town. Accommodation, stores, fuel. (*66/281*)

Undulating country provides views across heathlands. The countryside forms part of the Port Campbell National Park.
Loch Ard Gorge turnoff: (*75/272*) Turn **S** for Loch Ard Gorge** (an impressive sea gorge - beach access - and site of a tragic shipwreck) and Island Arch*. Short walking tracks lead to The Blowhole** (a 17m vertical shaft; 40m wide) and Thunder Cave* (a narrow sea gorge). Other tracks lead to Broken Head* and along the Sherbrook River valley. Picnic area near Sherbrook River crossing. Offshore lies the spectacular Muttonbird Island**.

Lookout: located just off the road. Stop here for a view of **The Twelve Apostles*** , a collection of sea stacks and probably one of the best coastal scenes in Australia. Mornings are best for photography. (*78/267*)

Glenample Homestead Interpretative Centre:* old restored homestead and vistors centre. The nearby Gibson Steps** provides access to the beach down the 90m high cliffs, and a tunnel leads through the cliff to the Twelve Apostles Beach** - do not walk here at high tide or in rough weather - dangerous swimming. (*79/268*)
Undulating country offers good distant views*.

Princetown (Alt 30m):* small township set on the Gellibrand River - good canoeing. Walking trail leads to Point Ronald. Accommodation, store, fuel. (*84/263*)

World* (located on Great Ocean Rd). Accommodation, stores, fuel. (*10/337*)

Great Ocean Road junction: (*12/335*) Turn **SE** for Port Campbell. *Turn **W** for Warrnambool.*
Plains and low rises offer distant views of farming and grazing country.
Nullawarre: locality. (*29/318*)
Nirranda: locality.
Undulating country provides sweeping views across farming country.
Bay of Islands is located in the Bay of Islands Coastal Park, a rugged cliff-lined coast with numerous stacks. A lookout** overlooks Boat Bay. (*48/299*)
Undulating country offers coastal views* as the route passes through part of the Bay of Islands Coastal Park. Just off the road lies Crofts Bay* (beach, island stacks), Massacre Bay* (fishing, spectacular cliffs), and Bay of Martyrs* (beach, stacks).

Peterborough (Pop 210):* small fishing township. Good swimming and fishing in Curdles River estuary. The lookout* near the river mouth is worth seeing. (*53/294*)

Undulating country offers sweeping views of the coast and hinterland. The route passes through Port Campbell National Park.
The Grotto:* lookout and walking trail into collapsed caves. Sea arch*. (*56/291*)

DAY SEVEN

WARRNAM-
BOOL

10

Allansford

2

Great Ocean
Road junction

0:50

41

Peterborough

London
13   Bridge

Port Campbell

Loch Ard
Gorge
18   Twleve
Apostles

Princetown

Melba Gully
31   SP

2:25

Lavers Hill

47

APOLLO BAY

45   Mt Defiance
Lookout

LORNE

Undulating country provides farmland views with the Otway Range in the background.

Gellibrand River crossing: a pleasant spot. From here a short alternative route connects with Princetown along the Gellibrand River - good birdwatching, wetlands. (*96/251*)

Hilly country supports farmlands and eucalypt forests. Occasional good views*.

Wattle Hill: former hotel* from the coaching days. From here a short unsealed road (about 13km return) leads to Moonlight Head*, an old settlement. Walking tracks lead to Wreck Beach* (sea anchors embedded in rocks) and the cliff-tops* (highest sea cliffs in Victoria) past Moonlight Head cemetery. (*99/248*)

Hilly country* supports eucalypt forests and rainforest gullies.

Melba Gully State Park:** considered to be the jewel of the Otway Ranges. This high rainfall area (over 2000mm pa) supports a dense rainforest of myrtle beech, blackwoods and tree ferns. Madsens Track Nature Walk takes you through the heart of the gully. Glow worms* are visible at night. No camping. (*112/235*)

Lavers Hill (Pop 250):** scenic township with a mountain-top atmosphere. Accommodation, stores, fuel. (*115/232*)

Beauty Spot Scenic Reserve:* picnic area with coastal views. Walking trail leads into mountain ash/tree fern forest. (*117/230*)

Johanna Road junction: (*124/223*) Turn S for the short drive (9km return; unsealed road) to Johanna*, a farming locality and surfing beach (swimming dangerous). Beach walking trails. Camping available. A lookout* is just south of the road junction.

Hilly country* and river flats supports a patchwork of very scenic dairy farms, forests and wetlands. The Otway National Park lies to the east, preserving mountainous tracts of eucalypt forests and rainforest gullies.

Cape Otway turnoff: (*142/205*) Turn S for the 26km return unsealed road to Cape Otway**. See the old lighthouse, cemetery, Telegraph Station and Signals Residence. En route a short track (about 12km return) leads to Blanket Bay Camp-

ing Area set within Otway National Park, with picnicking, camping, fishing, walking trails.

Maits Rest* delightful picnic area and cascades. Rainforest walk*. (*145/202*)

Hilly country is preserved in the Otway National Park.

Shelley Beach turnoff: (*157/190*) Turn S for Shelley Beach picnic area*. Walking trails.

Marpengo: locality.

APOLLO BAY (Alt 9m; Pop 2000):* attractive seaside settlement and mainland Australia's southernmost town. Worth seeing: Bass Strait Shell Museum*, Old Cable Station Museum*. Take the cliff walk across the headland. Full town facilities. (*162/185*)

Just out of town is the Barham Fernery* (off Apollo Bay-Beech Forest Rd), a fern reserve and Paradise picnic area. Crows Nest Lookout* (take the scenic Tuxion Rd) has great views.

Hilly country offers great views** of the coast, farmlands and high ridges. Hilly country continues past Lorne. Farmlands continue to Cape Patton.

Marriners Lookout turnoff: (*165/182*) Turn S for the short drive to Marriners Lookout*. Great views.

Skernes Creek: locality. Camping available. (*168/179*)

Wongarra: locality. (*174/173*)

Carisbrook Falls: picnic area.

Cape Patton: scenic lookout. Good views**

Angahook-Lorne State Park preserves parts of the Otway Coast through which the eastern leg of the Great Ocean Road passes for much of its length.

Kennett River:* locality - surfing and swimming beach. Caravan Park. (*185/162*)

Hilly country offers spectacular views**.

Wye River:** locality - surfing and swimming beach. Caravan Park. (*190/157*)

Hilly country offers spectacular views** between here and Lorne. Numerous lookouts**.

Artillery Rocks:* interesting rock formations resembling cannonballs located just off the road. Worth a look. (*194/153*)

Mt Defiance Lookout** incredible view - mornings are best.

Cumberland River crossing*: scenic valley - camping reserve. A walking track leads through a gorge to Cumberland Falls*. There is a cave west of the river mouth - take a torch. (*201/146*)

Sheoak Creek*: a short walk leads to to Sheoak Falls.

St George River crossing:* spectacular deep valley and inlet. Eastward the road is spectacular. Good views*.

LORNE (Alt 15m; Pop 1170):** popular tourist resort set in a spectacular location. Many things to see and do: picnic at the Foreshore Reserve*, see the historic society display and take in the view at Teddys Lookout*. Walking tracks lead from town up the Erskine River valley to The Sanctuary* or continue upstream (allow a day) to Erskine Falls. Full town facilities. (*207/140*)

Accommodation
Sandridge Motel, Cnr Mountjoy Pde/William St, ✆03 5289 2180, ✪$85-$200

Anchorage Motel, 32 Mountjoy Pde, ✆03 5289 1891, ✪$60-$130

Ocean Lodge Motel, 6 Armytage St (1kmS), ✆03 5289 1330, ✪$80-$160

Lorne Foreshore Reserve Caravan Park, Great Ocean Rd, ✆03 5289 1382, ✪Site: $22 Van: $75-$120

Just out of town, short drives lead into the hills and Angahook-Lorne State Park to Erskine Falls* - walking tracks; Blanket Leaf picnic area* - walking track; and Sheoak Creek picnic area.

Hilly country offers spectacular coastal views*. Good lookouts near Reedy Creek and Cinema Point**. In between these lookouts, Grassy Creek offers pleasant pools and cascades.

Eastern View marks the official eastern end of the Great Ocean Road, marked by a memorial arch. (*219/128*)

Moggs Creek: holiday locality. Just behind the settlement is Moggs Creek picnic area* - walking tracks. Just west of the settlement is Moggs Creek Lookout*, with good views.

Fairhaven: locality and beach.

Aireys Inlet (Alt 10m; Pop 680):* pleasant holiday settlement set among tea-tree scrub. Good swimming in the rock pools. There is a walking track* along the coast (see old volcanic formations) and to Moggs Creek. Split Point Lighthouse* is worth a look. Distillery creek picnic area (Bambra Rd), situated in the Angahook-Lorne State Park, is nice. Accommodation, stores, fuel. (*225/122*)

Hilly country provides good coastal views. Good lookout just west of Anglesea.

ANGLESEA (Alt Pop 2000): popular holiday centre. Good swimming. Worth seeing: Coogoorah Park - walking trails, a cliff walk across the heathland. Another walking track leads from Anglesea to Aireys Inlet. Full town facilities. (*236/111*)

Undulating country passes through woodlands and farmlands. An open cut brown coal mine and a power station lie to the west.

Point Addis Road junction: (*240/107*) Turn **S** for Point Addis* - surf beach, picnic area, good views*. Adjacent is Iron Bark Basin*, a tract of bushland - walking trails, old mine site, birdwatching.

Bells Beach turnoff: (*241/106*) Turn **S** for Bells Beach*, one of the world's famous surfing beaches. On good days, 3 to 4m hollow waves turn this place into a surfing paradise.

Torquay turnoff: (*247/100*) Continue straight ahead **N** along Anglesea Road for Geelong.

Plains and low rises cross farming country.

Princes Highway junction: (*263/84*) Turn **E** for Geelong and Melbourne then proceed **N**. *Turn S for Lorne.*

GEELONG (Alt 17m; Pop 145500):* largest provincial city in Victoria, set on Corio Bay. Many things to see and do: numerous historic buildings* dating from the gold rush days including Barwon Grange* historic house. National Wool Museum*, Mosaic Mural, Old Geelong Gaol*, Queens Park (walking trails, picnic area), Botanical Gardens*, Barwon Lookout (views overlooking Geelong), Customs House*, Western Beach,

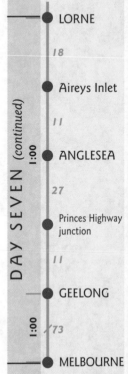

DAY SEVEN (continued)

LORNE

18

Aireys Inlet

11

1:00 ANGLESEA

27

Princes Highway junction

11

GEELONG

1:00 /73

MELBOURNE

Eastern Beach*, Geelong Maritime Museum**, Geelong Art Gallery*, Balyang Sanctuary (birdwatching, picnics), and Alden Lodge Coral Gardens* (shell and marine displays, massed flower gardens). Full town facilities. (**274/73**)

Accommodation

Corio Bay Motel, 292 Princes Hwy, ℡03 5275 1489, ✪$65-$75

Shannon Motor Inn, 285 Shannon Ave (1.5kmW), ℡03 5222 4355, ✪$70-$110

Kangaroo Motel, 16 The Esplanade South (1kmN), ℡03 5221 4022, ✪$60-$65

Rippleside Park Motor Inn, 67 Melbourne Rd, ℡03 5278 2017, ✪$65-$70

Riverglen Caravan Park, 75 Barrabool Rd, Belmont, ℡03 5243 5505, ✪Site: $15 Van: $45-$60

Barwon Caravan & Tourist Park, 153 Barrabool Rd, Belmont, ℡03 5243 3842, ✪Site: $18 Van: $55-$80

City Southside Caravan Park, 87 Barrabool Rd, Belmont, ℡03 5243 3788, ✪Site: $18 Van: $50-$70

Norlane: northern locality of Geelong - industrial area. (**281/66**)

Corio: locality. (**283/64**)

Plains and low rises offer broad distant views across grazing country.

Werribee turnoff: (**310/37**) Turn **NW** for **Werribee** (Alt 23m; Pop 24000), a former grazing settlement, nowadays an outer Melbourne suburb. Worth seeing is Werribee Park Mansion**, one of Victoria's great historic houses. The loop road rejoins the highway.

Plains support grazing country and scattered development.

Laverton turnoff: (**329/18**) Turn **NW** for Laverton, an outer Melbourne suburb.

From near the Laverton turnoff the route enters Melbourne's suburbs. Follow Highway 1 onto the Westgate Freeway.

Westgate Bridge:** one of Australia's great road bridges rises high over the Yarra River estuary. Good city views.

Stay on Westgate Freeway. Follow road signs for access to central Melbourne.

MELBOURNE (Alt 35m; Pop 3000000):** state capital of Victoria set on the banks of the Yarra River. For more information see Day 1. (**347/0**)

Road Trip 16
Corner Country Loop

Mildura-Broken Hill-Tibooburra-Innamincka-Lyndhurst-Arkaroola-Yunta-Burra-Renmark-Mildura

Total Distance: 2390km
Suggested Travelling Time: 8 days

Appreciate the harsh and beautiful aridity of the Corner Country

See the bush architecture of Tibooburra, the ruins at Milparinka, the remote settlement of Innamincka, sand dune country, the Barrier Range, Depot Glen, Sturt National Park, Cooper Creek, the northern Flinders Ranges, the spectacular arid mountain setting of Arkaroola, the historic mining town of Burra, Morgan river port, and part of the longest fence in the world.

Corner Country Loop

The Corner Country is the closest arid country to the major urban areas of south-east Australia, and as such it is perhaps the most visited area of the Australian outback. With the exception of the northern Flinders Ranges, this is unspectacular country, but it exudes an arid wildness than can be either harsh or beautiful, a fact that gives this region a sublime essence. Off the main highways and through-roads, this land still has a strong 'outback feel', country you can have almost to yourself, unlike some of the more popular destinations elsewhere. In this part of the world you can still experience the outback as it was before parts of it became popular tourist destinations.

The Climate

Travellers to the Corner Country will experience a variety of weather conditions, even extremes. During summer this area records some of the highest temperatures in Australia, with maximums up to the mid-forties. Normally though, most summer days are just hot, around 32C to 35C. Nights are generally mild (around 20C) but may occasionally be warmer. Unless staying on the major sealed highways, or within the southern districts when the odd cool change might relieve the heat, summer travel in this area is not recommended.

The time to travel this part of the country is during autumn or spring. Daytime temperatures are usually mild to warm, with only the odd hot (or cool) day. Nights are generally cool. Most years there will normally be little or no rain in autumn, and only the chance of occasional showers in spring. Winters are okay too, except that it can be cool during the day and quite cold at night.

Capital City Connections
Distances in kilometres

SYDNEY-MILDURA
via Hume/Sturt Highways

	Intermediate	Total
Sydney	0	0
Goulburn	191	191
Wagga	264	455
Hay	266	721
Mildura	286	1007

ADELAIDE-MILDURA
via Sturt Highway

	Intermediate	Total
Adelaide	0	0
Renmark	256	256
Mildura	153	409

MELBOURNE-MILDURA
via Calder Highway

	Intermediate	Total
Melbourne	0	0
Bendigo	149	149
Ouyen	300	449
Mildura	103	552

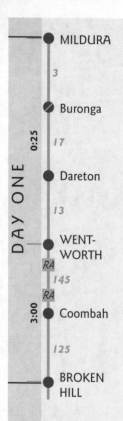

The Route
Distances in kilometres

	Intermediate	Total
Mildura	0	0
Broken Hill	303	303
Tibooburra	334	637
Innamincka	381	1018
Lyndhurst	471	1489
Copley	34	1523
Arkaroola	137	1660
Yunta	304	1964
Burra	158	2122
Renmark	115	2237
Mildura	153	2390

Silver City Highway
Mildura-Tibooburra

The Silver City Highway provides an easy and interesting route to Broken Hill, especially for those people coming from Victoria or southern New South Wales. This section of the route presents a variety of semi-arid landscapes. North of Broken Hill the real adventure begins, with stunning arid landscapes changing kilometre after kilometre. Conventional vehicles will find this a good road (when dry). It provides an easy and interesting route from Broken Hill to Tibooburra and Sturt National Park.

Warnings: beware of stock and kangaroos at night. Unsealed roads may be impassable after rain. Between Broken Hill and Tibooburra the road may be impassable after rain and subject to flooding. Avoid travelling this section at night. Make local enquiries before proceeding after rain or during summer months.

DAY 1: MILDURA-BROKEN HILL via Wentworth

Road to Take: Silver City Highway
Grade 1
Total Distance: 303km (3:25)

Intermediate Distances:

	Km	Hours
Mildura-Wentworth	33	(0:25)
Wentworth-Broken Hill	270	(3:00)

Average Vehicles per Day: 300 north of Wentworth
Regions Traversed: Western Plains (Lower Darling), Far West

▼

MILDURA (Alt 54m; Pop 21000):** large regional centre. For more information see Road Trip 15, Day 2. (*0/303*) Road Trip 15 connects. Head **NE** for Buronga.

Buronga (Pop 900): small town servicing irrigation farms. For more information see Road Trip 15, Day 2. (*3/300*) Turn **W** on Silver City Hwy for Buronga. *Turn **S** onto Sturt Hwy for Mildura.*

Dareton (Pop 650): small irrigation town set amid farms and belah scrub. Accommodation, stores and fuel. (*20/283*)

Cowanna: farming locality. Caravan park. (*27/276*)

WENTWORTH (Alt 37m; Pop 1500):* grazing and irrigation town on the confluence of the Murray and Darling Rivers (worth visiting*). Many historic buildings and museums including the Old Gaol. Also worth seeing is Weir and Lock No 10 (from here the Murray River falls 30.8m in its 827km journey to the sea!), and the Perry Sandhills* (5km along the Renmark road). Full town facilities. (*33/270*)

Plains south of Ana Branch support either dense growths of belah and rosewood, or sparse growth of belah with a ground cover of saltbush. Some low sandy rises. **Rest area.** (*59/244*)

Darling River Ana Branch: deep, occasionally water-filled channel which flows during moderate to high floods on the Darling River. Ana branches, unlike distributaries, rejoin the main channel further downstream. (*98/205*)

Floodplains to the east of the road, dotted with small, normally dry, lakes, some of which are visible from high points near Nialia Lake.

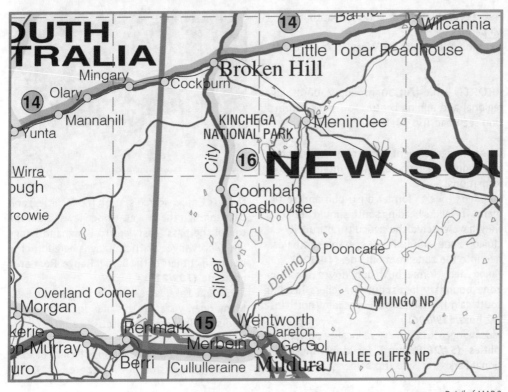

Detail of MAP 2

Popilta Lake:* normally a dry lake, visible from the road. A nearby parking area (**rest area**) allows views over the lake. The lake forms part of the flood-out country from the nearby Ana Branch of the Darling River. Some low sand dunes are nearby. (*161/142*)

Coombah (Alt 60m; Pop 5): roadhouse settlement. Limited stores, fuel. (*178/125*)

Low rises support belah woodlands.
Langwell Flats: broad plain on the edge of the saltbush country.
Plains: vast, mostly treeless plains offer expansive views* across the saltbush from the tops of low rises. Time zone boundary hereabout. Travellers heading north gain 1/2 hour, travellers heading south lose 1/2 hour.
Undulating country covered with a sparse growth of mulga forms part of the Barrier Range.

The interesting rock formations to the west are The Pinnacles.

BROKEN HILL (Alt 304m; Pop 25000): large mining and regional centre. For more information see Road Trip 14, Day 2. (*303/0*) *Road Trip 14 connects.*

DAY 2: BROKEN HILL-TIBOOBURRA
via Packsaddle

Road to Take: Silver City Highway
Grade 3 (lengthy sealed sections)
Total Distance: 334km (4:15)
Intermediate Distances:

	Km	Hours
Broken Hill-Packsaddle	177	(2:15)
Packsaddle-Milparinka turnoff	118	(1:30)
Milparinka turnoff-Tibooburra	39	(0:30)

Average Vehicles per Day: 60 south of Milparinka
Regions Traversed: Far West, Corner Country

BROKEN HILL (Alt 304m; Pop 25000): large regional and mining centre. For more information see Road Trip 14, Day 2. (*0/334*)

Barrier Range: ancient set of ranges, rocky hills and undulating lowlands. Many interesting rock formations.
Stephens Creek:* former bush pub and settlement. Travellers heading south should note that they have entered the agricultural fruit fly exclusion zone - no fruit or vegetables to be carried into the zone from outside. (*14/320*)
Yanco Glen:* former bush pub, now a ruin. Time zone boundary hereabout. Travellers heading south gain 1/2 hour, travellers heading north lose 1/2 hour. (*29/306*)
Mootwingee Road junction: locality only; no facilities. (*54/280*) Turn **E** for Mootwingee National Park - see Side Trip below.

Side Trip

Take the 154km return journey to Mootwingee National Park**, an interesting park set among the rounded domes and ridges of the Byngnano Range. Cypress pines are common on hilltops, contorted into fascinating shapes. Mulga occupies the intervening flats. Wild flowers are often present after good rains. Rocky gorges and waterholes abound. Self-guided walking tracks can be taken. It is worth spending two or three days exploring this area, as some localities have a powerful presence. There is restricted access to Mootwingee Historic Site** and Aboriginal paintings; enquire locally about tours. Good camping but no stores or fuel.

Byjerkerno Ridge:* interesting rocky ridge near the road, south of which is Mt Deering (449m). The area goes by the name of Euriowie. Many old mines are in this district (no public access). Low ranges and ridges line the western side of the road for many kilometres. Vegetation is mostly mulga shrublands.

Tibooburra buildings, NSW

Fowlers Gap: research station (no facilities) and pass through the ranges. Good views* from the top of the pass: eastward to Byngnano Range and Mootwingee district. Ranges here form the northern outliers of the Barrier Range. **Rest area** adjacent. (*109/225*)
Bancannia Lake: large salt lake lying to the east. Many open vistas in this area including views to distant low ranges. Saltbush country.

Packsaddle (Pop 5): roadhouse facility of some interest. Limited store, fuel. **Rest area**. (*177/157*)

Plains near Packsaddle support a covering of mulga. Koonenberry Mountain (408m) is visible to the east on the skyline.
White Cliffs Road junction: locality only; no facilities. (*224/110*)
Sand dunes form an outlier of the Strzelecki Desert. Covered in various acacias. Mulga occurs on the intervening flats.
The Salt Lake:* large, normally dry salt lake visible from the road.
Undulating country offers good views*. Mt Brown (310m) lies to the west.
Milparinka turnoff: (*295/39*) Turn **W** for Milparinka (3km return) and Depot Glen/Mt Poole (38km return). **Milparinka** (Alt 162m; Pop 5)* is a former gold mining settlement, today virtually a ghost town with photogenic historic stone buildings* and an interesting bush pub*. Accommodation, fuel. Nearby Depot Glen* is an attractive gorge and waterhole, site of explorer Sturt's enforced six month encampment due to high temperatures and drought.

DAY TWO

- ● BROKEN HILL
  - RA 2:15
  - *177 Yanco Glen*
- ● Packsaddle
  - RA 1:30
  - *118*
- Milparinka turnoff
  - 0:30
  - *39*
- ● Tibooburra

Detail of MAP 3

Plains and jump-up hills present a wild arid landscape. Saltbush is common on the plains. Lines of gidgees follow the creeks.

Tibooburra (Alt 183m; Pop 150):** interesting small grazing town surrounded by granite boulders. The main street has a 'wild west' appearance. Good examples of 'bush' architecture. It is worth spending half-a-day here at least. Also visit Sturt National Park headquarters for its displays and lots of info. Good camping at Deadhorse Gully, adjacent to Golden Gully* historic display. Accommodation, stores, fuel. (**334/0**)

Accommodation
Family Hotel, Briscoe St, ©08 8091 3314, ✪$45
Tibooburra Hotel, Briscoe St, ©08 8091 3310, ✪$45
The Granites Motel, Cnr Brown/King Sts, ©08 8091 3305, ✪$60
The Granites Caravan Park, Cnr Brown/King Sts, ©08 8091 3305, ✪Site: $16 Van: $30-$50

Corner Country
This route through the Corner Country provides access to Camerons Corner, Cooper Creek and Innamincka. The journey should not be undertaken lightly, and certainly not by inexperienced drivers in conventional vehicles, for it crosses harsh gibber plains and soft sand dunes. Looking benign, almost beautiful at dawn and dusk, these relentless, never-ending landscapes are harsh at midday, and potentially deadly in midsummer.

Nonetheless, many people do travel here, for it is just within reach during the cool season school holidays for those who live in Australia's southeast, making this area, and Cooper Creek, one of the most popular outback destinations.

Warnings: roads impassable in wet weather and subject to flooding. The route may be closed for weeks. Avoid travelling at night. In summer always make local enquiries before proceeding, and inform a reliable person of your travel intentions. Stay out of this area in sum-

mer unless experienced. The routes are suitable for experienced drivers of high clearance conventional vehicles, with extreme care. Sand dunes with clay caps (which may be broken) are encountered west of Camerons Corner.
Note: no fuel between Cameron Corner-Innamincka 241km.

DAY 3: TIBOOBURRA-INNAMINCKA
via Camerons Corner

Roads to Take: Tibooburra-Innamincka Road, Old Strzelecki Track
Grade 4
Grade 3 Tibooburra-Cameron Corner
Warning: Remote Route. No fuel 241km
Total Distance: 381km (5:40)
Intermediate Distances:

	Km	Hours
Tibooburra-Cameron Corner	140	(1:50)
Cameron Corner-		
Old Strzelecki Track junction	110	(1:50)
Old Strzelecki Track junction-		
Innamincka	131	(2:00)

Average Vehicles per Day: approximately 20 west of Camerons Corner
Regions Traversed: Corner Country, Strzelecki Desert

▾

Tibooburra (Alt 183m; Pop 150):** interesting town. For more information see Day 2.(*0/381*) Head **S** then turn **W** for Cameron Corner. *Continue **S** for Packsaddle.*

Grey Range: gibber plains and downs supporting saltbushes. In the distance jump-ups can be seen.
Sand dunes form part of the Strzelecki Desert. These dunes are lower than further west and richly vegetated with mulga, whitewood, emu-bushes, and other plants. Elsewhere are sandplains, similarly vegetated. Beware of the bags you see hanging from some shrubs; they contain caterpillars that spray irritating substances. At one point the road crosses a huge dune and broad Waka Claypan*.

Sturt National Park: large semi-arid park of former grazing leases. Preserves gibber plains, jump-ups and sand dune country.
Frome Swamp: seasonal wetland lying just north of the road.
Fort Grey:* former station building, now a ranger's residence. Nearby is a camping ground behind the dunes of Lake Pinaroo*. The lake is often full of water. The dead trees are coolabahs, killed by a massive flood. It is worth spending a few hours at least in this very photogenic area. Self-guided walks can be taken around the lake, but first inform someone of your intentions. (*105/276*)

Cameron Corner:* place where three states meet. Also marks a major bend in the direction of the dingo fence, part of the world's longest fence. The gate must be kept shut at all times. A short distance **NE** is the famous 'Corner Store'. Stop here for a chat, get local information and absorb the atmosphere. Store, fuel. (*140/241*) Continue **W** along Bollards Lagoon Rd for Innamincka. *Continue **E** for Tibooburra.*

Bollards Lagoon Station: working station; no facilities. (*155/226*)
Sand dunes form part of the Strzelecki Desert. The dunes here are lower and more vegetated than those further west.
Twilight Bore: open sandplain country hereabouts. (*189/192*)
Sand dunes** form part of the Strzelecki Desert. Those near the Merty Merty Station turn-off are large (up to 15m), mostly devoid of vegetation and very photogenic. Also the contrast between the rust red dunes and the black soil of the floodplain is astounding; the colour changes from one to another in a matter of metres. Good views* of the floodplain from atop the highest and most westerly dune. Elsewhere dunes support sand-hill canegrass, with emu-bushes (with fuchsia-like flowers) on their lower slopes. Between the dunes (swales) are sandy flats supporting emu-bushes and claypans.
Floodplain forms part of Strzelecki Creek system, a distributary of Cooper Creek. Black soil

Sand dune, south of Innamincka, SA

plains support a covering of coolabahs, with grasses after floods.

Merty Merty Station turnoff: (**250/131**) Continue **N** for Innamincka. Continue **S** for Tibooburra.

Floodplains form part of Strzelecki Creek system, a distributary of Cooper Creek. Black soil plains support a covering of coolabahs, with grasses after floods.

Strzelecki Track junction: locality only; no facilities. (**317/64**) Turn **E** for Innamincka. *Turn S for Cameron Corner.*

Della Gas Field: no services available. (**325/56**) Sand dunes line the road and form part of the Strzelecki Desert.

Innamincka (Alt 50m; Pop 10):* former droving township of which little remains, set on the banks of Cooper Creek. Present community dates from the 1970s. Interesting settlement, and only supply point in a large area. Enquire here for information regarding roads, camping and Innamincka Regional Reserve. River cruises. Accommodation, store, fuel. (**381/0**) *Road Trip 8 connects.*

Accommodation
Innamincka Hotel/Motel, Main St, ©08 8675 9901, ✪$65
Innamincka Trading Post Cabins, Main St, ©08 8675 9900, ✪$65

West of Innamincka, along the 15 Mile Track (Grade 4), are a number of camping areas set beside the waterholes of Cooper Creek, all within 20km of the settlement. Sites include Queerbidie Waterhole, Policemans Waterhole, Ski Beach, and Minkies Waterhole. Note that all camping areas

except Queerbidie (also called Town Common) require a Desert Parks Pass. East of Innamincka are other waterhole camping sites; see the notes to Road Trip 8.

The Strzelecki Track
Innamincka-Lyndhurst
Slicing a north-south route through the eastern arid regions of northern South Australia, the Strzelecki Track provides ready access to Cooper Creek and Sturt's Stony Desert. On its way it passes through some of Australia's driest country, which lies in the rain-shadow of the Flinders Ranges in the vicinity of Mt Hopeless. It also crosses The Cobbler and Strzelecki Deserts, passing within view of saltlakes and claypans. Formerly a droving trail, today's Strzelecki Track was reconstructed to service the Moomba Gas Fields. It is this route that provides the main tourist access to and from Cooper Creek.

The Strzelecki Track is suitable for drivers of conventional vehicles with care, although those travellers without outback unsealed road experience will find it quite an adventure.

Warnings: roads may be impassable when wet and subject to flooding. Avoid travelling at night. Always make local enquiries before proceeding, and inform a reliable person of your travel intentions. Stay out of this area in summer unless experienced - inform a reliable person of your intentions if travelling at this time. The roads are suitable for conventional vehicles if extreme care is taken - experienced drivers only; high clearance desirable. The main Strzelecki Track (Lyndhurst-Innamincka) is usually well-maintained, though drifting sand can cover the road.
Note: no fuel available between Innamincka-Lyndhurst 471km.

Tibooburra

1:50   140 *Fort Grey*

Cameron Corner

1:50   110

Old Strzelecki Track junction

67

2:00   Strzelecki Track junction

64

Innamincka

DAY THREE

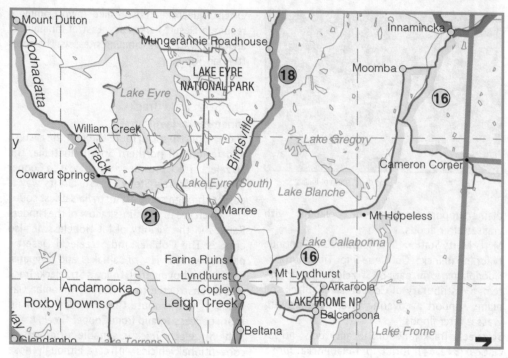

Detail of MAP 5

DAY 4: INNAMINCKA-LYNDHURST
via Strzelecki Crossing

Road to Take: Strzelecki Track
Grade 3
Warning: Remote Route. No fuel for 471km
Total Distance: 471km (6:50)
Intermediate Distances:

	Km	Hours
Innamincka-Strzelecki Crossing	197	(2:50)
Strzelecki Crossing-Lyndhurst	274	(4:00)

Average Vehicles per Day: 45 near Strzelecki Crossing
Regions Traversed: Strzelecki Desert, Saltlakes

Innamincka (Alt 50m; Pop 10):* former droving township. For more information see Day 3. (*0/471*)

Sand dunes line the road and form part of the Strzelecki Desert.

Della Gas Field: no services available. (*56/415*)
Old Strzelecki Track junction: locality only; no facilities. (*64/407*) Continue **W** for Moomba. *Continue E for Innamincka.*

Strzelecki Creek floodplain supports coolabah woodlands. Attractive after good seasons.

Floodplains support open tracts of country with a smattering of sand dunes.

Moomba: industrial complex and settlement lying 3km north. No facilities except for a telephone. Impressive, though alien-looking, gas plant. Natural gas is piped from here to Adelaide and Sydney. (*104/367*)

Sand dunes* form part of the Strzelecki Desert.

Merty Merty Road junction: locality only; no facilities. (*154/317*) Merty Merty lies 13km east. Continue **S** to Lyndhurst. *Continue N to Innamincka.*

Sand dunes* form part of the Strzelecki Desert. The dunes rise up to 20m above the plain. Acacias clothe the interdunal flats. Sand-hill canegrass occupies parts of the dunes. Grasses are common after rain.

Strzelecki Regional Reserve: large desert reserve preserving an arid wilderness.

Italowie Gorge, near Balcanoona, SA

Strzelecki Crossing: locality only; no facilities. Fairly pleasant area. (*197/274*)

Yaningurie Waterhole turnoff: (*200/271*) Turn **W** for Yaningurie Waterhole*. Camping area among the coolabahs.

Sand dunes* form part of the Strzelecki Desert. Various acacias occupy the interdunal flats. Sand-hill canegrass is found on the dunes. Grasses are common after rains.

Montecollina Bore:* flowing bore with adjacent wetland. (*249/222*)

The Cobbler Desert:* small bleached desert of clay nodules, stone and dunes. A bleak part of the countryside, very sparsely vegetated. Bulldust and sand drifts may occur here in very dry times. This section of the route is below sea level; near Moppa-Collina Channel the altitude is about -15m. The northern outliers of the Flinders Ranges can be seen in the distance.

Balcanoona turnoff: locality only; no facilities. (*276/195*) Balcanoona lies 150km south. Continue **W** to Lyndhurst. *Continue NE to Innamincka.*

Plains* support a sparse covering of saltbush. The countryside here is about as barren as it gets in Australia. This is also one of the driest spots in the country. Dry, rocky hills can be seen near Mt Hopeless (126m).

Blanchewater ruins:* old stone-built station buildings. Very photogenic in the afternoon light. Near Blanchewater ruins are mulga shrublands. Nearby Murnpeowie Station records the lowest average annual rainfall in Australia (128mm per annum). (*315/156*)

Plains supporting saltbush extend from the far distant Flinders Ranges, which lie on the southern skyline.

Dog Fence: part of the longest fence in the world.

Mount Freeling turnoff: (*397/74*) Mount Freeling (no facilities) lies 27km **E**. Continue **W** for Lyndhurst. *Continue N for Innamincka.*

Plains, low rises and rocky hills. Fair views from tops of rises. Saltbush dominates with occasional shrublands. Numerous mine sites are on northern side of the road near Mt Lyndhurst (286m). High peaks are visible to the east, including Mt Freeling (384m).

Plain covered with saltbush. Distant views to far ranges.

Lyndhurst (Alt 126m; Pop 30): bush township. For more information see Road Trip 18, Day 1. (*471/0*) *Road Trip 18 connects.* Head **NE** for *Innamincka.*

Flinders Ranges/Mid-North/Riverland
Lyndhurst-Copley-Arkartoola-Yunta-Burra-Morgan-Renmark-Mildura
The routes in the Flinders Ranges are accessible to all travellers, although the northern and easternmost areas could be difficult after rain. High summer temperatures in these areas might make for uncomfortable travelling too. Generally though, due to its elevation, the Flinders offers outback travellers moderate temperatures and an increase in rainfall - the region exists as a semi-arid peninsula virtually surrounded by a sea of aridity. Elsewhere, throughout the Mid-North, Riverland and Sunraysia districts the roads are in excellent condition and the countryside closely settled.

Warnings: beware of stock and kangaroos at night. Avoid travelling at night between Copley-Arkaroola-Yunta. Unsealed roads may be briefly impassable when wet. All routes are subject to flooding, especially flash-flooding, although such floods are usually short-lived. In summer, inform a reliable person of your travel intentions and make local enquir-

DAY FOUR

Innamincka

64

Old Strzelecki Track junction

2:50   90   Moomba

Merty Merty Road junction

43

Strzelecki Crossing

79

4:00   Balcanoona turnoff

195   Dog Fence

Lyndhurst

DAY FIVE

0:15 — Lyndhurst
34
1:25 — Copley
99 Camel Gap
— Arkaroola turnoff
I
0:30 — Balcanoona
I
— Arkaroola turnoff
30 Arkaroola-Mt Painter Sanctuary
— Arkaroola

ies before proceeding between Arkaroola-Yunta.

Note: no fuel available between Arkaroola-Yunta 304km.

DAY 5: LYNDHURST-ARKAROOLA
via Balcanoona

Roads to Take: Lyndhurst-Copley-Arkaroola Road
Grade 3
Total Distance: 165km (2:10)
Intermediate Distances:

	Km	Hours
Lyndhurst-Copley	34	(0:15)
Copley-Balcanoona	100	(1:25)
Balcanoona-Arkaroola	31	(0:30)

Average Vehicles per Day: 20 north of Yunta; 40 east of Copley
Regions Traversed: Flinders Ranges

Lyndhurst (Alt 126m; Pop 30): bush township. For more information see Road Trip 18, Day 1. (*0/165*) Head **S** for Copley.

For information on the route between Lyndhurst and Copley see Road Trip 18, Day 1.

Copley (Alt 238m; Pop 100): interesting township. For more information see Road Trip 18, Day 1. (*34/131*) *Road Trip 18 connects.* Turn **E** for Arkaroola. *Turn **N** for Lyndhurst.*

Low ranges* offer very good views of rolling saltbush-covered hills. Distant ranges are visible to the west.
Hilly country offers reasonable views across grasslands. Mt Jeffery (729m) is visible to the south.
Camel Gap:* watershed pass set between low rocky ranges; quite scenic. Interesting shale formations (climb a nearby hillslope for a look - take care on loose rocks). (*74/91*)

Iga-Warta:* store, camping area. Campbell Bald Hill (845m) is visible to the south. Adnyamathanha Cultural Tours are available. (*92/73*)
Nepabunna: no facilities. Aboriginal community of the descendants of the Adnyamathanha people. Northwards, Mt Rowe (900m) can be seen. (*97/68*)
Undulating country offers good views of ranges, especially the prominent Mt McKinlay (1050m) to the north.
Italowie Gorge:* attractive rocky gorge and creek bed. Photogenic cypress pines dot the ridges. Good spot for lunch or camping. Waterholes. It is worth walking a short distance upstream. River red gums provide shade. (*122/43*)
Balcanoona Plain offers good westward views.
Arkaroola turnoff. (*133/32*) Continue **E** for Balcanoona, 1km ahead. *Head **W** for Copley.*
Balcanoona: ranger station for Gammon Ranges National Park. No facilities except for park information, water and a telephone. (*134/31*) From Balcanoona an unsealed road (Grade 4) leads to Lake Frome - make local enquiries before proceeding.

Return **W** to Arkaroola turnoff (*135/30*) and turn **N**.

Weetootla Gorge turnoff: (*136/29*) Turn **W** for the 10km return (Grade 4) road to Weetootla Gorge, an attractive gorge and camping area. Walking trails lead from here deeper into the Gammon Ranges National Park. Grindells Hut is a long but fairly easy walk.
Undulating country offers good to great views* of the Munyalinna Valley and nearby ranges. The ranges are spectacular near Arkaroola.
Arkaroola-Mt Painter Sanctuary:** privately owned sanctuary preserving fine examples of arid mountain landscapes. Camping restricted to Arkaroola settlement.
Paralana Hot Springs turnoff: (*159/6*) Take this **NE** Grade 4 drive (maximum 54km return) to at least Welcome Pound*** one of the best arid mountain views in southern Australia. Further on is Paralana Hot Springs* sulphurous and

slightly radioactive springs with interesting algal formations. En route are fantastic ranges views**.

Arkaroola (Alt 488m; Pop 20):** privately-owned tourist settlement located in the spectacular arid mountain setting of the Arkaroola-Mt Painter Sanctuary. Geological formations, gorges, waterholes, lookouts, hot springs located in the area. Worth spending a few days here. 4WD tours available, walking trails. Accommodation, store, fuel. (*165/0*) *Head S for Balcanoona.*

Accommodation

Arkaroola-Mt Painter Sanctuary Resort, ©08 8431 7900, ⊙$45-$110

Arkaroola-Mt Painter Sanctuary Resort Caravan Park, ©08 8431 7900, ⊙Site: $17 Van: $90

A 25km return (Grade 4) journey to the west of Arkaroola will take you to The Pinnacles*, Bolla Bolanna Spring and smelter ruins*, and Noodoonooldoona Waterhole.

DAY 6: ARKAROOLA-YUNTA
via Balcanoona

Road to Take: Arkaroola-Balcanoona-Yunta Road
Grade 3
Warning: Remote Route. No fuel 304km
Total Distance: 304km (4:00)
Intermediate Distances:

	Km	Hours
Arkaroola-Balcanoona	32	(0:30)
Balcanoona-Yunta	272	(3:30)

Average Vehicles per Day: 20 north of Yunta
Regions Traversed: Flinders Ranges, Saltlakes, The North-East

Arkaroola (Alt 488m; Pop 20):** privately-owned tourist settlement. For more information see Day 5. (*0/304*) *Head S for Balcanoona.*

For details of the route between Arkaroola and Balcanoona see Day 5.

Arkaroola turnoff: (*30/274*) Turn **E** for Balcanoona. Turn **W** for Yunta turnoff.

Yunta turnoff: (*31/273*) Turn **S** for Yunta. *Turn E for Balcanoona/Arkaroola.*

Balcanoona Plain: broad plain supporting a cover of Mitchell grass, unusual in these parts. Good views*.

Plains: broad open plains support tracts of saltbush shrublands. Westward views to the ranges. En route an old grave is passed, as well as Prism Hill, recognisable by the dune sticking out of its side.

Blinman turnoff: locality only; no facilities. (*72/232*) Turn **SE** for Frome Downs. *Turn N for Balcanoona.*

Plains and low rises cross numerous creeks draining the mountains lying to the west. Open country provides expansive views* across the saltbush.

Dog Fence: gates to be kept closed at all times.

Frome Downs Station: working station; no facilities. (*135/169*)

Dog Fence: gates to be kept closed at all times.

Plains supporting open saltbush country with views to far distant ranges. Belah patches occasionally occur, providing some shelter from the winds. Elsewhere grow prickly wattles which always seem to be full of birds.

Low hills* support attractive tracts of bluebush and saltbush. The striking Mt Victor (465m) lies to the east.

Waukaringa ruins:* worth stopping here to explore the ruins (please do not disturb anything). Old gold mining township. The mine can be seen some distance away on side of the hill - no access. Very photogenic buildings and countryside. (*269/35*)

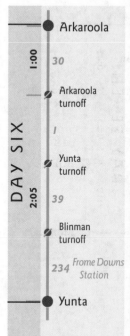

Road Trip 16

DAY SIX

1:00

● Arkaroola

30

⌀ Arkaroola turnoff

1

⌀ Yunta turnoff

39

⌀ Blinman turnoff

234 Frome Downs Station

2:05

● Yunta

Old ruin, Waukaringa, SA

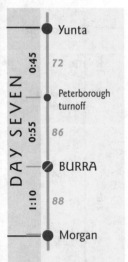

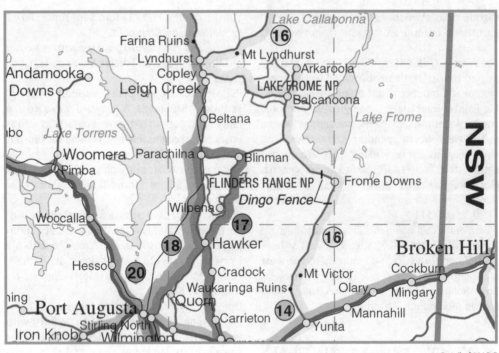

Detail of MAP 5

Low hills form part of the Olary Hills. The road climbs and dips, passing through attractive bluebush-covered slopes. Near Yunta is the immense bulk of Tappawuppa (611m). Good views* from the tops of the rises.

Yunta (Alt 303m; Pop 150): interesting township. For more information see Road Trip 14, Day 3. (**304/0**) *Road Trip 14 connects. /Head* **N** *for Frome Downs.*

DAY 7: YUNTA-MORGAN
via Burra

Roads to Take: Barrier Highway, Highway 64
Grade 1
Total Distance: 246km (2:50)
Intermediate Distances:

	Km	Hours
Yunta-Peterborough turnoff	72	(0:45)
Peterborough turnoff-Burra	86	(0:55)
Burra-Morgan	88	(1:10)

Average Vehicles per Day: 1000 near Peterborough turnoff
Regions Traversed: The North-East, Mid-North, Riverland

Yunta (Alt 303m; Pop 150): interesting township. For more information see Road Trip 14, Day 3. (**0/246**) Head **SW** along the Barrier Hwy for Burra.

For information about the route between Yunta and the Peterborough turnoff see Road Trip 14, Day 3.

Peterborough turnoff: (**72/174**) Peterborough lies 14km **W**. *Road Trips 14 and 17 connect.* Continue **S** to Burra. *Continue* **NE** *to Terowie.*

For information about the route between Peterborough turnoff and Burra see Road Trip 17, Day 4.

Detail of MAP 2

BURRA (Alt 474m; Pop 2000):** historic cop- per mining town. For more information see Road Trip 17, Day 4. (*158/88*) Turn **SE** onto Hwy 64 for Morgan. *Turn **N** for Yunta.*

Hilly country* offers good views. This treeless countryside supports grasslands and saltbush. Forms part of the Bald Hill Range. Stein Hill (605m) lies to the west.

Plains clothed in saltbush offer broad vistas. The countryside is suprisingly arid (around 220mm of rainfall a year) due to a rainshadow effect of the ranges visible to the west.

Whites Dam Conservation Park: belah and red mallee dominates the vegetation. No facilities.

Morgan (Alt 11m; Pop 450):** historic railway town and former Murray River port. Numerous photogenic stone buildings, especially along Railway Terrace*. Worth seeing: old railway area** and wharves, heritage trail*, ferry dock- yard (tours available), Port of Morgan Historic Museum*, Morgan-Whyalla Pumping Station

(tours available), fossil quarry* (1km south). On the opposite side of the river is the Morgan Con- servation Park*, an area of floodplain support- ing river red gums and wetlands. Accommoda- tion, stores, fuel. (*246/0*)

Accommodation

Colonial Motel, 1 Federal St, ©08 8540 2277, ✪$65
Terminus Hotel/Motel, Railway Tce, ©08 85402006, ✪$35-$55
Morgan Riverside Caravan Park, Main Rd, ©08 8540 2207, ✪Site: $18 Van: $35-$55

DAY 8: MORGAN-MILDURA via Overland Corner

Roads to Take: Highway 64
Grade 1
Total Distance: 268km (3:10)
Intermediate Distances:

	Km	Hours
Morgan-Renmark	115	(1:30)
Renmark-Mildura	153	(1:40)

DAY EIGHT

● Morgan

1:00

94

● Monash

6

⊘ Sturt Highway junction

15

— ● RENMARK

0:35

153

● MILDURA

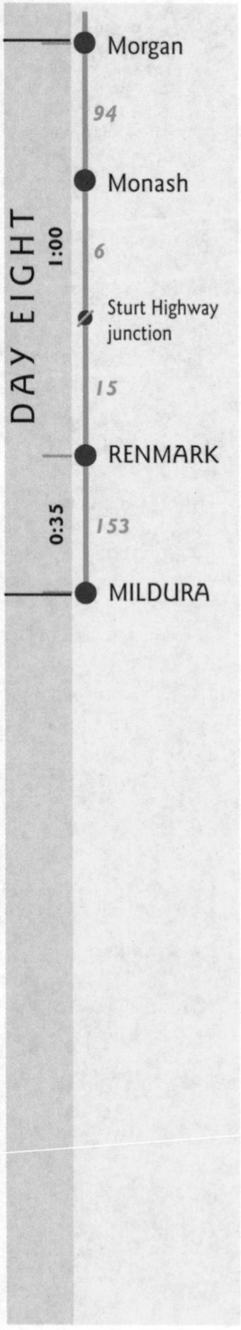

Average Vehicles per Day: 3000 near Mildura
Regions Traversed: Riverland, The Mallee, Sunraysia

Morgan (Alt 11m; Pop 450):* historic river port. For more information see Road Trip 7. (**0/268**) Stay on Hwy 64 heading **E** for Monash. *Stay on Hwy 64 heading **W** for Burra.*

Plains support mallee eucalypts and land cleared for grazing. Occasional river views*. Cliffs of limestone harbour numerous fossils. Eastward lies a fruit fly exclusion zone - no fruit or vegetables to be brought into the zone from outside.
Pooginook Conservation Park: small park preserving mallee eucalypts and regenerating land clearances. Limited facilities; camping.
Plains support tracts of mallee eucalypts; some grazing country.
Devlins Pound: amphitheatre of cliffs lining the river.
Overland Corner turnoff: (**69/199**) Turn here for the historic settlement of Overland Corner*, an historic hotel constructed of limestone. There is a museum here. The Overland Walking Trail* leads to a pioneers' cemetery, copper mine, Aboriginal campsites and canoe tree, and a lookout above the river. Nearby is Herons Bend Reserve*,

an attractive reserve of river cliffs and river red-gums; picnic area.
Plains support mallee scrubs. Some clearings are given over to grazing.

Monash: small irrigation township. Interesting playground*. Store, fuel. (**94/174**)

Plain supports vineyards and patches of mallee eucalypts.
Sturt Highway junction: (**100/168**) Nearby is the Big Orange Lookout:* popular tourist stop near a 16m orange-coloured sphere. A short distance **S** is the irrigation town of Berri. *Road Trip 15 connects.* Turn **NE** for Renmark. *Turn **W** for Monash.*
Plain supports irrigation farms.

RENMARK (Alt 20m; Pop 4250):* sizeable irrigation farming town. For more information see Road Trip 15, Day 3. (**115/153**) *Road Trip 15 connects.*

For details on the route between Renmark and Mildura see Road Trip 15, Day 3.

MILDURA (Alt 54m; Pop 21000):** large regional centre situated in Victoria's Sunraysia district. For more information see Road Trip 15, Day 2. (**268/0**) *Road Trip 15 connects.*

Road Trip 17
Flinders Ranges Loop

**Adelaide-Port Augusta-Hawker-
Parachilna-Blinman-Wilpena-
Peterborough-Burra-Adelaide**
Total Distance: 1042km
Suggested Travelling Time: 5 days

Soak up the scenic Flinders Ranges

See the magnificent Flinders Ranges, the at-
tractive former railway township of Quorn,
Pichi Richi pass, the ruins at Kanyaka,
Parachilna Gorge, the Blinman mine ruins,
Stokes Hill Lookout, Bunyeroo Valley,
Wilpena Pound, and Terowie historic village.

Flinders Ranges Loop

The Flinders Ranges is perhaps one of the most
scenic areas in South Australia. It is an area of
high, upstanding quartzite cliffs, undulating but
elevated shale lowlands, and gently sloping pied-
mont plains. Crossing this country are sealed
roads, and all-weather unsealed roads, that take
the traveller past high mountains and rocky
bluffs, or into deep valleys and narrow gorges.
Elsewhere are broad plains offering sweeping
views across cropping country.

The Climate

Temperatures in the Flinders Ranges are moderated by altitude. Summer visits may be okay (still
expect temperatures in the mid-thirties) but
nights are pleasantly mild. Autumn and spring,
with warm days and cool nights, are the best
time to visit. Winters are generally fine, though
showery weather and cool winds can be unpleasant; nights are generally freezing at this
time. In winter, snowfalls are not unusual on
high ground, although they rarely last for more
than a day.

Capital City Connections
Distances in kilometres
SYDNEY-PORT AUGUSTA
via Great Western/Mitchell/Barrier Highways/
Route 56

	Intermediate	Total
Sydney	0	0
Nyngan	57	578
Cobar	131	709
Broken Hill	444	1153
Peterborough	284	1437
Port Augusta	131	1568

MELBOURNE-ADELAIDE
via Western/Dukes Highways

	Intermediate	Total
Melbourne	0	0
Ballarat	111	111
Horsham	188	299
Adelaide	432	731

The Route
Distances in kilometres

	Intermediate	Total
Adelaide	0	0
Port Augusta	312	312
Hawker	107	419
Parachilna	89	508
Blinman	32	540
Wilpena	64	604
Hawker	52	656
Peterborough	144	800
Burra	86	886
Adelaide	156	1042

Flinders Ranges
**Adelaide-Port Augusta-Hawker-
Parachilna-Blinman-Wilpena-Hawker-
Peterborough-Burra-Adelaide**
Most of the Flinders Ranges is accessible to all
travellers, although the northern and easternmost
areas could be difficult after rain. High summer
temperatures in these areas might make for uncomfortable travelling too. Generally though, due
to its elevation, the Flinders offers outback travellers moderate temperatures and an increase in
rainfall - the region exists as a semi-arid penin-

ADELAIDE

5

ENFIELD & PROSPECT

5

GEPPS CROSS

38

Lower Light

12

Dublin

5

Windsor

8

Wild Horse Plains

12

Inkerman

14

Port Wakefield

32

Lochiel

DAY ONE 2:10

sula virtually surrounded by a sea of aridity. No-where else in this country can the traveller pass from dusty saltbush plains to park-like cypress pine woodlands dotted with grass-trees, all within the space of a few kilometres.

With its good network of roads and easy accessibility, the Flinders Ranges offers travellers a taste of spectacular mountainous country tinged with some far outback horizons. Destinations include Wilpena Pound, the old copper mining town of Blinman, the incredible Bunyeroo Valley, as well as numerous gorges.

Elsewhere the route passes through settled country and offers good driving conditions.

Warnings: beware of stock and kangaroos at night north of Hawker. Avoid travelling at night between Parachilna and Hawker via Wilpena. Unsealed roads may be briefly impassable when wet. All routes are subject to flooding, especially flash-flooding; such floods are usually short-lived.

DAY 1: ADELAIDE-PORT AUGUSTA via Crystal Brook

Road to Take: Highway One
Grade I
Total Distance: 312km via Crystal Brook (3:25)
Intermediate Distances:

	Km	Hours
Adelaide-Crystal Brook	198	(2:10)
Crystal Brook-Port Pirie turnoff	22	(0:15)
Port Pirie turnoff-Port Augusta	92	(1:00)

Average Vehicles per Day: 5000
Regions traversed: Adelaide Plain, Mid-North

▼

ADELAIDE (Alt 43m; Pop 1023000):** state capital of South Australia. For more information see Road Trip 15, Day 4. (*0/312*) Head **N** on Highway One for Port Pirie.

Parklands surround the city of Adelaide and North Adelaide. Attractive area.

ENFIELD & PROSPECT: Adelaide suburban areas. Full facilities.

Head **N** along King William Street, which becomes O'Connel Street in North Adelaide; follow Main North Road to Gepps Cross.

GEPPS CROSS: Adelaide suburb. Full facilities. (*10/302*)

Head **N** along Port Wakefield Road (Highway I).

Plain supports urban development to the east of the highway. Elsewhere are industrial areas. Caravan park en route.

Plains support market gardens and grazing from St Kilda turnoff to north of Wild Horse Plains.

Lower Light: small farming township. Store, fuel. (*48/264*)

Dublin: small farming township. Store, fuel. (*60/252*)

Windsor: small farming township. Store, fuel. (*65/247*)

Wild Horse Plains: farming township. Store, fuel. (*73/239*)

Plains cleared for grazing and cropping.

Inkerman: small farming community. Store, fuel. (*85/227*)

Port Wakefield (Alt 4m; Pop 500):* old gulf port with historic buildings. Heritage walk* Accommodation, stores, fuel. (*99/213*)

Accommodation

Port Wakefield Motel, Main Rd, ℂ08 8867 1271, ✪$60

Port Wakefield Caravan Park, Wakefield St, ℂ08 8867 1151, ✪Site: $13 Van: $20-$45

Plains and low rises support grazing and cropping. Kangaroo Hill (234m) is visible to the east

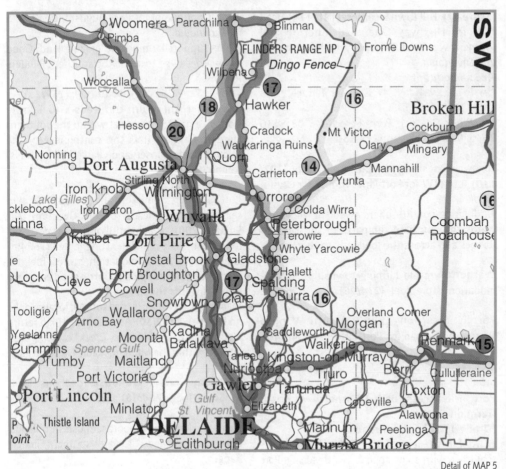

Detail of MAP 5

DAY ONE (continued)

2:10

● Lochiel

17

● Snowtown

26

● Redhill

13

● Merriton

5

⁄ Crystal Brook turnoff

6

● CRYSTAL BROOK

4

⁄ Highway One junction

0:15

12

● Warnertown

6

● Port Pirie turnoff

while South Hummock Range is visible to the west.

Lochiel: small farming township. Store, fuel. (*131/181*)

Plains and low rises given over to grazing and cropping. The normally dry Lake Bumbugga lies to the east. Saltworks located at the lake's southern end.

Snowtown (Alt 103m; Pop 500):* interesting small country town lying just off the highway. Accommodation, stores, fuel. (*148/164*)

Plains and low rises support grazing and cropping. Hummock Range lies to the west.

Redhill (Alt 92m): farming township located on the Broughton River. Store, fuel. (*174/138*)

Low rises support farmlands along the Broughton River. The Bluff is (365m) visible to the south.

Merriton: small township situated on the Broughton River. Store, fuel. (*187/125*)

Crystal Brook turnoff: locality only; no facilities. (*192/120*) Turn **NE** for Crystal Brook. *Turn **S** for Snowtown.*

CRYSTAL BROOK (Alt 111m; Pop 1700):* delightful town set at the end of the southern Flinders Ranges. Worth seeing: Crystal Brook Museum, Bowman Park Native Fauna Reserve

Road Trip 17

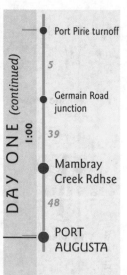

DAY ONE *(continued)*   1:00

- Port Pirie turnoff
- *5*
- Germain Road junction
- *39*
- Mambray Creek Rdhse
- *48*
- PORT AUGUSTA

(5km east). Full town facilities. **(198/114)** Head **NW** for Highway One road junction and Warnertown. *Head **SW** for Crystal Brook turnoff and Snowtown.*

Accommodation
Crystal Brook Hotel, 47 Railway Terrace, ©08 8636 2023, ✪$40
The Brook Caravan Park, Eyre Rd, ©08 8636 2640, ✪Site: $12 Van: $35-$50

Highway One road junction: locality only. **(202/110)** Turn **NW** for Port Pirie. *Turn **SE** for Crystal Brook.*
Undulating country offers sweeping views towards the southern ramparts of the Flinders Ranges and across the lowlands to the west.

Warnertown: old farming township. Accommodation, store, fuel. **(214/98)**

Port Pirie turnoff: **(220/92)** Turn **W** onto Warnertown Road for Port Pirie - see Side Trip below.

Side Trip
Port Pirie access roads (Warnertown Road/ Germain Road)
(Grade 1) 16km loop road
PORT PIRIE (Alt 4m; Pop 15500):* heavy industrial town with some appeal. Worth seeing: Port Pirie National Trust Museum*, Memorial Park*, Solomntown Beach, Arts Centre, Sampsons Cottage. Full town facilities.

Accommodation
Travelway Motel, 149 Gertrude St, ©08 8632 2222, ✪$60-$65
Abbacy Motel, 46 Florence St, ©08 8632 3701, ✪$50
Flinders Ranges Motor Inn, 151 MainRd, ©08 8632 3555, ✪$55-$95
Port Pirie Beach Caravan Park, Beach Rd, ©08 8632 4275, ✪Site: 15 Van: $30-$55
Port Pirie Caravan Park, Broughton Rd (3kmS), ©08 8633 0577, ✪Site: $12 Van: $30-$50

Germain Road junction: locality only - caravan park nearby. **(225/87)** Port Pirie lies 8km south-

west. Continue **N** for Port Augusta. *Continue **S** for Snowtown.*
Plains support farming and grazing land. Good eastward views* towards the southern Flinders Ranges.
Telowie Gorge access road turnoff: **(237/75)** An unsealed 16km return trip leads **E** to Telowie Gorge*, a narrow gorge set within the southern Flinders Ranges. It is the centrepiece of the Telowie Gorge Conservation Park. Walking trails, camping available.

Port Germein Road turnoff: **(243/69)** A 4km sealed loop road leads to **Port Germein** (Alt 9m; Pop 200)*, a delightful old wheat port surrounded by salt marshes. Long jetty* (1664m) is of interest. Accommodation, stores, fuel.
Plains support cropping country; good eastward views towards the ranges.
Mambrey Creek access road turnoff: locality only; no facilities. **(262/50)** An unsealed 10km return road leads **E** to the Mambrey Creek* camping area, located within the Mt Remarkable National Park.

Mambray Creek Roadhouse: roadhouse facility. Store, fuel. **(264/48)**

Plains and low rises support saltbush shrublands. Good eastward views* towards southern Flinders Ranges.
Highway 56 road junction: locality only; no facilities. **(288/24)** Continue **N** for Port Augusta. *Continue **S** for Port Pirie.*

PORT AUGUSTA (Alt 5m; Pop 14600):* large regional and industrial centre. For more information see Road Trip 14, Day 4. **(312/0)** *Road Trips 14, 18, 20 and 35 connect. Head **SE** for Port Pirie.*

▲

DAY 2: PORT AUGUSTA- PARACHILNA
via Hawker

Roads to Take: Port Augusta-Quorn-Hawker-Leigh Creek Road
Grade 1

Total Distance: 196km (2:20)
Intermediate Distances:

	Km	Hours
Port Augusta-Quorn	40	(0:35)
Quorn-Hawker	67	(0:45)
Hawker-Parachilna	89	(1:00)

Average Vehicles per Day: 180 north of Hawker
Regions Traversed: Flinders Ranges

PORT AUGUSTA (Alt 5m; Pop 14600):* large regional and industrial centre. For more information see Road Trip 14, Day 4. (*0/196*) Return **E** for Quorn turnoff.

Quorn turnoff: (*8/188*) Turn **N** for Stirling North and Quorn. *Turn **W** onto Hwy One for Port Augusta.*

Stirling North: small township. Store, fuel. (*9/187*)

Pichi Richi Pass:** narrow and steep valley negotiating the rugged western rampart of the Flinders Ranges. Occasional good views* if heading south. Keep an eye out for the Pichi Richi Railway.

QUORN (Alt 293m; Pop 1100):** attractive town with many fine photogenic old buildings, formerly a railway township. From here an historic railway runs regularly through the Pichi Richi Pass, following the old Ghan line. Railway workshop and museum** worth seeing. Museums and heritage walk. Enquire locally about walking trails to Dutchmans Stern and Devils Peak. A pleasant town to spend a few days. Full town facilities. (*40/156*)

Accommodation
The Mill Motel, 2 Railway Tce, ©08 8648 6016, ❂$85
Transcontinental Hotel, 15 Railway Tce, ©08 8648 6076, ❂$55
Quorn Caravan Park, Silo Rd, ©08 8648 6206, ❂Site: $17 Van: 35-$55

North of Quorn, within 35km along a Grade 3 unsealed road, lies Warren Gorge*, a pretty gorge with ribs of red rock. Nice spot for a picnic, with waterholes, and flowing creeks at the end of win-

ter. Camping is okay. Further north is Buckaringa Gorge,* a small attractive gorge where the surrounding hills are dotted with cypress pines.

Farming country offers distant views.
Willochra Plain: saltbush and grass-covered plain that has an air of desolation. Once this area was farmed for wheat, hence the number of township ruins. The aridity of the area could support neither farms nor close settlement. On the northern side of the Willochra Creek crossing (western side of road) are the ruins of Willochra*.
Gordon (Alt 235m): former township of which little remains. (*74/122*)
Kanyaka:* old station buildings. It is worth seeing these impressive ruins. (*81/115*)
Plains (forming part of the Willochra Plain) provides good views* to nearby ranges.
Wilson:* former settlement with scattered ruins. (*91/105*)

Hawker (Alt 315m; Pop 300):* small grazing and tourist town. Interesting old buildings including the railway station. Heritage walk and museum. Accommodation, stores, fuel. Farm accommodations are in the area. (*107/89*) Turn **NW** onto Leigh Creek Rd for Parachilna. *Turn **SW** for Quorn.*

Accommodation
Hawker Hotel/Motel, Elder Tce, ©08 8648 4102, ❂$40-$70
Outback Chapmanton Motor Inn, 1 Wilpena Rd, ©08 8648 4100, ❂$75
Flinders Ranges Caravan Park, Hawker-Leigh Creek Rd, ©08 8648 4266, ❂Site $18 Van: $35-$75
Hawker Caravan Park, Chaceview Tce, ©08 8648 4006, ❂Site: $18 Van: $65-$75

Ranges* offer great views of saltbush-covered hills and rocky ridges. Nearby Wonoka Hill rises to 630m.
Wonoka:* stone ruins set on an empty saltbush plain, very photogenic. Nearby abutments of a railway bridge are interesting. Distant ranges provide an attractive backdrop. (*125/71*)

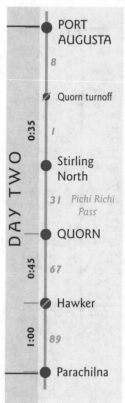

PORT AUGUSTA

8

Quorn turnoff

1

0:35

Stirling North

31 Pichi Richi Pass

QUORN

0:45

67

Hawker

1:00

89

Parachilna

DAY TWO

Road Trip 17

DAY THREE

0:35

Parachilna

18 *Parachilna Gorge*

Angorichina

14

1:05

Blinman

62 *Mt Flinders Ranges NP*

Wilpena turnoff

4

Wilpena

Lookout south of Moralana turn-off: worth a stop for excellent view of Mt Aleck (1128m), particularly interesting with uplifting clouds (common during winter). (*149/47*)

Plains and low rises covered with saltbush. At times, especially on the rises, there are excellent views* towards the Flinders Ranges, particularly near Edeowie Creek. When travelling south, the massive buttresses of Wilpena Pound seem to rise above the road. The highest mountain, St Marys Peak (1188m) is just visible. More obvious is Mt Abrupt (861m). An old railway line formation and scattered ruins line the road. En route Commodore Swamp, a seasonal wetland, is passed.

Branchina Gorge Road junction: locality only; no facilities. (*177/19*)

Commodore: ruins of old railway station. (*184/12*)

Parachilna (Alt 139m; Pop 20): small tourist and railway settlement. (*196/0*) Road Trip 18 connects. /Turn **S** for Hawker.

DAY 3: PARACHILNA-WILPENA via Blinman

Roads to Take: Parachilna-Blinman-Wilpena Roads
Grade 3
Total Distance: 96km (1:40)
Intermediate Distances:

	Km	Hours
Parachilna-Blinman	32	(0:35)
Blinman-Wilpena	64	(1:05)

Average Vehicles per Day: 180 north of Hawker
Regions Traversed: Flinders Ranges

Parachilna (Alt 139m; Pop 10): small grazing and railway township. For more information see Road Trip 18, Day 1. (*0/96*) Turn **E** for Blinman.

Plains support saltbush shrublands; good eastward views*.

Parachilna Gorge:** deep rocky defile with a sandy creek bed and shady river red gums. A good place to camp. Excellent views* of the ABC Range peaks. (*12/84*)

Angorichina: scenic area overlooking the ABC Range, the westernmost range of the Flinders. Accommodation, fuel. Camping available. (*18/78*)

Hilly country offers reasonable views.
Undulating country supports cypress pine woodlands.

Blinman (Alt 616m; Pop 120):* interesting old copper mining town. Former copper mining settlement and South Australia's highest township. Historic buildings, mine ruins* with walking track. Accommodation, store, fuel. (*32/64*)

Accommodation
North Blinman Hotel/Motel, Mine Rd, ℡08 8648 4867, ⬤$55-$65
Blinman Campground, Mine Rd, ℡08 8648 4867, ⬤Site: $12

Blinman South: small locality of a few houses. (*35/61*)

China Wall:* striking rock cliff. Photogenic in the afternoon light. The highest summit is Mt Emily (707m).

Flinders Ranges National Park:** spectacular rocky ranges, deep valleys, gorges, waterholes and attractive cypress pine-clad ridges. A popular area for scenic drives (especially Bunyeroo Valley and Brachina Gorge) and bushwalking. Includes St Marys Peak, the highest point in the Flinders, and Wilpena Pound, a virtually completely enclosed valley surrounded by rocky ranges. This park, like the spectacular country excluded from the park, is worth exploring for a few days. Good camping throughout the park - a permit is required and obtainable on access roads. The lookout* on the park's southern boundary has good views.

Dingley Dell Station ruins: camping area. (*62/34*)

Stokes Hill Lookout turnoff: (*79/17*) Turn **SE** for Stokes Hill Lookout**, probably the best, easily-accessible viewpoint in the Flinders Ranges.

The Bunkers Range, near Wilpena, SA

Most of the main ranges can be seen, taking in the geography of the central Flinders in one 360 degree view. The road to the summit is probably the highest in South Australia, approximately 750m.

Hucks Lookout* offer very good views towards the rugged ramparts of Wilpena Pound. Hilly country hereabouts. Grasstrees are common. (*82/14*)

Bunyeroo Valley turnoff: (*90/6*) Turn **NW** for ranges country** offering some of the best views in the Flinders Ranges. Big hills dotted with cypress pines and backed by rocky ridges. Mt Abrupt (861m) lies to the south-west. The road continues to Bunyeroo Creek*, a pretty, mostly dry, stream. Walking trails into Bunyeroo Gorge. Good camping nearby. Further on is Brachina Gorge**, a fascinating gorge cutting through the Heysen Range, lined with rocky cliffs, forming part of a geological trail. Camping is available. The road continues on to the main Hawker-Leigh Creek Road (see the notes above).

Wilpena turnoff: turn **W** for Wilpena. (*92/4*)

Wilpena (Pop 20):* tourist settlement at the entrance to Wilpena Pound**. Busy and popular bushwalking area on marked trails. Trails lead to St. Marys Peak, Wangara Lookout, Malloga Falls and Mt Ohlssen Bagge. Popular camping area. Accommodation, store, fuel. (*96/0*)

Accommodation

Wilpena Pound Resort, Wilpena Pound Rd, ℂ08 8648 0004, ✪$105

Wilpena Pound Camping and Caravan Park, Wilpena Pound Rd, ℂ08 8648 0004, ✪Site: $20

DAY 4: WILPENA-BURRA
via Peterborough

Roads to Take: Wilpena-Hawker-Orroroo Road, Highway 56, Barrier Highway
Grade 3
Grade 1 Wilpena-Hawker; Orroroo-Burra
Total Distance: 282km (3:35)
Intermediate Distances:

	Km	Hours
Wilpena-Hawker	52	(0:50)
Hawker-Orroroo	107	(1:25)
Orroroo-Peterborough	37	(0:25)
Peterborough-Burra	86	(0:55)

Average Vehicles per Day: 120 near Wilpena
Regions Traversed: Flinders Ranges, Mid-North

Wilpena (Pop 20):* tourist settlement. For more information see Day 3. (*0/282*)

Arkaroo Rock turnoff:* a short drive and walk leads to Aboriginal paintings. Very good views of the Wilpena Pound ramparts. (*11/271*)

Rawnsley Park turnoff: (*17/265*) Turn **W** for **Rawnsley Park** which offers a camping area and cabins, located at the foot of Rawnsley Bluff. Fuel available.

Elder Range Lookout:* great views of rocky ranges, excellent at sunset. (*27/255*)

Arkaba Hill Lookout:* more great views. (*30/252*) Plains suporting grasslands offer views* to the distant ranges. Chace and Druid Ranges are eastward, Elders Range and Hills of Arkaba are westward. The highest point in the Elders Range is Mt Aleck (1140m).

Hawker (Alt 315m; Pop 300):* small grazing and tourist town. For more information see Day 3. (*52/230*) Turn **SE** for Carrieton. *Turn **NE** for Wilpena.*

Undulating country offers good views over saltbush-clad grazing country.

Craddock (Alt 360m; Pop 5): former wheat farming township, now virtually a ruin, the area being unable to support farming. There are some

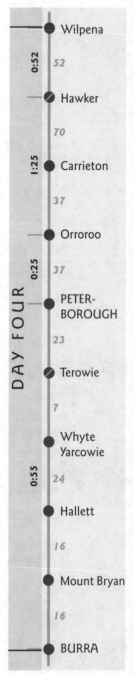

DAY FOUR

- Wilpena
- 0:52 | 52
- Hawker
- 70
- 1:25 | Carrieton
- 37
- Orroroo
- 0:25 | 37
- PETER-BOROUGH
- 23
- Terowie
- 7
- Whyte Yarcowie
- 0:55 | 24
- Hallett
- 16
- Mount Bryan
- 16
- BURRA

Road Trip 17

photogenic buildings; check to make sure they are unoccupied. Accommodation. (*80/202*)

Undulating country offers good views* of nearby hills. Saltbush country.

Carrieton (Alt 457m; Pop 200):* old wheat farming township that has survived. Many stone buildings. Accommodation, store, fuel. (*122/160*)

Eurelia (Alt 529m): former railway siding and present day terminus of an historic railway that runs from Peterborough. The Eurelia-Carrieton district is virtually the northern edge of the South Australian wheatbelt. (*136/146*)

Undulating country offers sweeping views across farmlands. Occasional ruins dot the landscape.

Orroroo (Alt 421m; Pop 650):* interesting small farming town. For more information see Road Trip 14, Day 4. (*159/123*) *Road Trip 14 connects.*

Black Rock: old farm ruins and railway siding. (*171/111*)

Undulating country offers broad vistas overlooking farming country. Distant range views.

PETERBOROUGH (Alt 533m; Pop 2300):* agricultural and railway town. For more information see Road Trip 14, Day 3. (*196/86*) *Road Trip 14 connects.*

Undulating country offers broad vistas across wheat cropping farmlands.

Terowie (Alt 498m; Pop 220):** former break-of-gauge railway town with numerous historic buildings* and a main street** little changed in one hundred years. Definitely worth visiting. Accomodation, stores, fuel. (*219/63*) *Road Trip 16 connects.* Turn **S** onto Barrier Hwy for Burra. *Turn **NW** onto Hwy 83 for Peterborough.*

Whyte Yarcowie (Alt 523m): farming township. Store, fuel. (*226/56*)

Undulating country supports wheat farms and grazing. Range views.

Hallett (Alt 602m): farming township; historic stone buildings. Store, fuel. (*250/32*)

Undulating country with range views. Wheat cropping and grazing. To the east lies Mt Bryan (936m).

Mount Bryan (Alt 519m): small farming township; interesting buildings. Store, fuel. (*266/16*)

Undulating country is given over to wheat farming and grazing. Broad vistas* toward ranges on either side of the route. Mt Cone (789m) lies to the east.

BURRA (Alt 474m; Pop 2000):** historic copper mining town. Numerous historic buildings, some dating back to the 1840s, with strong Cornish (and Welsh) influences. Many things to see such as the Thames Street Cottages*, Market Square* including Market Square Museum, Paxton Square* and Malowen Lowarth cottage museum*, the Dug Outs*, Unicorn Brewery Cellars*, old hotels*, Redruth Gaol*, various cottages, churches, railway station, smelter ruins*, the old mine site and buildings* (Australia's oldest), lookout*, and Ben Accord Mine Complex*. Full town facilities. (*282/0*) *Route 16 connects.*

▲

Paxton Square, Burra, SA

DAY 5: BURRA-ADELAIDE
via Riverton

Road to Take: Barrier Highway
Grade 1
Total Distance: 156km (2:00)
Intermediate Distances:

	Km	Hours
Burra-Riverton	62	(0:40)
Riverton-Adelaide	94	(1:20)

Average Vehicles per Day: 1000 near Burra
Regions Traversed: Mid-North, Adelaide Plain

BURRA (Alt 474m; Pop 2000):** historic copper mining town. For more information see Day 5. (*0/156*)

Undulating country offers good views*. Countryside given over to grazing and cropping.
Hanson: locality only. (*13/143*)
Portal Lagoon, a seasonal lake and wetland, lies to the east of the road. Mt North of Lake (670m) lies in the north-east.
Undulating country supports grazing and cropping. Tothill Range lies to the east.
Manoora: farming locality. (*43/113*)

Saddleworth (Alt 321m): small farming township. Store fuel. (*53/103*)

Riverton (Alt 269m; Pop 750):* pleasant farming town set on the Gilbert River. Interesting old buildings. Accommodation, store, fuel. (*62/94*)

Low rises offer reasonable views across the Gilbert River valley. Peters Hill lies to the east.

Tarlee (Alt 191m; Pop 200): old settlement of some interest. Accommodation, store, fuel. (*77/79*)

Undulating country provides pleasant views. The countryside is utilised for grazing and cropping. Light River crossing is of minor interest.
Low rises provide westward views across the northern Adelaide plain.
Roseworthy: locality. (*105/51*)
Sturt Highway junction: locality only. (*111/45*)
*Road Trip 15 connects. Turn **SW** for Adelaide. Turn **N** for Tarlee.*

For details of the route between Sturt Highway junction and Adelaide see Road Trip 15, Day 4.

ADELAIDE (Alt 43m; Pop 1023000):** state capital of South Australia. For more information see Road Trip 15, Day 4. (*156/0*) *Road Trips 15 and 20 connect.*

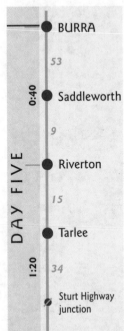

DAY FIVE

BURRA
53
0:40
Saddleworth
9
Riverton
15
Tarlee
34
Sturt Highway junction
1:20
45
ADELAIDE

Road Trip 18
Eastern Arid Connection

Port Augusta-Alice Springs via Birdsville
Total Distance: 2089km
Suggested Travelling Time: 6 days

> *Trek to Birdsville, Australia's most outback town*
>
> See the Afghan heritage of Marree, remote Birdsville, the old pub at Bedourie, the village of Beltana, Farina ruins, the Birdsville Track, gibber deserts, soaring sand dunes, Georgina River, Harts Range, the fossicking sites at Gemtree, and awesome arid landscapes.

Eastern Arid Connection

This road trip covers Australia's most arid country. If ever the expression 'Australia's dead heart' is apt, it is no more apt than here. For years at a time, low rainfall is the normal state of affairs. With rainfall less than 250mm per year on average, down to 125mm per year in parts of Sturts Stony Desert, this region presents a face of shimmering gibber plains, vivid red sand dunes and low barren jump-up hills. This is not unattractive country though; it presents to the traveller some of the best arid landscapes in the world.

Between those years of little or no rainfall are short periods, seasons almost, when torrential rains wheal in from the north-west, sometimes dumping the annual average precipitation overnight. Such wet periods correspond to vigorous monsoonal activity in the north of the country. Then flooding rains set the rivers of the Channel Country, and sometimes even the Central Australian rivers, flowing. Filling waterholes and river channels, their combined flows lead ultimately to Lake Eyre. Then the arid landscape turns into a garden of wildflowers, grasslands and brimming lakes.

This route can be undertaken by experienced drivers of 2WD vehicles in dry weather. Bear in mind that virtually the entire route north of Lyndhurst, a distance of nearly 1800km, is over unsealed roads.

The Climate

As befits the driest area in Australia, rainfall in this part of the country is low. Nonetheless light winter showers or heavy summer thunderstorms can be expected. Heavy rains during wet periods can close unsealed roads for weeks.

Stay out of the arid areas in summer. Maximum temperatures can be extreme, up to 48C with no shade. Nights can be very warm, around 26C. Best travel times are between autumn and spring. Though some warm to hot days can be experienced either end of this period, they rarely last for more than two to three consecutive days. Maximums will generally be in the low to high twenties. Nights are typically cool. In midwinter, cool days will be experienced, often with a wind. Maximums at this time are generally in the high teens. Nights are cold with occasional frosts. Springtime can be windy with the occasional duststorm.

Capital City Connections
Distances in kilometres
SYDNEY-PORT AUGUSTA
via Great Western/Mitchell/Barrier Highways/Route 56

	Intermediate	Total
Sydney	0	0
Nyngan	578	578
Cobar	131	709
Broken Hill	444	1153
Peterborough	284	1437
Port Augusta	131	1568

MELBOURNE-PORT AUGUSTA
via Western/Dukes Highways/Highway 1

	Total	Intermediate
Melbourne	0	0
Ballarat	111	111
Horsham	188	299
Adelaide	432	731
Port Pirie	215	946
Port Augusta	97	1043

Road Trip 18

The Route
Distance in Kilometres

	Intermediate	Total
Port Augusta	0	0
Quorn	40	40
Hawker	67	107
Leigh Creek	154	261
Marree	117	378
Birdsville	520	898
Boulia	380	1278
Jervois Station	463	1741
Alice Springs	348	2089

Flinders Ranges
Port Augusta-Marree
The Flinders Ranges exists as a semi-arid peninsula virtually surrounded by a sea of aridity. Nowhere else in this country can the traveller pass from dusty saltbush plains to park-like cypress pine woodlands dotted with grass-trees, all within the space of a few kilometres. With its good network of roads and easy accessibility, the Flinders Ranges offers travellers spectacular mountainous country tinged with some distant outback horizons.

Warnings: beware of stock and kangaroos at night. Avoid travelling at night. Unsealed roads may be briefly impassable when wet. All routes subject to flooding, especially flash-flooding; such floods are usually short-lived.

DAY 1: PORT AUGUSTA-MARREE
via Hawker

Roads to Take: Port Augusta-Hawker-Leigh Creek-Marree Road
Grade 3
Grade 1 Port Augusta-Lyndhurst
Total Distance: 378km (4:30)
Intermediate Distances:

	Km	Hours
Port Augusta-Quorn	40	(0:35)
Quorn-Hawker	67	(0:45)
Hawker-Parachilna	89	(1:00)
Parachilna-Copley	70	(0:45)
Copley-Lyndhurst	34	(0:25)
Lyndhurst-Marree	78	(1:00)

Average Vehicles per Day: 180 north of Hawker
Regions Traversed: Flinders Ranges, Saltlakes

▼

PORT AUGUSTA (Alt 5m; Pop 14600):* large regional and industrial centre. For more information see Road Trip 14, Day 4. (*0/378*) *Road Trips 14, 17, 20 and 35 connect.*

For information on the route between Port Augusta and Parachilna see Road Trip 17, Day 2.

Parachilna (Alt 139m; Pop 20): small tourist and railway settlement. (*196/182*) *Road Trip 17 connects.* Continue **N** for Leigh Creek. *Continue* **S** *for Hawker.*

Accommodation
Prairie Hotel, West Tce, ✆08 8648 4895, ✪$100-$230
Prairie Hotel Caravan Park, West Tce, ✆08 8648 4844, ✪Site: $12 Van: $65

Plains: good views* towards the western ramparts of the Flinders Ranges, especially in the late afternoon light; can also be attractive in the showery weather of winter. Saltbush is common.
Beltana turnoff: (*216/162*) Turn **NE** for **Beltana** (Alt 236m)**, an historic railway and Afghan township well worth visiting. All buildings are privately-owned and some are occupied - do not trespass. Information is available from Beltana roadhouse and the old police station. This 35km unsealed (Grade 3) loop road rejoins the main Hawker-Leigh Creek 10km south of Leigh Creek after passing through the scenic Puttapa Gap**, an attractive rocky gorge with old Ghan railway ruins and relics. The wild hops here are colourful during spring.

Beltana Roadhouse (Alt 200m; Pop 5): small roadhouse facility. Store, fuel. (*230/148*)

Lookout** south of Leigh Creek is definitely worth a stop. Excellent view of the flat-iron for-

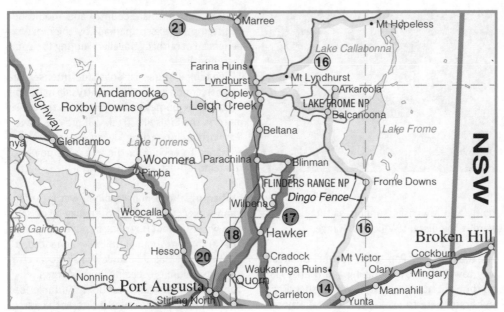

Detail of MAP 5

mations of the Mt Bayley Range (the best examples to be seen anywhere), and the broad saltbush plains leading to Mt Deception (691m). (*255/123*)

Aroona Dam turnoff: (*258/120*) Five unsealed kilometres **W** is Aroona Dam*, the water supply for surrounding townships. It is a pleasant area with picnic facilities set among rocky hills. Camping is okay.

LEIGH CREEK (Alt 260m; Pop 1800): modern mining town and district centre. Limited accommodation facilities (see Copley below). Stores, fuel. (*261/117*)

Copley (Alt 238m; Pop100):* former railway township with many interesting stone buildings. Today it is virtually a suburb of Leigh Creek. Accommodation, stores, fuel. (*266/112*) Road Trip 16 connects.

Accommodation

Leigh Creek Hotel, Railway Tce, ©08 8675 2281, ✪$50

Copley Caravan Park, Railway Tce, ©08 8675 2288, ✪Site: $20 Van: $30-$55

Coalfields: open cut mining has turned this landscape upside down.

Low ranges line the road, offering broad vistas. Plains mark the edge of the Flinders Ranges, whose purple jagged skylines mark the horizon. Saltbush is common.

Lyndhurst (Alt 126m; Pop 30): bush township with plenty of character. See the talc carvings. Five kilometres north, a short sidetrack leads to the Ochre Cliffs**, an ancient Aboriginal ochre mine. The cliffs here display numerous colours, and afternoons are best for photography. After rain, quartz crystals may be seen. Accommodation, store, fuel. (*300/78*) Road Trip 16 connects.

Accommodation

Lyndhurst Siding Hotel, Main Rd, ©08 8675 7781, ✪$55

Undulating country supports saltbush - good views*.

Farina:** ruined township, built as a wheat growing settlement. Many photogenic ruins, old equipment, railway relics, and more. Worth investigating, but please do not disturb anything. Camping area. (*325/53*)

Old House, Maree, SA

Plains and low rises support saltbush. Westward is the distant Willouran Range.

Marree (Alt 45m; Pop 150):** former Ghan railway township, now a grazing and tourist centre (but not at all touristy). Worth spending a few hours here to explore the old railway station*, a rebuilt mosque* (descendants of the Afghan cameleers still live here), and the Arabana Centre for its museum of artefacts and information about the surrounding district. Interesting buildings to photograph. Accommodation, stores, fuel. **(378/0)** *Road Trip 21 connects.*

Accommodation
Marree Hotel, Railway Tce South, ☎08 8675 8344, ✪$60
Marree Caravan and Campers Park, Cnr Birdsville Track (1kmE), ☎08 8675 8371, ✪Site: $14 Van: $30
Oasis Town Centre Caravan Park, Railway Tce South, ☎08 8675 8352, ✪Site: $12 Van: $35

▲

The Birdsville Track
Marree-Birdsville
The Birdsville Track, running between Marree and Birdsville, is outback Australia's most famous road, and leads to outback Australia's most famous town. This route is, in itself, a worthwhile travelling experience. A far cry from the days of lengthy 'horror stretches', today's Birdsville Track is a modern, upgraded, two-lane gravel and earth highway suitable for all vehicles in dry weather. Nonetheless, it crosses some of Aus-

tralia's most desolate country and should not be attempted, except perhaps by the most experienced of outback travellers, during the summer months.

High temperatures, lack of shade, intense glare and perception-distorting countryside make this a hazardous journey in hot weather. In the cooler months the Birdsville Track will provide travellers with an interesting 'desert experience' and a chance to encounter the awesome power of the remote Australian outback.

Warnings: road impassable in wet weather and subject to flooding; route may be closed for weeks. Avoid travelling at night. Stay out of this area in summer unless experienced; if travelling at this time always make local enquiries before proceeding, and inform a reliable person of your intentions. Suitable for drivers of conventional vehicles, with care.
Note: no fuel available between Marree-Mungerannie 205km; Mungerannie-Birdsville 315km.

DAY 2: MARREE-MUNGERANNIE
via Etadunna Station

Road to Take: Birdsville Track
Grade 3
Warning Remote Route between Marree-Mungerannie. No fuel Marree-Mungerannie 205km
Total Distance: 205km (3:30)
Average Vehicles per Day: 20 near Mungerannie
Regions Traversed: Saltlakes, Tirari Desert, Sturt's Stony Desert

▼

Marree (Alt 45m; Pop 150):* former Ghan railway township. For more information see Road Trip 1. **(0/205)**

Plains support a covering of saltbush. Low rises provide expansive views*. Numerous creek

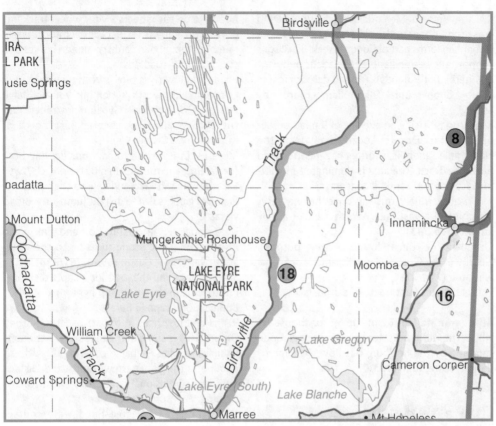

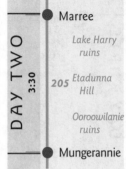

Detail of MAP 5

DAY TWO
3:30

- Marree
  - *Lake Harry ruins*
  - 205 *Etadunna Hill*
  - *Ooroowilanie ruins*
- Mungerannie

crossings and Frome River channels. Lake Marion is visible to the west.

Lake Harry ruins:* old stone building. Formerly a date palm plantation and camel trading post. A few date palms can still be seen. (**30/175**)

Jump-up hills: climb this stony mound (not when it is hot) for a vast view* of the saltbush plains and Lake Harry. Be careful on the steep slope.

Lake Harry: salt lake visible to the east.

Dog Fence: part of the longest fence in the world, separating sheep country from cattle country.

Clayton River: tree-lined watercourse. Adjacent is Clayton Station homestead - no facilities. (**53/152**)

Plains provide a barren, desolate landscape. Eastward lies country similar to Sturt's Stony Desert, westward lies vast empty plains occasionally interrupted by sand dunes. Sparse covering of saltbush.

Dulkinna Station: working station; no facilities. (**83/122**)

Plains and low rises offer sweeping views* across the saltbush plains and gibbers.

Cannuwaukaninna Bore: hot flowing bore. Be careful if investigating. (**110/95**)

Etadunna Hill, located near Etadunna Station, provides some vertical relief. A memorial cross commemorates the Aborigines and missionaries who ran and lived at the Killalpaninna Mission*, 20km to the north-west. Worth visiting when Lake Killalpaninna is full. At nearby Lake Kopperamanna is the site of a large Aboriginal trading centre where ochre, stone tools and other implements were traded for pituri, a plant used in sacred rituals. Traders converged here from across Australia in pre-European times. Permission for access is required from Etadunna Station. (**121/84**)

DAY THREE 5:00

● Mungerannie

Mungerannie Gap

315 *Mt Gason Bore*

State Border SA-QLD

● Birdsville

MV Tom Brennan Memorial:* small punt used to cross the Cooper in the old days. (*134/71*)

Floodplain forms part of Cooper Creek. Black soils support a low woodland of coolabahs and various herbs (after floods). A flood detour crosses nearby Cooper Creek/Lake Killamperpunna by ferry.

Sand dunes* rising an average of 9m, an outlier of the Tirari Desert. Locally known as the Natteranie Sandhills, a former hazard on the old Birdsville Track. The area is dominated by various acacias and sandhill canegrass.

Mulka Store ruins:* this was once the only service point in a vast area. Worth a bit of a look around. (*162/43*)

Ooroowilanie ruins:* former droving outpost. Nearby is the Ooroowilanie Swamp, a seasonal wetland. (*174/31*)

Plains support vast tracts of saltbush.

Mungerannie (Alt 62m; Pop 5): roadhouse facility. The old trucks* are worth seeing. Good camping by the hot bore overflow. Accommodation, store, fuel. (*205/0*)

▲

DAY 3: MUNGERANNIE-BIRDSVILLE
via Outside Track

Road to Take: Birdsville Track
Grade 3
Warning: Remote Route between Mungerannie-Birdsville
Total distance: 315km (5:00)
Average Vehicles per Day: 20 near Mungeranie
Regions Traversed: Sturt's Stony Desert, Channel Country

▼

Mungeranie (Alt 62m; Pop 5): roadhouse facility. For more information see Day 2. (*0/315*)

Mungerannie Gap: the major hill of the Birdsville Track. Good views from the top of the jump-ups. Area worth a brief exploration on foot, particularly in the late afternoon light. Please do not drive on the gibbers - your wheel track imprints will remain for decades. Unfortunately much of the gibber country along this road is scarred by off-road driving.

Plains and low rises offer sweeping views*.

Gypsum cliff:* worth a look but you will have to search for it on foot. Gypsum protrudes from the earthy cliff-face. Located just north of Kirrawadinna Creek.

Mirra Mitta Bore and ruins:* hot flowing bore (be careful) and ruins of an old station. (*35/280*)

Lake Howitt salt lake is visible to the west.

Plains of gibbers run to distant jump-ups. Broad vistas*.

Mt Gason Bore:* interesting bore and tank worth investigating. Old stone ruins lie to the west. Southward is Mt Gason (69m). (*81/234*)

Sand dunes* line the road for a short distance. Photogenic in the afternoon light.

Bodeys Bore: capped bore.

Plains and low rises form part of Sturt's Stony Desert. This is some of the most desolate country in Australia. A sparse covering of saltbush dominates the gibber-strewn landscape. Distant jump-ups. Occasional sand dunes* worth investigating. Awesome countryside**.

Damparanie Creek: tree-lined watercourse. Waterhole on the creek.

Plains of gibbers and the odd sand dune. Broad vistas*.

Floodplains* and sand dunes form part of the Diamantina (or rather Warburton Creek) floodout country. Plains supports a variety of grasses, herbs and saltbush, particularly after floods. Very scenic hereabout. About 85 kilometres south of Birdsville is Dead Mans Sandhill. Nearby are the graves of the Page family who perished in 1963.

Sand dunes* mostly run parallel the road. Various acacias and spinifex dominate the dunes. Floodplain country elsewhere. Coolabahs are common.

Floodplains support herbs and wildflowers after floods.

State Border between South Australia and Queensland. Time zone boundary - add 1/2 hour if heading south, subtract 1/2 hour if heading north.

Floodplains form part of the Diamantina River system.

Birdsville (Alt 43m; Pop 100):* Australia's most 'outback' town, though not necessarily its most remote, set by the Diamantina River. Interesting and historic droving settlement and customs post. Nowadays a tourist town. Worth seeing: Royal Hotel ruin; hot flowing bore*; Birdsville Hotel*, Birdsville Working Museum**, Burke and Wills tree, Pelican Point (picnics) and The Billabong (bird watching). Accommodation, store, fuel. (*315/0*) *Continue* **S** *on Birdsville Track for Mungerannie.*

Accommodation
Birdsville Hotel-Motel, Main St, ©07 4656 3244, ©$80
Birdsville Caravan Park, Florence St, ©07 4656 3214, ©Site: $17 Van: $60

An interesting side trip leads to Big Red*, also called Nappanerica Dune, 36km west of town on a Grade 4 road. It is probably the largest sand dune of the Simpson Desert. Climb to the top for great views. The track west of here is strictly 4WD only.

Channel Country Byway (Diamantina/ Birdsville Developmental Roads)
Birdsville-Boulia
This development road was constructed under the beef roads program to provide relatively easy access to far-flung cattle stations. As road trains replaced drovers, roads were upgraded, connecting remote stations to tiny bush townships and the outside world. This road virtually rings Queensland's Channel Country, passing through some of the most arid-looking country in Australia.

> **Warnings**: road impassable when wet; all roads subject to flooding. Avoid travelling at night. Inform a reliable person of your travel intentions and always make enquiries before proceeding. Stay out of this area in summer unless experienced. Recommended convoy travel only at this time. 4WD recommended between Birdsville and Bedourie; 2WDs okay with extreme care.

DAY 4: BIRDSVILLE-BOULIA via Bedourie

Road to Take: Channel Country Byway (Birdsville/Diamantina Developmental Road)
Grade 4
Grade 3 Boulia-Bedourie
Warning: Remote Route between Birdsville-Boulia
Total Distance: 380km (6:20)
Intermediate Distances:

	Km	Hours
Birdsville-Bedourie	189	(3:10)
Bedourie-Boulia	191	(3:10)

Average Vehicles per Day: 30 north and south of Bedourie
Regions Traversed: Channel Country

▼

Birdsville (Alt 43m; Pop 100):* Australia's most 'outback' town. For more information see Day 3. Continue **N** on Channel Country Byway for Bedourie.

Sand dunes* form part of the eastern edge of the Simpson Desert. Dunes support a sparse covering of sand-hill canegrass. Between the dunes are barren gibber flats. In some areas just north of Birdsville grow rare waddywood trees**; these slow-growing acacias are quite tall and worth having a look at. This is one of only three locations where they are found. Nearby is a rocky outcrop containing the Dingo Caves - good views from here at sunset. **Rest area** adjacent. (*14/366*)
Plains:* barren open country of gibbers, as desolate as it can get in the outback. The tops of rises offer fair views. Slight depressions support sparse saltbush and minor floodplains. Many areas contain nothing but rocks and sky, and are worth a brief walk around just to feel the immensity of the space, which can be quite awesome and belittling.
Cacoory ruins:* interesting stone-built ruin with a gidgee-lined creek nearby. There is also a bore and stock-watering facility. The low quartz ridge offers fair views. **Rest area**. (*80/300*)

DAY FOUR

3:10

● Birdsville
RA
168   Cacoory ruins
RA
Diamintina Dev. Road junction
21

● Bedourie
Georgina River
191

3:10

● Boulia

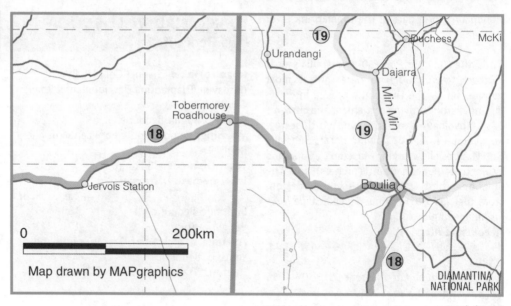

Detail of MAP 4

Plains and low rises support areas of saltbush on the plains with occasional low shrubs. The rises are quite barren, but offer expansive views*. Floodplains and flood-out lakes filling from the Georgina River/Eyre Creek. Dense growth of lignum (beware of cattle) and coolabah woodlands. Black soil country is completely impassable when wet. Glengyle Station (working station; no facilities) is passed en route.

Diamantina Developmental Road junction: locality only; no facilities. (**168/212**) Windorah lies 377km **E**. Turn **N** for Bedourie. *Continue* **S** *for Birdsville.*

Cattle Trough, Carcoory Ruins, Qld

Sand dunes set among saltbush (an uncommon plant at these latitudes). Acacias and spinifex dominate the dunes.

Bedourie (Alt 91m; Pop 100):* small bush township set upon low dunes. Interesting bush architecture, including the old pub*. Worth a couple of hours' exploration. Accommodation, store, fuel. (**189/191**)

Accommodation
Simpson Desert Oasis Motel, Herbert St, ©07 4746 1208, ✪$70
Simpson Desert Oasis Caravan Park, Herbert St, ©07 4746 1291, ✪Site: $14 (unpowered)

Plains with occasional sand dunes rise above sparsely covered gibber flats, while clay plains support Mitchell grass. Acacias and spinifex line the dunes.

Plains and low rises support a sparse covering of Mitchell grass. A range of jump-ups can be seen to the west. The jump-up, a flat-top hill, is called Twelve Mile Mountain. Occasional good views*. At the Breadalbane Station turn-off is a roadside grave. (**253/127**)

Georgina River:* multi-channelled stream supporting a coolabah woodland. River red gums are found near the main channels. Some waterholes form after floods. (*321/59*)

Plains* of clay stretch to the horizon, supporting a sparse covering of Mitchell grass.

Floodplain forms part of the Burke River. Some scattered trees break the horizon.

Boulia (Alt 143m; Pop 300):* small grazing town. For more information see Road Trip 19, Day 1. (*380/0*) Road Trip 19 connects.

▲

Donahue/Plenty Highways

Boulia-Alice Springs

This route offers the traveller the experience of solitude, and provides a mostly fair to good unsealed access between Central Australia and the Channel Country. The Donahue Highway connects Boulia to Tobermory Station via the Georgina River. The Plenty Highway has a variety of scenery: mulga-clad plains, endless vistas of Mitchell grass plains, attractive low sandstone hills and spectacular range country with some of the best fossicking sites in Australia.

Warnings: roads subject to flooding and impassable when wet. Avoid travelling at night. Always make local enquiries about conditions before proceeding. Stay out of this area during summer; if travelling at this time inform a reliable person of your travel intentions.

Note: no fuel available between Boulia-Tobermory Station 248km; Tobermory Station-Jervois Station 215km; Jervois Station-Gemtree 211km.

DAY 5: BOULIA-JERVOIS STATION
via Tobermory Station

Roads to Take: Donahue Highway, Plenty Highway

Warning: Remote Route between Boulia-Jervois Station. No fuel: Boulia-Tobermory

Station 248km, Tobermory Station-Jervois Station 215km

Grade 4

Grade 3 NT Border-Jervois Station

Total Distance: 463km (7:05)

Intermediate Distances:

	Km	Hours
Boulia-Tobermory Station	248	(4:15)
Tobermory Stn-Jervois Stn	215	(2:50)

Average Vehicles per Day: 25 east of Jervois Station

Regions Traversed: Channel Country, Sandover-Plenty River Basins

▼

Boulia (Alt 143m; Pop 300):* small grazing town. For more information see Road Trip 18, Day 1. (*0/463*) Head **NW** on Min Min Byway for Donahue Hwy junction.

Donahue Highway junction: (*9/454*) Turn **W** for Tobermory. *Turn **S** for Boulia.*

Plains support vast Mitchell grass grasslands. Broad views* from the tops of rises.

Plains support various low shrubs with an understorey of Mitchell grass. Elsewhere are sparse eucalypt woodlands with a spinifex understorey. Occasional vast views. Near the Herbert Downs Station turn-off (no facilities) are some sand dunes.

Georgina River* is a floodplain supporting a coolabah woodland. The main channels exhibit river red gums. (*128/335*)

Plains support Mitchell grass.

Low rises support tracts of Georgina gidgee.

Tobermory Station: working cattle station offering tourist facilities. Camping is available at the waterhole. Store, fuel. (*248/215*)

Urandangie Road junction: locality only; no facilities. (*252/211*) Continue **W** for Jervois Station. *Continue **E** for Tobermory Station.*

Plains and low rises support acacia shrublands on sandy flats. Georgina gidgee, a squat, contorted tree with deeply fissured bark, occupies the rises. The rises are limestone and offer only fair views.

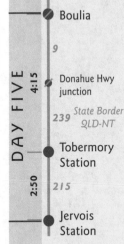

DAY FIVE

4:15

Boulia

9

Donahue Hwy junction

239   State Border
       QLD-NT

Tobermory Station

215

2:50

Jervois Station

Plains and low hills support vast tracts of mulga shrublands interspersed with sparse eucalypt woodlands. Some low hills are near the road, their virtually vegetation-free, gibber-strewn slopes offering good views*. This is an attractive area in the late afternoon light.

Low rises offer good views* southward towards the sandstone escarpments and flat-top hills of the Tarlton Range. Mt Guide (362m) is visible to the south. Good views* along the arrow-straight Plenty Highway.

Tall anthill*, about 4.5 metres high, on the south side of the road. This anthill is probably the largest in Australia.

Arthur Creek* offers a pleasant river red gum-lined sandy creek bed. (*65/398*)

Plains support the attractive mallee eucalypt known as blue mallee. The ground is covered with spinifex. Occasional low rises offer vast views* towards distant ranges: the Jervois Range to the north and the Tarlton Range to the east.

Jervois Station: working cattle station with limited facilities for travellers. Camping available at nearby **rest area**. Store, fuel. (*463/0*)

DAY 6: JERVOIS STATION-ALICE SPRINGS
via Harts Range

Roads to Take: Plenty Highway, Stuart Highway
Warning: Remote Route between Jervois Station-Harts Range
Grade 3
Grade 2 Gemtree-Alice Springs
Total Distance: 348km (4:50)
Intermediate Distances:

	Km	Hours
Jervois Station-Gemtree	211	(3:15)
Gemtree-Stuart Hwy junction	69	(0:50)
Stuart Hwy junction-Alice Springs	68	(0:45)

Average Vehicles per Day: 65 west of Gemtree
Regions Traversed: Central Australia, Sandover-Plenty River Basins

Harts Range Racecourse, NT

Jervois Station: working cattle station. For more information see Day 5. (*0/348*)

Marshall and Plenty River crossings* are quite attractive areas with river red gums. Waterholes form after rain. **Rest area** near Jervois Station.
Plains seem to extend forever on either side of the long straight road. Countryside is dominated by blue mallee shrubs with a ground cover of spinifex. Occasional mulga areas.

Stony ridge, barely 20 metres high, crosses the road, offering vast views* westward towards the Harts Range and other Central Australian ranges, eastward towards the Jervois and other low ranges. A short walk along the ridge (take care) provides an amazing panoramic view.

Low hills form quite an arid scene compared to the surrounding country. Flat-top hills and jump-ups are prominent. Tent Hill (482m) lies to the south. Reasonable views* northward from the tops of rises, overlooking the Plenty River valley.
Plain offers fair to good views southward towards the Harts Range. Mt Eaglebeak (770m) forms the eastern rampart of the Harts Range. Ironwood woodlands are common.

Atjere turnoff: (*134/214*) Turn **S** for Atjere.

Atjere (Alt 545m; Pop 120): small Aboriginal community of Eastern Arrernte people. Though on Aboriginal land, no permit is required for entry to the service area. The settlement (including nearby Harts Range) is known locally as Rltarlpelte. Store, fuel.

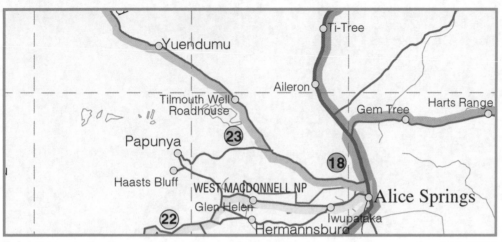

Detail of MAP 6

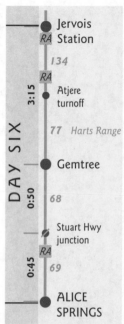

Harts Range:* a small locality and police station. Six kilometres south is the Harts Range racecourse*, set among dry, stony hills and ranges - an interesting place worth visiting. Behind stands Mt Brassey (1203m). (*135/213*)

Plains support acacia woodlands dominated by ironwood, a small tree with a droopy crown. Other trees to be seen include corkwoods and bloodwoods, and mulga shrubs. Good to excellent views* southward at intervals towards the higher ridges and peaks of the Harts Range, some of which rise over 500 metres above the plains. The Harts Range extends between Mt Riddock Station and Indiana Station turn-offs. Mt Riddoch (1094m) and Mt Campbell (1045m) are visible to the south.

Gemtree (Alt 650m; Pop 5):* small caravan park and roadhouse facility, of particular interest to gemstone fossickers. Enquire locally about fossicking areas, including the Zircon Field. A pleasant spot. Accommodation, limited stores, fuel. (*211/137*)

Accommodation
Gemtree Caravan Park, Plenty Hwy, ©08 8956 9855, ©Site: $20 Van: $55

Low hills (with higher ranges, including Mt Pfitzer (1063m), visible to the south, support a mixture of mulga shrublands and eucalypt wood-lands, typically bloodwoods. At intervals ironwoods can be seen. Reasonable views from the tops of rises.

Plains support extensive tracts of mulga. At intervals distant high hills can be seen to the south. Stuart Highway junction: locality only; no facilities. (*279/69*) Road Trip 20 connects. Turn **S** for Alice Springs. Turn **E** for Jervois Station.

Plains form part of the expansive Burt Plain, an area of sand plains and granitic plains supporting mulga shrublands. The mulga is quite dense along road verges. Fair views southward towards the northern rocky ramparts of the MacDonnell Ranges. Mt Everard (949m) is visible to the south-west. **Rest area** at the Tropic of Capricorn. (*317/31*)

Hilly country forms part of the MacDonnell Ranges, a complex of tall ranges and rocky hills. Numerous granite boulders can be seen just north of Alice Springs. Good views* southward towards the Heavitree Range. Elsewhere are banded metamorphic rocks exposed in road cuttings. The area supports mulga shrublands.

ALICE SPRINGS (Alt 547m; Pop 24000):** major regional centre. For more information see Road Trip 20, Day 5. (*348/0*) Road Trips 20, 22 and 23 connect.

DAY SIX

	Jervois RA **Station**
3:15	134 RA
	Atjere turnoff
	77 Harts Range
0:50	**Gemtree**
	68
	Stuart Hwy junction RA
0:45	69
	ALICE SPRINGS

Road Trip 19
Channel Country Connection

Winton-Mt Isa via Boulia
Total Distance: **655km**
Suggested Travelling Time: **2 days**

Enjoy the vast plains and desert scenery of western Queensland

See the Carters Ranges, the atmospheric pub at Middleton, Cawnpore Lookout, the mysterious Min Min Lights, gibber plains, the historic village of Dajarra, and wide open spaces.

Channel Country Connection

South of the uplands of North-West Queensland lies the northern districts of the Channel Country. The northern Channel Country is characterised by vast treeless plains, low jump-up hills and undulating lowlands coursed at intervals by multi-channelled streams, a characteristic from which the region takes its name. In the northern Channel Country these streams include the Diamantina, Burke and Georgina Rivers. Each river supports vast floodplains often innundated by floodwaters fed by monsoonal rains which fall upon their headwaters. These fairly reliable rains and floods (the monsoons do not always reach this far south) encourage the growth of grasses and herbs suitable for cattle grazing.

The Climate

This region is warm to hot throughout the year. Summers can be wet with monsoonal rains filling waterholes and flooding streams. The best time to visit here is during the dry season between April and October. Early in the season the days are still hot (low thirties) but the landscape is often green and the waterholes full after the wet season. As the dry season progresses, daytime temperatures fall (high twenties with the odd hot day) and nights are mild (low teens). Rainfall is very low or non-existant, producing endless sunny days.

Capital City Connections
Distances in kilometres
SYDNEY-NYNGAN
via Great Western/Mitchell Highways

	Intermediate	Total
Sydney	0	0
Bathurst	207	207
Dubbo	205	412
Charleville	821	1233
Barcaldine	408	1641
Winton	281	1922

MELBOURNE-GRIFFITH
via Northern/Newell Highways/Kidman Way

	Intermediate	Total
Melbourne	0	0
Shepparton	179	179
Griffith	266	445
Charleville	979	1424
Barcaldine	408	1832
Winton	281	2113

BRISBANE-CHARLEVILLE
via Warrego Highway

	Intermediate	Total
Brisbane	0	0
Toowoomba	129	129
Roma	352	481
Charleville	265	746
Barcaldine	408	1154
Winton	281	1435

The Route
Distances in kilometres

	Intermediate	Total
Winton	0	0
Boulia	360	360
Mt Isa	295	655

Min Min Byway (Kennedy and Diamantina Developmental Roads)
Winton-Mt Isa
This route, from Winton via Boulia to Mt Isa, presents the traveller with incredible desert

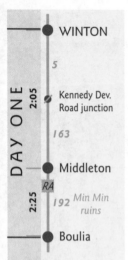

DAY ONE
2:05
2:25

● WINTON

5

Kennedy Dev.
Road junction

163

● Middleton

RA

192 *Min Min
ruins*

● Boulia

Tatta Hotel, Winton, Qld

scenery ranging from vast arid plains to intricate and endlessly fascinating eroded hills and jump-ups. As such it provides a much more scenic (and longer) route than the Matilda Highway, between Winton and Cloncurry and Mt Isa.

Warnings: take care on the narrow bitumen seal. Roads subject to flooding and may be closed for lengthy periods during the monsoon. Avoid travelling at night.

DAY 1: WINTON-BOULIA
via Middleton

Road to Take: Min Min Byway (Kennedy Developmental Road)
Grade 2
Total Distance: 360km (4:30)
Average Vehicles Per Day: 60 west of Middleton
Intermediate Distances:

	Km	Hours
Winton-Middleton	168	(2:05)
Middleton-Boulia	192	(2:25)

Regions Traversed: Mid-West, Channel Country

WINTON (Alt 187m; Pop 1150):** interesting grazing town. For more information see Road Trip 7, Day 6. (**0/360**) *Road Trip 7 connects.* Head **W** on Matilda Hwy for Kennedy Developmental Road junction.

Kennedy Developmental Road junction: (**5/355**) Turn **W** (Matilda Hwy veers north) for Middleton. *Continue **SE** onto Matilda Hwy for Winton.*
Plains and low rises are covered with Mitchell grass. The low shrubs are prickly mimosa. Expansive views* southwards, overlooking the Western River's eucalypt woodlands. Numerous single strand telephone lines (from the days when stations provided their own connections) give vertical relief to the scenery.
Diamantina River: multi-channelled stream supporting a eucalypt woodland. (**70/290**)
Jump-ups* eroded into a multitude of fantastic shapes: numerous mesas and buttes (pointy

mesas). Very photogenic in the right light. Worth investigating on foot, but be careful on the loose scree slopes and beware of rock falls.
Carters Range:** complex range of moderately high jump-ups, plateaux, mesas and buttes. Very photogenic in the dawn and dusk light. A variety of semi-arid vegetation: lancewood (an acacia) on the tops, spinifex on the slopes, Normanton box mallee (a eucalypt) on the lower slopes, river red gums lining the larger creeks. It is worth pulling over to spend some time in this very scenic area. (**135/225**)

Middleton (Alt 187m; Pop 5):* restored bush pub. Shady area for picnics. Stop a while and absorb the atmosphere. Accommodation, fuel. (**168/192**)

Plains support Mitchell grass grasslands. Jump-ups are visible on the horizon.
Cawnpore Lookout:** interesting lookout providing expansive views of the Cawnpore Hills jump-ups. Numerous mesa, butte and rocky pinnacle formations. Worth investigating. **Rest area**. (**221/139**)
Jump-ups rise near the road, providing an element of verticality.
Min Min Hotel ruins* located on Min Min Creek. Little to see, but the name is given to the Min Min lights, mysterious lights said to roll and hover just above the ground, similar to car headlights but sometimes appearing with a greenish tinge. They often approach the observer and then veer away. Although the lights have been sighted

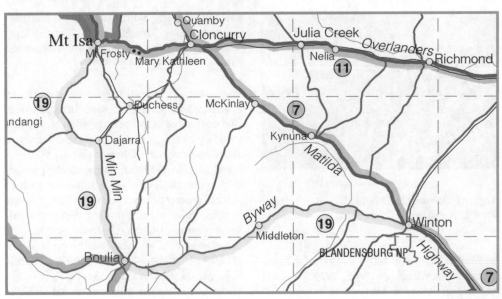

Detail of MAP 4

mostly in this area (hence the name), they may also be seen elsewhere on the open plains within the arid outback. Their silence and rolling movements are certainly eerie. (**252/108**)

Plains offer vast views* of distant jump-ups and low tablelands. The ground surface exhibits small gibber stones and is vegetated by a sparse covering of Mitchell grass. Camp out here and watch the road train headlights take an hour or so to reach you.

Floodplain forms part of the multi-channelled Hamilton River.

Hamilton Ruins:* old bush pub, now a ruin. Worth stopping for a brief look, but do not trespass. (**283/77**)

Plains with views* that reach to the horizon. You can feel mighty small in a place this big. Mitchell grass provides a sparse ground cover.

Coorabooka Road junction: locality only; no facilities. (**356/4**) A 20km return trip **S** down this unsealed (Grade 3) road leads to a grove of rare waddywood trees*, just one of three places in the world where they are found.

Boulia (Alt 143m; Pop 300):* small grazing town with interesting buildings to see. Set in a pleasant area on the banks of the dry Burke River. Boulia is the self-proclaimed capital of the Channel Country and has a small population of Pita Pita people. Worth seeing: Min Min Encounter*, Stone House Museum*, Corroboree Tree, The Red Stump. Accommodation, stores, fuel. (**360/0**) Road Trip 18 connects. Head **E** on Kennedy Developmental Road for Middleton.

Accommodation

Boulia Desert Sands Motel, Herbert St, ©07 4746 3144, ●$75-$90

Australian Hotel-Motel, Herbert St, ©07 4746 3144, ●$40-$60

Boulia Caravan Park, Winton Rd, ©07 4746 3135, ●Site: $12

DAY 2: BOULIA-MT ISA via Dajarra

Road to Take: Min Min Byway (Diamantina Developmental Road)
Grade 2
Total Distance: 295km (3:45)
Intermediate Distances:

	Km	Hours
Boulia-Dajarra	144	(1:50)
Dajarra-Mt Isa	151	(1:55)

Average Vehicles per Day: 90 near Dajarra

Donohues Store, Boulia, Qld

Regions Traversed: Channel Country, North-West Queensland

Boulia (Alt 143m; Pop 300):* small grazing town. For more information see Day 1. (*0/295*) Head **N** on Min Min Byway for Mt Isa.

Plains and low rises cross expansive Mitchell grass grasslands. Big views* from the tops of rises.
Plains and low rises support tracts of acacia shrublands with a grassy understorey. **Rest area** at Peak Creek. (*71/224*)
Plains support sparse woodlands with a grassy understorey. Ranges are visible on the western skyline.

Dajarra (Alt 333m; Pop 230):* attractive and interesting grazing township. Photogenic buildings including a wooden pub* (with risque paintings) and a vast corrugated-iron post office (now

a museum*). The old railway station precinct* is worth seeing. This is a good place to stop a while and absorb the atmosphere. Accommodation, store, fuel. (*144/151*)

Hilly country* passes through steep-sided rocky low ranges supporting a sparse eucalypt woodland dominated by white-trunked trees, perhaps snappy gums. Scenic area at its most attractive in the afternoon or early morning light.
Plains support yet more sparse eucalypt woodlands with spinifex but with occasional areas of Mitchell grass grasslands. Fair views from the tops of rises, especially towards the eastern ranges. Some open areas of quartz-strewn ground.
Urandangie turnoff: locality only; no facilities. (*212/87*) Uradangie lies 98km west. Continue **N** for Mt Isa. *Continue S for Boulia.*
Plains and low rises offer occasional views of ranges visible to the east. The usual eucalypt woodlands dominate the landscape.
Ranges* line the road exhibiting impressive ridgelines, rocky outcrops and bluffs. The countryside supports a sparse eucalypt woodland with a spinifex understorey. Enquire at Mt Isa as to the location of Aboriginal engravings* (approximately 10.5 kilometres south of town).

MT ISA (Alt 356m; Pop 22200):** large mining town and regional centre. For more information see Road Trip 11, Day 3. (*295/0*) *Road Trips 11, 12 and 24 connect.*

Road Trip 20
Stuart Highway

Adelaide-Darwin

Total Distance: 2997km

Suggested Travelling Time: 10 days

Cross the continent from coast to coast

See the opal fields at Coober Pedy and Mintabie, famous Alice Springs, the outback essence of Tennant Creek, the riverbank township of Adelaide River, Lake Hart, Breakaways Lookout, Finke River, the James Range, the colour-changing MacDonnell Ranges, the fascinating Devils Marbles, the historic villages of Barrow Creek and Daly Waters, Elsey National Park, Mataranka Thermal Pool, the waterfalls and gorges of Litchfield National Park, the grand Katherine Gorge, Berry Springs, Howard Springs, and the unique cultural blend of Darwin.

The Stuart Highway

The Stuart Highway is Australia's great north-south road slicing through the centre of Australia. It passes through a number of distinctive regions. Northern South Australia presents a face of shimmering gibber plains, vivid red sand dunes, and low barren jump-up hills. This rather attractive country provides some good arid vistas in the right light. Elsewhere are tracts of mulga.

Made famous in part by the watercolour artist Albert Namatjira, and symbolic of the Australian outback, Central Australia presents the traveller with a bewildering display of natural wonders. Everything you have heard about its landscapes and countryside is true. High rocky bluffs, deep gorges, long linear ridges, prominent peaks, cool waterholes, vivid red sand dunes, graceful desert oaks and magnificent colour changes on distant cliffs and ranges throughout the day, make Central Australia a magical place to visit.

Between Central Australia and the Top End lies the Barkly region, a huge tract of country supporting cattle stations, Aboriginal communities, and a few small townships. Space is the essential element of the Barkly region.

In the far north is Australia's Top End, a vast tract of monsoonal land. This is sparsely populated country extensively grazed by beef cattle. Elsewhere are large national parks and wilderness areas. Towns are few and far between. Those that exist are service centres for tourists, cattle stations or the mining industry.

The Climate

The climate of northern South Australia and Central Australia is primarily influenced by two features: a great distance from the sea (called continentality) and a moderate altitude (300m to 1500m). As a result it experiences wide variations in temperature. Summer maximums are hot to very hot (up to 45C) but with relatively mild nights. Winter maximums can be cool (14C to 22C) with cold to very cold nights (5C to -5C). Such extremes are most pronounced around Alice Springs and southwards. The northernmost districts, around Tennant Creek (Barkly region), are much milder in winter but experience very long and hot summers. The best times to visit Central Australia are in late autumn (April, May), or early Spring (mid-August, September). At these times the extreme heat of summer and cold of winter are for the most part avoided.

The Top End region is very warm to hot throughout the year. Maximum temperatures are extreme, especially in April and between August and November with temperatures reaching 35C-40C away from the coast. Night temperatures are also uncomfortable, with minimums often over 25C and accompanied by high humidity near the northern coast. While maximum temperatures are slightly cooler during the monsoon, due to the cloud cover, it is also very wet. Further south, maximums are very high (38C plus) throughout the warmer half of the year, although minimums are marginal cooler and rainfall is less.

The time to visit the Top End is between May and August (the dry season in the north). Note

DAY ONE

- ADELAIDE
  - 48
- Lower Light
  - 12
- Dublin
  - 13
- Wild Horse Plains
  - 26
- Port Wakefield
  - 49
- Snowtown
  - 50
- CRYSTAL BROOK
  - 22
- Port Pirie turnoff
  - 44
- Mambray Creek Rdhse
  - 48
- PORT AUGUSTA

2:10

0:15

1:00

that even then maximum temperatures may well be in the mid-thirties, though minimums are mild, falling to around 16C in the north, and 10C or less in the south. Rainfall is virtually non-existent at this time.

Capital City Connections

Distances in Kilometres

SYDNEY-PORT AUGUSTA
via Great Western/Mitchell/Barrier Highways/
Route 56

	Intermediate	Total
Sydney	0	0
Nyngan	578	578
Cobar	131	709
Broken Hill	444	1153
Peterborough	284	1437
Port Augusta	131	1568

MELBOURNE-ADELAIDE
via Western/Dukes Highways

	Intermediate	Total
Melbourne	0	0
Ballarat	111	111
Horsham	188	299
Adelaide	432	731

BRISBANE-TENNANT CREEK
via Warrego/Matilda/Barkly Highways

	Intermediate	Total
Brisbane	0	0
Roma	481	481
Longreach	698	1179
Cloncurry	516	1695
Mt Isa	118	1813
Tennant Creek	648	2461

The Route

Distance in Kilometres

	Intermediate	Total
Adelaide	0	0
Port Augusta	312	312
Coober Pedy	536	848
Marla	233	1081
Alice Springs	411	1532
Tennant Creek	507	2039
Katherine	642	2681
Darwin	316	2997

The Stuart Highway

Adelaide-Darwin

Cutting a swathe across northern South Australia and the Northern Territory, the all-sealed two lane Stuart Highway provides easy access for southerners heading to or from Central Australia and the South Australian opal fields of Coober Pedy. Covering a variety of landscapes, from mulga shrublands to vast never-ending saltbush plains, and culminating in the rocky grandeur of the Centralian mountains, this route is recommended for all outback travellers.

North of Alice Springs the Stuart Highway is the main access through the Northern Territory. Consequently it carries a fair degree of road-train traffic. The highway covers a variety of landscapes: mulga shrublands, rugged arid mountain ranges and scrub-choked sandplains. As usual the scenic highlights are interrupted by lengthy stretches of less interesting country that invites contemplation. While towns are few and far between (all worthy of a few days' exploration) there are many roadhouses and bush townships to intrigue the traveller.

Warnings: beware of stock and kangaroos at night; avoid night driving if at all possible. Road may be subject to flooding.
Note: no fuel available between Glendambo-Coober Pedy 252km.

DAY 1: ADELAIDE-PORT AUGUSTA
via Crystal Brook

Road to Take: Highway One
Grade 1
Total Distance: 312km via Crystal Brook (3:25)
Intermediate Distances:

	Km	Hours
Adelaide-Crystal Brook	198	(2:10)
Crystal Brook-Port Pirie turnoff	22	(0:15)
Port Pirie turnoff-Port Augusta	92	(1:00)

Average Vehicles per Day: 5000
Regions traversed: Adelaide Plain, Mid-North

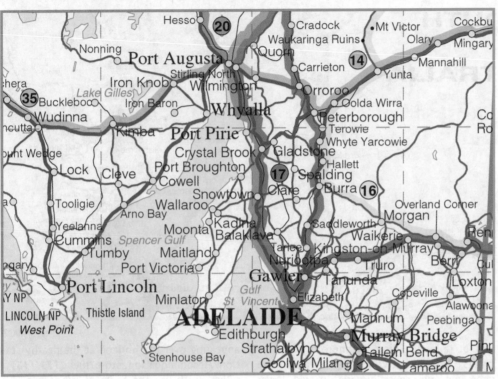

Detail of MAP 5

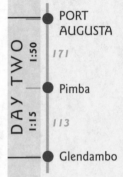

DAY TWO

1:50   ●   **PORT AUGUSTA**

     171

1:15   ●   Pimba

     113

  ●   Glendambo

ADELAIDE (Alt 43m; Pop 1023000):** state capital of South Australia. For more information see Road Trip 15, Day 4. (*0/312*) *Road Trips 15 and 17 connect.*

For information on the route between Adelaide and Port Augusta see Road Trip 17, Day 1.

PORT AUGUSTA (Alt 5m; Pop 14600):* large regional and industrial centre. For more information see Road Trip 14, Day 4. (*312/0*) *Road Trips 14, 17, 18 and 35 connect.*

DAY 2: PORT AUGUSTA-GLENDAMBO
via Pimba

Road to Take: Stuart Highway
Grade 1

Total Distance: 284km (3:05)
Intermediate Distances:

	Km	Hours
Port Augusta-Pimba	171	(1:50)
Pimba-Glendambo	113	(1:15)

Average Vehicles per day: 700 west of Port Augusta
Regions Traversed: Far North (Gairdner Plain)

PORT AUGUSTA (Alt 5m; Pop 14600):* large regional and industrial centre. For more information see Road Trip 14, Day 4. (*0/284*)

Plains gradually slope towards the head of Spencers Gulf. Numerous eastward views* toward the western ramparts of the Flinders Ranges. Many high residual hills are in the area, including Tent Hill (320m). Plains are mostly open with a saltbush covering west of Port Augusta.

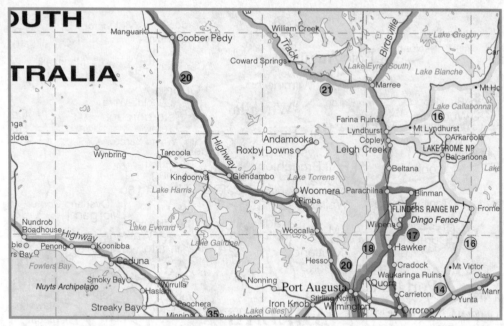

Detail of MAP 5

Hesso: railway siding. Numerous western myalls* hereabouts. Quite photogenic in the right light and especially eerie on cold, foggy mornings. (*51/233*)

Bookaloo: railway siding. (*79/205*)

Undulating country supports stands of mulga shrublands. Elsewhere are woodlands of western myall, a low acacia tree which looks like something lifted from the African savanna. Occasional views* eastward towards the Flinders Ranges.

Wirrappa:* railway siding in an interesting location. There is a saltlake on one side and a steep rocky bluff marking the edge of the Arcoona Plateau on the other. (*146/138*)

Nurrungar: no access. Former secret spy base. A quick view can be had from the highway where the road crosses a shallow valley just west of the old Island Lagoon Tracking Station turn-off. Radomes are clearly visible.

Pimba (Alt 187m; Pop 20): roadhouse facility and old railway settlement with some character, lying just north off the highway. Woomera town is visible in the distance. Rail buffs can get some good photographs of railway lines dis-

appearing over the horizon at the nearby station. Accommodation, store, fuel. (*171/113*)

7km north lies the town of **Woomera** (Alt 185m; Pop 1800), a former closed defence town. Worth exploring is the missile park* and the cemetery (why so many stillborns and dead babies?). Full town facilities.

Plains provide vast views of saltbush. The ground is strewn with gibbers.

Eucolo Bluff: lookout with good views* overlooking Island Lagoon saltlake. The bluff separates the sand plain from the gibber-strewn Arcoona Plateau. (*196/88*)

Lake Hart* can be clearly seen from the road to the north. A short walk (careful crossing the railway line) leads to the lake's edge and old salt works' ruins*. Very photogenic. On the far side (you need binoculars) is the ELDO rocket launching pad.

Plains support tracts of mulga. In some places, low sand dunes may be seen. Many saltlakes are in this area.

Wirraminna: railway siding. (*230/54*)

Coondambo: railway siding. (*267/17*)

Plains support mulga shrublands with areas of western myall woodlands, each with a ground cover of saltbush.

Glendambo (Alt 152m; Pop 30): relatively new settlement servicing the highway. Picnic area, fauna park*. Accommodation, store, fuel. (**284/0**)

Accommodation
Glendambo Tourist Centre Hotel-Motel, Stuart Hwy, ©08 8672 1030, ✪$80-$95
Glendambo Tourist Centre Caravan Park, Stuart Hwy, ©08 8672 1035, ✪Site: $17

DAY 3: GLENDAMBO-COOBER PEDY
via Stuart Highway

Road to Take: Stuart Highway
Grade 1
Total Distance: 252km (2:50)
Average Vehicles per Day: 350 north of Glendambo
Regions Traversed: Far North, (Gairdner Plain, Oodnadatta Tableland)

Glendambo (Alt 152m; Pop 30): highway settlement. For more information see Day 2. (**0/252**)

Plains with a covering of mulga and/or western myall. Occasional low sand dunes and claypans may be seen.
Gosse Range: low barren rocky range just visible above the tree tops.
Plains support a covering of mulga shrublands and western myall woodlands. These woodlands are attractive in the late afternoon light.
Phone for emergency use only. **Rest area**. (**84/168**)
Plains support vast tracts of mulga shrublands occasionally interspersed with patches of open saltbush country. At the McDouall Peak Station - Mirikata Station intersection, the old Stuart Highway can be seen.
Teal Hole: **rest area** and **emergency phone**. (**161/91**)

Stores, Coober Pedy, SA

Low rises offer good views* to the mulga-clad lowlands to the west and the barren saltbush plains to the east.
Sand dunes* stand isolated from one another on the saltbush plains, their relatively dense shrubby vegetation in stark contrast to the emptiness that surrounds them.
Low rises offer far-reaching views* across the empty saltbush plains. Occasionally distant jump-ups can be seen on the eastern horizon.
Stuart Range: really a long escarpment with jump-ups and mesas, known locally as breakaways. Barely visible from the highway, cliffs, rocky outcrops and shallow valleys may be seen to the east.

COOBER PEDY (Alt 213m; Pop 3500):** large and interesting opal mining town set upon the barren slopes of the Stuart Range. There are many underground residences, or dugouts. Worth spending a day or two in this area to visit mines, opal showrooms, underground churches*, Big Winch lookout*, wind turbines, Desert Cave* (underground hotel), Umoona Mine and Museum*, Opal Cave Lookout and the Old Timers Mine**. No permit is required to fossick on unclaimed mullock heaps, but owners' permission is required on occupied claims. Beware of hidden shafts - this is a real hazard. Multi-cultural population (over 45 nationalities) means a diversity of cafes, clubs and foodstuffs. Full town facilities. (**252/0**)

Accommodation
Mud Hut Motel, St Nichos St, ©08 8672 3003, ✪$90-$120

DAY THREE 2:50

Glendambo

RA

252

Teal Hole

RA

COOBER PEDY

DAY FOUR

1:50   ● COOBER PEDY
150

0:55   ● Cadney Park
83

2:00   ● Marla
RA   State Border
178   SA-NT

● Kulgera

Opal Inn Hotel-Motel, Hutchison St, ℂ08 8672 5054, ⊙$50-$90
The Underground Motel, Catacombe Rd, (1.5kmN), ℂ08 8672 5324, ⊙$95
Radekas Downunder Motel, Oliver St, ℂ08 8672 5223, ⊙$65-$80
Stuart Range Caravan Park, Cnr Hutchinson St/ Stuart Hwy, ℂ08 8672 5179, ⊙Site: $14 Van: $40-$50
Coober Pedy Oasis Caravan Park, Hutchison St, ℂ08 8672 5169, ⊙Site: $18 Van: $55-$75
Opal Inn Caravan Park, Hutchison St, ℂ08 8672 5054, ⊙Site: $17 Van: $35
Ribas Underground Camping and Caravan Park, William Creek Rd (5kmS), ℂ08 8672 5614, ⊙Site: $14

DAY 4: COOBER PEDY-KULGERA via Marla

Road to Take: Stuart Highway
Grade 1
Total Distance: 411km (4:45)
Intermediate Distances:

	Km	Hours
Coober Pedy-Cadney Park	150	(1:50)
Cadney Park-Marla	83	(0:55)
Marla-Kulgera	178	(2:00)

Average Vehicles per Day: 350 near Marla
Regions Traversed: Far North, Central Australia

COOBER PEDY (Alt 213m; Pop 3500):** large and interesting opal mining town. For more information see Day 3. (*0/411*)

Breakaways turnoff: (*22/389*) This 18km return unsealed (Grade 3) road leads **E** to a lookout** that provides excellent views over breakaway (jump up) country. There are some walks in this area, including one to The Castle, a prominent jump-up. Dusk or dawn is best for photography. Plains and low rises offer vast, awe-inspiring vistas*. Saltbush country.
Phone for emergency use only. (*75/366*)
Pootnoura: railway siding; no facilities. (*86/325*)

Plains supports tracts of mulga. the countryside forms the eastern edge of the Great Victoria Desert.

Cadney Park (Alt 310m; Pop 10): modern road-house facility set in the mulga scrub. A quiet place for an overnight stop. Accommodation, store, fuel. (*150/261*)

Jump-ups, of moderate interest in the late afternoon light, can be seen to the east near the Wintinna Station turn-off. Saltbush is common. Plains forms the eastern edge of the Great Victoria Desert. Mulga shrublands occupy the plains. Seasonal swamps supporting canegrass occupy shallow depressions. Occasional views from the tops of rises.

Marla (Alt 365; Pop 240): new and modern township servicing northern South Australia. Accommodation, store, fuel. (*233/178*)
Accommodation
Marla Travellers Rest Hotel-Motel, Stuart Hwy, ℂ08 8670 7001, ⊙$70-$85
Marla Travellers Rest Caravan Park, Stuart Hwy, ℂ08 8670 7001, ⊙Site: $15 Van: $20

Mintabie turnoff: (*235/176*) A 70km return journey on an unsealed (Grade 3) road leads **W** to **Mintabie** (Alt 400m; Pop 100)**, an unusual and rustic opal mining centre with plenty of character. Lack of civic control means plenty of unusual dwellings, no proper roads and a casual attitude - attributes the locals prefer. Well worth visiting. A permit is required for entry and these are easily obtainable from the Marla Police Station. Stores, fuel.

Pitjantjatjara Aboriginal Land: freehold land owned by members of the Pitjantjatjara people. No permit is required for travel on the highway. Low hills* of granite are attractive in the late afternoon light. The hills support saltbush and mulga.
Indulkana: Aboriginal settlement; no access without a permit. The township is visible on the slopes of Mt Chandler (551m), from near the Indulkana turn-off.

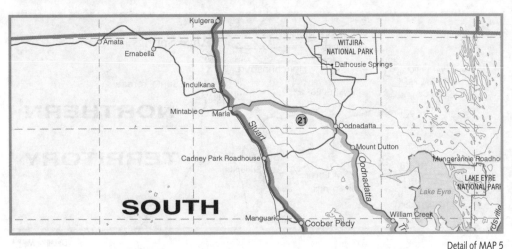

Detail of MAP 5

DAY FIVE

Kulgera

0:50 | 74

Erldunda

0:45 | RA | 69

Ernest Giles
Road Junction

RA | 39 | Finke River

Stuarts Well

1:25 | RA | 87

South
Alice Springs

4

ALICE
SPRINGS

Plains and low rises supports mulga shrublands. The tops of low rises offer fair views*. Occasional hills can be seen in the distance. Creek crossings, especially Marryat Creek*, provide shady areas for rest or picnic stops. **Rest area** and **emergency phone** at Marryat Creek. (*356/55*)

State Border between South Australia and the Northern Territory. **Rest area**. (*391/20*)

Mulga Park turnoff: locality only; no facilities. (*392/19*) Mulga Park lies 165km **W**. Continue **N** for Kulgera. *Continue S for Marla.*

Low rises offer wide vistas*. Low granite hills. Sparse shrublands cover the flats.

Kulgera (Alt 511m; Pop 20): roadhouse and small township with some character. A relaxing place worth stopping in for a while. Museum*. Accommodation, store, fuel. (*411/0*)

Accommodation
Kulgera Roadhouse Hotel-Motel, Stuart Hwy, ©08 8956 0973, ✪$65-$75
Kulgera Caravan Park, Stuart Hwy, ©08 8956 0973, ✪Site: $15

DAY 5: KULGERA-ALICE SPRINGS
via Erldunda

Road to Take: Stuart Highway
Grade 1

Total Distance: 273km (3:00)
Intermediate Distances:

	Km	Hours
Kulgera-Erldunda	74	(0:50)
Erldunda-Ernest Giles Rd jctn	69	(0:45)
Ernest Giles Rd jctn-Alice Springs	130	(1:25)

Average Vehicles per Day: 270 north of Kulgera

Regions Traversed: Central Australia (Amadeus Lowland, MacDonnell Ranges)

Kulgera (Alt 511m; Pop 20):* roadhouse and small township. For more information see Day 4. (*0/273*)

Low hills:* interesting low granite hills and outcrops. The hills rise 50m above the plain. Mulga shrublands are on the flats. One access point lies 8km north of Kulgera on eastern side of road (about a kilometre in), and is worth a quick look. Plains support mulga shrublands with a grassy understorey. Eileen Hill (484m) is visible to the east.

Karinga Creek: low lying flood country with saltpans and low dunes. (*65/208*)

Plains support mulga shrublands.

Erldunda (Alt 407m; Pop 30): roadhouse facility. The area abounds with desert oaks, a grace-

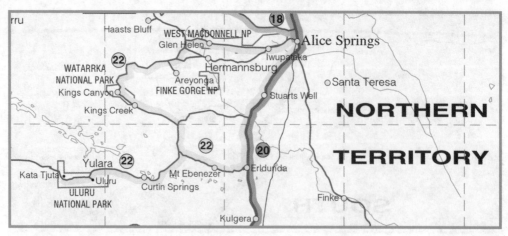

Detail of MAP 5

ful, willowy type of she-oak. Accommodation, store, fuel. **(74/199)** *Road Trip 22 connects.*

Accommodation

Desert Oaks Motel, Stuart Hwy, ✆08 8956 0984, ✪$85

Desert Oaks Caravan Park, Stuart Hwy, ✆08 8956 0984, ✪Site: $20

Seymour Range and Mt Sunday Range are just some of the low ranges and hills which loom as purple ridges in the distance. Between these low ranges are some minor sand dunes. Desert oaks and spinifex occupy the sandy country. Broad views*.

Plains and low rises support open grasslands with patches of mulga. Fair views. **Rest area**. **(106/167)**

Palmer River Crossing: pleasant area. **(124/149)**

Ernest Giles Road junction: locality only; no facilities. **(143/130)** Turn **W** for the 32km (Grade 3) drive to Henbury Meteorite Craters** - walking trails and camping available.

Finke River:* broad sandy riverbed lined with superb river red gums. This river is said to be the oldest in the world. Worth stopping for a short while. Occasionally food and snacks are available from a caravan nearby. **Rest area** adjacent. **(148/125)**

Maloneys Creek* is pleasant enough for a brief stop. A rough track on the western side of Maloneys Creek passes through a fossil locality.

This is an interesting area to explore on foot for an hour or two. The track leaves the highway at Maloneys Creek bridge.

Plain south of Hugh River supports open grassy areas. Fair views* to the south towards the flat-topped Chandlers Range.

Stuarts Well (Alt 485m; Pop 20): roadhouse facility. Adjacent is the Camel Outback Safari which also provides services to travellers. Caravan park. Store, fuel. **(182/91)**

James Range:* moderately rugged rocky ranges supporting spinifex and a variety of sparse, low-growing shrubs. Interesting views from the road. Photogenic in the right light.

Rainbow Valley turnoff: locality only; no facilities. **(196/77)** Turn **E** for the 44km return trip to Rainbow Valley**, an attractive area of multicoloured clifflines, best seen at dawn and dusk. Camping is available adjacent to claypans. The access road can be sandy (Grade 4). The centrepiece of Rainbow Valley Conservation Reserve. Plains support a mulga shrubland with eucalypt scrubs, dominated by blue mallees on the sandy sections. **Rest area (213/60)** just north of James Range. Mt Polhill (774m) forms a prominent ridgeline above the plain, and is a part of the Waterhouse Range. Reasonable views*.

Brewer Plain: stony plain supporting a mulga shrubland. Occasional views northward towards the MacDonnell Ranges.

South Alice Springs: scattered development on the outskirts of Alice Springs. Worth seeing: Old Timers Folk Museum*, Mecca Date Farm, Frontier Camel Farm (includes museum and reptile display), Transport Heritage Centre** (old Ghan railway paraphenalia and early road transport - incorporates a train ride** along the old railway line to Ewaninga), and the Pitchi Richi Aboriginal Cultural Experience* (includes William Ricketts sculptures and an animal sanctuary). Accommodation (see Alice Springs entry), fuel. **(269/4)**

Low ranges* and rocky outcrops line the road; quite scenic.
MacDonnell Ranges:** spectacular series of uplifted and tilted ranges which change colour during the day. Very photogenic, especially at dusk and dawn. The road passes through the narrow Heavitree Gap*.

ALICE SPRINGS (Alt 547m; Pop 24000):** major regional centre servicing pastoralists, Aboriginal communities and tourists. Spectacularly situated beneath the red quartzite bluffs of the MacDonnell Ranges. Though the town is mostly modernised and little remains of the 'old Alice', it still retains some character and charm. Worth seeing: Anzac Hill Lookout* and the Old Telegraph Station* (the walking trail from town is also the start of the Larapinta Trail that leads west across the MacDonald Ranges), School of the Air*, Olive Pink Botanical Reserve*, Museum of Central Australia*, Adelaide House (interesting architecture and early Flying Doctor memorabilia), Royal Flying Doctor Service, John Flynn Memorial Church, Panorama Guth (museum and art gallery), Ted Strehlow Research Centre*, Central Australian Aviation Museum*, memorial cemetery, and the Alice Springs Desert Park*. Full town facilities. **(273/0)** Road Trips 18, 22 and 23 connect.

Make enquiries here about the Larapinta Trail**, a trekking and bushwalking track that, when completed, will run the length of the Western MacDonnells. The trail between the old Alice Springs Telegraph Station and Standley Chasm,

and between Serpentine Gorge and the Ochre Pits, among other sections, are already completed.

Accommodation
Heavitree Gap Outback resort, Palm Cir (4.4kmSW), ℰ08 8950 4444, ◐$80
Desert Palms Resort, 74 Barrett Dr (1kmS), ℰ08 8952 5977, ◐$95
Elkira Court Motel, 65 Bath St, ℰ08 8952 1222, ◐$95-$115
Melanka Lodge Motel, 94 Todd St, ℰ08 8952 2233, ◐$55-$85
The Swagmans Rest Motel, 67 Gap Rd, ℰ08 8953 1333, ◐$80
Alice Motor Inn, 27 Undoolya Rd, ℰ08 8952 5144, ◐$75-$85
Mount Nancy Motel, Stuart Hwy (3kmN), ℰ08 8952 9488, ◐$75
Todd Tavern Hotel, Todd St, ℰ08 8952 1255, ◐$45-$55
MacDonnell Range Holiday Park, Palm Pl (4.8kmSW), ℰ08 8952 6111, ◐Site: $21 Van: $445-$100
G'Day Mate Tourist Park, Palm Cir (4.8kmSW), ℰ08 8952 9589, ◐Site: $20 Van: $45-$60
Wintersun Gardens Caravan Park, Stuart Hwy (2kmN), ℰ08 8952 4080, ◐Site $20 Van: $45-$85
Alice Springs Heritage Tourist Park, Ragonesi Rd (5kmSE), ℰ08 8953 1918, ◐Site: $17 Van: $35-$60
Stuart Caravan Park, Larapinta Dr, ℰ08 8952 2547, ◐Site: $19 Van: $45-$65
Heavitree Gap Outback Resort, Palm Cir (4.4kmSW), ℰ08 8950 4444, ◐Site: $18

DAY 6: ALICE SPRINGS-BARROW CREEK
via Ti Tree

Road to Take: Stuart Highway
Grade 1
Total Distance: 283km (3:10)
Intermediate Distances:

	Km	Hours
Alice Springs-Aileron	133	(1:30)
Aileron-Ti Tree	61	(0:40)
Ti-Tree-Barrow Creek	89	(1:00)

Average Vehicles per Day: 580 north of Aileron
Regions Traversed: Central Australia

DAY SIX

ALICE SPRINGS
RA
69 *Tropic of Capricorn*
1:30

Plenty Hwy junction
RA
64

Aileron
RA
61
0:40

Ti Tree
89
1:00

Barrow Creek

ALICE SPRINGS (Alt 547m; Pop 24000):** major regional centre. For more information see Day 5. (*0/283*)

Hilly country forms the northern part of the MacDonnell Ranges complex. Jagged hills, rocky gullies, granite boulders and reasonable south-ward views* towards the striking bluffs of the Heavitree Range will be seen.
Tanami Road junction (**W**): locality only; no facilities. *Road Trip 23 connects.* (*20/263*)
Tropic of Capricorn:* marked by a sign. Stand here at the summer solstice and have the sun directly over your head! **Rest area**. Mt Everard (948m) is visible to the south. (*31/252*)
Plains support tracts of mulga. They are part of the Burt Plain. Southward the high hills and ranges of the northern ramparts of the Mac-Donnell Ranges can be seen. The blue range visible to the north-east is Strangways Range - blue colouration is due to mulga scrubs. Mitchell grass grassland are hereabouts.
Plenty Highway junction (**E**): locality only; no facilities. (*69/214*) *Road Trip 18 connects.*
Plains support extensive tracts of mulga shrublands with a grassy understorey. Plains form part of the vast Burt Plain, an elevated plain set some 650 metres above sea level. The plain varies from sandy to granitic. Granite sheets and low rocky outcrops may be seen. **Rest area** at Conners Well. (*95/188*)
Native Gap Conservation Reserve:* interesting gap set within the narrow ridge known as the Hann Range. Very scenic spot. Camping is available. Mt Ewart (803m) is visible to the east. (*117/166*)
Ryans Well:* small historic reserve preserving a deep stock well and the ruins of Glen Maggie homestead. Worth a quick look. A good spot for a picnic. (*126/157*)

Aileron (Alt 656m; Pop 10): roadhouse facility. The old Aileron Hotel was unfortunately de-

stroyed by fire. Accommodation, store, fuel. (*133/150*)

Prowse Gap:* low gap surrounded, particularly on the west, by moderately high range country rising up to 240 metres above the plains. Mt Boothby (887m) lies to the west. These ranges form the eastern edge of the Reynolds Range. The red-flowering tall shrubs occasionally seen north of Reynolds Range are bean-trees. **Rest area** nearby.
Plains support extensive tracts of mulga shrub-lands. Southward are occasional views towards the hills surrounding Prowse Gap. Keep an eye out for an unusual sight in these parts: a farm!
Pmara Jutunta: Aboriginal settlement of Anmatyerre-speaking people situated just off the highway. Located on Ahakeye Aboriginal Land. (*186/97*)

Ti Tree (Alt 552m; Pop 60):* interesting small township with the usual characteristic road-house facility. Little remains of the old roadhouse some 300 metres to the west. Interesting art gallery. Accommodation, store, fuel. (*194/89*)

Central Mount Stuart Historic Reserve*: com-memorates the European discovery of Central Australia by John Stuart. Nearby is Central Mt Stuart (849m), once considered the supposed centre of Australia (no public access). Picnic facilities. A short distance west is the Hanson River. (*220/63*)
Plain supports an acacia shrubland with a spinifex understorey. This plain is an outlier of the Tanami Desert.
Stirling Swamp*, a floodout, created by creeks rising in the Forster Range, supports white-trunked coolabahs.
Forster Range offers an interesting landscape of flat-top hills and ranges with good views*, es-pecially from the tops of rises. Countryside sup-ports sparse woodlands of bloodwoods and corkwoods with spinifex. Mulga shrublands are common on the flats.

Barrow Creek (Alt 511m; Pop 15):* interest-ing older style bush pub and roadhouse facility

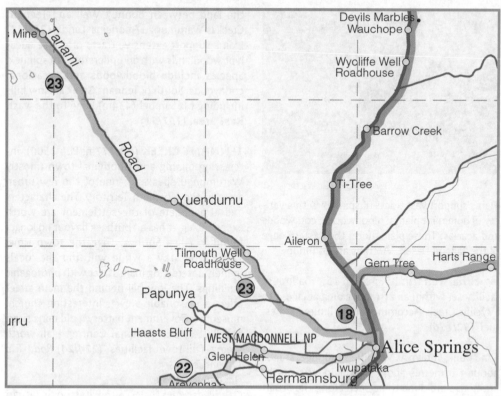

Detail of MAP 6

with plenty of character. Adjacent stone-built telegraph station* is quite photogenic, as are the low flat-top hills that surround the settlement. Good views* from hill tops, but be careful when scrambling up the loose scree slopes. Stop a while to absorb the atmosphere. Accommodation, store, fuel. (283/0)

Accommodation

Barrow Creek Hotel, Stuart Hwy, ©08 8956 9753, ©$45

Barrow Creek Caravan Park, Stuart Hwy, ©08 8956 9753, ©Site: $10

DAY 7: BARROW CREEK-THREE WAYS
via Tennant Creek

Road to Take: Stuart Highway
Grade 1

Total Distance: 248km (2:40)
Internmediate Distances:

	Km	Hours
Barrow Creek-Wycliffe Well	92	(1:00)
Wycliffe Well-Wauchope	18	(0:10)
Wauchope-Tennant Creek	114	(1:15)
Tennant Creek-Three Ways	24	(0:15)

Average Vehicles per Day: 550 south of Wauchope

Regions Traversed: Central Australia, Tanami Desert, Barkly region

Barrow Creek (Alt 511m; Pop 15):* interesting older style bush pub. For more information see Day 6. (0/248)

Plains support extensive tracts of mulga shrublands. Occasional ranges are visible to the east. Osborne Range:* striking range rising 120 metres above the plain. The summit lies at 523m.

Devils Marbles, near Wauchope, NT

Plains support vast tracts of spinifex with a variety of dominant plants: bloodwoods, corkwoods and acacias. These plains form the eastern edge of the Tanami Desert. Anthills are common.

Wycliffe Well (Alt 358m; Pop 15): roadhouse facility set within an attractive area adjacent to Wycliffe Creek. Accommodation, limited stores, fuel. (*92/156*)

Sand dune, known as Wycliffe Sandridge, stands about 7.5 metres above the plain, the northernmost sand dune to be seen along the Stuart Highway.

Wauchope (Alt 365m; Pop 5):* (pronounced walk-up) older style bush pub and roadhouse facility with plenty of character. Well worth visiting. Accommodation, fuel. (*110/138*)

Devils Marbles turnoff: (*120/128*) Turn **E** for the Devil's Marbles**. This feature should not be missed. More fascinating than spectacular, these rounded granite boulders are scattered in heaps across a shallow valley. Very photogenic, especially in the early morning or late afternoon light. It is worth spending half a day here. Walking tracks and fair camping areas. Nearby Davenport Range lies to the east (visible from just south of Wauchope) and is considered to be one of the oldest land surfaces in the world.
Bonney Well:* a pleasant spot for a picnic. Remains of an old well exhibit original stonework, worth a quick look at least. **Rest area**. Most of

the land between Bonney Well and Tennant Creek is Warumungu Aboriginal Land. (*137/111*) Plains support extensive tracts of sparse eucalypt woodlands with an understorey of spinifex. Species include bloodwoods and occasional corkwoods. South of Tennant Creek are low hills including Mt Samuel (434m) lying to the west. **Rest area**. (*197/51*)

TENNANT CREEK (Alt 377m; Pop 3500): interesting mining and Aboriginal town (mostly Warumungu speakers), one of the few urban areas in the Northern Territory. The characters and atmosphere of the settlement are worth experiencing; it has an outback flavour no longer found in Alice Springs. Give the town time. Those why stay a while will find the locals friendly. Interesting main street with photogenic buildings. The low hill behind the main street offers a reasonable view*. Interesting church, museum*, Government battery*, old mine sites, and Battery Hill Regional Centre* - all worth seeing. Full town facilities. (*224/24*) *Road Trip 11 connects.*

Accommodation
Goldfields Hotel-Motel, 603 Paterson St (Stuart Hwy), ⚲08 8962 2030, ⚲$75
Safari Lodge Motel, Davidson St, ⚲08 8962 2207, ⚲$80-$90
Bluestone Motor Inn, Paterson St, ⚲08 8962 2617, ⚲$75-$95
Outback Caravan Park, Peko Rd (1kmE), ⚲08 8962 2459, ⚲Site: $19 Van: $60
Tennant Creek Caravan Park, 280 Paterson St, ⚲08 8962 2325, ⚲Site: $16 Van: $40-$65

Two short return journeys lead east and west out of Tennant Creek. Eastwards is the Nobles Nob Road (24km return; Grade 2) leading to a lookout* and Nobles Nob*, an 82m deep open cut mine. Westward the Warrego Road (96km return; Grade 2) leads to Orlando Mine, an old mine under care and maintenance (nearby are old mining relics and ruins*) and Warrego, a modern mining township currently under care and maintenance. A short distance north of Warrego (4WD only) is a fossicking area; enquire locally.

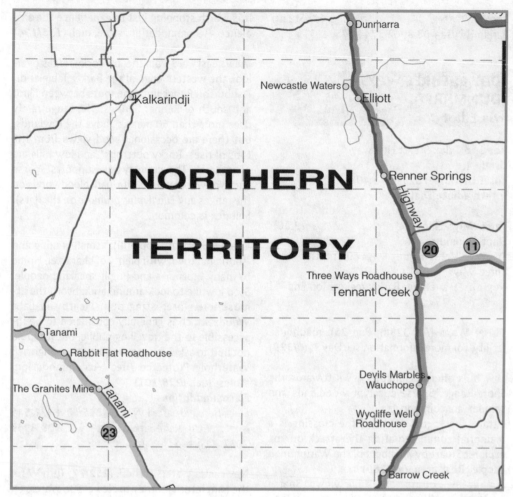

Detail of MAP 6

Hilly country* offers fair views across the low McDouall Ranges. Hills are clothed with snappy gums and spinifex.

Mary Ann Dam turnoff: (230/18) Turn **E** for Mary Ann Dam*, a pleasant spot if sufficient rain has filled the reservoir. Walking tracks lead into the nearby ranges.

Telegraph Station:* the original Tennant Creek, nowadays a restored, very photogenic building well worth seeing. Nearby are some graves. Opposite the old telegraph station, a 12km return unsealed (Grade 3) road leads to The Pebbles*, a collection of interesting granite boulders composed of large crystals and very pho-

togenic in the late afternoon light. An attractive area. (235/13)

Three Ways (Alt 328m; Pop 25):* interesting roadhouse facility with plenty of character. The lively bar is worth experiencing. Camping here is popular with travellers. There is a small monument to John Flynn ('Flynn of the Inland'), founder of the Royal Flying Doctor Service. Accommodation, limited store, fuel. (248/0) Road Trip 11 connects.

Accommodation

Threeways Roadhouse Motel, Cnr Stuart/Barkly Hwys, ℮08 8962 2744, ✪$55

DAY EIGHT

2:30

1:10

● Three Ways
RA
135

● Renner Springs
93

● Elliot
RA
101

● Dunmarra

Threeways Roadhouse Caravan Park, Cnr Stuart/Barkly Hwys, ©08 8962 2744, ✪Site: $15

DAY 8: THREE WAYS-DUNMARRA
via Elliot

Road to Take: Stuart Highway
Grade I
Total Distance: 329km (3:40)
Intermediate Distances:

	Km	Hours
Three Ways-Elliot	228	(2:30)
Elliot-Dunmurra	101	(1:10)

Average Vehicles per Day: 400 north of Three Ways
Regions Traversed: Barkly region, Top End

Three Ways (Alt 328m; Pop 25): roadhouse facility. For more information see Day 7. (*0/329*)

Low hills offer reasonable views towards the Short Range. Sparse eucalypt woodlands and spinifex are common.
Attack Creek: just south of the crossing is a memorial commemorating the attack on the explorer Stuart by members of the Warumungu people. **Rest area**. (*49/280*)
Undulating country offers fair views. Sparse eucalypt woodlands and spinifex are common.
Views* eastward overlooking the western edge of the Barkly Tableland.
Fossicking area on either side of the Helen Springs Station turn-off (eastern side of highway; park well off the road). Worth a quick look at least. The surface is strewn with smoky quartz and amethyst. (*117/212*)
Flat-top hill sometimes known as Lubras Lookout. Mt Willeray (369m) lies to the west.

Renner Springs (Alt 325m; Pop 5):* one of the more interesting roadhouse facilities along the highway. Plenty of character here. One of the few settlements left from the post-war period.

It is worth stopping just to experience the ambience. Accommodation, store, fuel. (*135/194*)

Views eastward from the low rocky ridges overlook the western edge of the Barkly Tableland. Ashburton Range lines the route between Elliot and south of Renner Springs. The range rarely rises more than 60 metres above the lowlands, but there are occasional good views from the tops of rises. Rocky outcrops* and low hills are of interest. The countryside supports sparse eucalypt woodlands (white-bark bloodwoods on the ranges and *Eucalyptus pruinose* on the flats). Spinifex is common.

Elliot (Alt 221m; Pop 600):* small grazing and Aboriginal town with plenty of character. Home to many Mutpurra and Jingili-speaking people. Stop a while to look around and absorb the atmosphere. Interesting pub. Nearby is Lake Woods which is generally considered to be inaccessible to the travelling public, but it would not hurt to ask. Also enquire about the Longreach Waterhole Protected Area. Accommodation, stores, fuel. (*228/101*)
Accommodation
Elliot Hotel, Stuart Hwy, ©08 8956 0984, ✪$45
Midland Caravan Park, Stuart Hwy, ©08 8969 2037, ✪Site: $16 Van: $50-$65

Newcastle Waters turnoff: (*252/77*) Turn **W** for the 6km return journey to Newcastle Waters**, an old droving township with many interesting historic buildings, some quite photogenic. Well worth visiting. The township is on private property so please respect the signs. Museum in the old store, old hotel, memorial park. Heritage walks. No other facilities. **Rest area** near turnoff.
Sturt Plain is a wide open tract of grasslands, predominantly bluegrass. The countryside hereabouts marks the north-western edge of the Barkly Tableland. Reasonable views are available from the causeways that cross the Newcastle Creek floodplain.
Plains support dense thickets of lancewood.
Monument commemorates the joining of the overland telegraph. (*302/27*)

Plain supports tracts of the acacia scrub known as lancewood, which forms quite dense thickets. Just south of Dunmarra is an open grassy plain, virtually the northernmost tract of open country along the Stuart Highway.

Dunmarra (Alt 205m; Pop 10): roadhouse facility with some character. Nearby are old buildings of an earlier roadhouse. Accommodation, store, fuel. (*329/0*)

DAY 9: DUNMARRA-KATHERINE
via Mataranka

Road to Take: Stuart Highway
Grade 1
Total Distance: 313km (3:25)
Intermediate Distances:

	Km	Hours
Dunmurra-Daly Waters Junction	44	(0:30)
Daly Waters Junction-Mataranka	164	(1:45)
Mataranka-Katherine	105	(1:10)

Average Vehicles per Day: 550 south of Cutta Cutta Caves
Regions Traversed: Top End

▼

Dunmarra (Alt 205m; Pop 10): roadhouse facility. For more information see Day 8. (*0/313*)

Buchanan Highway junction (**W**): locality only; no facilities. (*8/305*)
Plain supports a grassy eucalypt woodland. For northbound travellers this country is typical of what lies ahead. **Rest area** at Dingo Hill.

Daly Waters Junction (Alt 230m; Pop 10): modern roadhouse facility with some character. Accommodation, store, fuel. (*44/269*) *Road Trip 24 connects.*

Accommodation
Hi-Way Inn Motel, Cnr Stuart/Carpentaria Hwys, ©08 8975 9925, ✪$60
Hi-Way Inn Caravan Park, Stuart Hwy/Carpentaria Hwys, ©08 8975 9925, ✪Site: $14

Old house, Larrimah, NT

Daly Waters turnoff: (*48/265*) Turn **W** for **Daly Waters** (Alt 212m; Pop 20)*, an interesting historic settlement just off the highway and well worth visiting. The bush pub has plenty of character (and tourists!). Raised houses are typical of bygone Territory architecture. Nearby is the aerodrome and museum*, also worth seeing. Camping available. Accommodation, store, fuel. Plains support extensive tracts of grassy eucalypt woodlands. During the latter part of the wet season these grasses are tall and green. Their dry season appearance is due to drought at this time. Momument to the explorer Alexander Forrest. (*101/212*)
Ruin just off the road (concrete slabs mostly) is the remains of the wartime No.45 Australian hospital.
Low rises do not offer much in the way of views.

Larrimah (Alt 184m; Pop 25):* delightful and attractive township with plenty of character. There is a very interesting pub, a tourist complex behind the roadhouse (buffalo, crocodile and more), old houses and ruins, a museum, and old North Australian Railway yards* which are relatively intact and 'unmuseumised'. Enquire locally about access to Birdum ghost town. It is worth spending half a day here just to poke around. Accommodation, store, fuel. (*137/176*)

Gorrie turnoff: (*146/167*) Turn **W** for Gorrie, located just off the highway. Gorrie* was a highly secret World War II airfield and base of which little remains except for a lengthy runway and remains of an aircraft, machinery and the like.

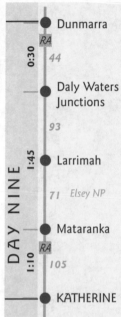

Road Trip 20

Dunmarra
RA
0:30   44
Daly Waters Junctions
93
1:45   Larrimah
71   Elsey NP
Mataranka
RA
1:10   105
KATHERINE

DAY NINE

Low rises support large tracts of eucalypt woodlands, principally bloodwoods, with a grassy understorey. A typical tropical woodland landscape.

Elsey Creek* (Warloch Ponds) embankment and bridge offer reasonable views. Eastward lies a lengthy railway bridge, part of the disused North Australian Railway. Numerous bauhinias will be seen hereabouts, recognised by their outer drooping branchlets and butterfly-like leaves. The tree is deciduous during the dry season, then the ground is carpeted with purple fallen leaves. At this time it has small orange-red flowers.

Elsey Graves turnoff: (195/118). Turn E for the 16km return, Grade 2 road to the Elsey graves*, where many of the We of the Never Never characters are buried. Nearby is the original Elsey Homestead site.

Roper Highway junction (E): locality only; no facilities. (201/112)

Elsey National Park turnoff: (206/107) This 32km return Grade 2 road leads E into Elsey National Park*, a very pleasant (and relatively quite) woodland park straddling the Roper River. Features include a thermal pool (see listing below), bush walks, safe swimming in the Roper River*, and tufa dams** (natural limestone spas). Camping is available at 12 Mile Yards (privately run; canoe hire). The majority of the park is dominated by grassy eucalypt woodlands and bauhinias. Anthills are common.

Mataranka Homestead turnoff: (206/107) Turn NE for Mataranka Homestead - see Side Trip below.

Side Trip

Mataranka Homestead access road (Grade 1) 12km return

Mataranka Homestead (Alt 130m; Pop 10):** busy but laid-back resort settlement with a relaxed feel. You do not have to stay here to enjoy the amenities. Numerous activities are available, including tours, bush walks and bike hire. There is a replica of the Old Elsey Homestead (it is better than it sounds) and, best of all, Mataranka Thermal Pool**, immediately adjacent in the Elsey National Park, which although crowded should not be missed. The pool is surrounded by pandanus palms, cabbage tree palms and melaleucas. Nearby is a glorious pool* in the Waterhouse River. Camping available. Accommodation, store, fuel.

Accommodation

Mataranka Homestead Motel, Homestead Rd, ©08 8975 4544, ©$85

Mataranka Homestead Caravan Park, Homestead Rd, ©08 8975 4544, ©Site: 19 Van: $90

Mataranka (Alt 136m; Pop 150):* small grazing and tourist township with an attractive main street. Calls itself 'Capital of the Never Never'. Interesting pub. Museum. Accommodation, stores, fuel. (208/105)

Accommodation

Territory Manor Motel, Martin Rd, ©08 8975 4516, ©$85

Mataranka Shell Roadhouse Motel, Roper Tce, ©08 8975 4571, ©$70

Territory Manor Caravan Park, Martin Rd, ©08 8975 4516, ©Site: $19

Mataranka Shell Roadhouse Motel, Roper Tce, ©08 8975 4571, ©Site: $14 Van: $70

Undulating country, with occasionally rocky rises, supports eucalypt woodlands with a grassy understorey.

Low rises and undulating country support wide tracts of grassy woodlands dominated by eucalypts. Rest area (265/48) nearby. At the King River crossing, the old railway bridge* can be seen south of the road.

Cutta Cutta Caves turnoff: (285/28) Turn SW for a short detour to Cutta Cutta Caves*, interesting tropical caves set within a low limestone ridge (similar rocky outcrops can be seen just south of Katherine). The caves themselves have the usual formations. Tours are available and often crowded during the tourist season. Interesting walking trails are among the outcrops (tower karsts). The area is part of a Nature Park. The woodland includes carbeen gums, bauhinias and native figs, with a grassy understorey.

Low rises support grasy eucalypt woodlands.

KATHERINE (Alt 107m; Pop 10500):* large regional centre and grazing town with a sizeable

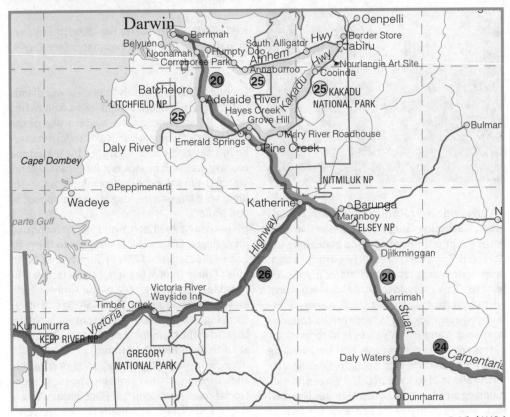

Detail of MAP 6

Aboriginal population of predominantly Jawoyn people. Nearby is a large RAAF Base (Tindel). Features worth seeing include Katherine Railway Station* (museum), O'Keeffe Residence* (interesting bush house), Katherine Museum*, Knotts Crossing (Overland Telegraph Station site), Katherine School of the Air, Katherine Low Level Nature Park* (good swimming - heed warnings), the World War II bomb craters, Springvale Homestead*, and thermal pool* (delightful). Full town facilities. (*313/0*) Road Trip 26 connects.

Accommodation

Riverview Motel, 440 Victoria Hwy (3kmSW), ©08 8972 1011, ✪$75

Crossways Hotel-Motel, Katherine Tce (Stuart Hwy), ©08 8972 1022, ✪$85-$100

Beagle Motor Inn Motel, Cnr Fourth/Lindesay Sts, ©08 8972 3998, ✪$70-$85

Pine Tree Motel, 3 Third Ave, ©08 8972 2533, ✪$95-$105

Katherine Low Level Caravan Park, Shadforth Rd (5kmW), ©08 8972 3962, ✪Site: $21 Van: $80

Riverview Caravan Park, 440 Victoria Hwy (3kmW), ©08 8972 1011, ✪Site: $19 Van: $40-$70

Knotts Crossing Resort Caravan Park, Cnr Giles/Cameron Sts, ©08 8972 2511, ✪Site: $18 Van: $65-$75

Red Gum Caravan Park, 42 Victoria Hwy (1kmW), 08 8972 2239, ✪Site: $18 Van: $65

Frontier Katherine Caravan Park, Stuart Hwy (3kmS), 08 8972 1744, ✪Site: $18

Shady Lane Caravan Park, Gorge Rd (6kmNE), 08 8971 0491, ✪Site: $19 Van: $55-$70

Katherine Gorge Caravan Park, Gorge Rd (31kmNE), 08 8972 1253, ✪Site: $19

Road Trip 20

Katherine Gorge, NT

A great side trip (60km return; Grade 1) leads **NE** to **Katherine Gorge****, an impressive deep gorge cut into the Arnhem Land plateau by the Katherine River. Sheer cliffs up to 60 metres high, deep waterholes, rapids and side canyons are features. This a very spectacular area well worth visiting. Note that the grandest scenery (second gorge and beyond) is best seen by canoe or boat tour. Various bushwalks lead to portions of this and other gorges (note that bushwalking is very hot and tiring in this countryside). Shorter bushwalks lead to lookouts. The gorge and surrounding area are contained in Nitmiluk National Park. A visit is highly recommended. Allow at least two days and expect a crowd. Accommodation, limited store, fuel.

DAY 10: KATHERINE–DARWIN via Pine Creek

Road to Take: Stuart Highway
Grade 1
Total Distance: 316km (3:30)
Intermediate Distances:

	Km	Hours
Katherine-Pine Creek	91	(1:00)
Pine Creek-Adelaide River	112	(1:15)
Adelaide River-Darwin	113	(1:15)

Average Vehicles per Day: 800 north of Pine Creek; 2,300 north of Acacia Store
Regions Traversed: Top End

KATHERINE (Alt 107m; Pop 8000):* large regional centre. For more information see Day 9. (**0/316**)

Low rises support eucalypt grassy woodlands with rocky outcrops. About eight kilometres north of Katherine, on the western side of the road, are rocky pinnacles*, two- to four-metre-high limestone tower karsts. In the limestone country keep a sharp look out for cycads, a short statured primitive-looking plant (about 2-3m high) with large metre-long leaves composed of stiff leaflets.

Hilly country: good northward view overlooking rocky ridges. O'Shea Hill (240m) lies to the east. Edith Falls turnoff: (**32/279**) Turn **NE** for Edith Falls* (38km return; Grade 1), an attractive waterfall located on the edge of the Arnhem Land escarpment - swimming, bushwalking and more. Camping is available. A good spot for a picnic. Located in the Nitmiluk National Park. **Rest area** at Edith River near the turnoff.

Hilly country offers good views* of nearby hills and ranges in what is probably the most spectacular countryside north of Alice Springs. Stony ridges and distant mountain scenes are common. One kilometre south of the Fergusson River crossing is a turn-off leading to a Telecom tower (two kilometres in, partially sealed access, incredibly steep road, not suitable for caravans, use at your own risk) offering excellent views** over the surrounding range country, an area commonly referred to as the Pine Creek Ridges. Fergusson River crossing: there is an old railway bridge*. Mt Giles (252m) lies to the west. (**58/258**)

Undulating country supports grassy eucalypt woodlands.

Pine Creek (Alt 189m; Pop 500): historic mining town currently undergoing a resurgence in mining. Good views of the open-cut mine and surrounding countryside from lookout*. Many historic buildings. The railway station and yards are in excellent condition (nowadays a museum*). Nearby is a National Trust museum*.

Small community of mostly Wakiman people. Accommodation, stores, fuel. (*91/225*) *Road Trip 25 connects.*

Accommodation
Pine Creek Hotel-Motel, 40 Moule St, ©08 8976 1288, ✪$85
Pine Creek Service Station Caravan Park, Moule St, ©08 8976 1217, ✪Site: $20
Kakadu Gateway Caravan Park, Buchanan Rd, ©08 8976 1166, ✪Site: $20 Van: $50-$110

Low hills offer fair views* from the tops of rises. Flat-top ridges are common, as are eucalypt woodlands partly dominated by fan-leaved bloodwoods, a type of eucalypt.

Emerald Springs (Alt 240m; Pop 5): interesting roadhouse facility with plenty of character. Accommodation, limited store, fuel. (*122/194*)

Low ranges offer scenic views* of flat-top hills and ridges. This area is known as Corkscrew Pass. Good views from the tops of rises. Eucalypt woodlands are common. The pinkish-purple flowering (June/July) shrubs in the understorey are turkey bushes.

Hayes Creek (Alt 190m; Pop 15): roadside inn set within a rocky landscape. Good views*. Camping and bushwalks available. A stroll to the nearby creek is worthwhile: beneath the riverine forest canopy are thousands of butterflies. Accommodation, limited store, fuel. (*145/171*)

Dorat Road junction (**W**): locality only; no facilities. (*151/165*) *Road Trip 25 connects.*
Undulating country supports eucalypt woodlands with a grassy understorey, commonly native sorghum which grows to three metres at the end of the Wet. Occasional low hills offer fair views.
Bridge Creek* bamboo thickets can be seen. **Rest area** adjacent (*169/147*). North of Hayes Creek, monsoonal rainforests line most streams.

Adelaide River (Alt 50m; Pop 150):* attractive township set on the banks of the Adelaide River. Worth stopping for a while. Much to see, including the War Cemetery** (a very moving experience), the old high level railway bridge*, old railway station (now a museum*), rest area, and the Snake Creek Arsenal (2km north of town). Interesting pub. Accommodation, stores, fuel. (*203/113*) *Road Trip 25 connects.*

Accommodation
Adelaide River Inn Hotel-Motel, Stuart Hwy, ©08 8976 7047, ✪$60-$75
Adelaide River Show Society Caravan Park, Dorat Rd (1kmSW), ©08 8976 7032, ✪Site: $14
Adelaide River Inn Caravan Park, War Memorial Dr, ©08 8976 7047, ✪Site: $15

Low ridges line the road offering an undulating skyline. Eucalypt woodlands are common. Strips of bitumen alongside the road between here and north of Noonamah are old World War II airstrips, many of which are indicated by informative signs - the observant may see scattered relics. From south to north the airstrips are Pell, Coomalie, Livingstone, Hughes, Strauss and Sattler.
Low ridges offer occasional views*. The countryside supports eucalypt shrubby woodlands presenting a generally green face.
Coomalie Creek: interesting waterhole* and **rest area**. Notice a change in the landscape here: the understorey northward is generally green most of the year, while southward it appears brown during the dry season. A caravan park is nearby. (*228/88*)
Litchfield National Park turnoff: (*230/86*) Turn **W** for Batchelor and Litchfield National Park.

Side Trip
Litchfield National Park access road (Grade 1) 156+km return
Batchelor (Alt 70m; Pop 600):* attractive settlement with incredible gardens. Accommodation, stores, fuel.
Rum Jungle: old uranium mine site currently undergoing reclamation. Little to see.
Finniss River crossing is of minor interest (beware of estuarine crocodiles). Nearby are two caravan parks set within an area of cleared farmlands and eucalypt woodlands. Eucalypts include Darwin box.

Road Trip 20

KATHERINE
RA
1:00   91

Pine Creek
31

Emerald Springs
1:15   23

Hayes Creek
RA
58

Adelaide River
RA
50   Litchfield NP
RA

Acacia Store
19

Noonamah
1:15   15

Coolalinga
16

Berrimah
13

DARWIN

DAY TEN

Magnetic anthill, Litchfield National Park, NT

Litchfield National Park: large national park preserving a scenic area centred on the sandstone Tabletop Range and adjacent black soil plains.
Anthills* found on the black soil flats are of the magnetic variety. Worth investigating and very photogenic. Up to two metres high but barely 40 centimetres thick, these anthills are aligned north-south, a temperature control mechanism.
Hilly country forms the escarpment of the Tabletop Range.
Florence Falls:** spectacular waterfall and gorge. Bushwalks. Like all waterfalls in the Top End, these are mostly a trickle during the dry but become a torrent during the wet. Camping is available nearby. En route is access to Buley Rock Hole where camping is available.
Tabletop Range forms a plateau that supports a eucalypt woodland with a shrubby tropical understorey.
Tolmer Falls:** spectacular lookout overlooking the falls, a deep gorge and the distant plains. Numerous rocky outcrops and cliffs can be seen. Bushwalks.
Wangi Falls:** a delightful area, probably the highlight of Litchfield. Large swimming hole set beneath high cliffs and a trickling (dry season) waterfall. Rainforests, bushwalks, lookout. Camping available.

Low hills supports tracts of eucalypt woodlands. Woodcutters Mine lies west of the road.
Manton Dam turnoff: (**244/72**) A short distance **E** is Manton Dam, a recreation area. Picnics, boating and swimming.

Acacia Store (Alt 50m; Pop 5): roadhouse facility set among the woodlands. Accommodation, store, fuel. (**253/63**)

Low rises support eucalypt woodlands.
Berry Springs turnoff: (**268/48**) A short detour leads **W** to **Berry Springs** (Alt 20m; Pop 100), a scattered settlement of small farms, rural allotments and eucalypt woodlands. Worth visiting: Berry Springs Nature Park* with its rainforest fringed swimming holes (no camping), and Territory Wildlife Park*, a type of open range zoo. Both of these features are highly recommended. Accommodation, stores, fuel.

Noonamah (Alt 40m; Pop 250): roadhouse facility and service centre servicing the surrounding rural farms and allotments. Nearby is a crocodile farm. Accommodation, store, fuel. (**272/44**)

Low rises have been partially cleared for farmlands. Elsewhere are eucalypt woodlands dominated by Darwin woollybutts and stringybarks, with a shrubby understorey. Sand palms are common. Some pandanus palms will be seen. These woodlands appear green for most of the year (unlike the grassy woodlands further south) even though they are regularly fired during the dry season. A smoke haze is not uncommon during July and August.
Arnhem Highway junction (**E**): (**280/36**) Just north of the junction is the Wishart Siding Museum*. Road Trip 25 connects.
Low rises support a mix of eucalypt woodlands and ribbon development along the highway.

Coolalinga (also known as 18 Mile): spread out settlement and ribbon development lining the highway. Numerous small farms, rural allotments and patches of eucalypt woodlands are features. Caravan park and roadhouse facilities. Store, fuel. (**287/29**)
Accommodation
Coolalinga Caravan Tourist Resort, Stuart Hwy, ☎08 8983 1026, ⊛Site: $18 Van: $70

Howard Springs turnoff: (**290/26**) A short detour leads **NE** to **Howard Springs** township (accommodation, store, fuel) and Howard Springs Nature Park**, where you can have a picnic lunch with the birds and swim (no saltwater crocodiles here) with the fish, including metre-long barramundis! Bushwalk through a monsoonal rainforest.

Palmerston turnoff: (**294/22**) A short distance **SW** is **Palmerston**, a new and modern satellite city built to take the overflow from Darwin. It is dominated by a tall water tower, which has fair views* overlooking Port Darwin in the distance. Full town facilities but with limited accommodation.

Berrimah: predominantly an industrial suburb and edge of the virtually continuous development of the Darwin Urban Area. Accomodation, store, fuel. (**303/13**)

Accommodation
Overlander Caravan Park, Cnr Stuart Hwy/McMillans Rd, ℂ08 8984 3025, ✪Site: $22
Palm Village Resort, 907 Stuart Hwy (4kmS), ℂ08 8931 2888, ✪Site: $22 Van: $45-$90
Sundowner Caravan Park, McMillans Rd, ℂ08 8947 0045, ✪Site: $21 Van: $50-$75
Shady Glen Caravan Park, Cnr Stuart Hwy/Farrell Cres, ℂ08 8984 3330, ✪Site: $22 Van: $55-$85

DARWIN (Alt 24m; Pop 75000):** is a tropical city with an 'Asian' feel - Australia seems to be a long way south. There are many tourist facilities and attractions. Worth seeing is Darwin Harbour and Wharf Precinct*, Smith Street Mall, old Government House*, State Square, artworks at the Supreme Court, Chinese Temple*, Tree of Knowledge*, Fannie Bay Gaol Museum*, Darwin Botanic Gardens**, Mindil Beach markets** (highly recommended - expect a huge crowd), Doctors Gully* (fish feeding frenzy), Museum and Art Gallery**, East Point** (good views), Lee Point (nice beach - swim at own risk, but not during the stinger season) and nearby Casuarina Coastal Reserve*, Holmes Jungle Nature Park*, wartime sites, and more. A few days spent here will be well worth it. Full town facilities. (**316/0**) Road Trip 25 connects.

Accommodation
Asti Motel, Cnr Smith/Plackard Sts (1.1kmNW), ℂ08 8981 8200, ✪$85-$100
Cherry Blossom Motel, 100 Esplanade, ℂ08 8981 6734, ✪$90
Palms Motel, 100 Mc Minn St (1.4kmN), ℂ08 8981 4188, ✪$75-$135
Value Inn Motel, 50 Mitchell St, ℂ08 8981 4733, ✪$65-$70
Don Hotel-Motel, 12 Cavenagh St, ℂ08 8981 5311, ✪$75-$90
Top End Hotel, Cnr Mitchell/Daly Sts, ℂ08 8981 6511, ✪$105-$130
Metro Inn Darwin Motel, 38 Gardens Rd, ℂ08 8981 1544, ✪$90-$145
Darwin Phoenix Motel, 63 Progress Dr, Nightcliffe (10kmN), ℂ08 8985 4144, ✪$85-$95
Paravista Comfort Inn Motel, 5 MacKillop St, Parap (5kmN), ℂ08 8981 9200, ✪$90-$120
Casablanca Motel, 52 Gregory St, Parap (5kmN), ℂ08 8981 2163, ✪$60-$90

Road Trip 21
Ooodnadatta Track

Marree-Marla
Total Distance: 615km
Suggested Travelling Time: 2 days

Venture along the ancient trail through Oodnadatta

See the enormous saltlake of Lake Eyre South, Old Ghan railway ruins, photogenic Curdimurka Railway Station, The Bubbler and Blanche Cup springs, William Creek historic village, desert landscapes, the ruins of Edwards Creek and Algebuckina, Mt Dutton, and the charismatic town of Oodnadatta.

The Oodnadatta Track

The unsealed but well-maintained Oodnadatta Track follows probably the world's most ancient trail, an Aboriginal pathway that led from mound spring to mound spring. These natural outlets of the Great Artesian Basin, often set upon a mound of their own making, were utilised by Aboriginal traders transferring goods (pituri, ochre, implements) and knowledge between southern and northern Australia. In their footsteps came European explorers, pastoralists and miners, the Overland Telegraph Line and the original Ghan railway, each making use of the reliable water supply in this, some of the most arid country in Australia.

The Climate

As befits the driest area in Australia rainfall in this part of the country is low. Nonetheless light winter showers or heavy summer thunderstorms can be expected. During wet periods, heavy rains can close unsealed roads for weeks.

Stay out of the arid areas in summer. Maximum temperatures can be extreme, up to 48C with no shade. Nights can be very warm, around 26C. Best travel times are between autumn and spring. Though some warm to hot days can be experienced either end of this period, they rarely last for more than two to three consecutive days. Generally maximums will be in the low to high twenties. Nights are usually cool. In midwinter, cool days will be experienced, often with a wind. Maximums at this time are generally in the high teens. Nights are cold with occasional frosts. Springtime can be windy with the occasional duststorm.

Capital City Connections
Distances in kilometres
SYDNEY-MARREE
via Great Western/Mitchell/Barrier Highways/
Route 56/Hawker-Leigh Creek Road

	Intermediate	Total
Sydney	0	0
Nyngan	578	578
Cobar	131	709
Broken Hill	444	1153
Peterborough	284	1437
Hawker	144	1581
Marree	271	1852

MELBOURNE-MARREE
via Western/Dukes Highways/Highway 1/
Hawker-Leigh Creek Road

	Intermediate	Total
Melbourne	0	0
Ballarat	111	111
Horsham	188	299
Adelaide	432	731
Port Pirie	215	946
Port Augusta	97	1043
Hawker	107	1150
Marree	271	1421

The Route
Distance in Kilometres

	Intermediate	Total
Marree	0	0
William Creek	204	204
Oodnadatta	202	406
Marla	209	615

Road Trip 21

DAY ONE

1:50

Marree

68   *Alberrie Creek*

Roxby Downs turnoff

Lake Eyre South

136   *Curdimurka ruins*

1:50

The Bubbler

William Creek

The Oodnadatta Track
Marree-Marla

Today's Oodnadatta Track provides access to northern South Australia, the Finke River Country, Central Australia and the Simpson Desert. Whilst commonly used by 4WDs, this route is accessible, when dry, to travellers in conventional vehicles, and is recommended to anyone who has an interest in Australia's history or a love of wide open spaces.

Warnings: road is impassable in wet weather and subject to flooding. Avoid travelling at night. Make local enquiries before proceeding; in summer, inform reliable person of your intentions if travelling between Marree and Marla. If inexperienced, stay out of this area in summer. A Desert Parks Pass is required to visit Lake Eyre National Park (but not required for Lake Eyre South). The road is generally well maintained but wash-outs can occur after rain and floods.
Note: no fuel available between Marree-William 204km; William Creek-Oodnadatta 202km; Oodnadatta-Marla 209km.

DAY 1: MARREE-WILLIAM CREEK via Coward Springs

Road to Take: Oodnadatta Track
Grade 3
Warning: Remote Route. No fuel Marree-William Creek 204km
Total Distance: 204km (2:40)
Intermediate Distances:

	Km	Hours
Marree-Roxby Downs turnoff	68	(0:50)
Roxby Downs t/off-William Creek	136	(1:50)

Average Vehicles per Day: 25 near William Creek
Regions Traversed: Saltlakes

Marree (Alt 45m; Pop 150):* former Ghan railway township. For more information see Road Trip

18, Day 1. (*0/204*) *Road Trip 18 connects.* Head **W** along Oodnadatta Track for William Creek.

Three kilometres west of Marree is a 174km return drive over unsealed roads (Grade 4 north of Muloorina Station - camping available) leading **N** to Lake Eyre South* (good views) and Lake Eyre North at Level Post Bay. Good views*; wildflowers in season. Forms part of Lake Eyre National Park. A Desert Parks Pass is required.

Callana ruins:* former old Ghan railway siding. The water hose and goods platform are still visible. (*16/188*)
Plains and low rises support vast expanses of saltbush. Fair views from the tops of rises. Willouran Ranges are visible in the south.
Wangianna ruins:* former old Ghan railway siding and railway station. (*36/168*)
Poole or Alberrie Creek: scenic valley with good views* from the western side. A short distance east is the Dingo Fence.
Alberrie Creek: old outback-style house (very photogenic). Do not trespass. Just to the east are a number of impressive sculptures** well worth a look. (*52/152*)
Low hills support a low open woodland, unusual in this part of the world. Structurally this country is a northern outlier of the Flinders Ranges. Hermit Hill lies to the north.
Roxby Downs turnoff: locality only; no facilities. Nearby are the ruins of Bocheepie railway siding. (*68/136*) Roxby Downs lies 115km south. Continue **W** for William Creek. *Continue* **E** *for Marree.*
Gregory Creek:* interesting old Ghan railway bridge crossing salt-encrusted creek.
Lake Eyre South:** low dunes provides a lookout (*85/119*) over the Lake Eyre South saltlake. Very photogenic area at dawn/dusk, or when full of water. Walk down the tracks to the lake's edge. Numerous wild flowers sping up after rains. The lake bed is part of Lake Eyre National Park. A walk over the salt surface is very interesting; look for the mounds of salt house small spiders which feed on wind-blown insects. Do not drive on the lakebed. Further west is another lookout.

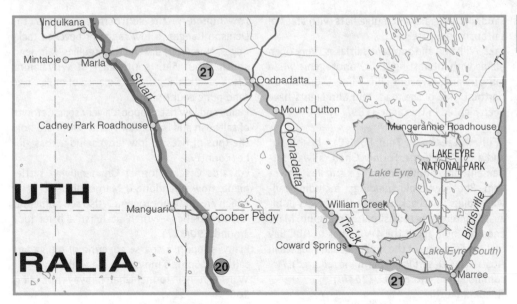

Detail of MAP 5

Curdimurka ruins:** preserved ruins and section of train line. A former fettlers' camp on the old Ghan railway - very photogenic. Please do not vandalise. Buildings, desalination plant, flowing bore, absolutely desolate countryside. This area is below sea level. (*99/105*)

Stuart Creek crossing: salt-encrusted creekline set 12m below sea level.

Bubbler and Blanche Cup turnoff: (*123/81*) Turn **S** for Blanche Cup*, a high mound spring with a reed-lined blue pool of water, and The Bubbler*, a mound spring that bubbles up sand and water creating endless patterns. Occasionally it bubbles up a metre or more in height. A small creek

runs to a wetland. Elsewhere the landscape comprises of barren salt flats. Six kilometres return. Features form part of the Wabma Kadarbu Conservation Park.

Coward Springs ruins:* former railway settlement ruins. The old house is quite photogenic. Beware of deep wells. The flowing bore to the north has formed a wetland. A line of Athol pines mark out the old hotel. Camping area; tours available. (*129/75*)

Plains extend between Warriners Creek and Curdimurka, supporting a cover of saltbush. Low ranges visible to the south are stony plains and jump-up country. Broad vistas*.

Beresford ruins:* former fettlers' camp on old Ghan railway. Desalination plant, ruined building, flowing bore and dam. Beresford Hill looms large, rising 44m above the open plains to the south. Nearby are Warburton Springs. (*153/51*)

Strangways ruins:* former overland telegraph repeater station and township, graveyard, flowing bore and mound springs, all on a low, reed-topped hill near Warriners Creek. Surrounded by open plains with vast vistas. (*166/38*)

Irrapatna ruin: stone ruin, formerly fettlers' hut on old Ghan railway.

Irrapatna Dunes: vivid red dunes interspersed with claypans make for an interesting area.

Lake Eyre South saltpan, west of Maree, SA

Road Trip 21

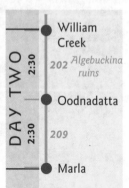

DAY TWO

● William
  Creek

2:30

202 *Algebuckina*
     ruins

● Oodnadatta

2:30

209

● Marla

Sandhill canegrass and mulga flats with areas of saltbush dominate.

Lake William* and adjacent saltlakes. Very open plains with interesting lakes, photogenic when full of water. Gypsum cliffs* line the lakes on northern side of the road. Min Min Lights have been sighted in this area. (*189/15*)

William Creek (Alt 74m; Pop 10):* bush pub* and a few dwellings. Former Ghan railway settlement, now South Australia's smallest township. Photogenic old buildings, including railway siding*; outback humour (Bill Rivers Boulevard); interesting tourist maps, museum. Make enquiries here about the 4WD track to ABC Bay on Lake Eyre, one of the most desolate places in Australia (a Desert Parks permit is required). Accommodation, store, fuel. (*204/0*)

Accommodation
William Creek Hotel, Oodnadatta Track, ©08 8670 7880, ©$60
William Creek Campground, Oodnadatta Track, ©08 8670 7880, ©Site: $6 (unpowered)

▲

DAY 2: WILLIAM CREEK-MARLA via Oodnadatta

Road to Take: Oodnadatta Track
Grade 3
Warning: Remote Route. No fuel William Creek-Oodnadatta 202km. Oodnadatta-Marla 209km
Total Distance: 411km (5:00)
Intermediate Distances:

	Km	Hours
William Creek-Oodnadatta	202	(2:30)
Oodnadatta-Marla	209	(2:30)

Average Vehicles per Day: 30
Regions Traversed: Saltlakes, Far North (Oodnadatta Tableland)

▼

William Creek (Alt 74m; Pop 10):* former Ghan railway township. For more information see Day 1.

Plain supports tracts of mulga.

Low hills form the southern portions of the Denison Ranges, a low range of bevelled rocky ridges. Numerous dry and rocky gullies. Fair view* south about 5km south-east of Wilyalallina Creek, overlooking a vast expanse of mulga-clad sand dune country.

Plains and low rises support a very sparse growth of saltbush and burrs. Fair views* eastward from the tops of rises to low ranges and across gibber country.

Edwards Creek:* former Ghan railway settlement, now abandoned. Many ruins, some of which are quite photogenic. Also see numerous railway srelics. Worth at least a brief look around. (*90/321*)

Plains support a sparse covering of mulga and saltbush. Some sand dunes are visible.

Warrina ruins:* former Ghan railway ruin. (*111/300*)

Sand dunes* provide a change in countryside. Sand-hill canegrass and spinifex grow on the dunes while mulga and saltbush occupy the intervening flats.

Algebuckina ruins:** definitely worth a stop as there is plenty to explore. See the stone ruins* connected with the old Ghan railway, and the large red railway bridge* over Neales River (very photogenic), one of the longest bridges in South Australia. Be very careful when walking on the bridge decking. An old gold mine is located near the northern end of railway bridge (west of the old railway line). Algebuckina Waterhole* is accessed through the gate east of the bridge, then by continuing a kilometre or so in. Good camping here, but little firewood. (*143/268*)

Ockenden Creek:* attractive valley with tree-lined creek. South of the creek, and west of the road, the reed-lined Ockenden Spring* can be seen. Between Mt Dutton and Ockenden Creek, purple and red gibbers cover the hills and low rises.

Mt Dutton ruin:* stone fettlers' cottage and water tank, part of the old Ghan railway. Located on private property, so do not disturb anything. (*158/253*)

Low hills line the road rising to the heights of Mount Dutton (176m) west of the road. Good views (no track) from the top. A sparse cover-

General Store, Oodnadatta, SA

Sand dunes visible to the north of the road form part of the Alberga Dunefield. Dunes support sand-hill canegrass and spinifex. Intervening flats are covered in mulga.

Coongra Creek flood-plain supports a low woodland of coolabahs. Jump-ups visible to the south rise 50m above the plain. Waterholes* are north of the road and approximately 3km west of Olarinna Creek.

Jump-ups* line the route. This saltbush-covered gibber country is attractive in early morning and late afternoon light.

Plains support mulga shrublands. This section of the route follows the old Stuart Highway. Near Welbourn Hill Station turn-off are gibber plains.

Marla (Alt 365; Pop 240): modern township servicing northern South Australia. For more information see Road Trip 20, Day 4. (*411/0*) *Road Trip 20 connects.*

ing of saltbush dominates the landscape. Good views from nearby Cadnaowie Lookout*.
Barton Gap: a low pass through a set of hills. Good views* to the south.

Oodnadatta (Alt 113m; Pop 180):* interesting and photogenic bush township with plenty of character. One of the outback's tidiest towns. Some ruins are connected with the old Ghan railway. A sizeable community of Yankunytjatjara people (pronounced "young goonjarrer") reside here; they refer to Oodnadatta as Tanytjipaka. It is worth spending some time exploring the town and area. Call into the Pink Roadhouse for local information. Accommodation, stores, fuel. (*202/209*)

Accommodation
Transcontinental Hotel, Oodnadatta Track, ✪$60
Oodnadatta Caravan Park, Oodnadatta Track, ✆08 8670 7822, ✪Site: $18 Van: $20-$60

Mt O'Halloran* (177m) has a rough track (better to walk) leading to a lookout. There are good views overlooking the Neales River. Nearby is the Angle Pole*, a turn in the old overland telegraph line. (*206/205*)
Dalhousie Springs turnoff: locality only; no facilities. (*219/192*) Dalhousie Springs lies about 140km north. Continue **NW** for Marla. *Continue* **SE** *for Oodnadatta.*
Plains and low rises provide vast vistas. Saltbush dominates the gibber-strewn countryside. To the south lies the northern branch of the Neales River, marked by a low coolabah woodland.

Edwards Creek ruin, south of Oodnadatta, SA

Road Trip 22
Central Australia Loop

**Alice Springs-Yulara-Kings Canyon-
Glen Helen-Alice Springs**
Total Distance: 1225km
Suggested Travelling Time: 5 days

Be moved by Australia's greatest geological treasures

See immense Uluru, the spectacular domed range of Kata Tjuta, the modern resort at Yulara, Mt Conner, superb Kings Canyon, Tylers Pass, Gosse Bluff, Ellery Creek Big Hole, Standley Chasm, Simpsons Gap, and the gorges: Redbank, Glen Helen, Ormiston and Serpentine.

Central Australian Loop

Made famous in part by the watercolour artist Albert Namatjira, and symbolic of the Australian outback, Central Australia presents the traveller with a bewildering display of natural wonders. Everything you have heard about its landscapes and countryside is true. High rocky bluffs, deep gorges, long linear ridges, prominent peaks, cool waterholes, immense rock domes, vivid red sand dunes, graceful desert oaks and magnificent colour changes on distant cliffs and ranges throughout the day, make Central Australia a magical place to visit. Bear in mind, though, that Central Australia covers a vast area and that many features of interest are separated by kilometres of plains country. Although the plains country may not seem interesting, after a week of exploring rocky gorges and mountain ranges, you may well appreciate the wide open spaces.

The Climate

The climate of Central Australia is primarily influenced by two features: a great distance from the sea (called continentality) and a moderate altitude (500 to 1500m). As a result it experiences wide variations in temperature. Summers maximums are hot to very hot (up to 45C) but with relatively mild nights. Winter maximums can be cool (14C to 22C) with cold to very cold nights (5C to -5C). The best times to visit Central Australia are in late autumn (April, May), or early Spring (mid-August, September). At these times the extreme heat of summer and cold of winter are mostly avoided.

Capital City Connections
Distances in Kilometres
SYDNEY-ALICE SPRINGS
via Great Western/ Mitchell/Barrier/Stuart Highways

	Intermediate	Total
Sydney	0	0
Dubbo	412	412
Broken Hill	741	1153
Port Augusta	415	1568
Coober Pedy	536	2104
Alice Springs	684	2788

BRISBANE-ALICE SPRINGS
via Warrego/Matilda/Barkly/Stuart Highways

	Intermediate	Total
Brisbane	0	0
Roma	481	481
Longreach	698	1179
Mt Isa	634	1813
Tennant Creek	648	2461
Alice Springs	507	2968

ADELAIDE-ALICE SPRINGS
via Highway One/Stuart Highway

	Intermediate	Total
Adelaide	0	0
Port Augusta	312	312
Glendambo	284	596
Coober Pedy	252	848
Kulgera	411	1259
Alice Springs	273	1532

The Route
Distances in kilometres

	Intermediate	Total
Alice Springs	0	0
Erldunda	199	199

Yulara	244	443
Kata Tjuta	73	516
Kings Canyon	356	872
Glen Helen	226	1098
Alice Springs	127	1225

Central Australia Loop

Alice Springs-Erldunda-Yulara-Kings Canyon-Glen Helen-Alice Springs

This road trip around Central Australia will provide the traveller with numerous scenic delights: the impressive ranges and gorges of the Western Macdonnell, the sand plains and saltlakes of the Amadeus Lowland, and the stupendous outcrops of Uluru, Kata Tjuta and Atila.

Most of the major tourist routes throughout Central Australia are accessible to all travellers, even for conventional vehicles on the unsealed roads, when dry. Nonetheless, relatively heavy traffic can make some of these unsealed roads rather corrugated and potholed. Also note that even where the main road is sealed, many of the shorter access roads to specific features may be unsealed and rough. Care will then be required, and caravans may not be accessible.

Warnings: roads subject to flooding (flash flooding in mountainous areas). Unsealed roads are often impassable when wet. Try to avoid travelling at night, especially on unsealed roads. Note that some unsealed roads may be rough due to relatively heavy usage. Travel according to road conditions, not to a timetable. Inform a reliable person of your intentions during the summer months on the following route: Mereenie Loop road between Kings Canyon-Glen Helen.
Note: No fuel between Kings Canyon-Glen Helen bypassing Hermannsberg 226km.

DAY 1: ALICE SPRINGS-YULARA
via Erldunda

Road to Take: Lasseter Highway
Grade 1
Total Distance: 443km (4:55)

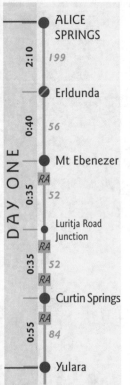

ALICE SPRINGS

2:10	199
Erldunda	
0:40	56
Mt Ebenezer	
RA 0:35	52
Luritja Road Junction	
RA 0:35	52
RA Curtin Springs	
RA 0:55	84
Yulara	

DAY ONE

Intermediate Distances:

	Km	Hours
Alice Springs-Erldunda	199	(2:10)
Erldunda-Mt Ebenezer	56	(0:40)
Mt Ebenezer-Luritja Road turnoff	52	(0:35)
Luritja Road turnoff-Curtin Springs	52	(0:35)
Curtin Springs-Yulara	84	(0:55)

Average Vehicles per Day: 300 east of Yulara
Regions Traversed: Central Australia (Amadeus Lowland)

ALICE SPRINGS (Alt 547m; Pop 24000):** major regional centre. For more information see Road Trip 20, Day 5. (*0/443*) *Road Trips 18, 20 and 23 connect.* Head **S** on Stuart Hwy for Erldunda.

For information on the route between Alice Springs and Erldunda see Road Trip 20, Day 5.

Erldunda (Alt 407m; Pop 30): roadhouse facility. For more information see Road Trip 20, Day 5. (*199/244*) *Road Trip 20 connects.* Turn **W** onto Lasseter Hwy for Mt Ebenezer. *Turn **N** onto Stuart Hwy for Alice Springs.*

Plains with a few low dunes support a mulga shrubland. Occasional fair views to the south. Desert oaks are common among the sand dunes.

Mt Ebenezer (Alt 457m; Pop 20):* roadhouse with some character. Owned by the Imanpa Aboriginal Community and an outlet for their artifacts. A pleasant place to relax from driving for a while. Accommodation, store, fuel. (*255/188*)

Plains support a covering of mulga shrublands with open grassy areas. Distant purple ranges seem to float in a grey-green sea. The Basedow Range and Mt Ebenezer are visible to the north. **Rest area**. (*300/143*)

Luritja Road junction (**N**): locality only; no facilities. (*307/136*) Continue **W** for Curtin Springs. *Continue **E** for Mt Ebenezer.*

Saltlakes* visible from the road. A short walk here is interesting. Park well off the road (not in wet weather). **Rest area** nearby. (*332/111*)

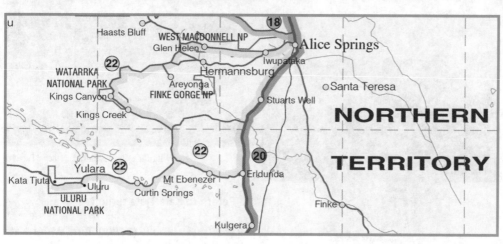

Detail of MAP 5

Lookout* and **rest area** gives an excellent and photogenic view of Mt Conner (863m), known as Atila to the Pitjantjatjara people. A short, steep path climbs a dune for further views of Atila and a saltlake - be careful crossing the road. (*338/105*)

Mulga Park turnoff: locality only; no facilities. (*348/95*) Mulga Park lies 68km **S**. Continue **W** for Curtin Springs. *Continue **E** for Mt Ebenezer.*

Curtin Springs (Alt 485m; Pop 10):* this road-house attached to a cattle station has plenty of character and characters. Provides good, cheap bush camping (saves spending at least one night at Yulara). Accommodation, store, fuel. (*359/84*)

Sand dunes line the road forming confused patterns and shapes. Having rarely, if ever, been grazed, the landscape is pristine. Spinifex is common on the dunes, desert oaks in-between.

Katiti Aboriginal Land: land belonging to Pitjantjatjara and Yankunytjatjara speaking people. No permit is required for entry.

Lookout* and **rest area** provides an excellent distant view of Uluru and Kata Tjuta from atop a sand dune (follow the footprints). At dusk you will find no better or more moving scene than this first glimpse of Uluru and Kata Tjuta. (*415/28*)

Yulara (Alt 510m; Pop 800): modern resort with a virtual monopoly on accommodation and services. Excellent for the fly-in fly-out tourists, bad news for budget travellers. As no camping is permitted in Uluru National Park, everyone must stay overnight here. Excellent national park displays* and information. Interesting architecture. Accommodation, store, fuel. (*443/0*)

Accommodation

Outback Pioneer Hotel, Yulara Dr, ✆02 9360 9099, ✪$60-$300

Spinifex Lodge, Yulara Dr, ✆02 9360 9099, ✪$135

Ayers Rock Campground, Yulara Dr, ✆08 8956 2055, ✪Site: $30 Van: $135

DAY 2: YULARA-ULURU/ KATA TJUTA-YULARA

Roads to Take: Uluru Road, Kata Tjuta Road
Grade I
Total Distance: 125km (1:30)
Intermediate Distances:

	Km	Hours
Yulara-Uluru	17km	(0:15)
Uluru-Kata Tjuta	56km	(0:40)
Kata Tjuta-Yulara	52km	(0:35)

Average Vehicles per Day: 300 south of Yulara
Regions Traversed: Central Australia (Amadeus Lowland)

Road Trip 22

DAY TWO

0:15   8   Yulara
           Sunset View-
           ing Area

           Kata Tjuta
           turnoff

       9

0:40   *Uluru*

       9

           Kata Tjuta
           turnoff

       43 *Sunset View-*
           ing Area

           Kata Tjuta

0:35   52 *Valley of the*
           Winds

           Yulara

Uluru, Uluru-Kata Tjuta National Park, NT

Yulara (Alt 510m; Pop 800): modern resort. For more information see Day 1. (*0/125*)

Uluru-Kata Tjuta National Park: large park preserving sand plain vegetation as well as the monoliths of Uluru and Kata Tjuta. Pay park fees at Park Entrance Station. (*4/121*)
Kata Tjuta turnoff: (*8/117*) Head **S** for Uluru.
Sunset Viewing Area:** highly recommended in order to see the fantastic changes of colour and light on Uluru. Stay after sunset (most people have left by then) for even more colour changes during twilight. (*12/113*)
Visitor Centre** provides fascinating information and displays, as well as kiosk facilities. Adjacent are Aboriginal artifacts on display and for sale. It is worth spending some time here. (*16/109*)

Uluru:*** probably the singularly most spectacular feature in Australia. Few people fail to be moved by its presence. Rising 348m above the plain, this nearly upstanding rocky range appears as a giant solitary rock. Walks are available, especially around the rock. The climb is exposed and hazardous, and considered inappropriate by the local Pitjantjatjara community. The Kantju Gorge walk is excellent in the late afternoon light. (*17/108*)

Kata Tjuta, Uluru-Kata Tjuta National Park, NT

Return to Kata Tjuta turnoff.

Kata Tjuta turnoff: (*26/99*) Turn **W** for Kata Tjuta.
Sand dunes support a cover of spinifex and shrubs, with desert oaks and mulga occupying the intervening flats.
Lookout* provides a viewing area overlooking Kata Tjuta. Best at dawn and dusk. (*51/74*)
Sunset viewing area** as good as that at Uluru, without the crowds. (*67/58*)

Kata Tjuta:*** spectacular range of conglomerate rocks forming high domes intersected by deep, narrow gorges. Of major spiritual significance to Pitjantjatjara and other Aboriginal people. Mt Olga rises 546m above the plain. Short walk into Olga Gorge**. (*69/56*)

Valley of the Winds:*** spetacular walk among the domes. Not to be missed. (*73/52*)

Return to Yulara via outgoing route.

Yulara (Alt 510m; Pop 800): modern resort. For more information see Day 1. (*125/0*)

DAY 3: YULARA-KINGS CANYON via Kings Creek

Roads to Take: Lasseter Highway, Luritja Road
Grade 1
Total Distance: 304km (3:25)

Intermediate Distances:

	Km	Hours
Yulara-Luritja Road junction	136	(1:30)
Luritja Rd jctn-Ernest Giles Rd jctn	68	(0:45)
Ernest Giles Rd jctn-Kings Creek	60	(0:40)
Kings Creek-Kings Canyon	40	(0:30)

Average Vehicles per Day: 100 east of Ranger Station
Regions Traversed: Central Australia (Amadeus Lowland)

Yulara (Alt 510m; Pop 800): modern resort. For more information see Day 1. (*0/304*)

For information on the route between Yulara and Luritja Road turnoff see Day 1.

Luritja Road junction: (*136/168*) Turn **N** for Kings Canyon. *Turn **W** for Yulara.*
Plain supports tracts of mulga.
Liddle Hills: interesting low range of stony hills. Good views* to the south of distant ranges that seem to float on a blue-green sea of mulga.
Plain* supports an attractive desert oak woodland. Spinifex forms the understorey. **Rest area** en route.
Ernest Giles Road junction: locality only; no facilities. (*204/100*) Continue **NW** for Kings Creek. *Continue **S** for Yulara.*
Wallara ruin: former roadhouse and accommodation facility which has been pulled down (a pity) set near the base of the striking Yowa Bluff (700m).
Plains* with low dunes support an attractive desert oak woodland with a spinifex understorey.
George Gill Range: flat-topped sandstone range rising 50m (in the east) to 250m (in the west) above the plain. The range parallels the road for some distance. In some places are smooth cliff-faces of Mereenie sandstone, the same rock that forms the walls of Kings Canyon.

Kings Creek (Alt 620m; Pop 5):* working cattle station which provides services for travellers. Pleasant place to camp or visit. Store, fuel. (*264/40*) Continue **W** for Kings Canyon. *Continue **E** for Yulara.*

Accommodation
Kings Creek Station Camping Ground, Luritja Road, ✆08 8956 7474, ✪Site: $20

Watarrka National Park: large national park of undulating sand plains and moderately high sandstone tableland edged by a prominent escarpment.
Ranger Station: call in here for displays and information about Watarrka National Park. (*279/25*)
Kathleen Gorge:* a short nature walk leads to an attractive waterhole, picnic area.
Lilla: homeland community of Luritja people.
Kings Canyon turnoff: (*299/5*) Turn **N** for the 6km drive to Kings Canyon***, a spectacular and deep canyon, well worth visiting. A strenuous climb to top of range offers superb views of the southern wall of the canyon (best in the late afternoon light). Interesting beehive domes** (the 'Lost City') and the 'Garden of Eden'** (a shady waterhole) are also of interest. At dusk the blazing red ridgelines are photogenic. Allow one full day, maybe two, to appreciate this Centralian highlight. Picnic area at Canyon car park.

Kings Canyon (Alt 600m; Pop 20): tourist style resort settlement. Aboriginal cultural tours available. Camping available. Accommodation, store, fuel. (*304/0*)
Accommodation
Kings Canyon Resort, Luritja Rd, ✆02 9360 9099, ✪$260-$370
Kings Canyon Resort Caravan Park, Luritja Rd, ✆08 8956 7442, ✪Site: $26 Van: $95

DAY 4: KINGS CANYON-GLEN HELEN
via Mereenie Loop Road

Road to Take: Mereenie Loop Road (Larapinta Drive)
Warning: Permit Required. Remote summer route. No fuel 226km.
Grade 3 All sealed route to Glen Helen via Kings Creek, Erldunda and Alice Springs

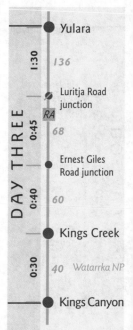

Road Trip 22

DAY THREE

Yulara
1:30 — 136
Luritja Road junction
RA
0:45 — 68
Ernest Giles Road junction
0:40 — 60
Kings Creek
0:30 — 40 — Watarrka NP
Kings Canyon

Road Trip 22

Total Distance: 226km (3:35)
Intermediate Distances:

	Km	Hours
Kings Canyon-Ipolera turnoff	154	(2:15)
Ipolera turnoff-Glen Helen	72	(1:20)

Average Vehicles per Day: less than 50
Regions Traversed: Central Australia

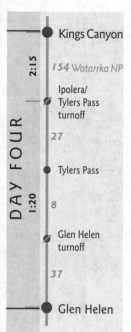

DAY FOUR

2:15

Kings Canyon

154 *Watarrka NP*

Ipolera/
Tylers Pass
turnoff

27

Tylers Pass

8

Glen Helen
turnoff

37

Glen Helen

1:20

Kings Canyon (Alt 600m; Pop 20): tourist style resort settlement. For more information see Day 3. (*0/226*)

Watarrka National Park: large national park of undulating sand plains and moderately high sandstone tableland edged by a prominent escarpment.

Carmichael Crag:* prominent rocky mountain (806m) rising above a mulga-clad plain. Very photogenic in the afternoon light.

Haast Bluff Aboriginal Land: Mereenie Loop Road permit required for entry.

Lookout* provides good views northward overlooking sand dune country. Just south is Morris Pass. To the south-east lies Hope Valley. No camping allowed. (*28/198*)

Plains support sparse woodlands of desert oaks with an understorey of spinifex. Low dunes can be seen. Southward and eastward ranges break the horizon. Camels Hump (921m) lies to the north. En route the Mereenie Gas Field is passed.

Katapata Pass:* scenic area near the Areyonga turn-off (no access) located in the attractive Gardiner Range. Mt Katapata (846m) lies to the north.

Low hills of sandstone can be seen to the south. Elsewhere is a plain supporting tracts of mulga and occasional desert oak groves. Gosses Bluff (914m) lies to the north.

Ipolera/Tylers Pass turnoff: (*154/72*) Turn **S** for the 22km return drive to Ipolera:* small Aboriginal community of Arrernte people set near the Krichauff Range. Cultural tours are available, including the large ground painting of the Spinifex Pigeon Dreaming**. Camping available. Store. Fuel may be available, check beforehand.

Turn **N** for Tylers Pass and Glen Helen (if necessary, continue straight on to Hermannsberg for fuel - 44km). *Turn **W** for Kings Canyon.*

Plains and low rises support desert oak woodlands and spinifex.

Gosse Bluff turnoff: (*166/60*) Turn here for Gosse Bluff* (12km return), a ring of mountains formed by a comet impact. Of major significance to Aboriginal people. Hills rise 200m above the plain. The area is known locally as Tnorala, and Gosse Bluff is located in the Tnorala Conservation Reserve. Picnic area.

Tylers Pass: locality only; no facilities. (*181/45*) Excellent views from nearby lookout** (**E**) in all directions. Southward is probably the best obtainable view of Gosse Bluff (914m). Northward, running east to west, are the MacDonnell Ranges, including the high peaks of Mt Sonder (1346m), Mt Razorback (1231m) and Mt Zeil (1531m). Attractive spinifex grasslands cover the nearby hills.

Glen Helen turnoff: (*189/37*) Turn **E** for Glen Helen. *Turn **S** for Tylers Pass.*

Amethyst Field:* fossicking area of amethysts and smoky quartz. Interesting outcrop of partially weathered crystals. Worth visiting. (*197/29*)

Redbank Gorge turnoff: (*206/20*) Turn **N** for the short drive to Redbank Gorge**, a very interesting gorge whose entrance is barred by a deep, cold waterhole. Though wet suit swimming or air-bed floating are the only ways to see the gorge properly, the sandy bed creek walk under river-red gums is certainly worthwhile. This is a very attractive area that is less busy than the other gorges in the Western MacDonnells. Camping available.

Glen Helen (Alt 631m; Pop 10):* interesting and atmospheric resort offering good services to travellers. Beautiful views of the Finke River and rocky bluffs. Nearby is Glen Helen Gorge**, probably one of the most attractive of the smaller Centralian gorges. A popular place during the tourist season. It is worth seeking a vantage point to view sunrise on nearby Mt Sonder (1346m). Accommodation, store, fuel. (*226/0*)

Accommodation

Glen Helen Resort Caravan Park, **Namatjira Drive**, ☏08 8956 7489, ✪Site: $22

DAY 5: GLEN HELEN-ALICE SPRINGS
via Namatjira Drive

Road to Take: Namatjira Drive
Grade 1
Total Distance: 127km (1:40)
Average Vehicles per Day: 180 east of Glen Helen
Regions Traversed: Central Australia (MacDonnell Ranges)

Glen Helen Gorge, MacDonnel Ranges, NT

Glen Helen (Alt 631m; Pop 10):* interesting resort settlement. For more information see Day 4. (*0/127*)

West MacDonnell National Park:*** large national park encompassing some of the finest arid scenery in Australia. The generally sparse vegetation cover allows for the rocky ranges and peaks to be clearly seen along with the daylight colour changes. The vegetation of the park is variable, though the following is typical: mulga dominates much of the valley lowlands along with other acacias, grevilleas (beefwood) and hakeas (corkwood). The southern sunny slopes are dominated by spinifex. The northern shady slopes support native figs, eromophilas (native fuchsias), cycads, ghost gums, with cypress pines on the ridgelines.

Ormiston Gorge turnoff: (*4/123*) A short detour leads **N** through spectacular country to Ormiston Gorge**, a large gorge with numerous walking tracks, one of which leads into Ormiston Pound**, a rocky valley surrounded by some of the finest arid mountain landscapes to be seen anywhere, including the high Mt Giles (1283m). Well worth visiting, although can be very crowded. Stacks of information and displays are at the visitors centre. Camping available.

Ochre Pits turnoff: (*19/108*) This short detour leads **N** to the Ochre pits*, an interesting ochre cliffs cut by a creek bed. Ochre still used by Aborigines today. Very photogenic. Walking track to Inarlanga Pass*.

Lookout* provides good views eastwards along the narrow Mereenie Valley and the high peaks of the Heavitree Range on the northern side of the road. **Rest area**. (*22/105*)

Serpentine Chalet access road turnoff: (*22/105*) Turn **N** for Serpentine Chalet ruin*. This feature gives some idea of tourism 1960s style. Numerous walks into the ranges. Camping available.

Serpentine Gorge turnoff: (*30/97*) A short detour **N** leads to Serpentine Gorge*, an interesting gorge in a scenic setting, certainly worth a look. Entrance is barred by a waterhole (not deep) beyond which the walker can see why the gorge was so named. A steep climb leads to a spectacular lookout**.

Low range* south of the road is a long linear ridge. This ridge parallels the road well to the west of Glen Helen.

Ellery Creek Big Hole turnoff: (*41/86*) Turn **N** for Ellery Creek Big Hole:* gorge with a large and attractive waterhole which is always very cold. Interesting rock formations. Camping available.

Lookout:** excellent views to the west. It is worth being here at sunrise to see the sunlight strike the high, jagged peaks while the valley below lies in darkness. Spinifex abounds here, very photogenic in the afternoon light. Good eastwards views* east of the lookout along the road - near sunset is the best time. **Rest area**. (*51/76*)

Larapinta Drive junction: locality only; no facilities. (*82/45*) Turn **NE** for Alice Springs. *Turn* **W** *for Glen Helen*.

Hugh River: broad sandy riverbed with attractive river red gums.

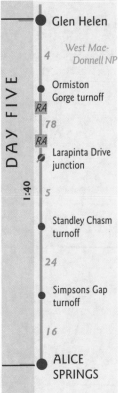

DAY FIVE
1:40

Glen Helen

4
West MacDonnell NP

RA
Ormiston Gorge turnoff
78
RA
Larapinta Drive junction
5
Standley Chasm turnoff
24
Simpsons Gap turnoff
16
ALICE SPRINGS

Iwupataka: formerly known as Jay Creek, this Aboriginal settlement is visible from the road. Various language groups live here, including Western Arrernte and Southern Luritja. No public access.

Iwupataka Aboriginal Land: freehold land occupied by Western Arrernte and Southern Luritja people. No permit is required for travel on the main road.

Standley Chasm turnoff: (87/44) An 18km return sealed road leads **N** to Standley Chasm**, a narrow gorge of red quartzite which positively glows for ten minutes as the sun passes quickly overhead at midday. Well worth seeing but expect a crowd. This narrow 5 to 9m wide gorge is worth seeing at other times. A walk is required to see the spectacle. Located on Iwupataka Aboriginal Land; no permit required for access. Kiosk facilities are available.

Twin Ghost Gums:* two ghost gums made famous by an Albert Namatjira painting. Scenic backdrop.

Honeymoon Gap turnoff: (110/17) Turn **N** for Honeymoon Gap*, a small and attractive gap in a narrow, rocky range. The sandy creek bed supports a shady river red gum woodland. A ridgeline of cypress pines is very photogenic in the afternoon light. The road through the gap provides an alternative route to Alice Springs.

Simpsons Gap turnoff: (111/16) A 14km return (Grade 1) drive **N** leads to Simpsons Gap**, a very popular gorge with a cathedral-like atmosphere in a spectacular setting. Interesting rock formations and a waterhole can be seen. Numerous walks lead into the ranges and to rocky bluffs and lookouts. The ranger station has lots of information and displays.

John Flynn's Grave:* grave of the founder of the Royal Flying Doctor Service, set near the foot of Mt Gillen.

ALICE SPRINGS (Alt 547m; Pop 24000):** major regional centre. For more information see Road Trip 20, Day 5. (127/0) *Road Trips 18, 20 and 23 connect.*

Road Trip 23
Tanami Connection

Alice Springs-Halls Creek
Total Distance: 1117km
Suggested Travelling Time: 3 days

Take the adventurous route through the Tanami Desert

See the northern MacDonnell Ranges, Aboriginal settlements, vast spinifex plains, the Rabbit Flat Roadhouse, Elskey Hills, Sturt Creek, the world's second-largest meteorite crater at Wolfe Creek, and isolated desert scenery.

Tanami Connection

The Tanami Connection offers travellers an adventurous short-cut between Central Australia and The Kimberley via the Tanami Desert. While most commentators suggest that the route can be driven in two days and that there is nothing to see, a traveller could easily spend five days on this road and see plenty. The southern sealed portion travels along the northern edge of the MacDonnell Ranges, offering some excellent desert mountain views. The grand scenery also takes in vast spinifex plains and rocky ranges and outcrops. The world's second largest meteorite crater and Australia's remotest roadhouse await the traveller. The Tanami Road is one of the few roads in Australia that crosses virtually uninhabited country for much of its length, so there are some awesome spaces to traverse. A journey along the Tanami Road must not be undertaken lightly.

The Climate

Summers maximums are hot to very hot (up to 45C). Nights are very warm. Winter maximums can be cool to mild (15C to 22C in the south) with cold to very cold nights (5C to -5C in the south). Milder conditions prevail in the north. The best times to travel the Tanami are in late autumn (May) or late winter/early Spring (mid-August, September). At these times the extreme heat of summer and the cold of winter can be largely avoided.

Capital City Connections
Distances in kilometres
SYDNEY-ALICE SPRINGS
via Great Western/Mitchell/Barrier/Stuart Highways

	Intermediate	Total
Sydney	0	0
Dubbo	412	412
Broken Hill	741	1153
Port Augusta	415	1568
Coober Pedy	536	2104
Alice Springs	684	2788

BRISBANE-ALICE SPRINGS
via Warrego/Matilda/Barkly/Stuart Highways

	Intermediate	Total
Brisbane	0	0
Roma	481	481
Longreach	698	1179
Mt Isa	634	1813
Tennant Creek	648	2461
Alice Springs	507	2968

ADELAIDE-ALICE SPRINGS
via Highway One/Stuart Highway

	Intermediate	Total
Adelaide	0	0
Port Augusta	312	312
Glendambo	284	596
Coober Pedy	252	848
Kulgera	411	1259
Alice Springs	273	1532

The Route
Distances in kilometres

	Intermediate	Total
Alice Springs	0	0
Tilmouth Crossing	187	187
Yuendumu	103	290
Rabbit Flat	308	598
Billiluna	282	880
Halls Creek	237	1117

Road Trip 23

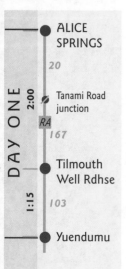

ALICE SPRINGS

2:00

20

Tanami Road junction

RA

167

1:15

Tilmouth Well Rdhse

103

Yuendumu

Tanami Road
Alice Springs-Halls Creek

The Tanami Road is a long, lonely route over mostly good roads, except for the Western Australian section immediately west of the state border (sandy with bulldust holes, bad corrugations - recommended only for experienced drivers of conventional vehicles). This is a remote road travelling through remote country. Heed the warnings below.

Warnings: road subject to flooding; impassable in wet weather. Avoid travelling at night. Make local enquiries before proceeding and inform a reliable person of your travel intentions. The road between WA-NT Border and Billiluna is rough; recommended only for experienced drivers of conventional drive vehicles. Stay out of this area in summer unless experienced; convoy travel for all vehicles recommended at this time. Monsoonal rains occasionally flood the route between Halls Creek and Balgo turn-off - road may be closed for months.

Note: no fuel available between Yuendemu-Rabbit Flat 308km; Rabbit-Flat-Billiluna 282km.

Important Note: Rabbit Flat Roadhouse is closed Tuesday, Wednesday and Thursday - the traveller will then require sufficient fuel for the Yuendumu-Billiluna leg (590km). Also note that Carranya Roadhouse does not sell fuel. Always make local enquiries regarding fuel before leaving Alice Springs or Halls Creek.

DAY 1: ALICE SPRINGS-YUENDUMU
via Tilmouth Well Roadhouse

Road to Take: Tanami Road
Grade 3
Total Distance: 290km (3:15)
Intermediate Distances:

	Km	Hours
Alice Springs-Tilmouth Well Rdhse	187	(2:00)
Tilmouth Well Rdhse-Yuendumu	103	(1:15)

Average Vehicles per Day: 50 north of Papunya turn-off
Regions Traversed: Central Australia

ALICE SPRINGS (Alt 547m; Pop 24000):** major regional centre. For more information see Road Trip 20, Day 5. (*0/290*) *Road Trips 19, 20 and 22 connect.* Head **N** on Stuart Highway for Tanami Road junction.

Hilly country forms the northern edge of the MacDonnell Ranges complex. Good views* from the tops of rises, especially southward towards the striking quartzite cliffline of the Heavitree Range. Granite boulders, dry valleys and jagged ridges can be seen.

Tanami Road junction: locality only; no facilities. (*20/270*) Turn **W** for Tilmouth Well. *Turn S for Alice Springs.*

Plains support extensive tracts of grassy mulga shrublands, known locally as the Everard Scrub. The plains themselves, like those further west, form part of the vast Burt Plain, a sand and granitic plain set over 600 metres above sea level. Good eastward views along the road towards Mt Everard (910m).

Plains offer excellent views southward towards Mt Hay (1249m), one of the higher peaks of Central Australia. The countryside here is devoid of mulga and supports a grassland. Wildflowers are common after rain. This would be one of the best sweeping views** available in Central Australia.

Low rises offer reasonable views* from their crests. Mt Chapple (1206m) is visible to the south-west. **Rest area.** (*125/165*)

Plains support grassy mulga shrublands. Southward is an impressive view of an unnamed range rising far above the plains. Its spinifex-clad slopes exhibit rocky outcrops.

Plains support tracts of mulga shrublands which unfortunately do not allow for views. The observant may glimpse Rembrandt Rock (661m), a granite hill rising above the plain. Patches of melaleucas grow on outwash plains. Other shrubs and trees include grevilleas and corkwoods.

Detail of MAP 6

DAY TWO

3:45   RA

308   *Chilla Well*

0:35   45

● Yuendumu

● Rabbit Flat

● *Tanami Mine*

Tilmouth Well Roadhouse (Alt 560m; Pop 5): roadhouse facility set by Napperby Creek. This river red gum-lined sandy creek is a delightful spot. Accommodation, limited stores, fuel. (*187/103*)

Stuart Bluff Range: a surprisingly narrow range of rock rising over 100 metres above the plain (710m above sea level). Worth pulling over and scrambling up the northern slope to the top (be careful of loose rocks) for excellent views* both north (endless mulga scrubs sliced by the Yuendumu road; Reynolds Range on the horizon) and south (highest peaks of the Western MacDonnells clearly visible as well as a large saltpan: Lake Lewis). Only fair views southward from the road pass.

Plains support extensive tracts of mulga shrublands with a grassy understorey. At intervals along the road are disused earth dams, bores and windmills, relics from the droving days.

Yuendumu and Yalpirakinu Aboriginal Land: no permit is required for entry, providing you stay on the road reserve. A permit is not required (this may change) for fuel or store purchases in Yuendumu. No alcohol allowed.

Hilly country exhibits rocky outcrops. Fair views* westward overlooking Yuendumu and the surrounding low ranges.

Yuendumu (Alt 665m; Pop 600-900): sizeable Aboriginal settlement of predominantly Warlpiri-speaking people, known locally as Yurntumu. If you find the place somewhat run down, consider that these people had little choice in its location, design, or whether or not they wished to live here. For most this is not their homeland, although many have since returned to their 'country camps'. Fascinating art gallery**. No accommodation. Stores, fuel. (*290/0*)

DAY 2: YUENDUMU-TANAMI MINE via Rabbit Flat

Road to Take: Tanami Road
Grade 3
Warning: Remote Route. No fuel for 308km
Total Distance: 353km (4:20)
Intermediate Distances:

	Km	Hours
Yuendumu-Rabbit Flat	308	(3:45)
Rabbit Flat-Tanami Mine	45	(0:35)

Average Vehicles per Day: 15 west of Yuendumu
Regions Traversed: Central Australia, Tanami Desert

▾

Yuendumu (Alt 665m; Pop 600-900): sizeable Aboriginal settlement. For more information see Day 1. (*0/353*)

Road Trip 23

Tanami Road, south of Tilmouth Crossing, NT

Yuendumu Aboriginal Land: Warlpiri land; no permit required for road access.

Low ranges lie north and south of the road interspersed with mulga-clad plains. Occasional fair to good views*.

Yarunganyi Hills:* attractive range of isolated hills, mountains and ridges separated by sandy flats and shallow valleys. Granite domes are common. Mulga shrublands and open grassy areas cover the lowlands.

Ruins* of an old mine and Mt Doreen Station. Located on private property. Numerous relics and old buildings which are very photogenic. Do not disturb anything. Enquire locally about access. Attractive country hereabouts. (*58/295*)

Sandplain of acacia shrubs and spinifex marks the edge of the Tanami Desert. Southward the sand plain grades into a mulga-clad plain. Good views* southward towards distant ranges.

Plain supports a mulga shrubland in the vicinity of Yaloogarrie Creek.

Sandplain covered with acacia shrublands and spinifex.

Mala Aboriginal Land: no permit required for road access. No alcohol allowed.

Jila: Aboriginal country-camp of Warlpiri people located just off the road. (*127/226*)

Chilla Well:* old windmill and bore, nowadays a ruin, located in a shallow valley. Worth a short walk to investigate. (*129/224*)

Low rise (about one kilometre north) offers vast views over the desert. Mt Theo can be seen in the far distance to the north-east.

Central Desert Aboriginal Land: no permit required for road access. No alcohol allowed.

Sandplain supports tracts of acacia shrublands with a spinifex understorey.

Renahans Bore: **rest area**. Only the graffiti on the water tank is remotely interesting. (*160/193*)

Ruin:* yards and an old bore (Refrigerator Well) worth inspecting. Area supports many bloodwood trees. Ruin difficult to see from the road. (*187/166*)

Sandplain supports acacia shrublands with a spinifex understorey. This plain is typical of the southern Tanami Desert. Note the variations in vegetation: relatively dense in the shallow valleys; much thinner on the higher ground.

Plain offers open views* (one of the few along the Tanami Road) over the spinifex. Large anthills are common. At times, smoke from fires may be seen in the far distance - perhaps of Aboriginal firestick farming.

Sandplain supports an acacia shrubland with a spinifex understorey.

Rocky outcrops of granite boulders lie adjacent to the road. No public access; sacred site.

The Granites Mine: working mine; no access or facilities for travellers. Assistance is given if required. Some ruins* of the old Granites mine can be seen upon a low ridge south of the road. (*253/100*)

Low ridge offers reasonable views* of The Granites Mine, an interesting place to take a short walk.

Sandplain supports an acacia shrubland with a spinifex understorey.

Low rise covered with white quartz, supports a mulga shrubland with a spinifex understorey.

Plain exhibits grassy areas, claypans and large anthills. Expansive views*.

Rabbit Flat*: Australia's remotest roadhouse. Nonetheless, the night time glow of mining operations in two directions makes the owner feel just a bit built-out! Interesting settlement. Note: no service available on Tuesday, Wednesday or Thursday. Camping available. Limited store, fuel. (*308/45*)

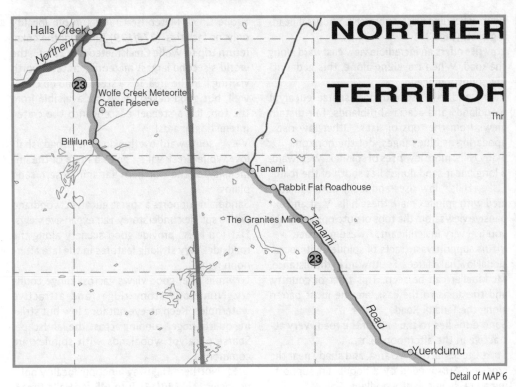

Detail of MAP 6

Low rise offers fair views. Spinifex and occasional shrubs cover its surface.

Plains support a sparse covering of acacias with a shrubby understorey.

Tanami Mine: a reworked old gold mine, currently closed. A view of the workings can be seen from the Lajamanu turn-off, which is set upon a rise. This mine, along with neighbouring mines (The Granites and Bullock Soak), developed in co-operation with the Warlpiri people, upon whose lands these mines are located. You will need to establish your own bush camp here. (**353/0**)

DAY 3: TANAMI MINE-HALLS CREEK
via Billiluna

Road to Take: Tanami Road
Grade 4
Grade 3 Billiluna-Halls Creek
Warning: Remote Route. No fuel for 237km

Total Distance: 407km (5:30)
Intermediate Distances:

	Km	Hours
Tanami Mine-Billiluna	237	(3:15)
Billiluna-Halls Creek	170	(2:15)

Average Vehicles per Day: approximately 10 south of the Balgo turnoff
Regions Traversed: Tanami Desert, The Kimberley

Tanami Mine: for more information see Day 2. (**0/407**)

Central Desert Aboriginal Land: Warlpiri Land. No permit is required, but stay on the road reserve.

Mt Tanami is marked by rocky outcrops set upon a rise and surrounded by undulating country and a few minor creeks. Interesting area.

Killi Killi Hills: another low rise offering distant westward views* along the road.

State border between Northern Territory and Western Australia. Time zone boundary: add 1.5

hours if heading west, subtract 1.5 hours if heading east. (**78/329**)

Low rise offers an incredible view eastward along the road. When travelling alone, this is daunting country indeed!

Plains and low rises support sparse eucalypt woodlands and acacia shrublands. Fair distant views from the tops of rises. Other low rises, appearing as blue ranges, dot the horizon.

Selby Hills: more low rises of spinifex. Westward, a long linear sand dune* lies south of the road.

Elskey Hills:* low rises and rocky outcrops covered with spinifex mark these hills. Vast and expansive views from the tops of outcrops will make you feel very insignificant. Awesome space.

Plains support vast tracts of spinifex with occasional low hakea trees. Southward in the distance, Mt Mueller can be seen. This tract of country, and the areas to the east, are the most barren along the Tanami Road.

Sand dune lies to the east of the road. Very attractive in the afternoon light.

Sturt Creek:* attractive area, and shady near the crossing. Surrounded by a floodplain supporting a grassy eucalypt woodland.

Billiluna (Alt 290m; Pop 100):* friendly Aboriginal township and cattle station of Walmatjarri and Kukatja people. No accommodation. Store, fuel. (**237/170**)

View * southwards overlooking vast plains.

Plains support a sparse eucalypt woodland with spinifex, sometimes shrubs, in the understorey.

Carranya Roadhouse: establishment that had no fuel during my visit and, last heard, was closed. (**277/130**)

Wolfe Creek Meteorite Crater turnoff: locality only; no facilities. (**278/129**) Turn **E** for the 46km return trip to Wolfe Creek Meteorite Crater*, the world's second largest meteorite crater - worth visiting if in the area. It's a steep climb up crater wall, but good desert views are available from the top. It's a steeper descent into the crater. Interesting lizards!

View* southward overlooking the broad, shallow Wolfe Creek valley, gives a taste of the immensity of the northern Tanami Desert sand plains.

Sandplain supports a sparse eucalypt woodland with a spinifex understorey. Fair expansive views.

Flat-top hills* provide good scenery along the roadside. Very striking features in the late afternoon light.

Low hills offer good views* across range country. Numerous stony ridges and attractive waterholes. Keep an eye out for a low but striking quartz ridge* running across the landscape. Sparse eucalypt woodlands with spinifex are common.

Great Northern Highway junction: locality only; no facilities. (**390/17**) Turn **NE** for Halls Creek. *Turn S onto Tanami Road for Alice Springs.*

Plains and low rises support sparse eucalypt woodlands with a grassy understorey. Distant views from the tops of rises northward towards the purple bulk of Mt Barrett (696m).

HALLS CREEK (Alt 409m; Pop 1250):* interesting grazing and Aboriginal town. For more information see Road Trip 26, Day 3. (**407/0**) *Road Trip 26 connects.*

Road Trip 24
Barkly Tableland Connection

Mt Isa-Daly Waters Junction
Total Distance: 1323km
Suggested Travelling Time: 4 days

Encounter sweeping plains, escarpment country and the Barkly Tableland

See the sandstone spires of Bukalara Rocks, Camooweal historic village, the endless vistas across the Barkly Tableland, Brunette Downs Racecourse, and the scenic area around Cape Crawford.

Barkly Tableland Connection

The Barkly region is a huge tract of country supporting cattle stations, Aboriginal communities, and a few small townships. Space is the essential element of the Barkly region, especially on the broad sweeping plains of the Barkly Tableland. This road trip provides a sealed alternative to the main Barkly Highway, and the unsealed Savanna Way further north. By travelling to Cape Crawford you will see spectacular escarpment country. At Borroloola you will have access to the McArthur River and Gulf of Carpentaria estuarine waters.

The Climate

The Barkly region is a very warm to hot land throughout the year. Maximum temperatures are extreme, especially in April and between August and November, with temperatures reaching 35C-40C away from the coast. Nightime temperatures are also uncomfortable with minimums often over 25C, and typically accompanied by high humidity. While maximum temperatures are slightly cooler during the monsoon, due to the cloud cover, it can also be showery.

The time to visit is between May and August (the dry season in the north). Note that even then maximum temperatures may well be in the low-thirties, though minimums are mild, falling to around 10C. Rainfall is virtually non-existant at this time.

Capital City Connections

Distances in kilometres

SYDNEY-MT ISA
via Great Western/Mitchell/Matilda/Barkly Highways

	Intermediate	Total
Sydney	0	0
Nyngan	578	578
Charleville	655	1233
Mt Isa	1150	2383

BRISBANE-MT ISA
via Warrego/Matilda/Barkly Highways

	Intermediate	Total
Brisbane	0	0
Roma	481	481
Longreach	698	1179
Cloncurry	516	1695
Mt Isa	118	1813

ADELAIDE-BARKLY RH
via Highway One/Stuart/Barkly Highways

	Intermediate	Total
Adelaide	0	0
Port Augusta	312	312
Coober Pedy	536	848
Kulgera	411	1259
Alice Springs	273	1532
Three Ways	531	2063
Barkly RH	187	2250

The Route

Distances in kilometres

	Intermediate	Total
Mt Isa	0	0
Camooweal	189	189
Barkly Roadhouse	260	449
Cape Crawford	377	826
Borroloola	113	939
Cape Crawford	113	1052
Daly Waters	271	1323

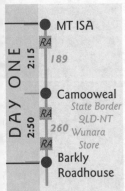

Road Trip 24

Detail of MAP 4

Barkly Highway

Mt Isa-Barkly Roadhouse

West of Mt Isa, vast expanses of Mitchell grass form the Barkly Tableland - big sky country. Further west lies a vast semi-arid landscape described by many travellers as dreary - slow down and enjoy the space.

Warnings: beware of stock and kangaroos at night; avoid night travel if at all possible. Road may be subject to flooding.

DAY 1: MT ISA-BARKLY ROADHOUSE via Camooweal

Road to Take: Barkly Highway
Grade 1
Total Distance: 449km (5:05)
Intermediate Distances:

	Km	Hours
Mt Isa-Camooweal	189	(2:15)
Camooweal-Barkly Roadhouse	260	(2:50)

Average Vehicles per Day: 200 east of Avon Downs
Regions Traversed: North-West Queensland, Barkly Tableland

MT ISA (Alt 356m; Pop 22200):** large mining town and regional centre. For more information see Road Trip 11, Day 3. (*0/449*) *Road Trips 11, 12 and 16 connect.*

For information on the route between Mt Isa and Camooweal see Road Trip 11, Day 4.

Camooweal (Alt 233m; Pop 360): interesting grazing town. For more information see Road Trip 11, Day 4. (*189/260*)

For information on the route between Camooweal and Barkly Roadhouse see Road Trip 11, Day 4.

Barkly Roadhouse (Alt 244m; Pop 5): roadhouse facility. For more information see Road Trip 11, Day 4. (*449/0*) *Road Trip 11 connects. Turn E onto Barkly Hwy for Camooweal.*

Tablelands/Carpentaria Highways

Barkly Roadhouse-Borroloola-Daly Waters Junction

The Barkly Tableland's two highways, the Carpentaria and Tablelands - both really beef roads - offer travellers a sealed alternative route between the Top End and north-west Queensland. Consequently they are moderately trafficked by out-back standards. While one would be stretched to call either route scenic, there are some exceptions, particularly in the Cape Crawford area where both routes leave the tablelands and pass through broken escarpment country before entering the Gulf Savanna region. Also, along the Tablelands Highway there are many broad vistas overlooking the vast Mitchell grass plains.

Warnings: roads subject to flooding. Avoid travelling at night. During the monsoon make local enquiries before proceeding. If travelling at this time carry water and food (as you always would) in case of being stranded by floodwaters.
Note: no fuel between Barkly Roadhouse and Cape Crawford (377km); Cape Crawford-Daly Waters Junction (271km).

DAY 2: BARKLY ROADHOUSE-CAPE CRAWFORD
via Tablelands Highway

Road to Take: Tablelands Highway
Grade 2
Total Distance: 377km (4:20)
Average Vehicles per Day: 50 north of Brunette Downs turnoff
Regions Traversed: Barkly Tableland, Gulf Country

Barkly Roadhouse (Alt 244m; Pop 5): roadhouse facility. For more information see Road Trip 11, Day 4. (*0/377*) Turn **N** onto Tablelands Hwy for Cape Crawford.

Plains support vast areas of eucalypt woodlands, typically bloodwoods, with a spinifex understorey. Plains support extensive tracts of Mitchell grass grasslands. Playford River crossing (*54/323*) of minor interest.
Lake Sylvester* lies **W** of the road. It is an ephemeral drainage depression. Fringing these 'lakes', sometimes referred to as dry bogs, are areas of bluebush shrublands. (*100/277*)

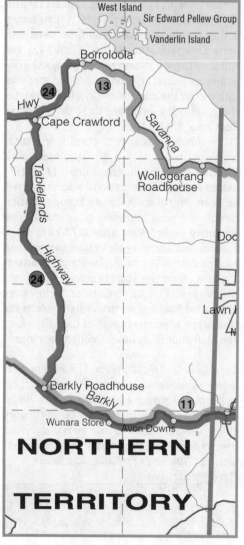

Detail of MAP 4

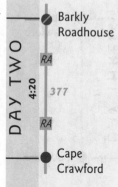

Plains exhibit broad vistas of Mitchell grass grasslands. Expansive views of little but open space from the tops of rises. These plains are mostly composed of clay underlain by limestone. A few outcrops and low limestone rises may be seen. The observant may notice differences in the Mitchell grass: barley Mitchell grass is widespread, occasionally in combination with Flinders grass; wetter areas (depressions) may

DAY THREE 1:15

Cape
Crawford

113

*Bukalara
Rocks*

Booroloola

exhibit weeping Mitchell grass. Grasses are usually green after monsoonal rains, turning brown during the dry season drought. Between Brunette Downs Station turnoff (*130/247*) and Anthony Lagoon Station turnoff (*225/152*), ribbon-stones* can be found along the roadside. Park well off the road (when dry), rest from travelling, enjoy the space and do some fossicking. **Rest area**. (*147/230*)

Plains support extensive tracts of sparse eucalypt woodlands with a grassy understorey. Corella Creek Community turnoff (*166/211*) passed en route. The occasional acacia shrub will be seen. North of Anthony Lagoon Station turnoff is a wide bluegrass grassland offering expansive views*. **Rest area**. (*270/107*)

Ranges, hills and rocky bluffs form the northern escarpment* of the Barkly Tableland, an attractive area supporting sparse eucalypt woodlands with a spinifex understorey. Note the low ridge of jumbled boulders on the western side of the road, a few kilometres south of Cape Crawford. The McArthur River flows through the range.

Cape Crawford (Alt 80m; Pop 5):* modern roadhouse settlement located in an attractive setting. Helicopter flights are available to the Abner Range, one of northern Australia's many 'hidden cities'. Ground tours may also be available. Turn here for Borroloola. Accomodation, limited store, fuel. (*377/0*) *Turn S for Barkly Roadhouse.*

Accommodation
Heartbreak Hotel, Carpentaria Hwy, ©08 8975 9928, ✪$55
Heartbreak Hotel Caravan Park, Carpentaria Hwy, ©08 8975 9928, ✪Site: $14

DAY 3: CAPE CRAWFORD-BORROLOOLA

Road to Take: Carpentaria Highway
Grade 2 (being upgraded to Grade 1)
Total Distance: 113km (1:15)
Average Vehicles per Day: 100 east of Cape Crawford
Regions Traversed: Gulf Country

Cape Crawford (Alt 80m; Pop 5):* modern roadhouse settlement located in an attractive setting. For more information see Day 2. (*0/113*) Turn **E** onto Carpentaria Hwy for Borroloola.

For details of the route between Cape Crawford and Borroloola see Day 4.

Borroloola (Alt 18m; Pop 800):* interesting settlement. For more information see Road Trip 13, Day 1. (*113/0*) *Road Trip 13 connects.*

DAY 4: BORROLOOLA-DALY WATERS JUNCTION via Cape Crawford

Road to Take: Carpentaria Highway
Grade 2 (being upgrade to Grade 1)
Total Distance: 384km (4:15)
Intermediate Distances:

	Km	Hours
Borroloola-Cape Crawford	113	(1:15)
Cape Crawford-Daly Waters Jctn	271	(3:00)

Average Vehicles per Day: 60 east of Daly Waters Junction
Regions Traversed: Gulf Country, Barkly Tableland, Top End

Borroloola (Alt 18m; Pop 800):* interesting settlement. For more information see Road Trip 13, Day 1. (*0/384*)

Narwinbi Aboriginal Land surrounds Borroloola. No permit is required for entry. Land and town are home to a sizeable population of Mara, Yanyula and Garawa people.

Plains and occasional low hills support a eucalypt woodland. Spinifex is common on hill slopes. Jump-up forms eastern edge of Bukalara Range and offers good views* eastward. The location is known as Frog Rock or Borroloola Jump-up. Numerous rocky ridges hereabout. The area supports a eucalypt woodland with a spinifex understorey.

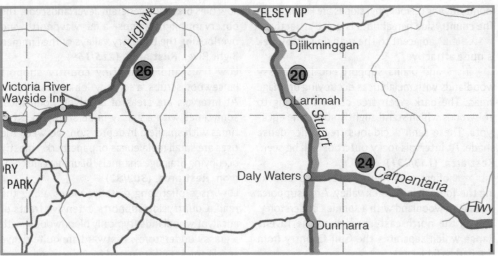

Detail of MAP 6

DAY FOUR

1:15

3:00

● Borroloola

113 Bukalara Rocks

RA

● Cape Crawford

271

RA

● Daly Waters Junction

Roper Bar turnoff (**N**): location only; no facilities. (**26/358**) About 2km down this road is Ryans Bend Store - interesting waterhole* nearby.

Low ridges rise above the general undulating level of the upland. The area supports a eucalypt woodland with an understorey of spinifex.

Bukalara Rocks:** a 'hidden city' of sandstone spires rising 25m in height. A fascinating and pristine area well worth investigating. Centrepiece of the Caranbirini Conservation Reserve. Camping is available. Adjacent is a pretty waterhole. (**41/343**)

Pandanus Jump-up: low jump-up or hill separating lower plains from stony uplands. Fair views* southward.

McArthur River Mine: large mine lying east of the road. (**62/322**)

Eight Mile Waterhole turnoff: (**71/313**) Turn **S** for the 3km return drive to Eight Mile Waterhole*, an attractive waterhole on the McArthur River.

Plains support eucalypt woodlands with a grassy understorey. Bauhinia woodlands can be seen at intervals. Bauhinias have blue-green paired leaves with drooping branchlets - trees are deciduous during the dry season. Plains offer fair to good views* of flat-top ranges and escarpments.

Leila Hill:* prominent hill set by the road, with good views southward towards the escarpment country. West of the hill is the Leila Creek

floodplain which supports a eucalypt woodland and minor wetlands.

Cape Crawford:* prominent headland and cliffline forming a portion of the Barkly Tableland escarpment.

Cape Crawford (Alt 80m; Pop 5):* modern roadhouse facility. For more information see Day 2. (**113/271**)

Roper Bar turnoff (**N**): locality only; no facilities. (**115/269**) Continue **W** for Daly Waters. *Continue **E** for Cape Crawford.*

Low hills* support eucalypt woodlands with a spinifex understorey. The large yellow flowers on the leafless (during the dry season) small trees

McArthur River, King Ash Bay, NT

found growing on rocky hill slopes are kapok bush. The countryside hereabouts is quite attractive. Waterhole* adjacent to the road on Little Creek is quite attractive.

Low rises and plains support eucalypt grassy woodlands with melaleucas occupying drainage areas. The dark green tree crowns belong to ironwoods which stand slightly above the eucalypts. These semi-deciduous trees offer dense shade. At intervals rocky outcrops will be seen. **Rest area**. (*153/231*)

Jump-up offers good views* eastward overlooking the Tooganginie Creek valley. Area supports a eucalypt woodland with a spinifex understorey. This is the north-eastern edge of the Favenc Range which separates the Gulf Country from the Barkly Tableland.

Undulating country supports a mixture of eucalypt woodlands with a variety of understoreys: grassy, shrubby and spinifex. Acacia shrublands are common.

Low hills break the generally level landscape. The observant might glimpse a fair view northward overlooking the tributary valleys of the Limmen Bight River. **Rest area**. (*215/169*)

Low rises and undulating country support lancewood scrubs, a scrappy-looking tall shrub. At intervals are areas of eucalypt woodlands, sometimes with a grassy understorey, at other times with spinifex. In depressions between the rises are small melaleucas or paperbarks, mostly occupying drainage channels. Bauhinias are common. **Rest area**. (*302/82*)

Low rises offer long distance views along the road. Countryside supports extensive tracts of eucalypt woodlands (typically bloodwoods) with a grassy understorey. Eastward are quite dense acacia thickets dominated by lancewood.

Daly Waters Junction (Alt 230m; Pop 10): modern roadhouse. For more information see Road Trip 20, Day 9. (*384/0*) *Road Trip 20 connects.*

Road Trip 25
Top End Loop

Darwin-Jabiru-Pine Creek-Grove Hill-Daly River-Darwin
Total Distance: 962km
Suggested Travelling Time: 4 days

Go through Kakadu

See the Adelaide and Mary Rivers, the tourist centre of South Alligator, the amazing Aboriginal rock art galleries at Ubirr and Nourlangie, laid-back Cooinda, Kakadu National Park, the Burrundie ruins, Grove Hill pub, the natural spa-baths at Douglas Hot Springs, and the delightful Daly River.

Top End Loop

Australia's Top End and Kakadu region is a vast tract of monsoonal land. It is sparsely populated country, extensively grazed by beef cattle, and supporting large reserves and wilderness areas such as the Kakadu and Litchfield national parks. Towns are few and far between - those that exist are service centres for tourists, cattle stations or the mining industry. Although a sparsely settled area, road connections - both sealed and unsealed - are very good, and along the main roads at least, services are available at regular intervals. Tourism has taken off here over the last 20 years.

The Climate

The Top End/Kakadu region is a very warm to hot land throughout the year. Maximum temperatures are extreme, especially in April and between August and November with temperatures reaching 35C-40C away from the coast. Night temperatures are also uncomfortable, with minimums often over 25C, accompanied by high humidity near the northern coast. While maximum temperatures are slightly cooler during the monsoon, due to the cloud cover, it is also very wet. Further south, maximums are very high (38C plus) throughout the warmer half of the year, though minimums are marginal cooler and rainfall is less.

The time to visit is between May and August (the dry season in the north). Note that even then maximum temperatures may well be in the mid-thirties, though minimums are mild, falling to around 16C in the north, and 10C or less in the south. Rainfall is virtually non-existant at this time.

Capital City Connections
Distances in kilometres
SYDNEY-KATHERINE
via Great Western/Mitchell/Matilda/Barkly/Stuart Highways

	Intermediate	Total
Sydney	0	0
Nyngan	578	578
Charleville	655	1233
Mt Isa	1150	2383
Three Ways	636	3019
Katherine	642	3661
Darwin	316	3977

MELBOURNE-KATHERINE
via Western/Dukes/Highway1/Stuart Highways

	Intermediate	Total
Melbourne	0	0
Adelaide	731	731
Port Augusta	312	1043
Alice Springs	1220	2263
Three Ways	531	2794
Katherine	642	3436
Darwin	316	3752

The Route
Distances in kilometres

	Intermediate	Total
Darwin	0	0
Jabiru	255	255
Pine Creek	308	563
Daly River	188	751
Darwin	224	975

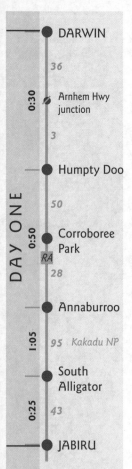

Kakadu National Park/Top End
Darwin-Jabiru-Pine Creek-
Daly River-Darwin

These Top End routes provide good travelling conditions during the dry season. The main roads are sealed, and many of Kakadu National Park's features are accessible even during the monsoon season. Elsewhere roads are unsealed - they provide good but dusty travelling conditions during the dry season, but can be washed out or scoured during and after the monsoon.

Kakadu landscapes are many and varied. Whilst undulating lowlands covered with tropical woodlands are the norm, there are places where the countryside is very scenic. The southern portions of Kakadu National Park offer some grand scenery within the escarpment country.

A special mention should be made about Kakadu National Park. Be aware that most of the park is tropical woodland and that it is a long way between specific features. Also note that virtually all the camping areas are located adjacent to wetlands which look scungy for much of the dry season but are loved by billions of vicious mosquitoes. To avoid the 'Kakadu peak-hour' at dusk, when unprepared travellers drive in all directions seeking respite from the biting irritants, you will need insect repellents and mozzie-proof tents (or indoor accommodation - ridiculously expensive) to provide the barest protection. Why the camping grounds are located next to these wetlands, I do not know. Fortunately camping grounds in the south of the park are okay.

Warnings: roads subject to flooding. Unsealed roads quickly deteriorate after monsoonal rains and may be closed for lengthy periods of time. Avoid travelling at night, but if it is unavoidable, beware of wandering stock.

DAY 1: DARWIN-JABIRU
via Annaburroo

Road to Take: Arnhem Highway
Grade 1
Total Distance: 255km (2:50)

Intermediate Distances:

	Km	Hours
Darwin-Humpty Doo	39	(0:30)
Humpty Doo-Annaburroo	78	(0:50)
Annaburroo-South Alligator	95	(1:05)
South Alligator-Jabiru	43	(0:25)

Average Vehicles per Day: 550 east of Adelaide River
Regions Traversed: Top End/Kakadu

DARWIN (Alt 24m; Pop 75000):** large tropical city. For more information see Road Trip 20, Day 10. (*0/255*) *Road Trip 20 connects.*

For information on the route between Darwin and Arnhem Highway Junction see Road Trip 20, Day 10.

Arnhem Highway junction: (*36/219*) *Road Trip 20 connects.* Turn **E** for Humpty Doo. *Turn **N** for Darwin.*

Humpty Doo (Alt 45m): small township servicing a large portion of the Darwin Rural Belt. The pub is worth visiting, especially when crowded. Accommodation, stores, fuel. (*39/216*)

Low rises support wide tracts of eucalypt grassy woodlands. Westward the countryside is partially cleared for rural allotments and small farms. Beatrice Hill has a visitors centre known as Window on the Wetlands*. Stop here for views, Aboriginal cultural and environmental information. (*66/189*)

Floodplains surround the Adelaide River offering good views*. Paperbarks are common on the plains as well as the introduced species, *Mimosa pigra*, which is causing infestation problems. Buffalo can be seen here (one of the few places left outside of zoos and enclosures).

Adelaide River:* wide attractive river lined with mangroves. River tours are available. Beware of estuarine crocodiles. (*68/187*)

Leaning Tree Lagoon:* centrepiece of a nature park of the same name. Good bird watching area. Camping is available, but access is unsealed.

DAY ONE

DARWIN

36

0:30

Arnhem Hwy junction

3

Humpty Doo

50

0:50

Corroboree Park

RA

28

Annaburroo

1:05

95   Kakadu NP

South Alligator

0:25

43

JABIRU

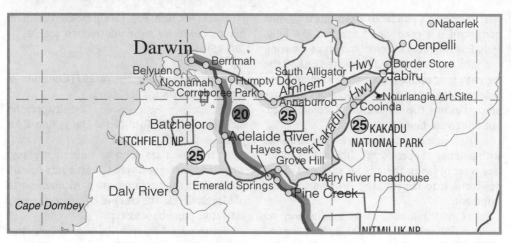

Detail of MAP 6

Supposedly no crocodiles! North of the road lies the Djukbinj National Park, an area of tropical woodlands and wetlands.

Corroboree Park (Alt 40m; Pop 5): roadhouse facility. Accommodation, fuel. (*89/166*)

Plains support tropical woodlands. Keep and eye out for the Cathedrals of the North Termite Mounds.

Hilly country offers good views* towards high wooded hills. Eucalypt woodlands are common.

Mary River:* pleasant river crossing and **rest area** - good spot for a picnic. Nearby is the Mary River National Park, a good area for fishing. Beware of estuarine crocodiles. A caravan park is nearby. (*114/141*)

Annaburroo (Alt 30m; Pop 15):* also known as Bark Hut. Roadhouse with plenty of interest. Stop here to absorb the atmosphere. The adjacent animal enclosure* is worth seeing. Accommodation, limited store, fuel. (*117/138*)

Accommodation

Bark Hut Inn Caravan Park, Arnhem Hwy, ©08 8978 8988, ◯Site: $17

Kakadu National Park:** vast national park and world heritage area preserving a range of monsoonal habitats, an amazing array of bird life, and housing a number of Aboriginal communi-

ties who have continually occupied this country for thousands of generations.

Ranger Station: entry fee to Kakadu National Park payable here. Information available. Enquire here about access to the Two Mile Hole and Four Mile Hole camping areas; unsealed access - Grades 3 and 5 respectively. (*172/83*)

Low rises are typical of virtually all of Kakadu's lowlands: vast tracts of eucalypt woodlands with patches of open forests (forests have touching crowns) with understoreys of shrubs and grasses. At the West Alligator River crossing (really a creek) are numerous paperbarks.

South Alligator (Alt 10m; Pop 10):* also known as Kakadu Holiday Village. Roadhouse facility and tourist centre. An attractive rainforest* is nearby on the south side of road. Accommodation, store, fuel. (*212/43*)

Accommodation

All Seasons Frontier Kakadu Village, Arnhem Hwy, ©08 8979 0166, ◯$135-$185

South Alligator River: worth a stop at the day-use area just north of the highway. Good views* overlooking the river (beware of estuarine crocodiles) and the road bridge. Huge mud banks at low tide. The tide here is about eight metres. Surrounding the river are wide floodplains offering expansive views (rare in Kakadu). (*215/39*)

Plain supports a pandanus palm forest*, while northward is a good view* towards low hills, including the rocky outcrop known as Binirrinj.

Mamukala turnoff: (222/33) Located just off the highway is Mamukala*, a nature trail and bird hide overlooking a wetland. Numerous birds are present during the dry season. Recommended, but bring your binoculars.

Low rises support eucalypt grassy woodlands with patches of open forest. About 15 kilometres west of Jabiru there is an eastward view* down the road towards the Arnhem Land escarpment.

Cahills Crossing Road junction: locality only; no facilities. This is the turn for Cahills Crossing and Ubirr - see Day 2. (250/5) Continue E to Jabiru. Continue W to South Alligator.

JABIRU (Alt 30m; Pop 1500): modern uranium mining town with some tourist facilities. Stock up here if spending time in Kakadu National Park. Accommodation, stores, fuel. (255/0)

Accommodation

Gagudju Crocodile Hotel Kakadu, Flinders St, ✆08 8979 2800, ✪$230

Kakadu Lodge and Caravan Park, Jabiru Dr, ✆08 8979 2422, ✪Site: $29 Van: $135-175

DAY 2: JABIRU-UBIRR-PINE CREEK
via Cooinda

Road to Take: Kakadu Highway
Grade 1
Total Distance: 295km (3:40)
Intermediate Distances:

	Km	Hours
Jabiru-Ubirr	42	(0:35)
Ubirr-Nourlangie Rock turnoff	58	(0:45)
Nourlangie Rock turnoff-Cooinda	33	(0:25)
Cooinda-Mary River Roadhouse	104	(1:15)
Mary River Roadhouse-Pine Creek	58	(0:40)

Average Vehicles per Day: 330 south of Jabiru; 230 east of Pine Creek.
Regions Traversed: Top End/Kakadu

JABIRU (Alt 30m; Pop 1500): modern uranium mining town. For more information see Day 1. (0/295)

Kakadu Highway junction: (4/291) Continue W for Ubirr. Continue E for Jabiru.

Cahills Crossing Road junction: locality only; no facilities. (5/290) Turn N for Ubirr. Turn E for Jabiru.

Plain and low rises support a eucalypt grassy woodland with good views* eastwards toward the Arnhem Land escarpment, particularly north of Magela Creek. The creek itself supports a very attractive paperbark forest*.

Merl Camping Area and Ranger Station: large camping ground. (40/255)

Border Store (Alt 5m; Pop 5):* small store. Accommodation, limited stores, fuel. (41/254) Nearby is Cahills Crossing*, a concrete causeway over the East Alligator River. Attractive area. Look for mud skippers (walking fish) on the causeway but beware of estuarine crocodiles. The road east to Arnhem Land requires permits. Nearby is a day-use area on the river and the Bardedjildji walk* among rocky outcrops.

Ubirr:*** Aboriginal rock art and location of probably one of the best scenic views in northern Australia. Many galleries have excellent rock paintings including the famous 'X-ray' style. Some paintings are up to 20,000 years old, among the oldest in the world. Climb Ubirr Rock for excellent views*** overlooking floodplain country and the Arnhem Land escarpment - late afternoons and sunset are best. This site should not be missed. (42/253)

Return to Kakadu Highway junction - see the notes above.

Kakadu Highway junction: (80/215) Turn S for Cooinda and Pine Creek. Turn W for Cahills Crossing Road junction - see the notes above.

Bowali: Information Centre and Park Headquarters for Kakadu National Park. Highly recommended for stacks of information, displays, enquiries, video shows and exhibitions. (82/213)

Old Territory-style building, Coomallee, NT

Malabanjbanjdju: camping area set by a billabong. Quiet area. (*94/201*)

Burdulba: camping area, quieter than most. Nearby, an attractive grove of grevilleas lines the road. (*96/199*)

Nourlangie Rock turnoff: (*100/195*) Turn **E** for Nourlangie Rock and other features - see Side Trip below.

Side Trip
Nourlangie Rock Road
(Grade 1) 26+km return

Nanguluwur Art Galleries** (three and a half kilometres return walk). Excellent paintings, similar to those at Nourlangie Rock, but without the crowds.

Gubara:* six kilometres return bush walk to waterholes set within a monsoon forest

Nawurlandja Lookout* provides one of the best view of the escarpment and surrounding lowlands (as well as of Nourlangie Rock) in the northern part of Kakadu.

Anbangbang Billabong:* great bird watching on this wetland.

Nourlangie Rock:*** very impressive sandstone hill with high rocky bluffs and sheer cliffs. A detached portion of the Arnhem Land escarpment and as close as most people will get to the 'stone country'. Excellent art sites (different to Ubirr) which should not be missed. Walking trails.

Low rises support grassy eucalypt woodlands. Notice the sand palms in the understorey. Anthills are common.

Muirella Park turnoff: (*107/188*) Turn **E** for Muirella Park: large camping area with an attractive waterhole* - beware of estuarine crocodiles.

Mirrai (Mt Cahill): isolated hill (152m) with a steep walking track (take water and wear a hat) offering expansive but somewhat restricted views* across much of the northern lowlands of Kakadu. An escarpment is visible on the southern horizon. (*109/186*)

Cooinda turnoff: (*129/166*) This short detour leads **W** to Cooinda.

Cooinda (Alt 10m; Pop 20)*, an attractive tourist facility with a relaxed laid-back feel about it. A good spot to rest a while. Nearby are camping areas as well as the Warradjan Aboriginal Cultural Centre* - displays, information, crafts, and more; and Yellow Waters*, a large, virtually permanent wetland supporting amazing birdlife. Boat tours** are available (highly recommended), and boardwalks** for viewing the wetlands on foot. Accommodation, store, fuel. (*133/162*)

Accommodation
Gagudju Lodge Cooinda, Cooinda Rd, ©08 8979 0148, ©$165

Gagudju Lodge Cooinda Caravan Park, Cooinda Rd, ©08 8979 0145, ©Site: $26 Van: $60

Mardugal: camping area on Jim Jim Creek. (*140/155*)

Low rises support eucalypt grassy woodlands. Anthills common.

Low hills provide a change in scenery and virtually mark the boundary between the wetter northern parts of Kakadu and the drier southern areas. Grassy woodlands here are lower in stature than further north, while anthills are larger.

Gungurul:* interesting lookout overlooking the South Alligator River. (*187/108*)

South Alligator River:* attractive area. The river bank supports a melaleuca forest. The white-trunked eucalypts away from the river are ghost gums. (*191/104*)

Plains support grassy eucalypt woodlands. Views* eastward towards sandstone cliffs, outliers of the Arnhem Land escarpment.

Bukbukluk Lookout* provides very good views over the 'stone country', attractive in the after-

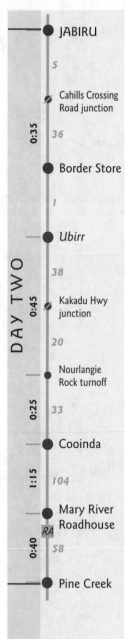

JABIRU

5

Cahills Crossing Road junction

0:35   36

Border Store

1

Ubirr

38

0:45   Kakadu Hwy junction

20

Nourlangie Rock turnoff

0:25   33

Cooinda

1:15   *104*

Mary River
RA **Roadhouse**

0:40   58

Pine Creek

DAY TWO

noon light. Numerous clifflines dominate. South-ward the plateau supports a eucalypt woodland somewhat taller than that immediately north. (**218/77**)

Gunlom Road junction: locality only; no facili-ties. (**225/70**) Turn **E** for Gunlom and other fea-tures - see Side Trip below.

Side Trip

Gunlom Road

(Grade 3) 74km return

Undulating country supports grassy eucalypt woodlands. Occasional eastward views* to-wards rugged hills and ridges.

Hilly country provides some of the best views** and wild country in Kakadu. Spectacular escarp-ments, rocky ridges, plunging cliffs and twisting valleys make this a very scenic area.

Kambolgie Creek is a camping area. Great east-ward views* towards Mt Callanan (afternoons are best for photography).

Yurmikmik:* walking track from here leads to lookouts and gorges.

Gunlom:** a pretty area of high cliffs, a deep pool and a trickling dry season waterfall. Great swimming. Bushwalks available. Popular camp-ing area.

Ranger Station: pay Kakadu National Park entry fees here. Information. (**227/68**)

Ikoymarrwa Lookout* provides reasonable views westward towards rocky hills. Mornings are best for photography. (**230/65**)

Kakadu National Park:** vast national park and world heritage area preserving a range of monsoonal habitats, an amazing array of bird life, and housing a number of Aboriginal com-munities who have continually occupied this country for thousands of generations.

Hilly country offers reasonable views* if head-ing west.

Mary River Roadhouse (Alt 113m; Pop 5): modern roadhouse facility. Accommodation, fuel. (**237/58**)

Low hills* feature rocky outcrops and granite boulders. Very attractive area.

Moline: old mining township. No public access to township or mine site, but keep an eye open for the now disused and overgrown Moline Golf Course*, an idiosyncratic worker-built construc-tion exhibiting a variety of features in their 'club-house' grounds.

Undulating country supports grassy eucalypt woodlands. At intervals low hills composed of granite boulders can be seen. **Rest area** at Harriet Creek. (**283/25**)

Grove Hill turnoff: (**305/3**) Grove Hill lies **W**. Continue **S** for Pine Creek. *Continue **N** for Mary River Roadhouse.*

Pine Creek (Alt 189m; Pop 500):* historic min-ing town. For more information see Road Trip 20, Day 10. (**308/0**) *Road Trip 20 connects.*

DAY 3: PINE CREEK-DALY RIVER via Grove Hill, Dorat Road

Roads to Take: Burrundie-Grove Hill Road, Dorat Road, Daly River Road

Grade 3

Total Distance: 188km (2:35)

Intermediate Distances:

	Km	Hours
Pine Creek-Grove Hill	61	(0:55)
Grove Hill-Stuart Hwy junction	18	(0:15)
Stuart Hwy jctn-Daly River Rd jctn	33	(0:25)
Daly River Road jctn-Daly River	76	(1:00)

Average Vehicles per Day: 50 north of Daly River

Regions Traversed: Top End

Pine Creek (Alt 189m; Pop 500):* historic min-ing town. For more information see Road Trip 20, Day 10. (**0/188**)

Grove Hill turnoff: (**3/185**) Turn **N** for Grove Hill. *Turn **W** for Pine Creek.*

Hilly country offers fair views. South of the Frances Creek turnoff a boulder field* of granite can be seen. The countryside supports a euca-lypt grassy woodland.

Old truck, Burrundie, NT

Undulating country supports a eucalypt woodland with a grassy understorey.

Burrundie:* old mining township and railway station of which little remains save for scattered relics. Railway lines and old platforms are still intact. Interesting. (*42/146*)

Grove Hill:* old railway station and an excellent example of a Top End style corrugated-iron hotel. The building currently holds an amazing collection of artefacts, and is very photogenic. A good place to meet 'bush characters'. Accommodation. (*61/127*) Head **W** then **S** to Stuart Highway junction. *Head **E** to Grove Hill turnoff.*

Fountain Head: old mining locality. (*68/120*)

Low rises support tracts of eucalypt woodlands.

Stuart Highway junction: locality only; no facilities. (*79/109*) *Road Trip 20 connects.* Continue **SW** along the short connecting road for Dorat Road junction. *Continue **NE** for Grove Hill.*

Dorat Road junction. Turn **W** for Daly River. *Turn **E** for Stuart Highway junction.*

Oolloo Crossing Road turnoff: (*83/105*) Turn **S** for the 65km return trip to Douglas Hot Springs**, thermal springs located in a nature park of the same name. A visit is highly recommended. Thermal springs issue through the sands of the waterholes, varying from very warm to hot - adjacent waters can be quite cool. Take care if bathing so as not to be scalded. The main spring area should be seen but not bathed in as you will be burnt. Camping available. Popular park.

Hilly country is very scenic with rocky outcrops, flat-top hills, rocky bluffs and ridges, and occasional good views*. The area supports a grassy eucalypt woodland.

Daly River Road junction: locality only; no facilities. (*112/76*) Turn **W** for Daly River. *Turn **S** for Grove Hill.*

Hilly country offers reasonable views* eastward towards a low range. Eucalypt grassy woodlands are common.

Woolianna Road junction: locality only; no facilities. (*182/6*) Turn **W** for Woolianna: store, caravan park and tourist features spread out along 20km of unsealed road, ending at Browns Creek Nature Reserve*, a small tract of monsonal rainforest; camping available.

Daly River Nature Park:* attractive area. (*183/5*)

Daly River (Alt 15m; Pop 250):* scattered township and Aboriginal settlement (Nauiyu Nanbiyu). A pleasant place to relax for a few days. Good fishing and boating area - beware of estuarine crocodiles. West of the river are two camping areas offering accommodation (Mango Farm and Perry's). Accommodation, stores, fuel. (*188/0*)

Accommodation

Daly River Pub, Daly River Rd, ℂ08 8978 2418, ✪$80

Woolianna on the Daly Tourist Park, **Woolianna Rd** (18kmN), ℂ08 8978 2478, ✪Site: $24

Daly River Mango Farm, 8kmNW over river, ℂ08 8978 2464, ✪Site: $22 Van: $80

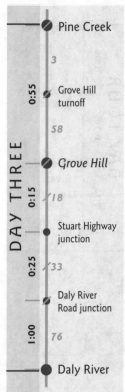

DAY THREE

	Pine Creek
3	
0:55	Grove Hill turnoff
58	
	Grove Hill
0:15	18
	Stuart Highway junction
0:25	33
	Daly River Road junction
1:00	76
	Daly River

Grove Hill pub, NT

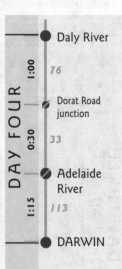

DAY FOUR

1:00   76

0:30   33

1:15   113

- Daly River
- Dorat Road junction
- Adelaide River
- DARWIN

DAY 4: DALY RIVER-DARWIN
via Adelaide River

Roads to Take: Daly River Road, Dorat Road, Stuart Highway
Grade 2
Total Distance: 224km (2:45)
Intermediate Distances:

	Km	Hours
Daly River-Dorat Rd junction	76	(1:00)
Dorat Rd junction-Adelaide River	33	(0:30)
Adelaide River-Darwin	113	(1:15)

Average Vehicles per Day: 50 north of Daly River
Regions Traversed: Top End

Daly River (Alt 15m; Pop 250):* scattered township. For more information see Day 3. (*0/224*)

For information on the route between Daly River and Dorat Road junction see Day 3.

Dorat Road junction: (**78/146**) Turn **N** for Adelaide River. *Turn **W** for Daly River.*

Hilly country composed of rocky bluffs and ridges, and occasional good views*. The area supports a grassy eucalypt woodland.
Robin Falls turnoff: (**97/127**) Turn **W** for the brief journey to Robin Falls*, a pleasant area set within a steep, rocky escarpment. Nice spot for a picnic. A short walk leads to the falls (barely a trickle during the dry season but good views of the rocky hills).

Adelaide River (Alt 50m; Pop 150):* attractive township set on the banks of the Adelaide River. For more information see Road Trip 20, Day 10. (*111/113*) *Road Trip 20 connects.* Turn **N** onto Stuart Hwy for Adelaide. *Turn **S** onto Dorat Road for Daly River.*

For information on the route between Adelaide River and Darwin see Road Trip 20, Day 10.

DARWIN (Alt 24m; Pop 75000):** large tropical city. For more information Road Trip 20, Day 10. (*224/0*)

Road Trip 26
Victoria River District/
Kimberley Connection

Katherine-Broome via Kununurra
Total Distance: 1553km
Suggested Travelling Time: 5 days

Marvel at the natural wonders of The Kimberley

See the great views around Timber Creek, the spectacular countryside near Kununurra, pleasant Wyndham, Sullivans Jump-Up, Victoria River, Gregory National Park, Keep River National Park, Lake Argyle, Five Rivers Lookout, the China Wall, Geike Gorge, the coastal town of Derby, popular and colourful Broome, and the extraordinary geological features of Purnululu National Park.

Victoria River District-Kimberley Connection

Australia's Victoria River District and Kimberley is a vast tract of monsoonal land. It is sparsely populated country extensively grazed by beef cattle. Elsewhere are large national parks and wilderness areas. Towns are few and far between; those that exist are service centres for tourists, cattle stations or the mining industry. Though a sparsely settled area, road connections are very good, and along the main roads at least, services are available at regular intervals. Tourism has taken off here over the last 20 years. Well prepared travellers will find this to be one of the most interesting areas in Australia to visit.

The Climate

This is a very warm to hot land throughout the year. Maximum temperatures are extreme, especially in April and between August and November with temperatures reaching 35C-40C away from the coast. Night temperatures are also uncomfortable, with minimums often over 25C, often accompanied by high humidity. While maximum temperatures are slightly cooler during the monsoon, due to the cloud cover, it is also very wet. Further south, maximums are very high (38C plus) throughout the warmer half of the year, though minimums are marginally cooler and rainfall is less.

The time to visit is between May and August (the dry season in the north). Note that even then maximum temperatures may well be in the mid-thirties, although minimums are mild, falling to around 16C in the north, and 10C or less in the south. Rainfall is virtually non-existent at this time.

Capital City Connections
Distances in kilometres
SYDNEY-KATHERINE
via Great Western/Mitchell/Matilda/Barkly/
Stuart Highways

	Intermediate	Total
Sydney	0	0
Nyngan	578	578
Charleville	655	1233
Mt Isa	1150	2383
Three Ways	636	3019
Katherine	642	3661

MELBOURNE-KATHERINE
via Western/Dukes/Highway1/Stuart Highways

	Intermediate	Total
Melbourne	0	0
Adelaide	731	731
Port Augusta	312	1043
Alice Springs	1220	2263
Three Ways	531	2794
Katherine	642	3436

The Route
Distances in kilometres

	Intermediate	Total
Katherine	0	0
Victoria River	194	194
Timber Creek	90	284
Kununurra	229	513
Halls Creek	359	872

Fitzroy Crossing	288	1160
Broome	393	1553

Victoria Highway

Katherine-Kununurra

Flat-top hills, endless grassy plains, sparse semi-arid woodlands, high red cliffs and deep waterholes provide a contrast of landscapes in this relatively quiet corner of Australia. With some outstanding plains-and-ranges scenery, interspersed with seemingly endless woodlands, the Victoria Highway offers the traveller some breathing space and solitude.

Warnings: roads subject to flooding; unsealed roads impassable when wet. Sections of road may be closed for during the monsoon.
Note: no fuel available Timber Creek-Kununurra 229km

DAY 1: KATHERINE-TIMBER CREEK
via Victoria River

Road to Take: Victoria Highway
Grade 1
Total Distance: 284km (3:15)
Intermediate Distances:

	Km	Hours
Katherine-Buntine Hwy jctn	126	(1:25)
Buntine Hwy jctn-Victoria River	68	(0:50)
Victoria River-Timber Creek	90	(1:00)

Average Vehicles per Day: 370 west of Katherine; 220 west of Victoria River.
Regions Traversed: Top End, Victoria River District

KATHERINE (Alt 107m; Pop 8000):* large regional centre. For more information see Road Trip 20, Day 9. (*0/284*) *Road Trip 20 connects.* Head W on Victoria Hwy for Timber Creek.

Undulating country supports extensive tracts of grassy eucalypt woodlands.
Rest area (*31/253*) east of King River.

Rest area east of Dry River Station turnoff. (*58/226*)
Low hills of flat-top plateaux break the otherwise undulating skyline. Fair distant views northward.
Undulating country supports eucalypt woodlands with a grassy understorey.
Low hills* of flat-top plateaux and mesas are reasonably scenic. A low rise west of Mathison Creek provides an expansive view* westward (mornings best). Eucalypt grassy woodlands are common. The open grassland areas are dominated by bluegrass. **Rest area** at 62 Mile Camp. (*102/182*)
Buntine Highway junction: locality only; no facilities. (*126/158*)
Views* near the Innesvale Station turn-off are excellent in a westward direction (very photogenic in the morning light). Flat-top hills and mesa formations abound.
Gregory National Park: large national park preserving spectacular scenery and a variety of environments ranging from broad plains to flat-top hills.
Ranges offer excellent views** (westward best) of high cliffs, scree slopes, rugged valleys and rocky outcrops. Spinifex is common on the steep slopes while Livistonia palms are common at the base of cliffs.
Sullivans Jump-Up: information centre and **rest area**. (*164/120*)
Hilly country follows Sullivans Creek with great views** beyond Victoria River.
Waterhole* on Sullivans Creek offers a **rest area**. Good spot for bird watching, picnicking and camping. (*177/107*)

Victoria River (Alt 38m; Pop 10): modern roadhouse facility set within a deep valley. Stop here to enjoy the view. A walk to the bridge (beware of traffic) provides excellent views up and down the river and to the rugged cliffs beyond. Boat tours are available. Beware of estuarine crocodiles. Accommodation, store, fuel. (*194/90*)

Accommodation
Victoria River Roadhouse Hotel-Motel, Victoria Hwy, ⓒ08 8975 0744, ◐$55
Victoria River Roadhouse Caravan Park, Victoria Hwy, ⓒ08 8975 0744, ◐Site: $20

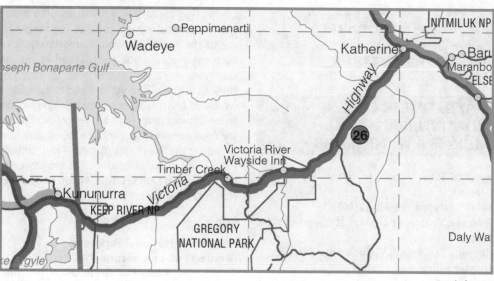

Detail of MAP 6

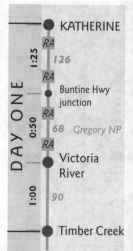

Walking track (rough but marked) provides great views** from the escarpment and identifies some vegetation. Westbound travellers will sight their first boab trees around here. Joe Creek picnic area nearby. (*196/88*)

Undulating country supports large tracts of eucalypt grassy woodlands. Occasional views southward towards the Stoke Range escarpments and northward views towards flat-top ranges. Boabs are common.

Kuwang Lookout:* set upon a low hill, this lookout provides good distant views towards the Stokes Range. Information boards and sighting 'scopes' locate natural features associated with Aboriginal stories. Interesting. (*251/33*)

Buchanan Highway junction: locality only; no facilities. (*257/27*)

Gregory National Park turnoff: locality only; no facilities. (*277/7*) Turn **S** for Gregory National Park - see Side Trip below.

Side Trip

A 74+km return unsealed (Grade 4) road leads **S** into Gregory National Park. Worth seeing is Limestone Gorge*, a rugged area of escarpments and waterholes, nutwood trees and boabs. Walking trail leads to good vantage points. Camping is available. At Bullita*, a ranger sta-

tion is located at a former outstation. The old yards and outbuildings are of interest. Camping is available here too. Nearby attractive waterholes and rock pools are good for swimming - only freshwater crocodiles here. Enquire locally about permits and access to use 4WD tracks running through the park. Tracks include: Bullita Stock Route, Humbert Track (exit park via Humbert River Ranger Station and Victoria River Downs), Wickham/Gibby Track (exits via Kalkarindji) and Broadarrow Track (exists to Buntine Highway).

Timber Creek (Alt 14m; Pop 100):* scattered grazing and Aboriginal township located in the attractive Newcastle Range. Aborigines are mostly Ngaringman people. The area is worth at least half-a-day. Relax around the township's roadhouses (very shady). Visit the old Victoria River Depot* (enquire locally), see the old police station (nowadays a museum*), take a Victoria River boat tour, drive part the way up the water tank road for good views** of the Newcastle Range, and drive up the range (4km west of town) for good views** of the Victoria River valley. Accommodation, stores, fuel. (*284/0*)

Accommodation
Timber Creek Hotel, Victoria Hwy, ©08 8975 0772, ✪$80

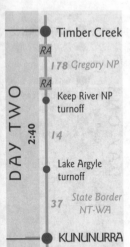

DAY TWO
2:40

Timber Creek

RA
178 Gregory NP

RA

Keep River NP
turnoff

14

Lake Argyle
turnoff

*37   State Border
NT-WA*

KUNUNURRA

Timber Creek Wayside Inn Hotel-Motel, Victoria Hwy, ©08 8975 0873, ✪$50-$90
Circle F Caravan Park, Victoria Hwy, ©08 8975 0722, ✪Site: $14 Van: $35-$70

▲

DAY 2: TIMBER CREEK-KUNUNURRA
via Keep River NP turnoff

Road to Take: Victoria Highway
Grade 1
Total Distance: 229km (2:40)
Average Vehicles per Day: 300 west of state border
Regions Traversed: Victoria River District, The Kimberley

▼

Timber Creek (Alt 14m; Pop 100):* scattered grazing and Aboriginal township. For more information see Day 1. (*0/229*)

Gregory National Park: large national park of former grazing leases preserving monsoonal and semi-arid environments and the rugged escarpments and ridges of the Newcastle and Stokes Ranges. Information is available in Timber Creek. Big Horse Creek:* attractive area and ready access to Victoria River (beware of estuarine crocodiles), good fishing, camping available. Part of Gregory National Park. A short distance west is a tree marked by the explorer Gregory. (*11/218*) Whirlwind Plains: vast plain supporting paperbark woodlands and areas of bauhinias. Ranges are visible to the north on the skyline. **Rest area** (*58/171*) at Auvergne Station turnoff. Westward, the northern ranges come closer into view. Grassland areas near the West Baines River. Pinkerton Range:* interesting, verging on spectacular, range of sandstone ridges, bluffs, pinnacles and cliffs, many of which exhibit intricate erosion features. Scattered boabs make this a scenic area. A **rest area** (*117/112*) in the vicinity offers the opportunity to see the range up close (no walking tracks, beware of spinifex, do not get lost).

Undulating country and low rises offer broad views*, particularly towards flat-top ranges lying to the north. The area supports tracts of eucalypt grassy woodlands. Bloodwoods are common.
Hilly country offers good views*, especially westward towards some stunning ranges. Sparse eucalypt woodlands with a spinifex understorey are common. A large concrete monument can be seen at the Halls Creek (Duncan Road) turnoff. Keep River National Park turnoff: locality only; no facilities. (*178/51*) Turn **N** for Keep River National Park - see Side Trip below.

Side Trip
Keep River National Park road (Grade 3) 62+km return
Keep River National Park:** interesting park preserving geological formations and Aboriginal heritage. Plenty of bushwalking and photographic opportunities.
Cockatoo Lagoon:* interesting wetland. A ranger station is located nearby.
Gurrandalng: camping area set among low rocky sandstone outcrops. An excellent walk leads from here to very spectacular viewpoints** overlooking beehive formations and intricately-eroded sandstone escarpments. The area is backed by high rocky bluffs. Walk highly recommended.
Gorge formed by the Keep River is of minor interest. Some Aboriginal paintings* worth seeing. Waterholes best after the end of The Wet.
Nganalam:*** excellent Aboriginal art site feature Wandjina figures; afternoons best. This site is very ancient and the presence of occupation has sculptured the gallery into an almost cathedral-like atmosphere with an awesome power. Highly recommended.
Jarrnarm:* pleasant camping area set beneath a high sandstone bluff. Bushwalks available.

Check Point: quarantine station located on the **state border** between the Northern Teritory and Western Australia. Border somewhat reminiscent of a customs post. No fruit, vegetables, etc. to be taken westward. Also a time zone boundary: add 1.5 hours if heading west, subtract 1.5 hours if heading east.

Lake Arygle turnoff: locality only; no facilities. (*192/37*) Turn **S** for Lake Argyle - see Side Trip below.

Side Trip
**Lake Argyle Road
(Grade 1) 68km return**
Ranges offer spectacular views** along a mountainous road. Plenty of photographic opportunities and viewpoints. The countryside supports tracts of sparse eucalypt woodlands with a spinifex understorey.
Lake Argyle (Alt 180m; Pop 20):** small tourist settlement overlooking the vast Lake Argyle impoundment. Spectacular area, especially westward towards the rugged Carr Boyd Ranges. Tours are available on the Lake; good fishing and boating. The Argyle Homestead museum* is nearby. An area worth visiting. Camping available. Accommodation, store, fuel.

Hilly country provides views* towards rugged ranges. Westward are large rocky outcrops. Elsewhere is undulating country supporting grassy eucalypt woodlands.

KUNUNURRA (Alt 46m; Pop 5000):* sizeable agricultural and tourist town set in spectacular countryside. There are many things to see in the Kununurra area. Excellent views from Kellys Knob Lookout* overlook the irrigated farms of the Ord Valley. Nearby Mirima National Park offers good walking among interesting rock formations** (no camping). Elephant Rock or the Sleeping Buddah (depending on viewpoint) is visible from around town. Ivanhoe Crossing* is a popular spot for fishing and sightseeing. Diversion Dam and impounded Lake Kununurra just west of town are of interest; tours available. Full town facilities. (*229/0*) Road Trip 27 connects.

Accommodation
Hotel Kununurra, Messmate Way, ©08 9168 1344, ©$100
Kimberley Court Motel, 2 Riverfig Ave, ©08 9168 1411, ©$85-$105
Kununurra Lakeside Resort, Casuarina Way (1kmS), ©08 9169 1092, ©$145

Ivanhoe Village Caravan Park, Cnr Ivanhoe Rd/ Coolabah Dr, ©08 9169 1995, ©Site: $18 Van: $65-$100
Kimberleyland Holiday Park, Victoria Hwy (1kmS), ©08 9168 1280, ©Site: $20 Van: $60-$90
Kona Lakeside Tourist Park, Lakeview Dr (1.8kmS), ©08 9168 1031, ©Site: $20 Van: $55-$100
Town Caravan Park, Bloodwood Dr, ©08 9168 1763, ©Site: $20 Van: $55-$100
Hidden Valley Caravan Park, Weber Plains Rd, (1.4kmNE), ©Site: $18
   Out of town are the Black Rock Falls (nearby is a stockman's grave) and Middle Springs located on Parrys Creek Road (west of town - 4WD only) - good swimming. Further on is Valentine Pool. On Webers Plain Road is the City of Ruins*, a series of sandstone pinnacles. Tours are available on the Lake, up the rugged Ord River to the Argyle Diamond Mine. For other features and tours, enquire locally.

▲

Victoria/Great Northern Highway: The Kimberley
Kununurra-Broome
The Victoria/Great Northern Highway in the Kimberley passes through interesting to spectacular countryside. The spectacular areas include the Durack and Ragged Ranges north of Warmun, the Bungle Bungles, the Wyndham and Kununurra areas, the King Sound mudflats and Roebuck Bay. Also of note are the interesting hills and ranges east of Halls Creek.

Warnings: roads subject to flooding. Beware of stock if travelling at night, especially near creek crossings. High temperatures will be experienced between October and March - always travel with water.
Note: no fuel available between Wyndham-Warmun 201km; Halls Creek-Fitzroy Crossing 288km; Fitzroy Crossing-Willare Bridge 229km; Fitzroy Crossing-Derby 256km.

DAY 3: KUNUNURRA-HALLS CREEK
via Warmun

Road to Take: Victoria Highway, Great Northern Highway
Grade 1
Grade 1 Wyndham Road
Total Distance: 359km (5:25)
Intermediate Distances:

	Km	Hours
Kununurra-Wyndham	101	(1:10)
Kununurra-Warmun	196	(2:15)
Warmun-Purnululu NP turnoff	53	(0:35)
Purnululu NP turnoff-Halls Creek	110	(1:25)

Average Vehicles per Day: 250 south of Kununurra turn-off
Regions Traversed: The Kimberley

▼

KUNUNURRA (Alt 46m; Pop 5000):* sizeable agricultural and tourist town. For more information see Day 2. (*0/359*)

Hilly country offers good views of nearby ranges, including the spectacular Carr Boyd Ranges to the south. Eucalypt woodlands are common.
Great Northern Highway junction: locality only; no facilities except for a **rest area**. (*45/314*) Turn **NW** for Wyndham - see Side Trip below. Turn **S** for Warmun. *Turn **E** onto Victoria Hwy for Kununurra.*

Side Trip

Wyndham Road
(Grade 1) 112km return
Ranges offer good views. Sparse eucalypt woodlands and spinifex dominate the countryside.
Gibb River Road junction (**W**): locality only; no facilities. *Road Trip 27 connects.*
The Grotto turnoff: turn **W** for a short drive to The Grotto*, an unplumbed swimming hole (beware of broken glass) set within a deep gorge. Good views from the top. Steep staircase descent. Unsealed access road.

Erskine Range: rugged range supporting a sparse eucalypt woodland with a spinifex understorey. Good views* along the road. **Rest area**.
Parrys Creek Road turnoff (**E**): this road provides access to Marlgu Billabong**, an excellent wetland bristling with birdlife (binoculars are handy). En route road crosses a low ridge offering the second best view** in northern Australia! Flat plains, abrupt ranges and scattered wetlands set in an immensity of space. The ruins of a telegraph station are located upon the ridge. Nearby Alligator Hole* is scenic. Further along Parrys Creek road are the fishing holes of Palm Springs, Crocodile Hole and Muggs Lagoon (4WD recommended; swimming not recommended due to saltwater crocodiles). En route, keep a lookout for the convict-built stone kerbing.
Mud flat seen to the west. Good views of nearby ranges. Lowlands support eucalypt woodlands with emergent boabs.
WYNDHAM - 3 MILE (Alt 5m; Pop 870):* main town centre. Numerous statues* are scattered around town, as well as a large concrete crocodile. The huge boab tree* is worth seeing, as is Three Mile Valley*, a pleasant place for a late afternoon walk. The location of the racecourse is also noteworthy. The Afghan cemetery is of interest. Make sure you visit Five Rivers Lookout**: probably the best view in northern Australia. Located 335m above sea level, it provides a relatively cool respite from the heat below. Early mornings offer clear views over the mud flats, the five rivers (Ord, King, Pentecost, Durack and Forrest), the true Kimberley plateau, The Gut (a narrow tidal race), the Cockburn Range, Cam-

Lee Tongs Store, Wyndham Port, WA

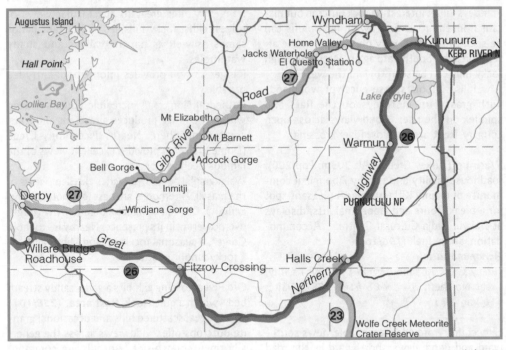

Detail of MAP 6

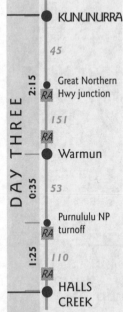

bridge Gulf and distant ranges to the north. Afternoon views tend to be hazy but atmospheric. Accommodation, stores, fuel.

Accommodation

Wyndham Community Club Hotel, Great Northern Hwy, ©08 9161 1130, ✪$60

Wyndham Town Hotel, O'Donnell St, ©08 9161 1003, ✪$90

Wyndham Caravan Park, Baker St (1kmN), ©08 9161 1064, ✪Site: $19 Van: $40

Mud flats separate 'Port' from '3 Mile', offering excellent views* towards The Bastion Range and overlooking Cambridge Gulf towards the spectacular Cockburn Range.

Wyndham Port:** historic township with a wonderful location beneath the towering slopes of The Bastion Range and fringed by mud flats and the blue waters of Cambridge Gulf. There are many old buildings, some quite photogenic. Get information about the heritage walk. Visit the museum. A kilometre north is Wyndham wharf* and port area, which has many old buildings and relics, as well as Crocodile Lookout*

set among the mangroves (take care). Nearby is the pioneer cemetery. Locals say there are no stray dogs in Wyndham due to the crocodile habitat directly behind the settlement's main street. The only dog I saw had three legs! Accommodation, stores.

Kingston Rest: camping area. (*67/292*)

Saw Ranges:** spectacular range of jagged hills and ridges. Very photogenic.

Dunham River crossing is a pleasant **rest area** close to attractive waterholes*.

Carr Boyd Ranges can be seen to the east, offering rounded bluffs, cliff faces and spectacular colour changes. Nearby country is undulating and supports grassy woodlands. Good views** abound. Hereabout and further south are some of the best Kimberley landscapes. Between the Dunham River and Glen Hill Station turnoffs are some intricately eroded cliff faces and ranges located close to the road.

Ranges are visible to the west, while eastward is a quite high range (apparently unnamed) lining the road. Continuous good to excellent views**.

Pompeys Pillar: interesting rock outcrop but distant from the road. Southward high bluffs can be seen to the east, very photogenic in the afternoon light. Southward again, interesting high rocky hills can be seen toward the west.

Low hills support sparse eucalypt woodlands with grassy understoreys on the flats and spinifex on the rises. Good views across open country. **Rest area** at Bow River crossing.

Warmun (Turkey Creek) (Alt 203m; Pop 200): roadhouse facility and nearby Aboriginal community of mainly Kitja people. A pleasant spot for a break. Tours and Aboriginal arts, displays at Daiwul Gidja Cultural Centre*. Accommodation, store, fuel. (*196/163*)

Accommodation

Turkey Creek Roadhouse and Caravan Facility, Great Northern Hwy, ©08 9168 7882, ✪Site: $16 Van: $75

Hilly country provides reasonable views southward and good views* northward as the road ascends/descends a very long hill. Violet Hill (524m) lies to the west. Eucalypts and spinifex are common.

Purnululu National Park turnoff (Bungle Bungles): locality only; no facilities except for a **rest area**. (*249/110*) Turn **E** for Purnululu National Park - see Side Trip below.

Side Trip

Spring Creek (Bungle Bungles) road (Grade 5) 110+km return

Purnululu National Park:*** extraordinary national park whose centrepiece is the Bungle Bungle massif, an intricately eroded sandstone plateau which has evolved into the grandest 'hidden city' of them all. A visit here should not be missed. Enormous canyons, spectacular beehive domes (southern end of park), sinuous river beds and an undulating sand plain make this one of Australia's great natural features. Entry fee payable. Low key camping grounds; walking tracks. Note that all features require short to moderately long walks. The park is closed January to March. **Warning:** access strictly 4WD.

Ranges** offer great to spectacular views of ridges, cliffs, rocky hillsides and distant panoramas as well as narrow valleys and shady waterholes.

Ranger Station provides information: entry fee payable.

Cathedral Gorge:*** incredible gorge set deep within the range produces a reverent and awesome atmosphere. Nearby Piccaninny Creek (Dome Walk***) provides excellent views of the famous beehive domes.

Walangindji Lookout* provides excellent views of the massif. Afternoons are best for photography.

Echidna Chasm:** spectacular narrow gorge, overpowering in its presence. Nearby is Froghole Gorge*, a seasonal rockhole, and Mini-Palms**, a rocky amphitheatre.

Ord River crossing exhibits a wide, sandy stream bed - worth a quick look. **Rest area**. (*258/101*) Low ranges, scattered hills and occasional granite outcrops offer wide views across the generally open countryside. Anthills are common. Sparse low eucalypt woodlands with a spinifex understorey dominate the landscape. Variable-barked bloodwoods are common.

Undulating country offers broad views from the tops of rises.

Low ranges can be seen to the east, very attractive in the late afternoon light.

HALLS CREEK (Alt 409m; Pop 1250): interesting grazing and Aboriginal town comprised mostly of Jaru and Kiji people. Information about Kiji and Jaru dreamtime places is obtainable from the Yarliyil Aboriginal Art Centre*. In town see the Russian Jack Memorial. Accommodation, stores, fuel. (*359/0*) Road Trip 23 connects.

Accommodation

Kimberley Hotel-Motel, Roberta Ave, ©08 9168 6101, ✪$100

Halls Creek Motel, Great Northern Hwy, ©08 9168 6001, ✪$85

Halls Creek Caravan Park, Roberta Ave, ©08 9168 6169, ✪Site: $14 Van: $45

East of town, along the Duncan Road, lies the China Wall* (afternoons best for photography),

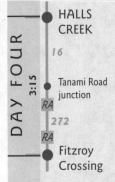

Caroline Pool*, and Old Halls Creek*, the original mining town. A return trip of around 35km (unsealed Grade 3 road) leads to these features. Further out along the Duncan Road lies Palm Springs* and Sawtooth Gorge* (about 80km return). Visiting these sites makes for a great day trip.

DAY 4: HALLS CREEK-FITZROY CROSSING
via Mary River

Road to Take: Great Northern Highway
Grade 1
Total Distance: 288km (3:15)
Average Vehicles per Day: 275 west of Halls Creek
Regions Traversed: The Kimberley

HALLS CREEK (Alt 409m; Pop 1250m):* interesting grazing and Aboriginal town. For more information see Day 3. (*0/288*)

Low rises and plains offer reasonable views across sparse grassy eucalypt woodlands. Northward lies the purple bulk of Mt Barrett (696m). Southward, a series of low ranges and hills can be seen.
Tanami Road junction (**S**): locality only; no facilities. (*16/272*) *Road Trip 23 connects.* Continue **SW** for Fitzroy Crossing. *Continue E for Halls Creek.*
Undulating country offers wide views across an ancient-looking landscape. Various low ranges and hills can be seen in the distance. Sparse low eucalypt woodlands dominate the landscape. Variable-barked bloodwoods, snappy gums and bean trees are common, with a spinifex understorey.
Mary River crossing is a pleasant spot for a break. **Rest area** with toilet adjacent. (*117/171*)
Plains and low rises support vast tracts of sparse eucalypt woodlands with a spinifex understorey. Variable-barked bloodwoods are common. The short white-trunked trees are snappy gums. Mt Bertram (382m) lies to the north.

Old fireplace, Old Halls Creek, WA

Lookout* provides good views across the countryside. Numerous distant hills and low ranges can be seen, including Mt Talbot (306m) to the south. Early mornings or late afternoons are best for photography. **Rest area**. (*183/105*)
Low hills offer good views. Scenic country hereabout including the Ngumban Cliffs (mornings best for photography). Westward is a scenic area* around Pinnacle Creek. Undulating country supports extensive tracts of sparse eucalypt woodlands with a spinifex understorey. The Mimbi Caves are in the vicinity - these may become accessible to the public during the currency of this book; make enquiries in Fitzroy Crossing.

Fitzroy Crossing (Alt 110m; Pop 1150):* sizeable Aboriginal community and grazing centre. Worth seeing: the rustic Crossing Inn*, the original township and its historic buildings*, the old Fitzroy River crossing*, and the pioneer cemetery*. Good fishing in the Fitzroy River (one of Australia's largest in terms of volume during The Wet); enquire locally. Also enquire here about access to Brooking Gorge and Mimbi Caves. Accommodation, stores, fuel. (*288/0*)
Accommodation
Fitzroy River Lodge, Great Northern Hwy (5kmE), ©08 9191 5141, ✪$160
Crossing Inn Hotel-Motel, Skulthorpe Rd, (4kmNE), ©08 9191 5080, ✪$90
Fitzroy River Lodge Caravan Park, Great Northern Hwy (5kmE), ©08 9191 5141, ✪Site: $21 Van: $120

DAY FOUR 3:15

● HALLS CREEK
16
● Tanami Road junction
RA
272
RA
● Fitzroy Crossing

A 42km return sealed road leads to Geikie Gorge**, a very interesting gorge and centrepiece of a national park of the same name. The gorge is located in what was once a coral reef that has been uplifted into a limestone range, an attractive area with cliffs that rise up to 30m. Boat tours are available. There are walking tracks to explore, and the western track is recommended in the late afternoon. Swimming is possible.

DAY 5: FITZROY CROSSING-BROOME
via Willare Bridge Roadhouse

Road to Take: Great Northern Highway
Grade 1
Grade 1 Derby Highway
Total Distance: 393km (4:20)
Intermediate Distance:

	Km	Hours
Fitzroy Crossing-Derby Hwy jctn	214	(2:20)
Derby Hwy jctn-Willare Bridge	15	(0:10)
Willare Bridge-Roebuck Rdhse	130	(1:25)
Roebuck Roadhouse-Broome	34	(0:25)

Average Vehicles per Day: 350
Regions Traversed: The Kimberley (Dampier Land, Fitzroy Plain)

Fitzroy Crossing (Alt 110m; Pop 1150):* Aboriginal community and grazing centre. For more information see Day 4. (*0/393*)

Plum Plain: broad plain supporting a bluegrass grassland. Oscar Range is visible to the north.
Leopold Downs Road turnoff (**N**): locality only; no facilities. (*42/351*)
Plains and low rises support sparse, low, grassy woodlands dominated by beefwoods, bean trees and boabs, with an understorey of ribbon grass. Occasional broad views available from the tops of rises. **Rest area**. (*87/306*)
Erskine Range:* low but impressive rocky range rising up to 65m above the plains. Good views along the road and to the south. Erskine Point (135m) is south of the road.

Road sign, Great Northern Highway, east of Derby, WA

Plains and low rises support extensive tracts of sparse eucalypt grassy woodlands. **Rest area**. (*152/241*)
Plains support tracts of pindan with occasional grassy eucalypt woodlands.
Derby Highway junction: locality only; no facilities. (*214/179*) Turn **N** for Derby - see Side Trip below.

Side Trip
Derby Highway
Grade 1 - 84km return
Plains and low rises supports tracts of pindan.
Gibb River Road junction: locality only; no facilities. *Road Trip 27 connects.*
DERBY (Alt 5m; Pop 3200):* sizeable grazing and regional town with some tourist attractions including the Boab Prison Tree (a sad place), Myall's Bore (both south of town on Derby Highway), town jetty** (good place to see the King Sound mud flats and observe the huge tides, up to 10.2m - also good high tide fishing), Wharfingers House museum*, Royal Flying Doctor Service, open air picture gardens, boab trees, pioneer cemetery and small botanic gardens. Get information here about the Pigeon Heritage Trail. Tours are available, including scenic flights along the Kimberley coastline (horizontal waterfalls, Buccaneer Archipelago, and more). Full town facilities. *Road Trip 27 connects.*
Accommodation
King Sound Resort Hotel, Loch St (1kmS), ☎08 9193 1044, ✪$120
Derby Boab Inn, Loch St (1.5kmS), ☎08 9191 1044, ✪$100

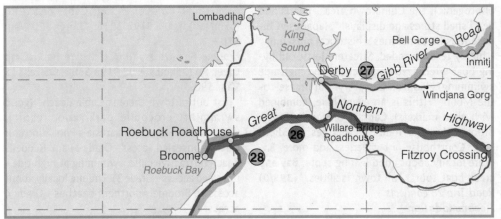

Detail of MAP 7

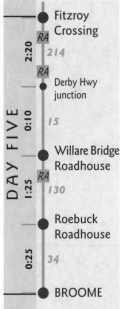

Spinifex Hotel-Motel, Clarendon St, ©08 9191 1223, ✪$60-$90

Kimberley Entrance Caravan Park, Cnr Sutherland/Stanley Sts (2.5kmS), ©08 9193 1055, ✪Site: $19

Willare Bridge Roadhouse (Alt 10m; Pop 5): modern roadhouse facility. Accommodation, limited store, fuel. (*229/164*)

Accommodation

Willare Bridge Roadhouse Caravan Facility, Great Northern Hwy, ©08 9191 4775, ✪Site: $15 Van: $50

Fitzroy River:* attractive crossing. Worth stopping for a look. **Rest area** adjacent, but no camping. Beware of estuarine crocodiles. The river's floodplain (including the Minnie River crossing) supports a eucalypt woodland and grassland.

Cable Beach, Broome, WA

Plains support grasslands. Note the field of anthills*. Distant view northward to King Sound mud flats across Jarrananga Plain.

Logue River: small stream marking the western limits of boabs*. Note the old telegraph poles nearby. (*261/132*)

Low rises support eucalypt grassy woodlands and bean trees. Distant northward view to Mt Clarkson.

Mt Jowleanga turnoff (**N**): site of Kimberley coloured stone rock shop. **Rest area**. (*283/110*)

Plains support vast tracts of pindan with occasional grassy eucalypt woodlands. Some minor anthills can be seen.

Roebuck Roadhouse (Alt 27m; Pop 5): modern roadhouse. Good place to see road-trains* close up. Accommodation, limited store, fuel. (*359/34*)

12 Mile: small rural locality set within the pindan scrub. No facilities. (*373/20*)

BROOME (Alt12m; Pop 12000):*** a colourful settlement with many historical associations that has, despite its recent rapid growth and popularity, managed to maintain its restful and laid-back atmosphere. To see the real Broome though, visit it during The Wet. During parts of The Dry it can become severely overcrowded and resources are pushed to the limit. Worth seeing: many old houses and stores (some quite photogenic), the Chinatown area*, pearls and pearl shell stores and displays**, Japanese/Chinese/Muslim cemeteries*, historical museum** - highly recommended, Streeters Jetty, old flying boat wrecks, Town Beach* (good high tide swimming), Pioneer Cemetery*, Staircase-to-the-Moon** (this is an event here, combined with night markets), Captain Gregory's House, Broome Heritage Trail, Sun Pictures*, Bedford Park, Courthouse, art galleries, and more. Enquire locally about good fishing spots. Bay and creek boat tours. Full town facilities. (**393/0**) *Road Trip 28 connects.*

Accommodation
Broome Motel, 51-57 Frederick St, ©08 9192 7775, ○$70-$100
Mangrove Hotel-Motel, 120 Carnarvon St, ©08 9192 1303, ○$145-$160
Roebuck Bay Hotel-Motel, Carnarvon St, ©08 9192 1221, ○$90-$130
Roebuck Bay Caravan Park, Walcott St (1.5kmS), ©08 9192 1366, ○Site: $20 Van: $50
Broome Caravan Park, Great Northern Hwy (4kmN), ©08 9192 1776, ○Site: $18 Van: $60
Cable Beach Caravan Park, Millington Rd (5kmNW), ©08 9192 2066, ○Site: $22

Palm Grove Caravan Resort, Cable Beach Rd (5kmNW), ©08 9192 3336, ○Site: $20 Van: $70+
Broome Bird Observatory Caravan Park, Crab Creek Rd (25kmE), ©08 9193 5600, ○Site: $15 Van: $90

Just out of town there is Cable Beach* (good swimming, crocodile park, zoo, resort), Gantheaume Point* (Anastasia's Pool, dinosaur tracks - unsealed access - Grade 3) and Reddells Beach (attractive cliffs, swimming at high tide - unsealed access - Grade 3). Enquire locally about access to Broome's northern beaches - Grade 4 access.

Further out of town is the Broome Bird Observatory:**, an interesting spot located on bird migration path. Bird hides, bush walks, tours, courses, and more. Accommodation, camping available. Access via unsealed (Grade 3) Crab Creek road (25km return; turnoff 9km east of Broome on highway. En route pull into one of the many Roebuck Bay beaches (be careful of deep sand) at high tide. Colourful rock formations** abound.

Road Trip 27
Gibb River Road

Kununurra-Derby
Total Distance: 705km
Suggested Travelling Time: 2 days

Clamber into the scenic gorges off the Gibb River Road

See Emma Gorge, the countryside around El Questro Station, the Cockburn Range, Pentecost River, Tunnel Creek, the plunging clifflines of King Leopold Range, and the gorges: Barnett River, Adcock, Bell, Lennard River and Windjana.

Gibb River Road

The Gibb River Road crosses a vast tract of monsoonal country. It is a sparsely populated area extensively grazed by beef cattle. Towns are non-existent along the route. A few small service centres provide limited services to travellers - these facilities may not be available during the wet season. Although a sparsely settled area, road conditions vary from fair to good during the dry season. Tourism has taken off here over the last 10 to 15 years and adequately prepared travellers will find this to be one of the most interesting areas in Australia to visit. The suggested travelling time is the barest minimum; allow up to 5 days if visiting most of the gorges.

The Climate

This is a hot part of the world, especially during summer or the dry season. Maximum temperatures are extreme at this time with temperatures regularly over 40C. Night temperatures are also uncomfortable, with minimums often over 25C, and accompanied by high humidity. It can also be wet at this time, with cyclonic rains in the south and monsoonal rains in the north.

The time to visit The Kimberley is between April and October (the dry season). Note that even then maximum temperatures may well be in the mid-thirties. Nights are generally cool to mild. Fortunately, in most years, rain is virtually absent in the dry season.

Capital City Connections
Distances in kilometres
SYDNEY-KUNUNURRA
via Great Western/Mitchell/Matilda/Barkly/Stuart Highways

	Intermediate	Total
Sydney	0	0
Nyngan	578	578
Charleville	655	1233
Mt Isa	1150	2383
Three Ways	636	3019
Katherine	642	3661
Kununurra	513	4174

MELBOURNE-KUNUNURRA
via Western/Dukes/Highway1/Stuart Highways

	Intermediate	Total
Melbourne	0	0
Adelaide	731	731
Port Augusta	312	1043
Alice Springs	1220	2263
Three Ways	531	2794
Katherine	642	3436
Kununurra	513	3949

PERTH-DERBY
via Brand/NW Coastal/Great Northern Highways

	Intermediate	Total
Perth	0	0
Geraldton	423	423
Carnarvon	478	901
Port Hedland	873	1774
Broome turnoff	576	2350
Derby	187	2537

The Route
Distances in Kilometres

	Intermediate	Total
Kununurra	0	0
Jacks Waterhole	172	172
Mt Barnett	226	398
Derby	307	705

Gibb River Road
Kununurra-Derby

The Gibb River Road is a mostly unsealed road that can be severely affected by monsoonal rains. While the route between Derby and the King Leopold Range and the side route to Windjana Gorge are usually in good condition during the dry season, and consequently passable to conventional vehicles driven with care, the rest of this route (the eastern portion of the Gibb River Road and its offshoots) is rough and stony - expect flat or shredded tyres and severe corrugations. During the dry season these roads are accessible to experienced drivers of conventional vehicles but a 4WD is recommended, as it is on all unsealed routes during the wet season.

Those travellers not wishing to endure the corrugations along the Gibb River Road could consider a return journey to the King Leopold Range from Derby before visiting Windjana Gorge and Tunnel Creek. Such a journey is readily accessible, during the dry season, for travellers in conventional vehicles prepared to travel on unsealed roads.

Warnings: unsealed roads quickly deteriorate after monsoonal rains (washouts, scouring, etc). The Gibb River Road between King Leopold Range and the Great Northern Highway via Mt Barnett is very rough; suitable only for experienced drivers of conventional vehicles. This road is very popular during the tourist season, consequently it is very dusty - drive slowly and take extreme care. Stay out of this area during the monsoon (December-March) and the monsoonal build-up (October, November - high temperatures and humidity) unless experienced. If travelling at this time inform a reliable person of your travel intentions. **Note:** no fuel available between Kununurra-Mt Barnett 403km: (fuel usually available at Jacks Waterhole, Home Valley and El Questro during the dry season); Inmitij-Derby 230km. Carry extra fuel (enough for 112km) for the return journey to Tunnel Creek.

DAY 1: KUNUNURRA-MT BARNETT
via Jacks Waterhole

Roads to Take: Gibb River Road
Grade 4
Total Distance: 398km (5:35)
Intermediate Distances:

	Km	Hours
Kununurra-Gibb River Rd jctn	53	(0:35)
Gibb River Rd jctn-Home Valley	63	(0:50)
Home Valley-Jacks Waterhole	56	(0:50)
Jacks Waterhole-Kalumburu turnoff	116	(1:40)
Kalumburu turnoff-Mt Barnett	110	(1:40)

Average Vehicles per Day: 45 west of Great Northern Highway
Regions Traversed: The Kimberley (Kimberley Plateau)

KUNUNURRA (Alt 46m; Pop 5000):* sizeable agricultural and tourist town. For more information see Trip 26, Day 2. (*0/398*) *Road Trip 26 connects.* Head **W** on Victoria Hwy for Great Northern Hwy junction.

Great Northern Highway junction: locality only; no facilities except for a **rest area**. (*45/353*) *Road Trip 26 connects.* Turn **N** for Gibb River Road junction. *Turn **E** onto Victoria Hwy for Kununurra.*
Gibb River Road junction: locality only; no facilities. (*53/344*) Turn **W** for Home Valley Station. *Turn **S** for Great Northern Hwy junction.*
King River crossing* attractive area. Excellent views westward towards the striking ramparts of Mt Cockburn South, which rise about 380m above the lowlands. The area is surrounded by undulating country and low ranges which support sparse grassy woodlands (including paperbark woodlands) and spinifex-clad slopes.
Emma Gorge turnoff: (*78/320*) Turn **N** for the short side trip to Emma Gorge*, a low key tourist resort (no camping) and attractive gorge with high red bluffs and cool waterholes. Mornings are best for photography. Fee payable for day use visitors.

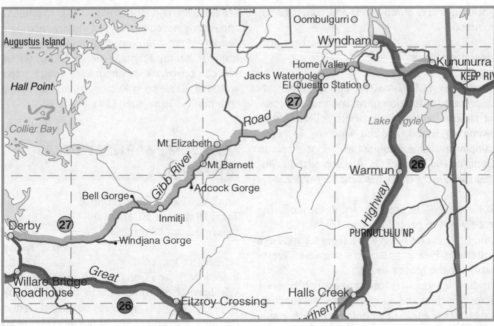

Detail of MAP 6

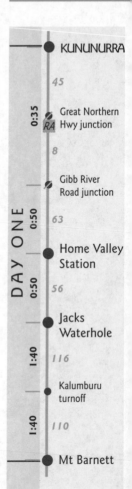

DAY ONE

KUNUNURRA

0:35   45

Great Northern
RA   Hwy junction

8

Gibb River
Road junction

0:50   63

Home Valley
Station

0:50   56

Jacks
Waterhole

1:40   116

Kalumburu
turnoff

1:40   110

Mt Barnett

El Questro Station turnoff: locality only; no facilities. (*86/312*) Turn **S** for El Questro Station - see Side Trip below.

Side Trip

El Questro Station (Alt 90m; Pop 10): a vast working cattle station and tourist facility located in very attractive countryside. Camping is available. Fee payable for day use visitors. Plenty to see. Highly recommended is Zebedee Springs** (thermal pools), El Questro Gorge* and Chamberlain Gorge** (boat tour). The Pentecost River crossing at the homestead is 4WD only. 32km return trip on a Grade 4 road. Accommodation, store, fuel.

Cockburn Range:* impressive and spectacular range of steep spinifex-clad slopes set beneath high red clifflines and rocky bluffs.

Fish Hole: attractive billabong marked by three impressive boab trees.

Pentecost River crossing* provides excellent eastward views towards the Cockburn Range which rises nearly 600m above river level. Good fishing downstream (beware of estuarine crocodiles).

Home Valley Station (Alt 35m; Pop 5): working cattle station and tourist facility with spectacular views of the Cockburn Range. Camping is available. Accommodation, limited store, fuel - check beforehand. (*116/282*)

Lookout* provides excellent views eastward towards the Cockburn Range. Late afternoons are best for photography. The Pentecost and Durack Rivers can also be seen. (*119/279*)

Undulating country provides views of low hills, ranges and valleys. Sparse eucalypt woodlands

Cockburn Range, near El Questro Station, WA

(including rusty bloodwoods and scarlet gums) common.

Gregory's Jump-Up: steep ascent/descent provides good views.

Jacks Waterhole (Alt 300m; Pop 5): former cattle property outstation nowadays mostly a tourist facility. Delightful waterhole* offers fishing, swimming, boating and bird-watching. Tours and camping available. Enquire here about access to Oomaloo and Durack Falls. Accommodation, limited store, fuel - check beforehand. (*172/226*)

Rollie's Jump-Up: steep ascent/descent offering good views of rugged hill country.

Durack River crossing:* attractive area and large waterhole. Pleasant place to rest a while. Westward rise the Mosquito Hills.

Undulating country offers reasonable views across low hills and outcrops. The area supports vast tracts of eucalypt woodlands (scarlet gums, rusty bloodwoods) with spear grass or curly spinifex, otherwise Darwin stringybarks and woollybutts. Occasional creek crossings are pleasant and may have waterholes until late in the dry season.

Low hills can be seen from the road (Gibb Range to the east). Tracts of open eucalypt woodlands with a grassy understorey.

Kalumburu turnoff: locality only; no facilities. (*288/110*) Kalumburu lies 270km **N**. Continue **W** for Mt Barnett. *Continue **E** for Jacks Waterhole.*

Low hills and undulating country support grassy eucalypt woodlands.

Mt Elizabeth Station turnoff: locality only; no facilities. (*360/38*) Turn **N** for Mt Elizabeth Station (60km return - Grade 4): a working cattle station, Ngariyin community and low key tourist facility. Tours to Aboriginal rock art sites and camping available. Accommodation, limited store, fuel.

Barnett River Gorge turnoff: (*376/22*) A short road leads **N** to Barnett River Gorge*, a small attractive gorge and waterfall; Aboriginal paintings* nearby. Good swimming. Worth seeing.

Low hills and undulating country support eucalypt woodlands.

Mt Barnett (Alt 400m; Pop 130): roadhouse and Aboriginal community of mostly Ngaringin people. Make enquiries and obtain permit to camp at nearby Manning Gorge (7km), where you can bushwalk, swim and see an attractive waterfall. Close by is Kupingarri, an Aboriginal community Store, fuel. (*398/0*)

DAY 2: MT BARNETT-DERBY via Inmitji

Road to Take: Gibb River Road
Total Distance: 307km (4:00)
Intermediate Distances:

	Km	Hours
Mt Barnett-Inmitji	77	(1:10)
Inmitji-Windjana Gorge turnoff	104	(1:20)
Windjana Gorge turnoff-Derby	126	(1:30)

Average Vehicles per Day: 90 east of Derby
Regions Traversed: The Kimberley (Kimberley Plateau, King Leopold Ranges)

Mt Barnett (Alt 400m; Pop 130): roadhouse facility. For more information see Day 1. (*0/307*)

Galvins Gorge:* attractive gorge located close to the road. A waterfall (20m) and rock pools are very photogenic. Good swimming. Aboriginal art including Wandjina figure*. Camping area nearby.

Phillips Range: rocky tableland supporting a eucalypt woodland with a spinifex understorey. Good views* northward from the top of the range at its northern end, likewise southward at southern end.

Adcock Gorge turnoff: (*32/275*) A short detour leads **S** to Adcock Gorge*, an attractive gorge with a great swimming hole. Gorge up to 30m deep with a small waterfall. Aboriginal burial ground nearby. A short walk to the gorge is required, and the last few hundred metres of the track are quite rough. Camping available.

Beverley Springs turnoff: (*48/259*) Turn **NW** for Beverly Springs (110km return -Grade 5): a working cattle station offering tourist facilities: birdwatching, bushwalks, swimming and fishing.

Access to Grenville Gorge. Darwin woollybutts and spear grass is common. Accommodation.

Undulating country offers reasonable views. Countryside supports extensive tracts of grassy eucalypt woodlands.

Inmitji: Aboriginal settlement and roadhouse. Store, fuel. (**77/230**)

Isdell Range: low rocky range lying to the west. Eastward, Precipice Range can be seen.
Silent Grove Road junction: locality only; no facilities. (**86/221**) Turn **W** for Bell Gorge** (60km return - Grade 4): a beautiful rugged gorge, considered to be one of the best in this part of the Kimberley. A short walk is required to reach it from the end of the tracsk. Camping is available along Bell Creek. The road is closed early December to late April.

King Leopold Range:** spectacular range of high peaks, bold bluffs, plunging clifflines and rocky outcrops - one of the scenic highlights of the Gibb River road. Great views. A short distance away is Mt Bell, one of the highest mountains in the Kimberley. Good lookout* at northern end of range (mornings best for photography); **rest area** at March Fly Creek*. The area supports a variety of vegetation including sparse snappy gum woodlands with curly spinifex and spear grass understoreys on the hillslopes, grey box woodlands in the valleys, and screw palms along the creeks. Keep an eye out for some contorted rock formations* (heading north). The range is located in the King Leopold Range National Park, as is Lennard River Gorge.
Lennard Gorge access road turnoff: locality only; no facilities. (**109/198**) Turn **S** for Lennard River Gorge** (16km return - Grade 5 track): a spectacular gorge 5km long, with sheer vertical walls. A small waterfall and pool provides good swimming.

Mt Hart turnoff: locality only; no facilities. (**112/195**) Turn **NW** for Mt Hart (120km return - Grade 5 track): a former cattle station home-

stead, nowadays offering full accommodation (bookings essential). No camping permitted.

Inglis Gap: rugged and rocky country hereabout. Good views* from the top of the range overlooking valleys and hills. The area supports a sparse eucalypt woodland.
Hilly country provides good views, particularly northward towards the main King Leopold Range. Numerous granite outcrops and rounded hills can be seen. Sheer-sided high granite domes are visible to the west. Interesting rock slabs* rise vertically from the hillsides. The vegetation cover includes sparse woodlands of snappy gums and twin-leafed bloodwoods, with an understorey of curly spinifex and spear grass.
Plains offer good views towards distant ranges. Grassy eucalypt woodlands and bean trees are common.
Yamarra Pass* (one of many spellings) cuts through the limestone Napier Range. Many boabs and cliffs make this area quite photogenic. On the western side of the pass is a rock silhouette resembling Queen Victoria. (**172/135**)
Lennard River crossing is a pleasant area. (**181/126**)
Windjana Gorge turnoff: locality only; no facilities. (**182/125**) Turn **SE** for Windjana Gorge - see Side Trip below.

Side Trip
Windjana Gorge-Tunnel Creek access road (Grade 3) 112km return
Windjana Gorge:** spectacular gorge with walls up to 90m high, the main feature of the Windjana Gorge National Park. Surrounding countryside includes the rocky escarpments of the limestone Napier Range. The gorge is over 3km long and offers good walking during the dry season. Numerous waterholes are home to freshwater crocodiles. Camping is available. This national park is highly recommended but can be crowded.
Lillimilura ruins*, a police outpost (100m north of the road). An interesting site.
Tunnel Creek:* centrepiece of a national park of the same name. Tunnel Creek flows through the Oscar Range. If you do not mind getting wet, a

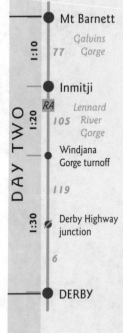

DAY TWO

Mt Barnett

1:10   77   *Galvins Gorge*

Inmitji

RA

1:20   105   *Lennard River Gorge*

Windjana Gorge turnoff

119

1:30   Derby Highway junction

6

DERBY

walk through is possible, but take a torch and do not enter during storms. The tunnel is 750m long, 12m high and 15m wide. Stalactites will be seen. The cave is home to many bats. No camping.

Plains support extensive tracts of pindan woodlands with a grassy understorey. Open grassland area, supporting ribbon and bluegrasses, presents sweeping views.

Meda Station turnoff: (264/49) Turn **N** for Meda Station, a working cattle station offering camping, fishing and picnicking on the May River. Beware of estuarine crocodiles.

Plains and low rises support wide tracts of Pindan, characterised by dense acacia shrubs and boabs with a tall grassy understorey. Great silhouettes at dusk.

Derby Highway junction: locality only; no facilities. (301/6) Turn **N** for Derby. *Turn **E** onto Gibb River Road for Mt Barnett.*

DERBY (Alt 5m; Pop 3200): interesting grazing town. For more information see Road Trip 26, Day 5. (307/0) *Road Trip 26 connects.*

Road Trip 28
The North-West Connection

Broome to Perth via Carnarvon
Total Distance: 2384km
Suggested Travelling Time: 5 days

Cruise down Australia's west coast from top to bottom

See Eighty Mile Beach, Cape Keraudren, the scenic town of Millstream, Cape Cuvier, Hearson Cove, the Blowholes near Carnarvon, Fortescue River, Murchison River in the Kalbarri National Park, the historic village of Greenough, and the tourist features of Geraldton.

The North-West Connection

Australia's North-West is a vast tract of land ranging from semi-arid deserts to monsoonal country. It is a sparsely populated land extensively grazed by cattle in the north and sheep in the south. Towns are few and far between; those that exist are service centres primarily connected with the mining industry. Elsewhere are small townships (most with a mining heritage) or roadhouses. Although a sparsely settled area, road connections, both sealed and unsealed, are very good, and along the main roads at least, services are available at regular intervals. Tourism has taken off here over the last 10 to 15 years and adequately prepared travellers will find this to be one of the most interesting areas in Australia to visit.

From the Murchison River southwards the countryside changes from outback rangelands to partially cleared cropping and grazing country.

The Climate

This is a hot part of the world, especially during summer or the dry season. Maximum temperatures are extreme at this time with temperatures regularly over 40C. Night temperatures are also uncomfortable, with minimums often over 25C, accompanied by high humidity in the north or along the coast. It can also be wet at this time with cyclonic rains in the south and monsoonal rains in the north.

The time to visit North-West Australia is between April and October (the dry season in the north). Note that even then, in the Kimberley, maximum temperatures may well be in the mid-thirties. Further south, coastal temperatures are generally mild to warm during the day (22C - 26C) and cool, sometimes cold, at night. Inland, cold night temperatures (around 5C or less) can be expected. Fortunately, in most years, rain is virtually absent in the north and limited to showers in the south.

Further south, around Geraldton for instance, winter maximum temperatures are cool to mild, nights can be cold, and showery weather is likely.

Capital City Connections

Distances in kilometres

SYDNEY-BROOME
via Great Western/Mitchell/Matilda/Barkly/
Stuart/Victoria/Great Northern Highways

	Intermediate	Total
Sydney	0	0
Nyngan	578	578
Charleville	655	1233
Mt Isa	1150	2383
Three Ways	636	3019
Katherine	642	3661
Kununurra	513	4174
Broome	1040	5214

MELBOURNE-BROOME
via Western/Dukes/Highway1/Stuart/Victoria/
Great Northern Highways

	Intermediate	Total
Melbourne	0	0
Adelaide	731	731
Port Augusta	312	1043
Alice Springs	1220	2263
Three Ways	531	2794
Katherine	642	3436
Kununurra	513	3949
Broome	1040	4989

SYDNEY-PERTH
via Great Western/Mitchell/Barrier/Highway56/
Eyre/Coolgardie-Esperance/Great Eastern
Highways

	Intermediate	Total
Sydney	0	0
Port Augusta	1568	1568
Ceduna	468	2038
Norseman	1210	3248
Coolgardie	168	3416
Merredin	295	3711
Perth	261	3972

The Route

Distances in Kilometres

	Intermediate	Total
Broome	0	0
Port Hedland	610	610
Carnarvon	873	1483
Geraldton	478	1961
Perth	423	2384

Great Northern Highway:
Great Sandy Desert

Slicing through pindan shrublands of varying
heights and densities, the Great Northern Highway crosses a vast and seemingly unending sea
of sand. Long low sandy waves rise and fall, the
crests barely 40 metres above the troughs, with
each crest ten or more kilometres apart. The road
provides distant views of the far off crests along
its lengthy straights. One would never describe
this route as scenic; it is, nonetheless, of some
interest for those travellers not in a hurry, especially Eighty-Mile Beach and Cape Keraudren.

Warnings: beware of stock, kangaroos and
camels at night. Some sections of road are
subjected to flooding.
Note: no fuel available Sandfire Roadhouse-
Roebuck Roadhouse 285km.

DAY 1: BROOME-
PORT HEDLAND
via Sandfire Roadhouse

Road to Take: Great Northern Highway
Grade 1
Total Distance: 610km (6:40)
Intermediate Distances:

	Km	Hours
Broome-Roebuck Roadhouse	34	(0:25)
Roebuck Rdhse-Sandfire Rdhse	285	(3:00)
Sandfire Rdhse-Pardoo Rdhse	138	(1:30)
Pardoo Roadhouse-Port Hedland	153	(1:45)

Average Vehicles per Day: 250 south of
Roebuck Roadhouse
Regions Traversed: The Kimberley, Great
Sandy Desert, Pilbara

BROOME (Alt12m; Pop 12000):*** a colourful settlement with many historical associations.
For more information see Road Trip 26, Day 5.
(**0/610**) *Road Trip 26 connects.*

12 Mile: small rural locality set within the pindan
scrub. No facilities. (**20/590**)

Roebuck Roadhouse (Alt 27m; Pop 5): modern roadhouse facility. A good place to view the
big road-train rigs* up close. Accommodation-
camping available, store, fuel. (**34/576**) Turn **S**
onto Great Northern Hwy for Sandfire Roadhouse. *Turn **W** onto Broome Hwy for Broome.*

Roebuck Plains: broad plain supporting a grassland. Expansive views.
Plains and low rises support a dense growth of
tall acacia wattles, typically Broome pindan
wattle, and a dense understorey of tall grasses,
typically native sorghum or curly spinifex. This
type of countryside is known as The Pindan.
Scattered amongst the pindan are taller trees,
sometimes eucalypts such as rough-leafed
bloodwoods or *E. dampieri*; occasionally helicopter trees (bleached-looking leafless trees in
the dry season). Long views down the highway.

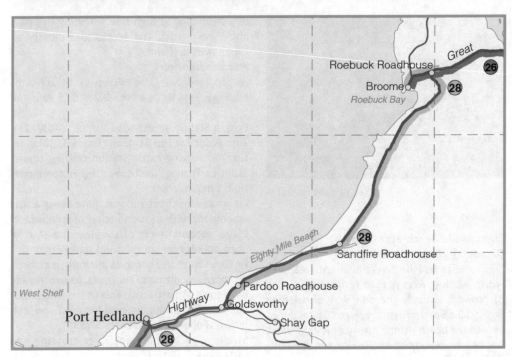

Detail of MAP 7

DAY ONE

- BROOME
  - 0:25 — 34
- Roebuck Roadhouse
  - RA
  - 3:00 — 285
  - RA
- Sandfire Roadhouse
  - 1:30 — 138
- Pardoo Roadhouse
  - RA — 142
- Dixons
  - 1:45 — 1
- Port Hedland turnoff
  - 10
- PORT HEDLAND

Cape Villaret Road junction: (*119/491*) Turn **W** for Cape Villaret (unsealed access -Grade 3) and Eco Beach Resort, a wilderness lodge offering accommodation. Good beach - day visitors okay.

Port Smith Road junction: (*141/469*) Turn **W** for Port Smith* (unsealed access Grade 3 - 46km return) a pleasant coastal area set on a tidal lagoon. Good fishing and swimming when the tide is in. Bird park and garden* worth visiting. Caravan park and camping able; limited stores.

Shamrock Vegie Stall: rustic roadside stall selling fresh vegetables. A short distance south is a **rest area**. (*143/467*)

Plains and low rises support Pindan wattles. Elsewhere are areas of eucalypt and acacia low woodlands with a spinifex understorey. Broad distant vistas. **Rest area**. (*213/397*)

Plains and low rises support acacia shrublands, typically pindan wattle with a spinifex understorey. The shrubs here are of a lower stature than those further north. On the flats between the rises are dense scrubs of paperbarks. Near the Anna Plains Station turnoff are distant views of Mt Phire.

Plains support treeless tracts of grasslands, samphires and small, normally dry, lakes. Vast views.

Sand dunes* line the road. Spinifex is common, with a sparse overstorey of desert walnuts. This fragment of country is typical of the western portion of the Great Sandy Desert proper.

Sandfire Roadhouse (Alt 30m; Pop 10): pleasant roadhouse facility with a small park. Accommodation, limited store, fuel. (*319/291*)

Accommodation
Sandfire Roadhouse Hotel-Motel, Great Northern Hwy, ☏08 9176 5944, ◐$35-$80. Camping available.

Sandplain with distant sand dunes supports a sparse desert walnut woodland with a ground cover of spinifex.

Eighty Mile Beach access road turnoff: locality only; no facilities. (*364/246*) Turn **W** for Eighty Mile Beach - see Side Trip below.

Dusk, Eighty-Mile Beach, WA

Side Trip
Eighty Mile Beach access road
(Grade 3) 20km return

Eighty Mile Beach:** very pleasant area, well worth visiting. Access road (unsealed - Grade 3) provides virtually the only way of reaching Eighty Mile Beach. There are huge coastal dunes behind the beach - climb one to enjoy the view. The beach area is good for walking and shell collecting, but swimming is unsafe due to sharks and other sea nasties. Excellent place to view sunsets, especially at low tide. The tides here travel a long way out, so be careful not to be caught by the incoming tide. Camping is available. Limited stores.

Low rises support quite dense but fairly low statured acacia-dominated scrubs including *Acacia pachycarpa*, with an understorey of spinifex. Glimpsed views of white coastal dunes.
Plains and low rises support acacia-dominated scrubs and spinifex. Desert walnuts can be seen on the rises. Some rocky outcrops and distant views to white coastal dunes.

Pardoo Roadhouse (Alt 5m; Pop 10): roadhouse facility. Accommodation, store, fuel. (*457/153*)
  Opposite the roadhouse is the turnoff to Cape Keraudren** (Grade 3 - 28km return) a scenic coastal area located at the end of Eighty Mile Beach. Worth visiting. Good fishing. Mangroves line the estuary. Intricately eroded limestone cliffs (take care if walking) provide good views. Beware of large tidal range. A sandy beach of-

fers swimming at high tide. Camping (fee payable - no shade). The access road crosses an expansive grassland.
Accommodation
Pardoo Roadhouse Caravan Facility, **Great Northern Hwy**, ©08 9176 4916, ✪Site: $15 Van: $50

Pardoo Station access road turnoff: (*489/121*). Turn **N** for **Pardoo Station** (Grade 3; 32km return) a working cattle station offering tourist facilities. Fishing, shell collecting. Accommodation, camping, fuel.
Plains and low rises support quite dense acacia woodlands with a ground cover of spinifex.
Plains support tracts of spinifex. The start of open country for southbound travellers.
De Grey River* area supports attractive grasslands and open woodlands of eucalypts, paperbarks and bean trees. An attractive area at the river crossing provides an opportunity for good rock collecting. Popular **rest area**. (*527/83*)
Strelley River:* pleasant river crossing and waterhole.
Marble Bar turnoff: locality only; no facilities. (*560/50*) *Road Trip 30 connects.* Turn here for Marble Bar - see Side Trip below.

Side Trip
A 306km return (short unsealed Grade 3 section) road can be taken to Marble Bar, Australia's hottest town. **Marble Bar** (Alt 173m; Pop 360)* is an historic mining town. There are many features worth seeing, including the Ironclad Hotel*, Government buildings*, Water Tank Lookout*, old cemetery, Old Ironclad Battery*, old mine workings and relics, as well as the Marble Bar** itself.
Accommodation
Marble Bar Travellers Stop Motel, **Halse Rd**, ©08 9176 1166, ✪$100
Marble Bar Caravan Park, **264 Contest St**, ©08 9757 2180, ✪Site: $20 Van: $55

Plains and low rises support tracts of sparse acacia shrublands (typically *Acacia translucens*) and spinifex. Broad vistas from the tops of rises. Excellent nighttime views** of Port Hedland.

There are interesting low hills near the Marble Bar turnoff.

Tjalka Waka (9 Mile): small Aboriginal community. No facilities.

Dixons: roadhouse facility and outer suburb of Port Hedland. Accommodation, store, fuel. (**599/11**)

Accommodation
Mercure Inn Port Hedland Airport, Great Northern Hwy, ©08 9172 1222, ©$125-$160
Dixons Caravan Park, Great Northern Hwy, ©08 9172 2525, ©Site: $20 Van: $60-$80

Port Hedland turnoff: (**600/10**) Turn **N** for Port Hedland. *Turn* **E** *onto Great Northern Hwy for Broome.*

PORT HEDLAND (Alt 6m; Pop 16000):* sizeable regional and industrial centre. Major iron ore port. Give this town time; there is more of interest here than you might think. The town is separated from the mainland by extensive tidal flats. Mangroves line tidal estuaries. Redbank Lookout, 1km north of the highway junction, overlooks the tidal flats and a saltworks, and is a good spot to see the 2km long iron ore trains*. Worth seeing: Observation Tower, shipping observation lookout* (see the world's largest ships close up and the large tidal fluctuations*), St Mathews Anglican Church, Two Mile Ridge Aboriginal Carvings (a key is available from Aboriginal Affairs office), Don Rhodes Mining Museum*, Pioneer and Pealers Cemetery*, Water Tower Lookout, Pretty Pool (nice when the tide is in), Staircase-to-the-Moon (visible around full moon at Cooke Point), turtle-watching* (Cooke Point, Pretty Pool - September to April), and whale watching (humpbacks - June to October). Tours of the BHP facilities. Good fishing - make local enquiries. Full town facilities. (**610/0**) *Road Trips 29 and 30 connect.*

Accommodation
Pier Hotel, The Esplanade, ©08 9173 1488, ©$85
Hospitality Inn, Webster St (4.5kmE), ©08 9173 1044, ©$160
Hedland Accommodation Centre, Hunt St, ©08 9140 2925, ©$40

Cooke Point Holiday Park, Athol St (8kmE), ©08 9173 1271, ©Site: $20 Van: $60-$100
South Hedland Motel, Court Pl, South Hedland (16kmS), ©08 9172 2222, ©$120
South Hedland Caravan Park, Hamilton Rd, South Hedland (16kmS), ©08 9172 1197, ©Site: 20 Van: $60-$80

North-West Coastal Highway
Port Hedland-Perth
Running virtually parallel to the west coast, the North-West Coastal Highway is the main outback route between Port Hedland and Geraldton. It is a moderately trafficked highway accessing the Exmouth Peninsula, and the Gascoyne and Pilbara hinterlands. This route provides access to some very interesting coastal areas west of the highway, in particular Shark Bay, Monkey Mia, Point Quobba, Ningaloo Marine Park, Cape Range National Park, Exmouth and Onslow. Between Nanutarra and Karratha the highway traverses scenic countryside.

Warnings: beware of stock and kangaroos at night. Extreme summer temperatures will be experienced; if travelling at this time carry plenty of water in the vehicle. Road may be subjected to flooding.
Note: no fuel available between Nanutarra Roadhouse-Minilya Roadhouse 229km.

DAY 2: PORT HEDLAND-FORTESCUE ROADHOUSE via Roebourne

Road to Take: North-West Coastal Highway
Grade 1
Total Distance: 339km (3:45)
Intermediate Distances:

	Km	Hours
Port Hedland-Roebourne	102	(2:15)
Roebourne-Fortescue Roadhouse	137	(1:30)

Average Vehicles per Day: 1100 east of Karratha/350 east of Roebourne
Regions Traversed: Pilbara

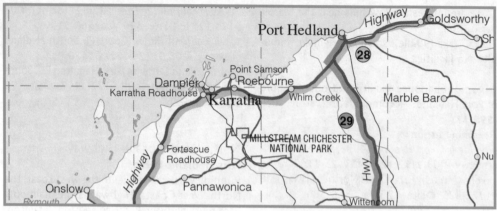

Detail of MAP 7

PORT HEDLAND (Alt 6m; Pop 16000):* large regional centre. For more information see Day 1. (*0/339*)

South Hedland turnoff. (*14/325*) Turn here for **South Hedland** (Grade 1; 4km return), a modern town development housing most of Port Hedland's population. Worth seeing: Shay Gap Memorial Park*. Full town facilities.

Plains support tracts of spinifex in association with a sparse acacia-dominated shrubland. Good nighttime views* of the lights of Port Hedland if heading east.

Great Northern Highway junction: locality only; no facilities. (*42/297*) *Road Trips 29 and 30 connect.*

Yule River:* attractive river crossing and waterhole lined with paperbarks and river red gums. **Rest area**. (*69/270*)

Plains and low rises offer vast views. Spinifex is common with scattered eucalypts and acacias. **Rest area** at Peewah River. (*92/247*)

Low hills and flat-top ranges support spinifex, occasionally with a variety of shrubs. In some places, black dolerite boulders* appear very striking in the landscape. Good views across scenic country.

Whim Creek (Alt 32m; Pop 15) :* old mining centre and bush pub. (The pub unfortunately was partially destroyed by a cyclone in late 1999). Accommodation - check beforehand, fuel. (*118/221*)

Adjacent to Whim Creek is the turnoff to Balla Balla (unsealed access - Grade 3; 40km return), an old port for the Whim Creek mines. Little to see along the mangove-lined estuaries but a good area for fishing. Shadeless camping is available. The route crosses a broad grassland with expansive views*, especially northward to the bulk of Depuch Island. Tidal flats near the coast.

Low hills provide expansive views. Sparse acacia shrublands and spinifex are common.

Plains support extensive tracts of grasslands, typically lovegrasses. In the distance, flat-top ranges with black bouldery faces can be seen. Expansive views* abound, some of which are impressive in the right light. At times, whirlwinds or willy-willies can be seen. **Rest area** at Sherlock River. (*145/194*)

Millstream turnoff: locality only; no facilities. (*175/164*) Turn **S** for Millstream - see Side Trip below.

Side Trip
Millstream Road
(Grade 3) 240km return
Warning: no fuel or services available. Carry sufficent fuel and water for your return journey; stay out of this area in summer.

Plains support wide sweeping grasslands. Expansive views abound. The horizon is lined with distant flat-top hills and ranges, including Mt Wellard (237m). Willy-willies may be seen.

Pyramid Hill:* interesting and photogenic conical hill west of the road.

Plains support vast tracts of lovegrass grasslands. Good views. The skyline is delineated by numerous flat-top hills. Southward, the Chichester Range escarpment can be seen. Near the escarpment are low rocky hills* and boulders - a wildly scenic area.

Millstream-Chichester National Park preserves a large portion of the Chichester Range escarpment and the adjacent plains, as well as a portion of the Fortescue River. Much of the park is wilderness.

Python Pool:* large rock pool set at the base of a high cliff and normally dry waterfall. A very pleasant spot, relatively cool and shady. Walking trails lead to the pool as well as Mt Herbert along the Camel Trail*. The surrounding countryside is very dry and rocky, and covered with virtually nothing but spinifex. Camping is available at Snake Creek.

Mt Herbert:* wide sweeping views across the spinifex-clad escarpment and the distant George River plain. Pyramid Hill can be seen in the distance. Walking trails lead to the summit of Mt Herbert* (344m - excellent views) or downhill to McKenzie Spring* (a camel watering hole) then along the Camel Trail* to Python Pool. The sparse low shrubs hereabout are kanji. South of Mt Herbert, the far distant escarpment of the Hamersley Range can be seen to the south.

Millstream:** definitely worth visiting - an oasis amid an expanse of aridity. Millstream itself is a former station homestead, nowadays a ranger station where camping, water, information and a telephone are available. Adjacent is Chinderwarriner Pool*, a tropical waterhole lined with Millstream fan palms, introduced date palms and paperbarks, covered with lilies, and edged with sedges. On the nearby Fortescue River are waterholes (Deep Reach* and Crossing Pool*) with camping facilities. These river red gum and bullrush-lined waterholes are very attractive. The scenic Snappy Gum Drive* encircles the waterholes. Walking tracks lead around the homestead and to Crossing Pool.

Roebourne (Alt 12m; Pop 1700):* historic town with plenty of interest. Numerous stone buildings, some of which are quite photogenic. Good views from Mt Welcome Lookout behind the town. Also worth seeing is the Old Roebourne Gaol* (historical museum and tourist bureau), where tours to Robe River's Cape Lambert facility depart. Enquire here about Emma Withnall Heritage Trail. Sizeable Aboriginal population. Spend some time here, first appearances can be misleading. Accommodation, stores, fuel. (202/137)

Accommodation

Harding River Caravan Park, Jiwuna Way (1kmE), ©08 9182 1063, ✪Site: $15 Van: $40

Wickham Lodge, 6 Wickham Drive, Wickham (10kmN), ©08 9187 1439, ✪$80

Point Samson Lodge, 56 Samson Rd, Point Samson (21kmN), ©08 9187 1052, ✪$125-$150

Port Samson turnoff: (204/135) Turn **N** for Port Samson - see Side Trip below.

Side Trip

Wickham (Alt 20m; Pop 2300), 10km from Roebourne, is a modern town connected with the shipment of iron ore. Worth seeing: Tank Hill Lookout*, Iron Ore Haul Truck display, and Robes Visitor Centre. A short distance away is Boat Beach. Nearby is the Cape Lambert wharf*, one of the longest and highest open ocean wharves in the Southern Hemisphere - 2.7km long and 17.9m high (no access unless on a tour - see Roebourne notes). Limited accommodation, stores, fuel.

Near Wickham is the turnoff to **Cossack****, an old ghost town and former port for the region. Numerous stone buildings, a few of whch are photogenic. Also worth seeing: Old Court House Museum*, Nanny Goat Hill, Tien Tsin and Mount Beach Lookouts (overlooking the settlement), old tramway ruins*, early settler's cemetery*, Settlers Beach and Reader Head Lookout*** (this last lookout offers one of the best coastal views in the Pilbara - highly recommended at low tide). Fish from the wharf. This

Road Trip 28

PORT HEDLAND

14

South Hedland turnoff

28

Great Northern Hwy turnoff

RA

76

RA

Whim Creek

RA

57

Millstream turnoff

27

Roebourne

29

Karratha turnoff

9

Karratha Roadhouse

RA

99

Fortescue Roadhouse

DAY TWO

2:15

1:30

Sturts desert pea, Hearson Cove, WA

old settlement is well worth visiting for an hour or two. The road to Cossack crosses salt flats and tidal estuaries. Accommodation, tearooms. **Point Samson** (Alt 2m; Pop 20)*, 21km from Roebourne, is a pleasant spot to relax for a few days. Good fishing in the tidal creeks. Nearby Honeymoon Cove* offers good swimming; snorkling. Reefs are exposed at low tide - good exploring (wear foot protection). Tank Hill Lookout* offers good views. Also worth seeing: Johns Creek boat harbour, Popes Nose (view from causeway south of town), old jetty site, *Solveig* wreck at Back Beach (southern end). Accommodation, store, fuel.

Low hills and undulating country line the road with good views from the tops of rises. Mt Marie (125m) lies to the south. The countryside is dominated by spinifex or lovegrass grasslands. Karratha turnoff: locality only; no facilities. (*231/104*) Turn **N** for Damiper via Karratha - see Side Trip below.

Side Trip
Dampier Road/Karratha Road
(Grade 1) 54km return
KARRATHA (Alt 5m; Pop 12000): large regional centre. Nearby beach on Nickol Bay is interesting; reasonable views from TV Hill Lookout; fishing at Nickol River (eastern end of town). The Jaburara Heritage Trail* is worth a look (interesting walk, good views, geological/flora/Aboriginal information). Full town facilities.

Accommodation
Mercure Inn, Searipple Rd, ©08 9143 9888, ○$130-$160
Pilbara Holiday Park, Rosemary Rd (4kmSW), ©08 9185 1855, ○Site: $25 Van: $55
Balmoral Holiday Park, Balmoral Rd (4kmW), ©08 9185 3628, ○Site: $25 Van: $55
Karratha Caravan Park, Moonligunn Rd (3kmS), ©08 9185 1012, ○Site: $18 Van: $40
Salt flats provide expansive views to nearby rocky ranges. East of the main causeway is the Dampier Salt Lookout (tours available of Dampier Salt), adjacent is the Pilbara Railways Museum**.
DAMPIER (Alt 5m; Pop 2500): modern iron ore port town located upon a rocky ridge overlooking some of the islands of the Dampier Archipelago. Most of the islands are part of a reserve: boating, swimming, fishing, bushwalking, camping, and more - enquire locally about access. In town the following are worth seeing: Red Dog Memorial*, William Dampier Lookout, Burrup Lookout (rough access), foreshore area*, Hamersley Iron Visitors Centre (tours available of Hamersley Iron Port Facility - fee payable). Accommodation, stores, fuel.

Accommodation
Dampier Transit Caravan Park, The Esplanade, ©08 9183 1109, ○Site: $16

North of the town (look for signs on way in) the Woodside industrial complex is very impressive, especially at night*. It forms a part of Australia's largest infrastructure, the North-West Shelf Gas Project. The Visitors Centre** is worth seeing.

Nearby Hearson Cove** is well worth visiting. With a very attractive cove set among rocky hills, this quiet area is worth exploring on foot. Staircase-to-the-Moon* is worth seeing. Good swimming and picnic facilities. Unsealed access (Grade 3). En route, hilly country* dominated by rocky outcrops of dolerite can be seen. These hills have the appearance of loosely jumbled boulders. In places throughout the Burrup Peninsula, these boulders have Aboriginal engravings** - enquire locally as to their location. Over 10,000 petroglyphs have been identified, making this the most prolific rock art gallery in Australia. 1km before Hearson Cove, a short track (100m - southern side of road) leads to a short walk (100m) into Deep Gorge* where numerous petroglyphs can be seen.

Karratha Roadhouse: modern roadhouse facility. Fuel. (*240/99*)

Maree Pool:* attractive waterhole located on the river red gum-lined Maitland River. Well worth visiting; numerous aquatic plants and melaleucas dominate the area. **Rest area.** (*258/81*)

Plains and low rises are covered with extensive grasslands. Southward are rocky ranges and hills including Mt Leopold (250m). Expansive views from the tops of rises, including one that encompasses the tidal flats and off-shore islands of the Indian Ocean coastline. Elsewhere are distant views toward the Dampier Archipelago.

Ranges* with impressive rocky outcrops can be seen to the north and south. They are rent with deep, rocky valleys and gorges. The hillsides support a sparse eucalpyt woodland with a spinifex understorey. This landscape is the most rugged through which the highway passes. Mt Virchow (255m) lies to the south.

Fortescue Roadhouse (Alt 70m; Pop 10): interesting roadhouse facility located within an attractive and rugged setting. Nearby is the river red gum-lined Fortescue River*. Well worth stopping to take a short walk, explore, fossick or to have a picnic. **Rest area** adjacent. Accommodation, fuel. (*339/0*)

Accommodation
Fortescue River Roadhouse and Caravan Park, NW Coastal Hwy, ©08 9184 5126, ©Site: $18 Van: $35

DAY 3: FORTESCUE R'DHOUSE-CARNARVON
via Nanutarra Roadhouse

Road to Take: North-West Coastal Highway
Grade 1
Total Distance: 534km (5:50)

Intermediate Distances:

	Km	Hours
Fortescue Rdhse-Onslow turnoff	120	(1:20)
Onslow turnoff-Nanutarra Rdhse	45	(0:30)
Nanutarra Rdhse-Burkett Rd jctn	112	(1:15)
Burkett Rd jctn-Minilya Rdhse	117	(1:15)
Minilya Roadhouse-Carnarvon	140	(1:30)

Average Vehicles per Day: 400 north of Carnarvon
Regions Traversed: Pilbara, The North-West, Gascoyne

Fortescue Roadhouse (Alt 70m; Pop 10): pleasant roadhouse on the banks of the Fortescue River. For more information see Day 2. (*0/534*)

Ranges are clearly visible to the east with rocky outcrops rising above the spinifex-clad lower slopes. A broad sweeping coastal plain falls westward with the Indian Ocean on the skyline.

Pannawonica Road junction: locality only; no facilities. (*43/491*) Turn **E** for the 94km return drive (Grade 1) to **Pannawonica**, a typical Pilbara-style iron mining town. Surrounded by high flat-top hills and ranges. Accommodation, stores, fuel.

Robe River:* pleasant spot; **rest area**. (*45/489*)
Low ranges visible to the east across the intervening lowlands. Spinifex is common.

Plains (mostly westward) support a sparse acacia shrubland dominated by various species, with an understorey of spinifex. Occasional expansive views.

Onslow Road junction: (*120/414*) Turn **NW** for Onslow - see Side Trip below.

Side Trip
Onslow road
(Grade 1) 164+km return
Plains support extensive tracts of spinifex and large anthills, some of which have formed into interesting shapes. Shrubs on the plains include *Acacia pyrifolia* and *A. ancistrocarpa* with and understorey of spinifex. Eastward views to distant ranges near the highway. En route is Bobbys Tree.

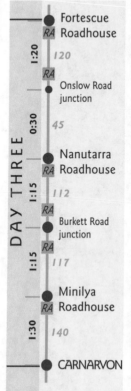

DAY THREE

Fortescue Roadhouse	RA
1:20	120
RA	
Onslow Road junction	
0:30	45
Nanutarra Roadhouse	RA
1:15	112
RA	
Burkett Road junction	
RA	
1:15	117
Minilya Roadhouse	RA
1:30	140
CARNARVON	

Old Onslow turnoff:* Old Onslow is the site of the former settlement, today marked by a number of stone ruins. Worth a brief visit at least, as is the Ashburton River* nearby (good fishing). Grasslands are common hereabout, with a smattering of eucalypts. Unsealed access road (Grade 3).

Salt flats line the road into Onslow, providing broad views. Near tidal creeks are mangrove formations, while on the edge of the flats there are low salt-tolerant shrubland communities. Keep an eye out for the Termite Town, an interesting spectacle.

ONSLOW (Alt 3m; Pop 650):* interesting older style 'north-west' town. Well worth visiting. A pleasant spot to relax for a while and to escape the tourist hordes. Good fishing at Four Mile Creek and Beaden Creek. Accommodation, stores, fuel.

Accommodation

Onslow Mackerel Motel, Second/Third Sts, ©08 9184 6444, ○$100-$120

Ocean View Caravan Park, Second Ave, ©08 9184 6053, ○Site: $18 Van: $55

Parry Range rises to the east, clearly visible across the spinifex-clad lowlands. Westward are lowlands dotted with isolated rocky hills and ridges. Good expansive views.

Nanutarra Roadhouse (Alt 100m; Pop 15): roadhouse settlement situated near the banks of the shady Ashburton River*. Good walks along bush tracks and in the river bed during the dry season. Note the bent melaleucas and incredible pothole formations. Good waterholes and rock collecting area. **Rest area** nearby. Accommodation, camping, fuel. (*165/374*) *Road Trip 30 connects.*

Undulating country* consisting of rocky rises and ridges as well as flat-top hills covered with spinifex. Expansive views from the tops of rises. Scenic countryside hereabouts. The tall mountain to the east is Mt Alexander (418m).

Barradale:* former roadhouse site of which, unfortunately, little remains. **Rest area** set by the normally sandy bed of the Yannarie River. (*234/305*)

Sand dunes* cross the road at regular intervals. Their vivid red crests are quite photogenic in the late afternoon light. Fair views from the tops of the dunes. Spinifex is common on the sand dunes, with a sparse covering of low trees, typically corkwood and *Grevillea pyramidalis*. At certain times a bright purple morrison will be seen in flower on the dunes.

Burkett Road junction: locality only; no facilities. (*278/261*) Exmouth lies 167km **NW**. *Road Trip 30 connects.* Continue **SW** for Carnarvon. *Continue **NE** for Nanutarra.*

Lake bed occupies a lowland east of the road. Desolate country hereabout with expansive views over the lake bed. Nearby are low hills and rises supporting a sparse shrub cover. Four kilometres north of the Winning Station turnoff is an **emergency phone**.

Undulating country includes plains, low rises and the distant Giralia Range (213m) visible to the west.

Plains support tracts of snakewood, dead finish and emu-bushes on the low rises, and *Acacia pyrifolia* with spinifex on sandy flats. Anthills are common north of the Lyndon River. **Rest area** at Lyndon River. (*345/189*)

Sand dunes form part of the Carnarvon Dunefield.

Minilya Roadhouse (Alt 40m; Pop 5): roadhouse facility and **rest area** set by the Minilya River*, an attractive river red gum-lined watercourse. Accommodation, fuel. (*394/140*) *Road Trip 31 connects.*

Accommodation

Minilya Bridge Roadhouse Caravan Park, NW Coastal Hwy, ©08 9942 5922, ○Site: $16 Van: 40-$45

Sand dunes form part of the Carnarvon Dunefield. The dunes with their bare red crests are quite photogenic in the right light. The dominant plant on the dunes is horse mulga, while *Acacia subtessarogona* can be seen on the flats. After rains these dunes support attractive wildflowers.

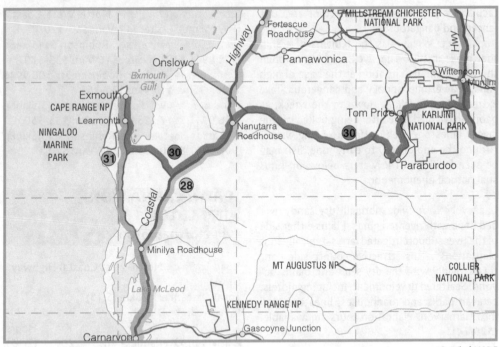

Detail of MAP 7

Plains support vast tracts of shrublands. What looks like saltbush is in fact emu-bush. Some open areas provide expansive views.

Blowholes Road junction: locality only; no facilities. (*510/24*) Turn **W** for Point Quobba and the Korean Star Wreck - see Side Trip below.

Side Trip
Blowholes Road.
This 190km return drive leads to Point Quobba (Grade 2) and the Korean Star wreck (Grade 3). Point Quobba* (no facilities; camping area): a rustic fishing settlement with an interesting if somewhat rundown character. It is a popular spot with the locals on weekends. Good fishing. The attractive beach is protected by a coral reef. A low hill gives good views across a coral lagoon to a small island. Good views* from the high dunes behind the beach. Nearby are the Blowholes*, eerily set upon a jagged limestone platform edged by a low seaward cliff. The ocean's swells bubble and seethe through narrow fissures within the rock, occasionally erupt-

ing through holes in the surface, blowing water to great heights (up to 20m). Only inspect closely during calm seas; even then there is the ever-present danger of king waves washing the platform. This is a dangerous place, but very impressive. Nearby, set upon a limestone ridge, is the Point Quobba Lighthouse*. Excellent views can be obtained from here.

North of Quobba is a memorial* to the sinking of the *HMAS Sydney** during World War II, a sinking that raises many unanswered questions. It is worth visiting just to experience the strange aura of the place.

Quobba Station: a working sheep station. Camping facilities may be available; make local enquiries.

Cape Cuvier*: port for a nearby salt mine. There is no public access to the mine, but the loading facilities can be seen from a nearby viewpoint (look for tracks heading towards the cliffs north of the salt mine's haul road). Cliffs provide excellent views** of the Cape and the wreck of the *Korean Star* - well worth visiting for the spectacular scenery. **Warning:** viewpoint area un-fenced and dangerous.

Korean Star Wreck** is the remains of a ship that broke in two. The swell washing through the wreck, and its situation at the base of high cliffs, is awesome, spooky and dangerous. Take extreme care if walking down to the wreck, as people have died here after being pulled off the jagged limestone rock platform by king waves. Around the end of May to early June, fish may be seen feeding in the waters below, an unu-sual natural phenomenon.

Gascoyne River:* wide, normally dry, sandy river bed lined with river red gums. Plains either side of the river support irrigated farms, typically fruit plantations*. This attractive countryside con-trasts vividly with the dry semi-arid plains be-yond. Scattered development, including motels, caravan parks and roadhouses, lines the road into Carnarvon. Plantation tours are available. (*520/14*)

CARNARVON (Alt 3m; Pop 5000): sizeable coastal town servicing fishing, pastoral and tour-ist industries. Some scenes of the old Carnarvon may be glimpsed in the side streets. Worth see-ing: One Mile Jetty*, old jetty railway, Lighthouse Keepers Cottage and Museum*, the Fascine, Tropical Bird Park* (fee payable), and Chinamans Pool* (picnic area, birdlife). Numerous fishing spots including Long Jetty, Dwyers Leap, Small Boat Harbour, Oyster Creek and Miaboolya Beach. Full town facilities. (*534/0*)

Accommodation
Carnarvon Hotel, Olivia Tce, ℂ08 9941 1181, ✪$50-$70
Port Hotel, Robinson St, ℂ08 9941 1704, ✪$30-$45
Gateway Motel, 379 Robinson St (3kmE), ℂ08 9941 1531, ✪$95
Hospitality Inn, West St (1kmW), ℂ08 9941 1600, ✪$105
Marloo Retiree/Senior Tourist Caravan Park, Wise St (3kmE), ℂ08 9941 1439, ✪Site: $17
Wintersun Caravan Park, Robinson St (4kmE), ℂ08 9941 8150, ✪Site: $18 Van: $45-$65

Capricorn Holiday Park, North-West Coastal Hwy (5kmE), ✪Site: $17 Van: $50-$70
Carnarvon Caravan Park, Robinson St (5kmE), ℂ08 9941 8101, ✪Site: $16 Van: $35-$70
Carnarvon Tourist Park, Robinson St, ℂ08 9941 1438, ✪Site: $16 Van: $35-$55
Norwesta Caravan Park, Robinson St (3.5kmE), ℂ08 9941 1277, ✪Site: $16 Van: $35-$50
Plantation Caravan Park, Robinson St (5.5kmE), ℂ08 9941 8100, ✪Site: $17 Van: $70

DAY 4: CARNARVON-GERALDTON
via Northampton

Road to Take: North-West Coastal Highway
Grade 1
Total Distance: 478km (5:15)
Intermediate Distances:

	Km	Hours
Carnarvon-Overlander Rdhse	200	(2:15)
Overlander Rdhse-Kalbarri t/off	177	(1:50)
Kalbarri turnoff-Geraldton	101	(1:10)

Average Vehicles per Day: 920 north of Geraldton/600 south of Overlander Roadhouse
Regions Traversed: Gascoyne, Murchison, Wheatbelt (Central-West)

CARNARVON (Alt 3m; Pop 5000): large town. For more information see Day 3. (*0/478*)

Sand dunes with saltbush flats line the road. The long dune east of the highway is called the Baxter Range. Upon it sits the old OTC Satellite Earth Station*. Good views*.

Plains support extensive tracts of acacia shrub-lands. While not scenic, the vivid red soils of the plains are impressive in the late afternoon sunlight. Small saltpans line the road.

Wooramel Roadhouse (Alt 20m; Pop 5): road-house. Accommodation, store, fuel. (*124/354*)
Accommodation
Wooramel Roadhouse Caravan Park, NW Coastal Hwy, ℂ08 9942 5910, ✪Site: $11 Van: $40

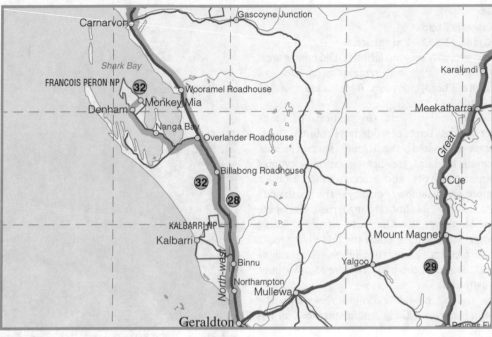

Detail of MAP 7

Plain supports an open treeless area of saltbush, one of the few such areas south of the Pilbara. Low hills and rises can be seen in the distance. Westward are distant views across Shark Bay. Low hills (would be called jump-ups in the Eastern States) line the road and a lookout (*150/228*) provides good views* overlooking the saltbush plains and Shark Bay beyond.

Sandplains support extensive tracts of acacia shrublands. Occasional long views down the dead-straight road from the tops of rises.

Overlander Roadhouse (Alt 80m; Pop 5): roadhouse. Notable for being centrally situated on a hundred kilometre or so stretch of straight road. Accommodation-camping available, fuel. (*200/278*) *Road Trip 32 connects.*

Sandplains support a relatively dense acacia shrubland with a shrubby understorey. From the tops of low rises the dead-straight highway can be seen vanishing near the horizon. These rises are very low limestone ridges.

Billabong Roadhouse (Wannoo) (Alt 120m; Pop 5): roadhouse. Accommodation, fuel. (*247/231*)
Accommodation
Billabong Homestead Hotel-Motel, NW Coastal Hwy, ©08 9942 5980, ©$60

Sandplains and low rises support acacia shrublands with a shrubby understorey. **Rest area**. (*293/185*)
Sandplains support a diversity of plant life, including mallee eucalypts and numerous shrubs and heaths. Worth stopping the car (well off the road) for a quick look at least.
Eurady Station turnoff (**W**): (*336/142*) Nearby station offers accommodation, camping.
Mary Springs Mine ruins are visible to the west of the road. (*358/120*)
Murchison River:* pleasant bridge crossing. **Rest area**. From just north of the Murchison River extensively cleared farming country ranges south towards Geraldton. (*364/114*)
Galena: locality only; no facilities. Old mining area.
Kalbarri turnoff: locality only; no facilities. (*377/101*) Turn **W** for Kalbarri - see Side Trip below.

Side Trip
Kalbarri Road
(Grade 1) 132+km return
Ajana: locality only; no facilities. Old mining area.
Warribano Chimney:* remains of an old lead smelter. Photogenic ruins. Access road unsealed - Grade 3.
Kalbarri National Park: large national park preserving vast tracts of wilderness country. Landscape dominated by heathlands; species include various banksias, grevilleas, grass trees, cypress pines, eucalypts, and acacias, which produce impressive wildflower displays. The heathlands are clearly visible from the main road. Elsewhere the Murchison River has cut a deep and scenic gorge, whilst on the coast the underlying rocks have produced a fantastic cliffline. No car camping allowed in the park. Enquire locally about bushwalks.
Lookouts** provide excellent views over the Murchison River Gorge. Interesting rock formations.
Z-Bend:** tall cliffs and colourful rocks line the 150m deep Murchison River Gorge. Very scenic area.
The Loop:** excellent views overlooking the Murchison River Gorge. The area exhibits colourful cliffs, waterholes and wildlife.
Kalbarri (Alt 3m; Pop 820):** low-key seaside resort settlement set by the mouth of the Murchison River. Very attractive and popular area; a nice place to relax for a few Days. Nearby are many scenic lookouts, including the Meenarra Hill Lookout* which provides good views over the Murchison River mouth and Kalbarri. Other features include coast and estuary cruises, Wildflower Centre, pelican feeding* (8:45am daily), and Rainbow Park (bird park). Good fishing hereabouts. Accommodation, stores, fuel.
Accommodation
Kalbarri Palm Resort, Porter St, ©08 9937 2333, ❂$65-$90
Anchorage Caravan Park, Anchorage Lne/River Road (1.4kmN), ©08 9937 1181, ❂Site: $16 Van: $35-$65
Kalbarri Tudor Caravan Park, Porter St, ©08 9937 1077, ❂Site: $18 Van: $35-$80

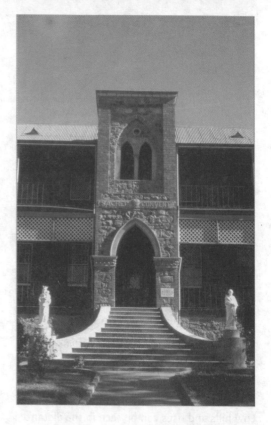

Northampton Monastery, WA

Murchison River Caravan Park, Grey St, ©08 9937 1005, ❂Site: $16
Red Bluff:** coastal tourist facility set at the northern end of the cliffed coastline. Excellent lookout nearby.
Accommodation
Red Bluff Caravan Park, Red Bluff Rd, ©08 9937 1080, ❂Site: $13 Van: $40-$50
Lookouts** extend to Bluff Point. Seek local advice before proceeding if travelling in a conventional car. Numerous vantage points are just off the main track. Sights include colourful plunging clifflines (best in the afternoon light), gorges, gullies, coves, arches and rock formations. Take care if walking.

Binnu: small roadhouse settlement situated within farming country. Store, fuel. **(388/90)**

Farming country occupies extensively cleared land given over to cropping and grazing. Landscape usually a lush green after winter rains, brown and dried after the summer drought. Fair views from the tops of rises.

Northampton (Alt 165m; Pop 750):* old lead mining town, nowadays a farming settlement. Many photogenic old buildings, including miners' cottages constructed in the 1860s. Interesting main street. The old Gwalla mine site is clearly visible east of the highway, south of the town. Museum. Accommodation, stores, fuel. (*416/52*)

Accommodation
Northampton Caravan Park, NW Coastal Hwy, ©08 9934 1202, ✪Site: $12

Farming country occupies cleared land given over to cropping and grazing. Good views* from hilltops across the rolling paddocks. **Rest area** (*445/33*) set amid the hills. Closer to Geraldton, the flat-topped Moresby Range can be seen to the east, the Indian Ocean to the west.

Glenfield: outlying suburb of Geraldton. Store, fuel. (*466/12*)

GERALDTON (Alt 5m; Pop 21000):* large regional centre with many tourist features. Worth seeing: Gregory Street historic buildings precinct*, Cathedral of the Holy Cross* (huge stained-glass window), St Francis Xavier Cathedral** (outstanding architecture by Father John Hawes - big name in these parts), The Hermitage*, The Residency* (old Governor's residence), Geraldton Museum, Sir John Forrest Memorial, Regional Art Gallery, Lighthouse Keepers Cottage, Fishermans Wharf, and various lookouts including Mills Park Lookout* on top of the nearby Moresby Range. Enquire locally for more details. Full town facilities. (*478/0*)

Accommodation
Hospitality Inn, Cathedral Ave (1.5kmS), ©08 9921 1422, ✪$100-$120
Batavia Motor Inn, 54 Fitzgerald St, ©08 9921 3500, ✪$70
Mariner Motor Hotel, 298 Chapman Rd (3kmN), ©08 9921 2544, ✪$50-$60

Geraldton Hotel, 19 Gregory St, ©08 9921 3700, ✪$35
Belair Gardens Caravan Park, Willcock Dve (2kmW), ©08 9921 1997, ✪Site: $17 Van: $30-$45
Sunset Beach Holiday Park, Bosley St (6kmN), ©08 9938 1635, ✪Site: $18 Van: $35-$70
Batavia Coast Caravan Park, 89 Hall Rd (10kmN), ©08 9938 1222, ✪Site: $13 Van: $30
Separation Point Caravan Park, Port Way (2kmS), ©08 9921 2763, ✪Site: $15 Van: $35-$60

Brand Highway
Geraldton-Perth
The Brand Highway is a direct route between Geraldton and Perth passing through the sandplain country north of Perth and the Central-West farming districts of the Wheatbelt. Of interest to travellers are the fantastic wildflowers during late winter/early spring.

Warnings: road subject to flooding. Beware of urban traffic between Bullsbrook and Perth.

DAY 5: GERALDTON-PERTH via Dongara

Road to Take: Brand Highway
Grade 1
Total Distance: 423km (5:00)
Intermediate Distances:

	Km	Hours
Geraldton-Dongara	65	(0:45)
Dongara-Badgingarra	154	(1:45)
Badgingarra-Muchea	149	(1:40)
Muchea-Perth	55	(0:50)

Average Vehicles per Day: 1700 south of Dongara
Regions Traversed: Wheatbelt (Central-West), Coastal Plain (northern sandplain)

GERALDTON (Alt 5m; Pop 21000):* large regional centre. For more information see Day 4. (*0/423*)

Old Store, Greenough, WA

GERALDTON

24

Greenough

6

S-Bend

35

Dongara

110

Halfway Mill
Roadhouse
RA
44

Badgingarra

43

Cataby

32

Moore River
RA

74

Muchea

0:45

1:45

1:40

DAY FIVE

Plains **offer good views**** over the Greenough Flats. Westward lies a prominent vegetated sand dune. Note the small, twisted or leaning trees*, a result of the high salt content in the air. This is a very scenic area.

Greenough (Alt 27m; Pop 100):** historic settlement well worth visiting. Scattered stone buildings form a National Trust conservation area. Worth seeing: Hampton Arms Inn*, Pioneer Museum*, Pioneer Cemetery, Greenough Wildlife and Bird Park*, scattered historic buildings including Clinchs Mill*. Store. **(24/399)**

Accommodation
Greenough Rivermouth Caravan Park, Hull St, ©08 9921 5845, ✪Site: $16 Van: $ 35-$50

Greenough Flats **offer great sweeping views****.

S-Bend: roadhouse facility. Store, fuel. **(30/393)**

Accommodation
S-Bend Caravan Park, Brand Hwy, ©08 9926 1072, ✪Site: $13 Van: $30-$45

Low rises **are mostly cleared for farming.**

Dongara (Alt 9m; Pop 1900):* interesting small town set on the Irwin River. Worth seeing: old flour mill*, Russ Cottage* (pioneer cotage), The Prioy Lodge* (historic inn), Old Dongara Police Station* (historic displays). A short distance away is Port Denison*; worth a look is Fishermans Lookout* with its old obelisk. Accommodation, stores, fuel. **(65/358)**

Accommodation
Old Mill Motel, Brand Hwy, ©08 9927 1200, ✪$65
Dongara Motor Hotel, Moreton Tce, ©08 9927 1023, ✪$80
Dongara/Denison Tourist Park, 8 George St, (2kmS), ©08 9927 1210, ✪Site: $15 Van: $35-$45
Seaspray Caravan Park, 81 Church St (1kmW), ©08 9927 1165, ✪Site: $15 Van: $35-$75

Low rises **support grazing and cropping.**
Sandplain **supports an amazing diversity of vegetation, typically heaths and scrubs. This countryside is virtually in pristine condition and forms part of the Red Book Flora Reserve. Excellent wildflowers**** at the end of winter/early spring. Good birdwatching.
Arrowsmith River: **crossing is of minor interest. Nearby is a caravan park where tours of wildflowers are available in season. (123/300)**
Sandplain **supports heaths and scrubs. Wildflowers**** **during season.**
Eneabba turnoff: (**145/278**) Turn here for **Eneabba** (Pop 350; 3km return), a small sand (rutile) mining town located just off the highway. Mineral sand mines are open by appointment - mining trail. Store, fuel.
Sandplain **supports scrubs and heaths.**

Halfway Mill Roadhouse: roadhouse facility. Store, fuel. (**175/248**)

Hilly country **offers good views***, especially northwards. Land partially cleared for grazing. Scenic **rest area** at Coomallo Creek. (**191/232**)
Undulating country **offers good views of nearby hills. Uncleared areas offer wildflowers during the season, otherwise countryside cleared for grazing.**

Badgingarra: small farming township. Opposite the roadhouse and caravan park, a walking trail leads into the Badgingarra National Park, a reserve protecting a diverse community of heaths and shrubs. Good wildflowers** in season. Store, fuel. (**219/204**)

Detail of MAP 8

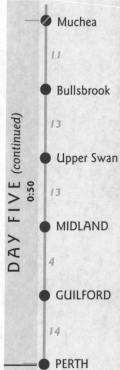

DAY FIVE *(continued)* 0:50

- Muchea
- *11*
- Bullsbrook
- *13*
- Upper Swan
- *13*
- MIDLAND
- *4*
- GUILFORD
- *14*
- PERTH

Accommodation

Badgingarra Caravan Park (behind roadhouse), ©08 9652 9184, ◎Site: $13

Hilly country offers good views over heathlands and cleared grazing country.
Undulating country has been mostly cleared for grazing.

Cataby: roadhouse facility. Store, fuel. (**262/161**)

Low rises, mostly cleared for grazing, offer fair views.
Sandplain supports tracts of heathlands; some clearings for grazing.

Moore River (Pop 5): roadhouse facility. Nearby Moore River* crossing (Regans Ford **rest area**) is pleasant. Accommodation, store, fuel. (**294/129**)

Moore River National Park lines the western side of the road. Extensive tracts of heathlands and scrubs with wildflowers** at the end of winter.

Plains support cleared grazing country dotted with grass trees.
Plains have been cleared for grazing and cropping. Fair eastward views towards the Darling Range escarpment.

Muchea: small farming township. Store, fuel. (**368/55**) Great Northern Highway junction. *Road Trip 29 connects.* Turn **S** onto Great Northern Hwy for Perth. *Turn **W** onto Brand Hwy for Moore River.*

Plains support farmlands. Eastward views towards the Darling Range. RAAF Pearce airbase lies to the west.

Bullsbrook: small town set at the foot of the Darling Range. Accommodation, stores, fuel. (**379/44**)

Plains support farmlands including vineyards. Eastward views* toward the Darling Range.

Upper Swan: scattered township set amongst vineyards. Accommodation, stores, fuel. (**392/31**)

Plains cleared for farming and vineyards. Eastward views. Parts of the plain are occupied by the suburbs of Herne Hill, Middle Swan and Midvale.

Midland and Guilford can be avoided by using the Roe Highway/Great Eastern Highway bypass. Turn **E** onto Roe Highway (*402/21*) then **W** onto Great Eastern Bypass (*408/15*) rejoining Great Eastern Highway (Midland Road) near Airport (*414/9*). *Reverse directions if heading **N** from Perth.*

MIDLAND area: forms part of the Perth suburban area. Full town facilities. (*405/18*)

Accommodation

Budget Motel, 51 Victoria St, ©08 9250 2688, ✪$55
Banksia Tourist Village & Caravan Park, 219 Midland Rd, ©08 9250 2398, ✪Site: 20 Van: $60-$80
Midland Caravan Park, 2 Toodyay Rd (1kmNE), ©08 9274 3002, ✪Site: $17 Van: $35-$45

GUILFORD:* attractive Perth suburb with interesting old buildings, set on the banks of the Swan River. Full services. (*409/14*)

Accommodation

Rose & Crown Hotel-Motel, ©08 9279 8444, ✪$70

Between Guilford and Perth is a continuous suburban area. Turn **W** onto Causeway - follow Perth sign. (*420/3*) *Turn **E** for Midland.*

Swan River precinct:* attractive parklands and river estuary edge the south-eastern corner of the city centre. Good skyline views of the city.

PERTH (Alt 19m; Pop 1097000):** state capital of Western Australia. For more information see Road Trip 33, Day 1. (*423/0*) *Road Trips 29, 33 and 34 connect.*

Road Trip 29
Great Northern Highway

Port Hedland-Perth
Total Distance: 1645km
Suggested Travelling Time: 3 days

Brave Western Australia's untamed interior

See the attractive mining town of Newman, the Chichester Range, the bush pub at Kumarina, the Murchison ghost towns, the historical buildings in Cue, wildflower displays, the attractive countryside around Bindoon, and the Spanish architecture and Benedictine monastery at New Norcia.

Great Northern Highway

This highway crosses the rump of Australia's North-West, a vast tract of land ranging from semi-arid country in the north to relatively benign farmlands in the far south. It is a sparsely populated land extensively grazed by cattle and sheep on outback rangelands. In the south the land has been cleared for cropping and grazing. South of Wubin, the towns are few and far between in the outback areas; those that exist are service centres primarily connected with the mining industry. Elsewhere there are small farming townships or roadhouses. Although this route crosses a sparsely settled area, road conditions are very good, and services are available at regular intervals.

The Climate

This is a hot part of the world during summer. Maximum temperatures are extreme at this time with temperatures regularly over 40C. Night temperatures are also uncomfortable, with minimums often over 25C, accompanied by high humidity in the north. It can also be wet at this time with cyclonic rains in the north.

The time to visit north-west Australia is between April and October (the dry season in the north). Temperatures are generally mild to warm during the day (22C - 26C) and cool, sometimes cold, at night. Inland, cold night temperatures (around 5C or less) can be expected. Fortunately, in most years, rain is virtually absent in the north and limited to showers in the south. In the far south, wintertime days can be cool and showery.

Capital City Connections
Distances in kilometres
SYDNEY-PERTH
via Great Western/Mitchell/Barrier Highways/
Route 56/Eyre/Coolgardie-Esperance/Great
Eastern Highways

	Intermediate	Total
Sydney	0	0
Nyngan	578	578
Broken Hill	575	1153
Port Augusta	415	1568
Norseman	1687	3255
Perth	724	3979

MELBOURNE-PERTH
via Western/Dukes Highways/Highway 1/Eyre/
Coolgardie-Esperance/Great Eastern Highways

	Intermediate	Total
Melbourne	0	0
Horsham	299	299
Adelaide	432	731
Port Augusta	312	1043
Norseman	1687	2730
Perth	724	3454

The Route
Distances in kilometres

	Intermediate	Total
Port Hedland	0	0
Munjina	261	261
Newman	197	458
Meekatharra	422	880
Mt Magnet	196	1076
Dalwallinu	318	1394
New Norcia	119	1513
Perth	132	1645

PORT
HEDLAND

42

2:50　North-West
Coastal Hwy
junction

RA

219

RA

Munjina

0:25　*RA*

35　Karajini NP

Karajini Drive
turnoff

RA

1:45　*162*

NEWMAN

DAY ONE

Great Northern Highway
Port Hedland-Perth

The Great Northern Highway passes through areas of what some people might descibe as dreary country, especially for those travellers in a hurry. Admittedly, the Meekatharra-Newman section of the highway is not particularly scenic, but during late winter/early spring the countryside can be carpeted with one of the world's best wildflower displays. Between Newman and Port Hedland, the route passes through the inland Pilbara, a splendidly scenic arid region of high mountains and desert plains. South of Meekatharra are many old mining towns and ruins.

South of Mt Magnet, the highway crosses undulating granite plains, sandplains, the wheatbelt and the northern hills district of the Darling Plateau. While some sections of this part of the route are quite scenic, it is the mass displays of everlastings in late winter/early spring between Paynes Find and Mt Magnet that make this portion of the road a magnificent drive.

Warnings: beware of stock and kangaroos at night. Avoid night driving north of Wubin if at all possible. Road may be subjected to flooding.
Note: no fuel available South Hedland-Munjina-244km; Kumarina-Meekatharra 256km.

DAY 1: PORT HEDLAND-NEWMAN
via Munjina

Road to Take: Great Northern Highway
Grade 1
Total Distance: 458km (5:00)
Intermediate Distances:

	Km	Hours
Port Hedland-Munjina	261	(2:50)
Munjina-Karijini Drive junction	35	(0:25)
Munjina-Newman	162	(1:45)

Average Vehicles per Day: 250 south of Munjina
Regions Traversed: Pilbara

PORT HEDLAND (Alt 6m; Pop 16000):* regional centre and iron ore port. For more information see Road Trip 28, Day 13. (*0/458*) *Road Trip 28 connects.*

For information on the route between Port Hedland and North-West Coastal Highway junction see Road Trip 28, Day 2.

North-West Coastal Highway junction: locality only; no facilities. (*42/416*) *Road Trip 28 connects.* Turn **S** on Great Northern Hwy for Munjina. *Turn **E** on Great Northern Hwy for Port Hedland.*
Plains support tracts of acacia shrublands. Occasional expansive grasslands offer wide vistas. The lights* of Port Hedland are visible for some distance at night. **Rest area**. (*74/384*) Nearby Indee Station offers camping and caravan facilities. Unsealed access (Grade 3).
Plains are formed on granite. The dominant vegetation is spinifex with kanji forming a sparse overstorey. Other species of shrubs include corkwoods and caustic trees. Grasses may be present after rains. Interesting solitary hill* on the side of the road.
Low hills are quite scenic and offer broad vistas. Nearby, just visible from the highway, is the Wodinga Mine. (*112/346*)
Rocky outcrops* of granite form a striking feature in the landscape. Very beautiful at dusk.
Marble Bar Road junction: locality only; no facilities. (*166/292*)
Yule River: fair spot for a picnic, with some shady paperbarks. Access is from the southern side. (*170/288*)
Plains and low rises support spinifex with scattered eucalypts and shrubby acacias such as kanji. Good views* heading south towards the Chichester Range.
Chichester Range:* long escarpment rising above the plains. The range rises gradually up to 150m above the lowlands. Good views. Rocky outcrops are common. Spinifex is the dominant vegetation, along with a smattering of mygums. A pretty valley* contains a **rest area** (*217/241*) with an **emergency phone**. On top of the range is an

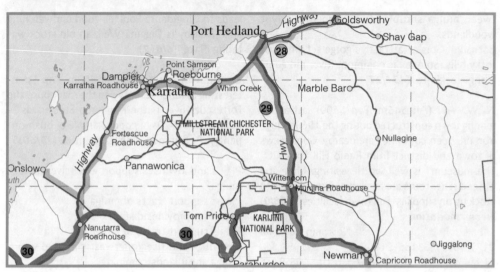

Detail of MAP 7

open tract of grassland, typically three-awn grass. The southern side of range provides scenic views* of rocky outcrops and distant views of the Hamersley Ranges. Spinifex is common.

Plains support extensive tracts of mulga shrublands.

Fortescue River forms a broad shallow valley with no distinct watercourse. Mulga shrublands are common.

Plains formed by outwash from nearby Hamersley Ranges. Good views of ranges to the south. Spinifex is common, with mulga and some eucalypts.

Munjina (Alt 490m; Pop 10): modern roadhouse facility set at the foot of the Hamersley Range escarpment; an attractive setting. Accommodation, limited store, fuel. (*261/197*) *Road Trip 30 connects.*

Ranges** form part of the Hamersley Range escarpment. The road traverses rugged gorge lands, passing numerous cliffs, bluffs and rocky residual outcrops. Spectacular area. Ranges rise over 200 metres above the lowlands.

Karijini National Park:** preserves a large area of the Hamersley Range, the roof of Western Australia. Rising above this undulating plateau are remnant hills and mountains. Edging its northern side is a long escarpment deeply incised by steep, rocky gorges. The park incorporates some of the most scenic country in Western Australia, and contains some of Australia's best arid mountain landscapes

Munjina East Gorge Lookout:* good views over the rugged and partially disected escarpment country. The attractive white-trunked trees are known as mygums. Spinifex is common. **Rest area. (*276/182*)**

Karijini Drive turnoff (**W**): locality only; no facilities. (*296/162*) *Road Trip 30 connects.*

Undulating country occupys a plateau some 700 metres high. Elsewhere are plains and low hills supporting either mulga with a spinifex understorey or open eucalypt woodlands, also with a spinifex understorey. Out of sight is Western Australia's highest mountain, Mt Meharry (1245m).

View:* (north of Packsaddle turnoff) excellent southward view towards Mt Robinson and The Governor. More excellent views* near Mt Robinson. **Rest area (*344/114*)** and an **emergency phone**.

Low hills provide reasonable views. Spinifex is common, with a sparse shrubby overstorey.

Hilly country provides good views, particularly of the Opthalmia Range. Vegetation varies between mulga shrublands and open eucalypt woodlands.

Cathedral Gorge:* attractive gorge set amongst rocky hills. Spinifex is common. River red gums along creeklines. (*431/27*)

NEWMAN (Alt 546m; Pop 5500): attractive mining town constructed during the 1960s. Huge iron ore open cut mines are nearby. Good views of town and district from Radio Hill Lookout*. The museum* is well worth visiting. Mine and other district tours are available. A good place to stock up on supplies. Full town facilities. (*458/0*)

Accommodation

All Seasons Newman Hotel, Newman Dr, ©08 9177 8666, ✪$155-$180

Mercure Inn Newman, Newman Dr, ©08 9175 1101, ✪$130-$150

Dearloves Caravan Park, Cowra Dr (1.5kmS), ©08 9175 2802, ✪Site: $19 Van: $45-$80

Newman Caravan Park, Kalgan Dr, (2kmSE), ©08 9175 1428, ✪Site: $18 Van: $50-$90

DAY 2: NEWMAN-MT MAGNET via Meekatharra

Road to Take: Great Northern Highway
Grade 1
Total Distance: 618km (6:45)
Intermediate Distances:

	Km	Hours
Newman-Kumarina	163	(1:45)
Kumarina-Meekatharra	259	(2:50)
Meekatharra-Mt Magnet	196	(2:10)

Average Vehicles per Day: 250 north of Meekatharra
Regions Traversed: Pilbara, Gascoyne, Murchison Goldfields

NEWMAN (Alt 546m; Pop 5500): iron ore mining town. For more information see Day 1. (*0/618*)

Fortescue River:* attractive area with plenty of shady river red gums. A good place to collect river stones. An access track on the eastern side leads to Ginginanra Pool*, a good birdwatching area. Nearby is Diggina Well, an old stock watering place. (*6/612*)

Capricorn Roadhouse (Alt 550m; Pop 5): interesting roadhouse. Between the roadhouse and Fortescue River is the Minderoo Stockyards* - built in the 1920s, a good example of bush carpentry. Accommodation, store, fuel. (*13/605*)

Plains and low rises support extensive tracts of mulga.

Plains support tracts of mulga.

Low ridge provides distant views.

Plains support tracts of mulga.

Low ridge and rises offer vast glimpsed views. Mulga shrublands dominate.

Little Sandy Desert: outlier of the Great Sandy Desert. Sand dunes, quite densely vegetated, line the road and can be photogenic in the late afternoon light. Elsewhere are sandplains supporting spinifex and shrubs.

Collier Range National Park: undeveloped wilderness park conserving areas of high ground known as the Collier Range. Areas of spinifex on the higher country, mulga on the lower country. Some hills are visible, rising above the general level. Distant flat-top hills and bluffs can be seen to the east.

Kumarina (Alt 600m; Pop 5): former copper mining area, nowadays a bush pub and roadhouse. Accommodation, fuel. (*163/455*)

Low rise offers distant views of Collier Range.

Plains and low rises support mulga shrublands. Occasional low ranges are visible in the distance.

Gascoyne River: the three branches of the Gascoyne are indicated by extensive sand flats and relatively tall trees of an acacia type known locally as gidgee (not to be confused with the eastern states' gidgee). The middle branch has an attractive waterhole* and **rest area (234/384)**. The southern branch has a very pretty waterhole* west of the road, with an old well and water trough also worth seeing. Unoffical **rest area**.

Ruin, Nanine, WA

Townscape, Cue, WA

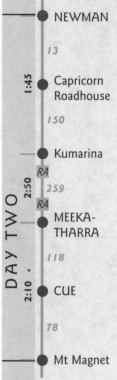

Plains and occasional low rises support a mulga shrubland. Robinson Range is visible to the west. Karalundi: former Aboriginal mission, now run as a school. Enquire locally about access. (*357/ 261*)

25 Mile Well: former stock route well. Worth a quick look. **Rest area**. (*381/237*)

Plains support tracts of mulga.

MEEKATHARRA (Alt 511m; Pop 1000): old mining town with some character. Mining is still in progress. Worth spending a short time here to absorb the atmosphere. The Royal Flying Doctor service is open to visitors. Accommodation, stores, fuel. Stock up here if heading north. (*422/196*)

Accommodation

Auski Inland Hotel-Motel, Cnr Main/Robert Sts, ©08 9981 1433, ✪$60-$105

Commercial Hotel, Main St, ©08 9981 1020, ✪$45

Meekatharra Caravan Park, Great Northern Hwy, ©08 9981 1253, ✪Site: $15

Low ranges are visible to the west. Elsewhere the country is slightly undulating, providing occasional views from the tops of rises. Mulga shrublands are common. A large mine is visible to the west.

Nanine:* old mining settlement where a few ruins remain. It is worth exploring on foot. The country hereabout has been degraded by mining, but is interesting nonetheless. Good views to the south overlooking Lake Anneen. (*463/155*)

Plains support mulga shrublands. Attractive countryside in this area. Small lakes and flood-plains support areas of grassland and saltbush. The old railway line on the eastern side is of interest.

Tuckanurra:* old mining settlement and railway ruins. (*501/117*)

Nallan Lake:* attractive area even when the lake is dry. When the lake is full, this place is a delight. Good wildflowers after winter rains (late August-September) - not a mass display, but pretty nonetheless. (*520/98*)

CUE (Alt 453m; Pop 320):** interesting old mining town with many photogenic historical buildings. Walk the streets and see the old buildings*. A good view of the town can be seen from the Kintore Blow*, a white quartz hill near the Fire Station. Ask for directions to the corrugated-iron Masonic Hall*, a very unusual building. Many ruins in the town offer good photographic opportunities. Accommodation, stores, fuel. (*540/78*)

Accommodation

Murchison Club Hotel-Motel, Austin St, ©08 9963 1020, ✪$45-$55

Cue Caravan Park, Austin St, ©08 9963 1107, ✪Site: $15

From Cue, take the unsealed road (Grade 3) to Wilgie Mia** , an old Aboriginal ochre mine (136km return), or Walga Rock**, a gallery of Aboriginal rock paintings (92km return) depicting snakes, emus, kangaroos and other creatures, as well as a Dutch ship that visited the Western

DAY TWO

NEWMAN

13

1:45

Capricorn Roadhouse

150

Kumarina

RA

2:50

259

RA

MEEKA-THARRA

118

2:10

CUE

78

Mt Magnet

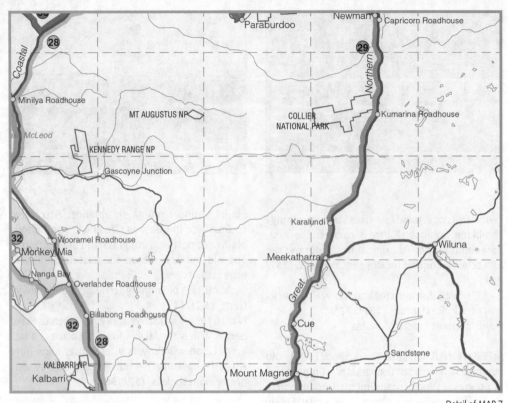

Detail of MAP 7

Australian coast in the 17th century! Climb the rock for excellent views.

Lake Austin: large saltlake (only a small portion seen from the road) crossed by a causeway.
Ruins form the old mining settlement of Austin. Little remains to be seen today, but it is worth taking a quick look among the scattered relics. (567/51)
Plains support a mulga shrubland with a shrubby understorey.

Mt Magnet (Alt 427m; Pop 620)*: old mining town with some character. Interesting main street with impressive buildings. The old open-air picture theatre is of interest. The town is undergoing a change, with new mining ventures in the area. This is a good area for gemstone prospecting - enquire locally. Just north of town is **Lennonville***, the ruins of an old mining settlement. Accommodation, stores, fuel. (618/0)

Accommodation
Commercial Club Hotel, 63 Hepburn St, ✆08 9963 4021, ✿$80
Grand Hotel, Hepburn St, ✆08 9963 4110, ✿$85
Mt Magnet Caravan Park, Hepburn St, ✆08 9963 4198, ✿Site: $17

DAY 3: MT MAGNET-PERTH via Dalwallinu

Road to Take: Great Northern Highway
Grade 1
Total Distance: 569km (6:40)
Intermediate Distances:

	Km	Hours
Mt Magnet-Dalwallinu	318	(3:40)
Dalwallinu-New Norcia	119	(1:20)
New Norcia-Perth	132	(1:50)

Average Vehicles per Day: 450 east of Milang

Regions Traversed: Murchison Goldfields, Wheatbelt, Darling Plateau, Coastal Plain

Mt Magnet (Alt 427m; Pop 620): old mining town. For more information see Day 2. (*0/569*)

Plain supports tracts of mulga shrublands. Low ridge and rocky outcrop provides reasonable views.

Low rises offer vast vistas from their tops. Occasional low ridges break the skyline. Excellent wildflower displays*** literally cover the plains as far as the eye can see; a staggering sight for first-timers. The flowers (mainly everlastings) come in a variety of colours. Wildflowers are usually present after winter rains (late August-September). Mulga shrublands are common.

Paynes Find (Alt 345m; Pop 10): a small old mining settlement with some character. Interesting bush pub. Accommodation, fuel. (*144/425*)

Plains and low rises offer fair views. Occasional low ridges dot the skyline. Very good wildflower** displays after winter rains (late August-September). Mulga shrublands are common, with an overstorey of eucalypts. Some patches of mallee eucalypts can be seen.

Low hills offer good southward views*. At times the high bulk of Mt Singleton (698m) is visible. **Rest area** at Mt Gibson. (*212/357*)

Sandplains and low rises, marked by orange-yellowy sand. Dense thickets of various acacias with patches of eucalypts are common. A variety of shrubs and heaths form the understorey. Good wildflowers** at the end of winter (not so much the mass displays of further north, but an incredible variety of different flowers - explore on foot but do not lose sight of the vehicle).

White Well:* an old stone circular well located by the road, probably made by the monks of New Norcia. **Rest area**. About 500m off the highway, a track leads through wattle thickets to a large exposed expanse of granite rock*, a good spot for a picnic. (*250/319*)

Undulating country supports tracts of sandplain vegetation. **Rest area**. (*265/304*)

Rabbit Proof Fence:* although barely noticeable, this fence ran for hundreds of kilometres and was built in an attempt to stem the tide of rabbits from the east. It roughly marks the boundary between farm and outback station country. Saltlakes edge the road. Fair views across the cleared countryside.

Undulating country supports wheat cropping. Reasonable views* from tops of rises. **Rest area**. (*290/279*)

Wubin (Alt 339m; Pop 50): small wheat-farming township. Worth seeing: Wubin Wheat-Bin Museum*. **Rest area**. Accommodation, store, fuel. (*297/272*)

Undulating country mostly cleared for cropping. Broad views.

Dalwallinu (Alt 335m; Pop 600): fairly large wheat-farming town serving the surrounding district. Worth seeing: the Old Well; pleasant park for picnics near the old railway station. **Rest area**. Accommodation, stores, fuel. (*318/251*)

Accommodation

Dalwallinu Hotel-Motel, Johnston St, ℗08 9661 1102, ☺$55-$75

Undulating country cleared for grazing and cropping; reasonable views* across the countryside. Between Dalwallinu and Bindoon, there are good early spring wildflowers** along the edge of the road reserve and on uncleared land; not massed displays but a diversity of types.

Pithara: small farming township. Store, fuel. (*331/238*)

Undulating country provides good views* overlooking cleared grazing and cropping country. **Rest area**. (*361/208*)

Miling:* small farming town with interesting buildings. Accommodation, store, fuel. (*368/201*)

Bindi Bindi (Alt 306m): small farming township. Store, fuel. (*384/185*)

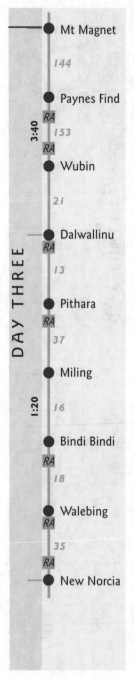

DAY THREE

Mt Magnet

144

3:40

Paynes Find

RA

153

RA

Wubin

21

Dalwallinu

RA

13

Pithara

RA

37

Miling

1:20

16

Bindi Bindi

RA

18

Walebing

RA

35

RA

New Norcia

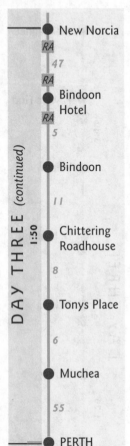

DAY THREE *(continued)* **1:50**

- New Norcia
  - *RA*
  - *47*
  - *RA*
- Bindoon Hotel
  - *RA*
  - *5*
- Bindoon
  - *11*
- Chittering Roadhouse
  - *8*
- Tonys Place
  - *6*
- Muchea
  - *55*
- PERTH

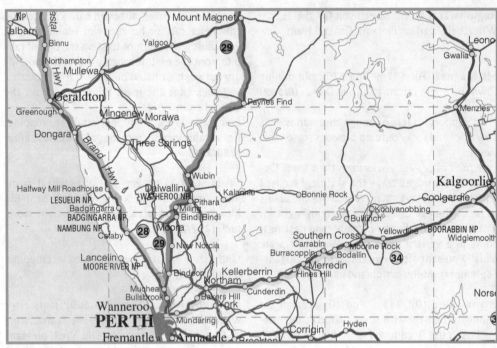

Detail of MAP 8

Undulating country supports grazing and cropping. **Rest area.** (*395/174*)

Waleebing: farming locality and roadhouse. Store, fuel. **Rest area.** (*402/167*)

Low hills* have been mostly cleared for grazing. Attractive countryside. **Rest area.** (*407/162*)

New Norcia (Alt 171m: Pop 150):** one of Australia's most unusual small towns - a Benedictine monastry town. Worth seeing: the unique Spanish architecture* of the church, monastry, colleges and other buildings; the art gallery** (one of the best outside of the state capitals) and museum** (fascinating); Marian Shrine*, cemetery, old flour mill, and more. Take the heritage trail*. Accommodation, store, fuel. (*437/132*)

Accommodation
New Norcia Hotel, Great Northern Hwy, ©08 9654 8034, ©$65

Low hills* have been partially cleared for grazing. This is attractive countryside, especially after winter rains. Good wildflowers (in season) at the **Flora rest area**. (*464/105*)
Rest area. (*475/94*)

Bindoon Hotel: accommodation, fuel. (*484/85*)

Low hills form attractive countryside. Between Bindoon and Dalwallinu there are good early spring wildflowers** along the road reserve. **Rest area.** (*485/84*)

Bindoon (Pop 200):* a pleasant small, spread-out farming town set within the Brockman River valley. Wineries are in the area. Worth seeing: Blackboy Ridge Park* which preserves grass trees and wildflowers, and has picnic areas and walking trails. Accommodation, stores, fuel. (*489/80*)

Undulating country offers good views* across the Brookman River valley.

City skyline, Perth, WA

Chittering Roadhouse: roadhouse facility. Store, fuel. (*500/69*)

Low hills offer good views* across the mostly cleared grazing country.

Tonys Place: roadhouse facility. Store, fuel. (*508/61*)

Muchea: small township and roadhouse. Store, fuel. (*514/55*) *Road Trip 28 connects.*

For details of the route between Muchea and Perth see Road Trip 28, Day 5.

PERTH (Alt 19m; Pop 1097000):** state capital of Western Australia. For more information see Road Trip 33, Day 1. (*569/0*) *Road Trips 28, 33 and 34 connect.*

Road Trip 30
Pilbara Connection

Munjina-Exmouth
Total Distance: 786km
Suggested Travelling Time: 3 days

> *Immerse yourself in grand arid-mountain landscapes*
>
> See Karijini National Park, arid mountains, Fortescue Falls, Joffre Falls, Oxers Lookout, the off-shore delights of Exmouth, and the stunning Knox, Kalamina and Weano gorges.

Pilbara Connection

Incorporating some of the grandest arid mountain country in Australia, the Pilbara is a region of vivid contrasts: high mountains, deep gorges, vast stony plains, expansive grasslands, huge tracts of spinifex, gently sloping coastal plains, gigantic iron ore mines, some of the longest trains in the world, modern suburban-looking towns, old mining townships, and some of the fiercest summer temperatures in Australia.

The Pilbara is a region definitely worth visiting, and, if time allows, for exploring in detail. It is a microcosm of the arid Australian outback. The Pilbara should be on every traveller's itinerary, for its huge size and relative isolation gives this region a grandeur that might otherwise be swamped if it were more visited or more populated.

The Climate

This is a hot part of the world, especially during summer. Maximum temperatures are extreme at this time, with temperatures regularly over 40C. Nighttime temperatures are also uncomfortable, with minimums often over 25C. It can also be wet, with cyclonic rains.

The time to visit the Pilbara is between April and October. The temperatures are generally mild to warm during the day (22C - 30C) and cool, sometimes cold, at night. Inland, cold night temperatures (around 5C or less) can be expected. Fortunately, in most years, rain is virtually absent at this time of year.

Capital City Connections
Distances in kilometres
SYDNEY-MUNJINA
via Great Western/Mitchell/Matilda/Barkly/Stuart/Victoria/Great Northern Highways

	Intermediate	Total
Sydney	0	0
Nyngan	578	578
Charleville	655	1233
Mt Isa	1150	2383
Three Ways	636	3019
Katherine	642	3661
Kununurra	513	4174
Broome	1040	5214
Port Hedland	610	5824
Munjina	261	6085

MELBOURNE-MUNJINA
via Western/Dukes Highways/Highway 1/Eyre/Coolgardie-Esperance/Great Eastern/Great Northern Highways

	Intermediate	Total
Melbourne	0	0
Horsham	299	299
Adelaide	432	731
Port Augusta	312	1043
Norseman	1687	2730
Perth	724	3454
Meekatharra	765	4219
Munjina	619	4838

The Route
Distances in kilometres

	Intermediate	Total
Munjina	0	0
Tom Price	153	153
Paraburdoo	81	234
Nanutarra	275	509
Exmouth	277	786

Road Trip 30

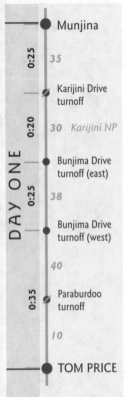

Karijini Drive/
Tom Price-Paraburdoo-Nanutarra Road
Munjina-Nanutarra

The main cross-country route, the all-sealed Karijini Drive/Tom Price-Paraburdoo-Nanutarra Road, provides access to one of the gems of the Western Australian outback, Karijini National Park, as well as to the iron ore mining towns of Tom Price and Paraburdoo. This route provides some of the best scenery in the Pilbara.

> **Warnings:** all roads subject to flooding. Beware of stock and kangaroos at night; avoid night travelling if at all possible. Unless travelling on sealed roads, stay out of this area in summer unless experienced (very high summer temperatures - always carry water in the vehicle). If travelling at this time inform a reliable person of your travel intentions.
> **Note:** no fuel between Paraburdoo-Nanutarra 270km; Nanutarra-Exmouth 277km.

DAY 1: MUNJINA-TOM PRICE via Karijini Drive

Roads to Take: Great Northern Highway, Karijini Drive
Grade 1
Grade 3 Bunjima Drive
Total Distance: 153km direct (1:45)
Total Distance: 264km via Bunjima Drive and all gorges
Intermediate Distances:

	Km	Hours
Munjina-Karijini Drive turnoff	35	(0:25)
Karijini Drive turnoff-Bunjima Drive (eastern) turnoff	30	(0:20)
Bunjima Drive (eastern) turnoff-Bunjima Drive (western) turnoff	38	(0:25)
Bunjima Drive (western) turnoff-Tom Price	50	(0:35)

Average Vehicles per Day: over 100
Regions Traversed: Pilbara (Hamersley Ranges)

▼

Munjina (Alt 490m; Pop 10): roadhouse settlement. For more information see Road Trip 29, Day 1. (*0/153*) *Road Trip 29 connects.*

For information on the route between Munjina and Karijini Drive turnoff see Road Trip 29, Day 1.

Karijini Drive turnoff: locality only; no facilities. (*35/118*) *Road Trip 29 connects.* Turn **W** onto Karijini Drive for Tom Price. *Turn **N** onto Great Northern Hwy for Munjina.*

Karijini National Park** (formerly Hamersley Ranges National Park) preserves a large area of the Hamersley Range, the roof of Western Australia. Rising above this undulating plateau are remnant hills and mountains. Edging its northern side is a long escarpment deeply incised by steep, rocky gorges. The park incorporates some of the most scenic country in Western Australia, and contains some of Australia's best arid mountain landscapes.

Ranges line the road providing good views*, especially of Mt Windell (1107m). Mulga shrublands are common.

Plains provide excellent views* of Mt Windell to the south.

Bunjima Drive turnoff (eastern end): (*65/88*) Turn **N** for Bunjima Drive and access to all Karijini National Park gorges - see Side Trip below.

Side Trip
Bunjima Drive - Hamersley Gorges Access Road
(Grade 3) 149km loop road (including all gorges)

Fortescue Falls:** well worth visiting - attractive area of weeping waterfalls, ferns and deep pools set within a steep-side gorge. Nearby is the normally dry Gordon Falls* and Circular Pool*. Walking tracks lead to lookouts, the falls and Dales Gorge beyond. Note the cypress pine woodlands, an unusual sight. Camping is available at this popular site.

Visitors Centre:* stop here for information on the national park.

Kalamina Gorge:** not as spectacular as the other gorges, but readily accessible and very attractive. Good for bushwalking. Springs, pools, ferns and river red gums all feature.

Knox Gorge:** spectacular gorge over 100m deep, lined with incredibly red cliffs. Good views

---

DAY ONE

- ● Munjina
- 0:25 — 35
- ⊘ Karijini Drive turnoff
- 0:20 — 30 *Karijini NP*
- ● Bunjima Drive turnoff (east)
- 0:25 — 38
- ● Bunjima Drive turnoff (west)
- 40
- 0:35 — ⊘ Paraburdoo turnoff
- 10
- ● TOM PRICE

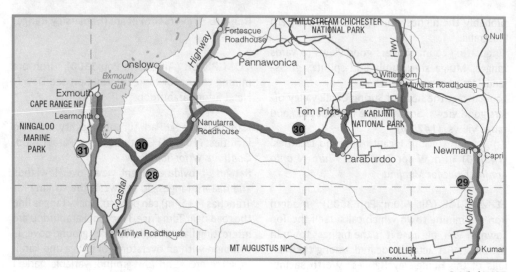

Detail of MAP 7

(best seen early morning or late afternoon). Nearby, a walking track leads into the gorge. On the road in, about 2km, is Joffre Falls*, an attractive weeping fall (best seen at midday) at the head of Joffre Gorge* (best seen in early morning). Camping is available nearby.

Weano Gorge:*** spectacular gorge that should not be missed. A steep track descends into Weano Gorge, a narrow chasm 100m deep and a few metres wide, that leads to a large rock pool. Above the gorge is Oxers Lookout***, an awe-inspiring lookout. Here Weano, Joffre and Hancock Gorges all meet to become Red Gorge. A rough trail leads into Hancock Gorge*. Camping is available nearby.

Hilly country offers good views*. South-west of Mt Vigors, on a low, rocky ridge, are excellent views* towards Mt Bruce.

Bunjima Drive turnoff (western end): locality only; no facilities. (**103/50**) Continue **W** for Tom Price. *Turn **N** onto Bunjima Drive for the Side Trip - see above.*

Ranges offer good views of surrounding countryside. Mulga is common.

Plains and low rises offer superb vistas**, especially of Mt Bruce (1235m), WA's second highest mountain, and the ranges around Mt Oxer

(1192m) to the north. Mulga shrublands are common.

Mt Bruce access road turnoff: (**102/51**) A short access road leads **S** to the base of Mt Bruce (Western Australia's second highest mountain), a spectacular high bluff rising over 500m above the lowlands. A walking track leads to lookouts* (unfortunately marred by the Marandoo mine) and the summit**.

Plains offers tremendous eastbound views** towards Mt Bruce and the ranges around Mt Stevenson (1172m) and, further west, Mt Frederick (1205m).

Range provides excellent westward views at the top of a pass* (limited parking). This pass is

Mt Stevenson, Hammersley Range, WA

Road Trip 30

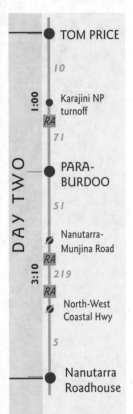

TOM PRICE

10

1:00

Karajini NP turnoff

RA

71

PARA-BURDOO

51

Nanutarra-Munjina Road

RA

3:10

219

RA

North-West Coastal Hwy

5

Nanutarra Roadhouse

probably the highest through-road in Western Australia.

Undulating country offers good views towards ranges. Mulga shrublands and spinifex grasslands are common.

Lookout* at the head of Spring Creek valley offers good views. South of the lookout are good range views. (*147/16*)

Paraburdoo turnoff: locality only; no facilities. (*143/10*) Turn **W** for Tom Price. *Turn **N** onto Karijini Drive for Munjina.*

TOM PRICE (Alt 740m; Pop 3500):* modern iron ore mining town which calls itself the Top Town in WA, because it is the highest town in the state. Attractively located among the high hills of the Hamersley Ranges. Worth seeing: Town Lookout and Kings Lake Park* (good spot for a picnic - no swimming). Drive up to Mt Nameless Lookout** (very steep access - 4WD recommended) on the highest road in the state at 1128m, or follow the walking track, which starts behind the caravan park, to the summit*. Mine tours. Full town facilities. (*153/0*)

Accommodation

Karijini Lodge Motel, Stadium Rd, ⓒ08 9189 1110, ✪$130

Mercure Inn Tom Price Hotel, Central Rd, ⓒ08 9189 1101, ✪$100-$130

Tom Price Caravan Park, Off Mine Rd (4kmW), ⓒ08 9189 1515, ✪Site: $19 Van: $85

DAY 2: TOM PRICE-NANUTARRA ROADHOUSE
via Paraburdoo

Roads to Take: Nanutarra-Paraburdoo-Tom Price Road
Grade 1
Total Distance: 356km (4:10)
Intermediate Distances:

	Km	Hours
Tom Price-Paraburdoo	81	(1:00)
Paraburdoo-Nanutarra Roadhouse	275	(3:10)

Average Vehicles per Day: 70 east of Nanutarra

Regions Traversed: Pilbara (Hamersley Range)

TOM PRICE (Alt 740m; Pop 3500):* iron ore mining town. For more information see Day 1. Head **E** for Paraburdoo.

Karijini National Park turnoff: locality only; no facilities. (*10/346*) Continue **SE** for Paraburdoo. *Continue **W** for Tom Price.*

Ranges* provide excellent views over lowlands and distant ranges. To the west, the striking Mt Trunchas (1154m) can be seen. Rocky ranges line the road near Tom Price. North of Paraburdoo are interesting flat-top hills. Spinifex ground cover is common with an overstorey of mulga and kanji. In some areas, on low ground, variable-barked bloodwoods (a eucalypt) will be seen. **Rest area** (*34/322*) at Halfway Bridge (attractive waterhole*). The small settlements near the road here are Aboriginal communities (no facilities). Mt Bennett (1094m) is visible to the east.

PARABURDOO (Alt 380m; Pop 2300): modern iron ore mining town set at the foot of the Paraburdoo Ridge. Interesting geological formations hereabout. Good views from Radio Hill Lookout*. Enquire locally about swimming holes. Accommodation, stores, fuel. (*81/275*)

Accommodation

Paraburdoo Inn, Cnr Tom Price/Rocklea Rd, ⓒ08 9189 5303, ✪$115-$150

Undulating country provides occasional good views, especially towards Paraburdoo Ridge and other ranges. The ground cover is spinifex with a sparse acacia overstorey that includes mulga. Ranges offer interesting distant views.

Hardey River crossing*. Excellent eastward views.

Nanutarra-Munjina Road junction: locality only; no facilities. (*132/224*) Turn **W** for Nanutarra. *Turn **S** for Paraburdoo.*

Ranges line the road. Good views.

Beasley River:* pleasant spot; stream bed lined with river red gums. **Rest area** adjacent.

Undulating country provides good views* across the lowlands to distant ranges, very attractive early or late in the day. Some far-flung purple peaks and ranges can be seen, including the prominent Mt Wall (948m). Countryside ranges from low hills and rocky rises to gently undulating plains and riverine valleys. Vegetation is mostly spinifex with overstoreys of mulga and other acacias. In some places eucalypts are present, forming a sparse covering. Good wildflowers after rain. Mt De Coucey (485m) and its attendant range are visible to the south. East of Mt De Coucey are tombstone rocks* - flat, vertical sheets rising a metre or two above the ground. Undulating country provides vast views across the spinifex-clad lowlands. The typical shrubby overstorey is absent in many places - where present it may be mulga or other acacias. Keep an eye out for unusual rock formations: low bouldery hills* rising like pyramids. Shady **rest area** at Duck Creek (*289/67*). Mt Stuart (351m) lies to the north.

Low ridges and rocky outcrops support spinifex and shrubs. A scenic area*.

North-West Coastal Highway junction: locality only; no facilities. (*351/5*) *Road Trip 28 connects.* Turn **S** for Nanutarra Roadhouse. *Turn **E** for Paraburdoo.*

Nanutarra Roadhouse (Alt 100m; Pop 15): pleasant roadhouse. For more information see Road Trip 28, Day 3. (*356/0*) *Road Trip 28 connects.*

DAY 3: NANUTARRA R'DHOUSE-EXMOUTH
via Burkett Road

Roads to Take: North-West Coastal Highway, Burkett Road, Exmouth Highway.
Grade 1
Total Distance: 277km (2:50)
Intermediate Distances:

	Km	Hours
Nanutarra Rdhse-Burkett Rd jctn	112	(1:10)
Burkett Rd jctn-Exmouth Hwy jctn	79	(0:50)
Exmouth Highway jctn-Exmouth	86	(0:50)

Average Vehicles per Day: 150
Regions Traversed: The North-West

Nanutarra Roadhouse (Alt 100m; Pop 15): pleasant roadhouse. For more information see Road Trip 28, Day 3. (*0/277*)

For information on the route between Nanutarra and Burkett Road junction see Road Trip 28, Day 3.

Burkett Road junction: locality only; no facilities. (*112/165*) Turn **NW** for Exmouth. *Turn **NE** onto North-West Coastal Hwy for Nanutarra Roadhouse.* Low rises support extensive tracts of acacia shrublands. Fair views from the tops of rises. Giralia Station: working sheep station. Basic accommodation and camping available available. Sand dunes* and broad sand plains support a low woodland of eucalypts with a spinifex understorey. The sand dunes are quite photogenic in the afternoon light. They support various shrubs such as *A. victoriae*, *A. coriacea* and *Grevillea stenobotrya* among others. Fair views from the tops of some dune crests.

Exmouth Highway junction: locality only; no facilities. (*191/86*) *Road Trip 31 connects.* Turn **N** for Exmouth. *Turn **E** for Nanutarra Roadhouse.*

For information on the route between Exmouth Highway junction and Exmouth see Road Trip 31, Day 1.

EXMOUTH (Alt 13m; Pop 3000):* originally a defence town connected with the Naval Communications Station. For more information see Road Trip 31, Day 1. (*277/0*) *Road Trip 31 connects.*

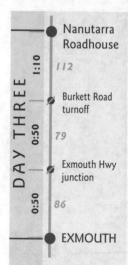

DAY THREE

Nanutarra Roadhouse

1:10

112

Burkett Road turnoff

0:50

79

Exmouth Hwy junction

0:50

86

EXMOUTH

Tombstone outcrop, east of Nanutarra, WA

Road Trip 31
Exmouth Peninsula Connection

Carnarvon-Exmouth/Yardie Creek
Total Distance: 902km
Suggested Travelling Time: 3 days

Gaze over Western Australia's own coral reef

See the coastal holiday town of Coral Bay, Shothole Canyon in Cape Range National Park, Pebbly Beach, Point Murat, the views across North-West Cape from Vlaming Head, Jurabi Coastal Park, Yardie Creek Gorge, and the extensive Ningaloo Reef system which rivals its better-known counterpart.

Exmouth Peninsula Connection

Surrounded by Exmouth Gulf and the Indian Ocean, the Exmouth Peninsula is an arid area of open sweeping plains and low limestone ranges, country partially protected in the scenic Cape Range National Park. Offshore is Ningaloo Marine Park, an area that preserves a series of coral reefs comparable to parts of the Great Barrier Reef. The advantage of visiting the Ningaloo Reefs is that they lie very close to the coast (often only a few hundred metres off-shore), making them accessible to anyone with a small boat. Other areas of interest in the Exmouth district make this a worthy region in which to take a brief respite from travelling.

The Climate

This can be a hot part of the world during the summer. Maximum temperatures are extreme at this time with temperatures climbing over 40C. Night temperatures are also uncomfortable, with minimums often over 25C. This area is sometimes subjected to tropical cyclones.

The time to visit the Exmouth Peninsula is between April and October. Conditions are generally mild to warm during the day (22C - 28C) and cool, sometimes cold, at night. Note that cool winds from the south-west can blow hard all day, producing a wind chill. Inland, cool night temperatures (around 7C or less) can be expected. Fortunately, in most years, rain is virtually limited to showers at this time.

Capital City Connections
Distances in kilometres
PERTH-CARNARVON
via Brand/North-West Coastal Highways

	Intermediate	Total
Perth	0	0
Muchea	55	55
Cataby	106	161
Eneabba	117	278
Geraldton	145	423
Carnarvon	478	901

The Route
Distances in Kilometres

	Intermediate	Total
Carnarvon	0	0
Coral Bay turnoff	227	227
Exmouth	137	364
Yardie Creek	87	451
Carnarvon	451	902

North-West Coastal Highway/ Exmouth Highway/Yardie Creek Road
Carnarvon-Exmouth-Yardie Creek

This is a good quality two-laned sealed road that crosses arid countryside to Exmouth. Glimpses of Exmouth Gulf be seen at intervals. Short, good quality unsealed roads lead to points of interest. Beyond Exmouth, the good quality but narrower Yardie Creek Road runs down the ocean side of Exmouth Peninsula, accessing Ningaloo Reef.

Warnings: beware of stock and kangaroos at night. Roads may be subject to flooding. Though coastal districts, these areas are subject to high summer temperatures; carry water in the vehicle.

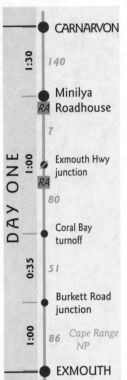

DAY ONE

1:30 — CARNARVON
140

1:00 — Minilya Roadhouse
RA
7 — Exmouth Hwy junction
RA
80 — Coral Bay turnoff

0:35
51 — Burkett Road junction

1:00
86 — Cape Range NP
EXMOUTH

DAY 1: CARNARVON-EXMOUTH via Coral Bay

Roads to Take: North-West Coastal Highway, Exmouth Highway
Grade 1
Total Distance: 364km (4:05)
Intermediate Distances:

	Km	Hours
Carnarvon-Minilya Roadhouse	140	(1:30)
Minilya Rdhse-Coral Bay turnoff	87	(1:00)
Coral Bay turnoff-Burkett Rd jctn	51	(0:35)
Burkett Road junction-Exmouth	86	(1:00)

Average Vehicles per Day: 165 north of Minilya Roadhouse
Regions Traversed: The North-West/Exmouth Peninsula

▼

CARNARVON (Alt 3m; Pop 5000): large town. For more information see the notes to Road Trip 28. **(0/364)** Head **N** on North-West Coastal Hwy for Minilya Roadhouse.

For details of the route between Carnarvon and Minilya Roadhouse see the notes to Road Trip 28.

Minilya Roadhouse (Alt 40m; Pop 5): roadhouse facility set by the attractive, sandy bed of the Minilya River*. **Rest area** adjacent. Accommodation, fuel. **(140/224)**

Exmouth Highway junction: locality only; no facilities. **(147/217)** Road Trip 28 connects. Turn **N** for Exmouth. Turn S for Minilya Roadhouse.
Low rises, forming the Gnargoo Range, provide vast views of spinifex country. The shrubs appear to be umbrella wattle.
Lyndon River:* countryside hereabout is sparse and open, providing expansive views. Distant views to the Giralia Ranges. **Rest area**. **(173/278)**
Plains support extensive tracts of snakewood, bramble wattle and desert oak (do not confuse with the desert oaks of Central Australia).
Low rises offer vast views across spinifex country.

Coral Bay turnoff: locality only; no facilities. **(227/137)** Turn **W** for Coral Bay - see Side Trip below.

Side Trip
Coral Bay Road
(Grade 1) 24km return
Coral Bay (Alt 5m; Pop 120):* small coastal tourist and holiday settlement. Tours are available to view the Ningaloo Reef, one of the world's major reef systems, located about 150m off-shore. A short distance away, off the road into Coral Bay past the landing ground, an unsealed access road leads to Maud Landing,* an interesting area with old jetty ruins, date palms and buried relics. Accommodation, stores, fuel.
Accommodation
Ningaloo Reef Resort, Robinson St, ©08 9942 5934, ©$105-$135
Bayview Caravan Park, Coral Bay Rd, ©08 9942 5932, ©Site: $19 Van: $45-$70

Low rises and occasional sand dunes support extensive tracts of bramble wattles, desert oaks and rattlepod grevilleas. Spinifex is common on rises. Anthills are common. Giralia Range is visible to the east. Broad vistas.
Burkett Road junction: locality only; no facilities. **(278/86)** This all-sealed two-lane road leads **E** to the North-West Coastal Highway. *Road Trip 30 connects*. Continue **N** for Exmouth. *Continue **S** for Minilya Roadhouse.*
Low hills, constituting the Rough Range, provide good views (especially southwards) across the open undulating lowlands. Vegetation is mostly sparse low shrublands and spinifex.
Plains and occasional dunes. Cape Range is visible to the north. Rough Range lies to the south.
Wapet Creek: good fishing. Beware of stonefish - wear heavy footwear if wading. **(329/35)**
Learmonth: airforce base. Nearby is the Learmonth Airport and Wapet Jetty, with good fishing and beachcombing. Visible from the road (no public access) is a solar observatory. **(332/32)**
Kailis Fisheries: seafood store and caravan park. Good fishing nearby. Also turn here for the lookout* located at the end of the very scenic** Charles Knife Road. This road runs along a ra-

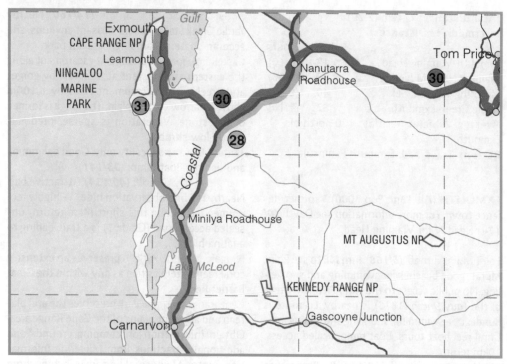

Detail of MAP 7

zorback ridge between two canyons. Good viewpoints along the escarpment; beware of loose cliff edges. Walking tracks at the end. An excellent place to watch sunrise over Exmouth Gulf. Forms part of the Cape Range National Park. Road unsealed (Grade 3) - 24km return. (343/21)

Plains, covered with snakewood and dead finish, offer good views westward towards Cape Range, and eastward overlooking Exmouth Gulf.

Shothole Canyon turnoff: locality only; no facilities. (353/11) Turn W for access to Cape Range National Park and Shothole Canyon**, an area of scenic arid valleys supporting only a sparse covering of vegetation. The colourful rock layers are very photogenic in the late afternoon light.

Pebbly Beach: good swimming and colourful pebbles. (253/11)

EXMOUTH (Alt 13m; Pop 3000):* originally a defence town connected with the Naval Communications Station, today it also services the tourist and fishing industries. A modern settlement rebuilt after the 1999 cyclone. Worth seeing: Town Beach and Sunrise Beach. Tours are available from here to see the parks, including off-shore tours to see whale sharks** (late autumn) and coral spawning** (March, April). Full town facilities. (364/0) Road Trip 30 connects.

Accommodation

Potshot Hotel Resort, Murat Rd, ✆08 9949 1200, ✪$110-$130

Sea Breeze Resort, 116 North St (5kmN), ✆08 9949 1800, ✪$100-$120

Exmouth Cape Tourist Village, Truscott Cres/ Murat Rd (1.5kmS), ✆08 9949 1101, ✪Site: $20 Van: $60-$90

Ningaloo Caravan & Holiday Resort, Murat Rd, ✆08 9949 2377, ✪Site: $23 Van: $70-$120

DAY 2: EXMOUTH-YARDIE CREEK-EXMOUTH via Vlaming Head

Road to Take: Yardie Creek Road
Grade 1

Road Trip 31

DAY TWO

- EXMOUTH
- 0:10 | 12
- Vlaming Head
- 0:30 | 35 | Ningaloo Marine Park
- Milyering
- 0:30 | 40 | Turquoise Bay
- Yardie Creek
- 1:10 | 87
- EXMOUTH

Total Distance: 174km (2:20)
Intermediate Distances:

	Km	Hours
Exmouth-Vlaming Head	12	(0:10)
Vlaming Head-Milyering	35	(0:30)
Milyering-Yardie Creek	40	(0:30)
Yardie Creek-Exmouth	87	(1:10)

Average Vehicles per Day: 120 north of Exmouth
Regions Traversed: Exmouth Peninsula

▼

EXMOUTH (Alt 13m; Pop 3000):* former defence town. For more information see Day 1. (*0/174*) Head **N** for Vlaming Head.

Point Murat turnoff: (*6/168*) Turn **NE** to see Point Murat: good beaches for swimming and snorkelling. No public access to the Navy Pier. The wreck of the *Fairy Queen* (1875) is nearby. En route is Bundegi*, a swimming, snorkling and fishing area. Coral reef boat tours. Boat ramp. Sealed access, 10km return.

Mildura Wreck turnoff. (*10/164*) An 8km return unsealed road leads **NW** to North-West Cape*, an interesting area, especially the nearby wreck of the *SS Mildura* (1907). Good beach fishing. Nearby (you cannot miss it) is the VLF Antenna Field, a prohibited area. The centre tower (Tower Zero) is 388m high!

Vlaming Head:* a low promontory near the head of Exmouth Gulf. The countryside hereabouts is arid, supporting a sparse, low shrubland. Nearby is the Vlaming Head Lighthouse*, with excellent views across North-West Cape. Adjacent are the ruins of a World War II radar site. Accommodation, limited stores, fuel - no fuel beyond this point. (*12/162*)

Accommodation
Lighthouse Caravan Park, Yardie Creek Rd, ©08 9949 1478, ©Site: $18 Van: $45-$60

Jurabi Coastal Park: narrow coast park preserving coastal dunes and adjacent plains. No camping. Plenty of beach access.

Yardie Creek Station turnoff: (*14/160*) Nearby Yardie Creek Station offers pleasant environs, and accommodation, camping, caravan park.
Cape Range forms a prominent escarpment along the eastern skyline, rent at intervals by gorges and creeks. The escarpment rises over 100m above a narrow coastal plain. The range is formed of limestone. Vegetation is sparse, predominantly low shrubs.
Tantabiddi Creek: locality only. Good swimming and fishing. Boat ramp. (*33/141*)
Mangrove Bay turnoff: (*40/134*) Attractive bay. Nearby is a bird observation hide** - highly recommended. Along this short (4km return) unsealed access road (Grade 3) is a trail leading to a fauna hide*.
Ningaloo Marine Park:** preserves an extensive coral reef system as rich as any within the Great Barrier Reef.
Cape Range National Park preserves the arid plateau and adjacent plains of the Cape Range area. Obtain information on camping grounds and additional attractions from Milyering Information Centre. Major snorkling areas include, from north to south, are Lakeside, Turquoise Bay, Oyster Bay and Pilgramunna.
Milyering: Information Centre* for the Cape Range National Park and Ningaloo Marine Park. Stacks of information, displays, videos, and more. Highly recommended. No other facilities are available. (*47/127*)
Turquoise Bay** a popular and pretty bay and beach, lies just off the road. Good swimming and snorkling. (*56/118*)
Mandu Mandu Creek: attractive inlet. Nearby is the Mandu Mandu Creek Gorge* with its scenic walking trail. Coral reefs are located just a few hundred metres off-shore. (*61/113*)
Yardie Creek:** spectacular gorge of deep blue water hemmed in by vertical cliffs. Worth visiting. Walking trails are along the cliff tops. A very popular scenic area. (*87/87*)

For details on the return journey to Exmouth see the notes above.

EXMOUTH (Alt 13m; Pop 3000):* former defence town. For more information see Day 1. (*174/0*)

▲

DAY 3: EXMOUTH-CARNARVON via Coral Bay

Road to Take: Exmouth Highway, North-West Coastal Highway
Grade 1
Total Distance: 364km (4:05)
Intermediate Distances:

	Km	Hours
Exmouth-Burkett Rd junction	86	(1:00)
Burkett Rd jctn-Coral Bay turnoff	51	(0:35)
Coral Bay turnoff-Minilya Rdhse	87	(1:00)
Minilya Roadhouse-Carnarvon	140	(1:30)

Average Vehicles per Day: 165 north of Minilya Roadhouse

Regions Traversed: Exmouth Peninsula/The North-West

EXMOUTH (Alt 13m; Pop 3000):* former defence town. For more information see Day 1. (*0/364*)

For information on the route between Exmouth and Carnarvon see Day 1.

CARNARVON (Alt 3m; Pop 5000): large town. For more information see to Road Trip 28, Day 3. (*364/0*)

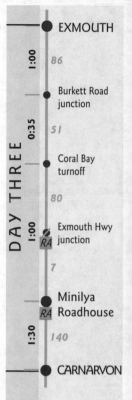

Road Trip 32
Shark Bay Connection

Geraldton-Monkey Mia
Total Distance: 864km
Suggested Travelling Time: 2 days

Slow down for the rugged coastline of the Shark Bay World Heritage Area

See the world's oldest lifeforms at Hamelins Pool, fascinating Shell Beach, Eagle Bluff, the attractive bayside town of Denham, Peron National Park, and bottle-nosed dolphins at Monkey Mia.

Shark Bay Connection

The Shark Bay World Heritage Area includes some of the finest coastal scenery in Western Australia, and is probably one of the best arid coastlines in Australia. This region is characterised by very scenic coastal and water views, the friendly semi-wild dolphins of Monkey Mia, and the sub-tropical settlement of Denham. There are other interesting features as well, including some of the richest marine environments of coastal Australia. Travellers should contemplate spending at least a few days in this area.

The Climate

This can be a hot part of the world, especially during summer. Maximum temperatures are extreme at this time with temperatures reaching over 40C. Night temperatures are also uncomfortable, with minimums often over 25C.

The time to visit the Shark Bay area is between April and October. Conditions are generally mild to warm during the day (22C - 24C) and cool, sometimes cold, at night. Inland, cold night temperatures (around 5C or less) can be expected. Rainfall is virtually limited to showers at this time of year.

Capital City Connection
Distances in kilometres
PERTH-GERALDTON
via Brand Highway

	Intermediate	Total
Perth	0	0
Muchea	55	55
Cataby	106	161
Eneabba	117	278
Geraldton	145	423

The Route
Distances in Kilometres

	Intermediate	Total
Geraldton	0	0
Overlander Roadhouse	278	278
Denham	129	407
Monkey Mia	25	432
Geraldton	432	864

North-West Coastal Highway/ Denham-Monkey Mia Road
Geraldton-Monkey Mia

This good quality two-laned sealed road passes through shrublands and quite arid countryside. Glimpses of the Shark Bay Loops (embayments) can be seen at intervals. Short, good quality unsealed roads lead to points of interest.

Warnings: beware of stock and kangaroos at night. Roads may be subject to flooding. Though coastal districts, these areas are subject to high summer temperatures along their inland access roads; carry water in the vehicle.

DAY 1: GERALDTON-MONKEY MIA
via Denham

Roads to Take: North-West Coastal Highway, Denham Road-Monkey Mia Road
Grade 1
Total Distance: 432km (4:40)

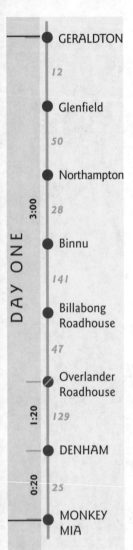

GERALDTON

12

Glenfield

50

Northampton

28

Binnu

3:00

141

Billabong
Roadhouse

47

Overlander
Roadhouse

1:20

129

DENHAM

0:20

25

MONKEY
MIA

DAY ONE

Intermediate Distances:

	Km	Hours
Geraldton-Overlander Roadhouse	278	(3:00)
Overlander Roadhouse-Denham	129	(1:20)
Denham-Monkey Mia	25	(0:20)

Average Vehicles per Day: 200 west of Overlander Roadhouse

Regions Traversed: Central-West, Murchison, Shark Bay

▼

GERALDTON (Alt 5m; Pop 21000):* large regional centre with many tourist features. For more information see the notes to Road Trip 28. (*0/432*) *Road Trip 28 connects.*

For information between Geraldton and Overlander Roadhouse see the notes to Road Trip 28.

Overlander Roadhouse (Alt 80m; Pop 5): roadhouse. Notable for being centrally situated on a hundred kilometre or so stretch of straight road. Accommodation-camping available, fuel. (*278/154*) *Road Trip 28 connects.* Turn **W** onto Denham Road for Denham. *Turn **S** onto North-West Coastal Hwy for Geraldton.*

Accommodation

Overlander Roadhouse Caravan Facility, NW Coastal Hwy, ©08 9942 5905, ⊙Site: $13 Van: $45

Low rises formed by old limestone ridges. The westernmost rises give good views over salt flats. Various shrubs dominate the landscape.

Hamelin Pool turnoff: locality only; no facilities. (*307/125*) Turn **W** for Hamelin Pool:** do not confuse with Hamelin Station (working sheep station; no access) passed on the way in. There is an old telegraph station*, nowadays a museum and tea shop, well worth visiting. Good views** from a nearby dune overlook the telegraph station on one side, and the still waters of Hamelin Pool on the other. Nearby Hamelin Pool* is incredibly salty. Stromatolites** may be seen at low tide. Whilst not scenically grand, these green-coloured objects which look like soft

rocks are the oldest surviving life forms known - they have existed for about 3,500 million years! Stromatolites are matted sheets of blue-green algae that trap sediment, thus forming mounds. (Grade 3 access; 10km return.)

Accommodation

Hamelin Pool Caravan Park, Hamelin Pool, ©08 9942 5905, ⊙Site: $13 Van: $45

Salt flats visible from the road. Some halophytes are present. Good views across the flats from a low rise to the east.

Views* overlooks a portion of Hamelin Pool.

Undulating country supports extensive tracts of shrublands and deep red dunes.

Nanga Bay turnoff: locality only; no facilities. (*355/77*) Turn **SW** for **Nanga Bay** (Alt 10m; Pop 10): working sheep station and low-key tourist facility. Some shell-block buildings*. An interesting place. Tours are available. Accommodation, fuel. (Grade 1 access; 6km return.)

Accommodation

Nanga Bay Resort, Nanga Bay, ©08 9948 3992, ⊙$65-$100

Nanga Bay Caravan Park, Nanga Bay, ©08 9948 3992, ⊙Site: $18 Van: $50-$90

Shell Beach:* a beach composed entirely of countless tiny shells up to 10m deep and 110km long! Well worth seeing. Take your sunglasses as it is very glarey. Just north of the beach there is a good view* overlooking Shell Beach and Lharidon Bight beyond. (*362/70*)

Undulating country provides good views across the low hills and towards Freycinet Reach. Low shrublands and spinifex dominate the landscape, giving this area an open feel.

Eagle Bluff turnoff. (*388/44*) Turn **W** for views from Eagle Bluff*, a high limestone headland well worth visiting. Good views across Freycinet Reach. On a clear day the Useless Loop saltworks can be seen. Numerous marine life, including turtles, should become visible if you patiently watch the waters. Eagles are common, hence the name. Short walks (be careful on the loose slopes) recommended. Unsealed access (Grade 3), 8km return.

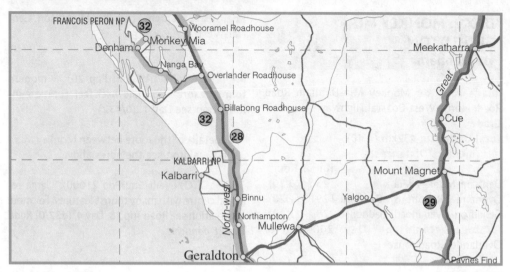

Detail of MAP 7

Undulating country supports extensive tracts of shrublands, of which numerous species are represented. Occasional views across the low hills.

DENHAM (Alt 2m; Pop 450):** attractive bayside town supported by fishing and tourist industries. The polyglot population includes Malay descendants. Interesting shell-block buildings*. Good views ares available from the old limestone dunes behind the settlement. This is Australia's westernmost town. It is worth spending a few days in this very relaxing place. Good fishing. Museum*. Accommodation, stores, fuel. (*407/25*)

A few kilometres away lies the Peron National Park*, a former sheep station. Access beyond the old station homestead requires a 4WD. Numerous coastal camping sites and fishing areas. No facilities available; carry sufficent fuel for at least 100kms.

Accommodation
Shark Bay Hotel-Motel, 43 Knight Tce, ©08 9948 1203, ✪$75-$90
Denham Seaside Caravan Park, Knight Tce, ©08 9948 1242, ✪Site: $18 Van: $55
Shark Bay Caravan Park, 4 Spaven Way, ©08 9948 1387, ✪Site: $16 Van: $45-$55
Blue Dolphin Caravan Park, Hamelin Rd, ©08 9948 1385, ✪Site: $16 Van: $40-$70

Undulating country supports dense shrubs. Open claypan areas, locally called birridas.

MONKEY MIA (Alt 2m; Pop 20):** modern tourist resort with a laid-back feel, set by the still waters of Shark Bay and backed by high red dunes and scrub. Famous for its (mostly) daily visits by semi-wild bottlenose dolphins*** who interact with people near the shoreline; an incredible experience and highly recommended. Local information is available about dolphin contact. Other activities include beach and bush walks, swimming and fishing. Motel, limited stores, fuel. (*432/0*)

Accommodation
Monkey Mia Dolphin Resort, Monkey Mia, ©08 9948 1320, ✪Site: $22 Van: $40-$160

Shell Beach, Shark Bay, WA

DAY 2: MONKEY MIA-GERALDTON
via Denham

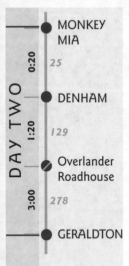

DAY TWO

MONKEY MIA
0:20
25

DENHAM
1:20
129

Overlander Roadhouse
3:00
278

GERALDTON

Roads to Take: Monkey Mia-Denham Road Road, North-West Coastal Highway
Grade 1
Total Distance: 432km (4:40)
Intermediate Distances:

	Km	Hours
Denham-Monkey Mia	25	(0:20)
Overlander Roadhouse-Denham	129	(1:20)
Geraldton-Overlander Roadhouse	278	(3:00)

Average Vehicles per Day: 200 west of Overlander Roadhouse

Regions Traversed: Shark Bay, Murchison, Central-West

MONKEY MIA (Alt 2m; Pop 20):** modern tourist resort with a laid-back feel. For more information see Day 1. (**0/432**)

For details of the route between Monkey Mia and Geraldton see the notes above.

GERALDTON (Alt 5m; Pop 21000):* large regional centre with many tourist features. For more information see Road Trip 28, Day 4. (**432/0**) *Road Trip 28 connects.*

Road Trip 33
The South-West Loop

Perth-Mandurah-Bunbury-Margaret River-Augusta-Nannup-Bridgetown-Bunbury-Perth
Total Distance: 740km
Suggested Travelling Time: 4 days

Weave through the lush countryside of the south-west corner

See the delightful state capital of Perth, the wildlife reserves at Bunbury, Busselton Beachfront, Tuart Forest National Park, the attractive holiday town of Augusta, Cape Leeuin, jarrah and karri forests, the timber town of Nannup, and the vineyards of the fertile Margaret River district.

The South-West Loop

The South-West of Western Australia is Perth's playground. In such a vast and dry area, only the south-western corner of the state is relatively humid and green. Here the traveller can find tall eucalypt forests, perennial streams, lush farmlands, wineries, beautiful beaches and a lush, scenic countryside. The South-West is Western Australia's toe-hold on 'the good life'.

The Climate

The climate of the South-West can be summed up as what climatologists call Mediterranean: hot, dry summers and mild, wet winters. Summer days range from very warm to very hot (it can be mild on the southern seaboard) with temperatures ranging from around 25C to 30C. Nights are generally mild (around 18C). Heatwaves can occur in January and Febuary with maximum temperatures in the low to mid-forties and warm nights in the mid-twenties. There is virtualy no rainfall between November and April, except for drizzle along the southern and south-western coasts.

Winters are generally cool to mild with showery weather. Perth, in fact, is Australia's wettest winter capital city. Showery weather may last for days, and along the exposed western and southern coastline gale force winds are common. The cooler days will have maximums around 15C to 18C with night temperatures around 5C to 10C.

The best time to travel the South-West is in autumn (dry, still, balmy days) or spring (little rain, some wind but lush, green landscapes and wonderful wildflowers).

Capital City Connections
Distances in kilometres
ADELAIDE-PERTH
via Highway One/Eyre Highway

	Intermediate	Total
Adelaide	0	0
Port Augusta	312	312
Ceduna	468	780
Norseman	1210	1990
Perth	724	2714

SYDNEY-PERTH
via Great Western/Mitchell/Barrier/Eyre Highways

	Intermediate	Total
Sydney	0	0
Port Augusta	1568	1568
Ceduna	468	2038
Norseman	1210	3248
Perth	724	3972

DARWIN-PERTH
via Victoria/Great Northern/North-West Coastal Highways

	Intermediate	Total
Darwin	0	0
Katherine	316	316
Port Hedland	2095	2411
Geraldton	1351	3762
Perth	423	4185

The Route
Distances in kilometres

	Intermediate	Total
Perth	0	0
Bunbury	185	185
Augusta	144	329

Road Trip 33

Bridgetown	134	463
Bunbury	92	555
Perth	185	740

PERTH
31
Thomas Road junction
7
Rockingham Road junction
6
1:05
Erin Road junction
19
Golden Bay
DAY ONE
10
Mandurah turnoff
4
MANDURAH
4
Highway One junction
1:10
4
Falcon
5
Wannanup

Highway One (Mandurah Road/Old Coast Road)

Perth-Bunbury

The main route to the South-West from Perth is via Highway One, also known as the Mandurah Road or the (old) Coast Road. It is 4 lanes over much of its length to Bunbury. From Perth it is possible to access this road via the Kwinana Freeway and Thomas Road (the route described below); via Canning Highway and Stock/Rockingham Road; or via either Canning or Stirling Highways, Fremantle, and Cockburn Road. All these routes join in the Kwinana Industrial area.

Highway One is a major road servicing the coastal developments of Rockingham, Mandurah, and the regional centre of Bunbury. It crosses coastal plains and passes coastal dunes though it is rarely in sight of the sea. It is the recommended quick route to The South-West.

Warnings: take care on the two-lane section of the highway between Mandurah and Bunbury. Take care in the urban areas around Kwinana, Rockingham and Mandurah.

DAY 1: PERTH-BUNBURY via Mandurah

Road to Take: Highway One (Mandurah Road, Old Coast Road)
Grade i
Total Distance: 181km (2:15)
Intermediate Distances:

	Km	Hours
Perth-Mandurah	77	(1:05)
Mandurah-Bunbury	104	(1:10)

Average Vehicles per Day: 22000 north of Mandurah
Regions Traversed: Coastal Plain

PERTH (Alt 19m; Pop 1097000):** state capital of Western Australia set on the Swan River estuary. Perth City is a delightful place and there are many things to see and do. Worth seeing: Art Gallery of Western Australia**, Kings Park and Botanic Gardens** (great views, picnic areas, wildflowers), Mineral Museum*, the Old Gaol*, Parliament House, Barracks Archway, Queens Garden*, Stirling Gardens, Supreme Court Gardens, Allan Green Conservatory*, Francis Burt Law Museum*, Perth Mint*, Western Australian Museum**, London Court*, Hay Street and Murray Street Malls. River cruises available on the Swan River and estuary. Full town facilities. (***0/181***) *Road Trip 28, 29 and 34 connect.*

Accommodation

Criterion Hotel, 560 Hay St, ©08 9325 0461, ✪$135
Emerald Hotel, 24 Mount St, ©08 9481 0866, ✪$115-$150
Perth Ambassador, 196 Adelaide Tce, ©08 9325 1455, ✪$100-$160
The Terrace Hotel, 195 Adelaide St, ©08 9492 7777, ✪$110-$220
Perth City Hotel, 200 Hay St, ©08 9220 7000, ✪$90-$110
The New Esplanade Hotel, 18 The Esplanade, ©08 9325 2000, ✪$65-$100
Wentworth Plaza Hotel, 300 Murray St, ©08 9481 1000, ✪$70-$130
Perth International Tourist Park, 186 Hale Rd, Forrestfield (12kmE), ©08 9453 6677, ✪Site: $20 Van: $70-$95
Kelmscott Caravan Park, 80 River Rd, Kelscott (24kmSE), ©08 9390 6137, ✪Site: $18
Crystal Brook Caravan Park, Kelvin Rd, Orange Grove (23kmSE), ©08 9453 6226, ✪Site: $17 Van: $45-$60
Perth Central Caravan Park, 34 Central Ave, Redcliffe (7kmE), ©08 9277 1704, ✪Site: $22 Van: $80
Scarborough Starhaven Caravan Park, 18 Pearl Pde, Scarborough (14kmNW), ✪Site: $17 Van: $35

Further out of town the following places and features are worth visiting. The **Northbridge** area is the centre of Perth's nightlife - numerous restaurants; **Crawley**: University of Western Australia's grounds**, the Berndt Museum of Antropology* (mainly Aboriginal arts and ar-

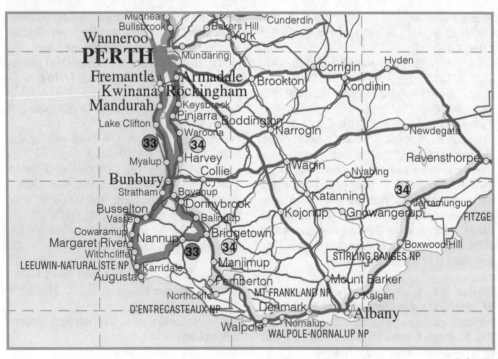

Detail of MAP 8

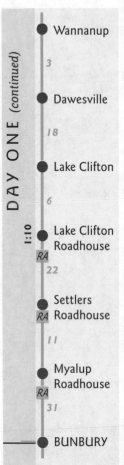

DAY ONE (continued)

Wannanup	
	3
Dawesville	
	18
Lake Clifton	
	6
Lake Clifton Roadhouse	1:10
RA	22
Settlers Roadhouse	
RA	11
Myalup Roadhouse	
RA	31
BUNBURY	

tefacts), scenic drive* along Riverside and Hackett Drives overlooking Matilda Bay; **Clermont**: Clermont Museum and picnic area and the Museum of Childhood* at Edith Cowan University; **Wembley**: Lake Monger's black swans* (symbol of Western Australia); **South Perth**: Perth Zoo*, the Old Mill* (old flour mill); **Subiaco**: Western Australia Medical Museum*; **Cottesloe** and **Scarborough**: excellent beaches* and coastal ambiance; **Ardross**: Wireless Hill Telecommunications Museum* and adjacent wildflowers* (in season); **Ashfield**: Rail Transport Museum**; **Guilford**: Guilford Museum* and historic buildings*; **West Swan**: Caversham Wildlife Park*.

Deserving of a special mention is **Fremantle****(23km **SW** along Mounts Bay Rd/ Stirling Hwy), a virtually intact Victorian sea port that has managed to maintain a separate identity even though it has been incorporated into the Perth suburban area. Freo, as it is called, is worth a day on its own. Recommended places to visit: Army Museum*, History Museum and Arts Centre*, Fremantle Prison*, Fremantle Wharves, War Memorial (good views*), Historic Boat Museum*, Samson House* (historic house), the Round House* (oldest building in Western Australia), numerous historic buildings*, Western Australia Maritime Museum*, The Esplanade Park, Fishing Boat Harbour*, Duyfken Replica*. River cruises on the Swan River; ferry ride to Rottnest Island. Full town facilities.

South Terrace, Fremantle, WA

Accommodation

The Flying Angel Club, 76 Queen St, ©08 9335 8188, ✪$95
Fremantle Hotel, Cnr High/Cliff Sts, ©08 9430 4300, ✪$80-$90
Rosie O'Gradys Hotel, 23 William St, ©08 9335 1645, ✪$70-$115
Fremantle Village Caravan Park, Cnr Cockburn / Rollinson Rds (3kmS), ©08 9430 4866, ✪Site: $26 Van: $65-$85

Between Perth and the southern end of the Kwinana Freeway the route passes through a continuous spread of Perth suburbs or scattered urban development. Good views* across Melville Water and around the Canning River just south of the city. Kwinana Freeway starts/ends at Thomas Road (at time of publication).

Thomas Road junction: locality. (*31/150*) Turn **W** - follow the signs for Mandurah/Bunbury.
Rockingham Road junction: locality. (*38/143*) Turn **S** - follow Mandurah/Bunbury signs. *Follow signs to Kwinana Freeway for Perth.*
Plain supports industrial complexes and heavy industry. Good light show* at night.
Erin Road/Paterson Road junction: (*44/137*) Turn **S** for Mandurah (follow Highway 1 signs - Rockingham straight on). *Turn **E** for Perth.*
Plain supports extensive urban development in the north and small land-holdings in the south.

Golden Bay: roadhouse facility. Store, fuel. (*63/118*)

Plain supports small land-holdings; old coastal dunes* visible to the west. Between Golden Bay and the Mandurah turnoff are four short detours leading to small coastal settlements and beaches. These include, from north to south, Golden Bay, Singleton, Madora and Sam Remo. Marapana Wildlife World* passed en route. Near Mandurah, urban development occupies the plain.
Mandurah turnoff: (*73/108*) Turn **SE** for the route through Mandurah. *Turn **N** for Perth.*

MANDURAH (Alt 5m; Pop 36000):* large coastal town set on Mandurah Estuary and Peel Inlet. Of interest is the Foreshore Reserve*, Christ's Church and James Service Anchor*, Mandurah Community Museum*, Peel Discovery Centre* (historical and natural history exhibits), Hall's Cottage. Numerous other holiday attractions. Full town facilities. (*77/104*)

Accommodation

Mandurah Foreshore Motel, 65 Ormsby Tce, ©08 9535 6633, ✪$60-$85
Mandurah Gates Resort, 110-116 Mandurah Tce, ©08 9581 1222, ✪$105-$125
Peninsula Caravan Park, Ormsby Tce (1kmNW), ©08 9535 2792, ✪Site: $16 Van: $35-$50
Lucky Caravan Park, 20 Henson St (2kmN), ©08 9535 3313, ✪Site: $22 Van: $55-$75
Belvedere Caravan Park, 153 Mandurah Tce, (1kmN), ©08 9535 1213, ✪Site: $16

Highway One junction: (*81/100*) Turn **S** for Falcon. *Turn **NW** onto Mandurah Road for Mandurah.*

Falcon: suburban area. Caravan Park. Stores, fuel. (*85/96*)

Wannanup: suburban area. Nearby Dawesville Cut is of interest - viewing area. Also of interest is the 12km long Estuary Scenic Drive loop road which provides good eastward views* across Peel Inlet and Harvey Estuary. Scattered development and bushland. Stores, fuel. (*90/91*)

Dawesville: suburban area. Caravan park. Stores, fuel. (*93/88*)

Low hills support dense coastal thickets and scattered urban development. Two short detours lead to coastal beaches.
Low rises support urban development. Glimpsed views of Harvey estuary. Fuel available nearby.

Lake Clifton: small settlement located besides Lake Clifton. Caravan park. Store, fuel. (*111/70*)

Lake Clifton Roadhouse: roadhouse facility. Store, fuel. (*117/63*)

Plain* supports peppermint woodlands and small land-holdings. **Rest area** at old Whittakers Mill. (*133/48*)

Settlers Roadhouse: roadhouse facility. **Rest area**. Store, fuel. (*139/42*)

Myalup Roadhouse: roadhouse facility. Store, fuel. (*150/31*)

Plains support farmlands and scattered woodlands. Fair views. Follow signs into the heart of Bunbury. **Rest area**. (*160/21*)

BUNBURY (Alt 4m; Pop 25000):* large regional centre located on Koombana Bay. Worth seeing: Marston Hill Lookout* (good views), Boulters Heights Lookout*, Bunbury Lighthouse, Dolphin Discovery Centre** (information and dolphin contact), the Twin Cathedrals (St Patricks and St Boniface), Anzac Park, Sir John Forrest Monument, Ocean Drive* (scenic drive along the coast), basalt rock outcrop (unusual in this part of the world), Mangrove Boardwalk** (mangroves and interesting wooden carvings), King Cottage Museum*, Centenary Gardens*, Big Swamp Nature Reserve* and Wildlife Park*, Maidens Reserve* (tuart forest), historic buildings* (includes the Old Railway Station, Customs House, Rose Hotel, Old Post Office, Paisley Centre, St Marks Church). Art galleries and craft outlets. Full town facilities. (*181/0*) Road Trip 34 connects.

Accommodation
Chateau La-Mer Motor Lodge, 99 Ocean Dr (1kmSW), ©08 9721 3166, ©$70-$85
Bunbury Motel, 45 Forrest Ave (2kmS), ©08 9721 7333, ©$65-$80
Ocean Drive Motel, 121 Ocean Dr, (1.5kmS), ©08 9721 2033, ©$65-$80
Welcome Inn Motel, ©08 9721 3100, ©$85-$150
Highway Hotel/Motel, Cnr Forrest Ave/Spencer St (1.3km S), ©$50-$75
Bunbury Accommodation Village, Cnr Bussell Hwy/Washington Ave (6kmS), ©08 9795 7100, ©Site: $20 Van: $50-$65
Koombana Bay Holiday Resort, Koombana Dr (1kmNE), ©08 9791 3900, ©Site: $18 Van: $55
Bunbury Glade Caravan Park, Bussell Hwy (4kmS), ©08 9721 3800, ©Site: $18 Van: $45-$55

A few kilometres north of town is **Australind** (Alt 3m; Pop 5700)*, an old settlement and growing urban area. Worth seeing: foreshore reserve* (picnics), St Nicholas Church* (probably Australia's smallest church), Henton Cottage* (historic house), Pioneer Cemetery, Pioneer Memorial, Rock and Gem Museum, and scenic drive along the estuary.

Bussell Highway-Brockman Highway
Bunbury-Bridgetown
This circular route passes through the highlights of The South-West region. The Bussell Highway is basically a coastal route giving access to Busselton, the Margaret River area, and Australia's south-western tip, Cape Leeuwin, south of Augusta. The Brockman Highway is a link road, joining Augusta with Nannup and Bridgetown. It passes through jarrah forests and follows, in part, the scenic Blackwood River valley.

Warnings: roads subject to flooding. At night beware of kangaroos and other animals in the forested sections.

DAY 2: BUNBURY-AUGUSTA via Busselton

Road to Take: Bussell Highway
Grade 1
Total Distance: 144km (1:45)
Intermediate Distances:

	Km	Hours
Bunbury-Busselton	54	(0:40)
Busselton-Margaret River	47	(0:35)
Margaret River-Augusta	43	(0:30)

Average Vehicles per Day: 1800 south of Margaret River
Regions Traversed: The South-West

BUNBURY (Alt 4m; Pop 25000):* large regional centre. For more information see Day 1. (*0/144*)

Plains supports mixed farming.

Stratham: roadhouse facility. Store, fuel. (*18/126*)

Plains support farmlands.
Tuart Drive turnoff: (*31/113*) Turn **W** for a delightful 13km loop drive through the Tuart Forest National Park, a small park preserving a stunning tuart forest** and wetland areas. Scenic drive. Picnic areas.
Plain supports mixed farmlands.

BUSSELTON (Alt 4m; Pop 6500):** attractive beachside holiday town. Many things to see and do including Old Butter Factory Museum*, St Mary's Church, Pioneer Cemetery*, Rotary Park (picnic area on the Vasse River), Ballarat Engine* (old steam locomotive) and the Busselton Beachfront** - includes the Oceanarium* and Busselton Jetty** (2km long and made from wood - jetty train rides). Full town facilities. (*54/90*)

Accommodation
Amaroo Motor Lodge, 31 Bussell Hwy (1kmW), ©08 9752 1544, ©$70-$95
Paradise Motel, Pries Ave, ©08 9752 1200, ©$60-$80
Restawhile Motel, 340 Bussell Hwy (4.5kmW), ©08 9754 4600, ©$50-$60
Riveria Motor Inn, 44 Bussell Hwy (1kmW), ©08 9752 1555, ©$65-$90
Busselton Motel, 90 Bussell Hwy, Cnr Bussell Hwy/Holgate St (1.5kmW), ©08 9752 1908, ©$40
Busselton Caravan Park, 163 Bussell Hwy (1.5kmW), ©08 9752 1175, ©Site: $17 Van: $40-$50
Kookaburra Caravan Park, 66 Marine Tce, ©08 9752 1516, ©Site: $17 Van: $35-$40
Beachlands Holiday Park, 10 Earnshaw Rd (3kmW), ©08 9752 2107, ©Site: $20-$30 Van: $45-$160

Plain supports scattered urban development and mixed farms.
Caves Road junction: (*63/81*) Turn **S** on Bussell Hwy for Margaret River. *Turn **E** on Bussell Hwy for Busselton.*

Vasse: small farming town. Store, fuel. (*65/79*)

Carbunup: farming township. Store, fuel. (*71/73*)

Undulating country has ben mostly cleared for mixed farming and grazing. Reasonable scenery.

Cowaramup:* small farming town servicing the surrounding dairying, grazing and viticultural countryside. In town the Country Store* is worth visting. Lions Pioneer Park is good for picnics. Numerous arts and craft outlets. Surrounding the town are many vineyards and wineries. Accommodation, stores, fuel. (*90/54*)

Undulating country has ben mostly cleared for mixed farming and vineyards.

MARGARET RIVER (Alt 90m; Pop 2500):* popular holiday centre set among forests and vineyards. Most of the attractions are spread out throughout the surrounding district. In the town itself is the Historic Settlement* (museum dedicated to land settlement), Rotary Park* (picnics, riverside walking trails, timber industry relics) and St Thomas More Church*. Numerous arts and craft outlets. Full town facilities. (*101/43*)

Accommodation
The Freycinet Inn, Cnr Bussell Hwy/Tunbridge St, ©08 9757 2033, ©$95-$125
Adamsons Riverside Motel, 71 Bussell Hwy, ©08 9757 2013, ©$75-$90
Edge of the Forest Motel, 25 Bussell Hwy, ©08 9757 2351, ©$80-$90
Margaret River Caravan Park, 36 Station St, ©08 9757 2180, ©Site: $18 Van: $35
Riverview Caravan Park, 8-10 Willmott Ave, ©08 9757 2270, ©Site: $18 Van: $50-$105

Witchcliffe: small rural township. Nearby is a Shell Museum. Store, fuel. (*110/33*)

Undulating country has been mostly cleared for farming. Good views*.

Karridale:* pleasant small farming township. Store, fuel. (*130/13*)

Low rises offer good views across mostly cleared farming lands.

Road Trip 33

DAY TWO

0:40
0:35
0:30

- BUNBURY
  18
- Stratham
  36
- BUSSELTON
  11
- Vasse
  6
- Carbunup
  19
- Cowaramup
  11
- MARGARET RIVER
  9
- Witchliffe
  20
- Karridale
  14
- AUGUSTA

Kuderdup: farming locality. (*137/6*)

Caves Road junction: locality only. (*141/2*) A short distance **W** is Jewel Cave** , a scenic cave exhibiting probably the largest straw stalactite in the world as well as fossil remains. Tours are available. Nearby is the Moondyne Adventure Cave, with tours also available.

AUGUSTA (Alt 10m; Pop 1100):* attractive holiday town located at the mouth of the Blackwood River. Good views* overlooking Hardy Inlet - boating, swimming. Seven kilometres west of town (Hillview Road) is the Hillview Lookout* offering broad vistas. The Historic Museum* is worth visiting. Full town facilities. (*144/0*) Head **N** on Bussell Hwy for Karridale.

Accommodation
Augusta Hotel/Motel, Blckwood Ave, ☏08 9758 1944, ✪$70-$120

Augusta's Georgianna Molloy Motel, 84 Blackwood Ave, ☏08 9758 1255, ✪$75-$95

Doonbanks Caravan Park, Lot 1 Blackwood Ave, ☏08 9758 1517, ✪Site: $16 Van: $30-$50

Westbay Retreat Caravan Park, Bussell Hwy (1kmN), ☏08 9758 1572, ✪Site: $17 Van: $35-$55

South of town, take the spectacular drive to Cape Leeuwin Lighthouse** on the south-western tip of Australia, a wild and windswept place. Climb* to the top of the lighthouse for great views. Lighthouse museum*. The nearby waterwheel* is of interest. An unsealed scenic drive leads back to the main road.

DAY 3: AUGUSTA-BRIDGETOWN
via Nannup

Road to Take: Brockman Highway
Grade 1
Total Distance: 134km (1:45)
Intermediate Distances:

	Km	Hours
Augusta-Nannup	88	(1:05)
Nannup-Bridgetown	46	(0:40)

Average Vehicles per Day: 250 west of Bridgetown
Regions Traversed: The South-West

AUGUSTA (Alt 10m; Pop 1100):* attractive holiday town. For more information see Day 2. (*0/134*) Head **N** on Bussell Hwy for Karridale.

For details of the route between Augusta and Karridale see the above notes.

Karridale: farming township. (*13/121*) Turn **E** onto Brockman Hwy for Nannup. *Head **S** on Bussell Hwy for Augusta.*

Low rises support farming country.

Alexandra Bridge: rural locality. Nearby is the Blackwood River: pleasant camping area surrounded by jarrah trees. (*23/111*)

Low rises support farmlands in the west. Eastwards are extensive tracts of jarrah forests. **Rest area.** (*57/77*)

Darradup: historic settlement with some old buildings located on the Blackwood River. Mixed farming area. (*68/66*)

Undulating country supports jarrah forests.

Nannup (Pop 520):* attractive timber and holiday town on the Blackwood River. Worth seeing: Old Templemore* (historic cottage), Blackwood River walking trail*, Casuarina Walking Trail, Town Arboretum*. Arts and craft shops. Accommodation, stores, fuel. (*88/46*)

Low hills have been cleared for farming.

Hilly country* offers good views.

Undulating country supports karri forests.

Karri Gully:* attractive picnic area set among the karri forests. (*107/27*)

Donnelly River turnoff: (*111/23*) Turn **S** for Donnelly River, an old timber milling town nowadays used as a holiday camp. Interesting old timber mill* and museum. Picnic area. Accommodation, store.

Bridgetown Jarrah Park:* scenic picnic area; walking trails. (*114/20*)

Hilly country* offers great views along the Blackwood River.

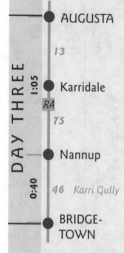

DAY THREE

AUGUSTA

13

1:05

Karridale

RA

75

Nannup

0:40

46 *Karri Gully*

BRIDGE-TOWN

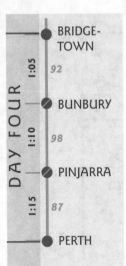

Kangaroo Paw, Wireless Hill, WA

BRIDGETOWN (Alt 155m; Pop 2150):** attractive country town. For more information see Road Trip 34, Day 6. (**134/0**) *Road Trip 34 connects.*

The South-Western Highway
Bridgetown-Perth
The South-Western Highway passes through a variety of landscapes: the grazing lands around Bridgetown, the orcharding country around Donnybrook, and the relatively green and lush pastures of the Harvey-Bunbury district.

Warnings: road subject to flooding. Beware of wildlife in the forested sections at night.

DAY 4: BRIDGETOWN-PERTH via Bunbury

Road to Take: South-Western Highway
Grade 1
Total Distance: 277km (3:30)
Intermediate Distances:

	Km	Hours
Bridgetown-Bunbury	92	(1:05)
Bunbury-Pinjarra	98	(1:10)
Pinjarra-Perth	87	(1:15)

Average Vehicles per Day: 5000 south of Byford
Regions Traversed: The South-West, Coastal Plain

BRIDGETOWN (Alt 155m; Pop 2150):** attractive country town. For more information see Road Trip 34, Day 6. (**0/277**)

For information on the route between Bridgetown and Perth see Road Trip 34, Days 6 and 7 .

PERTH (Alt 19m; Pop 1097000):** state capital of Western Australia. For more information see Day 1. (**277/0**) *Road Trips 28, 29 and 34 connect.*

Road Trip 34
Great Southern Loop

Perth-Merredin-Kalgoorlie-Norsemam-Esperance-Albany-Bunbury-Perth
Total Distance: 1710km
Suggested Travelling Time: 7 days

Count the many faces of the great south

See the old buildings at Coolgardie, the charm of Kalgoorlie and Boulder, the Darling Range, Mundaring Weir, the old mining town of Norseman, Peak Charles National Park, the port at Esperance, the many attractions of Albany on King George Sound, Torndirrup National Park, the quaint town of Denmark, William Bay National Park, Mt Frankland, Warren National Park, the Pemberton-Northcliffe Tramway, Manjimup Timber Park, the farmlands around Donnybrook, the pretty town of Harvey, and the most attractive town in the south-west: Bridgetown.

Great Southern Loop

The south-west quarter of Western Australia is a vast area ranging from scenic rural outlooks, tall karri forests, and rugged coastal landscapes to endless rolling wheatlands and salmon gum woodlands. This road trip skirts the settled corner of a very big state by taking in the eastern Goldfields and southern coastline.

The Goldfields is an outback region of sprawling plains clothed with very attractive salmon gums and gimlet trees, among which are hidden old mining sites, ghost towns and modern, huge open-cut mines. Here gold, and more recently nickel, has helped establish Western Australia's economic base. The Goldfields is a region worth considering for its mining heritage and subtle beauty.

The southern coastal region is a dramatic region of plunging cliffs, huge granite domes and vast, undulating sandplains. The countryside ranges from broadacre farmlands in the east to tall karri forests in the west.

The Climate

The climate of the south-west quarter of Western Australia and the Goldfields can be summed up as hot, dry summers and mild, wet winters. Summer days range from very warm to very hot (it can be mild on the southern seaboard) with temperatures ranging from around 28C to 36C. Nights are generally mild (around 18C) but can occasionally be warmer (up to 23C). Heatwaves are common in January and Febuary with maximum temperatures in the low to mid-forties and warm nights in the mid-twenties. As a rule the west coast (Perth) is generally hotter than the southern coast (Albany, Esperance), and the Goldfields are generally warmer than the coast. There is virtualy no rainfall between November and April except for drizzle along the southern coast. Nonetheless it can pour during rare cyclonic outbreaks from the north.

Winters are generally cool to mild with showery weather. Showery weather may last for days and along the exposed western and southern coastline gale force winds are common. The cooler days will have maximums around 15C to 18C. Nights can be cold at this time with temperatures around 0C to 5C. Along the Darling Range and higher portions of the Wheatbelt, sub-zero temperatures are recorded.

The best time to travel the south-west and Goldfields is in autumn (dry, still, balmy days) or spring (little rain, some wind but lush, green landscapes and wonderful wildflowers).

Capital City Connections
Distances in kilometres
ADELAIDE-NORSEMAN
via Highway One/Eyre Highway

	Intermediate	Total
Adelaide	0	0
Port Augusta	312	312
Ceduna	468	780
Norseman	1210	1990

SYDNEY-NORSEMAN
via Great Western/Mitchell/Barrier/Eyre
Highways

	Intermediate	Total
Sydney	0	0
Port Augusta	1568	1568
Ceduna	468	2038
Norseman	1210	3248

DARWIN-PERTH
via Victoria/Great Northern/North-West
Coastal Highways

	Intermediate	Total
Darwin	0	0
Katherine	316	316
Port Hedland	2095	2411
Geraldton	1351	3762
Perth	423	4185

The Route
Distances in kilometres

	Intermediate	Total
Perth	0	0
Northam	98	98
Merredin	163	261
Coolgardie	295	556
Norseman	168	724
Esperance	202	926
Albany	480	1128
Manjimup	368	1496
Bunbury	129	1525
Perth	185	1710

Great Eastern Highway
Perth-Kalgoorlie
The Great Eastern Highway runs east-west
across the southern portion of Western Australia. From Perth it cuts across the urbanised
coastal plain, the jarrah-clad escarpment and hill
country of the Darling Plateau, the undulating
plains of the Western Australian wheatbelt, and
the vast, virtually uninhabited sandplains of the
Yilgarn before reaching Coolgardie and Kalgoorlie.

Warnings: roads subjected to flooding. Ur-
ban traffic between Perth and Mundaring.
Beware of kangaroos and stock between
Southern Cross and Kalgoorlie.

DAY 1: PERTH-KALGOORLIE
via Merredin

Road to Take: Great Eastern Highway
Grade 1
Total Distance: 595km (6:45)
Intermediate Distances:

	Km	Hours
Perth-Northam	97	(1:20)
Northam-Merredin	164	(1:50)
Merredin-Southern Cross	108	(1:10)
Southern Cross-Coolgardie	187	(2:00)
Coolgardie-Kalgoorlie	39	(0:25)

Average Vehicles per Day: 1600 east of
Kellerberrin
Regions Traversed: Coastal Plain, Darling
Plateau, Wheatbelt, Goldfields

PERTH (Alt 19m; Pop 1097000):** state capital of Western Australia. For more information
see Road Trip 33, Day 1. (*0/595*) *Road Trips 28,
29 and 33 connect.*

From the city take St Georges Tce, which be-
comes Adelaide Tce, cross the Causeway, turn
NE onto Great Eastern Highway (Midland
Road) (*3/592*); turn **SE** onto Great Eastern
Bypass (*9/586*); turn **N** onto Roe Hwy (*15/
580*); turn **E** onto Great Eastern Hwy (*17/578*).
Reverse directions for Perth.

MIDVALE (Alt 16m): Perth suburb. Full town
facilities. (*17/578*) *Road Trips 28 and 29 connect.*

Hilly country forms the escarpment of the Darling Range. Good westward views* across the
coastal plain. The countryside supports urban
development (the suburbs of Greenmount and
Darlington) as well as jarrah forests.
Low hills support tracts of jarrah forest and scattered urban development. **Rest area.**
John Forrest National Park turnoff: (*26/569*) Turn
N for John Forrest National Park:* pleasant park
set within the jarrah forests. Worth seeing and
doing: scenic drives, swimming holes, walking
trails, picnic areas.

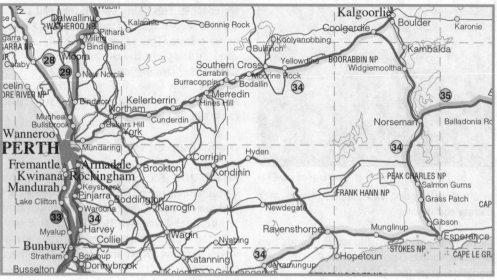

Detail of MAP 8

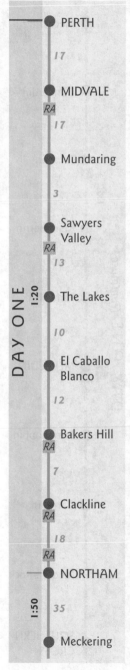

Mahogany Creek: rural hinterland of houses, small farms and jarah forests.

Mundaring (Alt 297m; Pop 1000):* pleasant hill suburb of Perth. Walking and bike trail* extends along an old railway line. Worth seeing is the Mundaring Community Sculpture Park*. Accommodation, stores, fuel. (*34/561*)
  A short distance away is Mundaring Weir*, an impressive dam and reservoir. Beneath the dam wall the interesting C. Y. O'Connor Museum** exhibiting aspects of the Mundaring-Kalgoorlie water pipeline. Picnic area.

Sawyers Valley: hills' settlement set among the jarrah forests. Store, fuel. (*37/558*)

Undulating country supports jarrah forests. **Rest area** at Forsayth Mill. (*46/549*)
Lake Leschenaultia turnoff: (*44/551*) Turn here for Lake Leschenaultia*, a popular lake and picnic area. Canoeing and swimming. Camping available.

The Lakes: locality and roadhouse. Store, fuel. (*50/545*)

Hilly country has been partially cleared for grazing and orcharding. Elsewhere are tracts of jarrah forests.

El Caballo Blanco: horse-based entertainment centre. Accommodation, store, fuel. (*60/535*)

Bakers Hill (Alt 293m): small farming township. **Rest area**. Accommodation, store, fuel. (*72/521*)

Clackline: small farming township. **Rest area**. Store, fuel. (*79/516*)

Undulating country has been mostly cleared for grazing. Reasonable views*. Scattered trees include wandoo, distinguished by its white bark. **Rest area** at Eadine Spring. (*81/514*)

NORTHAM (Alt 149m; Pop 6300): sizeable country town set on the banks of the Avon (pronounced Av-on) River. Many historical buildings. Worth seeing: pioneer graves, Island Farm Nature Reserve, Mt Ommanney Lookout*, Old Railway Station Museum*, the Suspension Bridge* (longest pedestrian suspension bridge in Australia). Full town facilities. (*97/498*)

DAY ONE

	PERTH
17	
RA	
17	MIDVALE
	Mundaring
3	
	Sawyers Valley
RA	
13	
1:20	The Lakes
10	
	El Caballo Blanco
12	
	Bakers Hill
RA	
7	
	Clackline
RA	
18	
RA	NORTHAM
1:50	35
	Meckering

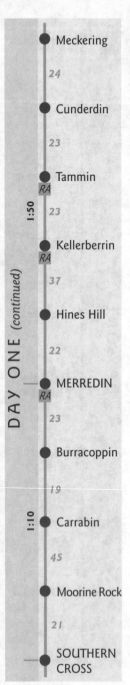

Road Trip 34

DAY ONE (continued)

- ● Meckering
  - 24
- ● Cunderdin
  - 23
- ● Tammin *RA*
  - 1:50
  - 23
- ● Kellerberrin *RA*
  - 37
- ● Hines Hill
  - 22
- ● MERREDIN *RA*
  - 23
- ● Burracoppin
  - 19
- ● Carrabin
  - 1:10
  - 45
- ● Moorine Rock
  - 21
- ● SOUTHERN CROSS

Cunderdin landscape, WA

Low hills offer good views across the cleared grazing countryside.

Meckering: small township made famous by a large earthquake experienced in 1968. Accommodation, store fuel. (*132/463*)

Low rises support expansive tracts of wheat cropping country. Attractive countryside* after winter rains.

Cunderdin (Alt 213m; Pop 700): small wheat-farming town. The Municipal Museum* is interesting, located in an old water pipeline pump house with a floodlite 31m chimney stack*. Accommodation, stores, fuel. (*156/439*)

Low rises support wheat farms. Broad vistas from the tops of rises.

Tammin (Pop 250): small wheat farming township. **Rest area**. Store, fuel. (*179/416*)

Undulating country supports wheat farms. Broad vistas.

Kellerberrin (Alt 247m; Pop 850):* pleasant wheat-farming town. Worth seeing: District Museum, heritage trail*, Pioneer Park* (picnics, early agricultural implements). **Rest area**. Accommodation, stores, fuel. (*202/393*)

Low rises mostly cleared for cropping. Saltlakes south of the road. These natural drainage channels have salty surfaces due, in part, to wholesale land clearances resulting in a raised water table. This rising table brings salt to the surface, rendering that land useless for grazing or agriculture. This saltation problem is widespread throughout the wheatbelt.
Doodlakine: farming locality. (*218/377*)

Hines Hill: locality and roadhouse. Store, fuel. (*239/356*)

Low rises support wheat farms.

MERREDIN (Alt 315m; Pop 2900): sizeable wheat farming town. Worth seeing: Hunt's Dam (old convict well), Cummins Theatre (interesting architecture), Mangowie Homestead* (old wayside stop and flora reserve), heritage trail, old railway water tower. **Rest area**. Full town facilities. (*261/334*)

Accommodation

Merredin Motel, 10 Gamenya Ave (1kmW), ©08 9041 1886, ○$60
Merredin Olympic Motel, Great Eastern Hwy (1kmW), ©08 9041 1588, ○$65
Potts Motor Inn, Great Eastern Hwy (1kmE), ©08 9041 1755, ○$80
Merredin Caravan Park, 2 Oats St (1.5kmW), ©08 9041 1535, ○Site: $16 Van: $35-$70

Low rises support wheat farms.

Burracoppin: wheat-farming locality. Store, fuel. (*284/311*)

Low rises offer sweeping views from tops of rises. Wheat cropping occupies the countryside.

Carrabin: small farming township. Accommodation, store, fuel. (*303/292*)

Low rises offer good views across the wheatlands.

Bodallin: small farming township. Store, fuel.

Low rises support broadacre cropping country.

Moorine Rock (Alt 405m): small cropping township. Store, fuel. (*348/247*)

Undulating country has been mostly cleared for cropping. Wimmera Hill offers good views*.

SOUTHERN CROSS (Alt 353m; Pop 1150):* interesting old gold mining town with some character. Today the town serves as a wheat-farming settlement. Worth seeing: Yilgarn History Museum*, the old cemetery, Hunts Soak (8km north of town). Enquire locally about old gold mines in the district. Full town facilities. (*369/226*)

Low rises support broadacre wheatlands. The countryside is extensively cleared, though some patches of native vegetation remain, particularly along the road reserve.

Yellowdine (Alt 367m; Pop 5):* old railway settlement. The current settlement has plenty of character and is worth stopping just to look. Accommodation, fuel. (*402/193*)

Sandplains support a wide variety of vegetation including casuarinas, grevilleas and hakeas. Good wildflowers** on the shrubs after winter rains (late August-September). Low rises provides fair distant views*. **Rest area**.
Boorabbin National Park: small park conserving sandplain vegetation. Good wildflowers** after winter rains.
Boorabbin: locality only, no facilities. Ruin* set near the highway. (*465/130*)
Low rises support very diverse sandplain vegetation, typically heath formations. Fair views from the tops of rises. **Rest area** and lookout. (*475/120*)
Woolgangie:* locality only, no facilities. Located just north of the highway. An old narrow gauge railway siding can be seen. Many rocky outcrops are in this area. Yardani Well **rest area** nearby. (*491/104*).
Plains and low rises support an attractive salmon gum woodland with a shrubby understorey.

Bullabulling (Alt 447m; Pop 5):* interesting bush pub and former railway station on the narrow gauge railway. Accommodation, fuel. (*526/69*)

Low rises* support attractive salmon gum and gimlet woodlands.

COOLGARDIE (Alt 427m; Pop 1500):** interesting historic mining town. Numerous old buildings, very photogenic. It is worth spending some time here exploring the streets. Visit Coolgardie Cemetery, Prior's museum**, C.Y. O'Connor Dedication (fountain), Gaol Tree, Goldfields Exhibition**, Waghorn's Bottle Museum, Old Pioneer Cemetery*, Railway Station Museum*, Warden Finnerty's House*, Lions Bicentennial Lookout*, Lindsay Pit Lookout, and the photogenic Catholic Church. Full town facilities. (*556/39*)

Accommodation
Coolgardie Motel, 49 Bayley St, ©08 9026 6080, ✪$70
Coolgardie Caravan Park, 101 Bayley St, ©08 9026 6009, ✪Site: $16 Van: $35
The Haven Caravan Park, Great Eastern Hwy (1kmW), ©08 9026 6123, ✪Site: $14 Van: $25-$30

Low rises support salmon gum woodlands.
Douglas Lake turnoff: (*583/12*) Turn here for short 4km drive to Douglas Lake*, a pleasant picnic area set among the salmon gums.

KALGOORLIE (Alt 376m; Pop 28000):** major mining town and regional centre with plenty of character. Grand buildings line a particularly impressive main street. The side streets too have a share of interesting and photographic buildings, including Kalgoorlie Town Hall* - heritage trail*. Also of interest is Kalgoorlie's sister settlement, Boulder**, with its many interesting buildings including Boulder Town Hall* - heritage trail*. Tourist features include mine tours, Museum of the Goldfields**, School of Mines Mineral Museum**, Goldfields War Museum, Hannans North Historic Mining Reserve*, Paddy Hannan's Statue*, Paddy Hannan's Tree, Mt Charlotte Lookout*, Karlkurla Bushland Park*, Royal Flying Doctor Service*, The Golden Mine Loop Line* (a restored railway in Boulder), the Arboretum* (picnic areas, walking trails), Super

Road Trip 34

DAY ONE (continued)

SOUTHERN CROSS

33

2:00 Yellowdine
RA
124 Boorabbin NP
RA

Bullabulling

30

COOLGARDIE

0:25 39

KALGOORLIE

Pit Lookout. Numerous tours available. Full town facilities. (**595/0**)

Accommodation

Hannans View Motel, 430 Hannan St (1kmSW), ©08 9091 3333, ◎$105-$150

Mercure Inn Overland Motel, Hannan St (2.5kmSW), ©08 9021 1433, ◎$80-$155

Star and Garter Motor Hotel, 497 Hannan St (1.3kmSW), ©08 9026 3399, ◎$85

Piccadilly Hotel, 164 Piccadilly St (1kmE), ©08 9021 2109, ◎$45

Boulder Accommodation Village Caravan Park, Lane St, Boulder, ©08 9093 1266, ◎Site: $20 Van: $75-$85

Kalgoorlie Accommodation Village Caravan Park, Burt St (2kmW), ©08 9039 4800, ◎Site: $20 Van: $70-$85

Prospector Holiday Park, Lower Hannan St (3kmW), ©08 9021 2524, ◎Site: $20 Van: $55-$80

Goldminer Tourist Caravan Park, Great Eastern Hwy (4kmW), ◎Site: $17 Van: $55-$75

Kambalda Road/ Coolgardie-Esperance Highway

Kalgoorlie-Esperance

The Coolgardie-Esperance Highway connects the Eastern Goldfields with the south coast port of Esperance, as well as providing access to the Eyre Highway at Norseman. The route pases through attractive salmon gum woodlands in the north and broadacre cropping country in the south.

Warnings: road subject to flooding. Beware of stock and kangaroos at night.

DAY 2: KALGOORLIE-ESPERANCE via Kambalda/Norseman

Roads to Take: Kambalda Road, Coolgardie-Esperance Highway
Grade 1
Total Distance: 391km (4:20)

Intermediate Distances:

	Km	Hours
Kalgoorlie-Kambalda	57	(0:40)
Kambalda-Norseman	132	(1:25)
Norseman-Esperance	202	(2:15)

Average Vehicles per Day: 600 north of Norseman
Regions Traversed: Goldfields, South Coast

KALGOORLIE (Alt 376m; Pop 28000):** major mining town and regional centre. For more information see Day 1. (**0/391**)

Breakaway:* attractive break in slope some 20m high and about 1km long. Numerous colours, notably pinks, yellows and browns, can be seen. Mornings are best for photography. Access by foot, approximately 150m from road. Park well off the road. (**23/368**)

Celebration Mine:* old mine ruins. Very photogenic, especially the headframe. Rusty tanks and dumps are in area and worth exploring. Look for the track in; the mine is roughly 600m from road. (**32/359**)

Low rises support salmon gums and gimlets. King Battery:* picnic area.
Kambalda turnoff: (**55/336**) Turn **E** for the 2km drive into Kambalda. *Turn **N** for Kalgoorlie.*

KAMBALDA (Alt 345m; Pop 2000): nickel mining town set among the salmon gums. Nearby is the large saltlake, Lake Lefroy. Good view over the lake from Red Hill Lookout. Full town facilities.

Kambalda West turnoff:(**57/334**) Turn **N** for Kambalda West. *Turn **E** for Kambalda.*

KAMBALDA WEST (Alt 350m; Pop 3000): modern mining town, developed to house the overflow from Kambalda. Unlike the hilly Kambalda, this settlement is built upon a plain. Worth a quick look. Full town facilities.

Low rises support gimlets and salmon gums.
Coolgardie-Esperance Highway junction: locality only; no facilities. (**77/314**) Turn **S** for Norseman. *Turn **E** for Kambalda West.*

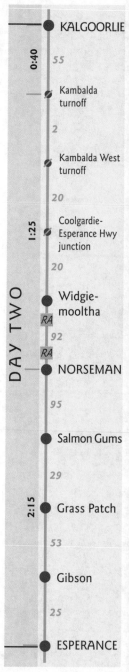

Emu Rocks: outcrops of granite. A pretty spot. (*81/310*)

Saltlake forms an arm of Lake Lefroy.

Widgiemooltha (Alt 321m; Pop 50): old mining township, now virtually a ghost town. Worth a quick look. Accommodation, store, fuel. (*97/294*)

Lake Lefroy:* an arm of the lake lies east of the road. (*102/289*)

Higginsville: old mining area and railway station. A pleasant spot for exploratory rambles. (*131/260*)

Lake Cowan* shoreline (careful crossing the railway line) is a good place to view the saltlake. Late afternoon best. **Rest area** adjacent. (*166/225*)

Low rises support salmon gums. Mt Thirsty (430m) lies to the west. **Rest area**. (*173/218*)

Lake Cowan: arm of a saltlake crossed by a causeway.

NORSEMAN (Alt 278m; Pop 1900):* old mining town with some character. Plenty of historical buildings, some very photogenic. A huge tailings' dump rises above the town. Worth investigating: Beacon Hill Lookout*, Heritage

Gimlet bark detail, near Peak Charles, WA

Trail*, Lions Park (picnics), Historic Collection (School of Mines), Bullen Decline*, gemstone leases (enquire locally). Full town facilities. (*189/202*) Road Trip 35 connects.

Accommodation

Norseman Eyre Motel, Cnr Eyre Hwy/Prinsep St (1.5kmN), ✆08 9039 1130, ✪$75-$90

Great Western Motel, Prinsep St (1kmN), ✆08 9039 1633, ✪$85

Gateway Caravan Park, Prinsep St (1kmN), ✆08 9039 1500, ✪Site: $19 Van: $30-$55

Plains support tracts of salmon gums.

Dundas Rocks turnoff: (*211/180*) This short drive (2km) leads to Dundas Rocks*, an interesting rocky outcrop set near the shoreline of Lake Dundas, a large saltlake.

Bromus Dam: old railway dam. **Rest area** adjacent. (*221/170*)

Plains covered with extensive tracts of salmon gum woodlands. Very attractive in the late afternoon light. Numerous other species are also present. This woodland is unusual insofar as it is such a tall woodland for such a low rainfall (around 280mm per annum).

Peak Charles National Park turnoff: (*243/148*) Turn **W** for the 100km return Grade 3 drive to Peak Charles National Park. Peak Charles** is a high rocky peak set upon a vast sand plain. Lower slopes of the Peak are easy to climb, higher portions of the Peak require care. Vast excellent views overlooking the Yilgarn Wilderness to the north. Also apparent are the in-roads made by the wholesale land clearances for wheat farming to the south and east.

Low rises support wheatlands. Uncleared remnants of natural vegetation, notably salmon gum woodlands. Peak Charles is clearly visible to the west. **Rest area**. (*261/130*)

Salmon Gums (Alt 249m; Pop 150): wheat-farming township set among salmon gums. Accommodation, store, fuel. (*284/107*)

Low rises support broadacre wheat farms. Little natural vegetation remains.

KALGOORLIE
0:40
55
Kambalda turnoff
2
Kambalda West turnoff
20
Coolgardie-Esperance Hwy junction
1:25
20
Widgie-mooltha
RA
92
RA
NORSEMAN
95
Salmon Gums
29
2:15
Grass Patch
53
Gibson
25
ESPERANCE

DAY TWO

Grass Patch (Alt 217m; Pop 50): small wheat-farming township. Mallee memorial is worth a quick look. Store, fuel. (*313/78*)

Scadden: locality set among the broadacre wheat farms. (*338/53*)
Plains support broadacre wheat farms. Attractive after winter rains, bleached and glary after the summer drought. Little natural vegetation remains, except along roadside reserves.

Gibson (Alt 157m; Pop 20): small wheat-farming township. Accommodation, store, fuel. (*366/25*)

Low rises offer fair broad views south of Gibson towards the coast.
Lookout* provides good views over Esperance, its surrounding saltlakes, and the granite islands and headlands of the coast. (*384/7*)
South Coast Highway junction: located on the outskirts of Esperance. (*388/3*) Continue into Esperance. *Head **N** on Coolgardie/Esperance Hwy Salmon Gums.*

ESPERANCE (Alt 10m; Pop 6500): large town and port servicing the surrounding hinterland, located on Esperance Bay. Worth seeing: Municipal Museum**, Museum Village, Lions Lookout*, Rotary Lookout*, The Esplanade and Foreshore* (swimming, picnics). Offshore cruises are available to Woody Island and other parts of the Recherche Archipelago. Full town facilities. (*391/0*)

Accommodation
Bay of Isles Motel, 32 The Esplanade, ©08 9071 3999, ●$100
Bayview Motel, 31 Dempster St, ©08 9071 1533, ●$75
Jetty Motel, 1 The Esplanade, ©08 9071 5978, ●$75-$85
Esperance Travellers Inn, Goldfields Rd (3kmN), ©08 9071 1677, ●$60
Pink Lake Tourist Park, Pink Lake Rd (2kmW), ©08 9071 2424, ●Site: $17 Van: $30-$70
Esperance Seafront Caravan Park, Cnr Goldfields/Norseman Rds (2kmNE), ©08 9071 1251, ●Site: $17 Van: $45-$90

Esperance Bay Caravan Park, Cnr The Esplanade/Harbour Rd, ©08 9071 2237, ●Site: $19 Van: $40-$70

Out of town, 50km to the east, is Cape Le Grande National Park**. This park preserves a variety of sandplain vegetation, high granite domes and a spectacular coastline. Ranger Station and information is near the entrance. Camping is available. Westwards is the 38km long Great Ocean Drive** loop road - highly recommended.

South Coast Highway
Esperance-Walpole
Running the length of Western Australia's southern coastline, the South Coast Highway passes through a variety of landscapes. In the west are tall karri forests interspersed with cleared grazing and dairying country - short detours lead to scenic coastal lookouts and settlements, or deep into forests to places such as the Ancient Empire and Tree Top Walk. Further east the country opens out into rolling farmlands dotted at intervals by high granite outcrops, centred around the historic town of Albany.

East of Albany the countryside is drier and the forests and farms are replaced by mallee scrubs and broadacre wheat farms. This more open landscape is dotted with high hills of granite, the vast sandplain country of the Fitzgerald River National Park, and the downlands west of Esperance. Short detours lead to a very scenic coastline of granite domes and blazing white beaches.

Warnings: roads subject to flooding. At night beware of kangaroos and other animal life in the forested sections.

DAY 3: ESPERANCE-ALBANY via Jerramungup

Road to Take: South Coast Highway
Grade 1
Total Distance: 480km (5:15)

Intermediate Distances:

	Km	Hours
Esperance-Ravensthorpe	186	(2:00)
Raventhorpe-Jerramungup	114	(1:15)
Jerramungup-Albany	180	(2:00)

Average Vehicles per Day: 550 west of Wellstead

Regions Traversed: South Coast

▼

ESPERANCE (Alt 4m; Pop 8650): large coastal town. For more information see day 2. (*0/480*)

South Coast Highway junction: located on the outskirts of Esperance. (*3/477*) Turn **W** for Ravensthorpe. *Head **S** for Esperance.*
Lake Warden lies to the north of the road.
Low rises are mostly cleared for farming; occasional views. **Rest area.** (*9/471*)
Dalyup: farming locality; no facilities. (*34/446*)
Undulating country supports broadacre wheat farms. Occasional fair views*. **Rest area.** (*54/426*)
Stokes Inlet turnoff: (*78/402*) Turn here for the 14km return (Grade 3) road leading to Stokes Inlet National Park*, a small park preserving coastal landscapes and the pretty Stokes Inlet. Camping is available on the inlet. Canoeing, swimming.
Undulating country supports broadacre wheat farms. Fair views* from the tops of rises.

Munglinup: small wheat farming township set by the Munglinup River. Store, fuel. (*105/375*)

Munglinup Wheat Bin: large wheat storage facility. (*109/371*)
Undulating country supports broadacre wheat farms. Broad vistas from the tops of rises. The area around Oldfield River provides views*.
Low hills* are quite scenic. Mt Desmond is visible to the south. **Rest area.** (*180/300*)

Ravensthorpe (Alt 234m; Pop 350):* old copper mining town, nowadays a farming community. Interesting historic buildings, very photogenic. Worth seeing: Catlin Creek Heritage Trail*

and the museum. Accommodation, stores, fuel. (*186/294*)

North of town (about 10km) is a lookout* in the Ravensthorpe Range - enquire locally. South of town a 100km return trip leads to **Hopetoun** (Alt 5m; Pop 320)*, a pleasant small coastal town, formerly an old port and railway terminus for the nearby copper mines. Good beaches. West of Hopetoun a good quality unsealed road leads to Fitzgerald River National Park* and tremendous views* around East Mount Barren.

Undulating country supports broadacre wheat farms. Occasional views. **Rest area** at the WA Time Meridian. (*190/290*)
West River Wheat Bin: large wheat storage facility. (*227/253*)
Undulating country given over to wheat farming. Good views* around Hamersley River crossing.
Fitzgerald: farming locality; no facilities. (*245/235*)
Undulating country supports broadacre wheat farms. Good views* in hilly country around Fitzgerald River crossing.
Jacup Wheat Bin: large wheat storage facility. (*272/208*)
Quiss Road junction: locality only; no facilities. (*281/199*) Turn **S** for access to Fitzgerald River National Park; ranger station nearby.
Undulating country supports broadacre farmlands. Gairdner River crossing is of minor interest.

Jerramungup (Pop 330): small wheat-farming town. Military Collection is worth seeing. Picnic and **rest area** at Lions Park. Accommodation, stores, fuel. (*300/180*)

Undulating country cleared for cropping; broad vistas.
Gairdner: farming locality and wheat bin; no facilities. (*333/147*)
Undulating country offers broad vistas across broadacre wheat farms.

ESPERANCE

3

South Coast Highway Jctn

RA

2:00

102

RA

Munglinup

RA

81

Ravensthorpe

RA

1:15

114

Jerramungup

RA

59

Boxwood Hill

RA

22

2:00

Wellstead

RA

56

Manypeaks

19

Kalgan

DAY THREE

DAY THREE (continued) 2:00

- Kalgan
- 12
- Bakers Junction
- 2
- King River
- 10
- ALBANY

Boxwood Hill (Pop 5): small farming township and roadhouse facility. Store, fuel. (*359/121*)

Turn **E** for the all-sealed 126km return journey to **Bremer Bay** (Alt 20m; Pop 220):* scenic coastal holiday settlement set on the Wellstead Estuary. Worth seeing: the lookout* and beachfront* (picnic area, swimming). Accommodation, stores, fuel.

Hilly country offers reasonable views*. At the Pallinup River crossing is a **rest area**. (*365/112*) Undulating country support tracts of mallee interspersed with cleared cropping lands.

Wellstead: small farming township. Store, fuel. (*381/99*)

Hassell National Park: long and thin national park preserving tracts of mallee along the highway. **Rest area**. (*410/70*) Plains and low rises support tracts of eucalypt mallee shrublands partially cleared for grazing and cropping.

Manypeaks: small farming township. Store, fuel. (*437/43*)

Low hills offer good views* across farmlands. Prominent granite peaks are visible to the south, including Mt Manypeaks (565m).

Kalgan (Alt 27m): small township set on the Kalgan River estuary. Store. (*456/24*)

Undulating country offers good views*. The countryside is cleared for grazing and cropping.

Bakers Junction: roadhouse facility. Store, fuel. (*468/12*)

King River (Alt 18m):* attractive small township set on the King River. Canoeing, swimming. Accommodation, store, fuel. (*470/10*)

Undulating country supports scattered hobby farms and vineyards. Occasional views.

ALBANY (Alt 13m; Pop 20500):** large regional centre situated on King George Sound. Worth seeing: Amity Replica* - an old ship, Dog Rock*, Lawley Park - good views of harbour, Middleton Beach*, Mt Clarence (186m) Lookout*, Mt Melville (157m) Lookout*, Wagon Rock Lookout, Patrick Taylor Cottage Museum*, Princess Royal Fortress* (old military installation), St Johns Church*, Strawberry Hill Farmhouse (built in 1836 - the oldest farmhouse in WA), Old Gaol Museum*, and Residency Museum*. Cruises are available on the harbour. Numerous other holiday attractions. Full town facilities. (*480/0*)

Accommodation

Ace Motor Inn, 314 Albany Hwy (3kmNW), ©08 9841 2911, ✪$85

Amity Motor Inn, 234 Albany Hwy (2kmNW), ©08 9841 2200, ✪$70-$80

Dog Rock Motel, 303 Middleton Rd, ©08 9841 4422, ✪$65-$100

Royal George Hotel/Motel, 62 Stirling St, ©08 9841 1013, ✪$75

Emu Point Motel, Cnr Mermaid Ave/Medcalf Pde (6kmE), ©08 9844 1001, ✪$65-$75

Middleton Beach Holiday & Caravan Park, 28 Flinders Pde (3kmE), ©08 9841 3593, ✪Site: $20 Van: $50-$85

Mt Melville Caravan Park, 22 Wellington St (1kmN), ©08 9841 4616, ✪Site: $20 Van: $45-$65

Emu Beach Holioday Park, Medcalf Pde (7kmNE), ©08 9844 1147, ✪Site: $17 Van: $40-$120

Albany Tourist Village Caravan Park, 550 Albany Hwy (4kmN), ©08 9841 3752, ✪Site: $16 Van: $35-$70

Ninety kilometres north of Albany lies the Stirling Ranges National Park, preserving the best mountainous country in the southern half of Western Australia. Allow one full day to take the Stirling Range scenic drive** (drive against the rising or setting sun) and Bluff Knoll*** - both these features should not be missed. En route the Porongurup National Park* is worth a look.

South of Albany the Frenchman's Bay Road leads to Torndirrup National Park, a popular park featuring fantastic granite cliffs as well as The Gap** (a deep cleft in the coastal cliffs); the Natural Bridge** (an interesting granite formation); a short distance away is an impressive lookout*;

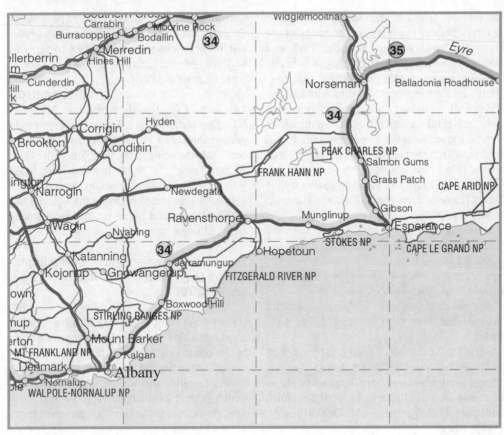

Detail of MAP 8

and the Blowholes (walking required). Also of interest is the Whaleworld Museum** (whaling museum and site of Australia's last whaling station). This drive is approximately 45km return.

Other places of interest include the 56km mostly sealed return drive via Lower King and Lower Kalgan to Two Peoples Bay Nature Reserve**, a scenic park of granite domes, scrubby heathlands, beautiful lakes and azure bays. Preserves habitat of noisy scrub birds. Interpretative Centre. No camping.

DAY 4: ALBANY-WALPOLE
via Denmark

Grade 1
Total Distance: 120km (1:30)

Intermediate Distances:

	Km	Hours
Albany-Denmark	54	(0:40)
Denmark-Walpole	66	(0:50)

Average Vehicles per Day: 600 east of Walpole
Regions Traversed: South Coast

ALBANY (Alt 13m; Pop 20500):** large regional centre situated on King George Sound. For more information see Day 3. (**0/120**)

Plains and low rises support grazing country. Fair views from tops of rises.
Hay River: locality only, situated on the paperbark-lined Hay River. Good canoeing. (**43/77**)
Undulating country cleared for farming. Reasonable views.

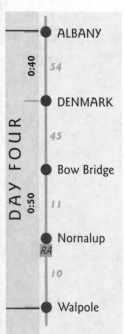

DAY FOUR

ALBANY

0:40   54

DENMARK

45

Bow Bridge

0:50   11

Nornalup

RA

10

Walpole

DENMARK (Alt 5m; Pop 2000):** attractive and hilly holiday town set on the banks of the Denmark River. Norm Thornton Park and Berridge Park* (either side of the highway bridge crossing) are good places for picnics, canoeing. Worth seeing: Historical Museum, Mokare Heritage Walk* - passes through karri trees and paperbark scrubs along the eastern bank of the Denmark River, Karri Walk* passes through karri forests, Wilson Inlet Heritage Walk Trail* follows the old railway line around Wilson Inlet, and Poison Point Lookout (just south of town on Inlet Drive). Numerous arts and craft outlets. Full town facilities. (*54/66*)

Accommodation
Denmark Unit Hotel/Motel, Holling Rd, ©08 9848 2206, ●$80
The Denmark Waterfront Motel, 63 Inlet Dr (3kmS), ©08 9848 1147, ●$85
Ocean Beach Caravan Park, Ocean Beach Rd (8kmS), ©08 9848 1105, ●Site: $18 Van: $45-$65
Rivermouth Caravan Park, Inlet Dr (1kmS), ©08 9848 1262, ●Site: $16 Van: $35-$45

Some short drives lead from Denmark to places of scenic interest. These include Mt Shadforth Lookout* (18km return) and Ocean Beach* (16km return).

Lookout* offers good views towards Point Hillier. (*71/49*)
William Bay National Park turnoff: (72/48) Turn **S** for the short unsealed drive to Green Pool* (popular swimming area set amongst granite boulders), Elephant Rocks* (spectacular granite rock formation looking somewhat like elephants) and a great lookout** that provides stunning westward views towards Point Hillier.
Hilly country* supports farms and karri forests.
Undulating country* has been partially cleared for farming. Elsewhere are karri patches with tea-tree and paperbark scrubs on the flats. Scenic area.
Kenton: locality located on the Kent River. No facilities. (*90/30*)

Bow Bridge: roadhouse facility situated on the Bow River. Store, fuel. (*99/21*)

Conspicuous Cliffs turnoff: (*105/15*) Turn **S** for Conspicuous Cliffs*, a scenic area with a whale-watching** viewing platform (June to September). No swimming. Red-flowering gums in this area (summer months).
Valley of the Giants access road turnoff: (*106/14*) Turn **N** for the short drive to Walpole-Nornalup National Park. The park preserves old growth forests of karris, red tingles and marri trees. Worth seeing is the Tree Top Walk** and Ancient Empire** - highly recommended forest walks. Tree Top Walk provides an elevated (up to 40m high - no steps) pathway through the forest's crown. Ancient Empire is a boardwalk among giant red tingle trees. Kiosk.

Nornalup:* attractive farming township situated on the Frankland River. **Rest area**. Store, fuel. (*110/10*)

Hilltop Road turnoff: (*117/3*) Turn here for the short, unsealed one-way loop road that leads to the Giant Tingle Tree*, a huge tree, rated as one of the ten biggest living things in the world. This is certainly the world's biggest eucalypt, with a girth of 24m. Short walking track.
Walpole-Nornalup National Park preserves tracts of karri forersts.
Hilly country* supports karri forests.

Walpole (Alt 5m; Pop 340):* small farming and holiday town located on Walpole Inlet. **Rest area** at Pioneer Park. Accommodation, stores, fuel. (*120/0*)

Accommodation
Walpole Hotel/Motel, South Coast Hwy, ©08 9840 1023, ●$65
Tree Top Walk Motel, South Coast Hwy, ©08 9840 1444, ●$100
Coalmine Beach Caravan Park, Coalmine Beach (3kmE), ©08 9840 1026, ●Site: $18 Van: $45-$65
Rest Point Tourist Centre, Rest Point Rd (5kmW), ©08 9840 1032, ●Site: $18 Van: $45-$80

About 25km north of Walpole lies Mt Frankland**, a tall and imposing granite mountain (422m) surrounded by beautiful karri forests*. Excellent views** overlook the distant

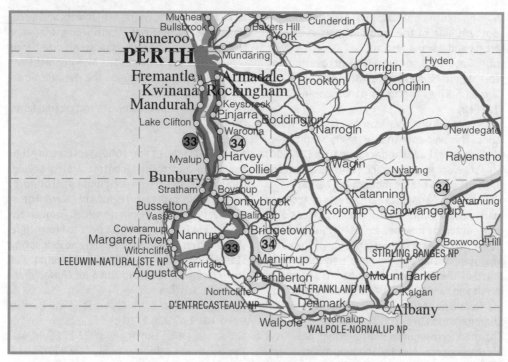

Detail of MAP 8

southern coastline and wild country to the north. There is a walking trail to the top and around the granite outcrop. Camping is available. Forms part of the Mt Frankland National Park.

South-Western Highway

Walpole-Perth

Running across the south-western rump of Western Australia, this route connects Perth and the west coast with the southern coast and Albany. It connects with the South Coast Highway (really just a continuation of this route) at Walpole.

The South-Western Highway passes through a variety of landscapes: the tall karri forests of the Shannon-Walpole area, the grazing lands around Bridgetown, the orcharding country around Donnybrook, and the relatively green and lush pastures of the Harvey-Bunbury district.

Warnings: road subject to flooding. Beware of wildlife in the forested sections at night.

DAY 5: WALPOLE-PEMBERTON via Northcliffe

Roads to Take: South-Western Highway, Northcliffe-Pemberton Road
Grade I
Total Distance: 124km (1:30)
Intermediate Distances:

	Km	Hours
Walpole-Northcliffe turnoff	69	(0:50)
Northcliffe turnoff-Northcliffe	27	(0:20)
Northcliffe-Pemberton	28	(0:20)

Average Vehicles per Day: 500 west of Walpole
Regions Traversed: The South-West

Walpole (Alt 5m; Pop 340):* small farming and holiday town. For more information see Day 4. **(0/124)**

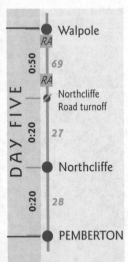

Walpole

RA
0:50   69
RA
        Northcliffe
        Road turnoff
0:20   27

        Northcliffe

0:20   28

        PEMBERTON

DAY FIVE

Walpole-Nornalup National Park lies on the southern side of the road and preserves karri forests and coastal features.

John Rate Lookout:* viewpoint overlooking Nornalup Inlet. **Rest area**. (*5/119*)

Crystal Springs: national park camping area. (*12/112*)

Hilly country supports karri forests and heathlands. This wild countryside is very scenic.

Mt Burnet **rest area** and walking trail. (*24/100*)

Mt Pingerup: walking track (4km return) leads to the summit of this mountain. (*26/98*)

Hilly country* supports karri forests mixed with marri trees. Some jarrah forests. Occasional rocky outcrops may be seen. Mt Frankland National Park lies on the eastern side of the road.

Shannon National Park: large park preserving most of the Shannon River basin, an area of jarrah and karri forests. Worth seeing: Great Forest Trees Drive (48km circuit - enquire locally in Shannon) and Great Forest Trees walk.

Shannon: former timber mill township, nowadays a camping area. Nearby Shannon offers swimming, canoeing, walking trails. **Rest area** adjacent. (*66/58*)

Northcliffe Road turnoff: locality only; no facilities. (*69/55*) Turn **W** for Northcliffe. *Turn **S** for Walpole.*

Undulating country has been cleared for farming. Further east the road passes through some very attractive stands of karri forests**.

Northcliffe (Pop 240):* nice old timber town and terminus of the Pemberton-Northcliffe tramway. Worth seeing: Northcliffe Forest Park* - walking trails, Pioneer Museum*, and George Gardner Rock Collection* at the Tourist Centre. Accommodation, stores, fuel. (*96/28*)

A sealed (Grade 2) road heads south for 29km to Windy Harbour* and Point D'Entrecasteaux (great views*).

Hilly country supports jarrah and marri forests with karris in the wetter areas.

Brockman National Park: small park preserving karri trees*. Picnic area. (*114/10*)

Warren National Park turnoff: (*116/8*) Turn **W** for the short drive to Warren National Park*, an attractive park preserving karri forests and a section of the Warren River. Worth seeing: Marianne North Tree*, lookouts, riverside scenic drive* (one way west to east), Dale Evans Bicentennial Tree* (climbing tree). Canoeing on the river. Picnic areas; camping areas.

Hilly country supports forests and cleared farmlands.

PEMBERTON (Alt Pop 1000):* interesting timber town and tourist centre. Worth seeing: Gloucester Tree* (can be climbed), Founders Forest (70m tall karri regrowth), Karri Forest Discovery Centre*, Pemberton Pool, Pemberton-Northcliffe Tramway** (train rides to Northcliffe, Warren River Bridge, Lyall Siding) and Pemberton Station Precinct**, and Pioneer Museum. Full town facilities. (*124/0*) *Head **S** for Northcliffe.*

Accommodation

Karri Forest Motel, Widdeson St (1kmN), ©08 9776 1019, ✪$85-$120

Gloucester Motel, Ellis St, ©08 9776 1266, ✪$65

Pemberton Hotel, Brockman St, ©08 9776 1017, ✪$60

Pemberton Caravan Park, Pump Hill Rd, ©08 9776 1300, ✪Site: $18 Van: $50-$110

DAY 6: PEMBERTON-BUNBURY via Manjimup

Roads to Take: Vasse Highway, South-Western Highway

Grade 1

Total Distance: 160km (2:00)

Intermediate Distances:

	Km	Hours
Pemberton-Manjimup	31	(0:25)
Manjimup-Bridgetown	37	(0:25)
Bridgetown-Bunbury	92	(1:10)

Average Vehicles per Day: 2000 north of Manjimup

Regions Traversed: The South-West, Coastal Plain

PEMBERTON (Alt Pop 1000):* interesting timber town and tourist centre. For more information see Day 5. (*0/160*) Head **NE** for South-West Hwy junction.

Undulating country* supports jarrah and karri forests.

South-West Highway junction: (*16/144*) Turn **N** for Manjimup. *Turn **SW** for Pemberton.*

Diamond Tree:* tall (51m) karri tree once used as a fire tower, which can be climbed. **Rest area** adjacent. (*22/138*)

MANJIMUP (Alt Pop 5000): large timber town and farming centre. Worth seeing: Manjimup Timber Park** (walking trails, picnic areas, fire tower lookout, historical hamlet, timber museum, Bunnings Age of Steam Museum), Forests Visitor Centre* (historical displays). Full town facilities. (*31/129*)

A 46km return journey along the sealed Ralston and Graphite Road leads to One Tree Bridge*, an attractive picnic area set with karri forests. Nearby is Glenoran Pool and the Four Aces*, four impressive tall karri trees in a row - walking trail. Three kilometres off the highway, along Perup Road, is the King Jarrah Tree*, a big old jarrah estimated to be 500 years old. Picnic area and walking trail. The turnoffs are 1km north of town along the highway.

Palgarup: small timber mill township. No facilities. (*41/119*)

Undulating country is utilised for grazing. At the Donnelly River crossing is the old Donnelly Well*, a pioneer watering place. (*53/107*)

Hilly country has been mostly cleared for grazing. Good views*.

BRIDGETOWN (Alt 155m; Pop 2150):** probably the most attractive town in the South-West, set deep within the Blackwood River valley. Interesting main street with photogenic buildings. Worth seeing: Blackwod River Park* (**rest area**, picnicing, canoeing), Suttons Lookout*, Local History Collection at the Tourist Office, St Pauls Church*, Bridgedale House - historic cottage, and Blackwood River Railway Bridge*. Full town facilities. (*68/92*) *Road Trip 33 connects.*

Accommodation
Nelsons of Bridgetown Motel, 38 Hampton St, ©08 9761 1641, ○$70-$160
Bridgetown Caravan Park, South-Western Hwy (1.5kmW), ©08 9761 1053, ○Site: $17 Van: $35-$40

Hilly country offers good views*.

Undulating country supports jarrah forests and grazing lands.

Greenbushes turnoff: (*85/75*) Turn here for the old tin mining town of **Greenbushes** (Alt 289m; Pop 400)*. The Greenbushes Historic Park* has relics from the old tin mines. A viewing platform overlooks the open cut mine. Heritage trails. Accommodation, store, fuel.

Hilly country supports jarrah forests and pine plantations. Occasional good views*.

Balingup (Pop 150):* attractive small town with some historic buildings. Worth seeing: Ballingup Pool, the oak trees in the Avenue of Remembrance*. Numerous arts and craft shops. Accommodation, stores, fuel. (*94/66*)

Mullalyup: roadhouse facility and historic hamlet. Nearby is the old Blackwood Inn* and a war memorial. Store, fuel. (*100/60*)

Undulating country has been mostly cleared for farming.

Kirup: small farming and timber township. Enquire locally about access to Kirup Falls. Store, fuel. (*107/53*)

Low hills have been mostly cleared for farming, grazing, and orchards near Donnybrook. Patches of jarrah forests remain.

DONNYBROOK (Alt 63m; Pop 1650):* interesting orcharding and farming town. Many historic buildings, such as the Anchor and Hope Inn and the Anglican Church. Picnic area at Trigwell Place at the southern end of town. Canoeing on the Preston River. **Rest area**. Full town facilities. (*124/36*)

Road Trip 34

PEMBERTON

16

0:25   South-West
RA   Highway Jctn

15

MANJIMUP

0:25   37

BRIDGE-
RA   TOWN

26

Balingup

6

Mullalyup

7

1:10   Kirup

17

DONNY-
RA   BROOK

15

Boyanup
RA

21

BUNBURY

DAY SIX

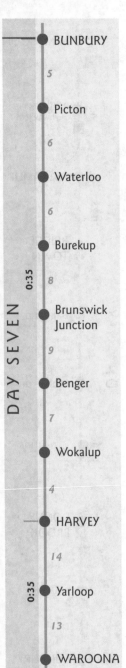

Undulating country supports jarrah forests interspersed with orchards. Fair views.

Boyanup: pleasant small farming township. Boyanup Transport Museum* (trains, cars, farm machinery) worth seeing. Store, fuel (*139/21*)

Plains have been cleared for farmlands.

BUNBURY (Alt 4m; Pop 25000):* large regional centre. For more information see Road Trip 33, Day 1. (*160/0*) *Road Trip 33 connects.*

DAY 7: BUNBURY-PERTH via Pinjarra

Road to Take: South-Western Highway
Grade 1
Total Distance: 185km (2:25)
Intermediate Distances:

	Km	Hours
Bunbury-Harvey	45	(0:35)
Harvey-Pinjarra	53	(0:35)
Pinjarra-Perth	87	(1:15)

Average Vehicles per Day: 5000 south of Byford
Regions Traversed: Coastal Plain

BUNBURY (Alt 4m; Pop 25000):* large regional centre. For more information see Road Trip 33, Day 1. (*0/185*)

Picton: outer suburb of Bunbury. Store, fuel. (*5/180*)

Waterloo: roadhouse facility. Store, fuel. (*11/174*)

Plains support farming country.

Burekup: roadhouse facility. Store, fuel. (*17/168*)

Roelands: farming locality.

Brunswick Junction (Alt 32m; Pop 850):* pleasant small farming town set on the Brunswick River. Of interest is the Cow Statue and Brunswick Pool* - swimming, picnic area. (*25/160*)

Plains support grazing country.

Benger: roadhouse facility. Store, fuel. (*34/151*)

Plains support grazing country. Eastward views.

Wokalup: small township with an interesting pub*. Accommodation, store, fuel. (*41/144*)

HARVEY (Alt 37m; Pop 2570):* pretty farming and irrigation town. Worth seeing: Stirling Cottage (local history display), Internment Camp Shrine*, Harvey Historical Museum*, picnic areas at Apex Park, Stirling Park and Snell Park. Full town facilities. (*45/140*)

Undulating country supports grazing country.

Yarloop: * interesting old timber township. Worth seeing is the Yarloop Workshop Museum*, heritage walk. Two kilometres southwest, on Clifton Road, is Yarloop Pool - swimming, picnic area. Stores, fuel. (*59/126*)

Undulating country supports farmland. Reasonable views.

WAROONA (Pop 1850):* pleasant small dairying and farming town set on low hills. Worth seeing: Drakebrook Weir* - swimming, canoeing, picnic area. Enquire locally about bushwalking trails. Full town facilities. (*72/113*)

Plains support farmlands. Eastward views*.

Coolup: small farming township. Store, fuel. (*85/100*)

Placid Park: roadhouse facility. Store, fuel. (*88/97*)

Plains support farmlands. Eastward views towards the Darling Range escarpment. Old Blythwood* historic property is passed en route.

PINJARRA (Alt 10m; Pop 1900):* interesting historic town set on the banks of the Murray River. Worth seeing: Edenvale historic house*, Heritage Rose Garden*, Pioneer Memorial Park* on the banks of the river - picnic area, Pinjarra Heritage Trail*, Hotham Valley Railway** (steam train rides to Dewellingup), Suspension Bridge, St John's Church. Full town facilities. (*98/87*)

Accommodation
Pinjarra Motel, South-Western Hwy (1kmS), ©08 9531 1811, ✪$60-$80
Pinjarra Caravan Park, Lot 95 Pinjarra Rd (2kmW), ©08 9531 1374, ✪Site: $16 Van: $50-$60

Turn here for the 23km sealed drive to **Dwellingup** (Alt 264m; Pop 400)*, a pleasant timber town set within the jarrah forests. Many things to see including the Dwellingup History and Visitors Centre*, Forest Heritage Centre* (displays, short walking trail), old Dwellingup Railway Station** (picnic area, Hotham Valley Railway depot, Etmilyn Forest Tramway terminus), Dwellingup Pharmacy Museum*. Accommodation, stores, fuel.

North Dandalup: farming township. Store, fuel. (*114/71*)

Plains and low rises offer views* across grazing country and the Darling Range escarpment. Attractive Christmas trees (short trees in otherwise bare paddocks) flower in early summer.

Keysbrook: small township. Store, fuel. (*123/62*)

Serpentine (Alt 32m): small rural township (the main body of the settlement is located west of the highway). Worth seeing: Turner Cottage (historic house, family park and mini-railway) and the Tractor and Machinery Museum*. Caravan Park nearby. A short distance away is Serpentine Falls. Store, fuel. (*132/53*)

Plains and low rises support grazing and mixed farming. Eastward views* towards the Darling Range escarpment. Tumbulgum Farm (large rammed earth-building, numerous other attractions) is passed en route.

Byford (Alt 62m): small rural township and growing suburb. Store, fuel. (*148/37*)

ARMADALE (Alt 55m): outer Perth suburb. Worth seeing: Armadale Reptile and Wildlife Centre*, Enchanted Forest of Light* (pixie lights - nighttime only), History House Museum*, Minnawarra Historic Precinct. Full town facilities. (*156/29*)

Accommodation
Heritage Country Motel, Cnr South-Western/Albany Hwys, ©08 9399 5122, ✪$80
Hillside Garden Caravan Park, 270 South-Western Hwy (2kmS), ©08 9399 6376, ✪Site: $18 Van: $45

The route between Armadale and Perth forms a part of the Perth suburban area. Follow South-Western Highway (Armadale Road) to the Causeway (*182/3*); turn **W** for Perth City.

PERTH (Alt 19m; Pop 1097000):** state capital of Western Australia. For more information see Road Trip 33, Day 1. (*185/0*) *Road Trips 28, 29 and 33 connect.*

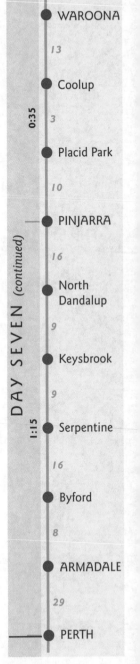

DAY SEVEN (continued)

WAROONA
13
Coolup
0:35   3
Placid Park
10
PINJARRA
16
North Dandalup
9
Keysbrook
9
Serpentine
16
1:15   Byford
8
ARMADALE
29
PERTH

Road Trip 35
Nullarbor Crossing

Norseman-Port Augusta
Total Distance: 1687km
Suggested Travelling Time: 4 days

> *Conquer the mighty Nullarbor*
>
> See the Newman rocks outcrop, isolated roadhouses, Madura Pass, Eucla Pass, Head of Bight, the wheat-farming town of Penong, Ceduna on Murat Bay, Mt Wudinna, the Gawler Ranges Historic Museum at Kimba, the Mining Museum at Iron Knob, and the contrasting landscapes of the Nullarbor Cliffs and the Nullarbor Plain.

The Nullarbor

The Nullarbor holds a certain mystique for Australians: it denotes the great Australian emptiness. As a major geographical barrier that divides eastern and western Australia, it makes Western Australians feel separated from the Eastern States, as though they are a different people, as if the state were another country. This feeling is tangible and Western Australians, more than any other Australians, see it in this light. Blame it on the Nullarbor. The Nullarbor is not an empty region though; it is simply a vast area of arid country that is similar in extent and aridity to many other Australian regions. It is definitely worth experiencing.

The Climate

The climate of the Nullarbor and northern Eyre Peninsula is mostly a semi-arid one with hot, dry summers and mild, occasionally showery winters. Summer temperatures can be very hot (up to the mid-forties) but these days are always relieved, eventually, by cool changes bringing cloudy skies and drizzle, and making daytime temperatures drop to the low twenties. Nights correspond to the days: warm nights follow hot days and cool nights follow mild days.

Winter sees days of sunshine with cool winds and showers, or days of cloud with drizzle. Maximum temperatures range from the mid-teens to high teens; minimum temperatures from 0C to 8C. The best time to travel this area is in autumn (clear, still days) or spring (light winds, green tinges in the landscape).

Capital City Connections
Distances in kilometres
SYDNEY-PORT AUGUSTA
via Great Western/Mitchell/Barrier Highways/
Route 56

	Intermediate	Total
Sydney	0	0
Nyngan	578	578
Cobar	131	709
Broken Hill	444	1153
Peterborough	284	1437
Port Augusta	131	1568

MELBOURNE-PORT AUGUSTA
via Western/Dukes Highways/Highway 1

	Intermediate	Total
Melbourne	0	0
Ballarat	111	111
Horsham	188	299
Adelaide	432	731
Port Pirie	215	946
Port Augusta	97	1043

PERTH-NORSEMAN
via Great Eastern/Coolgardie-Esperance
Highways

	Intermediate	Total
Perth	0	0
Northam	98	98
Merredin	163	261
Coolgardie	295	556
Norseman	168	724

The Route
Distances in kilometres

	Intermediate	Total
Norseman	0	0
Balladonia	193	193
Eucla	522	715

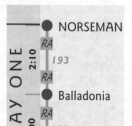

Ceduna	495	1210
Wudinna	211	1421
Port Augusta	257	1687

DAY ONE
2:10 · RA · 193 · RA
2:00 · RA · 182 · RA

NORSEMAN

Balladonia

Caiguna

Eyre Highway
Norseman-Port Augusta

The Eyre Highway is the major and only readily accessible route between the southern portions of South and Western Australia. While no longer a rugged adventure, today's crossing on the all-sealed road is still a major travelling experience, particularly for those people crossing the Nullarbor for the first time. While the route cannot boast a major hill, and flat to slightly undulating landscapes are the order of the day, there are some dramatic surprises, the Nullarbor cliffs being one. Elsewhere are more subdued but still interesting features, such as the treeless section of the Nullarbor Plain, limestone caves, giant sand patches, rocky gullies, old ruins, attractive woodlands, areas of uninhabited country, and so on. Also of note is the longest length of straight roadway in the world - about 145km!

East of Nundroo the countryside changes into one of broadacre farmlands characteristic of the northern Eyre Peninsula.

Give the Eyre Highway the time it deserves. If driven too fast, this crossing will seem boring. It is the little things that make the seemingly mediocre country interesting. By slowing down you will not miss them.

> **Warnings:** beware of stock, kangaroos, camels and wombats at night.
> **Note:** if visiting the cliff side lookouts between Border Village and Nullarbor Roadhouse, stand well back in strong winds. Visit only sign-posted lookouts; other tracks to the cliff tops may be sandy. All lookouts are about a kilometre or so from the highway. These lookouts provide good spots for whale and seal watching.
> **Also note** that sections of the highway are used as emergency landing strips for the Flying Doctor - heed appropriate warnings.

DAY 1: NORSEMAN-CAIGUNA via Balladonia

Road to Take: Eyre Highway
Grade 1
Total Distance: 375km (4:10)
Intermediate Distances:

	Km	Hours
Norseman-Balladonia	193	(2:10)
Balladonia-Caiguna	182	(2:00)

Average Vehicles per Day: 400 west of Balladonia
Regions Traversed: Goldfields, Nullarbor Plain

NORSEMAN (Alt 278m; Pop 1500):* old mining town. For more information see Road Trip 34, Day 2. (*0/375*) *Road Trip 34 connects.*

Jimberlana Hill: interesting lookout just off the road. Good views* over Lake Cowan. (*7/368*)
Undulating country* supports an attractive woodland of salmon gums. Two **rest areas** are near Southern Hills Station turnoff. (*83/292*)
Fraser Range: low range of hills rising above the general level of the plains. Good views from the tops of ridges (you will need to walk) of a vast, seemingly endless blue-grey scrub.
Old road* south of today's highway offers the chance for a quiet bushwalk. Interesting rocky hills form part of the Fraser Range. (*105/270*)
Low hill offers reasonable westward views towards the Fraser Range. Wildflowers may be seen in this area. **Emergency telephone**. (*108/267*) Keep an eye out for the turnoff (*140/235, N*) to Newman Rocks* (4km return): interesting rocky outcrops and granite sheets. Rockholes of water after rain. A pretty area worth investigating. Salmon gum woodlands are common.
Undulating country* presents the traveller with far-reaching views along the highway. Salmon gum woodlands abound, attractive in the afternoon light. Adjacent to the road are numerous claypans. This very photogenic area is worth exploring on foot, but park well off the road. Be-

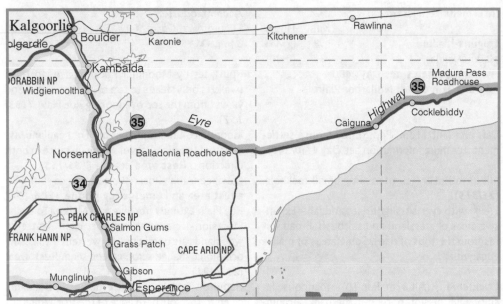

Detail of MAP 8

yond the road lies uninhabited wilderness country. **Rest area**. (*166/209*)

Balladonia (Alt 153m; Pop 10):* roadhouse facility in an attractive setting. Note the time zone boundary: add 3/4 hr heading west, lose 3/4 heading east. (This part of the Eyre Highway, between the state border and Balladonia, runs on Central-Western Time). Accommodation, store, fuel. (*193/182*)

Accommodation
Balladonia Hotel-Motel, Eyre Hwy, ©08 9039 3453, ✪$80
Balladonia Caravan Facility, Eyre Hwy, ©08 90339 3453, ✪Site: $18

Undulating country: if coming from the east this will seem like hilly country! The country hereabout is granite, and occasional rocky outcrops may be seen. Vegetation is a eucalypt woodland dominated by salmon gums, with a shrubby understorey that includes saltbush. Long vistas down the road.
Ruins of an old telegraph station are visible from road. (*221/154*)
Plains with ever-so-slight rises and falls. On the rises grows an open woodland dominated by sugarwoods, with a saltbush understorey. On the falls is open saltbush country. Two **rest areas**. (*241/134* and *301/74*)
Emergency telephone and **rest area** situated virtually in the middle of what is the longest straight stretch of roadway in the world: approximately 145km. Uninhabited country hereabout. (*318/57*)
Plains support sugarwood woodlands with some mallee eucalypt shrublands near Caiguna. Two **rest areas**. (*336/39* and *323/52*)
Blowhole:* underground cavity and opening set within the limestone plain, located 10m off the side of the road. (*370/5*)

Caiguna (Alt 113m; Pop 5): roadhouse facility with friendly birdlife. Accommodation, store, fuel. (*375/0*)

DAY 2: CAIGUNA-EUCLA via Madura

Road to Take: Eyre Highway
Grade 1
Total Distance: 340km (3:45)

Road Trip 35

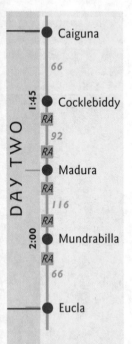

DAY TWO

1:45

2:00

- Caiguna
- 66
- Cocklebiddy
  - RA
  - 92
  - RA
- Madura
  - RA
  - 116
  - RA
- Mundrabilla
  - RA
  - 66
- Eucla

Intermediate Distances:

	Km	Hours
Caiguna-Madura	158	(1:45)
Madura-Eucla	182	(2:00)

Average Vehicles per Day: 400
Regions Traversed: Nullarbor Plain

Caiguna (Alt 113m; Pop 5): roadhouse settlement. For more information see Day 1. (*0/340*)

Jillbunya Rockhole: interesting small rockhole. (*21/319*)
Plains with ever-so-slight rises and falls. Expansive areas of grassland and saltbush. Broad vistas from the tops of rises. Some areas of mallee eucalypts.

Cocklebiddy (Alt 82m; Pop 10):* roadhouse facility. Old mission ruins out the back. Accommodation, store, fuel. (*66/274*)

Accommodation
Wedgetail Inn, Eyre Hwy, ©08 9039 3462, ✪$55-$80
Cocklebiddy Caravan Facility, Eyre Hwy, ©08 9039 3462, ✪Site: $16

Moonera Tank: earth dam. **Rest area**. (*110/230*)
Claypans occupy the lower portions of the plain, their surfaces covered in saltbush. Elsewhere are extensive tracts of eucalypt mallee shrublands. Plains support tracts of mallee. **Rest area**. (*132/208*)
Lookout* at the top of Madura Pass provides good views overlooking the Roe Plain. **Rest area** adjacent. (*157/183*)

Madura (Alt 21m; Pop 10): roadhouse set at the base of the Baxter Cliffs. An interesting walk can be taken along the old narrow-sealed Madura Pass* - good views from top of the escarpment. The Pass leaves the highway just east of the settlement. Western myalls are common. Woodlands on the base of the escarpment take advantage of run-off from a nearby hillslope. Accommodation, store, fuel. (*158/182*)

Accommodation
Madura Pass Oasis Motel, Eyre Hwy, ©08 9039 3464, ✪$95

Ruin* set by Moondini Rockhole; rough track (walkers only) leads to top of escarpment. Good views* from the top overlooking Roe Plain. (*183/157*)
Moondini Bluff: prominent bluff or headland visible from the highway for a long distance in both directions. **Rest area** nearby. (*185/155*)
Carlabeencabba Rockhole: quite a nice spot with a **rest area** and **emergency phone**. (*206/134*)
Roe Plain extends from west of Madura to Eucla. Occasional claypans may be seen. Scattered woodlands are dominated by western myalls. The occasional mallee scrub can be seen. **Rest area**. (*219/121*)
Hampton Tableland lies to the north, the name given to the southern edge of the true Nullarbor Plain. Claypans, caves, sinkholes and rockholes are common, set upon or within limestone rock. The tableland edge is marked by rocky limestone outcrops. Mallee scrubs are common. The escarpment is referred to as the Baxter Cliffs, and forms part of the presumed longest unbroken cliffline in the world (375km). Numerous limestone outcrops and bluffs are passed, as well as minor rocky creeklines.
Jillah Rockhole: small rockhole. **Rest area**. (*261/79*)
Kuthala Pass: rough walking trail to top of Hampton Tableland. Good views*. (*271/69*)

Mundrabilla (Alt 27m; Pop 5):* roadhouse facility with an interesting aviary and murals. Accommodation, store, fuel. (*274/66*)

Accommodation
Mundrabilla Motor Hotel, Eyre Hwy, ©08 9039 3465, ✪$60
Mundrabilla Caravan Facility, Eyre Hwy, ©08 9039 3465, ✪Site: $13

Plains support tracts of western myall. Northwards views towards the Baxter Cliffs.
Najada Rockhole: small rockhole. **Rest area**. (*304/36*)

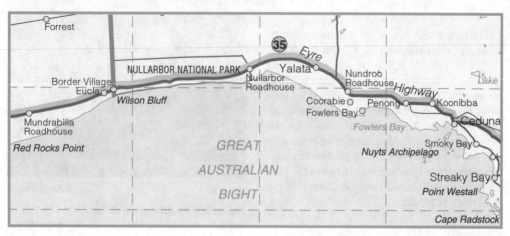

Detail of MAP 5

Ruin:* remains of old stone building. A good views over Roe Plain from near the ruin. Beware of the deep, uncovered well. Fair views eastward along the highway towards the white Eucla dunes (Delisser Sandhills). (*320/20*)

Eucla National Park preserves the old telegraph township of Eucla and surrounding sand dunes. Ruins* of the former telegraph station are now mostly covered by sand. The old stone buildings are very photogenic. About a kilometre away on the coast (walk slightly west of south) are the remains of the old Eucla jetty*. A stroll through the dunes is interesting, especially in the early morning (before footprints mar the landscape). Note the interesting ripple patterns in the sand. Looking inland from atop a high dune towards the Baxter Cliffs and Roe Plain provides awesome views*. (*335/5*)

Eucla Pass:* interesting rocky valley through which the highway ascends/descends the Baxter Cliffs. The illuminated white cross nearby is dedicated to all Christians.

Eucla (Alt 87m; Pop 30):* large roadhouse settlement, virtually a township. Good views* from the settlement overlooking the Roe Plain and Delisser Sandhills. Visit the museum* at the motel. Accommodation, store, fuel. (*340/0*)

Accommodation
Eucla Motor Hotel, Eyre Hwy, ©08 9039 3468, ✪$70-$80
Eucla Caravan Park, Eyre Hwy, ©08 9039 3468, ✪Site: $12

Eucla telegraph station ruins, Eucla, WA

DAY 3: EUCLA-CEDUNA
via Nullarbor Roadhouse

Road to Take: Eyre Highway
Grade 1
Total Distance: 495km (5:30)
Intermediate Distances:

	Km	Hours
Eucla-Nullarbor Roadhouse	198	(2:10)
Nullarbor Roadhouse-Penong	224	(2:30)
Penong-Ceduna	73	(0:50)

Average Vehicles per Day: 500 near Nundroo
Regions Traversed: Nullarbor Plain, Eyre Peninsula

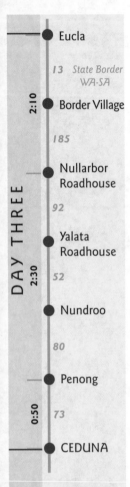

DAY THREE

- **Eucla**
- 2:10
- *13 State Border WA-SA*
- **Border Village**
- *185*
- **Nullarbor Roadhouse**
- *92*
- 2:30
- **Yalata Roadhouse**
- *52*
- **Nundroo**
- *80*
- **Penong**
- 0:50
- *73*
- **CEDUNA**

Eucla (Alt 87m; Pop 30):* roadhouse settlement. For more information see Day 2. (*0/495*)

State Border between South Australia and Western Australia. Agricultural check point for travellers heading west - no fruit or vegetables beyond this point. The crossing is somewhat akin to a customs post. Also time zone boundary: add 3/4 hr heading west, lose 3/4 heading east. (This part of the Eyre Highway, between the state border and Balladonia, runs on Central-Western Time). (*13/482*)

Border Village (Alt 95m; Pop 5): roadhouse facility set right on the state border. Main feature is a giant red kangaroo. Accommodation, store, fuel. (*13/482*)

Nullarbor National Park: large national park of former grazing leases, conserving the southern portion of the Nullarbor Plain.
Lookout: good views* overlooking the Great Australian Bight and the large dunes called the Merdayerrah Sandpatch. (*26/469*)
Plains form the southern part of the Nullarbor Plain. The vegetation here is dominated by mallee eucalypts and quite dense due to its proximity to the ocean. Stunted shrubs are near the cliff top. Wildflowers are often seen in this area.
Lookout:* expansive views from atop a high cliff, overlooking the southern margin of the Nullarbor Plain. Its a sheer 85m drop to ocean, so stand well back in winds. (*55/440*)
Diamond Bore: locality only. **Emergency telephone**. (*73/422*)
Lookout: excellent views** of cliffline and ocean. Very dangerous sheer drop. This is a powerful place. (*88/407*)
Lookout:* good views overlooking the Great Australian Bight. Beware of strong winds. (*117/378*)
Lookout:* good views of cliffline and ocean. Be careful in winds. **Emergency phone** nearby. (*146/349*)
Plains support a shrubland of mallee eucalypts.
Plains support a low shrubland of saltbush. This is part of the true treeless Nullarbor Plain.

Nullarbor cliffs, SA

Nullarbor Roadhouse (Alt 78m; Pop 10):* small settlement set upon the treeless Nullarbor Plain, marked by a Big Whale. Centre for the adjacent Nullarbor National Park; make enquiries here about access to Murrawijinia Cave* and the condition of the old (unsealed) Eyre Highway that leads to Bunabie Blowhole and Koonalda Cave. Accommodation, store, fuel. (*198/297*)

Accommodation

Nullarbor Hotel-Motel, Eyre Hwy, ©08 8625 6271, ✪$85
Nullarbor Caravan Park, Eyre Hwy, ©08 8625 6271, ✪Site: $10 Van: $30

Plains covered with saltbush offer expansive views*. Here, and west of Nullarbor, is the only stretch of treeless plain on the highway. The plain has slight rises and falls producing an undulating effect. Vast vistas from the tops of rises, including the vivid white sand patch of the head of the bight.
Yalata Aboriginal Land: no permit required for access.
Head of Bight access road turnoff: locality only; no facilities. (*212/283*) Turn **S** for the 24km return sealed access road to the Head of the Bight*. Access to beach and cliffs. Whale watching** in winter (May to October). Offshore is the Great Australian Bight Marine Park. A permit is required, obtainable at White Well: ranger station, Nullarbor Roadhouse, Yalata Roadhouse, Ceduna tourist centre.
Dick Plain tower: emergency telephone. (*257/238*)

Undulating country is formed by old limestone dune ridges. The countryside is dominated by a eucalypt shrubland of mallees with a shrubby understorey, notably saltbush.

High ridge* presents a long vista westward down the road. From its base, looking eastward, the ridges appear as a high hill.

Yalata Roadhouse (Alt 110m; Pop 5):* Aboriginal-owned roadhouse set among the old limestone dune ridges. Artefacts for sale. Enquire about access to coastal fishing spots - permit required. Accommodation, store, fuel. (*290/205*)

Plains and low rises covered with large mallee eucalypts. Long road vistas from tops of rises. Eastward the country is cleared for grazing.

Nundroo (Alt 35m; Pop 20): roadhouse facility set upon a cleared plain used for grazing. A few stone ruins are located west of the roadhouse. Enquire here about access to coastal fishing areas at Scotts and Mexican Hat Beaches. Accommodation, store, fuel. (*342/153*)

Accommodation
Nundroo Hotel-Motel, Eyre Hwy, ©08 8625 6120, ©$75
Nundroo Caravan Park, Eyre Hwy, ©08 8625 6120, ©Site: $15

Undulating country offers vast views from the tops of rises. Northward are occasional glimpses of uncleared country, the southernmost dunefields of the Great Victoria Desert. Countryside is used for grazing and some cropping.
Bookabie: locality only, no facilities. A few stone ruins dot the plain.

Penong (Alt 25m; Pop 250):* small attractive wheat-farming town. Many interesting stone buildings to see. Numerous transportable windmills surround the town, extracting water from the limestone beneath. The Woolshed Museum is worth visiting. South of town on a good unsealed road (42km return) is Point Sinclair*, an attrac-

tive bay and jetty (fishing). Nearby is Cactus Beach*, a famous surfing beach located in a spectacular setting; worth visiting - basic camping available. Accommodation, store fuel. (*422/73*)

Accommodation
Penong Hotel, Eyre Hwy, ©08 8625 1050, ©$45

Undulating country supports broadacre wheat farms. Little natural vegetation remains except for the mallee eucalypts growing along the road reserves.

Agricultural Check Point: agricultural check point. No fruit, vegetables or plants to be carried eastwards.

CEDUNA (Alt 5m; Pop 2900):* major town of Eyre Peninsula's west coast. An attractive place with white stone buildings* set beside Murat Bay. The adjacent park* is pleasant. Nearby is the port and older style settlement of Thevenard (the local fishing spot), worth a quick visit for views* back towards Ceduna. Also see the Big Oyster and Old Schoolhouse Museum. Full town facilities. (*495/0*)

Accommodation
East West Motel, 66 McKenzie St, ©08 8625 2101, ©$75-$90
Highway One Motel, Eyre Hwy (2kmEW), ©08 8625 2208, ©$55-$70
Ceduna Foreshore Community Hotel-Motel, South Tce, ©08 8625 2008, ©$65-$85
Pine Grove Motel, 49 McKenzie St, ©08 8625 2201, ©$65
Ceduna Caravan Park, 29 McKenzie St, ©08 8625 2150, ©Site: $22 Van: $30-$55
Ceduna Foreshore Caravan Park, South Tce, ©08 8625 2290, ©Site: $18 Van: $40-$65
Ceduna Shelly Beach Caravan Park, Decres Bay Rd (3kmE), ©08 8625 2012, ©Site: $14 Van: $50-$70
Ceduna Airport Caravan Park, Eyre Hwy, ©08 8625 2416, ©Site: 12 Van: $25-$40

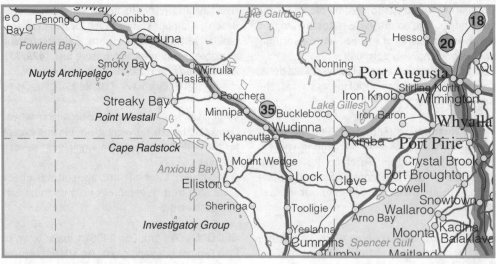

Detail of MAP 5

DAY 4: CEDUNA-PORT AUGUSTA
via Kimba

Road to Take: Eyre Highway
Grade 1
Total Distance: 468km (5:15)
Intermediate Distances:

	Km	Hours
Ceduna-Wirrulla	93	(1:00)
Wirrulla-Wudinna	118	(1:20)
Wudinna-Kimba	102	(1:10)
Kimba-Iron Knob	89	(1:00)
Iron Knob-Port Augusta	66	(0:45)

Average Vehicles per Day: 660 east of Kimba
Regions Traversed: Eyre Peninsula

CEDUNA (Alt 5m; Pop 2900):* farming town and coastal community. For more information see Day 3. (*0/468*)

Kongwirra Hill: notable if only for its Telecom tower. Vast views westward towards Ceduna.
Undulating country supports broadacre farmlands. The area is virtually devoid of natural vegetation, except along road reserves.

Wirrulla (Alt 78m; Pop 50): small wheat-farming township and railway station. Accommodation, store, fuel. (*93/375*)

Yantanabie: railway siding, no facilities. (*106/362*)
Cungena: railway siding, no facilities. (*120/348*)

Poochera (Alt 82m; Pop 50): small wheat-farming township. Accommodation, store, fuel. (*140/328*)

Low rises support broadacre farmlands. Little natural vegetation remains except along the roadside. Mallee eucalypts are dominant.
Karcultaby: railway siding and school; no facilities. (*153/315*)
Condada: farming locality; no facilities. (*162/306*)

Minnipa (Alt 149m; Pop 190): small wheat-farming township. **Rest area**. A 30km return unsealed drive north of town leads to the interesting Yarwondutta Rock* and the 'wave-like' granite formation of Pildappa Rock, with a picnic area adjacent. Accommodation, store, fuel. (*173/295*)
Accommodation
Minnipa Hotel-Motel, Railway Tce, ©08 8680 5005, ◎$50-$70

Minnipa Hotel Caravan Park, Eyre Hwy, ©08 8680 5175, ◎Site: $10

Yaninee: railway siding, no facilities. Interersting Lutheran Church*. Nearby, to the south, is the saltlake Lake Yaninee. (*189/279*)

Wudinna (Alt 88m; Pop 650): small wheat-farming town, larger than most in this part of the country. Accommodation, store, fuel. (*211/257*)
Accommodation
Gawler Ranges Motel, Eyre Hwy, ©08 8680 2090, ◎$60-$80
Wudinna Hotel-Motel, Burton Tce, ©08 8680 2019, ◎$45
Gawler Ranges Caravan Park, Eyre Hwy, ©08 8680 2090, ◎Site: $18 Van: $35

A 26km unsealed loop road leads **N** to the interesting granite outcrops of Polda Rock*, Little Mt Wudinna*, Turtle Rock*, Pygery Rocks*, and Mt Wudinna** - follow the sign-posted route. Mt Wudinna (261m) is the second largest granite outcrop in Australia. Excellent views from the sides and top. To the north lies the peaks of the Gawler Ranges. Elsewhere are vast expanses of wheatbelt, very attractive after winter rains. Picnic facilities and shade at base.

Lake Wannamana: saltlake lying south of the road.

Kyancutta (Alt 58m; Pop 30): small farming township. Polkdinney Park is a pleasant **rest area**. Store, fuel. (*224/244*)

Undulating country supports broadacre wheat farms. Fair to good views* from the tops of rises of occasional granite outcrops. Very attractive country after winter rains.
Koongawa: locality only, no facilities. South of the road nearby, a monument commemorates the death of explorer John Drake in 1844. Of interest is the granitic Waddikee Rocks*, with a good view from the top of the rise. There are interesting crystals in the rock, which is 2.4 billion years old! (*255/213*)

Kimba (Alt 263m; Pop 800): small wheat-farming town. Worth seeing: the Big Galah - you can not miss it, Halfway-Across-Australia* sign, Kimba and Gawler Ranges Historic Museum** (one of the best), Lions Memorial Park and Apex Central Park. Enquire about the Roora Walking Trail* leading to White Knob Lookout. Accommodation, store, fuel. (*313/155*)
Accommodation
Kimba Community Hotel-Motel, High St, ©08 8627 2310, ◎$70
Kimba Motel Roadhouse, Eyre Hwy (1kmW), ©08 8627 2040, ◎$70
Kimba Motel Caravan Park, Eyre Hwy (1kmW), ©08 8627 2092, ◎Site: $14 Van: $30-$35

Undulating plains support wheat cropping, land formerly covered in mallee eucalypts.
Lake Gilles Conservation Park: large wilderness park conserving numerous plant and animal species. Mallee eucalypts dominate the countryside, covering an area of longitudinal sand dunes. Limited 4WD access to Lake Gilles saltpan. No facilities.
Undulating country supports mallee eucalypts. Long distance views along the road from the tops of rises. Views include Middleback Ranges, visible to the east.

Iron Knob (Alt 180m; Pop 330):* small former iron ore mining town of some character situated at the foot of the Middleback Ranges. Good views northward, in the late afternoon light, towards the Gawler Ranges. Worth seeing: BHP Mining Museum*. Accommodation, store, fuel. (*402/66*)
Accommodation
Iron Knob Roadhouse Motel, Eyre Hwy, ©08 8646 2058, ◎$35

Undulating country covered with low saltbush shrubs offer vast vistas*. Distant ranges on the skyline. At intervals, groves of western myalls may be seen.
Pandurra Station: caravan park and camping area. Station tours are available. (*431/37*)

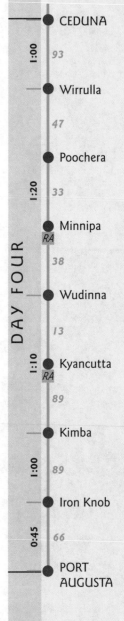

Road Trip 35

DAY FOUR

1:00	CEDUNA
93	
	Wirrulla
47	
1:20	Poochera
33	
	Minnipa
RA	
38	
	Wudinna
13	
1:10	Kyancutta
RA	
89	
	Kimba
1:00	89
	Iron Knob
0:45	66
	PORT AUGUSTA

Hilly country lines the road either side of Lincoln Gap. Good views* northward towards the head of Spencer Gulf and the western ramparts of the Flinders Ranges.

Undulating country provides broad vistas* eastwards towards the Flinders Ranges. Goat Hill (275m) lies to the west.

PORT AUGUSTA (Alt 5m; Pop 14600):* large regional and industrial centre. For more information see Road Trip 14, Day 4. (*468/0*) *Road Trips 14, 17, 18 and 20 connect.*

Connecting Routes

Connecting Route A
SYDNEY-GILGANDRA
via Bathurst, Dubbo

Roads to Take: Great Western, Mitchell & Newell Highways
Grade I
Total Distance: 506km (6:05)
Intermediate Distances:

	Km	Hours
Sydney-Bathurst	219	(2:50)
Bathurst-Dubbo	230	(2:30)
Dubbo-Gilgandra	65	(0:45)

Regions Traversed: Sydney region, Blue Mountains, Central Tablelands, Central-West
Facilities en route:

SYDNEY: state capital of New South Wales - full town facilities. (*0/506*) Take the Great Western Hwy **W** for Bathurst.
Glenbrook: outer Sydney suburb - stores, fuel. (*74/432*)
Blaxland: outer Sydney suburb - full town facilities. (*76/430*)
Numerous settlements line the route until Mt Victoria.
Rest area at Bulls Camp. (*92/414*)
Rest area/lookout at Mt Boyce - highest point on road: 1093m. (*131/375*)
Mt Victoria: mountain town - accommodation, stores, fuel. (*137/369*)
Hartley: historic township - store, fuel. (*146/360*)
Lithgow turnoff: large town - full town facilities. (*157/349*)
Rest area near Wallerawang turnoff. (*168/338*)
Meadow Flat: locality. (*187/319*)
Yetholme: locality. (*197/309*)
Kelso: township - store, fuel. (*216/290*)
BATHURST: regional centre - full town facilities. (*219/287*) *Connecting Route F connects.* Take

the Mitchel Hwy **W** for Orange. *Take the Great Western Hwy **E** for Sydney.*
Rest area at The Rocks. (*237/269*)
Lucknow: historic township - store, fuel. (*261/245*)
ORANGE: regional centre - full town facilities. (*272/234*)
Molong: country town - full town facilities. (*310/196*)
Rest area at Cundumbul. (*340/166*)
Rest area near Wellington Caves turnoff. (*369/137*)
Wellington: country town - full town facilities. (*378/128*)
Geurie: township - accommodation, store, fuel. (*399/107*)
Rest area west of Geurie. (*401/105*)
DUBBO: regional centre - full town facilities. (*449/57*) *Connecting Route E connects.* Take the Newell Hwy **N** for Gilgandra. *Take the Mitchell Hwy **S** for Orange.*
Talbragar: township - store, fuel. (*456/50*)
Eumungerie turnoff (**E**): township - store, fuel. (*479/27*)
Gilgandra: country town - full town facilities. For more information see Road Trip 2. (*506/0*) *Road Trip 2 connects. Take the Newell Hwy **S** for Dubbo.*

Connecting Route B
BRISBANE-ROCKHAMPTON
via Gympie

Road to Take: Bruce Highway
Grade I
Total Distance: 644km (7:40)
Intermediate Distances:

	Km	Hours
Brisbane-Gympie	162	(2:10)
Gympie-Maryborough	93	(1:00)
Maryborough-Gin Gin	117	(1:20)
Gin Gin-Rockhampton	272	(3:10)

CONNECTING ROUTE A

2:50 2:30 0:45

- SYDNEY
  74
- Glenbrook
  2
- Blaxland
  61
- Mt Victoria
  9
- Hartley
  41
- Meadow Flat
  10
- Yetholme
  19
- Kelso
  3
- BATHURST
  42
- Lucknow
  11
- ORANGE
  38
- Molong
  68
- Wellington
  21
- Geurie
  50
- DUBBO
  7
- Talbragar
  50
- Gilgandra

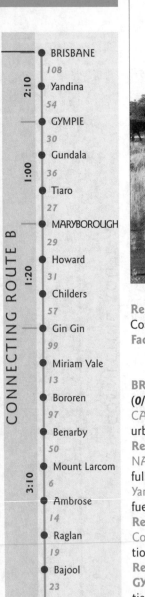

CONNECTING ROUTE B

	●	BRISBANE
2:10	*108*	
	●	Yandina
	54	
	●	GYMPIE
1:00	*30*	
	●	Gundala
	36	
	●	Tiaro
	27	
1:20	●	MARYBOROUGH
	29	
	●	Howard
	31	
	●	Childers
	57	
	●	Gin Gin
	99	
	●	Miriam Vale
	13	
	●	Bororen
	97	
	●	Benarby
	50	
3:10	●	Mount Larcom
	6	
	●	Ambrose
	14	
	●	Raglan
	19	
	●	Bajool
	23	
	●	Gavial
	14	
	●	ROCKHAMPTON

Regions Traversed: Brisbane region, Sunshine Coast, Mary-Burnett, Capricornia
Facilities en route:

BRISBANE: state capital - full town facilities. (*0/644*)
CABOOLTURE turnoff (**W**): outer Brisbane suburb - full town facilities. (*44/600*)
Rest area: Wild Horse Mountain (*61/583*)
NAMBOUR turnoff (**W**): large country town - full town facilities. (*101/543*)
Yandina: small town - accommodation, store, fuel. (*108/536*)
Rest area: north of Yandina. (*110/534*)
Cooroy turnoff (**E**): small town - accommodation, store, fuel.
Rest area: south of Gympie. (*156/488*)
GYMPIE: large country town - full town facilities. (*162/482*)
Gunalda: township - store, fuel. (*192/452*)
Tiaro: small town - accommodation, store, fuel. (*228/416*)
MARYBOROUGH: large country town - full town facilities. (*255/389*)

Howard: small town - accommodation, store, fuel. (*284/360*)
Rest area at Isis River. (*304/340*)
Childers: small town - accommodation, store, fuel. (*315/329*)
Gin Gin: small town - accommodation, store, fuel. (*372/272*)
Rest area north of Gin Gin. (*374/270*)
Rest area south of Miram Vale (*435/209*)
Miriam Vale: small town - accommodation, store, fuel. (*471/173*)
Bororen: township - store, fuel. (*484/160*)
Rest area near Tannum Sands turnoff. (*512/132*)
Benaraby: township - store, fuel. (*518/126*)
Calliope turnoff (**W**): small town - accommodation, store, fuel. (*534/110*)
Mount Larcom: small town - accommodation, store, fuel. (*568/76*)
Ambrose: township - store, fuel. (*574/70*)
Raglan: township - store, fuel. (*588/56*)
Bajool: township - store, fuel. (*607/37*)
Gavial: township - store, fuel. (*630/14*)
ROCKHAMPTON: large regional centre - full town facilities. (*644/0*) For more information see Road Trip 3. *Road Trips 3, 4 and 9 connect.*

Connecting Route C
MELBOURNE-GRIFFITH
via Shepparton

Road to Take: Hume/Goulburn Valley/Newell Highways/Kidman Way
Grade 1
Total Distance: 456km (5:25)
Intermediate Distances:

	Km	Hours
Melbourne-Shepparton	179	(2:25)
Shepparton-Jerilderie	138	(1:30)
Jerilderie-Griffith	139	(1:30)

Regions Traversed: South-Central Victoria, North-Central Victoria, Riverina
Facilities en route:

MELBOURNE: Victorian state capital - full town facilities. (*0/456*) For more information see Road Trip 15. *Road Trip 15 connects.*
Craigieburn: outer Melbourne suburb - store, fuel. (*25/431*)
Kalkallo: township - accommodation, store, fuel. (*32/424*)
Wandong small town - accommodation, store, fuel. (*55/401*)
Goulburn Valley Highway junction: (*101/355*) Turn **N** for Shepparton. *Turn SW onto the M31 for Melbourne.*
Nagambie: country town - accommodation, store, fuel. (*123/333*)
Murchison East: township - store, fuel. (*145/311*)
SHEPPARTON: regional centre - full town facilities. (*179/277*)
Numurkah: country town located just off the highway - full town facilities. (*211/245*)
Murray Valley Highway junction: (*231/225*) Turn **E** for Strathmerton. *Turn S onto Goulburn Valley Highway for Shepparton.*
Strathmerton: small town - accommodation, store, fuel. (*235/221*)
Newell Highway junction: (*245/211*) Turn **N** for Tocumwal. *Turn W for Strathmerton.*
Murray River: **state border** between New South Wales and Victoria. (*259/197*)

Tocumwal: small town - accommodation, store, fuel. (*260/196*)
Finley: country town - full town facilities. (*281/175*) Riverina Hwy Junction. Continue **N** for Jerliderie. *Continue S for Tocumwal.*
Jerilderie: country town - full town facilities. (*317/139*)
Kidman Way turnoff: (*334/122*) Turn **NW** for Coleambally and Griffith. *Turn S for Jerilderie.*
Coleambally: small town - accommodation, store, fuel. (*390/66*)
Waddi: township - store, fuel. (*416/40*)
Darlington Point: small town - accommodation, store, fuel. (*419/37*)
Rest area south of Hanwood. (*450/6*)
Hanwood: small town - accommodation, store, fuel. (*453/3*)
GRIFFITH: regional centre - full town facilities. (*456/0*) For more information see Road Trip 7. *Road Trip 7 connects.*

Connecting Route D
BRISBANE-ROMA
via Toowoomba

Road to Take: Warrego Highway
Grade 1
Total Distance: 480km (5:35)
Intermediate Distances:

	Km	Hours
Brisbane-Toowoomba	128	(1:25)
Toowoomba-Dalby	83	(1:00)
Dalby-Roma	269	(3:10)

Regions Traversed: Brisbane region, Darling Downs, Western Downs
Facilities en route:

BRISBANE: Queensland state capital. Full town facilities. (*0/480*)
Marburg turnoff: township - accommodation, store, fuel. (*55/425*)
Hatton Vale: township - accommodation, store, fuel. (*70/410*)
Gatton turnoff (**S**): small town - accommodation, store, fuel. (*86/394*)

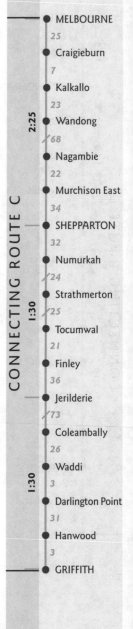

MELBOURNE
25
Craigieburn
7
Kalkallo
23
Wandong
68
Nagambie
22
Murchison East
34
SHEPPARTON
32
Numurkah
24
Strathmerton
25
Tocumwal
21
Finley
36
Jerilderie
73
Coleambally
26
Waddi
3
Darlington Point
31
Hanwood
3
GRIFFITH

2:25

CONNECTING ROUTE C

1:30

1:30

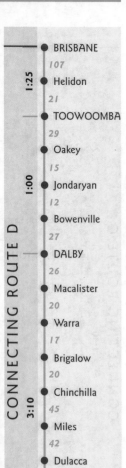

CONNECTING ROUTE D

1:25	● BRISBANE
	107
	● Helidon
	21
	● TOOWOOMBA
	29
	● Oakey
1:00	*15*
	● Jondaryan
	12
	● Bowenville
	27
	● DALBY
	26
	● Macalister
	20
	● Warra
	17
	● Brigalow
	20
3:10	● Chinchilla
	45
	● Miles
	42
	● Dulacca
	38
	● Yuleba
	19
	● Wallumbila
	42
	● ROMA

Helidon: township - accommodation, store, fuel. (*107/373*)

Rest area just west of Helidon. (*108/372*)

TOOWOOMBA: regional centre - full town facilities. (*128/352*) Stay on the Warrego Hwy **NW** to Dalby. *Stay on the Warrego Hwy* **E** *to Brisbane.*

Oakey: small town - accommodation, store, fuel. (*157/323*)

Jondaryan: small town - accommodation, store, fuel. (*172/308*)

Bowenville: township - store, fuel. (*184/296*)

DALBY: large country town - full town facilities. (*211/269*) For more information see Road Trip 8, Day 7. *Road Trip 8 connects.*

Macalister: township - store, fuel. (*237/243*)

Warra: township - store, fuel. (*257/223*)

Brigalow: township-store, fuel. (*274/206*)

Chinchilla: country town - full town facilities. (*294/186*)

Miles: country town - full town facilities. (*339/141*)

Rest area west of Miles. (*360/120*)

Dulacca:township - store, fuel. (*381/99*)

Yuleba: township - store, fuel. (*419/61*)

Wallumbila: township - store, fuel. Rest area nearby. (*438/42*)

Rest area located east of Roma. (*474/6*)

ROMA: large country town - full town facilities. (*480/0*) For more information see Road Trip 2, Day 2. *Road Trips 2 and 8 connect.*

Connecting Route E
SYDNEY-BOURKE
via Dubbo

Road to Take: Mitchell Highway

Grade 1

Total Distance: 814km (9:35)

Intermediate Distances:

	Km	Hours
Sydney-Bathurst	219	(2:50)
Bathurst-Dubbo	230	(2:30)
Dubbo-Nyngan	164	(2:00)
Nyngan-Bourke	201	(2:15)

Regions Traversed: Sydney region, Blue Mountains, Central Tablelands, Central-West, Western Plains

Facilities en route:

SYDNEY: state capital of New South Wales - full town facilities. (*0/814*)

For information about the route between Sydney and Dubbo see the notes to Connecting Route A.

DUBBO: regional centre - full town facilities. (*449/365*) *Connecting Route A connects.*

Narromine: country town - full town facilities. (*488/326*)

Trangie: small town - accommodation, stores, fuel. (*523/291*)

Nevertire: small town - accommodation, stores, fuel. (*556/258*)

Nyngan: country town - full town facilities. (*613/201*) *Road Trip 14 connects.*

Girilambone: township - store, fuel. (*656/158*)

Coolabah: township - store, fuel. (*686/128*)

Rest area north of Coolabah. (*715/99*)

Byrock: township - accommodation, store, fuel. (*737/77*)

Rest area south of Bourke. (*792/22*)

Bourke: country town - full town facilities. (*814/0*) For more information see Road Trip 7, Day 2. *Road Trip 7 connects.*

Connecting Route F
SYDNEY-HAY
via Bathurst, West Wyalong

Roads to Take: Great Western/Mid-Western Highways

Grade 1

Total Distance: 737km (8:45)

Intermediate Distances:

	Km	Hours
Sydney-Bathurst	219	(2:50)
Bathurst-West Wyalong	273	(3:10)
West Wyalong-Goolgowi	138	(1:30)
Goolgowi-Hay	107	(1:15)

Regions Traversed: Sydney region, Blue Mountains, Central Tablelands, Central-West, South-West Slopes, Riverina

Facilities en route:

SYDNEY: state capital of New South Wales - full town facilities. (*0/737*)

For information about the route between Sydney and Bathurst see the notes to Connecting Route A.

BATHURST: regional centre - full town facilities. (*219/518*) *Connecting Route A connects.* Head **SW** on the Mid-Western Highway. *Head **E** on the Great Western Highway.*

Rest area south-west of Bathurst. (*243/494*)

Blaney: country town - full town facilities. (*256/481*)

Rest area north of Carcoar. (*267/470*)

Carcoar turnoff: historic town - accommodation, stores, fuel. (*269/468*)

Mandurama: township - store, fuel. (*278/459*)

Lyndhurst: small town - accommodation, stores, fuel. (*282/455*)

COWRA: large country town - full town facilities. (*330/407*)

Rest area near Bumbaldry. (*354/383*)

Grenfell: historic town - full town facilities. (*386/351*)

Rest area at Bogolong. (*395/342*)

Caragabal: small town - accommodation, store, fuel. (*432/305*)

West Wyalong: country town - full town facilities. (*492/245*)

Weethalle: township - store, fuel. (*540/187*)

Rankin Springs: township - accommodation, store, fuel. (*572/165*)

Connecting Routes

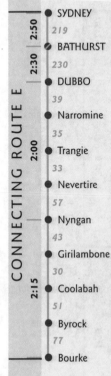

CONNECTING ROUTE E

2:50		SYDNEY
	219	
2:30		BATHURST
	230	
		DUBBO
2:00	39	
		Narromine
	35	
		Trangie
	33	
		Nevertire
	57	
		Nyngan
2:15	43	
		Girilambone
	30	
		Coolabah
	51	
		Byrock
	77	
		Bourke

Connecting Routes

Goolgowi: township - accommodation, store, fuel. (*630/107*) For more information see the notes to Road Trip 7. *Road Trip 7 connects.* **Rest area** west of Goolgowi. (*633/104*)

Gunbar: locality only; no facilities. (*662/75*) **HAY**: country town - full town facilities. (*737/ 0*) For more information see Road Trip 15. *Road Trip 15 connects.*

CONNECTING ROUTE F

● SYDNEY
2:50
219
◉ BATHURST
37
● Blaney
22
● Mandurama
4
● Lyndhurst
3:10
48
● COWRA
56
● Grenfell
46
● Caragabal
60
● West Wyalong
48
● Weethalle
1:30
32
● Rankin Springs
58
● Goolgowi
32
1:15
● Gunbar
75
● HAY

Before You Go

Transport: How to Go

Driving is not the only way to travel around Australia. Those who do not wish to sit for hours behind the wheel might like to consider the fly-drive option, flying from home to a large town or regional centre, then hiring a vehicle to do a road trip. South-east Australians often do fly-drives to Tasmania, Perth, Cairns or Alice Springs. This can be an expensive way of travelling, but does at least save the time of travelling long distances.

Joining a coach tour is another option. This can be either very expensive, if staying in overnight accommodation and having all meals bought or prepared for you, or moderately expensive if on a camping tour where you are expected to contribute to meal preparation, setting up camp, and so on. An advantage of these options is that most of the work is done for you, but disadvantages include not having the flexibility to linger in places which appeal to you, and being stuck with the same group of people, some of whom you may not like. It also limits your interaction with the local population. These types of tours come into their own when they are of a short duration or when visiting relatively inaccessible areas.

Non-driving, independent-minded people might like to consider using ground-based public transport. For instance, bus lines operate along all the main highways across and around Australia as well as to popular tourist destinations. Likewise, passenger trains run along the inter-capital city routes and to major regional centres. As most bus and train services originate from the state capitals or regional centres, getting to these destinations is not a problem. An advantage of this type of travel is that one is free to move, within the constraints of the timetable, from any one point to another at will. A disadvantage is that you will travel from settlement to settlement; to visit the country in between you would have to hire a vehicle or join a tour, either of which is not always possible.

Flying is another option, but negates the purpose of this book, inasmuch as one flies over the country and does not pass through it. It is also very expensive.

Travelling by mountain bike is not as ridiculous as it sounds, especially during the cooler months and if using sealed roads. Although basically for the fit, bike travel is very cheap and fair distances can be covered each day. Thought must be given to food, water and camping requirements, for these services may not always be available at the end of a cycling day. Motor bikes are another alternative, particularly on the sealed roads.

The principal means of travelling the country is by motor vehicle, whether conventional (2WD) or four-wheel drive (4WD). Each of the routes has been graded (*see under How To Use This Book*), indicating which unsealed roads are okay for conventional vehicles, which are suitable for experienced drivers of conventional vehicles, and which are strictly 4WD.

A compromise between conventional vehicles and 4WDs is the campervan. These high clearance vehicles also offer comfortable accommodation. A disadvantage is that you have to pack everything up even if you are just travelling down the road to pick up some supplies.

Preparing your Vehicle

The most important thing you can do for your peace of mind if travelling long distances is to make the vehicle mechanically sound. Attend to all those nagging doubts - every squeak, rattle and leak - before you depart.

Have the vehicle thoroughly inspected beforehand by your mechanic. Tell him or her where you are going and have the vehicle's suspension, tyres, fuel system, cooling system and brakes checked. Replace the wheel bearings and universals (if still okay, keep the old ones for spares), replace any dodgy items and those due for renewal (some replaced items might do for spares), have a tune-up, change the oil and filters, and grease the nipples. Add coolant to the cooling system, and replace the battery if it is more than a year old. If travelling in outback country, pack all the spares required (*see the Appendices*); chances are you will not need any of them. Even if you do not know how to replace them yourself (it would help your self-confidence if you did), and there is no mechanic or road service nearby, someone passing by will probably be able to help you.

An important point, especially for conventional vehicles, is ground clearance. For peace of mind, an adequate ground clearance is necessary if travelling extensively on unsealed roads. One way of controlling this is by not overloading the vehicle and carrying only what is absolutely necessary. Height can also be gained by attaching helper springs or air shock absorbers (there are arguments for and against this last option).

If you are intending to travel on Grade 4 roads (*see under How To Use This Book*) in a 2WD vehicle, fit sump and fuel tank guards, and plastic hosing (cut along one edge) over the brake and fuel lines.

Preparing Yourself

Having decided how to go and when, have you thought about yourself? Unless travelling on an all-expenses tour, you will need to think about food and water.

Always travel with some food with you wherever you decide to go. Being held up by floodwaters or a breakdown, even on the busiest roads, may see you stranded for a short time. These inconveniences are better handled on a full stomach. If travelling in *outback country*, unless you intend to stay entirely on the main sealed highways, do not count on being able to buy all your meals. It is cheaper and more reliable to prepare your own, be it a lunchtime picnic or three meals a day. Stock up beforehand and replenish wherever possible. If travelling in *remote outback country* you will have to prepare most of your meals. In these cases always carry enough food to last everyone in your vehicle for at least 3 to 5 days.

Likewise, always carry some water, even on the busiest roads. During summer it can be very hot and it is crucial in avoiding dehydration. At any time in *remote outback country*, always carry sufficient water to last for five days, roughly four litres per person per day. Remember that this amount, 20 litres per person, will be a major contribution to your load.

On long and extended journeys that take you to the outback, be prepared to camp out. Unless on a tour, do not count on getting indoor accommodation every night in hotels or motels, especially during the school holidays. For this you will need either bedrolls (swags) or a lightweight tent, plus bedding or sleeping bags.

Cheap accommodation can usually be found at caravan parks (on-site vans or cabins) or at backpacker lodges. The cheapest accommodation is, of course, bush camping (*see under On The Road*).

Supply yourself with a good set of road maps and other maps in order to get an overview of the country you plan to visit (this book is good for the close-up details). The road service organisations' state and district maps are usually the most reliable. The more information you can assemble, the more interest you will get out of your travels. Try to include everyone who is accompanying you in the pre-trip planning so that they too feel a part of the venture.

You will also need money. While the larger centres have automatic teller machines, most of the smaller ones do not, even if they have a bank (which may not be your brand). In addition, in the outback, many establishments do not have credit card facilities, though most nowadays do have EFTPOS. You will need to carry some cash (replenish supplies in the larger centres or through EFTPOS facilities) or travellers cheques, or perhaps open a bank account which allows you to withdraw limited amounts at post offices (Commonwealth Bank).

Permits and Access

Travel within Australia is not quite as unrestricted as you might think. All of the continent

has some form of land tenure, ranging from un-alienated Crown land through to freehold land, and also including Aboriginal land, pastoral leasehold land, mining leases, national parks and reserves, restricted areas, military reserves, and others. With these forms of tenure come a number of restrictions with regard to access. These are detailed as follows:

National Parks and Reserves
In order to visit or camp within national parks you will have to obtain a permit or pay a park user's fee. Conditions vary from state to state.

New South Wales and Victoria
No special restrictions. Some parks will require you to pay for overnight stays, usually on a self registration system.

Queensland
In Queensland you will require a camping permit to stay overnight at any of the national parks. Fees are paid either in advance (around $2 to $5 per person per night) or on a self-serve registration system. Send advance paid fees to the Queensland National Parks and Wildlife Service.

South Australia
A *Desert Parks Pass*, costing around $80 and lasting for a year (or $18 per day), will give you access and the right to camp in the Innamincka Regional Reserve as well as other South Australian desert national parks such as Lake Eyre and Witjira. The annual fee includes an information handbook. Note that you do not need a Desert Parks Pass to travel on public highways or roads, or if not camping overnight within these parks. Desert Parks Passes are available from numerous outlets throughout South Australia, western Queensland and western New South Wales, but it is better to apply in advance as the information which accompanies the pass is useful in planning your journey.

In addition, a *Desert Parks Camping Permit* is available for one or two nights within the desert national parks. These permits are available at Desert Parks Pass outlets. Other national parks (ie in the Flinders Ranges) require camping permits for overnight stays. These are usually available at or near national park entry stations or on a self registration system within the campground.

Western Australia

Some parks require payment for admission, others do not. These payments can be made on an individual basis (which can be expensive) or as multiple entries over a period of time (which is cheaper in the long run). Most parks will require you to pay for overnight stays, usually on a self registration system.

Tasmania

All Tasmanian national parks require a pass or permit whether overnighting or not. A fee is charged on a daily, monthly or yearly basis. The two month holiday pass represents the best value for visitors; approximately $30. Passes are available at park entrances, tour operators and local stores.

Northern Territory

Note that there are two park systems in the Northern Territory. Uluru-Kata Tjuta and Kakadu National Parks are administered Federally; the remainder are Territory-based.

At *Uluru*, camping is not permitted. Daytime access is possible by paying a park user's fee, payable at the park entrance station. At *Kakadu*, permits for access cost around $15 per person and last for 14 days. Fees are payable at park entrance stations. Camping fees are payable each night, the price depending on the facilities available. If you wish to bushwalk and camp overnight another permit is required - seek information at park ranger stations.

In Territory-administered national parks, access fees are payable in some parks. Fees are payable for overnight camping, usually on a self-registration system.

Fossicking

Different states have different regulations regarding fossicking. Note that fossicking is different to noodling. Fossicking usually involves the use of hand tools for digging; noodling is picking over mullock heaps or selecting rocks off the ground by hand. Generally, specific areas are set aside for fossicking and noodling. Check to see that local authorities differentiate between fossicking and noodling.

If intending to noodle make local enquiries first. Some miners may allow you to noodle on their mullock heaps. Never fossick or noodle on a miner's claim without the permission of the claimholder. Claims are normally marked out by white pegs in the ground. The best time for noodling and fossicking is after rain.

New South Wales: no special noodling requirements. Enquire locally about fossicking.

Queensland: fossicking requires a permit or licence (available for 1 to 12 months - fees vary accordingly). Licences are available locally from mining registrars' offices. Fossicking is not permitted on any miner's claims.

South Australia: you require a prospecting permit to fossick, obtainable from the Department of Mines and Energy.

Western Australia: fossickers require a miner's right, obtainable locally from mining registrars atached to the Department of Minerals and Energy.

Northern Territory: permit required for fossicking, enquire locally.

Fishing

Fishing regulations vary from state to state. Most states require an inland fishing licence to fish inland waterways, and some states (New South Wales for example) require a licence for ocean fishing. Note that there are rules regarding the size of the catch, bag limits and season times, and these vary from state to state. Also special licences may be required for such activities as lobstering, marron fishing, or using fishing nets. Licence prices vary, ranging from around $5 a day, up to about $50 for a season or year. Make further enquiries at relevant State Fisheries offices.

Aboriginal Land

Virtually all of the routes contained herein do not require permits for access to Aboriginal Land, even if that road crosses such land. These routes have their own road reserves and you are permitted free access and usage of that road, and within the road reserve boundaries, usually around 20 to 50 metres either side of that road.

Roads requiring permits are as follows:

Mintabie Road (*Road Trip 20*): permit easily obtainable at Marla Police Station.

Mereenie Loop Road (*Road Trip 22*): souvenir permit readily obtained from tourist outlets in Alice Springs, Glen Helen, King Canyon, and others. This permit also allows access to Gosses Bluff.

Head of Bight access road (*Road Trip 35*): permits readily available at Nullarbor Roadhouse, Yalata Roadhouse or White Well Ranger Station.

Entry to some communities will require permits or permission from land holders. Enquire locally or in the nearest main town. It is illegal for uninitiated people to enter designated sacred sites. Such sites are clearly signposted.

Freehold and Leasehold Land

This is private property and should be respected as such. If you wish to enter such land, permission should be sought from the owner, occupier or leaseholder. Note that most roads occupy their own road reserve (up to 50m either side of the road) and offer unrestricted travel. In some rare cases short side roads cross private lands to reach a tourist feature. In cases where such usage is allowed, no permission is required, but heed any notices (including leaving gates as you find them) and respect the property rights of the landholder.

Restricted Areas

These include military bases, hazardous mining sites, telecommunication areas, and so on. Forget about access. An exception is the Woomera Prohibited Area that occupies a significant portion of northern South Australia. No permit is required for access along the Stuart Highway or along the William Creek-Coober Pedy Road. If deviating from these routes, you will need a permit obtainable from the Department of Defence, Woomera.

Loading the Vehicle

How you pack the vehicle and have access to its contents will have a major bearing on how well you enjoy your travels. While the load list seems endless, individual items often take up surprisingly little space, and after a week on the road everything should have its place. It will surprise you, on your return, how much spare space there seems to be!

Following are some loading hints.

1. Think light. Ask yourself, 'Is this thing I am holding really necessary?' The list in the *Appendices* will give you an idea, but you will probably need to make your own list.

2. Compartmentalise things into, for instance, clothes and personal items, food, cooking utensils, camping gear, spare parts, tools, etc. Cardboard boxes are ideal for many of these 'compartments' as they flex, are light, and are replaceable.

3. Load so that each 'compartment' is relatively accessible. This saves double handling. For instance, emergency food and water can be buried deep in the vehicle whereas lunch-time tucker and water should be easily accessible. Let each 'compartment' have its own position. It may take a few days on the road to determine this.

4. Have one person in charge of loading: then any 'compartment' or item therein that is missing will be noticed. Insist that items are replaced immediately after use. If this habit is established early, then the ease of travelling, stopping for lunch, setting up camp, and moving on again, is greatly enhanced.

5. Distribute the load evenly, with heavier items stored low to keep the vehicle's centre of gravity low. This is especially important on rough roads, sand dunes, and the like.

6. If using a roof rack, make sure it is strong and only store lightweight gear on it.

7. Do not store jerry cans of fuel in the cabin or on the roof rack. Store safely away from cigarette smokers. Beware of static build-up: earth the can against bare metal on the car before opening. Jerry cans of fuel are potential bombs.

8. Pack the load tightly so that items do not become missiles in the event of sudden stops or accidents.

On The Road

In this chapter we will look at some of the things you might need to do to make your travels more enjoyable.

Road Conditions

For travelling peace-of-mind, knowing what the road conditions are like is important. Generalised road conditions are displayed on road service organisation or petrol company maps. More detailed road conditions are given in this book (*see under How to Use This Book*). Current road conditions for major roads, updated as required, are available on the following telephone numbers:

New South Wales: 1300 131 122
Victoria 03 9882 8111
Queensland: 07 3219 0900
Northern South Australia: 1300 361 033
Western Australia: 1800 013 314
Northern Territory: 1800 246 199

For local or shire roads ring the local council. Of course, for the latest road conditions, ask fellow travellers or roadhouse operators.

Travelling and Outback Etiquette

One way of enjoying your travels is to be a pleasant traveller, one who respects other travellers, road users and locals.

The first step is to *slow down*. By travelling slowly (which may mean doing a shorter trip if your time is limited) you will give yourself more time to absorb your surroundings and to appreciate the countryside, its towns and people.

Likewise, consider other road users on *narrow-sealed and unsealed roads*. Slow down. By slowing down when passing or overtaking other vehicles, you will reduce the dust hazard and likelihood of windscreen breakages.

It is generally considered bad form (even illegal) to travel on *naturally formed unsealed roads* in wet conditions. These roads are readily cut-up by vehicle usage, resulting in deeply gouged wheel tracks which dry to form imbedded ruts, making travel after rains uncomfortable at least. Though you may pass along a road but once, a local may have to travel the same road regularly. Stay off wet, unsealed roads unless absolutely necessary. Either find an alternative all-weather route, or wait until the road dries out. This usually takes only one sunny day.

Do not camp on private property without permission. It is usually okay to camp on road reserves or at rest areas for a night or two.

In all cases, leave *gates* as you find them. Never leave a closed gate open, even if you know someone is behind you. They might turn off, turn around, or even break down before reaching you.

In the outback, *station homesteads*, unless providing facilities for travellers, should not be approached except in absolute emergencies. Whilst most station people are friendly, they get sick of having to pull people out of bogs, supply them with petrol, or answer silly questions. The days when station people eagerly awaited the arrival of strangers for company have long gone.

In the outback it used to be customary to *wave* at fellow travellers, and in many places it still is. Though no longer necessary on the busiest roads, make the effort on the quieter routes and unsealed roads. It acknowledges the presence of others as equals and denotes friendliness. It is these people who will come to your aid if required.

Be careful with *photography* in some remote townships. Not everyone likes having their picture taken, especially Aborigines or those who have moved there in order to start new lives. If you want to take photographs, spend some time in the township, talk to a few locals and do not hide the camera. If the locals think you are really interested in the area they will relax when you start taking photographs. If you want to take photographs of people, ask first and establish a relationship.

If you wish to talk to *Aborigines*, and they will certainly enrich your travels, then stand at a visible distance. Individuals may wander by and say hello, or a member of a group will eventually saunter up to see what you want. Do not expect to be invited to the next initiation ceremony, but asking questions or showing interest in their culture will elicit responses. You will be expected to pay for photographs, as reciprocity is a strong cultural attribute.

In *remote country*, herein defined as any unsealed cross-country outback route with less than 30 vehicles per day, always inform a reliable person of your travel intentions. Do not forget to inform them of your safe arrival. Carry five days supply of food and water and avoid summer travel.

Environmental Impact

An aspect of life is that we all have an impact on the environment. As more people travel, environments are impacted upon more regularly and with a greater chance of permanent damage. There are ways of reducing your impact and consequently the total environmental impact.

If you do not like feeling the crush of people in your travels, avoid travelling during the autumn, winter and spring school holidays, when roads are much busier, accommodation is more limited, and tourist sites are crowded. By travelling outside these times you can experience the countryside almost as though it was your own.

Another way of reducing your impact is by staying on the roads and tracks at all times, including walking tracks. Vehicles leaving the road not only destroy the vegetation but also imprint the landscape with wheel tracks and gouges. These imprints can last for up to twenty years in arid areas! If looking for a bush campsite, do it in daylight by either following another person's tracks (preferably an established track) or by turning off onto hardpan surfaces (scalds, dry claypans, old road alignments) which leave no imprint.

Please do not throw litter or food scraps from a moving vehicle, and always take all your rubbish with you, including cigarette butts and tissue papers, and deposit them at approved sites. While cigarette smokers seem to be more conscious nowadays about where they throw their butts, the paper tissue brigade still mar many a bushwalk or camping site with dropped tissues. Please take them with you. These items take years to rot in arid country. A small plastic bag in the vehicle serves well as a litter bag.

With toilet deposits in the bush, dig a small hole, do your business, then either carefully burn the toilet paper or take it, suitably wrapped, with you.

Maintaining your Sense of Humour

This is crucial if you are to enjoy your journey. Bear in mind that travelling is an experience and an adventure, and at times it will be tiring. If you suffer easily from environmental stress, or lack a sense of humour, then perhaps extended touring is not for you. There are ways, though, of reducing these stresses.

Try to avoid travelling west (north-west in winter) during the late afternoon, or east in the early morning. The incoming sun and glare will be blinding, making travel hazardous as well as tiring. If you do not hit a kangaroo or cow, you will probably still end up with headache. Likewise, travelling in a northerly direction is more tiring than heading south as the sun, especially in winter, will strike the windscreen at an angle, increasing the glare and giving the landscape a washed-out look. This can make travelling dreary. Also, be aware of the fatigue-producing and hypnotic effect of running for hours over dead-straight bitumen roads.

Much of the tiredness and fatigue experienced on the 'boring stretches' is due to dehydration. That lethargic feeling and slowness of thinking can be overcome by regularly sipping water. In dry climates you will be losing moisture by sweating, even though you do not notice it due to rapid evaporation. Always carry water in the vehicle cabin. Soft drinks and alcohol only increase the problem.

When parked in the bush and there is no shade, throw an old rug, blanket or tarpaulin over the vehicle. By placing it over the roof and covering some of the windows (hold it in place with the doors) you can shade the car, making it feel cooler. It also reduces glare.

Wear a shady hat and sunglasses at all times when you are outside the vehicle during daylight hours. If walking, always carry drinking water. On extended walks carry some food, walk with company, and inform a reliable person of your intentions. At least leave a note on the windscreen mentioning date, time, direction or destination, and expected return.

Bush Nasties

Whether bush camping, bush walking or just strolling through the bush, you may encounter some nasty things, most of which can be avoided.

In the plant world, be aware of *stinging nettles*, common along bush tracks in moist areas, or on disturbed ground. These small plants with their roughly triangular serrated leaves have stinging hairs that can cause some pain. This pain may linger for some days if your skin gets wet. A useful antidote is the dock plant that usually grows nearby. Squeeze the plant's juices over the sting. Related to stinging nettles is the *stinging tree*, found only in rainforests, and usu-

ally on disturbed ground. These trees are large and have large, heart-shaped leaves. Brushing against these leaves will inflict severe stings that may last for days or weeks. As the trees are usually large, it is unlikely that you will brush against them. Rainforest areas have a number of other nasty plants as well, though if you stay on established paths and tracks you should be okay.

Among the animal kingdom are a few animals worth avoiding. *Snakes* are usually quite shy and will move away from you if given the chance. Be careful when stepping over logs and walking around at night without adequate footwear. Also be careful when picking up firewood, or around fallen logs. Most people are bitten by snakes when trying to kill or handle them. Snakes are often seen during spring when they are sluggish and might be warming themselves on a walking track. If bitten by a snake, seek medical advice immediately.

Other things worth avoiding are *funnel-web spiders*. Do not go sticking your fingers in any holes and be careful picking up wood. Funnel web spiders are most common in the eastern coastal districts and will move about after rain.

Check clothes and footwear before putting them on. The same goes for *red back spiders*. They are found in drier country throughout the continent and like to hide under wood, in old buildings, under toilet seats, and so on. If bitten by either a funnel-web or red back spider, seek medical advice immediately. Many other spiders (including trapdoors, wolf spiders, white-tails) should be avoided. While they will not kill you, they can make you feel very sick. In addition, some people may have adverse allergic reactions to their bites.

Other land based nasties are found in rainforests or moist gullies. *Ticks* are tiny burrowing animals that itch like mad when disturbed. They can be removed by applying tea-tree oil (aftershave lotion will do), waiting a minute, and pulling the creature out with tweezers. Leaving a tick in your body can make you very sick, and may kill you after a week. Found in the same type of country, *leeches* respond to body heat and attach themselves to your clothing, boots or body, usually the legs. If attached to your skin, apply a flame or cigarette to them.

In arid areas beware of *scorpions*. While they will not kill you they can inflict a painful sting. Similarly, in all areas, *bees*, *wasps* and *hornets* should be guarded against, especially by those people allergic to their stings.

Probably the biggest potential threat to life exists in the tropics. Within a hundred kilometres of the tropical coast, between Port Hedland and Rockhampton, are found *estuarine or salt-water crocodiles*. They live along the coastline, in estuaries, and in or near freshwater coastal streams and waterholes. Generally any tropical coastal river or estuary, and its environs, downstream from a rocky bar or rapids, will house these deadly reptiles. In estuarine crocodile country, observe the following: heed crocodile warning signs (a lack of signs does not guarantee crocodile-free waters); do not camp within 50m of a stream or waterhole; stand well back from river banks if sightseeing, fishing or collecting water (use a bucket on a rope); do not clean fish or leave food scraps near a river bank; do not return to the same part of a river bank

day after day; do not swim or wade; keep your eyes open. *Freshwater crocodiles* occupy tropical freshwater habitats. While not deadly, do not disturb them for they can inflict a nasty bite.

Along the coastline are many rock pools full of sea creatures. Most are harmless, many are not nice, and some are very deadly. The small and attractive *blue-ringed octopus* (no blue rings appear unless it is disturbed) can kill you in minutes if you touch it. Leave all octopuses, and other marine creatures, alone.

In the ocean waters are many nasty things, but chances are you will never encounter them. The obvious ones are *sharks*, which may eat, or at least take a bite out of you (unlikely but not impossible). Swimming in tropical coastal waters is downright deadly during the *marine stinger* (sea wasp or box jellyfish are other names) season between October and May. To be stung by these creatures is to die an agonising death. Swim either out of season or in marine stinger safety enclosures.

In temperate ocean waters, the biggest concern when swimming or surfing is the *bluebottle* or jelly-fish. These creatures have nasty blue stingers dangling from their glutinous bodies and are virtually impossible to see in the water. They can also sting you if handled when washed up on the sand. Bluebottles seem to be at their worst when on-shore winds are blowing.

Bush Camping

Try to look for a campsite before dusk and try to camp where others have been. If this is not possible, look for old road alignments, gravel pits or a hardpan surface (scalds, dry claypans, etc). These surfaces are usually level, hard, clean, safe for small fires, and leave virtually no imprints.

Always choose your *campsite* on foot, not through the windscreen of a moving vehicle travelling in ever-increasing circles (I have seen people do this!). Never camp in creek beds, by flooding rivers, or under large trees (especially river red gums) - there may be dead limbs about to fall. Flash floods can kill (it may be dry where you are but raining upstream) and flooding rivers may rise rapidly overnight. Also do not camp near stock watering places, homesteads or outstations. Remember that mosquitos like water too.

Where possible use camping stoves for cooking. Firewood is scarce in many areas, and in popular areas it may be non-existent. When making a *campfire*, dig a shallow trench and use wood sparingly; the dry timber of inland trees emits considerable heat. A small stick fire is sufficient to boil a billy and a few sticks placed on a bed of coals will produce that fireside ambience considered desirable by campers. When finished, bury the fire by filling in the trench.

If it is very cold, do what the Aborigines do: make a couple of small stick fires and sit between them. Raging blazes waste wood and only heat part of you. Select your wood carefully as it may harbour animal or insect life. Please do not burn our national heritage; old wooden fence posts, signs and railway sleepers are a part of our history.

In popular camping sites there may be a shortage of wood. Sharing campfires may be possible in these instances.

When camping, do all your *washing* and cleaning away from waterholes, creeks, etc, as soap, shampoo and detergent will pollute or contaminate them. For your *toilet*, dig a pit well away from the camp and any water, and bury the waste. It is preferable to burn the toilet paper on a campfire, but not whilst cooking! Also give some thought as to where to use your generator, radio or portable television. In quiet places this not only disturbs stock, but wildlife and other campers as well. Beware of broken bottles and glass in or near waterholes, and at picnic and rest areas.

If no facilities are available, take all of your *rubbish* with you for later disposal on a town tip. Buried rubbish will soon be dug up and scattered by wildlife. If camping for a few days, or if leaving camp for a part of the day, put food well away; thieving crows have been known to wreck a campsite and to demolish a large amount of food. In many places there may already be a lot of litter. Although unpleasant, you can feel virtuous by cleaning up and properly disposing of other people's rubbish. Not only will your campsite be cleaner but a clean campsite generally stays clean when other travellers arrive.

Where to Camp

Rest areas (some with toilets and water) are located on most highways and main roads. While good for rests, lunch stops, etc, they are generally not the best place to camp. On busy roads they are often filthy from litter and are close to the highway. If using them, settle down near other travellers. In the outback and northern Australia, rest areas are popular for overnight camping among travellers. Be aware that in some states rest areas are not intended for overnight stops.

Road reserves consist of the land lying usually about 15 to 50 metres either side of the road. While not much good on busy highways or in cleared country, road reserves are quite okay for a night or two on quiet outback roads.

Reserves include crown land reserves, local council reserves, and the like. Many local councils set aside areas for bush camping at popular stopovers, for example, beside streams or at river crossings. These tend to be more common in forested or outback country.

National parks and reserves mostly offer camping facilities ranging from basic (cleared ground, fireplace) to elaborate (fireplaces, picnic tables, toilets, even cold and hot showers). In popular parks you may need to book in advance. Elsewhere these camping areas operate on a first come-first served basis. Normally an overnight payment is required and a camping permit may be necessary (*see under Before You Go*).

State forests offer similar camping options to those listed above. These have the added advantage that your pet dog, under control, may be welcome too. Conditions vary from state to state. There are few restrictions in New South Wales, Victoria and South Australian state forests. Queensland has pet restrictions and a permit may be required (enquire locally). Western Australia has only a few state forest camping areas due to dieback quarantine restrictions.

Private establishments and **local councils** offer a broad range of camping areas (and caravan parks) from basic to elaborate, with fees to match. Note that it is illegal in Western Australia to camp within 16km of an established camping area or caravan park.

Breakdowns

You can avoid virtually all breakdowns by thoroughly preparing your vehicle before departure, and you can avoid most accidents by travelling safely and slowly, and by being extra careful when travelling at dawn, dusk or at night.

If you have broken down in a small or remote settlement and spare parts are not available, one of the quickest ways of getting the part is to ring a friend back home, have them buy the item and post it to you as soon as possible.

In outback country, avoid night travelling if at all possible. If you must travel at this time, keep your speed under 70 kilometres per hour. That should be slow enough to stop a kangaroo from landing in your lap via the windscreen. This is a real problem, as many outback roads are unfenced. Remember that during dry times, animals, especially cattle and kangaroos, will use bitumen and other hard road surfaces as water catchments from which to drink. They will also gather near creek crossings.

If your car breaks down in the remote outback, or if you have an accident, stay with the vehicle. As long as someone knows where you are, and that you have not arrived when you said you would, someone will be along eventually to help you. While you have spare food and water, you will be okay. If you must leave the vehicle, leave a note on the inside of the windscreen stating date, time, direction of destination, and expected return. If it is hot or shadeless, make shade with your spare rugs and blankets, or lie under the car (you may have to dig a trench first). Do not exert yourself during the heat of the day. If the situation is desperate, light a smokey fire by day (use spinifex, engine oil, spare tyres) and a bright fire by night.

Getting Lost

Getting lost can range from taking a wrong turn down a city street to being stranded for weeks behind floodwaters on a dead-end track that nobody knows you have gone down. By following the road trips in this book you should not get lost (wrong turns in towns notwithstanding). All routes are on gazetted roads ranging from freeways to unformed earth roads. Signage is mostly good. If you heed the warnings and note the road grading then you can plan your drive to within you and your vehicle's capabilities, and have a safe journey.

People get lost, or run into serious trouble, by leaving the road or travelling along a little-used track without telling a reliable person where they have gone. If leaving the beaten path, by either vehicle or foot, *seek and heed local advice before setting out, and inform a reliable person of your plans*. Keep a log of turns and distances if driving.

If you are actually lost, stop and consider the situation. Look for your tracks and retrace them, taking note of the lay of the land from high points - look for prominent features. A log of turns and distances will get you back into known territory. If your are completely lost, stay put (heed the breakdown information above). As long as that reliable person knows where you were going, help will eventually arrive.

Glossary

Bauhinia: a deciduous tropical shrub or small tree with oval-shaped leaves.

Beefwood: a sizeable tree with rough fissured bark found in semi-arid areas.

Belah: a tree species of *Casuarina* exhibiting needle-like branchlets and a rather shaggy and untidy crown; found on some plains in southern and eastern semi-arid country.

Bimble box: a type of eucalypt exhibiting thin, fibrous bark; often grows with cypress pines in eastern semi-arid country.

Bluebush: an attractive blue-tinged low shrub often found growing with saltbush; popular sheep fodder; common in South Australia - found in northern Australia around dry bogs.

Bluegrass: tall tropical grass growing on clay plains.

Blue mallee: attractive blue-tinged mallee eucalypt less than three metres tall found growing on plains in arid areas of Central Australia, often with spinifex.

Boab: sizeable deciduous tree characterised by its bulbous trunk; found growing in the Kimberley and Victoria River District. Leafless during dry season.

Boree: attractive acacia tree with a silvery crown found growing in Mid-West Queensland.

Bottle tree: large tree with a bulbous trunk (do not confuse with boabs) which appears as an emergent tree in the dry woodlands of North-West and central Queensland.

Breakaways: local Western Australian term describing a long, low escarpment that often separates a higher level plain or plateau from a lower level plain. Height rarely more than 30m. Western Australians also refer to jump-up hills (mesas) as breakaways as are the jump-up hills in the Coober Pedy district.

Brigalow: a species of acacia with a shaggy crown. Once widespread throughout eastern inland Queensland it has been extensively cleared for farming.

Canegrass: a 'reed-like' grass that grows in semi-arid areas on inundated land.

Claypan: a clay-covered depression that holds water after rain.

Clay plains: flat to undulating plain of clay particles often supporting a grassland.

Collapsed doline: a depression in the surface of limestone country whereby that surface has collapsed into a cave cavity beneath; common on the Nullarbor Plain.

Coolabah: a species of eucalypt found on floodplain country.

Corkwood: small tree with corky bark and needle-like leaves found in arid areas.

Country camps: small clan-sized Aboriginal community set up, usually on their own initiative, on that clan's traditional land.

Cypress pine: species of *Callitris* with a Christmas tree appearance found growing on sand dunes or on arid, rocky hills (sometimes with a gnarled appearance).

Darwin box: a medium-sized tree of the tropical woodlands exhibiting rough, compact bark that covers the whole tree.

Desert oak: a tree species of *Allocasuarina*, often large, with a graceful rounded crown. Common in the Amadeus Lowland area of Central Australia and in parts of the Great Sandy Desert.

Desert walnut: smallish tree found growing in the western portion of the Great Sandy Desert.

Dry bogs: term used to describe depressions that contain water after seasonal rains; common in parts of the Barkly Tableland. Supports a variety of herbs and often ringed with bluebushes. Good cattle grazing country.

Flat-iron: a roughly triangular-shaped hillside bounded by gorges and located on tilted rock strata. Common along the western side of the Flinders Ranges.

Floodouts: floodplains located at the terminus of inland rivers subjected to inundation; often good cattle grazing country.

Georgina gidgee: squat unattractive tree often less than 3m high with a large crown compared to its height; common on the Tobermory Plain in the eastern Sandover-Plenty River Basins region.

Ghost gum: attractive gum-like eucalypt with a vivid white trunk found growing in northern Australia in both semi-arid country and tropical woodlands.

Gibbers: small stones found scattered over plains.

Gidgee: a species of acacia found growing on floodplain country, drainage lines, etc, in eastern semi-arid and arid areas.

Gnamma holes: small spherical rock holes found in granite that often contain water; common in the Eastern Goldfields.

Granite dome: rounded hill of granite rock standing up above a plain; heights vary from a few metres to over a hundred metres.

Granite plain: plain exhibiting slabs, outcrops or domes of granite; elsewhere sandy.

Grasslands: a tract of country supporting little else but grasses.

Hakeas: refers herein to small trees (usually needlewoods and corkwoods) found growing in semi-arid and arid country.

Halophytes: salt tolerant shrubby plants usually found growing around the edge of saltlakes or in saline coastal areas.

Homelands: an Aboriginal occupied traditional area usually supporting a small clan-based community or country camp.

Ironwood (desert areas): an attractive acacia with a large drooping crown; common in the northern areas of Central Australia.

Ironwood (tropical areas): a large semi-deciduous tree with a dark green crown found growing in the tropical woodlands.

Jump-ups: (referred to as breakaways in the Coober Pedy district) name given to low ranges, isolated hills or low tablelands exhibiting a flat-top or upper surface and bounded by steep sides. The upper crust is formed by a hard crust called silcrete. Would normally be called breakaways in Western Australia, but are different features to the 'breakaways' defined above.

Kapok bush: deciduous shrub or small tree found alongside many roads in the tropical woodlands. During the dry season it has large, yellow flowers.

Lagoon: northern Australian term for waterhole.

Lake plain: plain, often of alluvium (flood-deposits) adjacent to a lake.

Lancewoods: a species of acacia that forms dense thickets up to 10m high in the dry tropical regions, often growing on gravelly-red soils. Smaller, less dense versions may occupy the upper levels of jump-ups in semi-arid areas of western Queensland.

Laterite: a reddish rock, common in tropical regions, exhibiting a hard crust, underlain by mottled and white clays. Hard crust forms widespread low tablelands.

Leopardwoods: small tree found in eastern semi-arid areas with a trunk that exhibits leopard-like spots.

Lignum: a thicket of the species *Muehlenbeckia* which grows adjacent to outback waterholes and on floodplain country

Local relief: difference in height between a hill top and adjacent valley, or between high and low points in undulating country.

Lunette: a crescent-shaped dune located on the downwind side of a lake bed.

Mallee: either a multi-stemmed shrub of a eucalypt species, or the name given to the countryside dominated by the same.

Melaleucas: varying sized trees with a papery bark found in wet depressions, river banks, etc.

Mesas: another name for jump-up hills.

Mill: Western Australian term for windmill.

Mitchell grass: a widespread tussocky grass found growing mostly on clay or black soil plains.

Mulga: a widespread species of acacia exhibiting either a shrubby or treed form, found growing in most types of semi-arid and arid country, especially south of the Tropic of Capricorn.

Mygums: once called snappy gums (these are a different species found in tropical semi-arid areas) - have white trunks and are common in the Pilbara region.

Native sorghum: common understorey grass in the tropical woodlands growing up to 3m tall. It is green during the wet season; broken and brown during the dry season.

Normanton box: a low mallee eucalypt found growing in the northern parts of the Channel Country (North-West Queensland), often at the base of jump-ups.

Nutwood: a moderate-sized tree of the tropical woodlands characterised by the prominent tesselated bark on its trunk.

Outwash plains: plains located near the base of a range built up from material eroded from that range.

Paperbarks: another name for melaleuca trees and shrubs; found in wet areas.

Pedimont plain: gently sloping plain found adjacent to high and thrusted ranges; common on the western side of the Flinders Ranges.

Pool: Western Australian term for waterhole.

Prickly mimosa: a shaggy-looking spiky acacia, believed to be introduced, found growing on the Mitchell grass plains of Queensland.

Quartz blows: a small area of stony plain dominated by white quartz; has the appearance of recently fallen hail.

Rainforest: dense stand of forest exhibiting a diversity of life forms: vines, epiphytes (eg staghorns), palms, ferns, buttressed trees, emergent trees (rise above the canopy), etc. Notable for its absence of eucalypts. In drier areas they may be called *dry rainforests*; in monsoonal areas they are called *monsoonal rainforests* - these latter types have less species and diversity.

Rainshadow: dry country in the lee of a range that lies in the path of moisture-laden winds.

River red gum: a species of eucalypt characterised by gum-like bark; often possesses a large trunk. Very common along river channels, sandy creek beds and waterholes.

Rolling downs: slightly undulating country of low rises and shallow valleys normally associated with black soil plains or clay plains. Common in Central-West and Fitzroy Basin regions of Queensland as well as the Barkly Tableland.

Saltbush: common low-growing shrub with a bluish-grey appearance found in the understorey of many woodlands and shrublands, or dominating the landscape in its own right, e.g. on the Nullarbor Plain. May grow in conjunction with bluebush. Common in semi-arid and arid western New South Wales, South Australia and south-east Western Australia.

Saltlakes: lake bed covered with a surface of salt. In some areas these lakes may support vegetation such as saltbush, samphires, etc.

Samphire: squat salt-tolerant plants of different species commonly found adjacent to, or even on, saltlakes.

Sand-hill canegrass: a species of *Zygochloa* characterised by a tangled mass of herbage, found growing upon sand dunes, e.g. Simpson Desert.

Sandplains: plains covered with a surface of sand, or exhibiting sand dunes and intervening interdunal areas or swales. In the southwest of Western Australia is a typical Western Australian version of sand plains: light-covered deep sands usually supporting a dense growth of shrubs and heaths.

Savanna woodlands: a type of tropical woodland exhibiting low well-spaced trees with a grassy understorey.

Snappy gums: attractive small white-barked eucalypts commonly found on the stony hills in tropical semi-arid country. *Also see mygums.*

Spinifex: a widespread native spiky grass common on sand plains, rocky hills, etc.

Stony plains: flat to undulating plains covered with stones or gibbers; often found in jump-up country or adjacent to ranges.

Tropical woodlands: widespread tracts of tropical country supporting trees with a parkland-like appearance. Grassy understoreys common but shrubs and lesser trees may be present.

Undulating country: plains country exhibiting low rises, ridges or undulations.

Variable-barked bloodwood: very common eucalypt growing throughout much of the northern semi-arid regions. Bark is variable, the crown somewhat open.

Western myall: attractive tree species of acacia exhibiting a flattish crown somewhat reminiscent of the trees of the African savanna; common in saltbush country in the southern semi-arid regions.

Whitewood: a small to medium sized tree (sometimes a shrub) which often has two trunks. Flowers are white, leaves are waxy; fairly common in semi-arid country.

Wilga: dense low tree with a rounded crown sometimes reaching the ground; found in southern semi-arid areas.

Woodlands: widespread tracts of country supporting trees with a parkland-like appearance. Understoreys vary from grass or spinifex to shrubs.

Further Reading

Absalom J, 1992, *Safe Outback Travel*, Five Mile Press, Melbourne.

ACF, *Daintree-Where the Rainforest Meets the Reef*, ACF-Kevin Weldon and Associates, Sydney.

Andrews B, 1994, *Explore Australia's Great Inland*, Child and Henry, Sydney.

Beard J, 1990, *Plant Life of Western Australia*, Kangaroo Press, Sydney.

Blombery A, 1985, *The Living Centre of Australia*, Kangaroo Press, Sydney.

Bohemia J, 1996, *Nyibayarri: Kimberley Tracker*, Aboriginal Studies Press, Canberra.

Breeden S & Wright B, 1989, *Kakadu: Looking after the Country*, Simon and Schuster, Sydney.

Breiter M, 1996, *Kakadu and the Top End*, Kangaroo Press, Sydney.

Brennan K, 1986, *Wildflowers of Kakadu*, KG Brennan, Jaibiru.

Clark M & Traynor S, 1987, *Plants of the Tropical Woodland*, Conservation Commission of the Northern Territory, Darwin.

Costermans L, 1994, *Native Trees and Shrubs of South-East Australia*.

Cowan J & Beard C, 1985, *Starlight's Trail*, Doubleday, 1985, Sydney.

Cusack M & S, 1989, *Our Year in the Wilderness*, Australian Geographic, Sydney.

Dempsey, F, 1980, *Old Mining Towns of North Queensland*, Rigby, Adelaide.

Douglas M & Farwell G, 1976, *Across the Top & Cape York to Kimberley*, Seal Books, Sydney.

Duffield R, 1979, *Rogue Bull: The Story of Lang Hancock - King of the Pilbara*, Collins, Sydney.

Durack M, 1997, *Kings in Grass Castles*, Bantam

Durack M, 1983, *Sons in the Saddle*, Corgi.

Edwards H, 1991, *Kimberley: Dreaming to Diamonds*, self-published, Perth.

Firth, D & C, 1995, *Cape York: A Natural Legacy*, Reed Books, Sydney.

Gerritson J, 1981, *Tibooburra-Corner Country*, Tibooburra Press.

Gordon, M, 2001, *Outback Australia*, Little Hills Press, Sydney.

Hardy B, 1976, *Lament for the Barkindji*, Rigby, Adelaide.

Harmer J, *Northern Australian Plants, Volume 1: Wildflowers of the Top End*, Society for Growing Australian Plants.

Henderson S, 1995, *From Strength to Strength*, Bolinda Press.

Hill E, 1995, *The Territory*, Angus and Robertson, Sydney.

Holthouse, H, 1995, *Cape York*, Australian Geographic, Sydney.

Holthouse, H, 1967, *River of Gold: The Story of the Palmer River Goldrush*, Angus and Robertson, Sydney.

Honeywill B & Plumb T, 1990, *Wild Country*, Sunbird Publishing, Brisbane.

Idriess I, 1951, *The Cattle King*, Angus and Robertson, Sydney.

Jarver P, 1988, *Kakadu Country*, Thunderbird, Darwin.

Learmouth N & A, 1971, *Regional Landscapes of Australia*, Angus and Robertson, Sydney.

Lowe P, & Pike J, 1990, *Jilji, Life in the Great Sandy Desert*, Magabala Books, Broome.

Lunney B, 1997, *Fifteen Hundred Down the Murranji*, Crawford House Publishing, Bathurst

Maloney B & Blombery A, 1995, *Kakadu to Broome: A Guide to Northern Australia*, Angus and Robertson, Sydney.

Mathews, A, 1992, *The Matilda Highway*, QTTC, Brisbane.

McGregor A, 1992, *The Kimberley*, Hodder and Stoughton, Sydney.

McKellar H, 1984, *Matya-Mundi*, Cunnamulla Aust. Native Welfare Association.

Moon, R & V, 1995, *Cape York: An Adventurers Guide*, Kikarra Adventure Publications, Melbourne.

Mowaljarlai D, & Malnic J, 1993, *Yorro Yorro, Spirit of the Kimberley*, Magabala Books, Broome.

Neidjie B, 1985, *Kakadu Man*, Mybrood, Sydney.

O'Keefe, C, 1990, *Discover Lawn Hill National Park*, Robert Brown and Associates, Carina.

Osterstock A, 1983, *Andamooka Opal*, Roling Press.

Petheram R & Kock B, *Plants of the Kimberley Region of Western Australia*, UWA Press, Perth

Pike, G, *Wings Over the Cape*, Pinevale Publications, Mareeba.

Readers Digest, 1991, *Discover Australia*, Sydney.

Read I, 1999, *Australia's Eastern Outback: The Eco-Touring Guide*, Little Hills Press, Sydney.

Read I, 1994, *The Bush: A Guide to the Vegetated Landscapes of Australia*, UNSW Press, Sydney.

Read I, 1999, *Outback Western Queensland: The Eco-Touring Guide*, Little Hills Press, Sydney.

Ritchie, R, 1995, *North Queensland's Wet Tropics: A Guide for Travellers*, Rainforest Publishing, Sydney.

Roberts C, 1995, *Australia's Kimberley: Visions of a Lasting Wilderness*, C & K Roberts, Broome

Roe P, 1983, *Gularabulu*, Fremantle Art Centre Press, Fremantle.

Ryan J, *Aboriginal Art of the Kimberley*, National Gallery of Victoria, Melbourne.

Sheedy B, *Outback on a Budget*, Viking O'Neil, Melbourne.

Taylor G, 1994, *Whale Sharks: Giants of Ningaloo Reef*, Angus and Robertson, Sydney.

Thomas A, 1997, *A Toast to the Kimberley*, Darlington Publishing Group, Perth.

Tyler I, 1996, *Geology and Landforms of the Kimberley*, Bush- Books, Perth.

Urban A, 1990, *Wildflowers and Plants of Central Australia*, Portside Editions, Melbourne.

Wheeler J (ed), *Flora of the Kimberley Region*, CALM, Perth.

Web Sites

Below is a list of some web sites that might be useful.

Adelaide Hills: www.adelaidehills.net.au
Atherton Tableland:
www.athertontableland.com
Auslig (government maps):
www.auslig.gov.au

Australia: www.walkabout.com.au
Barrossa Valley: www.barossa-region.org
Beachport: www.thelimestonecoast.com
Birds: www.birdsaustralia.com.au
Bowen: www.bowentourism.com.au
Broken Hill/Western NSW:
www.murrayoutback.org.au
Bunbury: www.bunburytourism.org.au
Burketown: www.burkeshirecouncil.com
Busselton: http://capeweb.com.au/escape
Bureau of Meteorology (weather information): www.bom.gov.au
Cardwell: www.gspeak.com.au/cardwell
Coober Pedy:
www.opalcapitaloftheworld.com.au
Flinders Ranges/Hawker:
www.hawker.mtx.net
Geelong: www.gstr.org.au
Great Ocean Road: www.greatoceanrd.org.au
Gulf Savanna: www.internetnorth.com.au/gulf/
Gulf Savanna: www.savannah-guides.com.au
Hema Maps: www.hemamaps.com.au
Hinchinbrook Island:
www.hinchinbrookferries.com.au
Innisfail: www.gspeak.com.au/Innisfail
Kingston SE: www.thelimestonecoast.com
Kuranda: www.kuranda.org
Main Road Western Australia:
www.mrwa.wa.gov.au
Margaret River: www.margaretriverwa.com
Melbourne: www.visitvictoria.com
Mildura: www.murrayoutback.org.au
Millicent: www.thelimestonecoast.com
Mt Gambier: www.thelimestonecoast.com
Nannup: www.compwest.net.au/~nannuptb/
Nelson: www.thelimestonecoast.com
Northern Lands Council: www.nlc.org.au
Outback Queensland:
www.outbackqld.net.au
Parks Tasmania: www.parks.tas.gov.au
Parks Victoria: www.parks.vic.gov.aus
Pemberton: www.pembertontourist.com.au
Pichi Richi Railway: www.prrps.com.au
Port Douglas: www.portdaouglas.com
Port MacDonnell:
www.thelimestonecoast.com
Queensland Dept of Environment and Heritage: www.env.qld.gov.au

Queenstown: www.queenstown.tco.asn.au
RAA: www.raa.net
Renmark: www.murrayoutback.org.au
Robe: www.thelimestonecoast.com
Robinvale: www.murrayoutback.org.au
Tasmania: www.discovertasmania.com.au
The Coorong: www.thelimestonecoast.com
Townsville: www.townsvilleonline.com.au
Transport South Australia:
www.transport.sa.gov.au/northern.htm
Undara Lava Tubes:
www.undara-experience.com.au
Victoria: www.visitvictoria.com
Warrnambool: www.gstr.org.au
Wentworth: www.murrayoutback.org.au
Whitsundays:
www.whitsundayinformation.com
Winton: www.matildacentre.com.au

Tourist Offices, Visitor Centres and Tourist Information

Below is a list of places where Tourist Information is available. They range from official local council or government tourist offices to private establishments.

Adelaide
South Australian Travel Centre
1 King William St, Adelaide, SA 5000
Phone: 08 8303 2033

Airlie Beach Tourist Information Centre
277 Shute Harbour Rd, Airlie Beach, Qld 4802
Phone: 07 4946 6665
Fax: 07 4946 7902
Email: abtic@whitsunday.net.au

Albany Tourist Bureau
Old Railway Station
Proudlove Pde, Albany, WA 6330
Phone: 1800 644 088
Fax: 08 9842 1490
Email: albanytb@omninet.net.au

Alice Springs
Central Australian Visitor Information Centre
60 Gregory Terrace, Alice Springs, NT 0870
Phone: 08 8952 5800
Fax: 08 8953 0295

Anakie (Gemfields)
The Big Sapphire
Anakie Rd, Anakie, Qld 4702
Phone/Fax: 07 4985 4525

Apollo Bay Visitor Information Centre
Great Ocean Rd, Apollo Bay, Vic 3233
Phone: 03 5237 6529
Fax: 5289 2492

Aramac Post Office and Tourist Information
Gordon/Lodge Sts, Aramac, Qld 4726
Phone/Fax: 07 4651 3147

Armadale Tourist Centre
40 Jull St, Aramadale, WA 6112
Phone: 08 9497 3543

Atherton
Tropical Tableland Promotion
Bureau, Herberton Rd, Atherton, Qld 4883
Phone: 07 4091 4222

Augusta Tourist Information Centre
70 Blackwood Ave, Augusta, WA 6290
Phone: 08 9758 1695
Fax: 08 9758 0172
Email: aupro@netserv.com.au

Australind Tourist Information Centre
Mardo Ave, Australind, WA 6230
Phone: 08 9721 7322

Babinda Visitor Centre
Bruce Hwy/Munro St, Babinda, Qld 4861
Phone: 07 4067 1008

Ballingup Tourist Information Centre
Old Cheese Factory Craft Centre
Nannup Rd, Balingup, WA 6253
Phone and Fax: 08 9764 1018

Barcaldine Tourist Information Centre
Oak St, Barcaldine, Qld 4725
Phone: 07 4651 1724
Fax: 07 4651 2243

Barossa Valley Wine and Visitors Centre
66-68 Murray St, Tanunda, SA 5352
Phone: 08 8563 0600
Fax: 08 8563 0616

Bendigo Visitor Information Centre
51 Pall Mall, Bendigo, Vic 3550
Phone: 03 5444 4445
Fax: 03 5444 4447

Bindoon
Chittering Tourist Centre
Great Northern Hwy, Bindoon, WA 6502
Phone: 08 9576 1100

Birdsville
Wirrarri Centre, Billabong Bvd, Birdsville, Qld
Phone: 07 4656 3300
Fax: 07 4656 3302

Blackall Tourist Information Centre
Short St, Blackall, Qld 4472
Phone/Fax: 07 4657 4637

Blackwater/Bluff
Duaringa Shire Council
Phone: 07 4935 7101

Borroloola
Gulf Regional Tourist Information Centre,
Borroloola, NT 0854
Phone: 08 8975 8601

Boulia Information Centre
Herbert St, Boulia, Qld 4829
Phone: 07 4746 3386
Fax: 07 4746 3387

Bourke Tourist Information Centre
Old Railway Station, Anson St, Bourke, NSW
2840
Phone: 02 6872 1222
Fax: 02 6872 2305
Email: Tourinfo@lisp.com.au

Bowen Tourist Information Centre
42 Williams St, Bowen, Qld 4805
Phone: 4786 4494
Fax: 4786 4499
Email: info@bowentourism.com.au

Bridgetown Tourist Centre
Hampton St, Bridgetown, WA 6255
Phone: 08 9761 1740
Fax: 08 9761 1105

Broken Hill Visitor Information Centre
Cnr Blende St/Bromide St
Broken Hill, NSW 2880
Phone: 08 8087 6077
Fax: 08 8088 5209
Email: tourist@pcpro.net.au

Broome Tourist Bureau
Broome Hwy/Bagot Rd, Broome, WA 6725
Phone: 08 9192 2222
Fax: 08 9192 2063

Bunbury Tourist Bureau
Old Railway Station
Carmody St, Bunbury, WA 6230
Phone: 08 9721 7922
Fax: 08 9721 9224
Email: welcome@bunburytourism.org.au

Burdekin Tourism Association Incorporated
Bruce Hwy, Ayr, Qld 4807
Phone: 07 4783 5988

Burketown Tourist Information Centre
Musgrave St, Burketown, Qld 4830
Phone: 07 4545 5111
Email: burkesc@bigpond.com

Burra Visitors Centre
2 Market Sq, Burra, SA 5417
Phone: 08 8892 2154

Busselton Tourist Bureau
38 Peel Tce, Busselton, WA 6280
Phone: 08 9752 1288
Fax: 08 9754 1470
Email: bsntb@highway1.com.au

Cairns
Tourism Tropical North Queensland
51 The Esplanade, Cairns, Qld 4870
Phone: 07 4051 3588

Camooweal
Barkly Tableland Heritage Centre
Camooweal, Qld 4828
Phone: 07 4748 2160
Fax: 07 4748 2133

Cardwell Information Centre
Bruce Hwy, Cardwell, Qld 4816
Phone: 07 4066 8468

Carnarvon Tourist Bureau
Civic Centre, 11 Robinson St
Carnarvon, WA 6701
Phone: 08 9941 1146

Ceduna Gateway Visitor Information Centre
58 Poynton St, Ceduna, SA 5690
Phone 1800 639 413
Fax: 08 8625 3294
Email: travelce@tpg.com.au

Charleville Information Centre
Cunnamulla Rd, Charleville, Qld 4470
Phone: 07 4654 3057
Fax: 07 4654 2284

**Charters Towers and
Dalrymple Tourism Association**
74 Mossman St,
Charters Towers, Qld 4820
Phone: 07 4752 0314

**Chillagoe Information Centre and
Heritage Museum**
Chillagoe, Qld 4871
Phone: 07 4094 7109

Cloncurry
Mary Kathleen Park
Daintree St, Cloncurry, Qld 4824
Phone: 07 4742 1361
Fax: 07 4742 1712

Cobar
Great Cobar Outback Heritage Centre
Barrier Hwy, Cobar 2835
Phone: 02 6836 2448
Fax: 02 6836 1818

Coober Pedy Tourist Information Centre
District Council Offices
Hutchison St, Coober Pedy, SA
Phone: 1800 637 076
Fax: 08 8672 5699

Coolgardie Tourist Bureau
62 Bayley St, Coolgardie, WA 6429
Phone: 08 9026 6090

Coral Bay Tourist Information Centre
Shopping Arcade, Coral Bay via Carnarvon,
WA 6701
Phone: 08 9942 5988

**Cradle Mountain-Lake St Clair National Park
Visitors Centre**
Cradle Valley Road, Cradle Valley, Tas 7306
Phone: 03 6492 1133

Croydon
Croydon Shire Council
Croydon, Qld 4871
Phone: 07 4745 6125
Fax: 07 4745 6147
Email: croydon@bigpond.com.au

Cue Tourism Centre
Lot 2 Austin St, Cue, WA 6640
Phone: 08 9963 1041

Cunderdin Tourist Information Centre
Museum Building
Forrest St, Cunderdin, WA 6407
Phone: 08 9625 1257

Cunnamulla Tourist Information Centre
Centenary Park, Cunnamulla, Qld 4490
Phone: 07 4655 2481
Fax: 07 4655 1120
Email: cunnamulla_tourism@bigpond.com.au

Cynthia Bay
Cradle Mountain-Lake St Clair National Park
Visitors Centre
Lake St Clair Rd, Cynthia Bay via Derwent
Bridge, Tas, 7140
Phone: 03 6289 1115

Dalby Tourist Information Centre
Thomas Jack Park
Cnr Warrego/Bunya Hwys, Dalby Qld 4405
Phone: 07 4662 1066

Dalwallinu Tourist Information Centre
Johnson St, Dalwallinu, WA 6609
Phone: 08 9661 1001

Darwin & Top End Tourism
Mitchell St/Knuckey St, Darwin, NT 0801
Phone: 08 8981 4300
Fax: 08 8981 0653

Denham
See Shark Bay below

Deniliquin Tourist Centre
Peppin Heritage Centre
George St, Deniliquin, NSW 2170
Phone: 03 5881 2878

Denmark Tourist Bureau
60 Strickland St, Denmark, WA 6333
Phone: 08 9848 2055
Fax: 08 9848 2271

Derby Tourist Bureau
1 Claredon St, Derby, WA 6728
Phone: 08 9191 1426
Fax: 08 9191 1609

Devonport
Devonport Showcase
5 Best St, Devonport, Tas 7310
Phone: 03 6424 8176

Dongara Tourist Information Centre
5 Waldeck St, Dongara, WA 6525
Phone: 08 9927 1404

Donnybrook Tourist Information Centre
Old Railway Station, Donnybrook, WA 6239
Phone: 08 9731 1720
Fax: 08 9731 1728

Dunsborough Tourist Bureau
Seymour Blvd, Dunsborough, WA 6281
Phone: 08 9755 3299
Fax: 08 9756 8065
Email: bsntb@highway1.com.au

Dwellingup History &
Visitor Information Centre
Marrinup St, Dwellingup, WA 6213
Phone: 08 9538 1108

Emerald
Central Highlands Tourist Information Centre
Clermont St, Emerald, Qld 4720
Phone: 07 4982 4142

Esperance Tourist Bureau & Travel Centre
Museum Village
Dempster St, Esperance, WA 6450
Phone: 08 9071 2330

Echuca Visitor Information Centre
2 Heygarth St, Echuca, Vic 3564
Phone: 03 5480 7555
Fax: 03 5482 6413

Exmouth Tourism
Payne St, Exmouth, WA 6707
Phone: 08 9949 1176

Fitzroy Crossing Tourist Bureau
Flynn Drive, Fitzroy Crossing, WA 6765
Phone: 08 9191 5355
Fax: 08 9191 5085

Fremantle Tourist Bureau
Town Hall/Kings Sq, Fremantle WA 6160
Phone: 08 9431 7878
Fax: 08 9431 7755
Email: holzwart@wantree.com.au

Gawler Tourist Information Centre
2 Lyndoch Road, Gawler, SA 5118
Phone: 08 8522 6814

Geelong Visitor Information Centre
Stead Park Princess Hwy, Geelong, Vic 3214
Phone: 03 5275 5799
Email: ecurtain@geelongcity.vic.gov.au

Geraldton Tourist Bureau
Bill Sewell Complex
Chapman Rd, Geraldton, WA 6530
Phone: 08 9921 3999

Gilgandra Visitors Centre
Coo-ee March Memorial Park
Newell Hwy, Gilgandra, NSW 2827
Phone: 02 6847 2045
Fax: 02 6847 1292

Griffith Visitors Centre
Cnr Kidman & Burley Griffin Ways, Griffith,
NSW 2680
Phone: 1800 681 141
Fax: 02 6962 7319
Email: griffith@webfront.net.au

Gulf Savanna Tourism
74 Abbott St, Cairns, Qld 4870
Phone: 07 4051 4658

Halls Creek Tourist Information Centre
Great Northern Highway
Halls Creek, WA 6770
Phone: 08 9168 6262
Fax: 08 9168 6467

Harvey Tourist & Information Centre
South-West Hwy/James Stirling Place
Harvey, WA 6220
Phone: 08 9729 1122

Hay Visitors Centre
407 Moppett St, Hay, NSW 2711
Phone: 02 6993 4045
Email: haytouristcentre@bigpond.com

Herberton Handicrafts
49 Grace St, Herberton, Qld 4872
Phone: 07 4096 3333

Hillston Visitor Information Centre
High St, Hillston, NSW 2675
Phone: 02 6967 2555

Hobart
Tasmania Tourist Information Centre
Cnr Davey & Elizabeth Sts, Hobart, Tas 7000
Phone: 03 6232 6300

Hughenden Visitor Information Centre
Gray St, Hughenden, Qld 4821
Phone: 07 4741 1021
Fax: 07 4741 1029

Ingham
Hinchinbrook Visitor Centre
Bruce Hwy/Lannercost St, Ingham, Qld 4850
Phone: 07 4776 5211
Fax: 07 4776 3039

Innisfail
See Mourilyan below

Iron Knob Community Tourist Centre
Phone: 08 8646 2129

Kalbarri Tourist Bureau
Allen Community Centre,
Grey St, Kalbarri, WA 6536
Phone: 08 9144 4600
Fax: 08 9144 4620

Kalgoorlie Tourist Bureau
250 Hannan St, Kalgoorlie, WA 6430
Phone: 08 9021 1966

Kambalda Tourist Bureau
Cnr Emu Rocks Rd/Marianthus Rd, Kambalda
West, WA 6442
Phone: 08 9027 1446

Karratha Tourist Bureau
Karratha Rd, Karratha, WA 6714
Phone: 08 9144 4600
Fax: 08 9144 4620
Email: tourist.bureau@kisser.net.au

Katherine Visitors Information Centre
Katherine Terrace/Lindsay St,
Katherine, NT 0851
Phone: 08 8972 2650
Fax: 08 8972 2969
Email: krta@nt-tech.com.au

Kellerberrin Tourist Information Centre
Shire Office
110 Massingham St, Kellerberrin, WA 6410

Kimba
The Sturt Pea Shoppe
Eyre Hwy, Kimba, SA 5641
Phone: 08 8627 2622

Kingston Tourist Information
Big Lobster, Princess Hwy, Kingston, SA 5275
Phone: 08 8767 2555

Kununurra Tourist Bureau
East Kimberley Tourist House
Coolabah Drive, Kununurra, WA 6743
Phone: 08 9168 1177
Fax: 08 9168 2598

Kuranda Envirocare Information Centre
Kuranda Rainforest Resort, Kuranda, Qld 4872
Phone: 07 4093 7570

Kynuna
Kynuna Roadhouse and Caravan Park
Kynuna, Qld 4823
Phone: 07 4746 8683
Fax: 4746 8871

Launceston
Tasmanian Tourism Information Centre
Cnr St John & Paterson Sts, Launceston, Tas
7250
Phone: 03 6336 3133s

Leigh Creek Regional Visitors Information Centre
Blackoak Drive, Leigh Creek, SA 5731
Phone: 08 8675 2723

Longreach Tourist Information Centre
Qantas Park, Longreach, Qld 4730
Phone: 07 4658 3555
Fax: 07 4658 3733
Email: visitinf@longreach.qld.gov.au

Lorne Visitor Information Centre
144 Mountjoy Pde, Lorne, Vic 3232
Phone: 03 5289 1152
Fax: 03 5289 2492

Mackay Tourism and Development Board
320 Nebo Rd, Mackay, Qld 4740
Phone: 07 4952 2677
Fax: 07 4952 2034
Email: info@mtdb.org.au

Malanda Environment Learning Centre
near Malanda Falls, Malanda, Qld, 4885
Phone: 07 4096 6957

Mandurah Tourist Bureau
Mandurah Tce, Mandurah, WA 6210
Phone: 08 9550 3999

Manjimup Tourist Bureau
Rose St/Edward St, Manjimup, WA 6258
Phone: 1800 023 388
Fax: 08 9777 1001

Marble Bar Tourist Information Centre
Travellers Stop
Lot 232 Halse Rd, Marble Bar, WA 6760
Phone: 08 9176 1166

Mareeba Information and Heritage Centre
Centenary Park, Kennedy Hwy,
Mareeba, Qld 4880
Phone: 07 4092 5674

Margaret River Tourist Bureau
Bussell Hwy, Margaret River, WA 6285
Phone: 08 9757 2911
Fax: 08 9757 3287
Email: amrta@netserv.net.au

McKinlay
Walkabout Creek Hotel
McKinlay, Qld 4823
Phone: 07 4746 8424
Fax: 07 4746 8768

Meekatharra Shire Council
Main St, Meekatharra, WA 6642
Phone: 08 9981 1253

Melbourne Tourist Information Centre
Melbourne Town Hall
Cnr Swanston/Collins Sts, Melbourne, Vic 3000
Phone: 03 9658 9658
Fax: 03 9658 9166

Merredin Tourist & Information Centre
Barrack St, Merredin, WA 6415
Phone: 08 9041 1666

Mildura
Sunraysia Tourism
180-190 Deakin Ave, Mildura, Vic 3500
Phone: 03 5021 4424

Millaa Millaa
The Falls Teahouse and Information Centre
Millaa Millaa Falls turnoff, via Millaa Millaa,
Qld 4886
Phone: 07 4097 2237

Millicent Tourist Information Centre
1 Mount Gambier Rd, Millicent, SA 5280
Phone: 08 8733 3205

Mission Beach Visitor Centre
Porters Promenade, Mission Beach, Qld 4852
Phone: 07 4068 7099
Fax: 07 4068 7066

Mitchell Tourist Information Centre
Kenniff Courthouse, Mitchell, Qld 4465
Phone: 07 4623 1133
Fax: 07 4623 1145

Mourilyan Information Centre
Bruce Hwy, Mourilyan, Qld 4858
Phone: 07 4063 2000
Fax: 07 4063 2022
Email: ccdb@znet.com.au

Mt Gambier Tourist Information Centre
Jubilee Hwy East, Mt Gambier, SA 5290
Phone: 08 8724 9750
Fax: 08 8723 2833

Mt Isa
Riversleigh Centre
Centenary Park, Mt Isa, Qld 4825
Phone: 07 4749 1555
Fax: 07 4743 6296

Mt Surprise
Old Post Office Museum, Mt Surprise, Qld
4871
Phone: 07 4062 3126

Murray Bridge Visitor Information Centre
3 South Tce, Murray Bridge, SA 5253
Phone: 08 8532 6660
Fax: 08 8532 5288

Nannup Tourist Information Centre
4 Brockman St, Nannup, WA 6275
Phone/Fax: 08 9756 1211
Email: nannuptb@compwest.com.au

Newman Tourist Information Centre and Museum
Newman Drive/Fortescue Ave, Newman, WA 6753
Phone: 08 9175 2888
Fax: 08 9175 2964

New Norcia Tourist Information Centre
New Norcia Museum and Art Gallery
Great Northern Highway
New Norcia, WA 6509
Phone: 08 9654 8056

Normanton Tourist Information Centre
29-33 Haig St, Normanton, Qld 4870
Phone: 07 4745 1166
Fax: 07 4745 1340

Norseman Tourist Bureau
Historic Museum,
68 Roberts St, Norseman, WA 6443
Phone: 08 9039 1071

Northam
Avon Valley Tourist Bureau
2 Greg St, Northam, WA 6401
Phone: 08 9622 2100

Northampton Tourist Bureau
Hampton Rd, Northampton, WA 6535
Phone: 08 9934 1488

Northcliffe Tourist Centre
Wheatley Coast Rd, Northcliffe, WA 6262
Phone/Fax: 08 9776 7203

Oatlands
Central Tasmania Tourism Information Centre
77 High St, Oatlands, Tas 7120
Phone: 03 6254 1212

Onslow Tourist Information
Second Ave, Onslow, WA 6710
Phone: 08 9184 6644

Orroroo
Orroroo/Carrieton District Council
Second St, Orroroo, SA 5431
Phone: 08 8658 1260

Pemberton Tourist Centre
Brockman St, Pemberton, WA 6260
Phone: 1800 671 133
Fax: 08 9776 1623
Email: pemtour@karriweb.net.au

Perth
Western Australia Tourist Centre
Forrest Place, Perth, WA 6000
Phone: 08 9483 1111

Peterborough Tourist Information Centre
Main St, Peterborough, SA 5422
Phone: 08 8651 2708
Email: peterborough@telstra.easymail.com.au

Pinjarra Tourist Centre
Cnr Henry St/George St,
Pinjarra, WA 6208
Phone: 08 9531 1438

Port Augusta
Flinders Ranges and
Outback Tourist Information
41 Flinders Terrace, Port Augusta, SA 5700
Phone: 08 8641 0793
Fax: 08 8642 4288
Email wadlata@wadarid.mtx.net

Port Campbell Visitor Information Centre
26 Morris St, Port Campbell, Vic 3269
Phone: 03 5598 6089
Fax: 03 5237 6194

Port Douglas Tourist Information Centre
23 Macrossan St, Port Douglas, Qld 4871
Phone: 07 4099 5599

Port Fairy Visitor Information Centre
22 Bank St, Port Fairy, Vic 3269
Phone: 03 5568 2682
Fax: 03 5568 2833

Port Hedland Tourist Bureau
13 Wedge St, Port Hedland, WA 6721
Phone: 08 9173 1711

Portland Visitor Information Centre
Lee Breakwater Rd, Portland, Vic 3305
Phone 03 5523 2671
Fax: 03 5521 7287

Quilpie Tourist Information Centre
Brolga St, Quilpie, Qld 4480
Phone: 07 4656 2166
Fax: 07 4656 1016

Quorn
Flinders Ranges Visitor Information Centre
Quorn, SA 5433
Phone/Fax: 08 8648 6419

Ravensthorpe Tourist Bureau
Ravensthorpe Community Centre,
Ravensthorpe, WA 6346
Phone: 08 9838 1277

Renmark/Paringa Visitors Centre
Murray Ave, Renmark, SA 5341
Phone: 08 8585 6704

Richmond
Kronosaurus Korner Fossil Centre
Flinders Hwy, Richmond, Qld, 4822
Phone: 07 4741 3429
Fax: 07 4741 3802

Robe Tourist Information Centre
Mundy Tce, Robe, SA 5276
Phone: 08 8768 2465

Robinvale Tourist Information Centre
Bromley Rd, Robinvale, Vic 3549
Phone: 03 5026 1388

Rockhampton-Capricorn Tourism
The Spire, Gladstone Rd, Rockhampton, Qld
4700
Phone: 07 4927 2055

Rockhampton Tourist Information Centre
208 Quay St, Rockhampton, Qld 4700
Phone: 07 4922 5339

Rockingham Tourist Centre
43 Kent St, Rockingham, WA 6168
Phone: 08 9592 3464
Fax: 08 9592 2778
Email: rtc@iinet.net.au

Roebourne Tourist Bureau
Queen St, Roebourne, WA 6718
Phone: 08 9182 1060
Fax: 08 9182 1257

Roma Regional Information Centre
Warrego Hwy, Roma, Qld 4455
Phone: 07 4622 4355

Ross
Tasmania Wool Centre
Church St, Ross, Tas 7209
Phone: 03 6381 5466

Sarina Tourist Art and Craft Centre
Railway Square, Sarina, Qld 4737
Phone: 07 4956 2251

Serpentine/Jarradale Tourist Information Centre
Council Office
Mundijong, WA 6202
Phone: 08 9525 5255
Fax: 08 9525 5441

Shark Bay Tourist Bureau
71 Knight Tce, Denham, WA 6537
Phone: 08 9948 1253
Fax: 08 9948 1065

Southern Cross Tourist Information Centre
Shire Office, Southern Cross, WA 6426
Phone: 08 9049 1001

South Hedland Tourist Bureau
Lotteries House
Leake St, South Hedland, WA 6722
Phone: 08 9172 5177

St George Regional Information Centre
Balonne Shire Council
Cnr Victoria/Grey Sts, St George, Qld 4487
Phone: 07 4625 3222

Strahan Visitors Centre
The Esplanade, Strahan, Tas 7468
Phone: 03 6471 7622

Surat Regional Information Centre
Cobb & Co Changing Station
Burrowes St, Surat, Qld 4417
Phone: 07 4626 5136

Tennant Creek Regional Tourist Association
Battery Hill Regional Centre, Peko Rd
Tennant Creek, NT 0860
Phone: 08 8962 3388
Fax: 08 8962 2509

Thargomindah
Thargomindah General Store
Dowling St, Thargomindah, Qld 4492
Phone 07 4655 3232
Fax: 07 4655 3222

Tom Price Tourist Bureau
Central Rd, Tom Price, WA 6751
Phone: 08 9188 1112
Fax: 08 9189 1441

Torquay Visitor Information Centre
Surf City Plaza, Beach Rd, Torquay, Vic 3228
Phone: 03 5261 4219
Fax: 03 5261 4756

Torrens Creek Information Centre
Old Post Office, Torrens Creek, Qld 4816
Phone/Fax: 07 4741 7272

Townsville
Highway Information Centre
Bruce Hwy, Stuart, Qld 4810
Phone: 07 4778 3555

Townsville
The Mall Information Centre
The Mall, Townsville, Qld 4810
Phone: 07 4721 3660

Tully Information Centre
Bruce Hwy, Tully, Qld 4854
Phone: 07 4068 2288
Fax: 07 4068 2858

Walpole Tourist Information
Pioneer Cottage, South Coast Hwy
Walpole, WA 6398
Phone: 08 9840 1111
Fax: 08 9840 1355

Warrnambool Visitor Information Centre
600 Raglan Pde (Princess Hwy)
Warrnambool, Vic 3280
Phone: 03 5564 7837
Fax: 03 5561 2133

Waroona Tourist Information Centre
Cnr South-West Hwy/Millar St
Waroona, WA 6215
Phone: 08 9733 1506

Wentworth Tourist Association
Adam St, Wentworth, NSW 2648
Phone: 08 5027 2076

Whitsunday Information Centre
Bruce Hwy, Proserpine, Qld 4800
Phone: 1800 801 252

Winton
Waltzing Matilda Centre
50 Elderslie St, Winton, Qld 4735
Phone: 07 4657 1466
Fax: 07 4657 1886
Email: matilda@thehub.com.au

Wudinna
District Council of Le Hunte
Burton Terrace, Wudinna, SA 5652
Phone: 08 8680 2002

Wyndham Tourist Information Centre
Kimberley Motors
Great Northern Highway, Wyndham, WA 6740
Phone: 08 9161 1281
Fax: 08 9161 1435

Yungaburra
Garden City Villa Information Centre
Cnr Gillies Hwy/Lake Barrine Rd, via
Yungaburra, Qld 4872
Phone: 07 4095 3541

List of Vehicle Spares and Tools

Vehicle Spares

* if travelling in remote country carry these items

- 2/3 spare wheels with tyres*
- silicone rubber gasket
- 1/2 jacks*
- radiator leak sealant
- wooden base for jack
- a few small corks (for holes)
- tow rope
- carburettor kit*
- fan belt/drive and compressor belts
- lengths of wire
- radiator/heater hoses

- air filter
- spare ignition key
- oil filter
- set of fuses
- vulcanising clamp*
- 2 spark plugs
- patches*
- light globes
- two tyre levers*
- headlamp
- valve key
- distributor points
- clutch cyclinder kit*
- condenser
- brake cyclinder kit*
- distributor cap
- air pressure gauge
- rotor
- spare nuts and bolts
- coil
- workshop manual
- 4 litres of engine oil
- bleeding spanner
- brake fluid
- 2m plastic hose
- lubricating spray
- 2m low tension wire
- tyre pump
- shackles for leaf springs
- fuel pump kit*
- jerry can
- insulating tape
- jumper leads
- plastic hand pump
- fire extinguisher

In addition you should carry any spares that your vehicle may specifically require.

Tools

- hacksaw
- file
- soft hammer
- cold chisel
- set of ring/open spanners
- lube gun
- feeler gauge

- socket set and handle
- set of screwdrivers
- wire brush
- pliers
- rags
- pointy pliers
- plus specific tools for your vehicle

A Suggested List of Personal Requirements, Camping Equipment, Food and Other Items

Camping Equipment

- tent
- knives
- detergent
- spade
- forks
- pan scourers
- grate
- spoons and teaspoons
- washing line
- toasting fork, griller
- spatula
- pegs
- camping stove
- sharp knife
- scissors
- gas bottle and fittings
- can opener
- folding chairs
- gas lamp and spare mantles
- tongs
- table
- camp oven
- tea towels
- hand broom
- frying pan
- oven mitt
- torches (one for everyone)
- billy
- chopping board
- Esky or portable fridge
- aluminium foil
- plates
- drinking water bottles
- matches

- bowls
- drinking water
- spare plstic bags
- tea mugs
- needle and thread
- plastic bowls with lids
- bucket
- old rug or tarpaulin

Bedding

- swag
- thermal mat
- sheets, blankets
- sleeping mat
- sleeping bags
- pillows

Toiletries

- soap and container
- shampoo, conditioner
- ladies requisites
- hard-water soap
- deodorant
- nail clippers
- towels
- washing detergent
- tweezers
- hand towel
- shaving gear
- toothbrush and paste

Clothing

- few shirts or T-shirts
- woollen jumpers
- boots, casual shoes
- lots of socks, undies, etc
- few pants and shorts
- overalls
- skivvies
- shady hat
- bathers
- If wintertime, consider the following
- wind cheater
- beanie
- raincoat
- scarf

Personal Items

- money
- insurance papers
- necessary permits
- cashcard, credit card
- address book
- camera and film
- travellers cheques
- pens and pencils
- spare camera battery
- wallet or purse
- notebook
- binoculars
- licence, registration
- maps and guide books
- Medicare/Health Care cards

Medical Kit

- tweezers
- antiseptic cream
- salt tablets
- insect bite applicator
- band-aids, bandages
- sunscreen 15+
- insect repellent
- burn cream
- prescription items
- pain killers
- small scissors
- other personal items

Food

- museli, breakfast cereal
- dried beans, lentils, etc
- carrots
- bread, dry buscuits
- dried peas
- pumpkin
- tea, tea bags, coffee
- self-raising flour
- parsley
- powdered milk
- tinned meat
- garlic
- sugar
- stock cubes
- lemons

- butter, margarine
- selection of herbs, spices
- oranges
- cheese
- baking powder
- apples
- peanut butter, jam, spreads
- cooking oil
- pears
- sardines, tinned fish
- dried fruits
- bananas
- baked beans, etc
- potatoes
- chocolate
- dried tomatoes
- onions
- sweets, desert items

Include a few tins of cooked vegetables, meals, etc, for your emergency rations; these do not require water for cooking. Stock up when possible on perishable items, bread and meat. The above items will keep for a fair while, especially during cooler weather, saving on refrigeration. If wrapped in newspaper and stored in a cool place, cheese, margarine, etc, will keep for up to a week in all but the northernmost areas.

Keep camping items in a lidded box where possible, and store cooking implements in plastic bags to avoid soiling other items with charcoal, sand, etc.

Keep clothes in a heavy-duty clear plastic bag with a fold-over top; it makes it easy to find stray items without having to remove everything from a case.

Bedrolls (swags) means your bed can stay permanently made and also means you do not have to erect a tent each night. Save the tent for extended camps or in mosquito-prone areas. A sleeping mat means you do not have to pump up air mattresses each night.

Before beginning the day's travels, cover the load with an old rug or tarpaulin to reduce the dust. This item can also be used as a means of producing shade over the car (lay over roof and hold in place with the doors) at lunchtime stops, or when going for walks.

Store camera, film and binoculars in a cool place within plastic bags. This will reduce the likelihood of dust entering the equipment.

Budget Form

This budget form will help you budget your road trip.

Road Trip Number:	
Basic Distance:	km
Side Trips, etc. (allow 10%):	km
Connecting Route Distance:	km
Total Distance:	km

TOWN	Distance	Fuel	Car Service	Accomm.	Food	Fees, Charges	Other Expenses
TOTAL							
GRAND TOTAL =							

NOTES:

Budget Form

This budget form will help you budget your road trip.

Road Trip Number:	
Basic Distance:	km
Side Trips, etc. (allow 10%):	km
Connecting Route Distance:	km
Total Distance:	km

TOWN	Distance	Fuel	Car Service	Accomm.	Food	Fees, Charges	Other Expenses
TOTAL							
GRAND TOTAL =							

NOTES:

Trip Log

List your expenditures here.

Date	Town	Speedo	Fuel $	Accom $	Meals $	Other Expenses $
	TOTALS=					

Photo Log

Roll 1	Roll 2	Roll 3
1	1	1
2	2	2
3	3	3
4	4	4
5	5	5
6	6	6
7	7	7
8	8	8
9	9	9
10	10	10
11	11	11
12	12	12
13	13	13
14	14	14
15	15	15
16	16	16
17	17	17
18	18	18
19	19	19
20	20	20
21	21	21
22	22	22
23	23	23
24	24	24
25	25	25
26	26	26
27	27	27
28	28	28
29	29	29
30	30	30
31	31	31
32	32	32
33	33	33
34	34	34
35	35	35
36	36	36

Town and Settlement Index

Use this index to find cities, towns, townships, roadhouse and other settlements that provide basic services including water, telephone, fuel, (limited) store, and accommodation.

- Map references refer to the colour maps at the front of the book. 2-E1, means map 2, grid reference E-1.
- Page numbers in bold refer to the entries with the most information on the town or township mentioned.
- Page numbers in italics refer to a town or township appearing on a Strip Map.

General Index

Use this index to find national parks and other conservation and nature reserves, major tourist features, major geographical features, and tourist-based information.